KOREA
LEADING DEVELOPING NATIONS

*Economy,
Democracy,
&
Welfare*

Sung Moon Pae, Ph.D.
Chair, Division of Social Sciences
Bellevue College

UNIVERSITY
PRESS OF
AMERICA

Lanham • New York • London

Copyright © 1992 by
University Press of America®, Inc.
4720 Boston Way
Lanham, Maryland 20706

3 Henrietta Street
London WC2E 8LU England

All rights reserved
Printed in the United States of America
British Cataloging in Publication Information Available

Library of Congress Cataloging-in-Publication Data

Pae, Sung M.
Korea leading developing nations : economy, democracy and
welfare / Sung Moon Pae.
p.   cm.
Includes bibliographical references and index.
1. Korea (South)—Economic conditions.   2. Democracy—Korea
(South)   3. Public welfare—Korea (South)   I. Title.
HC467.P22   1992   330.95195'043—dc20   92–16787 CIP

ISBN 0-8191-8742-9 (cloth : alk. paper)
ISBN 0-8191-8743-7 (pbk. : alk. paper)

™ The paper used in this publication meets the minimum requirements of American National Standard for Information Sciences—Permanence of Paper for Printed Library Materials, ANSI Z39.48–1984.

For my wife and companion, Sue
and my children
Bill, Suzan & Jeanne

CONTENTS

Foreword xi

Preface xiii

Introduction: Characteristics of The Korean People 1

Chapter 1 Korea as the Land of Morning Calm 3

Passiveness and Submissiveness Caused by Foreign Invasions 3
    Invasions from the North 4
    Invasions from the South 5
Lengthy Period of National Division 11
Passiveness and Submissiveness Reflected in Culture 13
Conclusion 15
Notes 16

Chapter 2 Korea as the Land of Determination 17

The Origins of Dynamism and Determination 18
Korea's Principal Historical Traits 19
    Reflections on the Korean Culture 19
    Indefatigable Struggles for National Defense 20
    Determined Enlightenment Movements 26
    Commitment to Struggles for Independence 27
Conclusion 33
Notes 33

Part I Economic Development 35

Chapter 3 Korea: Leader of the Nations in Economy 37
The Gloomy Economic Outlook for Third World Countries 37
    Economic Satellites 39
    One or Two Export Items vs. Diverse Import Items 39

The Terms of Trade   40
Erosion of Productivity Gains   41
Demand Inelasticity Against Cartel Formation   42
Foreign Loans and Investment   46
Investment by Multinational Corporations   50
The Radical vs. Conventional Development Theory   52
Korea Leading the Nations in Economic Development   57
Conclusion: Strengths of the Korean Economy   63
Notes   65

Chapter 4 The Korean Model of Economic Development   67

Factors Influencing Korean Economic Development   67
    Internal Factors   67
    External Factors   70
The Korean Economic Development Model   73
    The Traditional Import-Oriented Economy (1945-1953)   79
    Import-Substituting Economy (1953-1962)   81
    Labor-Intensive Light Industries (1963-1973)   83
    Capital-Intensive Heavy Industries (1973-1982)   89
    Technology-Intensive Intermediate Industries
       and Reinforcing Other Industries (1983-)   98
Prospects for Continued Economic Development   105
Conclusion   117
Notes   127

Part II Democratization   129

Chapter 5 The American Role in Democratization   131

The American Moral Mission   131
Realism: A Model of the American Role   136
Changes in the American Policy of Democratization in Korea   141
    Open Diplomacy (1950s-1960s)   141
    Quiet Diplomacy (1970s)   147
    Korea of the 1980s: Vital to U.S. National Interest   153
    Korea of the 1980s: Equal Partnership with the USA   161
    U.S. Policy of Cooptation (1980s-)   166
A Quantitative Approach   174
Conclusion   180

Notes   181

Chapter 6 Korea: Leader of the Nations in Democratization   185

Definition of Democracy   185
    The Fallacy of Its Substantive Definition   185
    Variety of Democratic Institutions and Practices   190
    The Procedural Definition of Democracy   202
Comparative Studies of Democratization   205
    A One-Time Static Approach   205
    A Longitudinal, Dynamic Approach   211
Conclusion: Korea Leading the Nations in Democratization   217
Notes   219

Chapter 7 Patron-Client Politics and the Democratic Legacy   221

Patron-Client Politics   221
    The Patriarchal Bureaucracy   221
    The Patriarchal Legislature   230
    The Patriarchal Political Parties   235
    Carrot and Stick Techniques   245
The Fallacy of Dichotomy between Patronage and Group Politics   253
The Democratic Legacy as an Unextinguished Flame   257
    The Legacy of Political Philosophy Advocating Democracy   258
    The Literature Advocating Democracy   260
    Struggles for Democracy   264
    The Implementation of Democratic Principles   266
Conclusion   268
Notes   269

Chapter 8 The Korean Model of Democratization   271

A Political Satellite Model   272
    The First Republic   277
        The Anti-Democracy Patron-Client Coalition   277
        The Pro-Democracy Coalition   281
    The Military Regime and the Third Republic   283

            The Anti-Democracy Patron-Client Coalition   283
            The Pro-Democracy Coalition   290
      The Fourth Republic   293
            The Anti-Democracy Patron-Client Coalition   293
            The Pro-Democracy Coalition   297
      The Fifth Republic   303
            The Anti-Democracy Patron-Client Coalition   303
A Pro-Democracy Coalition Entering into the Threshold in 1987
            311
A New Emerging Political Satellite Model in the Sixth Republic
            325
      A Small Left-Wing Coalition   326
      A Small Right-Wing Coalition   327
      A Broad Moderate Pro-Democracy Coalition   330
Conclusion: Democratic Accomplishments and Unfinished Tasks
            344
Notes   363

Part III Social Welfare Services   347

Chapter 9 Korea: Leader of the Nations in Social Welfare
            349

Liberal Economy as the Root Cause of Welfare Services   349
      Liberal Economy   349
      Problems of Liberal Economy   352
      Three Types of State Intervention   355
The Fallacy of the Furniss and Tilton Welfare State   358
The Outcome-Based Evaluation of Welfare Services   366
      The INSP   367
      The Physical Quality of Life Index (PQLI)   369
Korea Leading the Third World in the PQLI   371
Conclusion   392
Notes   394

Chapter 10 The Korean Model of Social Welfare Services
            395

Pensions   395
      Expansion of Pensions Based on Financial Feasibility   397
      Pension Types and Amount of Benefits   403

Contents ix

    Criticisms on the Pension Program 404
    Merits of the Pension 412
Medical Care Security 413
    Medical Insurance 413
    Criticisms on the Medical Insurance 420
    Merits of the Medical Insurance 424
    Medical Protection and Assistance 428
Public (State) Support for the Elderly, the Handicapped and the Poor 430
Private Sector Contributions 432
    Medical Professionals and Organizations 432
        The Association of Physicians for Humanism 433
        Medical Students 436
        Keimyung University Medical Center 437
        Yeo Sung-Sook, MD 441
Education by the Private and Public Sector Contributions 442
Housing by the Private and Public Sector Contributions 454
    Housing Status 454
    Housing Development by Joint Efforts 459
    Public Ownership of Housing and Land 461
    Public and Private Partnership 465
Conclusion 469

Chapter 11 Life, Liberty, and the Pursuit of Happiness 473

Interdependence Among Economy, Democracy and Welfare 473
Continued Democratization 474
Continued Economic Development 479
Continued Welfare Services 485
Conclusion 487

Appendix A Percent Central Government Expenditures for Economic Services, Welfare Services, and Physical Quality of Life 489

Bibliography 493

Index 515

Foreword

Most people love a success story, whether in sports, politics, business, or life in general. Few modern-day successes can rival the story that continues to unfold in South Korea. In four decades since the Korean War, South Korea's economy has become a shining example, a regional marvel made so much the brighter when contrasted with the Communist system which pervades neighboring North Korea.

To some extent, stories about politics and economics are told through numbers as well as words. And the numbers on Korea are impressive. Sung Pae's book presents some of the most telling numbers on his native country. But as an "insider," he goes beyond mere statistics to the people, events, and context. He paints a clearer picture of the catalytic forces at work there and looks ahead to what is likely to happen in the future.

As Westerners, we have grown up with an attitude that "Everything's up-to-date in Kansas City, USA." We have always been on the "cutting edge." I believe you will find in Dr. Pae's manuscript a more Eastern view of the world, the global village and marketplace in which we all must move, negotiate, compete, and live. It is at once a more ancient view, yet equally contemporary to our own--and equally relevant.

Dr. Pae presents a "model," implying something which can, and perhaps should, be learned from and emulated. Certainly, there are lessons we can learn and things we can, and probably should, do to be more like the Koreans. Yet Korea is not without warts. The picture of South Korea which the world sees via the media is too often that of a relatively small proportion of its population, oftentimes college students, clambering for instant change in confrontational ways--going toe to toe with what is portrayed as a somewhat rigid and authoritarian government. Dr. Pae's work shows us that this is by no means the whole story.

Change itself is perhaps the definitive reality of our time. South Korea has much to teach about adapting and persevering in a context of rapid social, economic, and political change. The Koreans have shown, and continue to show, great resilience and innovative spirit that has enabled them to come a long way in a short while.

We in the West inhabit the same dynamic world and must be equally innovative and resilient if we are to enjoy a standard of living and a quality of life comparable to our forebears. I hope that readers of this book will glean from it some valuable insights to that end. That, after all, is why we write books, and why we read them.

Dr. John B. Muller
President
Bellevue College

PREFACE

The right to life, liberty, and the pursuit of happiness, the very essence of human endeavor throughout the history of Eastern and Western civilizations, is precisely the cause toward which those civilizations' efforts in economics, democratization, and social welfare are aggressively and energetically bent in both the government and private sectors. But, dedication to these lofty goals notwithstanding, many developing Asian, African, and Latin American nations have been unable to achieve them. In consequence, large numbers of people in many countries are plagued by poverty, hunger, disease, homelessness, and deprivation of basic human rights and civil freedoms.

Amid this despair and loss, South Korea stands out as one of few rapidly developing countries. South Korea raised the per capita annual income from less than $100 in 1960 to $6,300 in 1991 as the outcome of the implementation of a series of successive five-year economic development plans. Her canny investment of human and other resources accelerated industrialization and reduced foreign debts through trade expansion. The agony of annual grain shortages and spring famines has been replaced by agricultural surpluses and the rapid rise of grain storage maintenance costs. Democratization reached a belated climax on June 28, 1987, based upon principles of peaceful transfer of power, civilian control of the armed forces, fair and open partisan competition, majority rule, protection of minorities, and guarantees of basic freedoms and civil rights. During the same brief period, South Korea adopted and implemented comprehensive medical care and significant improvements in pensions, education, and housing through the combined efforts of the private sector and, at a moderate level, the government.

In seeking understanding of the rapid economic development, democratization, and social welfare gains in South Korea, I have found myself torn between the two contending foci of inquiry in the social sciences: the universal and the particular--parsimony and "thick description." Lucian Pye has observed a steady pendulum swing between the two:

> At one time or another most of the fields have experienced the exhilaration of being in possession of elegant formulations promising universalistic knowledge. But then came the process of amendment, elaboration, and qualification to ever-greater complexity. In the end, the only alternative seems to be to seek understanding through in-depth analysis of particular cases; for, as the novelists say, "God is in the details."
>
> In time, however, "thick description" becomes tedious and the mind craves the power and elegance of generalizable theories. Clear logical theories then have their attractions for a while until they lose their charm for being too simplistic and mechanical. It is said that Niels Bohr never trusted a purely formal or mathematical argument. "No, no," he would say. "You are not thinking; you are just being logical." (Pye, 1990: 4)

In my search for a serviceable analytical approach that would advance understanding of the Korean developmental experience, I too have confronted the agony of choosing the one path or the other: whether "the universal or the particular," whether "parsimony or thick description." However, I at last came to realize that these two types of inquiring were not mutually exclusive but rather reinforced one another. Lucian Pye seems to admit as such:

> Healthy advances on two fronts should follow. First, we might expect greater sophistication in the art of describing particular cases, so that there will be fewer attempts to overwhelm with details and more effort given to fitting the details to theoretical concepts of causality. Second, our theory building would have stronger empirical foundations and seem less artificial to those with detailed knowledge of the concrete situations in the particular countries. (Pye, 1990: 14-15)

This book attempts to encompass both lines of inquiries: the first as a cross-national comparative study that seeks parsimony and universalistic knowledge; and the second as an in-depth case study of Korea which is based on detailed empirical data. The first two short introductory chapters examine major characteristics of Koreans--

negative and positive--which have played significant roles for rapid development. Beyond the introduction, the material is divided into three parts, each of which is divided into further chapters. Part I focuses on economic development. The cross-national study in Chapter Three examines to what extent Korea leads developing nations in economic development. Chapter Four explores how Korea leads them and suggests a Korean model of economic development.

Part II examines democratization. Some politicians and scholars insist that the success of democratization in Korea, as well as in many developing countries, must be attributed to the role of the United States. Hence, Chapter Five reviews the American idealistic and moral mission, suggests instead a model of the American role not idealistically but realistically played in developing countries, and examines why the United States would not and could not force the leaders in foreign countries to adopt democracy. A cross-national comparative study in Chapter Six reveals that Korea leads the developing nations in democratization despite the lukewarm attitude of the United States government and a tight grip of the South Korean authoritarian leaders on the pro-democracy citizens and leaders in Korea. The remaining two chapters examine the case of Korea. Chapter Seven explores to what extent Korea has inherited nondemocratic values, norms, and behaviors centered around a patron-client political culture and, nevertheless, cherished a democratic legacy. Chapter Eight suggests a Korean model of democratization on the basis of a "political satellite approach."

Part III deals with social welfare services. Chapter Nine rejects the Furniss and Tilton thesis that a welfare state is far superior to both a corporate-oriented positive state and a social security state in the delivery of welfare services. Chapter Nine rather pursues a cross-national study to compare countries not in terms of the type of state but in terms of the physical quality of life index (PQLI) as the ultimate outcome of the welfare services delivered to the people. A cross-national study reveals that Korea, with a modest percentage of the state expenditures dedicated to social welfare services, has accomplished one of the highest PQLIs among the developing economy-priority states. In fact, Korea has rapidly caught up with the high PQLI enjoyed among the advanced welfare-priority states. Chapter Ten examines how and why Korea became a leading nation and suggests a Korean model of social welfare services. Chapter Eleven concludes with a summary of major points presented in preceding chapters and outlines the prospects for continued economic development, democratization, and delivery of welfare services in Korea.

A number of people should be acknowledged for their contributions and support in making this book a reality. Dr. John B. Muller, President, and Dr. Harold F. Carpenter, Vice President for Academic Affairs, of Bellevue College provided me with generous professional growth funds and continued encouragement from the embryonic stage to the final completion of this manuscript. A ConAgra Distinguished Professorship and research grant enabled me to travel to Korea to collect first-hand data, government documents, and other information not readily available in the United States.

Dr. Kurt V. Rachwitz, an English professor at Bellevue College, kindly agreed to edit the manuscript and offered valuable comments. Many of my friends in the academic community were willing to spend their time and provide me with comments for improvement. They include Dr. Hy Sang Lee, Acting Dean, Graduate School, the University of Wisconsin at Oshkosh, Dr. H. Carl Camp and Dr. Joong Gun Chung at the University of Nebraska at Omaha, Dr. Jong Oh Ra at Hollins College, and Dr. Judd Patton at Bellevue College.

Dr. In Duk Kang, Director of the Institute for East Asian Studies (IEAS) in Korea, kindly allowed me to use the facilities of the institute during my research in Seoul. Miss Eunju Lee, a member of the editorial staff on *East Asian Review* assisted me in collecting data and in securing information on various voluntary contributions to health services by medical professionals in the private sector. Mr. In Hwan Oh, *Korea Time's* editor-in-chief, and Mr. Chul Sun Im, his associate editor, prepared a set of newspaper clips on various subjects related to my research. Dr. William A. Grubb collected the data on the voluntary, free medical treatment and services to needy patients made available by the Keimyung University Medical Center. Admiral James A. Lyons, Commander of the Pacific Fleet, kindly made a copy of his speech available. The Washington Institute for Values in Pulblic Policy kindly approved copyright permission to use parts of my chapter in *Korean Challenges and American Policy* (1991) edited by Ilpyong Kim. Heldref Publications also gave me a copyyright permission to use parts of my article in the Spring 1992 issue of *Asian Affairs*.

Ms. Elizabeth Wall of Bellevue College and Jeanne Pae, with consummate skill at the word processor, shepherded the manuscript through numerous revisions to this final version, which includes many tables and figures. They were ably assisted in their computer and data processing needs by Mr. James Verebely, Mr. Dick Mathews, and Mr. Roy Smith, Jr. Two of my students, Ms. Sharon Mears and Mr. Kevin Cho, assisted me in organizing the tables, figures, and newspaper clips.

Sung Moon Pae
Bellevue, Nebraska
August 1992

Introduction: Characteristics of The Korean People

Since the 1970s, the Republic of Korea (hereafter "Korea," for the sake of simplicity), has been depicted as an economically miraculous country by leaders of both developed and developing nations. During the 1960s and 1970s, Korea overcame various of its major difficulties such as lack of natural resources and insufficient funds for investment, and achieved one of the fastest rates of economic growth anywhere in the world. Korea is now envied by many developing countries and is seen by the developed nations as an emerging "second Japan."

From the beginning of the 1980s, Korea has been striving for democracy and finally established the Sixth Republic in 1988 in accordance with democratic reforms. Democratization has been attended by: constitutional amendments in 1987 that called for direct presidential elections; the subsequent peaceful transfer of power from the Fifth to the Sixth Republic; the popular election of the National Assemblymen; changes in the status of the Legislative and Judicial branches from their traditional roles of subservience to the Executive to that of mutual checks and balances on an equal basis; the promoting of the freedoms of speech, press, assembly, and religion; and the adoption and implementation of various welfare programs including health, housing, pensions, and balanced regional development.

Some have wondered: what are the key motivating factors that have caused Koreans to strive for rapid economic growth, democratization, and the promotion of welfare services? In order to answer that question, the characteristics of the Korean people and culture must be explored and understood from a historical perspective.

The first two chapters, therefore, focus on major characteristics of the Koreans. Chapter One examines to what extent Korean people have characteristics of passiveness and submissiveness, which may be the product of sufferings and humiliation from a series of foreign invasions and subsequent colonization, as most developing countries experienced until the end of World War II. Chapter Two suggests instead that Korean people have determination, perseverance, and dedication that have laid the foundation for economic development, democratization, and delivery of social welfare services.

Chapter 1 Korea as the Land of Morning Calm

The people living in Korea or Choson, meaning the Land of Morning Calm, were characterized by their progenitor, Hwan Ung (Heavenly bear) as being "very gentle, humble, and peace-loving."[1] Ironically, however, Hwan Ung's favorable description could also imply that Korean people lacked aggressiveness, dynamism, and determination. In fact, passiveness and submissiveness have been identified with the Korean people throughout their history.

These alleged characteristics of the Korean people are examined here from three perspectives: (1) a sequence of humiliation and suffering due to numerous foreign invasions, (2) a long period of division of the national territory, and (3) their incorporation into Korean culture as reflected in sculpture, painting, calligraphy, and literature.

Passiveness and Submissiveness Caused by Foreign Invasions

The "gentle, humble, and peace-loving, but passive and submissive" attitudes of the Korean people seem undeniably linked to the suffering and humiliation they have experienced as a consequence of 936 invasions from foreign countries over the past four thousand three hundred years (C. S. Lee, 1983: 16). This long record of vulnerability to the aggressive ambitions of others means that foreign invasions have been inflicted upon the Korean people on the average at least once every 4.6 years. Review of a few salient cases of foreign invasion will serve to highlight the impact of these violent events on Korea in terms of great loss of human life, enormous damage to property, depletion of natural resources, destruction of precious cultural artifacts, and deprivation of the Korean people of freedom, liberty, and self-determination.

Invasions from the North

The first major foreign invasion into the Land of Morning Calm by Yen of the northeastern section of China caused Ancient Choson to lose the territory west of the Liao River in the 3rd century B.C. Later Wi Man, who entered the service of Ancient Choson as a military commander in a base near the Yalu River, drove King Chun to the south and usurped power. Taking advantage of the domestic power struggle in Ancient Choson, Emperor Wu Ti of Han invaded the peninsula in 109 B.C. with an army of sixty thousand men and a navy numbering seven thousand. This brought about the collapse of Ancient Choson (KOIS, 1979: 76).

The second major invasion occurred in 285 A.D. The Hsien-pei tribes of the Manchurian area attacked Puyo. The invaders were initially expelled with the help of the Chinese Chin state, but in 346 A.D., the Hsien-pei tribes made another major attack and overpowered the Puyo defense forces. They carried off 50,000 prisoners including the Puyo leaders and brought an end to Puyo as an independent state (W. K. Han, 1971: 23).

The earlier Yen state also invaded Puyo's neighboring state, Koguryo, and took its capital in 342 A.D. The Queen and her mother were captured, along with the royal treasury, which had contained royal objects handed down from the royal ancestors. Contemporary accounts reveal that "more than 50,000 Korean people were captured and taken away to China" (W.K. Han, 1971: 43).

The invasion of the Khitan tribes (993 A.D.) and the ensuing Mongol invasions of Koryo further led to defeat, submission, and deep humiliation to the Land of Morning Calm. Some of the Khitan tribes who failed to re-establish their kingdom on the Liaotung peninsula because of the resistance from the Mongols fled across the Yalu River into Korea. They indiscriminately pillaged and burned as they made their way to Pyongyang.

The second invasion of Khitan refugees, which occurred in 1218, however, was stopped by the Mongols upon a request for help from Koryo. But, the Mongol demands for compensation for their sacrifices in helping Koryo drive out the Khitan refugees became excessive and unbearable for the Koryo government. Koryo's lukewarm response justified yet another Mongol invasion. The Mongols steadily pressed southward as far as Chungju against some scattered resistance, and General Choe U had no choice but to seek negotiations before the kingdom was completely conquered.

The Mongol peace terms, however, amounted to an unbearable level of reparations: 10,000 otter skins, 20,000 horses, 10,000 bolts of skin, clothing for 1,000,000 soldiers, and numerous Korean children and artisans to be taken as slaves. In order to enforce the terms, the Mongols sent seventy-two officials to be stationed in some of the country's major cities (W. K. Han, 1971: 167).

Although the Koryo government was forced to accept the humiliating terms and to honor the peace treaty, its leaders did not give up the hope of organizing an effective resistance. By 1232, when Mongol supervision relaxed, plans for resistance were put into effect. In order to increase their safety, the Koreans removed the entire court and government to Kanghwa Island off the west coast to be safe from Mongols' relative weak naval forces. The capital city, Kaesong, was also evacuated. The island's coast was fortified with a double wall and all available ships were commandeered for the transportation of supplies from the mainland.

As a result of the preparations, General Sartai of the Mongol forces returned to Koryo. In the ensuing military campaign, Kaesong and the Kingdom north of the Han River were quickly subdued. However, when General Sartai was killed by Kim Yun-ha, the leading Korean monk, who was also a skillful archer, the demoralized Mongol troops began to retreat from the peninsula.

During the four separate invasions between 1235 and 1257, destruction, ransacking and thievery were commonplace: a nine-story pagoda at Hwang Yong-sa Temple was destroyed; thousands of wood blocks used for printing the Buddhist Tripitaka, that were kept at Puin-sa Temple, were burned; all the major cities were ransacked, as were temples and palaces; and many precious works of art and historical documents were stolen (W. K. Han, 1971: 167-68).

Invasions from the South

Since 400 until 1910 Japan undertook a series of piracies along the southern part of the Korean peninsula, which were as rapacious as the northern invasions. Japan finally colonized Korea in 1910 until 1945. Japan first invaded Korea in 400. At that time, Kwang Gaeto, the King of Koguryo in the northern part of Korea, sent an army to Saro (later to be known as Silla), another independent state in the southern part of Korea. The combined forces defeated and drove out the invading army from Japan in an engagement in the Naktong River (W. K. Han, 1971: 44-47).

During the reign of King Kongmin (1351-1372), Koryo faced an increasingly severe problem of Japanese piracy. Many of the people of northern Kyushu and the islands off its coast had turned to piracy. They regularly plundered the coasts of Korea. The raids increased in frequency, territorial extent, and aggressiveness during King Kongmin's reign. The Japanese pirates no longer confined themselves to attacking southern coastal areas but marched overland and sailed up rivers to attack cities as far north as Kongju and Chonju.

When the pirates took towns, they indiscriminately destroyed houses and killed everyone who did not escape. "Farmland was left fallow in many coastal areas, and the transportation of tax grain to the capital was slowed. At one point, the pirates attacked Kanghwa Island, and the court seriously considered transferring the capital to a safer place" (W. K. Han, 1971: 180).

By 1370, Japanese piracy was no longer a matter of hit-and-run raids. Rather, the pirates had established permanent bases, not only on the southern coasts, but also on the coast of the northeastern areas of the Korean peninsula. The Japanese desire to secure grain and natural resources and, in turn, to export their goods became so strong that attempts were renewed to open Korea to Japan by force. In 1875, a Japanese envoy appeared in Tongnae, a southern city near Pusan, carrying formal proposals from the Japanese Emperor. Once again, the local Korean officials turned down the messages, indicating that they were not written in sufficiently respectful terms. That same year, the Japanese battleship *Unyo* and five other naval vessels approached Kanghwa Island. The Japanese delivered an ultimatum: negotiations must begin without delay. The Korean officials were convinced that the rejection of negotiations would cause Korea to face Japan's formidable power. A treaty of amity was reluctantly drawn and signed in Kanghwa Island in February 1876.

The Kanghwa Treaty read that the Korean dynasty called Chosen entered a treaty as a "free and sovereign state on an equal basis with Japan." Additionally, the independence and sovereignty of Korea, free from any interference from the Chinese, were to be guaranteed by Japan. In substance the treaty, however, provided Japan with various advantages.

First, Japan could detach Korea from its traditional relationship with China so as to have a full and free hand in the exploitation of Korea. Second, Japanese merchants were allowed to trade unhindered in three major Korean ports: Pusan, Wonsan, and Inchon. The three ports had been forcefully opened in the period between 1880 to 1883 (see Table 1-1). Consequently, the Japanese merchants, followed by emigrants, flocked to the ports and, in a few years, enjoyed a near monopoly of trade. The Korean merchants suffered serious losses. Third, financial and economic losses were further exacerbated because all articles imported from or exported to Japan were to be free of duty for several years, which made it impossible for Koreans to protect their domestic industries. Fourth, Japanese merchants were also given the right to lease buildings and land for housing and business purposes. Agents of Japanese firms began to acquire Korean properties. Fifth, Japanese nationals in Korea were granted the right of extraterritoriality, which placed them outside the legal jurisdiction of Korean courts (W. K. Han, 1971: 371-78).

Table 1-1 Number of Foreign Commercial Offices as of 1896

Countries	Inchon	Pusan	Wonsan	Total	Percent
Japan	26	132	52	210	81.4
China	46	14	12	42	16.2
Germany	2	0	0	2	0.8
U.S.A.	2	0	0	2	0.8
England	1	0	0	1	0.4
France	1	0	0	1	0.4
Total	78	146	64	258	100.0

Source: W. K. Han (1986: 478)

On the heels of exploitation unleashed under provisions of the Kanghwa Treaty, Japan was determined to gain exclusive control of Korea, first, in competition with China and then with Russia. The Japanese victory in the Sino-Japanese War (1894-1895) enabled Japan to exclude China from the Korean peninsula. Ignoring warnings from Japan, Russians in 1903 crossed the Korean border at Yong Ampo near the mouth of the Yalu River and began to purchase land, construct buildings, and erect telephone lines. On February 8, 1904, Japanese ships opened fire on the Russian warships at Port

Arthur. The Russo-Japanese War (1904-1905) was officially declared on the tenth of February.

The Korean government immediately and vainly declared complete neutrality. Ignoring the claim, Japanese troops landed at Inchon and marched into Seoul. On February 23, 1904, Japan forced the Korean government to sign the Korean-Japanese Protocol. Afterwards, Japan stationed six- and one-half battalions of its armed forces on Korean soil. They proceeded to lay military railways, seized Korean telegraph and telephone networks, and pre-empted land for military purposes. Making use of the Korean territory for military operations, Japan began decisively to defeat Russia. In March of 1905, the strategically important Manchurian city of Mukden finally fell. Russia was not able to send her Baltic fleet all the way to Asia.

The defeat of Russia brought about the exclusion of not only Russia but also of the United States and Britain from Korea. In July of 1905, Japanese Prime Minister Katsura Taro met secretly with William Howard Taft, the American Secretary of War, in Tokyo. The Taft-Katsura Agreement fully recognized Japan's interest in Korea in return for a Japanese promise not to interfere or raise objections over American rule in the Philippines. In August of 1905, a similar agreement was exchanged between Japan and Britain. In the agreement, Britain recognized Japan's full control of Korea and Japan promised to support British rule in India. "In every thing but name," Korea became a "part of the Japanese Empire" (W. K. Han, 1971: 445-47).

In October of 1905, the Japanese presented the Korean government a new agreement which consisted of five articles. The new agreement represented a major step toward Japan's eventual colonization of Korea and its absorption into the Japanese Empire in 1910. The key operational principle evident in all five provisions was Japan's intent to deprive Korea of its sovereign prerogatives in domestic affairs no less than in international relations.

In the international arena, Korean foreign relations were to be controlled and supervised by the Japanese Foreign Affairs Ministry, and the lives and interests of Koreans residing abroad were supposed to be protected by Japanese consuls. The Japanese Ministry was to fulfill the conditions of all existing treaties between Korea and other nations. And, henceforth, Korea was no longer allowed to enter into any new international agreements except through the mediation of Japan. These two provisions raised no doubt that Korea had lost sovereign control over its foreign affairs. The new agreement read that a Japanese Resident-General was to reside in Seoul and could consult the Korean Emperor whenever he deemed it necessary. Japanese commissioners under the Inspector-General's supervision were to reside in the open ports or any other place thought necessary. Overall, the consequences of this agreement included deep humiliation, loss of sovereignty, deprivation of rights and freedoms, and economic deprivation on the part of the Koreans.

In December of 1905, Ito Hirobumi was named Resident-General of Korea. By the end of January 1906, twelve commissioners had assumed their posts--one in Seoul and the rest in the provinces. In March of 1906, when Ito himself arrived, all the foreign legations were withdrawn from Korea, and the Resident-General was fully charged with overseeing foreign relations on behalf of Korea. He was under the direct authority of the Japanese Emperor and empowered to use Japanese troops at his discretion. The Korean armed forces were disbanded. In foreign relations, Ito protected and advanced the interests of Japan instead of Korea.

With the help of an intermediary, U.S. missionary-diplomat Homer B. Hulbert, Emperor Kojong of Korea sent a personal letter to U.S. President Theodore Roosevelt in which he declared the illegitimacy of the Korea-Japan treaty. In June 1907, the emperor also dispatched an emissary to the Hague Peace Conference to expose to the world Japan's aggressive policies. Immediately, the Office of the Resident-General "forced the monarch to abdicate the throne" (KOIS, 1979: 133).

Once it had consolidated its political control, Japan began to pursue a course of economic exploitation in Korea. Japanese merchants, with the support of generous loans from their home government, intruded into the Korean market and expanded their activities. This was evidenced by the increase in the number of Japanese residents: 126,000 in 1908; 210,000 in 1911; and 336,812 by 1919.

The Japanese began an aggressive program of coercive land purchase. They began first in the Honam Plain in Cholla Province, known as the Korean granary, and then expanded their purchases nationwide. After the implementation of a land registration system, they also seized state-owned, unclaimed land and military farms formerly cultivated by the Korean troops. Within a year, the Japanese Oriental Development Company, for example, had seized 30,000 chongbo (75,000 acres) and confiscated land from about

25,000 farmers and 12,000 others who had failed to pay farmland and additional taxes, respectively.

Table 1-2 Amount of "Export" of Rice and Beans to Japan and Their Price Increase in the Market for Korean Consumers (units= thousand *suk** and Mexican$)

	Rice		Bean	
	Export to Japan	Domestic Price for Koreans	Export to Japan	Domestic price for Koreans
Year	Amount %	Price %	Amount %	Price %
1885	9.8 100	15.6 100	28.0 100	28.8 100
1886	8.4 86	12.1 77	46.9 157	51.7 179
1887	67.5 688	90.0 579	304.5 1087	335.4 1164
1888	16.0 163	31.8 139	443.5 1583	471.5 1637
1889	34.5 352	77.5 496	447.3 1597	645.4 2241
1990	374.6 3822	2037.8 13062	659.5 2355	1005.0 3489

Source: Adapted from W. K. (1986: 435)
*One *suk* is equivalent to 4.9626 bushels.

Another way to demonstrate the extent of the exploitation of Koreans can be seen in the amount of Korean rice "exported" to Japan. "Exports" increased from 9,800 *suk* in 1885 (base year=100%) to 374,600 *suk* in 1890, an increase of 3,822.4% over the six year period (see Table 1-2). Still later, in 1912, the rice "export" to Japan accounted for only 4.3 percent of the total production in Korea. By 1933, over fifty percent of total rice production in Korea was delivered to Japan (Han, 1987: Part Seven). At that time, many Koreans suffered from malnutrition and starvation due to shortages of rice and other grain. To make the matters worse, the price of rice and beans invaluable for Korean domestic consumers accelerated geometrically due to the sky-rocketing rate of "exports" to Japan. These developments ruined the Korean economy in general and the lower and middle classes in particular.

Lengthy Period of National Division

The Korean people have long been characterized as "humble, gentle, peace-loving, but submissive, and passive." Throughout much of their history, they have inhabited a territory often invaded and divided. In fact, a historical survey extending from the inception of the Ancient Choson in 2333 B.C. to the present suggests that Korea has been divided for much longer periods of time than it has been unified.

Korea was unified under the Silla Kingdom in 668 A.D. as a single political entity with a common language and culture. However, Silla's unified state secured the territory only up to the southern shore of the Taedong River.

In 935 A.D., during the Koryo Dynasty, Korea's territory was expanded northward beyond the border of the Silla kingdom. But the northeastern part of the Korean peninsula, which is the current area of the Hamgyung provinces and part of North Pyongyang, was not incorporated due to the occupation of the area by the Juchen and Khitan tribes.

Over the span of its four thousand three hundred years, the Yi Dynasty by 1392 A.D. had succeeded in unifying the entire Korean peninsula up to the Yalu River on the west and the Tumen River on the east. Not encompassed, however, was the whole of Manchuria, which was part of the Korean territory under the Koguryo kingdom.

Upon the defeat of Japan by the Allied forces in World War II, Koreans were anxious to recover their independence following thirty-six years of Japanese colonial rule and to see the entire Korean peninsula unified as a single national territory. However, that dream did not come true. On December 1, 1943, at the Cairo Conference, the leaders of the United States, Great Britain, and China agreed that after the surrender of Japan, Korea would become an independent state "in due course" (U.S. DOS, 1951: 10).

At the Yalta Conference, President Roosevelt informally proposed to Stalin on February 8, 1945, a 20 to 30 year trusteeship arrangement for Korea, which provided an indefinite period during which foreign troops would be stationed in the country. The Roosevelt plan, however, did not materialize due to his death on April 12, 1945 (S. S. Cho, 1967: 10).

Similar to events which attended the end of the Sino-Japanese War and the Russo-Japanese War, Korea again became a victim of power politics in the international arena. In the Potsdam Conference that was held on July 29-August 2, 1945, the leaders of the United States, Great Britain and the Soviet Union reached a secret agreement that the Korean peninsula would be divided into two zones along the 38th parallel to facilitate the surrender and disarming of the defeated Japanese military forces. They agreed that the Soviet Union would occupy the northern zone and the United States the southern zone (U.S. DOS, 1947: 3). In accord with this agreement the Soviet Union entered the war against Japan eight days prior to the Japanese surrender and dispatched armed forces to the area north of the 38th parallel.

The United States claimed that the 38th parallel was not intended as a political demarcation but as a temporary expedient to facilitate military operations. Hence, the foreign ministers of the three powers met in Moscow on December 21, 1945. They arrived at an agreement that Korea would become independent after five years under the joint trusteeship of the United States, Great Britain, the Soviet Union, and China. The Joint Commission of the United States and the Soviet Union again convened in Seoul, Korea in March 1946 in order to assist in the establishment of a unified government of Korea (U.S. Congress, 1949: 118-19).

The onset of the Cold War, however, developed stalemate between the U.S. and U.S.S.R. On August 26, 1947, the United States, for example, proposed the re-convening of the Moscow Agreement, but the proposal was rejected by the Soviet Union. Therefore, the United States brought the Korean question to the United Nations. The United Nations finally adopted a United States resolution on November 14, 1947, which stated that a general election would be held under the supervision of a United Nations commission. However, the nine-member United Nations Temporary Commission was not allowed by the Soviet Union to apply the U.N. resolution to the northern part of Korea. On February 26, 1948, the United Nations General Assembly re-affirmed its previous resolution by calling for a general election in areas accessible to the United Nations Commission (Gordenker, 1959: 11-21).

In short, Korea has remained divided and separated for about 3,200 out of 4,300 years, which accounts for slightly less than three quarters of the entire history of Korea.[2]

Passiveness and Submissiveness Reflected in Culture

There is no doubt that the adverse fates of experiencing foreign invasions, division of the national territory, and the subsequent exploitation and suffering have influenced Korean people to have the deep-seated culture of the Land of Morning Calm. That may be characterized as "gentle, humble, peace-loving, harmony-seeking, but submissive and lacking dynamism."

Korean people have had a tendency to lead happy lives despite such unfavorable circumstances and environments. They wanted to live in "deep recesses of unapproachable mountains" and to "immerse themselves in the beauty of their land, their rivers, and the four seasons that visit them every year" (KOIS, 1979: 169) without aggressive pursuit of the expansion of territory, or commerce and trade with foreign countries.

These characteristics were expressed in painting, calligraphy, poetry, and literature. Korean arts, for example, are "clearly distinguished from the strong bold strokes of the continent, or from the dazzling colorations and excessive refinement that mark the art of island nations" (KOIS, 1979: 171). The pale colors which characterize many of Korea's celadons reflect "nothing strong or positive" (KOIS, 1979: 171). They rather mean "something passive or negative." "The magical effect of those strokes and lines seem, at a closer look, to reflect the ardent yearning for the life of the Son In, the hermit, who enjoyed sitting on a rock, seeking harmony with nature, appreciating the landscape of villages and clear skies, and viewing the waterfall" (KOIS, 1979: 171).

Ch'ang, a style of folk singing, also might be characterized as a "voice of crying in agony and sadness. Upon hearing and reading Korean lyrics and writings, foreigners may wonder whether this is not the true characteristics of the people" (KOIS, 1979: 171).

Static rather than dynamic characteristics were also clearly observed in various century-long typical Korean paintings such as "Yangban at home" or "at Sarang bang" (men's living room or quarters), and the "Interior of the Anbang" (women's quarters). Submissiveness and passiveness rather than aggressiveness and energetic endeavors in pursuit of goals might be equally identified in poetry and literature. Kim So-wol's "Azaleas" may depict a typical, passive attitude of Koreans in the past. While hating to see ". . . you leave, weary of me," So-wol continued, "I will quietly let you go . . . . I will bite my lip to stop my tears." So-wol as a typical male Korean, in his mind, might never conceive of the dynamic, passionate attitude of kissing, hugging, and taking a firm grip of his beloved one rather than of quietly letting her leave him. Let me introduce Kim So-wol's "Azaleas" and Han Yong-un's "Mountain Hut" as two poetries characterizing submissiveness and passiveness of the Koreans.

Azaleas

by
Kim So-wol (1903-1934)

When you leave,
weary of me,
I will quietly let you go.

An armful of azaleas
from Yaksan, Yongbyon
I will gather to strew your path.

Tread softly,
Step by step,
Upon the flowers as you go.

When you leave,
Weary of me
I will bite my lip to stop my tears.

Note: "Yaksan, Yongbyon" is a place in North Korea, famous for azaleas in spring.

Mountain Hut
by
Han Yong-un

Forsake this dusty world, they said
And I would achieve oblivion.
So I hewed the crags to build a hut
And delved the rocks to dig a well.

The clouds are entertained as guests,
Who freely come and freely go;
And the moon, although no sentinel,
Keeps watch all night above the gate.

The song of birds my music is,
and the wind among the pines my lyre--
As they were wont from ancient times.

None but my pillow knows
My rue for love of thee, which stays
And haunts me through the sleepless nights.

O solitude of the vacant heights!
Whence do you bring this silent grief?

Rather give me that tranquil grief
Without the song of nightingales!
O solitude of the vacant hills!

Conclusion

Passiveness and submissiveness, reflected in painting, calligraphy, poetry, and literature, characterize the Korean people. These negative characteristics may be rooted in a number of traumatizing events and influences. Paramount among them are: constant foreign invasions from the north and the south, humiliation, human sufferings from the damage of their properties and loss of lives, and a long period of national division. Koreans were not often free of outside influences, nor were they immune from the realities of international power politics. However, as Chapter Two will demonstrate, passiveness and submissiveness do not entirely characterize the Korean people.

Notes

    1. The Tangun mythology was introduced in *Samguk Yusa* (Memorabilia of the Three Kingdoms) which was edited by Il Yun during the reign of King Choong Yol (1274-1308) of Koryo Dynasty. It was translated and annotated by Lee Byung-do (1969). Professor Nae-hyun Yun, on the basis of a study of various Chinese documents, also claimed that the Ancient Choson emerged as a nation-state in the age of bronze culture in which Tangun was the religious and political leader of the nation while feudal lords dominated in local areas. See N. H. Yun (1987).

    2. Korea was ruled under a unified territory for a total 1,100 years: 23 years (676-699) in the Silla Dynasty, 457 years (936-1392) in the Koryo Dynasty, and 519 years (1392-1910) in the Yi Dynasty.

Chapter 2 Korea as the Land of Determination

Korea is no longer considered to be the Land of Morning Calm or the Hermit Kingdom but the Land of Dynamics and Determination. During the 1970s and 1980s, Korea was one of the fastest growing nations in the world. A recent World Bank report witnessed the fact that Korea had accomplished one of the most rapid rates of economic development: "From a position uncomfortably close to the bottom of the international income scale and without the benefit of significant natural resources, Korea embarked on a course of industrial growth that became one of the outstanding success stories in international development" (KOIS, 1979: 463).

The rationale for the description of Korea as the Land of Determination can be seen not only by its record of rapid economic development, but also in the increasingly bold struggle of hundreds of thousands of Koreans--intellectuals, university students, journalists, clergymen, and laymen--for democratization. The desire of Koreans to promote democratization was demonstrated as early as April 1960 by bold and energetic student protests against the dictatorial Rhee regime. In the 1970s, as record economic growth provided relief from the unrelenting struggle for the necessities of survival, larger numbers of Koreans became less consumed by economic concerns and more politically active in the fight for democracy. Of perhaps even greater importance, the republic of the 1980s successfully completed several five-year economic development plans, and has finally entered into the status of a newly industrializing country (NIC). The determination of the people seem reinforced by a rising educational level in which about 98 percent of the population are literate. Moreover, the rising urbanization means that about 70 percent of the population now live in urban areas (Pae, 1986, Ch. 3).

The ever-increasing desire for democracy and protection of human rights has recently been heightened by the struggles of intellectuals, students, and even the mass of middle-class Koreans. These struggles finally reached their climax on June 29, 1987. The outcome was the emergence of a bold, energetic blueprint for democratization which included major amendments to the Constitution that required direct, popular election of the president as well as a host of other democratic reforms.

The Origins of Dynamism and Determination

Throughout much of its history observers have characterized Korea as the Land of Morning Calm, which conjures such imagery as "passive, humble, submissive, static, gentle, and peace-loving." Some may wonder, therefore, how it is possible that Korea could experience spectacular economic growth over the past three decades and now take a giant step toward democracy.

It must be remembered, however, that Koreans have shown the qualities of perseverance, dedication, and determination over the hundreds of years they have struggled, against great odds, for survival. Consequently, they seem equally to merit the characterization as the Land of Determination for they manifest appropriate norms, values, and expectations.[1] These characteristics may be the result of the intermixture of Tangun mythology, Taoism, Confucianism, and Christianity together with the experiences of ordeals and human suffering from endless invasions by foreign powers.

The Tangun mythology provides the Korean people with special meanings and values. The mythology, no matter how unscientific and legendary, has provided the Korean people with a strong sense of national identity and cohesion as a single race speaking the common language of the descendants of Tangun (KOIS, 1979: 169). No matter how severely pained and humiliated the Koreans were made by foreign invasions, they have consistently demonstrated the determination to resist foreign exploitation and humiliation with perseverance, sincerity, and self-determination.

Following the ideals of Taoism, Koreans might have learned the values of patience, simplicity, contentment, and harmony. Buddhism taught Koreans compassion, perseverance, and national defense.[2] Confucianism praised "discipline, hard work, achievement-oriented education, dedication to duty, and responsibility" (I. J. Kim, 1986: xii). And Christianity inculcated among Koreans the values of hard work, aggressiveness, entrepreneurship, and the importance of commerce and trade from an economic point of view. From the political perspective, Christianity taught the Koreans the values of human dignity, equal opportunities, freedom, human rights, and democracy.

Korea's Principal Historical Traits

The Korean people's characteristics of perseverance, commitment, and hard work in the Land of Determination may be examined from the following vantage points: (1) the Korean culture; (2) the history of indefatigable struggles for national defense; (3) the bold enlightenment movements; and (4) the never-ending series of struggles for independence, freedom, and democracy.

Reflections on the Korean Culture

The characteristics of perseverance, faithfulness, loyalty, and aggressiveness may be identified, first of all, in Korean art of painting, calligraphy, and sculpture. Two subjects that frequently appear in paintings and calligraphy throughout a long period of history are the pine and the bamboo trees.

Besides their innate usefulness in meeting daily needs and serving ecological ends, pine and bamboo trees seem to symbolize Koreans. The trees retain green leaves throughout all four seasons, resisting cold temperatures in the winter and hot temperatures in the summer. Similarly, the Korean people have managed to survive harsh periods of suffering and humiliation inflicted upon them by foreign invasions on over 900 occasions. As they have not only survived, but preserved, they have accomplished an economic miracle that may enable them to enhance democracy as well.

Koreans have loved pine and bamboo trees so much that they have been a constant in their art. Professor Yushin Yoo did not exaggerate the importance of these two in the hearts and minds of the Koreans when he stated, "Take the bamboo out of Korean painting. Then half the pictures in the land would be ruined" (Y. Yoo, 1987: 40).

The Rose of Sharon (Hypericum Calcycinum), unlike the evergreens, does not blossom year-round, but it is in bloom for the longest period of time among all wild flowers. They are borne singly at the end of the shoots and appear in profusion over a prolonged period from June to the end of October, from the beginning of summer to the end of fall (Morley, 1970: 45). Surviving over an extended period of time, the Rose of Sharon may equally represent the symbol of perseverance and faithfulness. Therefore, it is accepted as the Korean national flower. The Rose of Sharon, indeed, represents Korea, the land of perseverance and determination.

Perseverance, dynamism, valor and aggressiveness, which characterize Koreans living in the Land of Determination, may also be identified in murals and paintings found in the ancient tombs of the Three Kingdoms period (from 57 B.C. to A.D. 935). Over the period of 700 years, the Three Kingdoms waged war with one another regularly in competition for power and dominance. Adventurous characteristics are clearly in evidence, especially from the people of the Koguryo Kingdom in their fine arts. A few examples, of many, are murals of the "Hunting Scene," the "Dragon God," the "War Horse," the "Four Gods," the "Dance by Three Women," and "Korean Wrestling" (Tae Kwondo).

The ceilings of these tombs are also lavishly decorated with Tae Kwondo duels and figures of fancy animals and cocks, together with symbols of the sun and of the moon. As two stout men engage themselves in a Tae Kwondo duel, which is detail depiction from a Koguryo tomb decoration, Professor Yoo claims that Tae Kwondo is a Koguryo Kingdom-originated self-defense art. These examples clearly show the "masculinity of the powerful Koguryo people" (Y. Yoo, 1987: 102).

Indefatigable Struggles for National Defense

The adventurous spirit of the Koguryo people enabled them to occupy a wide area extending north and south of the Yalu River. They were ultimately able to absorb the entire area of Manchuria into the Koguryo territory.

Kwang-gaeto Wang (391-412 A.D.) was the first King in Koguryo, who launched a military attack on the north while remaining friendly with Silla in the south. He defeated the Hsiao Sin in the northeast and took a number of fortresses and towns in the process, thus extending the power of Koguryo into the Liaotung area. In 400, he also sent troops to aid Silla. In combined operations with Silla's armed forces, he was victorious over invading Japanese forces in an engagement at the Naktong River. Kwang-gaeto Wang means "the king who expanded the country's territory" (W. K. Han, 1987: 45-48 and 64).

During the first six hundred years of the Three Kingdoms period in Korea, China had been politically divided by chronic internal strife. Chinese states and dynasties appeared and disappeared with confusing rapidity. Meanwhile, the Three Kingdoms in Korea were able to consolidate their territories. In 589, however, China was once again united by the Sui Dynasty.

Predicting a Sui attack, Koguryo in 598 A.D. took the initiative and secured the Liao River and its neighboring strategic bases for defensive purposes. As expected, a Chinese force of some 300,000 men attacked Koguryo but the offensive proved to be in vain. When the Sui Emperor Yang Ti succeeded his father Wen Ti, he determined to clear his borders of all states. In 612 A.D., he invaded Koguryo again and marched southward, this time with 1,130,000 troops. The invading column stretched for 1,000 li (about 240 miles). Korean General Ulchi Mun-dok held the Chinese forces at bay on the Liaotung peninsula for several months. Finding he was unable to conquer the Koreans, Emperor Yang Ti supplied 300,000 additional forces for a surprise attack on Pyongyang; however, that attempt failed. As Yang Ti was planning the third surprise attack, General Ulchi Mun-dok ambushed the Chinese forces at the Salsu (now the Chongchon) River and annihilated them. Only 2,700 out of 300,000 Chinese were able to escape.

Following its devastating defeats, the Sui Empire collapsed and was succeeded by the Tang Dynasty. In 644, Emperor Tai-tsung attacked Koguryo with a ground force of 200,000 and a naval force of 43,000. Fierce fighting occurred, especially at the Ahn Si-song fortress, where the siege lasted for sixty days. Ultimate victory again went to Koguryo, this time under the leadership of General Yon Kae-so-mun. Three additional Chinese offensives in 647, 648, and 655 were all repulsed.

Equally aggressive and determined as the Koguryo Kingdom was the Silla Kingdom in the south. One of her most impressive developments was the Hwarangdo (Flower of Youth Corps or Flower of Knights), a military academy of sorts. Handsome and intelligent young men from upper class families were recruited and received not only military training, but also learned Chinese classics, history, philosophy, and religion to foster well-rounded leadership based on Taoism.

The basic objectives of education and training in this academy were: 1) to serve the king with loyalty; 2) to serve one's parents with filial piety; 3) to be faithful to one's friends; 4) not to retreat in battle; and 5) not to kill indiscriminately.[3] It is obvious that these commandments were also derived partly from the Buddhist injunctions against taking life and partly from the Confucian virtues of loyalty, filial piety, and faithfulness.

A spirit of chivalry and patriotism resulted from such education. In time of war, Hwarang members fought valiantly. It was with the influence of the Hwarangdo spirit and the subsequent efforts of Hwarang-educated leaders such as Kim Yu-sin, the military leader, and Kim Chun-chu, later King Muyol that the Korean peninsula was unified for the first time since the Tangun era.

The very same determination to defend the national territory was also observed in the Koryo Kingdom. In 1010, the Liao King led 400,000 troops to the Koryo border. This attack was beaten off by General Yang Kyu. In December 1018, the Liao General Hsiao Pai-ya attempted a second major invasion with an army of 100,000. When the Liao army crossed the Yalu River, it was ambushed by General Kang Kam-chan's troops and badly mauled. Those who managed to escape were then further harassed by General Kang Min-Chom. It was recorded that only a few thousand of the 100,000 Liao troops survived to return home in 1019. That was the final result of thirty years of war.

Perseverance and determination of the Korean people were evidenced not only in their effort to resist military invasion from foreign countries, but also in their prayers for divine protection of their fatherland. Foreign invasions had destroyed not only the national shrines, the royal palace, and libraries, but also natural resources and residential homes. Therefore, the desire for the protection of the kingdom, properties, and lives of the people became heightened. It was the earnest desire of the Buddhist-oriented court to seek divine assistance; thereafter, the immense project of carving wooden blocks and printing some 6,780 volumes about Buddhism was undertaken. In a sense, this project provides a measure of the will to preserve and the depth of dedication to the defense of the fatherland for it took sixty years to complete. The whole undertaking was indeed a great stimulus to the development of the art of printing in Korea and led eventually to the invention of movable metal type in 1234, which preceded Gutenberg's (1450) by some 220 years.

The hand-carved wooden blocks, one for each page of a book, were then kept in Puinsa Temple in Taegu with the sincere prayer for the protection of their fatherland. However, the temple was destroyed during the Mongol invasions between 1233 and 1237, and the blocks and books printed from them vanished.

By 1238, all of Korea except Kanghwa Island was ravaged by a succession of foreign invasions and related depredations. In that year Koreans, in the hope of invoking the protection of Buddhist deities to assist the hard-pressed country, began once more to carve wooden blocks in a project to print the best of all Buddhist scriptures. This is the so-called Tripitaka Koreana. A total of 86,600 large wooden printing blocks, which represent the most outstanding compilation of Buddhist scriptures in the world, was completed in sixteen years. This fiat was accomplished even though the Koryo court took refuge at the Kanghwa Island during the foreign invasions and subsequently experienced severe economic difficulties. The Tripitaka Koreana was preserved in Kanghwa Island until it was moved to the Haeinsa Temple in the late 15th century, where it remains today.

Of course, the act of piety did not bring about the defeat of the Mongols. Instead, Koryo was ultimately forced to be a vassal state. However, one must note the value of perseverance and determination exhibited by those Koreans who, for the protection of their Kingdom, committed a total of 76 years to developing the original blocks and then to restoring them all over again after their complete destruction.

The same kind of perseverance and determination may be equally associated with the giant, stone-carved image of Maitreya Buddha, which consists of two massive pieces of granite more than 15.3 meters in height. The sculpture took 38 years to complete. It was undertaken under the same premise as underlay the hand-carved wooden blocks: the pious hope that protection would be accorded the kingdom by Buddhist deities.

Perseverance, commitment, and persistence of the people of the Land of Determination were similarly reflected in the events that occurred when Toyotomi Hideyoshi of Japan invaded Korea with an army of 150,000 in the spring of 1592. Korea had enjoyed two centuries of peace in which it pursued cultural rather than military activities. The government was not prepared to repel the Japanese forces. Most farmers gained exemption from military service by paying an in-kind tax with textiles, whereas most soldiers were employed on public works and had little real military training. Some active units were deployed to guard the northern border and others to repel Japanese pirates in the south, but there were no full-scale field forces. Furthermore, Korea did not possess the technology for manufacturing muskets and firearms at this time.

Subjected to surprise attack, outnumbered, and daunted by the Japanese use of firearms, the garrison in the southern port city of Pusan quickly fell. Within two weeks, Seoul followed in defeat. Although outnumbered by the better equipped Japanese regular forces with their modern weapons of gunpowder and firearms, the Koreans were still determined to resist the Japanese forces by means of guerrilla warfare. In defense of their territory, they relied upon swords, bows, arrows, and spears.

Led by Confucian scholars and Buddhist monks, voluntary guerrilla forces sprang up all over the country. The list of these patriotic leaders is too long to be listed here, but a selected list of these outstanding men would surely include: Kwak Chae-u, who defeated enemy troops in Kyongsang Province and recovered the Chinju fortress; Ko Kyong-myong, who led a guerrilla force in Cholla Province and died fighting at the Kumsan fortress; Cho Hon, who, together with the Buddhist leader Yong Gyu, drove the enemy out of Chongju and died at Kumsan; the aged Buddhist monk, Hyu Jong, who rallied all the monks of Pyongan Province into a fighting force and recaptured Pyongyang, while another leading Buddhist monk, Yoo Jong, fought the Japanese forces in Mt. Kumgang; and General Kwon Yul, who was besieged in the mountain fortress of Haengju near Seoul but beat off numerous attacks and inflicted heavy casualties on the Japanese invaders.

Plagued by the mounting guerrilla resistance offered by the Koreans, the Japanese sought a peace agreement. However, the negotiations failed to produce a settlement. Therefore, Hideyoshi launched another major invasion in 1597. This time he was repelled by the Korean naval forces led by Admiral Yi Sun-shin.

Admiral Yi's victories were attributed partly to his ingenious tactics and partly to the first ironclad warship in history. The *Kobukson* was constructed in the shape of a turtle. Admiral Yi's tactics were threefold: first, to hit and destroy the Japanese fleet; second, to exterminate additional Japanese vessels that stood as reinforcements off Hansan Island; and, finally, to destroy the Japanese troops when they began to withdraw from Korea.

Perseverance, commitment, and persistence can be seen as salient characteristics of the residents of the Land of Determination in the resistance offered by the Koreans ranging from intellectuals to the grassroots population against the Japanese annexation of Korea. Manifestations of resistance to foreign domination date from the Sino-Japanese War (1894-1895) and the Russo-Japanese War (1904-

1905) right on into World War II era, which ended in 1945. During this Korean "dark age," the Japanese made every effort to erase any trace of Korean national identity by pursuing such demeaning and humiliating policies as: forcing the Koreans to worship the Japanese Shinto god in 1937; adopting the so-called voluntary military service system and coercively mobilizing Korean youth in 1938; prohibiting the study of Korean history and the Korean national language; forcing the Korean children to learn the Japanese language at school and correspondingly punishing those who used their native language in conversation among themselves in 1939; requiring the Koreans to substitute Japanese names for all personal Korean names in 1939; burning all the books written in Korean; suppressing the freedoms of speech, press, assembly, and religion; closing the Korean daily newspapers, including the *Dong-A* and the *Choson*; and mobilizing Korean males into forced labor in mines, manufacturing factories, and military construction. By the end of the war, 2,616,900 Koreans were engaged in forced labor, while 723,900 were sent abroad. Additionally, in 1942, Korean men were conscripted into the Japanese army.

The coercive means of control and suppression of Koreans by the Japanese were further documented by the ever-increasing number of police, military police, and military civilian police in Korea. They were distributed among 640 civilian and 480 military stations. By 1914, the number of military stations had increased to 528, whereas the number of civilian police stations had declined to 108. The number of police officers increased from 1,120 in 1910 to 1,825 in 1918. Beginning in 1906, one- and one-half infantry divisions of the regular Japanese army were stationed in Korea on a rotation basis. This contingent was increased to two divisions in 1915. These police and military forces were held responsible for implementing a series of repressive policies, among them: the Peace Law (1907), outlawing independence movements of the Koreans; the Assembly Control Act (1910), prohibiting nationalist movement assemblies; and the Guns and Ammunition Control Act (1912), denying the possession of weapons by Koreans. However, the mighty force and legal restrictions of the Japanese could not control the spirit of determination and commitment to freedom and independence indefatigably pursued by the Koreans.

Determined Enlightenment Movements

Over the years, the Korean people had been inculcated with the principles of self-determination, independence, and democracy by a variety of bold and energetic enlightenment movements. Of special note is the important role of newspapers as one of the major agents for enlightenment. The first regular newspaper that appeared in 1883 was the *Hwangson Sunbo*. It was followed by the *Independent* that was sponsored by the Independence Association. This newspaper made a significant contribution to "fostering among the Koreans a spirit of independence and democracy," to "making them aware of civil rights," and to "creating a spirit of nationalism" (Han, 1987: 454). Equally aggressive and determined to enlighten the Korean people were *The Hwangsong News* (1898), *The Imperial News* (1898), and *The Taehan Daily News* (1905).

Newspapers were aided in the task of developing the national consciousness and the desire for freedom with the appearance of a number of political organizations dedicated to the study and dissemination of democratic ideals and resistance to the Japanese. The Constitutional Government Research Body that was established in 1905 endeavored to extend civil rights. The Korean Struggle Society that appeared in April 1906 challenged pro-Japanese organizations. The Struggle Group of 1907 inspired a true mass movement against the Japanese. Sinminhoe (New People's Society) of 1910 and Kugminhoe (People's Assembly) were engaged in cultivating nationalism in education, business, and culture.

Equally significant in the contribution to enlightenment movements was the establishment of modern educational institutions. Credit should go to many American missionaries who established schools following American models. Paejae Boys' School was the first modern high school in Korea. It was followed by Ehwa Girls' School and Kyongsin Boys' School in Seoul and a host of schools in other major cities. They were made available to students without regard to class or status, and began to educate young Koreans on modern subjects such as ethics, history, geography, law, economics, and mathematics as well as the spirit of democratic independence. Many Korean leaders who were blocked in direct efforts to resist the Japanese during the years from 1905 (the New Agreement concluded) to 1910 (the annexation implemented) began to turn to education as a means of fostering the national spirit. Thus, numerous schools were established. In 1905, Posong, Yangjong, and Hwimun

Schools were founded in Seoul, as many schools were established in other major cities as well. By 1910, some 3,000 private schools had been established.

A significant result of these educational endeavors was that a number of studies were published about Korean language and culture, the American and French revolutions, the rise and fall of nationalism and the exposure to foreign civilization, and biographies of national heroes. These efforts enhanced the stubborn determination of Koreans to fight for national independence, life, liberty, and the pursuit of happiness.

Korean determination was further encouraged by the famous speech of President Woodrow Wilson to the U.S. Congress on January 8, 1918. Among the Fourteen Points that deeply touched the minds of the Koreans was the principle of "self-determination of people." "An evident principle," which "runs through the whole program," he outlined, was that "of justice to all people and nationalities, and of their right to live in equal terms of liberty and safety with one another whether they be strong or weak." His principle of self-determination refers to: "Free open-minded, and absolutely impartial adjustment of all colonial claims, based upon a strict observance of the principle that in determining all such questions of sovereignty the interests of the populations concerned must have equal weight with the equitable claims of the government whose title is to be determined" (*The New York Times*, January 9, 1918: 1).

Commitment to Struggles for Independence

Enlightened by the educated leaders through newspapers, schools, mass rallies, and organized groups, and heartened by Wilson's declaration of self-determination, Koreans began to join popular resistance to Japanese rule. They were led by various leaders in many regions such as Choe Ik-hyon in protest spread to Kyongsang and Kangwon Provinces against the Kanghwa Treaty of 1876; and, Min Chong-sik in North Choong Chong Province with a force of about five hundred men and seventy-five old cannons in the spring of 1906. The rebels quickly spread to many different provinces and received considerable support from the people. They continued to harass the Japanese throughout 1907 and into 1908. However, they were unable to match the well-armed Japanese in pitched battles. Therefore, they confined their efforts to guerrilla warfare. In the end, many of them crossed the border into Manchuria to continue their war against the Japanese there.

Korean popular resistance was not limited to Korea and Manchuria. A surprise demonstration occurred even in Japan on February 8, 1919. As impossible as Salman Rushdie attending the Ayatollah's birthday party, about 600 Korean students who were studying in Japan gathered at the Korean Y.M.C.A. in Tokyo and attempted to present a manifesto proclaiming Korean independence from the Japanese government. They were immediately overpowered by the Japanese police.

Until March 1, 1919, Japanese authority had assumed that "the Koreans were a spiritless people lacking the intelligence, energy, and determination" to fight for independence and self-determination. Therefore, the Japanese believed that there might be at best minor protests such as those by a few Confucian scholars in 1876, the Korean soldiers in 1882, or the Tonghak in 1894 for the purpose of championing specific limited interests. But, they were confident there would be no major nationwide protests. Who would dare challenge the mighty power of Japan with mere fists and spears?

Their naive assumption turned out to be wrong. On March 1, 1919, thirty-three leaders risked their lives by signing their names to the Declaration of Independence. They proclaimed that Korea had the right to exist as a free and independent nation, and that she had been forcefully annexed to Japan unjustly and against her will. Inspired by the declaration and influenced by the leaders, demonstrators assembled in Pagoda Park. Copies of the Declaration were printed and sent all over Korea and also to the Paris Peace Conference, to the President of the United States, and even to the government of Japan. What was truly unbelievable was that: the signers of the declaration made no attempt to hide; the demonstrators embraced people of all classes, occupations, ages, and sexes; they marched into the streets not only in Seoul but in every community in Korea; the demonstration was an act of peaceful civil disobedience in which no armed revolt, resistance, or violence had been planned or waged; and Koreans began to envision a modern, independent state with a democratic government which would guarantee personal freedom.

The Japanese were shocked and frightened by the nationwide civil demonstrations. They began to fire into unarmed crowds and indiscriminately killed and wounded many civilians. It was estimated that about two million Koreans took part in some 1,500 demonstrations; about 7,000 were killed and 15,000 wounded; about 715 private houses, 47 churches and two school buildings were destroyed; about 46,000 people were arrested and 10,000 of them, including 186 women, were tried and convicted (see Table 2-1). "People in every occupation were involved in the uprisings as a truly national movement" (Y. S. Kim, 1983: 50).

Table 2-1 Number of Participants in the March 1st Movement, Casualties, and Punishments

Province	Number of Demonstrations	Number of Participants (1,000)	Number Killed	Number Wounded	Number Arrested	Church	School	House
Kyunggi	297	666	1,472	3,142	4,680	15		
Hwanghae	115	63	238	414	4,218	1		
Pyongan	315	515	2,042	3,665	11,610	26	2	684
Hamkyung	101	59	135	667	6,215	2		
Kangwon	57	99,	144	645	1,360			15
Chung Chung	154	121	590	1,116	5,233			
Cholla	222	249	384	767	2,900			
Kyongsang	228	154,	2,470	5,295	10,085	3		16
Kando & Hwatae (China)	51	489	34	157	5			
Total	1,548	2,021	7,509	15,850	46,306	47	2	715

Source: Han (1987: 530)

The very same determination to demonstrate a spirit of national unity and pride and to resist exploitation and inhumane treatment was also witnessed ten years after the Independence Movement in October 30, 1929. In Kwangju, South Cholla Province, a group of Japanese students attempted to force their attentions on some Korean girls. Korean boys dared to come to their defense. The Japanese police who intervened, however, arrested the Koreans and released the Japanese students unpunished. The news spread quickly throughout the entire city of Kwangju and practically every Korean student in the city participated in demonstrations. Sympathetic demonstrations spread like wildfire across the whole country. Disorder lasted for five months and involved 54,000 students from 194 schools. About 1,642 of them were imprisoned, 2,330 were suspended from school indefinitely, and 582 were permanently expelled (Han, 1987: 487).

The stubborn determination to fight for independence, freedom, and democracy could be observed not only from collective, popular uprisings and resistance but also in the behavior of many individual heroes on different occasions.

1. When Emperor Kojong was coerced to sign the second Korea-Japan Agreement on November 17, 1905, which deprived Korea of national sovereignty in diplomatic relations with foreign countries, Min Yong-hwan could not be content with mere protests. He preferred suicide to living under the Japanese rule.

2. The Korean consul to Great Britain, Yi Han-ung also committed suicide as a protest against the Agreement.

3. Yi Chun and two other delegates were sent as envoys secretly to plead Korea's cause in the second World Peace Conference to be held at The Hague in 1907. However, they were denied permission to participate in the conference as representatives of Korea on the grounds that Korea had no rights to diplomatic representation. In protest against the loss of national sovereignty and the denial of an opportunity to denounce Japan as an aggressor before the delegates at the conference, Yi Chun committed suicide.

4. In 1908, in San Francisco, Chon Myong-un and Chang In-hwan shot and killed D. W. Stevens, an American who had been employed by the Japanese in setting up the Resident-General's government and had thereafter praised the Japanese control of Korea.

5. On October 26, 1906, at the Harbin railroad station, An Chung-gun assassinated Ito Hirobumi, the elder statesman who had master-minded the Japanese takeover and become the first Resident-General in Seoul.

6. Yu Kwan-sun, a young student, led her fellow women compatriots in the Independence Movement and died in prison in 1920 at the age of 17 following the most inhumane treatment by the Japanese police.

7. In 1932, Yi Bong-chang attempted to assassinate the Japanese Emperor who walked out of his palace in Tokyo to receive a military parade.

8. In April 1932, in Shanghai, Yun Bong-gil threw bombs at Japanese army generals performing a ritual and caused casualties.

Now facing overt and widening opposition, the Japanese plan to assimilate Korea into the Japanese Empire was intensified. Japanese officials prohibited the publication of 142 articles and 96 editorials in Korean newspapers during 1929 and 1930. They overwhelmed the Korean-run magazines by establishing 582 Japanese-run counterparts. The Japanese authorities suppressed summer schools, which taught and encouraged the use of Hangul, the Korean language. They dissolved the Chindan Hakhoe (Korean Academic Society), which was organized by Korean scholars for the express purpose of conducting and publishing research on Korean history. However, after 36 years of Japanese colonial imperialism, the Korean culture emerged intact despite Japan's intense efforts to obliterate it. That it survived is due mainly to "its durability and stubborn loyalty" and "determination of the Korean people" to preserve their identity, independence, and culture.

Korea's strong determination was recently demonstrated in sports. In the 1976 Summer Olympics, for example, Korea achieved distinction as the 19th-ranked nation in terms of the number of medals received (see Table 2-2). Thereby, Korea exceeded not only all of the developing countries of the Third World but also many developed countries including Switzerland, Norway, Denmark, Australia, and Canada. However, in the 1988 Summer Olympics Korea rose to the fourth place in the ranking. This feat surprised people of many countries as well as the Koreans themselves.

As a consequence of the nation's rapid economic growth, Koreans of the 1980s could enjoy plentiful and nutritious food. They also began to emphasize sports and physical fitness. The Korean government expended an impressive sum of money to build the highly sophisticated sports complexes for the 1988 Summer Olympics in Seoul. According to a correspondent of *The Chinese People's Daily* who visited Korea during the 1988 Seoul Olympics, all of the elementary and high schools in Korea were equipped with playgrounds and sports facilities. He also commented on the many tennis courts and public parks in convenient locations where children and the general public enjoyed exercising (*Korea Times,* October 8, 1988). Upon being asked if the Korean girls' handball team's gold medal was the result of sheer luck, the coach replied:

Korea Leading Developing Nations

Table 2-2 Medal Standings of Summer Olympics

1976					1988				
Country	Ranking	G	S	B*	Country	Ranking	G	S	B
USSR	1st	47	43	35	USSR	1st	55	31	46
E. Ger.	2nd	40	25	25	E. Ger.	2nd	37	35	30
U.S.A.	3rd	34	35	25	USA	3rd	36	31	27
W. Ger.	4th	10	12	17	**S. Korea**	**4th**	**12**	**10**	**11**
Japan	5th	9	6	10	W. Ger.	5th	11	14	15
Poland	6th	8	6	11	Hungary	6th	11	6	6
Bulgaria	7th	7	8	9	Bulgaria	7th	10	12	13
Cuba	8th	6	4	3	Romania	8th	7	11	6
Romania	9th	4	9	14	France	9th	6	4	6
Hungary	10th	4	5	12	Italy	10th	6	4	4
Finland	11th	4	2	0	China	11th	5	11	12
Sweden	12th	4	1	0	Britain	12th	5	10	9
Britain	13rd	3	5	5	Kenya	13th	5	2	2
Italy	14th	2	7	4	Japan	14th	4	3	7
France	15th	2	2	5	Austral.	15th	3	6	5
Yugo.	16th	2	3	5	Yugo.	16th	3	4	5
Czecho.	17th	2	2	4	Czecho.	17th	3	3	2
N. Zeal.	18th	2	1	1	N. Zeal.	18th	3	2	8
S. Korea	**19th**	**1**	**1**	**4**	Canada	19th	3	2	5
Switzer.	20th	1	1	2	Poland	20th	2	5	9
Jamaica	21st	1	1	0	Norway	21st	2	3	0
N. Korea	22nd	1	1	0	Nether.	22nd	2	2	5
Norway	23rd	1	1	0	Denmark	23rd	2	1	1
Denmark	24th	1	0	2	Brazil	24th	1	2	3
Mexico	25th	1	0	1	Finland	25th	1	1	2
Trinidad	26th	1	0	0	Spain	26th	1	1	2
Austral.	27th	0	1	4	Turkey	27th	1	1	0
Canada	28th	0	5	6	Morocco	28th	1	0	2
Nether.	29th	0	2	3	Portugal	29th	1	0	0
Brazil	30th	0	0	2	Austria	30th	1	0	0
Total	88 Countries					161 Countries			

Source: *The World Almanac and Book of Facts* (1989: 862); *Korea Times* (October 1, 1988)
*G, S and B stand for gold, silver, and bronze medals.

Since we were defeated by the Soviet Union in the 1984 Los Angeles Olympic game, we have been constantly haunted day and night by the sense of humiliation. Dwarfed and overwhelmed by the Russian girls in size, height, and physical strength, we have yet never given in. Strong determination to win, which we have inherited from the time immemorial, has encouraged us to keep in practice several thousand times, preparing for the 1988 Seoul Olympics. I believe we outnumber the Russian counterpart in practices. Practice makes perfect. There is no luck (*Korea Times,* October 1, 1988).

Conclusion

People of every nation-state have negative and positive cultural characteristics. Koreans have both, too. Properly motivated and stimulated by domestic and external challenges, Koreans began to minimize negative characteristics and maximize positive cultural characteristics to modernize their economy, democratize their century-old authoritarian political system, and enhance welfare services. A correct understanding of positive national characteristics such as perseverance, dedication, determination, value of education and inquiry, and hard work helps readers grasp the reasons why Korea leads the world's developing nations in economic growth, democratization, and welfare services.

Notes

1. There is a school of thought which suggests a hypothesis that submissive and passive characteristics may not be the "original traits" inherited in the Korean people, see KOIS (1979: 173).

2. Buddhism came to Korea as early as 372 A.D. The Confucian classics entered the peninsula during the era of Three Kingdoms by the fourth century A.D. Christianity began to spread among the Yangban during Chongjo's reign (1776-1800). For detailed discussion on the impact of religion on the Korean culture, see KOIS (1979: 190-210).

3. The five commandments were included in a book called *Sesok Ogye* (Five Commandments), which was written by the monk Won Gwang Popsa.

Part I Economic Development

Introductory chapters have examined the proposition that Koreans, on the one hand, have humble, gentle, and peaceful characteristics as well as passive and submissive ones from the influences generated by frequent foreign invasions and exploitation. On the other hand, however, they often display such characteristics as perseverance, dedication to national defense, loyalty, discipline, and determination for achievement. These norms, values, and expectations, which were originated from the Tangun mythology, Taoism, Buddhism, Confucianism, and Christianity, are reflected in the Korean culture--in its paintings, sculpture, art, and sports. The dynamic qualities have been further reinforced throughout Korea's history of indefatigable struggles for national defense, enlightenment movements for the masses, and struggles for independence and freedom.

At the inception of the Republic of Korea in 1948, Koreans have continued to exert the very same dedication and determination, but in the post-World War II era in the pursuit of economic development, democracy, and welfare services. Part I of this study inquires into the extent to which Korean determination, dedication, and hard work have been invested in a variety of development strategies. As Jon Woronoff pointed out in his book, *Korea's Economy (1983: 9)*, the Korean economy was by no means perfect. The Koreans made mistakes but changed policies accordingly to "get more things right than wrong. . . . Seen in this light, Korea's economic growth unquestionably was a miracle!" Woronoff used four criteria to measure the economic miracle in Korea. They are height (quantitative growth), breadth (diversification), depth (accumulation of wealth and the ability to pay foreign loans), and time (the fastest growth rate in a short period of time).

In Chapter Three the question to be examined is the extent to which developing countries in the 1960s, 1970s and 1980s experienced economic decline, stagnation, or slow growth, while Korea led them in all categories of growth. In Chapter Four a Korean model of economic growth is presented and answers are sought to the question of how Korea has successfully, and successively, passed through each stage of economic development.

Chapter 3 Korea: Leader of the Nations in Economy

The Gloomy Economic Outlook for Third World Countries

England was claimed the harbinger for the epoch of modern economic growth on the basis of the advance of science and technology during the last quarter of the nineteenth century. The United States soon achieved a similar pattern of growth. They were then respectively followed by Germany, Canada, and Japan. In the early twentieth century, the Soviet Union and Eastern Europe joined them. The baton recently was passed over to the countries of the Third World. Those countries which started the economic race early in the nineteenth century have already reached an advanced economy like Rostow's High Mass-Consumption Stage, whereas, among the later starting countries, some have entered into the Take-off Stage, others in the Pre-Take-off, and some still lagging behind in the Traditional Stage.

The conventional theory suggests that economic development is a linear progress in which every economy--regardless of the economic and political systems--has to pass through the sequential stages of growth. Despite the facts that the pace of passing through those stages varies from state to state and that the stage theory incorporates negative stages, namely, retrogression, no state can bypass the sequence of stages. The rationale is that one economic stage becomes a prerequisite for the next higher stage (Rostow, 1960).

To the conventional theorist, the developed countries have progressed ahead of their counterparts of the Third World because of dedication, hard-work, advances in science and technology, better management skills, investments, and the promotion of trade. But developing countries of today lack these requisites. However, if developing countries can correct their domestic deficiencies and make up the gap in these requisites, coupled with foreign aid, investment, and technical assistance, then their economies will grow. The conventional theory focuses on the factors primarily indigenous to Third World nations in relation to international comparative advantage in their efforts to understand the impediments to economic development, and recommends ways of overcoming them.

The radical theory, on the other hand, attributes the causes of underdevelopment and economic stagnation of Third World nations less to their domestic economic and social problems and more to their relationships with advanced capitalist countries of the North. The world is, according to this theory, divided into "core," "semi-periphery," and "periphery" in a hierarchical order. Hence, one global economic system, with advanced countries on the top as the core and Third World nations on the bottom as the periphery, is causally connected in a global division of labor. Therefore, underdevelopment is not a temporary stage which the developing countries can pass through, but they are structured to be permanently penetrated by and dependent on the advanced core countries.

The radical school of thought casts doubts on the conventional theory's basic assumption that there is essential similarity between the developmental problems of the poor countries today and the problems successfully coped with by the now-rich in earlier periods. To the radical, the people of the North have achieved prosperity, "not by the laws of the market, but by a particular sequence of World conquest and land occupation" (Ward, D'Anjou, and Runnals, 1971: 152-64). Underdeveloped countries have been robbed of their land, natural resources, and other primary products. Therefore, upon the heels of exploitation, the Third World countries of today have additional causes for economic stagnation or slow growth. They include: 1) the entrance into the world economic race of the poor countries as mere "subsystems of global capitalism," 2) their subsequent destiny to forcefully become "economic satellites" of the rich; 3) having only one or few major primary products for export; 4) disadvantageous terms of trade; 5) the erosion of productivity gains; 6) demand inelasticity of their primary products; 7) remote possibility to duplicate the OPEC's one-time cartel implementation, 8) financial dependency on foreign banks and international monetary banks, a mounting debt burden, and the subsequent drain of money into the current account deficit on the merchandise balance of trade, resulting in endlessly borrowing money from Peter to pay Paul part of principal and interest in the international money market; and 9) further encroachment upon domestic economy by foreign investment.[1] Let us briefly examine these factors which may explain the gloomy economic outlook for the Third World countries.

Economic Satellites

Developing countries complain that the economies of the advanced capitalist states embarked on their growth in the nineteenth century under domestic control of their respective markets relatively autonomously and independently of foreign economic forces. In this century, the Third World nations, which belatedly attempt to pursue economic development, become aware of the fact that they have already been deeply penetrated by foreign interests, becoming economic satellites of the dominant capitalists of the North. For example, the countries in Latin America, Africa, and Asia are inevitably forced into dependency economies: they export primary products such as minerals, lumber, rubber, and grain and, in return, import products manufactured by the advanced countries.

This pattern persists today as a general description of the structure of trade relationships between developed and developing nations. In 1980, the developing nations as a whole relied on the export of primary agricultural products and mineral resources including fuel for 79 percent of their export earnings. The developed nations depended on primary products for only 24 percent of their earnings. Inversely, manufactured products of the developing countries accounted for only 20 percent of their total exports, while those of the developed nations explained 75 percent (Lewis and Kallab, 1983: 248). Once their economy becomes foreign-oriented and dependent on the advanced countries, it becomes unlikely that they can escape from dependency and pursue their own independent economic development.

One or Two Export Items vs. Diverse Import Items

Many developing countries have a single export commodity: coffee, for example, accounts for nearly 90 percent, 70 percent, and 51 percent of the total exports of Burundi, Rwanda, and Colombia, respectively; alumina explains 50 percent for Jamaica; sugar 63 percent for Mauritius; copper 89 percent for Zambia; live animals 85 percent for Somalia; petroleum 100 percent for Saudi Arabia, 97 percent for Iran and Libya, 90 percent for Venezuela.

Countries whose exports of two raw materials explain more than 50 percent of their total exports are Burma (rice and teak), Mauritania (iron ore and fish), Zaire (copper and coffee), Bolivia (natural gas and tin), Costa Rica (coffee and banana), Dominican Republic (sugar and coffee), Jamaica (alumina and bauxite), and Bangladesh (jute and jute goods).[2]

While the value of the primary products exported by developing countries declines or remains at best the same, the types of manufactured import products become more diverse and sophisticated, and range from daily necessities such as clothes, footwear, radios and transistors to more expensive, luxurious items, such as color T.V.s, stereos, VCRs, computers, automobiles, refrigerators, air-conditioners, and others. This results in an increased trade deficit as there is decrease in purchasing power of a limited number of primary products in their exports for the import of more diverse and more expensive manufactured products from the advanced countries. In order to enhance the balance of payments, the developing countries have no other options but to increase the quantity of their primary products as a desperate measure to reduce the trade gap.

The Terms of Trade

A deficit in the balance of payments and the shortage of foreign currency often tend to encourage the developing countries of the same primary products to increase the quantity of the products without consideration of the formation of agreement like a cartel.

The consequence is the wild fluctuation in the price of such primary products as rubber from Southeast Asia, oil from the Middle East countries, and coffee and fruits from Latin American countries. This inevitably results in "price decay." The period between 1950 and 1986 saw a steady decline in real prices for nonfuel primary commodities. The prices for foods declined from the index of 155 in 1950 to less than 80 in 1986. Metals and minerals had a similar decline in their prices. Nonfood agricultural commodities fell in their prices to record lows from the index of 275 in 1950 to 80 in 1986. This shows more than 5.19 times as much decline (see Figure 3-1).

The World Bank identified four main reasons for the price decline of primary products. They are: the weakening demand for commodities in the industrial states, especially for agricultural raw

Figure 3-1 An Index of Third World Primary Product Export Prices Measured against Industrial Product Import Prices, 1950-1986

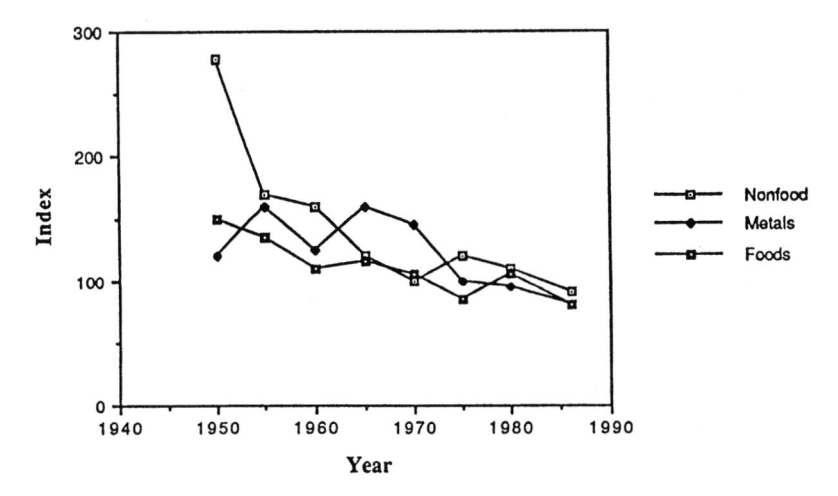

Source: The World Bank (1987: 17)

materials and metals; the over-expansion of supply in several important raw materials; the domestic agricultural price support programs of the industrial states and the subsequent outcome of large surpluses; and changes in taste, increased use of synthetic substitutes, and the production processes which become increasingly less intensive in raw materials (The World Bank, 1987: 17-18).

While primary product export prices vary erratically in the short-run and fall in the long-run (see Figure 3-1), manufactured product import prices tend to rise steadily. Measured as the ratio of export value divided by import value which is called "terms of trade," the World Bank has suggested an "unstable boom-and-bust cycle" in the short-run and a "steadily deteriorating disadvantage" of the primary product countries in the long-run.[3]

Erosion of Productivity Gains

Productivity gains refer to the increase in the quantity of production of export items with the level of labor force remaining the same or reduced. Saving in production cost is the key to economic growth, resulting in higher wages and higher living standards. However, in many developing countries productivity gains are not able to exceed price decays. This situation is exemplified as follows:

> Malaysia, for example, increased its rubber exports almost 25 percent from 1960 to 1968--from 850 to 1,100 thousand tons--while reducing its plantation labor force significantly. This is a notable gain in productivity. But its income from rubber sales declined by about 33 percent during these years as prices fell (Jones, 1985: 205).

Price erosion is further exacerbated by the continued increase of productivity gains because the increased quantity in export leads to additional declines in prices. Productivity gains also call for a reduction in the number of employees, thereby at least temporarily contributing to the increase in the number of the unemployed and the underemployed in developing countries.

Demand Inelasticity Against Cartel Formation

Demand inelasticity is another major disadvantage of primary products against manufactured goods. Once the foreign markets are saturated, no additional primary products such as bananas or apples will be exported. Nor can they be stored for an extended period of time. A mere increase in the production of the same primary goods among the developing countries causes reduction of prices, thereby benefiting only foreign consumers.

The only way to get rid of demand inelasticity is to form a cartel to control the amount of production and to increase the price of the primary products. An outstanding example of success is the Organization of Petroleum Exporting Countries (OPEC). The OPEC member nations were able to reach an agreement on pricing and production policies. The cartel resulted in raising the world price of crude oil more than 900 percent between 1973 and 1982. Consequently petroleum exporters were able to accumulate huge and unprecedented financial surplus.

Since 1980, however, the cartel has been unsuccessful. One may wonder, then, how OPEC was very successful during the periods of 1973 and 1979 and why it failed thereafter to restrict production level and to maintain or raise the price.

The success of the OPEC cartel may be attributed to several favorable conditions (Krasner, 1974: 68-90). Oil was a very special commodity. It was the energy foundation for everything in the advanced countries--manufacturing plants, transportation, offices, military operations, and a vast number of average households. Since substitutes for oil were not readily available, the demand for petroleum became absolute and, therefore, relatively unresponsive to the price increases. Price elasticity of demand became the key condition for the OPEC's successful cartel.

The relatively small number of producers became another condition for mutual cooperation. Sharing a sense of mutual interdependence and accepting short-term sacrifices for long-term gains, the members became collusive, while the petroleum consuming countries were not cohesive for effective collective countermeasures.

These positive conditions were favorably available to the OPEC members from 1972 to 1979, but began to gradually erode. Advanced states became clearly aware of the long-term effect of the oil embargo and began to take a range of measures to alleviate the ever-increasing level of "strangulation." They began to expand buffer stockpiles. They shifted energy policies away from heavy dependence on petroleum to nuclear energy, coal, and other nonfuel raw materials available from non-OPEC countries like Australia, Brazil, Canada, Rhodesia, and South Africa. They sought consumer coalitions to challenge the producer cartels, employing various methods such as fair distribution and even the possibility of threatened or actual military intervention to assure access to supplies. Active campaigning for energy conservation was simultaneously pursued by means of car pool, lowering the heating temperature, and reducing the speed limit of automobiles on the highways. As shown in Figure 3-2 oil imports by advanced countries subsequently declined rapidly from 1979. In 1989, the amount of imports was reduced to sixty-five percent that of 1979.

The seed of friction among the OPEC member nations, however, began to sprout between the moderate and radical members. Being conscious of the impact of pricing and production policies on the advanced countries and on the world economy, the more moderate members like Saudi Arabia argued for modest price increases without reduction in production to avoid a possible economic recession. The more radical members rather insisted on steep increases in price and reduction in production.

Moreover, the long history of ethnic and religious antagonism finally brought about the war between Iran and Iraq. The war forced

Figure 3-2 Comparison of OPEC and Non-OPEC Oil Exports and Oil Imports by Industrial Economies, 1973-1989, Expressed in Millions of Barrels per Day

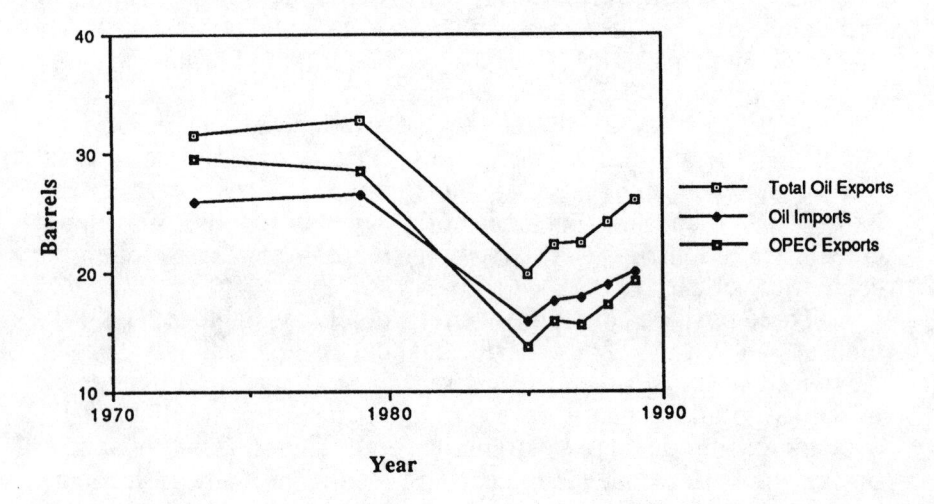

Source: International Monetary Fund (1990: 95)

both nations to increase the export of petroleum to purchase weapons. Being threatened by the possible military closure of the Strait of Hormuz by Iran, oil-exporting Arab countries became conscious of the necessity for cooperation and help from the United States and other advanced countries for the continued flow of oil from the Persian Gulf through the strait to the open sea.

Another dimension of insecurity and uncertainty was caused by the Soviet invasion into Afghanistan. Concurrently, the constant threat of war among Syria, Lebanon, the Palestine Organization, and Israel loomed ominously. Disintegration of OPEC was clearly evidenced by invasion into Kuwait in 1990, which fired oil prices into another skyrocketing rate of increase. But the neighboring states, especially Saudi Arabia, felt threatened by the Iraqi forces and desperately sought help from the United States and other U.N. members, thereby increasing oil production and compensating for the loss of oil production from Kuwait and Iraq. So, due to different factors--political, economic, military, and social--the unity, forged a decade earlier under the theme of the common interest in rapid

Figure 3-3 Crude Oil Production by OPEC and Non-OPEC, 1973-1989, Expressed in Millions of Barrels per Day

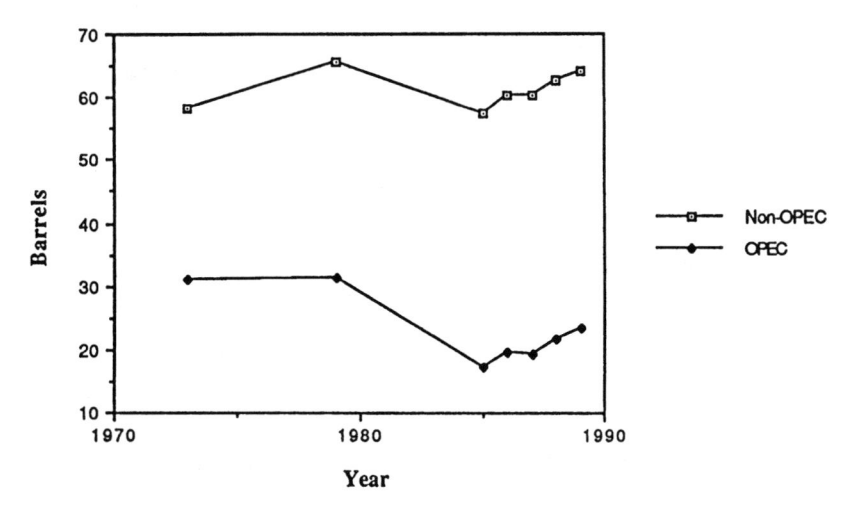

Source: International Monetary Fund (1990: 95)

capital gains and subsequent economic development, began to disintegrate.

Nor has the principle of price elasticity of demand worked very well since 1979 because the advanced countries were able to reduce oil imports much less than the level of total oil production. OPEC's share of the world's crude oil production dwindled from 53.3 percent in 1973 to 36.8 percent in 1989 because industrial states reduced the amount of oil imports and because non-OPEC nations like Bahrain, Colombia, Malaysia, Mexico, the Soviet Union, and China increased production. OPEC finally had to reduce oil prices and production (see Figures 3-2 and 3-3).

The OPEC experience demonstrates that a Third World cartel in a primary product, if monopolized by a few countries and essential to the industrial economies of the West and Japan, may pave an advantageous road to economic development for a certain period of time. However, a Third World cartel in a primary product is not able to exploit the same advantage over a sustained period of time because proper measures or alternatives can be explored and taken by advanced countries. Also, it may be rare that any primary product becomes so essential to the developed countries and yet monopolized by a few developing countries. Therefore, the prospect for cartel formation may not be very bright for other raw material producing organizations such as: the Intergovernmental Committee of Copper Exporting Countries, the International Tin Council, the Union of Banana Exporting Countries, and a host of other primary commodity groups.

Foreign Loans and Investment

Developing countries would need foreign loans and foreign investment in building industries either for import-substitution of goods or for the export of goods domestically manufactured at cheaper prices due to their comparative advantage. However, their initial optimism on the contribution of foreign loans to investment and subsequent economic growth often turned out to be bleak for several reasons. They include: the drop in export commodity prices, the decline in demand for their products due to worldwide economic recession following the oil embargoes, the rise in oil prices for non-oil-exporting developing nations and the subsequent decline of profits on their exports, the appreciation of the dollar in foreign exchange markets, variable rate loans, and the wild fluctuation of interest rate designed primarily for ensuring the lending banks their own profitability in a period of uncertainty.

The major consequences are the rolling over of foreign debts, the foreign debt amounting to an ever-increasing percentage of both the gross national product and total exports of the developing countries, and the subsequent question of their ability to pay the debt. Figure 3-4 and Table 3-1 show the amount of the total indebtedness of the Third World--long-, medium-, and short-term debts altogether. Their debts were only $65 billion in 1970 but geometrically increased to $1 trillion in 1985 and $1.3 trillion in 1988. Table 3-2 lists a few large debtor nations, together with the accumulated debt over the period of time from 1970 to 1988. Brazil and Mexico, for example, borrowed $3.2 billion each in 1970, but their cumulative debt as of the end of 1988 reached over $100 billion.

The exponential increase in debt may call for a critical question: Are these Third World countries able to pay their debt? In order to examine their ability to serve debt (repayments of principal

Korea: Leader of the Nations in Economy 47

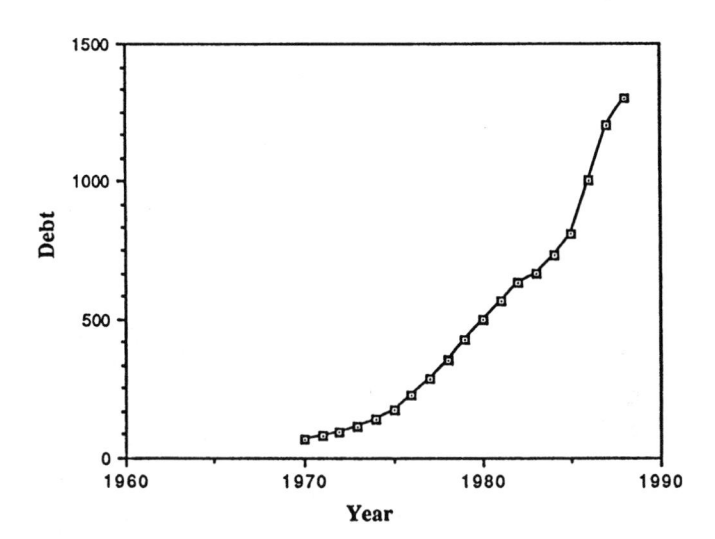

Figure 3-4 Cumulative Debt of the Third World (unit=$billions)

Source: For 1970-1981, *The Wall Street Journal*, January 29, 1981; for 1982-1983, *International Monetary Fund* (1983: 201); for 1984-1986,
The World Almanac (1988: 95)

Table 3-1 Cumulative Debt of the Third World (unit=$billions)

Year	Debt	Year	Debt	Year	Debt	Year	Debt
1970	65	1975	175	1980	495	1985	810
1971	79	1976	225	1981	565	1986	1,000
1972	90	1977	287	1982	628	1987	1,200
1973	110	1978	355	1983	665	1988	1,300
1974	140	1979	427	1984	730		

Source: see Figure 3-4

and interest on outstanding debts), two types of debt service indicators are chosen and computed. They are the ratio of debt service payments to exports of goods and services, and the ratio of debt service payments to GNP value in terms of U.S. dollars. The former indicates a country's ability to make payments on schedule,

Table 3-2 Increase in Medium- and Long-Term Foreign Debt for Selected Countries (units= $billions)

Country	1970	1981	1983	1985	1986	1988
Brazil	3.2	43.8	92	106.7	107.8	120.1
Mexico	3.2	42.7	87	97.4	102.0	107.4
Argentina	1.9	10.5	37	48.4	53.0	59.6
Venezuela	0.7	11.4	35	32.0	34.1	36.0
Chile	2.1	4.4	18	20.2	21.2	16.8
Nigeria	0.5	4.7	14	18.3	22.1	30.5

Source: For 1970 and 1981, The World Bank (1983: 178-79); for 1983, *The Washington Post,* Sept. 25, 1983, p. H1; for 1985, The World Bank (1985: 232-33); for 1986, *The World Almanac & Book of Facts* (1988: 95); for 1988, *U. S. News & World Report,* July 24, 1989: 20-21

whereas the latter measures its capacity to produce outputs with which to service its debts. These two indicators are presented in Table 3-3.

Table 3-3 gives a gloomy outlook. The gross national product (GNP) of Nigeria, Chile, and Venezuela decreased from 1981 to 1988, while that of Argentina, Brazil, and Mexico stagnated with a marginal gain of 12.2, 8.8, and 5.4 percent, respectively. However, their foreign debt increased geometrically. Brazil's total debt amassed until 1970 was $3.2 billion, which was equivalent to 7.0 percent of its GNP. In 1988, its total debt increased to $120.3 billion, which accounted for 38.2 percent of its GNP. During the same period of time, the debts of Venezuela, Mexico, Argentina, and Nigeria were less than ten percent of their GNP in 1970 to a range of sixty to 100 percent in 1988. The most serious case was Venezuela whose GNP decreased from $59.9 billion in 1981 to $59.4 billion in 1988, while debt increased from $11.4 billion to $36.0 billion. Therefore, its debt as the percent of GNP increased from 19.0 percent in 1981 to 60.6 percent in 1988. Its exports radically declined from $16.4 billion in 1981 to $1.9 billion in 1988. Therefore, the debt as the percent of the total exports in 1988 was 1,894.7. This clearly demonstrates that the chances to pay its foreign debts from exports of goods and services seem very low. Table 3-3 suggests that foreign loans did not enhance increase in export and the subsequent growth of the economy of these Third World countries.

James Baker, former U.S. Treasury Secretary during the Reagan administration and Secretary of State during the Bush administration, proposed the so-called Baker Plan in 1985. Its main objective was to provide a long-term solution to the debt crisis. The

Table 3-3 Total Debt, Its Percent of GNP, and Its Percent of Exports for Selected Countries (units=$billions & %)

Year	Items	Brazil	Mexico	Argentina	Venezuela	Chile	Nigeria
1970	Debt(1)	3.2	3.2	1.9	0.7	2.1	0.5
	GNP(2)	41.2	35.6	27.5	11.1	7.5	6.7
	Export(3)	2.7	1.3	1.7	-	-	-
	(1)/(2)	7.0	8.9	6.9	6.3	28.0	7.4
	(1)/(3)	118.5	246.1	111.7	-	-	-
1981	Debt(1)	43.8	42.7	10.5	11.4	4.4	4.7
	GNP(2)	289.0	144.0*	66.4*	59.9	24.0	77.0*
	Export(3)	23.2	21.5**	7.6	16.4**	3.7	16.6**
	(1)/(2)	15.1	29.6	15.8	19.0	18.3	6.1
	(1)/(3)	188.7	198.6	138.1	69.5	118.9	28.3
1983	Debt(1)	92.0	87.0	37.0	35.0	18.0	14.0
	GNP(2)	246.1	162.0*	90.3	70.8	23.6	65.0
	Export(3)	21.8	21.5	7.8	13.4	3.8	11.7
	(1)/(2)	37.3	53.7	40.9	49.4	76.2	21.5
	(1)/(3)	422.0	404.6	474.3	261.1	473.6	119.6
1985	Debt(1)	106.7	97.4	48.4	32.0	20.2	18.3
	GNP(2)	206.8	167.1	60.6	48.5	14.2	70.7
	Export(3)	25.6	21.8	8.3	12.2	3.7	12.5
	(1)/(2)	51.5	58.2	79.8	65.9	142.2	25.8
	(1)/(3)	416.7	446.7	583.1	262.2	545.9	146.4
1986	Debt(1)	107.8	102.0	53.0	34.1	21.2	22.1
	GNP(2)	250.0	126.0	72.9	57.0	18.4	66.2
	Export(3)	22.3	16.0	6.8	1.4	4.2	9.0
	(1)/(2)	43.1	80.9	72.7	59.8	115.2	33.3
	(1)/(3)	483.4	637.5	779.4	2435.7	504.7	245.5
1988	Debt(1)	120.3	107.4	59.6	36.0	16.8	30.5
	GNP(2)	314.6	151.8	74.5	59.4	16.5	31.8
	Export(3)	33.8	20.6	8.9	1.9	7.0	29.6
	(1)/(2)	38.2	70.7	80.0	60.6	101.8	95.9
	(1)/(3)	355.9	521.3	669.6	1894.7	240.0	103.0

Source: *The World Almanac and Book of Facts*, various years; for 1988, *U.S. News & World Report*, July 24, 1989, pp. 20-21, and *The Europa World Year Book 1990*
* As of 1980
** As of 1982

plan called for $29 billion of new loans from commercial banks and other lending institutions as long as the debtor nations decided to modernize their economies and institutionalize financial reforms. The underlying assumption was that economic growth based upon new loans would generate sufficient capital for debtor nations to repay their loans. Nevertheless, *Time* dramatizes the ever-increasing debts which the Third World countries are facing today:

> In three years the debt has only grown, increasing from $950 billion to $1.2 trillion. Brazil, Mexico and Argentina owed $283 billion at the end of 1987, some $30 billion more than they had when the plan was announced. In the meantime, economic growth has stagnated for most debtor countries (Rudolph, 1988: 86-87).

In February and March 1989, more than 300 people in Venezuela died during protests against the government's austerity program aimed at reducing the foreign debts. Argentina, with $60 billion of foreign debt, "has made no payment since April 1988." For the first five months of 1989, Argentine wages increased by 117 percent for construction workers and 173 percent for government employees. But prices increased by 441 percent for milk, 466 percent for eggs, 554 percent for bread, 993 percent for cooking oil, 1,000 percent for fresh cheese, and 2,850 percent for coffee. Money supply out of control and the subsequent hyper-inflationary price increases "have left even middle-class citizens unable to afford food and other necessities" (*Time,* June 12, 1989: 47).

Investment by Multinational Corporations

A majority of the Third World countries in the United Nations began to share concerns about financial dependency, a mounting debt burden, economic stagnation, and subordination to multinational corporations (MNCs). Raul Prebisch of Chile took the initial leadership in chartering the United Nations Conference on Trade and Development (UNCTAD) and held its first meeting in Geneva in 1964. That was followed by UNCTAD II in Dehli in 1968, UNCTAD III in Santiago in 1972, UNCTAD IV in Nairobi in 1976, UNCTAD V in Manila in 1979, and UNCTAD VI in Belgrade in 1983.[4] Despite diversity and disunity among the developing countries, their shared concern has been the emergence of "neo-imperialism," which was envisioned by Lenin in 1916 and seems to be actually witnessed in the Third World today. Neo-imperialism is evidenced by James O'Connor, Harry Magdoff, Paul Sweezy, Franze Fanon, Cheryl Payer, and a host of scholars as:

1. Growing foreign investment in manufacturing in developing countries, exploiting cheap labor.
2. A growing role of foreign governments and international banks such as the International Monetary Fund and the World Bank in the economies of Third World countries.
3. The concentration and centralization of capital and the integration of the world capitalist economy into the structures of the giant multinational corporations (MNCs).
4. Growing collaboration of the Third World bourgeoisie with Western capital.
5. Raising of self-financing from internal funds for expansion abroad by the major MNCs.
6. The flow of profits from the Third World to the West greater than that of new investment to the Third World.
7. Increase in sales of foreign, sophisticated weapons in developing countries.[5]

Michael Parenti contends that the United States is not less imperialistic than its counterparts in the West. The U.S. empire cannot be seen on a map, but the USA was and is the "most consummate practitioner of neo-colonialism, that is, the practice of direct exploitation without the burden of direct rule" (1989: 66). The Philippines and Brazil are two typical examples which he examined in detail to depict the United States as an earlier and a contemporary imperialist country.

Upon the passage of the Bell Act by Congress in 1946, the Philippines was granted political "independence," but American citizens were given equal rights with Filipinos in the exploration of the Philippines's natural resources, the operation of public utilities, and the establishment of manufacturing companies, banking, and credit institutions. A free trade relationship also was set up between the two nations. Parenti dramatized the consequences of the American imperialistic exploitation of the Filipinos:

> What occurred in the years that followed resembles a classical imperialist situation--minus the flag. U.S. companies engaged in competitive dumping of commodities. They put up competing factories and drove out scores of pioneering Filipino entrepreneurs. American businesses acquired control of key industries, siphoned off large amounts of local credit to finance their investments, and used U.S. banks to channel

Filipino savings to foreigners. American military bases and PX stores became among the biggest exporters--free from customs duties and regulations (1989: 67-68).

Parenti suggests that Brazil shows a recent reincarnation of American imperialism as manifested in the use of the Philippines in the past. When President Joao Goulart announced his plan to redistribute millions of acres of farmland to the poor and nationalize seven U.S. oil companies, his regime was soon overthrown in 1964, by a "U.S.-trained and financed right-wing military." The new regime immediately created very favorable conditions for foreign investment in Brazil such as tight restrictions on labor unions, the outlawing of labor strikes, generous tax rebates, and tax-free export earnings for foreign investors. These measures brought about the "Brazilian miracle within the next ten years." The gross national product tripled, growing faster than any in the world including Japan's. Nevertheless, Brazil faces the same imperialistic consequences.

> The growth reached only a small segment of the population. The real income of the poorest 80 percent declined by over half in the decade after Goulart. One-third of the population had tuberculosis; one-half of the children had no schools; and the infant mortality rate climbed to the second highest in the hemisphere. Hunger and starvation increased as vast acreages of farmland were converted to export crops.
> Two multinational corporations controlled 80 percent of Brazil's electronics industry, as Brazilian firms were driven out of business. American and other foreign companies controlled 60 percent of heavy industry, 90 percent of pharmaceuticals, and 95 percent of automobile production. All this new investment was of no benefit to Brazilian workers. Under the military dictatorship, the twelve-hour day was instituted; the unemployment rate climbed; and Brazilian workers had the highest industrial accident rate in the world (Parenti, 1989: 22).

The Radical vs. Conventional Development Theory

Radical theorists, therefore, point out that none of the now wealthy nations of the West was industrialized by investment by foreign governments or foreign business firms. The modernization of each economy was financed and managed overwhelmingly by the industrial capitalist class of each individual country. The theory holds true in Japan, too. Japan began to embark upon economic modernization in the late Nineteenth Century, first by fighting off Western imperialism and prohibiting foreign investment from coming into Japan. Therefore, radical theorists recommend that the Third World nations should kick out the MNCs, resist the temptation to import many Western-style consumer goods, and pursue, rather, self-development.

The Chinese economy under the leadership of Mao Tse-tung (Mao Zedong) provided an example of the radical theory of economic development. China, as late as 1935, was under a near-complete dependency economy such that 95 percent of China's iron, three-quarters of its coal, half of its textile production, and most shipping, public utilities, banking, insurance, and trade were controlled and managed by foreigners. Most industrial workers were hired by foreign firms. Under the helmsmanship of Mao Tse-tung since 1949, collective measures had been taken and the dependency economy was completely replaced by a self-reliant economy.

This may be attributed to the "century of humiliation" that Chinese people had suffered from imperialism of such European countries as Great Britain, France, the United States, Portugal, and Germany. As early as 1793, the Chinese emperor refused to have trade with European countries partly because of their "cultural inferiority and barbarianism" and partly because of China's self-sufficiency in a vast landmass and its suzerainty of many neighboring countries. His refusal to trade with England was clearly seen in the following letter:

> The virtue of the Celestial Dynasty having spread far and wide, the kings of myriad nations come by land and sea with all sorts of precious things. Consequently, there is nothing we lack, as your principal envoy and others have themselves observed. We have never set much store on strange or ingenious objects, nor do we need any more of your country's manufacturers (Fairbank and Teng, 1954: 19).

Amidst the relative lack of the Chinese interest in Western products, the European businessmen discovered that opium was a major marketable item. Despite the Chinese authority's attempts to restrict opium delivery by decrees, opium was smuggled into China beyond expectations. In 1729, when the first decree was announced, there were only 200 chests of pure opium smuggled into China. By 1830, it increased to about 19,000 chests and by 1838, to 30,000. After the European coercive trade reached its peak, in some communities as much as 50 percent of the population were addicted. This alarmed the Chinese authority so that serious efforts were pursued to halt the opium transactions. The Chinese forces seized $11 million worth of opium, drove the drug traffic out of Canton, and stopped the contraband.

The British government contended that the Chinese government interfered with international freedom of trade and initiated a battle that resulted in the destruction of the Chinese forts at Canton. China was, of course, defeated by the modern British naval forces and forced to sign the Treaty of Nanking in 1842. The treaty included the following provisions to: pay $21 million in reparations equivalent to the American federal budget at that time, give Hong Kong to Britain "in perpetuity," reopen Canton for opium trade, allow four additional treaty ports to the Europeans, and grant the European powers the privilege of extraterritoriality. It was followed by similar treaties with other European powers, including Cushing's Treaty of 1844. The Opium War was the first in a long series of national defeats including the T'aiping Rebellion (1861-1865) and the Boxer Rebellion (1900) that lasted from 1840 to 1945. This is called the Century of Humiliation, for which Mao justified the adoption of the radical theory of self-development.

One may wonder, then, whether the Chinese example of the radical theory can be emulated and imitated by other Third World nations. A firm negative answer is explained by the economic performance of China itself. Despite the ambitious launching of a self-reliant economy, China was by no means able to match Taiwan, Singapore, Hong Kong, and South Korea, its Far Eastern neighboring nations, in terms of speed and scope of economic dynamics. China's invasion into Vietnam in 1979 was not able to achieve its objective to "teach Vietnam a lesson." Far from that objective, China learned the painful lesson that it lacked the military strength and the industrial power to exert its power on a small neighboring country even a few hundred miles beyond its own border, which was ironically under the Chinese suzerainty in the past.

Table 3-4 Inflow of Foreign Direct Investment, 1970-1985 (units=$millions & %)

Category	1970	1972	1974	1976	1978	1980	1983	1985
Developed Countries	7,906 81.2%	10,314 79.9	17,930 97.2	11,238 79.8	22,425 75.1	42,099 80.6	33,828 76.7	37,837 76.7
Developing Countries:								
Latin America & Caribbean	815 8.4%	1,019 7.8	1,894 10.2	1,749 12.4	4,059 13.6	6,219 11.9	3,478 7.9	4,530 9.2
Africa	511 5.2%	762 5.9	-2,868 -16.0	-655 -4.6	1,420 4.6	243 0.4	1,609 3.6	1,727 3.5
South & East Asia	486 4.9%	780 6.0	1,445 7.8	1,690 12.0	1,888 6.3	3,197 6.1	4,720 10.7	4,495 9.1
Others	22 0.2%	23 0.1	39 2.1	46 0.3	78 0.3	446 0.8	458 1.0	723 1.5
Subtotal	1,834 18.8%	2,585 20.1	508 2.8	2,830 20.2	7,446 24.9	10,105 19.4	10,265 23.3	11,475 23.3
Total	9,740 100%	12,899 100%	18,438 100%	14,069 100%	29,872 100%	52,204 100%	44,093 100%	49,312 100%

Source: United Nations (1981: 286); United Nations (1988: 504-07)
*A minus sign (-) indicates reduction in the stock of foreign direct investment in the country.

Being clearly aware of backwardness, Deng Xiaoping (Teng Hsiao-ping) was determined to accelerate the pace of modernization. His four modernizations in the areas of agriculture, industry, technology, and defense, which were announced in 1978, called for $600 billion in capital investment for 128 industrial projects. China, which led the Third World countries in promulgating and pursuing the self-reliance-based radical model of economic development in the early 1950s, ironically betrayed the Third World nations in the late 1970s by denouncing the self-reliant radical theory of economic development, breaking the policy of isolationism, actively seeking foreign investment, and promoting trade with capitalist countries.

Foreign direct investment (FDI) is often blamed as a method for imperialistic countries to exploit developing nations. However, Table 3-4 demonstrates a consistent pattern of about an average of 81 percent of the total FDI from 1970 to 1985 into the developed

Table 3-5 Inflow of Profits on Foreign Direct Investment : 1975-1985
(units=$millions & %)

Category	1975	1980	1981	1982	1983	1984	1985
Developed Countries	24,989 99.4	58,191 97.4	50,645 95.6	36,924 95.1	39,582 96.3	43,589 97.7	53,034 98.9
Developing Countries:							
Latin America & the Caribbean	47 0.2	296 0.5	306 0.6	374 0.9	88 0.2	46 0.1	136 0.2
Africa	17 0.1	106 0.2	171 0.3	158 0.4	209 0.5	134 0.3	116 0.2
South & East Asia	46 0.2	82 0.1	801 1.5	657 1.7	320 0.8	117 0.3	115 0.2
Others	15 0.1	1,064 1.8	1,042 1.9	719 1.8	888 2.2	714 1.6	267 0.5
Subtotal	125 0.5	1,548 0.5	2,320 4.4	1,908 4.8	1,505 3.7	1,011 2.3	643 1.2
Total	25,115 100%	59,739 100%	52,965 100%	38,831 100%	41,087 100%	44,601 100%	53,668 100%

Source: United Nations (1988: 511-13)

countries in the regions of Western Europe, the United States, Japan, Australia, Canada, and New Zealand. Only about an average of nineteen percent of the FDI flowed into the developing nations. An average four-to-one ratio of direct foreign investment in advanced economies *vis-a-vis* all other countries for the past two decades does not support Parenti's neo-imperialism as the main objective for multinational corporate investment overseas.

Moreover, Table 3-5 shows the inflow of profits on FDI, namely, inflows of reinvested earnings on direct investment. Tables 3-4 and 3-5 give us an interesting insight on FDI. For example, the annual inflow of about eighty percent of the total foreign direct investment into economically advanced countries since 1975 (see Table 3-4) shows the inflow of over 95 percent of the total profits on FDI of foreign affiliates, which were not remitted outside the advanced host countries (Table 3-5). On the other hand, inflow of about twenty percent of FDI into developing countries demonstrates shockingly less than five percent of the total profits as the earnings of foreign affiliates which were not remitted outside the developing host countries. This clearly indicates that an annual average of four-fifths of the FDI has been invested so far in advanced countries and over ninety-five percent of the profits on the FDI reinvested in the advanced countries. But reinvestment in the host developing countries declined from 4.4 percent in 1981 to 1.2 percent in 1985. The continued heavy investment and reinvestment of multinational corporations in Europe and other advanced countries rather than in developing countries are encouraged by several favorable factors:

> The economic recovery of Europe, which provided an attractive market; the return to convertibility of European currencies, which enabled the unrestricted repatriation of earnings and capital; greater political stability both internally and internationally; and the formation of the EEC with its promise of a large market and its discrimination against third-party imports (Spero, 1985: 138).

In short, foreign direct investment of a relatively small amount in the developing countries *vis-a-vis* a large amount in advanced countries cannot be blamed as the imperialistic nature of foreign funds. This explains, not exploitation of the developing countries by the developed nations, but mutual exploitation of the developed countries among themselves.

Korea Leading the Nations in Economic Growth

Amidst the gloomy economic outlook for the Third World countries, Korea emerged, whose speed and quality of economic development distinguish it not only from these developing countries but also from three other East Asian "miracle economies" or three of the "Far Eastern Gang of Four"--Taiwan, Singapore, and Hong Kong.

Contrary to the radical theory of economic development, Korea has not been forced to become a "satellite" to advanced countries. She has not been dictated to import their manufactured goods and services. Her economy has not been eroded because of continued productivity gains. Unlike many developing countries, which have abundant natural resources, Korea does not inherit any significant amount of natural resources and, therefore, has no other options but to concentrate herself on trade for her survival and prosperity.

Table 3-6 Medium- and Long-Term Debts of Korea*
(units= $billions except in Per Capita GNP and %)

Year	Debt (1)	GNP (2)	Per Capita GNP	(1)/(2) =%	Exports (3)	(1)/(3) =%	Imports (4)
1970	$2.9	$7.4	$235	27.0%	$8.3	24.0%	$19.8
1981	32.4	67.2	1,870	48.2	21.2	152.8	26.1
1982	37.1	70.8	1,910	52.4	21.8	170.1	24.2
1983	40.4	75.3	2,010	53.6	24.4	165.5	26.1
1984	43.1	81.0	2,110	53.2	29.2	147.6	30.6
1985	46.8	83.1	2,200	56.3	34.7	134.8	31.5
1986	44.5	90.6	2,296	49.1	33.9	131.2	29.7
1987	35.6	118.6	2,826	30.0	47.3	75.2	41.0
1988	31.0	154.0	3,600	20.1	57.5	53.9	52.5
1989	27.1	184.0	4,270	14.7	64.0	42.3	61.0
1990	24.5	210.0	4,840	11.6	70.5	34.7	68.0
1991	23.0	240.0	5,500	9.6	79.5	28.9	76.5
1992	22.0	280.0	6,200	7.8	89.5	24.5	86.0

Source: *Dong-A Ilbo,* August 22, 1987; *Korea Herald,* November 21, 1987; *Korea Times* (Hankuk Ilbo), July 30, 1988; The World Bank (1987, Table 16: 232-33, 277)
*Data from 1988 to 1992 are estimated by the Economic Planning Board.

Korea borrowed a large amount of money and became the fourth largest debtor nation next to Brazil, Mexico, and Argentina up until 1985. But Korea's foreign debts have been decreasing much faster than scheduled due to payments of large portions of the principal and interest well in advance (see Tables 3-3 and 3-6).

While six major debtor nations show geometrical increases in debts as a percent of their GNP from 1981 to 1988, Korea indicates gradual increases in debt from 1970 until its peak in 1985, and then shows exponential decreases since 1985 (see Figure 3-5). Korea's foreign debts, measured as a percent of its export, also show geometrical increases similar to the six debtor nations, but decline after 1982 (Figure 3-6).

The gloomy prospect for the payment of foreign debts for these debtor nations can be predicted because of only moderate growth in GNP for Brazil and Mexico and the continued decrease of GNP for the remaining four nations. On the other hand, South Korea's total foreign debt was $46.8 billion in 1985 but declined to $44.5 billion in 1986, $35.6 billion in 1987, and $22.0 billion estimated in 1992 along with the increase of GNP from $67.2 billion in 1981 to $118.6 billion in 1987 and to $280 billion estimated in 1992. The Sixth Five-Year Economic Development Plan estimates

Korea: Leader of the Nations in Economy 59

Figure 3-5 Total Debt of Selected Countries as Percent of GNP

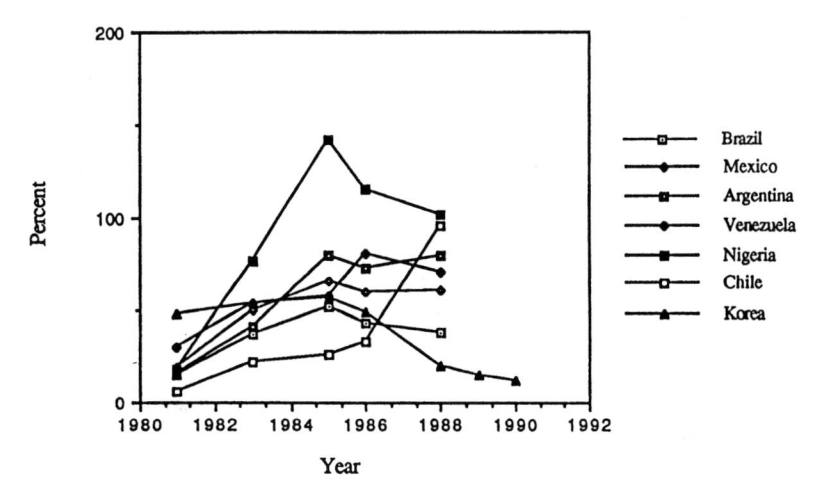

Source: Tables 3-3 and 3-6

Figure 3-6 Total Debt of Selected Countries as Percent of Exports

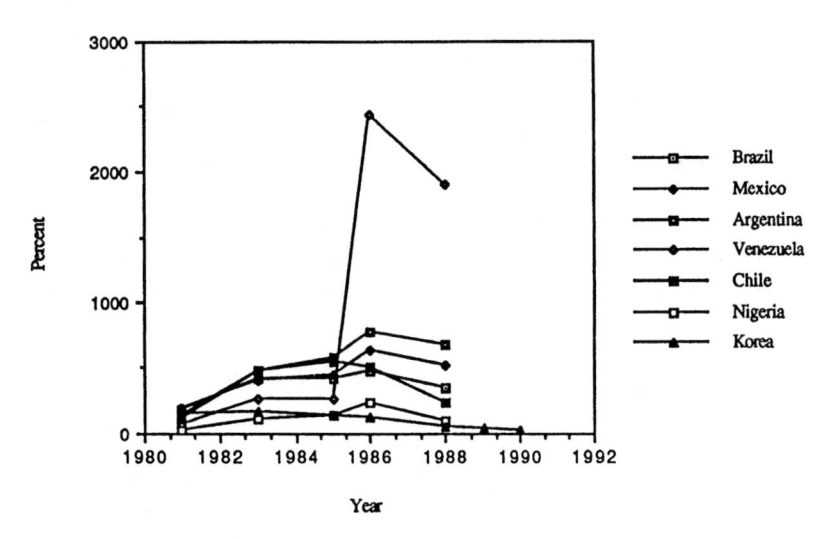

Source: Tables 3-3 and 3-6

that Korea's foreign debts will decrease from thirty percent of its GNP in 1987 to 7.8 percent of the GNP in 1992 (see Table 3-6). It is generally understood that Taiwan, Singapore, and Hong Kong have made "economic miracles" on the basis of different backgrounds and different strategies.[6] For example, economic assistance was made available to Taiwan and Korea by the United States and Japan, whereas assistance was not available to Singapore and Hong Kong. "The monetary and physical as well as human capital all originated in" the latter two countries (Klein, 1986: 119).

Singapore and Hong Kong were noted for harbors and shipping. Since they lie in major shipping lanes, both of them were "among the largest and busiest ports in the world. Thousands of oceangoing ships, coastal steamers, junks, and mechanized vessels of all sorts" populated their harbors (Klein, 1986: 96). Commerce became their economic mainstay. Taiwan and Korea were also surrounded by the ocean but did not lie in the main shipping lanes.

Laissez-faire economy became the basic guidelines and foundation for economic development in Singapore and Hong Kong, whereas positive intervention and an entrepreneurial role of the state in building, opening, establishing, initiating, patronizing, and taking risks in a wide variety of light and heavy industries as well as infrastructures prevailed in Taiwan and Korea. Commerce became the basic economic orientation for Singapore and Hong Kong, while agricultural growth laid the basic foundation for building import-substituting industries in Taiwan and Korea. Expenditure of at least five or more percent of the GNP/GDP was of absolute necessity for national defense and survival for Korea, Taiwan, and Singapore. Hong Kong, on the other hand, was almost free of such an important burden.

It is clear at this point that, despite the major differences, these four countries have all accomplished "economic miracles." Therefore, no one model of economic development is suitable for all developing nations. Indeed, there are many roads to economic growth.

Although they took different routes to economic development, these four Asian countries did have common denominators: 1) high values on education and hard work; 2) willingness to study, to use creative ideas and ingenuity, and to work to the maximum; 3) paucity of natural resources; 4) subsequent pursuit of no other alternatives but the emphasis of trade for economic survival and prosperity; 5) exposure to the West by former colonial rule; 6) lack of strong unions and relatively low wages thus far; 7) and emphasis on savings and investment in the future rather than current consumption.7

By the same token, Korea was equally distinguished from these three Asian "miracles." Korea alone suffered from a major war that lasted for three years from 1950 to 1953 and claimed loss and injuries of hundreds of thousands. It also caused near complete damage of all major infrastructures such as roads, railroads, bridges, harbors, manufacturing plants, schools, and communications.

Historian Han dramatized the aftermath of the Korean War:

> The casualties and damage inflicted by the war were heavy. . . . About 150,000 Korean people were killed, 250,000 wounded, 100,000 kidnapped to the north, 200,000 missing, several million homeless, . . . over 100,000 became orphans. . . . Taken and retaken four times, Seoul lay in ruins, as did most of the other cities of the south. More than half of all industrial facilities were inoperative, countless numbers of roads and bridges were destroyed, and whole villages had been wiped out in many areas (Han, 1987: 569).

The Korean War caused two million to run away from the North Korean, Orwellian type of government to the democratic one of South Korea. President Rhee also made a unilateral decision to release four million prisoners-of-war (POWs) who refused to return to North Korea. This caused a flood of two million refugees and four million POWs that exacerbated the level of unemployment and underemployment in South Korea (MOE, 1979: 295). The division of the Korean peninsula between North and South along the 38th parallel crippled the economy of South Korea more severely than that of North Korea because of the latter's monopolistic control of natural resources, industries, and electricity. Korea is much larger in the scope and extent of economy and the size of population than the other three and consequently "has had to overcome larger problems" (Kuznets, 1986: 37).

In the early 1960s when the First Five-Year Economic Development Plan was being undertaken, the Korean economy was much more at a disadvantage than the other three in terms of the amount of domestic savings available for investment. Korea alone had to rely on foreign loans for domestic investment, and, therefore, experienced more constraints and the mounting pressure

Figure 3-7 Industrial Performance and Economic Growth by Level of Income and Trade Orientation

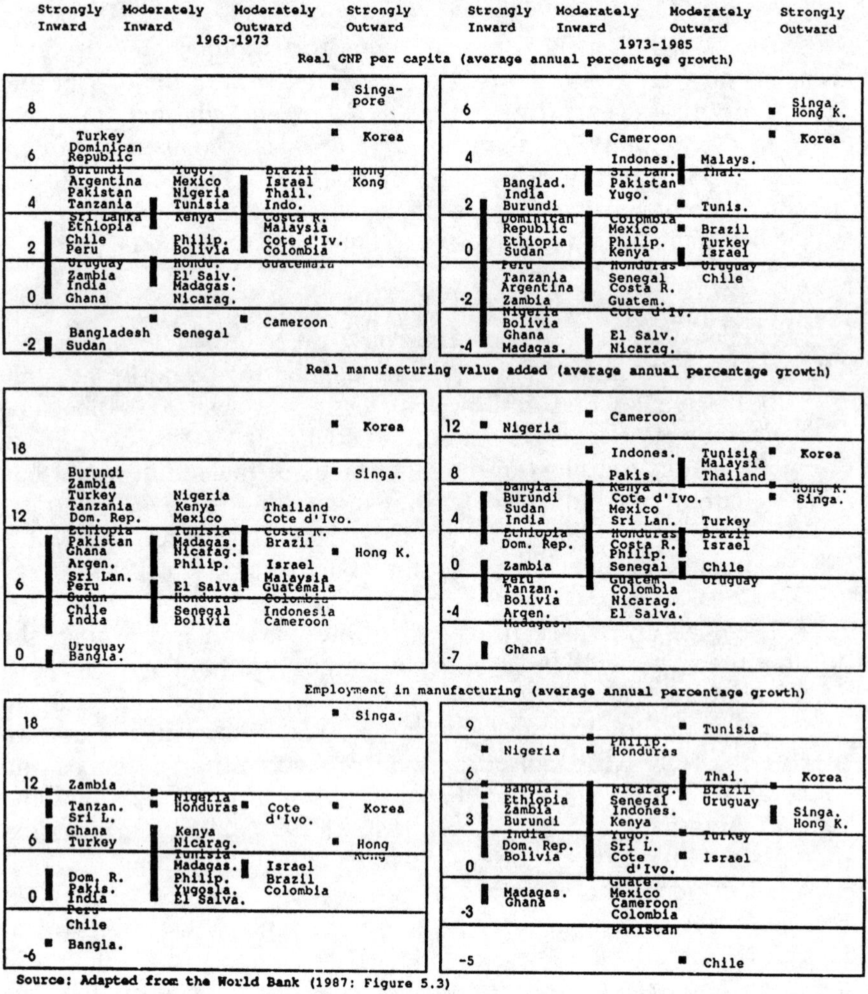

[Figure showing Real GNP per capita, Real manufacturing value added, and Employment in manufacturing growth rates by country groups classified as Strongly Inward, Moderately Inward, Moderately Outward, and Strongly Outward for periods 1963-1973 and 1973-1985.]

Source: Adapted from the World Bank (1987: Figure 5.3)

of the obligation to pay the principal and interest. Business leaders in Korea have been frequently forced to make donations to political leaders for organizing political parties and campaign expenditures. The more frequently the regime is changed, the more political money is diverted from investment. The other three have been nearly immune from such political burdens.

Korea: Leader of the Nations in Economy

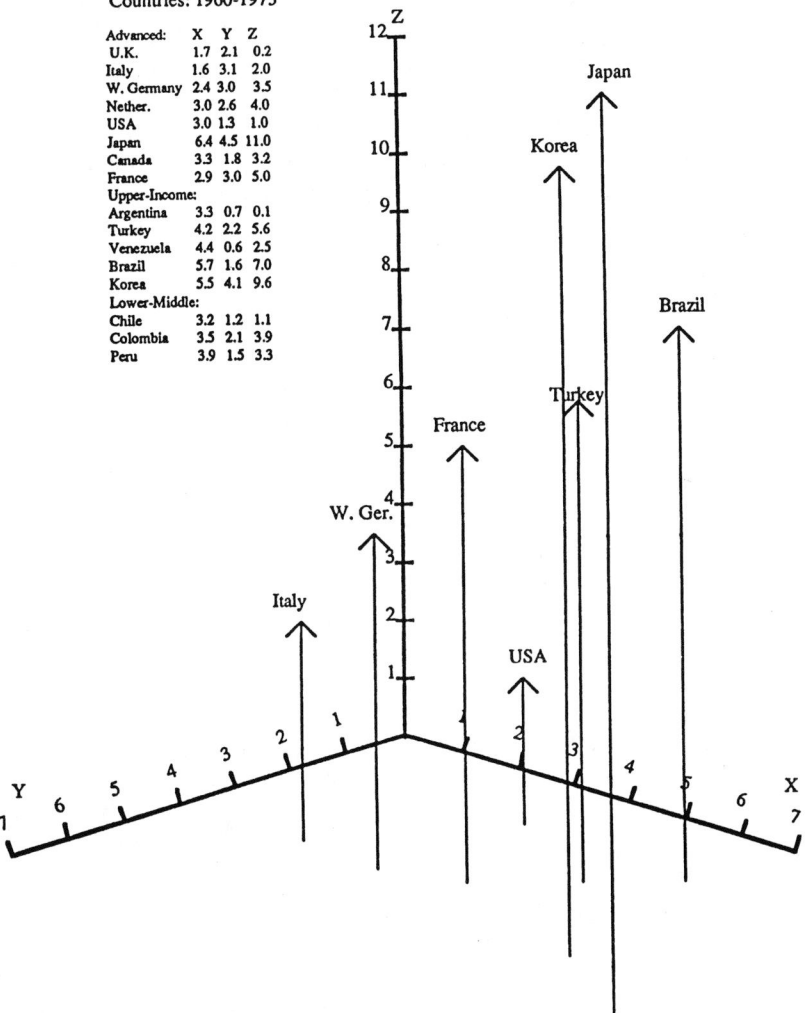

Figure 3-8 Contribution of Total Factor Input Growth Rate (X) and Total Factor Productivity Growth Rate (Y) to Real GDP Growth Rate (Z) in Selected Countries: 1960-1973

	X	Y	Z
Advanced:			
U.K.	1.7	2.1	0.2
Italy	1.6	3.1	2.0
W. Germany	2.4	3.0	3.5
Nether.	3.0	2.6	4.0
USA	3.0	1.3	1.0
Japan	6.4	4.5	11.0
Canada	3.3	1.8	3.2
France	2.9	3.0	5.0
Upper-Income:			
Argentina	3.3	0.7	0.1
Turkey	4.2	2.2	5.6
Venezuela	4.4	0.6	2.5
Brazil	5.7	1.6	7.0
Korea	5.5	4.1	9.6
Lower-Middle:			
Chile	3.2	1.2	1.1
Colombia	3.5	2.1	3.9
Peru	3.9	1.5	3.3

Source: Data for X and Y from Chenery, Robinson, and Syrquin (1986: Table 2-2); data for Z from the World Bank (1987)

Conclusion: Strengths of the Korean Economy

Transcending these disadvantages, Korea has committed itself to extensive growth in various manufacturing industries (thereby accumulating such input factors as land, labor, and capital) and productivity growth. Rapid growth rates can usually be achieved with expansion in factor inputs at early stages of industrialization. But with the growth and increase of labor wages, the comparative advantage, which was available at the early stage, was greatly reduced. Therefore, advance of technology and science, improvement in efficiency, and management skill in the use of all physical inputs become the imperatives for productivity growth.

As shown in Figure 3-7, the average annual percentage growth of real GNP per capita indicates that Korea together with Singapore, which was "strongly outward oriented," was leading all of the developing countries during 1963-1973. A consistent pattern may be equally observed during 1973-1985. Accumulation of factor inputs, increased employment in manufacturing, and enhancement of productivity growth were such that, in both real manufacturing value added and employment in manufacturing, Korea has led Singapore and Hong Kong as well as all upper middle-income countries such as Malaysia, Brazil, Israel, Uruguay, Mexico, and Argentina.[8]

Korea's economic success can also be witnessed when the real GDP growth rate is compared among a few selected countries-- advanced, upper- and lower-middle income ones. The level of real GDP growth (Z axis) is compared among these countries in relation to their growth of "total factor input" of land, labor, and capital in terms of extensive growth in various industries (X axis) and to their growth of "total factor productivity" in terms of intensive (efficiency) growth after subtracting the contributions of labor and capital growth from GDP (Y axis)(see Figure 3-8).

The higher the level of the total factor productivity growth becomes, the greater is the relative contribution of productivity to real GDP growth. The higher the level of the total factor input growth, the more extensively is the country committed to building various manufacturing industries. Differences in the stage of industrialization may explain part of the differences in performance among the countries shown. But Figure 3-8 shows that, although total factor inputs grew at about the same rate of six percent in Brazil and Korea in 1960-1973, Korea's real GDP growth rate was about three percent higher than that of Brazil due to the differences in productivity growth (Chenery et al., 1986: Table 2-2). Overall, Japan and Korea have achieved the highest level of both total factor productivity growth and total factor input growth, and the subsequent highest rate of GDP growth, almost twice as high as most of the selected advanced, upper middle-income and lower middle-income countries in the figure. There is no doubt that Korea leads all of the nations in economic development.

Notes

1. For detailed discussion on the radical theory, see Baran (1968); Amin (1976); Baran and Sweezy (1969); Caporaso (1978); Bergesen (1980); Smith (1979); Higgins (1979); Ward (1979); Myrdal (1972); Todaro (1981); Nagle (1987: ch. 12). Concerning a gloomy outlook of the South, see the South Commission (1990: ch. 2).

2. Considerable evidence has been marshaled to support this view. See Prebisch (1964); Hanson (1976: 178); Pirages (1978: 239); and International Monetary Fund (1983).

3. For further information, see Arghiri Emmanuel (1972); the United Nations Conference on Trade and Development (1964), widely known as the Prebisch Report.

4. For summary description of UNCTAD I through UNCTAD V, see Burney (1979: 18); for UNCTAD VI, see Burki (1983: 18-19).

5. Imperialism as the latest stage in development of capitalism was explained by Lenin (1969). Concerning further information on neo-imperialism, see O'Connor (1971); Baran and Sweezy (1971); Magdoff and Sweezy (1971); Cockcroft, Frank, and Johnson (1972); and Payer (1972).

6. The term "miracle economies" was used by Little in discussing Taiwan's economic growth in a comparative perspective. See Little (1979: 448-49). The "Far Eastern Gang of Four" was a term used by Fei. See Fei (1986: 71).

7. A comparative study among four Asian countries in this section is mainly based on chapters 2, 3, and 4 in Ilpyong Kim (1986) and World Bank (1987).

8. Cameroon as a low-income country in 1973-1985 showed almost the same growth rate as Korea in real manufacturing value added and real GNP per capita growth. But Cameroon was reversed in its orientation from export to import substitution. Its growth rate of employment, therefore, decreased to be near zero.

Chapter 4 The Korean Model of Economic Development

Chapter Four will examine two major questions: (1) What factors have contributed to rapid economic development in Korea? and (2) What model of economic development has Korea adopted and carried into execution? This chapter will then be concluded with an analysis of the prospect for her continued economic development in the future.

Factors Influencing the Korean Economic Miracle

Factors for rapid economic development in Korea can be examined in terms of internal (domestic) and external (foreign) perspectives. Both internal and external factors can also be explored from long-term and short-term perspectives (see Figure 4-1).

Internal Factors

Major long-run internal (domestic) factors which may be conducive to rapid economic development in Korea upon the inception of its republic can be examined from a brief review of the cultural characteristics. First of all, different cultures and religions prevailing in different dynasties in the past played important roles in shaping values, norms, and expectations of the Korean people and their leaders. Specifically salient are the virtues of the Tangun mythology, Taoism, Buddhism, Confucianism, Neo-Confucianism, Christianity, and Taejonggyo (Grand Religion) in chronological order. Each of these had its own peculiar and occasionally mutually-exclusive characteristics. However, none of the earlier accepted religions or thoughts was completely replaced by the later ones. Rather they were amalgamated and reinforced into the mainstream of the Korean culture--hard work, discipline, determination, and commitment to the national defense; the desire for independence from foreign colonialism; and recently, to economic development (Shim, 1987).

Figure 4-1 Causes for Economic Development in Korea

Internal (Domestic)		External (Foreign)
Long-Term: Perseverance, Commitment and Dedication		
Tangun	*The spirit of Hwarangdo	*Exposure to modern countries
Taoism	*Struggles for national defense:	*Colonial influences
Confucianism	Voluntary forces to expell foreign invaders 78 years of carving woodblocks	*Stimulus of Japan's growth
Buddhism		*Foreign aids and loans
Neo-Confucianism	*Creative ideals in: Military strategies by: Gen. Kwang Gaeto Gen. Ulchi Mun-dok	*American commitment to Korea's defense and subsequent political stability
Christianity	Gen. Yon Kae-so-mun Gen. Kang Kam-chan	
Taejonggyo (Grand Religion with Tangun as the founder	Gen. Kwon Yul Adm. Yi Sun-shin Scientific inquiries: Han-gul, Korean alphabet Rain gauge Kobukson (Turtle warship)	*Competition with North Korea *International environment for promotion of trade (GATT)
Short-Term:	*Enlightenment movement and education *Sense of survival imperative; paucity of resources; surplus of labor	*Generalized System of Preferences (GSP)

Amalgamation and mutual reinforcement may be witnessed in the institution of Hwarangdo (the Elite Youth Corps) in the Silla Dynasty (57 B.C.-935 A.D.), which may be equivalent to modern military academies. The institute trained and produced many excellent leaders who ultimately made possible unification of the Korean peninsula in 661 for the first time in history and brought about economic prosperity. The spirit of Hwarangdo was mainly influenced by Taoism. However, it also incorporated both "the value of saving lives" on the basis of Buddhism and "the virtue of loyalty" and "no retreat on the battlefield" based on Confucianism. Even today, Taejonggyo (the Grand Religion), which claims Tangun as its founder, advocates the very same principles of Hwarangdo and accepts its five commandments as the virtues of importance: the first commandment of "loyalty to one's king" was replaced by "loyalty to one's country," whereas the four others--"filial piety," " faith to friends," " no retreat in the battlefield," and "judiciousness in taking life"--remain the same. The very same values of Hwarangdo are included in textbooks for educating young Koreans today. In fact, the Educational Institute of Elite Youth was recently established at Kyongju, the former capital of Silla, where Hwarangdo was originated and fully implemented.

Perseverance and determination as the mainstream of the Korean culture were demonstrated by a variety of activities: the carving of wooden printing blocks for 78 years in prayer, asking for Buddha's protection of the fatherland; the developing of creative ideas and ingenuity in military strategies by kings, generals, and admirals against numerous invasions by the Chinese, Mongols, and Japanese; the promoting of science in astronomy and meteorology by developing rain gauges and building Chomsongdae, one of the oldest astronomical observatories; the developing of Hangul, the Korean alphabet, in 1443; and the building of Kobukson, the first iron-clad warship. Each of the major foreign invasions brought forth voluntary participation from tens of thousands of Koreans for regular and guerilla forces. In the case of struggles for independence from Japan, over two million Koreans from all walks of life volunteered to participate in demonstrations on the streets, resulting in 7,000 killed and 15,500 wounded.

Discipline, hard work, perseverance, and determination, which were concentrated on national defense and independence in the past, began to focus on economy since the 1960s. These positive characteristics are clearly manifested among Koreans by their longest hours of work per week, commitment to education and training, quality of production, productivity gains, making the most of comparative advantages, and the subsequent exponential increase in trade (see Table 4-3 and Figure 4-3).

Listed in terms of a short-term internal (domestic) perspective may be the paucity of financial and natural resources, surplus of labor aggravated by the refugees from the North and the prisoners-of-war released free without repatriation to the North, and the long experience of suffering and exploitation. Because of these factors, the Koreans have gained a strong sense of survival imperatives. The increase in literacy for the general public and the emphasis on higher education for the leadership group were also blended together for a cooperative endeavor to plan and achieve economic development.

One has to keep in mind that a large amount of literature on the success of the Korean economy and supposed causes for success abounds. The literature, however, mainly stresses macro-economic policies of the government--monetary, fiscal, and export orientation.[1] The economic success may well be greatly attributed to these elements in terms of a macro-level perspective, but more profound causes may be equally or perhaps more attributed to the national spirit as well as discipline, perseverance, and determination of each and every Korean who has been inculcated throughout Korean history, culture, and life experience.

External Factors

In terms of external (international) factors, we may consider the importance of Korea's exposure to the successful, market-oriented capitalistic economic system of modern countries such as the United States, West Germany, Japan, and Taiwan.

Alice H. Amsden played down the role of the United States and Japan in their contribution to economic development in Korea. The United States preferred stability to growth, expended over seventy percent of its economic aid on consumption goods rather than on machines and equipment, and promoted the subsequent increase of the dependency of Korea upon the American economy. Japan also began to stop transferring technological know-how when Korea was rapidly catching up with and seen as a formidable challenger to Japan in international trade (1989: Chapter Two).

Nevertheless, generous economic assistance from the United States since the inception of the republic and much more after the Korean War became the basic technical and financial source for building the infrastructure and economic rehabilitation. As is shown in Table 4-1, the American nonmilitary government grants and credits, which accounted for an average of almost thirteen percent of Korea's GNP during the period of 1953-1963, helped Korea build domestic industries for import substitution of foreign goods. However, Steinberg reminds readers that Korea did not blindly follow American advice for economic development. In fact, Korea pursued some programs on the basis of its own plans and strategies *against* the American advice. Two very well-known cases were the

Table 4-1 U.S. Economic Aid to Korea, 1945-1980   (unit=$millions)

Year	Total	GARIOA	ECA	PL480	AID	CRIK	UNKRA
1945	4.9	4.9					
1946	49.9	49.9					
1947	175.4	174.4					
1948	179.6	179.6					
1949	116.5	92.7	23.8				
1950	58.7		49.3			9.4	
1951	196.5		32.0			74.4	0.1
1952	161.3		3.8			155.4	2.0
1953	194.2		0.2		5.6	158.8	29.6
1954	153.9				82.4	50.2	21.3
1955	236.7				205.8	8.7	22.2
1956	326.7			33.0	271.0	0.3	22.4
1957	382.9			45.5	323.4		14.1
1958	321.3			47.9	265.6		7.7
1959	222.2			11.4	206.3		2.5
1960	254.4			19.9	225.2		0.2
1961	199.2			44.9	154.3		
1962	232.3			67.3	165.0		
1963	216.4			96.8	199.7		
1964	149.3			61.0	88.3		
1965	131.4			59.5	71.9		
1966	103.3			38.0	65.3		
1967	97.0			44.4	52.6		
1968	105.9			55.9	49.9		
1969	107.3			74.8	32.4		
1970	82.6			61.7	20.9		
1971	51.2			33.7	17.6		
1972	5.1				5.1		
1973	2.1				2.1		
1974	1.0				1.0		
1975	1.2				1.2		
1976	1.7				1.7		
1977	0.9				0.9		
1978	0.2				0.2		
1979	0.2				0.2		
1980	0.4				0.4		

Source: U.S. Department of Commerce, *Foreign Grants and Credits by the U.S. Government,* various years

construction of the Seoul-Pusan highway and the Rural Revitalization (Saemaul) Movement.

All donors were against the Seoul-Pusan highway, which was regarded as flamboyant, uneconomic waste, yet it proved to be highly successful. If the "new directions" of 1973 were in place earlier, the United States would have tried to convince Korea to expand its rural sector, not its urban, industrial base, and would have objected to the high rate of subsidization of much of Korean rural and industrial development. Yet in both cases Korean policies proved to be highly efficacious (Steinberg, 1988: 20).

An annual average of over $240 million of military aid during the early period of 1953-1963 (equivalent to over twelve percent of Korea's GNP) and the continued American commitment thereafter to the defense of South Korea helped the latter concentrate its energy and resources on economic development. The American guarantee also provided other advanced countries with a sense of security to commit to South Korea credits for further investment. Korean military units' equipment, supplied by the American military assistance, had undertaken the construction of roads, bridges, and other infrastructure. None of these contributions should be ignored.

The military assistance programs also provided Korean military personnel with training in organization, management, and technical skills. After their service, many enlisted men joined in industrial and service occupations, whereas many officers took senior management positions, especially in the government-owned enterprises (Mason, 1980: 183).

Japanese compensation for its Korean occupation and exploitation should not be brushed aside. The amount was equivalent to half the foreign currency required for the Second Five-Year Economic Development Plan (1967-1971).

The international environment, which was favorable toward the promotion of free trade, also helped Korea in economic development. The desire for free international trade was shared, first, by 23 countries. The General Agreement on Tariffs and Trade (GATT), an international code of tariff and trade rules, was drawn up and signed in 1947, effective as of January 1, 1948. It was dedicated to three basic principles for the promotion of international trade: (1) equal, nondiscriminatory treatment for all trading nations on the basis of the most-favored-nation principle, (2) reduction of tariffs by negotiations, and (3) prohibition of the use of quantitative restrictions such as import quotas except for the balance-of-payment reasons (Dam, 1970; Snape, 1986). Since then, GATT has been a major instrument for free trade in international markets, eliminating or negotiating such issues as tariffs, quantitative restrictions, and discriminations.

The Generalized System of Preferences (GSP) was another external factor favorable to the economic development of Korea. The GSP was adopted by the developed countries in the United Nations Conference on Trade and Development (UNCTAD) in Geneva in 1964 to grant trade preferences to the developing countries without violating GATT's rules regarding most-favored-nation nondiscrimination. The GSP in fact has helped developing nations including Korea to export their goods to the developed countries with less tariff on their goods until the former reach high levels of development and "graduate" from such preferences.

The Korean Economic Development Model

These factors--internal (domestic) and external (foreign)--were well combined to formulate and implement a series of export-oriented five-year economic development plans under the energetic initiative of the government with the cooperation of business firms and the general public. The characterization of economic development in Korea shows several phases of growth and transition.

Each of these stages does not necessarily have to be consummated before the next one takes over; however, each of them was, is, and will become a dominant economic mode of activities and operations. The emphasis of a specific economic stage is based on the "law of diminishing relative marginal utility" of individuals if they stagnate in one stage (Rostow, 1971: 8-9), and the "law of maximizing the amount of surplus in international trade" in accordance with comparative advantage. These stages include: 1) the "traditional import-oriented economy" (1945-1953); 2) the "import-substituting" of daily necessities, while basic preparations were made for light and heavy industries and their products continued to be imported (1953-1963); 3) the export-oriented economy focused on "labor-intensive light industries," while the basic foundation for heavy and high technology medium industries embarked on the basis of the foreign licenses and technical agreements, for example, with Ford to assemble the Cortina passenger car in 1967, and the adoption and implementation of such legislation as the Electronic Industry Promotion Law of 1969[2], during which stage, products of heavy and high-tech industries still had to be continuously imported (1963-73); 4) the export-oriented phase based on "capital-intensive chemical and

Figure 4-2 The Korean Model of Economic Development

1990s-
*Strengthening high-tech industries
*Improvement in heavy industries
-Example: From very large crude carrion (VLCCs) to samller higher value-added ships
*Improvement in light industries
-Example: higher value-added footwear

5th 5-yr. Plan 1985-
*Technology intensive intermediate industries for export

3rd & 4th 5-yr. Plan 1973-
*Capital intensive heavy industries
*Import of high-tech industry products
*Import substitution of some high tech products
*Preparation for high tech industries
-Examples:
1. The Blue House Project of 1983
2. The Long-Range Automobile Industry Promotion Plan of 1984

1st & 2nd 5-yr Plan 1963-
*Labor intensive light industries
*Import of heavy & medium industry products
*Preparation for heavy & high tech industries
-Examples:
1. Foreign licenses technical agreements with Ford in 1967
2. Electronics Industry Promotion Law of 1969

Reconstruction Period 1953-
*Import-substituting of daily necessities
*Import of other products
*Preparation for light industries

1945-
*Import-oriented economy

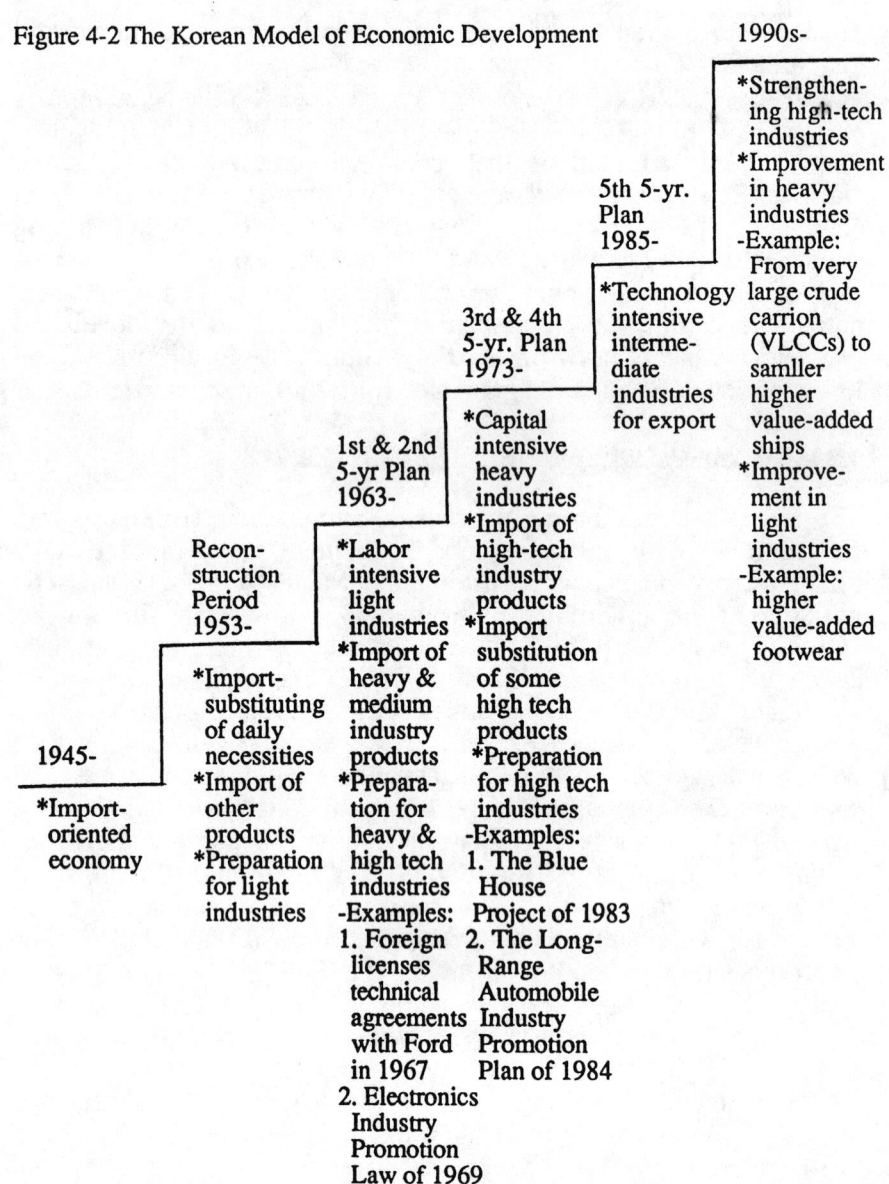

heavy industries," whereas basic plans and projects like the Long-Range Automobile Industry Promotion Plan of 1974 and the Blue House Project of 1983[3] for the establishment of high technology medium industries were engaged in and their products continued to

Table 4-2 The Korean Model of Economic Development

Primary Product Export, Manufactured Product Import (PPEMPI)	Import Substitution Industries (ISI)	Labor-Intensive Light Industries (LILI)	Capital-Intensive Heavy Industries (CIHI)	Technology-Intensive Intermediate Industries (TIII)	Simultaneous Improvement of All Three Industries (SIATI)
+_____	+_____	+_____	+_____	+_____	+_____
Time 1945	1953	1963	1973	1985	1990s

Major Characteristics

*Import of manufactured products with -Tariff -Quota -Preferential export rate system *Export of primary products: -Grain -Maritime products -Mineral resources *Investment in infrastructure *Land redistribution	*Import substituting industries: -Footwear -Textile -Sugar refineries -Processed food *Import of producer goods *Investment in infrastructure *Modernizing agriculture *Intersectoral financing for capital accumulation	*Investment in light industries for export: -Plywood -Food processing -Wig -Footwear -Accessaries *Investment in infrastructure: -Harbor -Roads -Electricity *Export promoting measures: -Export zone -Tariff rebate -Preferential loans	*Investment in heavy industries: -Iron & steel -Shipbuilding -Construction -Machinery -Military hardware -Chemical *Mechanization of farming *Further liberalization *Expansion in investment in infrastructure -Tax concession scheme -Liberalizing import items for exports	*Investment in high technology industries: -Automobile -Computer -Electronics -Appliances *R & D *Further liberalization *Further privatization	*Application of R & D to all three industries *Emphasis on R & D

be imported (1973-1984); and 5) the "technology-intensive export-oriented phase" relying on "intermediary industries" (1985-). From this stage on creativity, science, and technology apply to all three

Table 4-3 Key Indicators of Korea's Rapid Economic Development

Year	Exports (1)	Imports (2)	(1)/(2)	Cumulative foreign loans	GNP ($millions)	Per Capita ($)
Traditional Economy:						
1946	0	0	3.20			
1947	1	2	1.88			
1948	7	9	1.23			
1949	11	15	1.30			
1950	33	52	1.57			
1951	46	122	2.65			
1952	195	704	3.61			
1953	398	2237	5.61			
Import Substituting Economy:						
1954	24	243	10.12		1790	$84
1955	18	341	18.94		2033	$94
1956	25	386	15.44		1940	$89
1957	19	442	23.26		1950	$87
1958	17	378	22.23		2900	$128
1959	20	304	15.20		2200	$95
1960	33	344	10.42		1850	$74
1961	41	316	7.70		2300	$90
1962	55	422	7.67	77	2400	$92
Labor-Intensive Light Industries:						
1963	87	560	6.43	147	2700	$97
1964	119	404	3.39		2815	$102
1965	175	463	2.64	301	3085	$108
1966	250	716	2.86	347	3303	$113
1967	320	996	3.11		3713	$124
1968	455	1463	3.21		4071	$133
1969	623	1824	2.92		4575	$149
1970	835	1984	2.37		7318	$235
1971	1067	2394	2.24	3724	8057	$252
1972	1624	2522	1.55	4554	12242	$378
Capital-Intensive Heavy Industries:						
1973	3225	4240	1.31	5627	15017	$445
1974	4460	6852	1.53	7614	16218	$447
1975	5081	7274	1.43	10459	18509	$532
1976	7715	8776	1.13	13070	27092	$765
1977	10046	10815	1.07	15697	35040	$965
1978	12711	14976	1.17	18887	47189	$1279
1979	15756	20313	1.28	25903	64560	$1597
1980	17505	22292	1.27	34374	61250	$1503
1981	21254	26131	1.22	41669	67210	$1870
1982	21853	24251	1.10	37100	70840	$1910
Technology-Intensive Intermediate Industries:						
1983	24450	26192	1.07	40400	75320	$2010

The Korean Model of Economic Development 77

1984	29245	30631	1.04	43100	81080	$2110
1985	34700	31500	.90	46800	83120	$2200
1986	33900	29700	.87	44500	90600	$2296
1987	47300	41000	.86	35600	118600	$2826
1988	57500	52500	.91	31000	154000	$3600
1989	64000	61000	.95	27000	184000	$4270
1990	70500	68000	.96	24500	210000	$4840
1991	79500	76500	.96	23000	240000	$5500
1992	89500	86000	.96	22000	280000	$6200

Source: Data for 1946-53, Frank et al. (1975: Table 2-3); for the remaining years, The World Bank (1987:); for 1988 to 1992, *Dong A Ilbo* (8/22/1987; *Korea Herald* (11/21/1987); *Korea Times* (4/12/1988 and 7/30/1988)

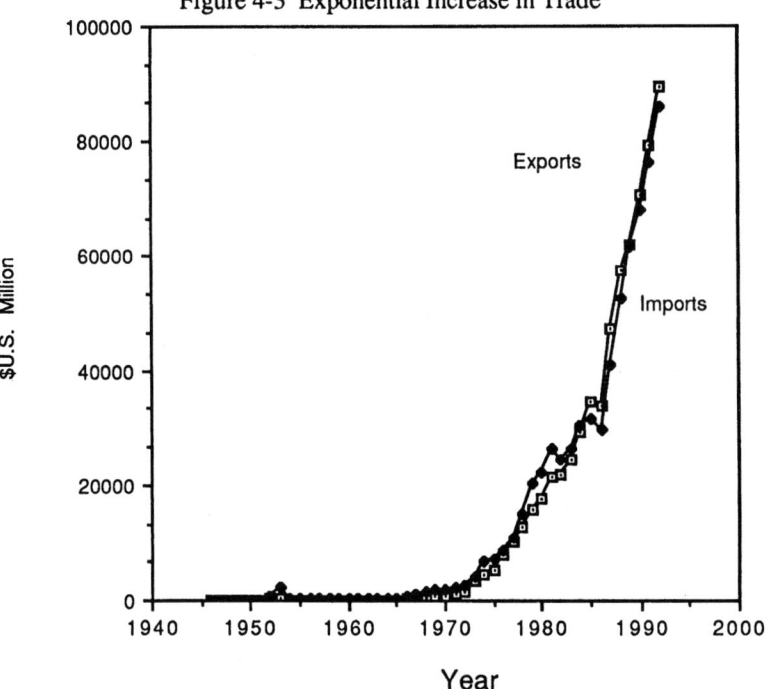

Figure 4-3 Exponential Increase in Trade

industries--light, heavy, and medium--to enhance higher value added productivity (see Figure 4-2 and Table 4-2).

The Korean model of economic development demonstrates the successful and successive completion of each of the first four stages of economic development. Since 1985, Korea has concentrated its talent, energy, and financial resources on the production and export

Table 4-4 Production Indexes of Major Commodities, 1946-1953
(1946=100, Index unweighted)

Commodities	1947	1949	1951	1953	Overall Increase (1953/1947)
Agricultural & Fisheries:					
Rice	115	122	94	117	101.7%
Wheat & Barley	90	123	74	125	138.8
Processed marine products	72	118	61	78	108.3
Cigarettes & Tobacco	237	367	316	433	182.7
Raw silk	100	92	66	112	112.0
Cotton yarn	109	247	111	257	235.7
Average	**121**	**178**	**120**	**187**	**147**
Nonagricultural Products:					
Anthracite coal	169	347	44	269	159.1
Tungsten ore	353	413	327	2,347	664.8
Salt	87	225	99	238	237.5
Cotton cloth	119	230	116	216	181.5
Paper & Paper Products	83	213	62	261	314.4
Laundry soap	7	197	268	310	442.8
Chinaware	107	419	274	330	308.4
Cement	172	225	68	390	226.7
Nails	598	865	225	1,114	186.2
Electric Power	109	291	140	327	300.0
Average	**180**	**343**	**162**	**580**	**305**

Source: Adapted from Charles Frank et al. (1975: Table 2-2)

of technology-intensive intermediate goods and services such as electronics, audio-visual, computers, VCRs, sophisticated TVs, automobiles, and the like. The Korean model brings about three significant outcomes. They are an exponentially increasing rate of trade, increase in the level of exports exceeding or balancing that of imports since 1984, and the fastest growth rates of GNP and per capita GNP in the world (see Figures 3-7, 3-8, 4-3, and Table 4-3). We will examine how each stage was accomplished, by whose efforts, with what outcomes, and toward which direction the Korean economy continues to gear.

The Traditional Import-Oriented Economy (1945-1953)

The export of primary products and the import of manufactured goods were the major economic characteristics of Korea during the period of 1945-1953, mainly due to the lack of industrialization. Nearly all of its exports during this period were agricultural products and unmanufactured natural resources (see Table 4-4). Agricultural and fishery products, for example, accounted for about eighty percent of the total annual exports in the early part of that period but declined to only ten to fifteen percent during 1951-1953. The two main reasons for the decline of grain and fishery exports were the increase in their domestic consumption by the increased population resulting from refugees flooding from the North and from the repatriation of overseas Koreans from Japan and China.

Because the population increase exceeded the agricultural output, about 670 thousand metric tons of food including wheat, barley, rice, and powdered milk had to be imported from May 1946 to January 1948. "In 1946, 1952, and 1953, food grain imports accounted for 34 to 44 percent of total non-arid imports." In other years, when grain imports were not so high, "manufactured goods imports accounted for 39 to 59 percent of total imports " (Frank et al., 1975: 10). Consequently, the ratio of imports to exports increased from 3.20 in 1946 to 5.61 in 1953 (see Table 4-3).

Starting from a very low base in 1946, the post-World War II recovery of nonagricultural natural resources extraction, on the other hand, began to increase about three-fold from 1947 to 1953. Hence, exports of such mineral products as tungsten, copper, graphite, kaolin, and talc, increased from about ten percent of the total in 1946 to about eighty percent in 1951-1953.

Nevertheless, due to slow industrial growth, mounting increases in imports, and the subsequent deficit in the balance of payments, the government began to take various measures such as tariffs, import controls, and export promotions. In 1946, a uniform tariff rate of ten percent was originally imposed on all imports except those financed by foreign assistance. In 1949, the Korean government adopted a stringent tariff reform program that became effective as of January 1950. Its major provisions of tariff structures included:

1. No duties on the imports of food grains, noncompetitive equipment, and raw materials required for industrial, educational, cultural, and sanitation facilities.
2. A ten percent duty on essential goods for which domestic production was small relative to demand and on unfinished goods not produced in Korea.
3. A twenty percent duty on unfinished goods produced in Korea.
4. A thirty percent duty on finished goods not produced in Korea.
5. A forty percent duty on finished goods produced in Korea.
6. A range of fifty to ninety percent duties on semi-luxury goods.
7. More than 100 percent duty on luxury goods (Frank et al., 1975: 36-37).

To discourage the import of nonessential manufactured goods and to encourage the exports of domestic primary products, the government took a series of measures. The first one was an import and export licensing system of 1946. It contained a list of imports that should be licensed and/or prohibited. The second measure was an import quota system in 1949 as a mechanism to control both the types and quantities of imports in accordance with a comprehensive commodity demand-and-supply program. The third action was the adoption of a preferential export system in 1951, which provided the exporters of domestic products with the right to use a range of one to ten percent of the export earnings for importing about forty different popular items thus far not readily approved for import (Frank et al., 1975: 37-38).

The deficit resulting from the amount of imports exceeding that of export was paid by the American aid programs called the GARIOA (Government Appropriations for Relief in Occupied Areas). During the period of 1945-1949 the GARIOA appropriated more than $500 million for the purpose of short-run emergency measures to prevent starvation and disease and to allow massive importation of commodities to overcome the shortage of consumer goods (see Table 4-1).

About fourteen percent of the aid program was allocated for an intermediate-term priority to raise agricultural products, especially rice, so as to make Korea self-sufficient in food. With this aim, more than half a million metric tons of fertilizer were imported.

This recorded the "highest application of commercial fertilizer to Korean soil" (Mason et al., 1980: 168).

Added to the massive application of fertilizer which contributed to the increase in agricultural output was land redistribution. The expropriation of Japanese-held land and the "purchase" of large Korean-owned estates with a modicum of compensation resulted in a "relative equality of agricultural assets" (Mason et al., 1980: 10) among the farmers. Such an efficient land reform could not to be found in most of the less-developed world at that time.

The outcome was that the number of tenants fell to only 5-7 percent of the total cultivators and that the amount of rented land fell from sixty percent to fifteen percent of the total farm land. Since the farmers no longer had to pay half of the total crop to their former landlords, the farmers had a greater incentive to maximize their production. This resulted in rapid increases in farm output.

Import-Substituting Economy (1953-1962)

The ever-increasing trade deficit and the continued dependence on foreign countries for manufactured goods, coupled with surplus labor forces tended to generate an alarming awareness of economic backwardness and called for the government to take decisive action for national economic independence. This became the main reason for the transformation of Korea from an import-oriented economy to an import-substituting economy of the daily necessities.

The import-substituting economy was facilitated by the government's intersectoral financing by artificially protecting domestic industries and augmenting their profits by means of various strategies such as import control, a low interest rate policy, high tariff protection, and an overvalued foreign exchange rate. Profits accrued from these measures were then invested together with foreign aid funds in establishing industries which would substitute manufactured goods thus far imported from other countries. The government also embarked on building infrastructure for the import-substituting industries. The policy for establishing import-substituting industries incorporated additional measures such as increases in the printing of money, high tariffs on manufactured import goods, tariff exemptions on items essential for domestic industries, import quotas, and benefits from favorable foreign exchange rates.

In an open market, the interest rate was supposedly determined by the flow of savings to finance investment, but, to assist the import-substituting entrepreneurs in rapidly augmenting voluntary savings and investment, the government provided them with loans with an interest rate much lower than that which prevailed in the free or black market. Such assistance was made through the government-controlled commercial banks and usually accompanied by printing more paper money, which caused price inflation. Low interest rates and inflation lowered the repayment burden of the borrowing entrepreneurs while increasing the burden of higher prices to the consumers, farmers, and wage earners.

Since a uniform tariff rate of ten percent on all foreign goods was adopted in 1946, the tariff rate increased an average of 40 percent in 1950 again. In 1957, changes in tariff rates resulted in an average 4.1 percent additional increase. The high tariff was able to protect domestic industries in the embryonic stage from foreign competition. The government, on the other hand, exempted tariffs on imports of machinery and equipment essentially required for building such import-substituting industries as metal work, machinery, sugar refining, textiles, mining, fishing, and chemicals (Frank et al., 1975: 36-37).

The government, of course, took measures for import controls with an import and export licensing system and an import quota system. Simultaneously, export promotion was encouraged with preferential access of exporters to foreign exchange loans, an export credit system with a lower interest rate than that prevailing in the market, and export subsidies of a certain amount of money per ton of export items, for example, 50 won per ton of Kaolin exports, and 1,500 won per ton of dried anchovies (Frank et al., 1975: 39).

Overvaluation of the foreign exchange rate was another income-transfer strategy. Due to a wide margin between the official rate and that of the black market, favorably lower official exchange rates were applied to the importers of machinery and equipment for building import-substituting industries and to the importers of raw materials for manufacturing. Overvaluation was combined with a multiple exchange rate system, which also favored import-substituting industries and penalized the importers of manufactured goods and their domestic consumers.[4]

Various governmental strategies as listed above for intersectoral transfer of the capital to the private business sector partially explained the establishment of many import-substituting industries in textiles, mining, footwear, electric power, sugar refineries, processed foods, and others. But the import of producer goods such as machinery, equipment, and raw materials for domestic production required a large amount of capital. As shown in Table 4-3, the total amount of imports during 1954-1962 reached $3.176 billion, whereas that of exports accounted for only $252 million. Thus, the amount of imports exceeded more than 12.6 times that of exports on average. This showed the highest skew in balance throughout the different phases of the economy in Korea. Nevertheless, the import of machinery, equipment, and raw materials was of absolute necessity for import-substituting industries.

For the development of import-substituting industries, $77 million of foreign loans was secured cumulatively as of 1962. The U.S. foreign aid, of course, took a lion's share of the loans. The United Nations Korean Reconstruction Agency (UNKRA) assistance and U.S. aid together amounted to $2.603 billion (See Table 4-1), explaining about 82 percent of the total loans during 1953-1962. "Of this amount, a large proportion was allocated to private traders and end-users for imports of raw materials, semi-finished products and investment goods" (Frank et al., 1975: 29).

For import-substituting industries to be successful, establishment and expansion of the infrastructures were inevitable. Therefore, the government was committed to effectively building electric power plants and improving communications, transportations, and dam construction. Agricultural improvement was moderately pursued to attain self-sufficiency with the purchase of about sixty percent more grain processing units, (for example, 62,209 in 1955 and 64,054 in 1960, as compared with 40,111 in 1951) and with the import of about sixty percent more of fertilizers (for example, 279.42 thousand metric tons in 1960 as opposed to 200.3 thousand metric tons in 1949) during this period (Mason et al., 1980: 213, 221-23).

Labor-Intensive Light Industries (1963-1973)

Post-war reconstruction and the subsequent establishment of manufacturing industries were able to produce enough goods to meet the demands of the domestic consumers. By 1960, the domestic market for manufactured consumer goods was almost completely supplied by domestic outputs; therefore, industries were no longer able to expand their production beyond the maximum level of

Figure 4-4 Classification of Forty-One Developing Economies by Trade Orientation, 1963-1973 and 1973-1985

Period	Outward Oriented		Inward Oriented	
	Strongly Outward Oriented	Moderately Outward Oriented	Moderately Inward Oriented	Strongly Inward Oriented
1963-73	Hong Kong Korea Singapore	Brazil Cameroon Columbia Costa Rica Cote d'Ivoire Guatemala Indonesia Israel Malaysia Thailand	Bolivia El Salvador Honduras Kenya Madagascar Mexico Nicaragua Nigeria Philippines Senegal Tunisia Yugoslavia	Argentina Bangladesh Burundi Chile Dominican Republic Ethiopia Ghana India Pakistan Peru Sri Lanka Sudan Tanzania Turkey Uruguay Zambia
Total	3	10	12	16
1973-85	Hong Kong Korea Singapore	Brazil Chile <- Israel Malaysia Thailand Tunisia <- Turkey <- Uruguay <- Kenya Mexico Nicaragua Pakistan Philippines Senegal Sri Lanka <- Yugoslavia	-> Cameroon -> Columbia -> Costa Rica -> Cote d'Ivoire El Salvador -> Guatemala Honduras -> Indonesia -> Madagascar Nigeria -> Peru Sudan Tanzania Zambia	Argentina Bangladesh Bolivia Burundi Dominican Republican Ethiopia Ghana India
Total	3	16	14	8

Source: Adapted from the World Bank (1987: Figure 5.1)
The arrow directions indicate the movement of the countries from the 1963-1973 period into either more inward or outward orientation during the 1973-1985 period.

domestic consumption. Nor were they able to hire more people from the ever-increasing labor force. In consequence the import-substituting economy began to face slow growth. At the same time the U.S. government announced that the American "assistance would be terminated in the near future" (Mason et al., 1980: 95). In fact, the amount of the U.S. nonmilitary government grants and credits was reduced from $382.9 million in 1957 to $149.3 million in 1964, a 61 percent decrease (see Table 4-1). Continuation of the import-substituting strategy could have worsened the shortage of foreign exchange in cases of the substantial reduction and the ultimate termination of the U.S. assistance. The shortage of domestic natural resources, a sluggish economy, and the mounting demand for employment were such that the import-substituting strategy had to be replaced by the export-oriented strategy. One has to keep mind, however, that such a shift at that time was rare in a global perspective. During the period of 1963-1973 among 41 selected developing countries, Korea was one of the three that became "strongly outward oriented," whereas ten countries were "moderately outward oriented" and a whopping 28 countries remained "inward oriented" (see Figure 4-4).

The essential strategy was the promotion of trade by means of a proper combination of liberalization and restriction. "Liberalization" refers to the lessening of government controls so as to allow and encourage entrepreneurs to invest in labor-intensive light industries, maximizing low wage and surplus labor, and concentrating on light industries that did not require sophisticated skills and technology beyond apprenticeship on the operation of machines and equipment purchased from advanced foreign countries. Comparative advantages in terms of cheaper and yet well-trained labor and the improvement in quality of products through learning and creative extensions and applications became the economic rationality in this stage. "Restriction" refers to active government control over economic activities that might hinder the growth of labor-intensive light industries.

Major policy innovations for export promotion included 1) raising the interest rate to a realistic level to encourage savings in banks for investment, 2) securing loans from foreign countries for additional investment, 3) liberalizing import items essential for labor-intensive light industries--modern machinery, equipment, and raw materials, with concurrent restriction on the importation of

Table 4-5 Preferential Bank Loans for Exports* (units= % & $ millions)

Objectives of Loans	Percent Annual Allocation of Loans for Different Objectives							Average Annual Interest Rate
	1964	1965	1966	1967	1968	1969	1970	
Credit for import of raw materials for export	66.6%	52.1%	60.2%	54.9%	46.6%	46.7%	46.2%	3.0
Import of capital goods & equipment for export industries		4.9	6.1	10.4	23.1	18.8	22.4	12.5
Export credit	18.5	31.8	21.9	20.4	18.6	17.3	17.7	6.5
Export industry promotion loans	0.8	0.5	0.2	0.2	0.8	0.0	0.0	26.0
Export industry operating loans	1.9	1.4	1.1	0.6				18.0
Loans for export specializing industries			0.6	0.9	1.3	1.1	0.7	12.5
Others export related	12.2	9.3	10.1	12.6	9.6	16.1	13.0	
Total: %	100.0	100.0	100.0	100.0	100.0	100.0	100.0	
$	39.2	44.6	61.0	120.9	154.1	220.1	355.1	

Source: The Bank of Korea; The Medium Industry Bank
*Blanks indicate the absence of data.

items not conducive to export, and 4) subsidizing export-oriented industries by the government.

There had been a wide discrepancy between the official interest rate that was made available by the bank and the interest rate prevailing in the curb market. The greater the discrepancy between the two, the less money was put into savings in banks because of relatively lower interest to be accrued from the banks.

In September 1965, the government finally made a bold decision to raise the interest rate on bank deposits. For example, the ceiling on commercial bank lending rates was raised from 16 to 26 percent. This resulted in the increase of domestic loanable funds due to the saving of more money in the safe banks away from the high risk curb market. Moreover, the government took a calculated risk to borrow foreign loans for additional investment. The cumulative foreign loans up until 1962 totalled $77 million. In 1963 alone, Korea borrowed $70 million and had accumulated a total of $147 million in loans. The amount of foreign loans as of 1971 reached $3,791 million, that is, about 26 times as much money as the total loans as of 1963 (see Table 4-3).

Devaluation was coupled with an increase of exports relative to imports. For example, the ratio of imports to exports was 6.43 in 1963 but improved to 3.39 in 1964 and 2.64 in 1965 (Table 4-3). This enabled the government to decide to further liberalize trade restrictions. The number of items eligible for importation increased from about 500 to 1,500 during the second half of 1964 and the first half of 1965 (Mason et al., 1980: 49). The number of automatic approvals of import items (a positive list system) had been increasing quickly, for example, from 5.2 percent of the 30,000 commodities as specified in the Standard International Trade Classification (SITC) during the first half of 1961 to 52.1 percent in the second half of 1967 (Mason et al., 1980: 44-46, 58-61).

Import of capital goods and equipment with tariff rebates was allowed mainly to build up such export-oriented light industries as textiles, clothing, electrical, machinery and apparatus, plywood, plates and sheets of iron and steel, footwear, and wigs. The import of related raw materials was greatly expanded. Tax concessions also were devised to exempt business firms from paying income taxes for new investment projects.

The government was equally enthusiastic about making financial credit available to private industries. Table 4-5 shows that preferential bank loans for exports had an exceptionally low interest rate of three percent on average. In the beginning of this economic phase, about 67 percent of the total loans of $39.2 million in 1964 were allocated for the import of raw materials. But the amount of loans for the import of raw materials gradually declined to only 46 percent of the total in 1970. Instead, over twenty percent of the total loans, that is, $355.1 million in 1970, were spent for the expansion and modernization of those industries. On the other hand, increase of tariff rates and restrictions on import were imposed on the items that would hurt the domestic light industries.

The outcome of these strategies was very "positive" and "challenging." The term "positive" means that those export strategies brought about only $87 million of exports in 1963, when the export-oriented light industries were initiated. But the exports reached a record of $3,225 million in 1973 when the light-industry stage was almost completed (see Table 4-3). The export of 1973, indeed, increased about 37 times as much as that of 1963. One may wonder, then, what made contributions to the spectacular increase in exports such that the ratio of imports to exports, which was 23.26, the highest level of imbalance in payments in 1957, decreased to only 1.31 in 1973. (see Table 4-3).

The answer was the contribution of labor-intensive light industries. While the overall amount of exports increased about 37 times during 1963-1973 (Table 4-3), the amount of exports by the labor-intensive light industries increased 290 times, for example, from $6.0 million in 1962 to $1,739.7 million in 1973 (see Table 4-6). To state it differently, the amount of exports by the labor-intensive light industries explained only 10.9 percent of the total exports in 1962 but increased to account for 53.9 percent of the total exports in 1973 (Table 4-6). Export-oriented, labor-intensive light industries maximizing the comparative advantage of cheap surplus labor forces with less sophisticated technology in the early phase of economic growth explains the success of the Korean economic model.

The term "challenging" means that the importance of labor-intensive light industries in its contribution to the overall amount of exports had been declining since 1968. For example, the export of plywood products explained 4.1 percent of the total exports in 1962, but gradually increased to 11.7 percent in 1966, and reached the pinnacle of 13.1 percent in 1968. Since then its percentage declined to only 8.3 percent in 1973. Wigs showed a similar pattern, reaching the peak of export in 1970 followed by decline. This declining pattern, which represented plywood, cotton, wigs, plates, and sheets, ultimately reflected the light industries in general. The exports of light industries accounted for 60.5 and 61.9 percent of the total exports in 1970 and 1971 and since then began to decline to 59.4 and 53.9 percent in 1972 and 1973, respectively (see the last column of Table 4-6). This trend, in fact, began to challenge both entrepreneurs and government economic leaders, because labor-intensive light

Table 4-6 Percent Exports of Major Labor-Intensive Light Industries, 1963-1973

Year	Ply-wood	Cotton	Wigs	Plates & Sheet of Iron & Steel	Foot-wear	Elec-trical, Machi-nery, Appara-tus	Clo-thing	Sum %	$ (millions)	% of Total Exports
1962	4.1	3.3	0.0	0.0	0.4	0.2	2.0	9.9	6.0	10.9
1963	7.5	5.1	0.0	9.8	0.8	1.1	5.5	29.8	25.1	28.8
1964	9.4	9.2	0.2	1.7	0.7	1.3	5.5	28.0	33.9	28.8
1965	10.0	5.8	1.3	5.7	2.3	1.8	11.5	38.4	69.2	28.5
1966	11.7	3.9	4.7	2.8	2.2	3.2	13.1	41.6	106.3	39.5
1967	10.2	3.5	6.3	0.3	2.3	2.6	16.5	41.7	149.2	42.5
1968	13.1	2.7	7.0	0.2	2.2	4.4	22.4	52.0	259.8	46.6
1969	11.3	2.6	8.6	0.5	1.5	6.0	22.9	53.4	375.2	60.2
1970	9.1	2.6	10.1	0.8	1.7	4.8	21.3	50.4	505.7	60.5
1971	9.2	2.3	5.2	1.5	2.8	5.5	22.5	49.0	661.3	61.9
1972	8.5	1.9	4.1	3.8	3.1	7.6	24.5	53.5	965.3	59.4
1973	8.3	1.7	2.5	4.0	3.3	10.6	23.0	53.4	1,739.7	53.9

Source: Economic Planning Board, *Major Economic Indicators*, various years; Percent of total exports is measured by the sum of the exports by these light industries divided by the total amount of exports.

industries in Korea began to show their limit in exports in competition with less developing countries, which could produce such products with the same quality at much cheaper wages and subsequent cheaper unit prices.

Capital-Intensive Heavy Industries (1973-1984)

The government had long adhered to the policy of low grain prices by importing large amounts of U.S. grain under the Public Law 480 (see Table 4-1). The suppression of grain prices was designed to catch two birds simultaneously: the humanitarian and political objective of relieving low-income people from the specter of starvation by insuring that food be available to them at low prices and the economic objective of maximizing comparative advantages in the labor-intensive light industries in export by maintaining the low urban wages commensurate with low staple prices.

The continued low grain price policy and the subsequent agricultural sacrifice for industrialization were such that the ratio of the average farmers' income to urban wage earners' income substantially declined to 79 percent. The farmers, who made much less income than their urban counterparts and yet, ironically, had traditionally remained loyal to the government and the government party, could not be politically ignored any longer. Support from the farmers had been the main source for government leaders and the government party to maintain their political power. Moreover, a large portion of the amount of exports from industries in trade had to be greatly offset by the ever-increasing amount of grain imports.

In 1968 the government adopted a two-tier grain pricing policy that purchased grain from farmers at higher prices than the market prices and sold them to urban wage earners at much cheaper prices. This new policy raised the income of farmers without increasing the market price of grains. This, in turn, became the lion's share of the government expenditures and a main cause for increases in the money supply.

The Korean farm society up until the early 1970s was characterized by small, fragmented land holdings centered around farm families; the lack of farm roads conducive to mechanization; shortage of skilled labor; little marketable surplus; and the lack of training in cooperation for mechanized and commercial orientation. In 1971, the government belatedly began to launch the ambitious New Community Movement (NCM) with three main objectives; 1) spiritual enlightenment which would "create and cultivate the spirit of self-reliance, independence, and hard work;" 2) social development; and 3) economic development.

The NCM promoted four major activities primarily in sequential order. At the initial stage, the government provided farmers with grants and credits so as to improve their living environments including roofs, kitchens, and toilets. Upon the cultivation of the self-help spirit in a more favorable environment, the farmers were encouraged to take up projects to create infrastructure as the foundation for the increase in agricultural production. The projects included the construction of small bridges leading to the villages, farm roads for the access of motor transport to the farmland, running-water facilities, power plants, and the establishment of cooperative credit unions. The third major area was income generating projects, which included group farming, common seedbeds, cultivation of commercial crops, diversification of production such as vegetables, fruits, horticulture, dairy farming, and community forestation. Small-scale rural manufacturing factories using local resources, materials, and labor were the fourth and last goal of the ambitious project.

Domestic chemical industries began to substantially increase their fertilizer output, which led to large decreases in their imports. For example, the chemical fertilizer consumption was 393 thousand metric tons in 1965, of which 81 percent was imported. In 1975, fertilizer consumption increased to 886.2 thousand metric tons, more than twice as much as that of 1965 but 97 percent of it was domestically produced.[5]

To facilitate these projects, the NCM Central Consultative Council was organized under the chairmanship of the Minister of Home Affairs. Similar organizations were established at each successive level--province, county, township, and village--to be in charge of training and education, planning, implementation, and evaluation of those projects. The share of the government's contribution to these projects accounted for 34 percent of a total of $25 million in 1971, and then increased to 54 percent, amounting to $1,308 million in 1978. The success of these projects was witnessed by the increase of farm income, for example, from 79 percent of the average income of the urban workers in 1971 to 102.0 percent in 1977 (Mason et al., 1980: 223; Pae, 1986: 98-100).

While the NCM was under full swing in the rural sector, the government's main emphasis in the urban sector during this period shifted from light industries to heavy and chemical industries. The reason for the government's shift was explained very well by Paul Kuznets on the basis of the imperative of division of labor in the international market. He stated, "Just as exports of labor-intensive products like plywood, textiles, and apparel from Korea, Taiwan, and other low-wage, newly industrializing countries reduced Japan's world-market share of labor-intensive manufacture" during the 1960s, growing competition from China, the Philippines, and other, even lower-wage countries began to have the same effect on Korea's more labor-intensive exports (Kuznets, 1986: 55).

Korea was able to shorten the phase of labor-intensive light industries to a decade and was ready to move to the capital-intensive heavy industries. This was possible by several main factors: 1) rapid economic growth; 2) subsequent accumulation of capital stock for investment; 3) heavy investment in education and training so as to enhance a sense of confidence in being committed to the calculated risk in heavy industries; 4) lack of any alternatives but the pursuit of further outward orientation; 5) the necessity of laying the industrial foundation for meeting the demand for intermediary goods resulting from the rapid growth of manufacturing goods; 6) the advantage of large, skilled, labor-intensive forces, which could be employed in the assembly process in some heavy industries like shipbuilding and steel; 7) willingness of advanced countries to transfer low-level-technology-related heavy industries like chemical and steel while monopolizing their own advanced technology; 8) concern of industrialized countries about the environmental impact of the high pollution of water and air upon their quality of life and the subsequent decision to transfer some heavy industries like chemical and petrochemical industries to the newly industrializing countries.[6] Let us briefly examine these factors.

The beginning of labor-intensive light industry-based economy in 1963 showed $92 of the per capita GNP. But by the year of 1973, it had reached $445. The rapid increase was attributed to the promotion of export. The export in 1973, for example, amounted to $3,225 million, about 37 times as much as that of 1963 ($87 million), whereas the import in 1973 ($4,240 million) increased only seven times as much as that of 1963 ($560 million). The ratio of import to export, which was 6.4 in 1963 improved to 1.31 in 1973 (see Table 4-3).

The rapid economic growth and improvement in the balance of payment helped entrepreneurs accumulate capital stock for investment. The Korean government took a series of additional measures for the increase of loanable funds, investment, and further export. Devaluations were taken in 1964 and again in 1971 and 1974 to maintain purchasing power parity and to stimulate exports further. Contrary to most developed countries, Korea rejected a floating exchange rate system because of the uncertainties of exchange rate movements resulting from the absence of domestically well-developed money and credit markets. Instead, Korea continued to peg its exchange rate to the U.S. dollar. The government began to adopt a "cheap money" policy, thereby reducing nominal interest rates from 21.3 percent to 17.4 percent in January 1971 and further down to 12.6 percent only seven months later. Thereafter, the rates continued to be low, with intermittent increases and decreases. Another important measure was to reduce the differentials in interest rates between short-term and long-term maturities such that much lower interest rates for short-term maturity could be greatly enhanced. This measure encouraged and mobilized both short-term and long-term savings (Kwack, 1986: 112).

The government took a bold and decisive measure to freeze all informal market loans and required them to be reported to the government, and then to be converted into five-year short-term loans after a three-year grace period. The so-called Third Emergency Measure of August 1972 facilitated the establishment of short-term financial companies such as investment and finance companies and mutual savings companies to replace and take over Korea's existing informal market transactions. The outcome was the integration of the informal market into formal financial institutions.

The actual size of the informal market had never been fully exposed and therefore not perfectly accurate. However, according to Koo, Hong, and Shin (1982) of the Korean Economic Institute, over the period of 1972-1981, the size of the underground market relative to total lendings by deposit money banks, money supply (M1), household assets, and total corporate debts declined from 0.29 to 0.07, from 0.67 to 0.27, from 0.19 to 0.07, and from 0.15 to 0.04, respectively.

To further mobilize domestic savings, the Public Ownership Inducement Law of 1972 was enacted. Additional measures were taken in 1974: the Regulations on Business Financing and Concentration of Business Ownership, the Agreements for Financing Control of Subsidiary Companies, and the Comprehensive Capital Market Development. These measures required large companies to open up public ownership. The government also introduced an installment security savings plan to promote investments by small investors. The outcomes were: an increase in the number of companies listed in the securities market from 24 in 1967 to 343 in 1981; and the increase of the amount of stock transactions from 25 billion won (U.S. $90 million) in 1967 to 2,534 billion won (U.S. $3.72 billion) in 1981. The ratio of nominal gross capital formation to nominal GNP increased from 24.0 percent in 1973 to 32.7 percent in 1980 (Kwack, 1986: 104-06).

As Figure 4-4 shows, by 1973 more developing countries began to revert from outward orientation back to inward orientation. Madagascar and Nigeria, for example, were "moderately inward-oriented" during 1963-1973 but became "strongly inward-oriented" in 1973-1985. While four countries like Chile, Tunisia, Turkey, and Uruguay became "moderately outward-oriented, six countries like Cameroon, Colombia, Costa Rica, Cote d' Ivoire, Guatemala, and Indonesia shifted from export-orientation to inward-orientation. This indicates that these countries might not have completed the stage of import-substituting economy, perhaps with adequate natural resources available.

Table 4-7 Structure of Commodities Exports by Industries (% of Total Exports)(units=% & $billions)

Goods	1975	1976	1977	1978	1979	1980	1981	1982	1983	1984	1985	1986	1987	1988
Primary & Processed Goods:	15.2	12.2	14.4	11.2	7.0	5.0	4.9	4.1	3.5	3.1	2.7	3.4	3.2	2.9
Light Industries:														
Textile & Clothing	35.8	32.4	31.0	31.6	37.3	34.8	34.4	31.0	27.8	23.4	25.3	28.4	28.0	25.3
Footwear	3.8	5.1	4.8	5.4	6.3	6.4	6.0	6.4	6.0	5.6	5.9	7.2	7.0	7.7
Wood Products	4.8	4.7	4.4	3.9	2.8	3.5	3.7	1.6	1.8	2.0	1.7	1.8	1.6	0.8
Others	11.1	12.7	12.3	12.6	6.2	7.4	6.3	5.2	5.3	6.0	5.5	6.7	6.9	3.0
Subtotal	55.5	54.9	52.5	53.5	52.7	52.1	49.5	44.2	40.9	37.0	38.6	44.2	43.6	43.9
Heavy and Chemical:														
Metal, Iron & Steel	7.2	4.6	3.7	4.3	9.3	12.2	10.9	10.8	9.3	8.6	7.1	6.8	6.1	6.9
Machinery	5.7	3.3	1.8	2.0	3.9	4.4	5.1	5.0	6.0	6.4	7.1	7.2	7.5	7.9
Ships	2.7	3.6	5.3	6.3	5.9	4.7	9.9	17.3	19.1	6.4	2.1	7.2	4.0	4.0
Petrochemical	3.8	0.8	.09	0.9	3.6	4.3	3.3	3.8	4.6	5.4	5.4	3.9	3.3	2.8
Others	2.0	7.3	13.8	12.8	0.9	1.7	2.0	1.8	1.0	0.5	0.4	0.4	0.4	0.3
Subtotal	21.4	19.5	25.5	26.3	23.8	27.3	31.3	38.7	40.0	41.8	40.7	25.6	21.4	21.8
High Tech:														
Electric & Electronics	8.0	10.3	8.3	8.7	15.4	14.6	13.3	12.0	14.4	16.3	14.7	20.1	22.8	23.5
Automobile	-	-	-	-	0.5	0.4	0.4	0.3	0.4	0.7	2.0	4.6	7.1	5.7
Others	-	3.1	-	0.3	0.7	0.6	0.7	0.7	0.8	1.0	1.2	2.0	1.8	1.9
Subtotal	8.0	10.3	8.3	8.7	16.5	15.6	14.4	13.0	15.6	18.0	17.9	26.8	31.7	31.4
Total Exports ($)	5.1	7.7	10.0	12.7	15.7	17.5	21.2	21.8	24.4	29.2	34.7	33.9	47.3	57.5
%	100	100	100	100	100	100	100	100	100	100	100	100	100	100

Source: Adapted from Korean Overseas Information Service (KOIS)(1979: 504); for 1979-1988, *Dong-A Annual* (1989: 606)

To the contrary, Korea had no option but to pursue further export-orientation following the speedy completion of the labor-intensive light industry economy. It was made possible by well-trained labor and management. Heavy training and education, in fact, enhanced a sense of confidence in labor forces by the government

Figure 4-5 Relative Importance of Different Industries by Percent Exports

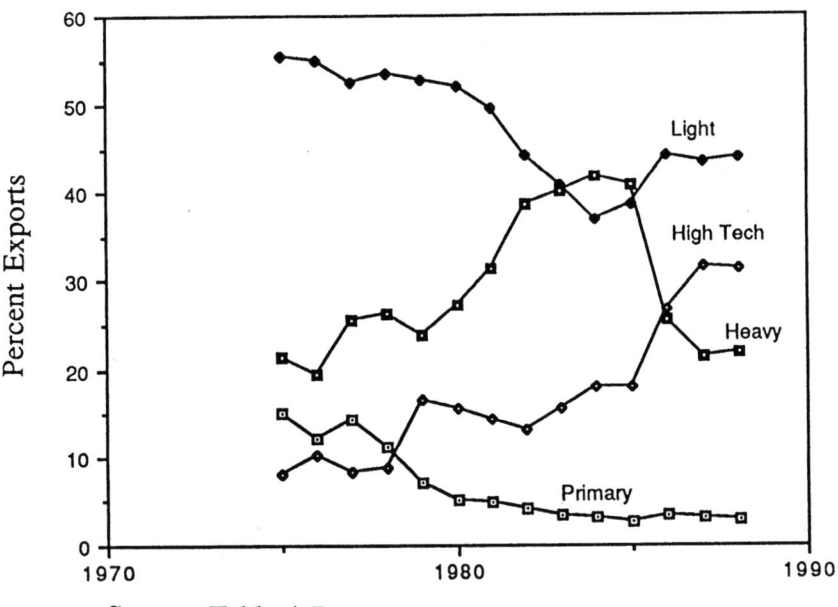

Source: Table 4-7

and business leaders. They soon took a calculated risk of committing themselves to investment in capital-intensive heavy and chemical industries such as electrical machinery, transport equipment, iron and steel, chemicals, petroleum, and shipbuilding.

Heavy industries have often been subject to criticism for being a political symbol of liberation from backwardness and economic violation of comparative advantage. In fact, Denmark did not pursue heavy industries. Some heavy and chemical industries, however, became more attractive to Korea than others. Shipbuilding, iron, and steel industries, for example, continued to depend on the skilled, labor-intensive assembly process, in which Korea was able to enjoy greater comparative advantage over industrialized countries because of the availability of a well-trained, large labor pool. Chemical and petrochemical industries were equally attractive because of greater domestic need of chemical fertilizers for the improvement of agricultural productivity and self-sufficiency and because of the importance of petrochemicals as an energy foundation for other industries in Korea. But due to high levels of pollution in the water, soil, and air, these industries became less favorably accepted in the advanced countries. The advance of technology was such that, while high technology continued to be monopolized by the advanced countries, low-level technology industries such as chemical, petrochemical, steel, and shipbuilding were then to be exported to the newly industrializing countries. Korea began to focus on these three groups of industries.

Capital-intensive heavy industries, however, were not likely to be built up by funds domestically mobilized alone. Therefore, foreign loans--long-term, short-term, and direct foreign investment (the least attractive option among these three with less than five percent of the total foreign loans thus far)--were actively sought and made available due to the increasing economic strengths and the potential for further growth in Korea.

The Korean government also provided heavy-industry entrepreneurs with a variety of benefits and assistance such as tariff rebates, favorable loans on low interest rate, tax concession schemes, and free export-manufacturing zones near major harbors like Masan and Iri where the exports of manufactured products and imports of raw materials and equipment were allowed duty free and without inspection. The cumulative foreign loans were $5.627 billion in 1973 but increased to $37.100 billion by 1982 and $46.8 billion by 1985 (Table 4-3).

Haggard and Moon sharply criticized the Korean government's Heavy and Chemical Industry Plan for its contribution to the increase in inflationary pressures. They also contended that the Korean government's ever-increasing financial and other benefits further exacerbated the concentration of wealth on a few giant conglomerates such that the top fifty *chaebol* accounted for 32 percent of the GDP in 1973 but 49 percent in 1980. The plan caused the credit squeeze to small- and medium-sized industries which "had been the backbone of Korea's successful export of labor-intensive manufactures." They blamed the big push for the "widening gap between rural and urban incomes, the growth of urban marginalism, and--perhaps most important--sharp increases in the prices of basic necessities and housing in the urban areas" (1990: 217-18). Their criticism of the government's "economic mismanagement" was dramatized:

> In 1979, the South Korean economy faltered. Growth rates that had averaged almost 10 percent a year between

1962 and 1978 fell to just over 2 percent between 1979 and 1981. . . . At the same time, inflation rose to 26 percent from an annual average of 16 percent between 1962 and 1978. Exports fell from a 27 percent average annual rate of real growth between 1962 and 1978 to 7.5 percent between 1979 and 1982. The current account deficit widened from $1.1 billion in 1978 to $4.4 billion in 1981 (Haggard and Moon, 1990: 216).

Therefore, Haggard and Moon stated that the new economic cabinet made a "fundamental break" with the style of economic management of the past (1990: 217).

I would rather suggest that the economic slump during the period of 1979 and 1981 was attributed partially to the cheap money policy of previous years and primarily to domestic exogenous variables such as the assassination of incumbent President Park and the subsequent lack of political stability and international exogenous variables such as the second oil shock, rising interest rates, the subsequent increase in Korea's debt service burden, and yet the decline of the overall international trade. I would also point out that there was no fundamental break with the past economic management but a temporary stabilization policy for adaptation and adjustment to the unexpected discrepancy resulting from these non-economic factors. The Korean government soon began to resume "fundamental continuity" rather than institute a "fundamental break" with the economic development plans. Haggard and Moon ironically admit later in the same article that the institutions of the new Fifth Republic exhibited "fundamental continuities with the Yushin system." "Economic policy making was again centralized in the Economic Planning Board" (1990: 220). They also admit that by contrast, "the very weight of the *chaebol* in the economy made it extremely difficult for the government to disengage from past patterns of support." (1990: 220). They finally concede that "the government remained bound by prior commitments to the weak financial structures of the largest firms, and a set of development goals that demanded the private sector's cooperation" (1990: 226).

Despite their growing concern about the ever-increasing amount of foreign debts, the heavy and chemical industries began to make positive contributions to more rapid economic growth during this phase. First of all, the gradual loss of the amount of money from export by labor-intensive light industries was more than fully compensated for by the exports of capital-intensive heavy industries. In fact, gains by the heavy industries exceeded relative percent losses of light industries in the years of 1983-1985. The export by light industries accounted for 55.5 percent of the total exports in 1975 but gradually declined to 40.9 percent in 1983, showing a loss of 14.6 percent of the total exports. But the export by heavy industries explained only 21.4 percent in 1975 but increased to 40.0 percent, thereby gaining 18.6 percent (see Table 4-7 Figure 4-5). This clearly indicates that the gains by the heavy industries exceeded the losses by light industries. Gains by the heavy industries also helped narrow the gap between imports and exports, for example, from 1.31 in the ratio of import to export in 1973 to 1.10 in 1982 (see Table 4-3).

Technology-Intensive Intermediary Industries and Reinforcing Other Industries (1983-   )

A decade-long commitment to investment in heavy industries and the production of iron, steel, and machinery facilitated in 1983-1985 the foundation for and the embarkation of technology-intensive intermediary industries such as electronics, automobiles, appliances, audio-visual products, and computers. As Table 4-7 and Figure 4-5 show, labor-intensive light industries and capital-intensive heavy and chemical industries began to face decline in the exports of their products not in terms of the absolute amount but in terms of their percentages of the total exports, starting from 1983-1985. On the other hand, technology-intensive intermediate industries soon began to accelerate the export of their products at a much higher rate, thereby compensating for the the relative decline of the other two, becoming the third dynamic engine of economy after the light and heavy industries.

Alice H. Amsden also emphasizes "learning" rather than "invention or innovation" as Korea's basis of industrialization.

> Learners do not innovate (by definition) and must compete initially on the combined basis of low wage, state subsidies (broadly construed to include a wide variety of government supports), and incremental productivity and quality improvements related to existing products (1989: 5).

Her thesis is valid because Korea heavily relied upon foreign technologies transferred into domestic industries. However, crucial in the phase of high-technology intermediary industrialization became the issue of domestic research and development (R and D) as equally important as or perhaps more important than foreign technology. As new challenges emerged, the Korean government began to take policy actions in at least six major areas: technology transfer, domestic emphasis on R & D not only by the government but also by the private sector, intersectoral cooperation, the promotion of high-technology industries, and internationalization of science and technology (S & T).

The importance of S & T was called to attention first when Korea began to enter into the stage of labor-intensive, export-oriented light industries. The government gradually laid a solid foundation of scientific and technological infrastructure by means of strengthening S & T education, promoting foreign technology import through foreign direct investment, and securing licensing agreements primarily on the transfer of electrical, chemical, and machinery technologies.

The Korean government, in the initial stage of economic growth, did not aggressively pursue foreign direct investment. This was evidenced by the amount of only $96 million of foreign direct investment in Korea under the stage of the labor-intensive light industries, namely an annual average of $9.6 million for ten years from 1963-72. But during the period of 1973-82, under the stage of heavy industry, foreign direct investment reached $1,152 million. The ever-increasing importance of S & T under the stage of technology-intensive intermediate industries can be witnessed by a rapid increase of direct foreign investment, amounting to $1,407 million for a short period of 1983-85, a whopping $469 million on average per year. The number of licensing agreements also indicates a substantial increase from an annual average of 166 agreements in the period 1973-1982 to 390 in the years of 1983-1985 (see Table 4-8).

Korea faces three fronts of challenge: the demand for increase in wages from domestic wage earners; increased competition in low wage, low technology production from other newly industrializing countries (NIC's); and the ever-increasing average annual amount of royalty payment from $1.7 million in 1963-72, to $54.7 million in 1973-82, to $194 million in 1983-85 and yet the reluctance of the developed countries to transfer their advanced technology for higher value-added production for fear of increased competition.

Table 4-8 Science and Technology for Economic Development (units=$millions & %)

	Labor-Intensive Light Industries 1963-1972	Capital-Intensive Heavy Industries 1973-1982	Technology-Intensive Industries 1983-	Number of (as of 1985) Research Institutes	Korean: Researchers
Strategies to:	Promote foreign technology import, Deepen scientific & technological infrastructure Strengthen S & T	Expand technical training Improve institutional mechanism for adapting imported technology Promote research applicable to industrial needs	Develop & acquire top-level scientists & engineers Perform R & D projects by private & public sectors		
Foreign direct investment overall:	$96	$1,152	$1,407		
Japan	$42(44%)	$591(51%)	$738(52%)		
USA	$42(35%)	$272(24%)	$461(52%)		
Others	$20(21%)	$285(24%)	$208(33%)		
Licensing Agreements on:					
Food	8(3%)	37(2%)	84(5%)	21(11%)	548(6%)
Textile	14(4%)	65(4%)	103(7%)	10(5%)	324(3%)
Chemical	83(26%)	315(19%)	266(17%)	49(27%)	1,542(17%)
Metal	41(13%)	193(12%)	131(8%)	38(21%)	2,606(28%)
Electric/ Electronic	88(28%)	364(22%)	386(25%)	16(9%)	372 (4%)
Machinery	65(20%)	573(35%)	470(30%)	42(27%)	3,834(42%)
Others	19(6%)	108(6%)	119(8%)		
Total	318(100%)	1,655(100%)	1,559(100%)	183(100%)	9,226(100%)
Licensed by:					
Japan	214(67%)	909(55%)	808(52%)		
USA	74(23%)	391(24%)	358(23%)		
Others	30(10%)	355(21%)	393(25%)		
Royalty Paid	$17	$547	$774		
Domestic R & D Investment					
Total	$40.5	$480	$1,768		
Gov't(G)	$31.0	$325	$460		
Private(P)	$9.5	$155	$1,308		
Ratio (G/P)	77:23	68:32	26:74		
as of	1970	1980	1986		

Source: Adapted from the MOST (1988)

Accordingly, Korea has begun to attend to the development of domestic S & T capabilities with renewed vigor. Domestic R & D investment accounted for only 0.48 percent of Korea's GNP in 1970 but increased to 0.86 percent in 1980, and finally reached 1.99 percent in 1986. In the embryonic stage of private industries, the government took a lion's share in R & D, for example, 77 percent of the total R & D investment in 1970. But slowly emerging giant conglomerates in the private sector gradually took over more, contributing to 74 percent of the total in 1986. Domestic research institutes numbered 183 in 1985 with 9,226 researchers specialized in electronics, electric, machinery, metal, and chemical fields (Table 4-8). Many researchers returned home after securing a degree in universities and working in industries and research institutes abroad.

The Korean government deliberated and recently announced "the Long Range Plan for Science and Technology Toward the 2000's." The grandiose blueprint for continued economic growth has nine major targets. They can be divided into two: specialization in domestic industries to be competitive with foreign ones on the basis of cooperation among the governmental, industrial, and academic sectors; and international cooperation for joint research (MOST, 1988).

To promote specialization in domestic industries the government established a Presidential S & T Advisory Committee and continues to hold the national Technology Promotion Conference. The conference is held once every three months and brings together some 250 leaders related to S & T from the government, industries, and the research community for exchanging information and policy recommendations. The plan also calls for expanding the size of the S & T manpower pool from 54,000 scientists and engineers (S & E) equivalent to 13 S & E per 10,000 people in the entire population in 1987 to 150,000 equivalent to 30 S & E per 10,000 in 2001.

Graduate school programs in major universities--public and private--play a significant role for increasing the number and enhancing the quality of scientists. Masters and doctoral degree recipients in engineering numbered only 723 in 1976 but increased to 5,337 in 1987. The Korean Advanced Institute of Science and Technology (KAIST) concentrates on the training of high level manpower. From its inception in 1970 until 1986 it had graduated 495 Ph.D.'s and 4,753 M.S.'s. During the period of 1987-1991, the KAIST planned to produce 1,055 additional Ph.D.'s and 3,040

M.S.'s. At the same time, continued efforts have been devoted to attracting Korean overseas scientists and engineers with generous financial and research benefits. Since the late 1960s some 1,400 have returned.

To encourage R & D in the private sector, the government legislated the Technology Development Promotion Act of 1972. The law allows: (1) tax exemption on the setting aside of "technology development research funds" and on new R & D equipment (ten percent of the total costs); (2) accelerated depreciation on ninety percent of the initial investment in R & D and testing facilities; (3) government grants to industries which gear toward national projects; (4) low interest loans on technology development projects; (5) tax deductions on income from patent and technological know-how; and (6) a range of 65 to 70 percent tax deduction on R & D equipment imported by industrial research institutes. The plan calls for continued increases in R & D expenditures from 1.99 percent of GNP in 1986 ($1.8 billion) to 3 percent in 1991 and a whopping 5 percent in 2001.

In order to reduce redundancy in research and promote intersectoral cooperation, the government embarked on building an "Academic Research-Industry Cooperation Center" in Daejeon City called "Daeduck Science Town." Already relocated into the town are nine government research institutes, five private institutes, and three universities. The plan called for a total of forty institutes to settle in the town by 1991.

To provide venture capital for new entrepreneurial initiatives, special government financial corporations were chartered. Four of them, Technology Development Corporation (established in 1981), Korea Technology Advancement Corporation (1974), Korea Development Investment Corporation (1982), and Korea Technology Finance Corporation (1984) have committed loans and investments worth more than $580 million.

It is generally understood that the government's active role in supervising major industries enhances efficiency. However, this is an overstatement. Many industries that had previously been under direct government control began to be privately owned because of revealed inefficiency. This indicates that creative ideas, ingenuity, and hard work could be greatly enhanced by entrepreneurs when government regulations and intervention were reduced. Government control of commercial banks in decisions involving lending and personnel matters greatly reduced the objective and efficient allocation of investment funds for industries. Banks and credit institutions began to claim their own autonomy for sound management and efficiency without political factors being taken into account.

By the same token, technology-intensive intermediary industries could be equally successful and competitive by small and medium-size industries. Monopolistic tendencies of giant conglomerates were not the answer to the new challenges. Hence, small- and medium-size technology-intensive firms were and continue to be promoted.

The Korean government equally pays attention to a keen sense of the growing internationalization of S & T. The rationale for international cooperation is revealed:

> The new technologies are also profoundly expensive to develop, and often have product life cycles which are quite short. The extremely high up front R & D and product development costs are often daunting even for the largest of the world's corporations. We are thus beginning to see an increasing number of "strategic alliance" between large firms in different countries (Suttmeier, 1988: 33).

Therefore, Korea has committed approximately $4 million to some 69 international joint projects with the United Kingdom on information technology, France on oceanography and aviation, West Germany on automation and robotics, and Sweden on precision machinery, to name a few. The application of science and technology is not only limited to technology-intensive intermediate industries but also to light and heavy industries.

Change in the employment composition in Korea, as shown in Table 4-9, further shows the change in emphasis of the specific type of industries during the different periods of time. During the 1960s, when labor-intensive light industries prevailed, the blue-collar labor forces working in various light industrial firms such as textiles, wigs, plywood, foot wear, and the like accounted for 84.9 percent of the total work force in the manufacturing sector. But the number gradually declined to 82.2 percent in 1970 and further down to 78.9 percent in 1980 due to the shift into capital-intensive heavy and technology-intensive industries with more extensive use of machinery and automated assembly lines. On the other hand, the number of clerical and sales employees continuously increased

Table 4-9 Change in the Work Forces in Relation to Different Industrial Stages in the Manufacturing Sector*

Employment Category	1960 Number & %	1970 Number & %	1980 Number & %	Increase '70/'60	'80/70
Production	404,735(84.9)	1,188,406(82.2)	2,206,851(78.9)	2.9	1.8
Clerical	17,330(3.6)	143,849(9.9)	356,362(12.7)	8.3	2.5
Sales	5,025(1.1)	27,778(1.9)	68,716(2.5)	5.5	2.5
Services	13,660(2.9)	22,740(1.6)	49,522(1.8)	1.7	2.2
Engineers (E)	4,425(0.9)	16,252(1.1)	44,999(1.6)	3.6	2.8
Managers (M)	31,350(6.6)	47,166(3.3)	69,585(2.5)	1.5	1.5
Total	476,525(100)	1,446,191(100)	2,796,035(100)	3.0	1.9
E / M	0.14	0.34	0.65		
White-/Blue-collar**	0.18	0.22	.027		

Source: Korea Institute for Educational Development (1983)
*Includes communications and transportation workers in the manufacturing sector.
**White-collar includes all of the above categories excluding production.

primarily due to increase in demand for data processing, filing and documentation, receiving orders and sales of goods and services. Hence, clerical personnel constituted 3.6 percent of the total manufacturing work force in 1960 but increased to 9.9 percent in 1970 and further to 12.7 percent in 1980.

Second to the production workers in terms of the overhead expenses are the administrative and managerial groups, who are usually paid more than three times as much as the average wage for all occupations (Pae, 1986: 98-100). It goes without saying that the increase in the number of administrators and managers increases the overhead expenses, the organizational hierarchy, red tape, and the potential for conflict with engineers and scientists (Simon, 1966: 22-26). Commensurate with these concerns, the number of administrators and managers had the lowest rate of increase from 1960 to 1980. Moving aggressively into technology-intensive intermediate industries such as information and telecommunications, semiconductors, computer and systems, and consumer electronics required increase in the number of engineers and scientists. In fact, they increased at the fastest rate among all types of work forces, namely 2.8 times from 1970 to 1980, followed by clerical and sales employees. Production workers, administrators and managers had the lowest rate of increase of 1.8 and 1.5, respectively. The importance of engineers and scientists vis-a-vis general administrators and managers is further evidenced by the rapidly increased ratios of engineers to administrators from 0.14 (14 percent) in 1960, 0.34 in 1970, and a whopping 0.65 in 1980.

Prospects for Continued Economic Development

Taiwan is one developing country that is equally competitive and successful as Korea. Korea and Taiwan are larger than Hong Kong and Singapore in both the size of population and the GNP. After World War II Korea and Taiwan, like most developing countries in Asia, Africa, and Latin America became independent of the foreign rule. Korea and Taiwan also are the late-starters of economic development and have followed through each of the economic growth phases--import substitution, light industries, heavy industries, and high technology intermediary industries--almost concurrently. Therefore, the Korean and Taiwan models may be much more emulated and suitable for reference by the developing countries.

However, one may identify significant differences in the economic environment and growth strategies between the two countries (see Table 4-10). Both Korea and Taiwan became Japanese colonies. But "the Japanese seemed to have concentrated especially on Taiwan," where the colonial rule lasted for fifty years instead of thirty-six years and, moreover, "the rulers and subjects got along somewhat better than in Korea" (Scitovsky, 1986: 155). As discussed in detail in Chapter Two, the Koreans engaged in a series of protests and demonstrations against the Japanese. But, such a spirit of national pride and independence and subsequent massive protests were not demonstrated in Taiwan. Therefore, the Japanese were able to concentrate their energy and efforts on full colonization and development of infrastructure--roads, railroads, and harbors. They also instituted agricultural experiment research stations and extension services, and utilized the machines, equipment, and fertilizers in Taiwan to a much greater extent than in Korea.

The subtropical, favorable climate enabled Taiwanese farmers to have double-cropping and even triple-cropping in the south, whereas in Korea double-cropping was possible only by alternating rice with an unpopular grain, barley. The increased practice of

Table 4-10 Economic Differences between Taiwan and Korea

	Item	Taiwan	Korea
1.	Savings	More	Less
2.	Emphasis of Industries	Small & Medium	Emphasis of Over-investment in Heavy Industries
3.	Income	Greatly Equitable	Less
4.	Foreign Loans	Light	Very Heavy
5.	Role of Agriculture for Economic Growth	Great	Moderate
6.	Role of Japan	Greater	Less
7.	Public Ownership	Few	Many
8.	Foreign Direct Investment	Heavy	Light
9.	Regulation and Control over Industries	Light	Heavy
10.	Foreign Exchange Rate	Less Adjustment	Frequent Overvaluation
11.	Credit	Easy + Open	Difficult + Closed
12.	Unemployment	Very Low	Low
13.	Market	Free	Controlled
14.	Rural Manufacturing	Under Full Swing	Initial Stage
15.	Investment	Less on Real Estate	Speculation on Real Estate

multiple-cropping in Taiwan became an important source of money for investment in import-substituting industries without large debts incurred from foreign loans in the early 1950s. Korea was not granted favorable weather conditions, and even the modicum infrastructure of roads, railroads, and harbors as the legacy of the Japanese colonialism was almost completely destroyed during the Korean War. Therefore, Taiwan was ahead of Korea from the very beginning of their economic growth. Estimated by the annual growth rate and per capita GNP as of the early 1980s, Korea still lagged behind Taiwan by eight to ten years (K.S. Kim and Roemer, 1979: 147; Little, 1979: 455).

Enterprises in Taiwan were predominantly small and medium, whereas Korean counterparts were large. The difference might be examined in term of the annual sales of the largest firms of the two countries, the number of manufacturing firms, and the number of their employees.

In 1981, Korea's largest conglomerate, Hyundai, earned the gross receipts of $10 billion, nearly three times as big as Taiwan's ten largest privately owned corporations. As of mid-1983, Hyundai and Samsung conglomerates in Korea showed annual sales of $8 billion and $5.9 billion and employed 137,000 and 97,384, respectively. Taiwan's largest privately-owned corporation, Formosa Plastics, posted annual sales of $1.6 billion and employed 31,211 (*Fortune*, August 20, 1983). For the past ten years from 1966 to 1976, 41,808 new manufacturing firms were added to 27,709 existing ones. This indicated an increase of 150 percent in Taiwan, while there was only a ten percent increase in Korea. As of 1976 their average employment size was markedly different, on average-- 34.6 and 68.8 persons in Taiwan and Korea, respectively (Scitovsky, 1986: 146).

The advantages of small and medium-size firms over large-size ones in Taiwan and, therefore, the relatively healthier economy of Taiwan than that of Korea are clear. First of all, the smaller the size of the firms, the more easy and cheap new firms can enter the market. The greater the number of firms newly incorporated, the greater the degree of competition among the firms, consequently the greater the level of productivity growth. The smaller the size of firms, the more adaptable they become to the changing demands and expectations of the external environment on their products; subsequently, the more competitive they are in the international markets. The greater the size of firms, the more diverse they become in the kinds of their products, the less vulnerable they are to particular purchasers.

What might have facilitated the emergence of small and medium-size industries in Taiwan? First of all, land reform that was enforced by the government tended to equalize the wealth of the farmers in general, resulting in neither too-rich nor too-poor farm households. The farmers in Taiwan were able to gain the export of their products. A higher personal savings rate was equally observed among urban residents who were employed in many small firms.

Table 4-11 Percentage Composition of Manufactured Output: Korea and Taiwan

	Light Industries		Heavy Industries	
Year	Korea	Taiwan	Korea	Taiwan
	Food, Beverages, & Tobacco		Chemicals, Petroleum, and Coal	
1960	19.3	44.5	7.7	10.1
1965	26.5	34.8	15.0	17.4
1971	24.6	20.9	23.5	20.8
1975	21.2	18.8	21.8	21.3
1979	16.5	13.0	17.4	19.0
	Textiles, Clothing, & Footwear		Nonmetallic Mineral Products except Petroleum and Coal	
1960	28.6	14.9	9.2	7.2
1965	19.8	15.0	5.0	6.5
1971	17.5	18.0	4.7	4.5
1975	22.0	15.8	4.7	4.7
1979	19.6	15.5	7.9	3.9
	All Light Industry		Basic Metal Products	
1960	70.0	71.2	2.4	3.1
1965	61.8	51.2	5.0	2.2
1971	54.7	50.7	4.7	2.9
1975	51.6	46.7	4.7	3.5
1979	44.7	44.4	7.9	6.7
			Machinery, Equipment, and Fabricated Metal Products	
1960			10.7	8.5
1965			11.5	13.3
1971			12.2	21.2
1975			16.3	23.7
1979			24.2	26.0
			All Heavy Industry	
1960			30.0	28.0
1965			38.2	39.8
1971			45.3	49.3
1975			48.4	53.3
1979			55.3	55.6

Source: Adapted from Scitovsky (1986: Table 5)

Perhaps the most important factor was the desire of many overseas Chinese to immigrate to Taiwan with their capital and establish independent enterprises of their own. This was the reason the Taiwanese government decided to promote small enterprises and welcomed overseas Chinese, who brought with them 34 percent of the total inflow of foreign capital. The success of small and medium-size industries became the imperative for Taiwan's survival and prosperity. It was with this strategy that Taiwan established forty-nine industrial parks and districts. The Taiwanese government established infrastructural facilities and encouraged new investors to open their business by renting rather than buying land and building, and provided them with generous loans (Scitovsky, 1986: 146-47).

The greater the number of people hired to the ever-increasing small firms, the more equitable the employees' income and the more stable the economy became. The need for strong government rules and regulations, restriction on loans, and the foreign exchange rate was gradually reduced. No large amount of loans was needed, either. The principle of market economy began to prevail. Economic decentralization became triumphant except for the public ownership of some heavy industries due to greater economies of scale and the lack of sufficient private resources and interests. Once small and medium-size industries were almost saturated in the urban areas, they began to absorb people in the rural areas.

No such comparable favorable factors were made available in the case of Korea. Farming in Korea was not so successful and the climate not so favorable as in Taiwan. No significant saving for loanable funds was made by farmers and urban workers. Nor was there any significant number of overseas Koreans who made a fortune and wanted to return to open their own business in their motherland.

Given these unfavorable conditions, the imperative for the energetic role of the Korean government was self-explanatory. The government embarked on establishing the machinery of economic planning, which was "larger, more elaborate, more centrally and prominently placed" in the top of the administrative hierarchy, and more efficiently "provided with channels of communication for consultation with business than that of Taiwan" (Scitovsky, 1986: 152). The Prime Minister chaired the Central Economic Committee, whereas the Deputy Prime Minister held a firm grip on the Economic Planning Board. They were further supported by a Product Evaluation Board and the Korean Development Institute for market research, profitability estimation, planning, and evaluation of the implemented plans.

In a comparative study between Taiwan and South Korea, Tibor Scitovsky became schizophrenic between the negative and positive aspects of the Korean economy. On the one hand, he was concerned with such negative factors of Korea as 1) relatively lower levels of domestic savings than Taiwan, 2) over-investments in heavy and chemical industries, which resulted in the phenomenal increase of foreign debts, 3) underutilization of their capacities, 4) the concentration of wealth and power on a few giant conglomerates at the expense of small and medium-size industries, which could have been equally efficient as large ones in terms of the different economies of scale in the market of intermediary, technology-intensive products.

On the other hand, he was stunned by the "economic miracle" which Korea has accomplished, despite all these disadvantageous factors, successfully and sequentially moving to each of these export-oriented economic growth phases in the fastest pace with nearly exactly the same rate of spectacular growth as Taiwan (see Table 4-11). The growth of manufactured output of all light industries accounted for 71.2 and 70 percent in 1960 in Taiwan and Korea, respectively, and steadily declined to 44.4 and 44.7 percent in 1979. A similar rate of output growth in all heavy industries also was witnessed, for example, in 28.8 and 30.0 percent in 1960 in Taiwan and Korea, respectively, but it increased to 55.6 and 55.3 percent in 1979.

Scitovsky flatly admitted:

> It seemed standard for Korean development planners always to project, aim for, and actively encourage more investment than seemed feasible on the basis of expected domestic savings and expected foreign capital inflows. The hope was that the economy would somehow accommodate itself to those overambitious plans, and the hope was usually fulfilled--very often overfulfilled (1986: 178).

The puzzle which bothered him most was the "economic miracle" hardly conceived of in his evaluation of Korea under "chronic inflation," "its disappointing domestic savings rate," "its continued dependence on foreign capital" reaching $46 billion in 1981, and "seriously mistaken decisions" of over-investment in heavy and chemical industries at the end of the 1970s on the threshold of world depression (Scitovsky, 1986: 178; Woronoff, 1983: 162-63).

As an old proverb states, the horse may be coercively dragged to a river but not forced to drink water. The imposition by the state of "performance standards on private firms" (Amsden, 1989: 8) does not warrant the performance as expected, unless the private firms are capable of meeting the standards. Business firms, labor, and Korean people in general are by no means careless bystanders in the Korean economic miracle.[7] No matter how overambitious the Korean government leaders were, the economic miracle was less likely to be accomplished without calculated risk and sound management based on the emphasis on: training and securing more engineers rather than general managers; apprenticeship beyond imitation; and the adoption of Theory Y, often referred to as "shop floor management" (Amsden, 1989: 321) so as to promote self-direction of the workers, two-way free and open communications between management and labor, and a sense of common destiny and interest in their enterprises without allowing foreign ownership and intervention as manifested in many large steel, shipbuilding, automobile, and other enterprises.[8]

Of course, not all Korean business firms have been equally successful. There were some large firms which were very successful and thriving once but went bankrupt due to poor management. They include Shinjin Motors, Taihan Electronics Industrial Group, Kyungnam and Samho Construction companies, Korea Shipbuilding and Engineering Company, and Kukje-ICC group (Amsden, 1989: 15-16). However, there were and still are a number of large business firms in Korea which have shown dedication and commitment to the survival imperative on the basis of "learning," improvement, productivity, and comparative advantage.

Economic success is also attributable to the "perseverance, commitment, and strong determination" of Korean people as fully examined in Chapter Two. These characteristics of the Koreans are clearly seen in "the world's largest working week" not just for a few days but over a long, sustained period of time. While "the working week has become shorter just about everywhere else," the length of their working week "increased substantially over time" (Scitovsky, 1986: 179). According to the survey by the Korean Department of Labor, the average monthly working hours were 221.5 in 1978 rather than 160 hours. In fact, the working hours increased from 221.5 in 1978 to 226.1 in 1983 (Pae, 1986: 93). While Korea lagged behind Taiwan in the increase of the number of small and medium-size firms (an annual average of 0.9 percent increase in Korea vis-a-vis 9.6 percent in Taiwan between 1966 and 1976), Korea's manufacturing production over the same time period ironically increased at an average annual rate of 22.7 percent vis-a-vis 17.8 percent in Taiwan (Scitovsky, 1986: 175).

Korea equally leads Taiwan in education and training of human resources. As Scitovsky admitted himself, "School enrollment rates at the primary and secondary levels are almost equally high in the two countries and only slightly lower than the average in the advanced industrial countries." What impressed him was the fact that modernization in Korea started later, "compulsory education ends sooner, and public expenditure on education is lower, averaging 3.5 percent of the GDP as against Taiwan's 4.5 percent (1986: 140).

As the Korean forefathers were deeply committed to education and enlightenment movements during the Japanese colonial period, a relatively smaller percentage of budget allocated by the government for education was reinforced by private expenditures paid by parents and donated by philanthropic educators for private schools. The total private and public expenditures on education in Korea reached "astonishingly high 9 percent of the GNP" on an annual average that was twice as much as that of Taiwan (Scitovsky, 1986: 140).

Higher education may be equally important for managerial and planning level as for research and development. Recent statistics indicated that over thirty percent of senior high school graduates were admitted to college, while over ten thousand college graduates at higher educational institutions go abroad for further study (U.S. Kim, 1986: 66).

The seemingly serious and mistaken over-investment in heavy and chemical industries at the end of the 1970s on the threshold of an acute and protracted world recession especially in shipbuilding, their underutilization, and the subsequent economic stagnation may be an accurate description of the Korean economy in terms of Scitovsky's near-sighted, short-run perspective. However, what he underestimated was the importance of heavy industries becoming the foundation for building technology-intensive intermediary industries. The continued economic growth would not be expected without its own sources of steel, metals, petrochemicals, and other essential materials for many industries. The economies of scale are such that the mass production of automobiles and intermediary industry products needs strong support from heavy industries. Investment by foreign loans--excessive and risky--is paid off after worries and agonies over the mounting increase of debt service. Since 1985 exports began to balance or exceed imports. Foreign debts began to decrease from $46.8 billion in 1985 to $44.5 billion in 1986, to

$35.6 billion in 1987, to $22 billion estimated in 1992 (see Table 4-3).

The overemphasis of large-size enterprises (*chaebol*) may have many shortcomings as fully discussed above. By the same token, "Korea is ahead of Taiwan on the research and development (R & D)" thanks principally to the size of many of its "giant manufacturing firms" that can afford the allocation of more funds for R & D. More than fifty large firms committed themselves to their own R & D and, therefore, expect further improvement in productivity (see Table 4-8). While conglomerates (*chaebol*) are huge compared with ordinary firms, they are still small compared with the foreign multinationals. Size is needed to make them competitive. Size may be perhaps even more important when they enter joint ventures with foreign partners. Otherwise, they may be dominated by the foreign ones.

Chaebol are more diversified into mutually unrelated enterprises and more centrally coordinated than their counterparts of foreign countries. However, as Amsden noticed, they have strengths in terms of the "economy of scope:" "accumulated experiences in the areas of feasibility studies, task force formation, purchase of foreign technical assistance, training, equipment purchase, new plant design and construction, and operation start-up" of totally unrelated enterprises (1989: 128). The economy of scope can be further extended to training of the best qualified personnel, facilitating intragroup transfer of money and personnel, the reduction of duplication of supporting and recording systems, sharing sophisticated statistical, research, and other staff services ruinously expensive for smaller firms, obtaining credit on more advantageous terms, and a uniform group culture.

Korea is equally sensitive to the economic strength of Taiwan's promotion of small and medium-size industries and strengthening of market economy. To promote small (less than twenty employees) and medium-size (20 to 300) enterprises, the Korean government began to enact the Anti-Monopoly Law of 1981, which reinforced the Fair Trade Act of 1976. The law required conglomerates to promptly pay subcontractors in cash, and geared toward establishing special banks like the Small and Medium Industry Bank for loans, and the Small and Medium Industry Promotion Corporation for management and technical assistance. However, the outcomes thus far seem still meager. Ironically, giant conglomerates have been accumulating more wealth and taking larger portions of the total production, employment, and exports than small and medium-size industries. The Korean Development Institute (KDI) reported that thirty conglomerates increased their percentages of the total manufactured production from 34.1 percent in 1977 to 40.2 percent in 1985, a 6.1 percent increase. But their exports suggested only 2.8 percent increase, namely, from 38.5 percent of the total exports in 1977 to 41.3 percent in 1985 (see Table 4-12).

Table 4-12 Trend of Economic Concentration in South Korea

Conglomerates (*chaebol*)	Manufacturing Companies incorporated into the Conglomerates		Percent of Total Production		Percent of Total Employment		Percent of Total Exports	
	1977	1985	1977	1985	1977	1985	1977	1985
5 Major Ones	99	94	15.7	23.0	9.7	9.7	24.2	27.0
10 Major Ones	158	147	21.2	30.2	12.5	11.7	29.0	32.2
20 Major Ones	267	218	29.3	36.0	17.4	15.5	35.3	38.3
30 Major Ones	337	270	34.1	40.2	20.5	17.6	38.5	41.3

Source: *Korea Times*, July 7, 1988

This indicates that giant conglomerates took ever-increasing amounts of manufactured production but relatively lower amounts of exports. This suggests that large-size conglomerates are by no means more efficient and advantageous than small and medium-size industries in exports. Therefore, the Korean government began to adopt 23 kinds of products exclusively designated for small and medium-size industries to manufacture in 1979, 103 items in 1983, 205 kinds in 1984, and 130 additional items in 1988. The government plans to expand more items for small and medium-size industries to produce, together with favorable financial loans available to them (*Korea Times*, July 7 & 16, 1988). According to the Ministry of Commerce and Industry, nineteen banking and credit institutes were chartered in January 1987 in accordance with the Law of 1986 for Supports of Small and Medium-Size Industries. These credit institutes provided 348 newly-established, small- and medium-size industries with about $97 million for the past one and a half years. By the end of 1988 they made loans of $142 million to about 600 new small- and medium-size industries which were primarily engaged in technology-intensive industries such as electronic,

Table 4-13 Average Annual Growth Rate of Upper Middle-Income Countries

Country	GDP 1965-80	GDP 80-85	Agriculture 65-80	Agriculture 80-85	Industry 65-80	Industry 80-85	Manufacturing 65-80	Manufacturing 80-85	Services 65-80	Services 80-85
Iran	6.2	-	4.5	-	2.4	-	10.0	-	13.3	-
Iraq	-	-	-	-	-	-	-	-	-	-
Romania	-	-	-	-	-	-	-	-	-	-
Trinidad & Tobago	4.8	-4.1	0.1	1.4	3.8	-4.0	-	-4.8	5.7	-4.5
Uruguay	2.4	-3.9	1.0	-1.3	3.1	-1.8	5.9	1.4	6.6	-1.9
Venezuela	5.2	-1.6	4.0	1.5	3.5	-1.8	5.9	1.4	6.6	-1.9
Argentina	3.3	-1.4	1.4	2.8	3.3	-2.5	2.7	-1.6	3.9	-1.8
Poland	-	0.5	-	-	-	-	-	-	-	-
Mexico	6.5	0.8	3.2	2.3	7.6	0.3	7.4	-	6.6	0.8
Yugoslavia	6.1	0.8	3.1	1.3	7.8	0.6	-	-	5.5	0.9
South Africa	4.0	0.8	-	-	-	-	-	-	-	-
Portugal	5.3	0.9	-	-0.7	-	0.9	-	-	-	1.3
Greece	5.8	1.0	2.3	-0.7	7.1	-0.6	8.4	-0.9	6.2	2.4
Brazil	9.0	1.3	4.7	3.0	10.0	0.3	9.8	-	9.4	1.8
Israel	6.7	1.7	-	-	-	-	-	-	-	-
Hungary	5.5	1.8	2.7	3.5	6.4	2.0	-	-	6.2	0.9
Panama	5.5	2.4	2.4	2.7	59	-2.2	4.7	-0.3	6.0	3.6
Oman	12.5	4.0	-	-	-	-	-	-	-	-
Algeria	7.5	4.9	5.8	2.1	8.1	5.3	9.5	9.0	7.1	4.9
Malaysia	7.3	5.5	-	3.0	-	6.7	-	6.1	-	5.9
Hong Kong	8.5	5.9	-	-	-	-	-	-	-	-
Singapore	10.2	6.5	3.1	-1.8	12.2	5.9	13.3	2.1	9.7	6.9
Korea	9.5	7.9	3.0	6.3	16.6	9.6	18.8	9.0	9.4	6.7

Source: Adapted from the World Bank (1987: 205)

electric, machinery, metallic and chemical ones (*Korea Times*, August 30, 1988). In fact, the promoting of small- and medium-size industries and the strengthening of the market economy have become the main economic objectives of the Sixth Republic of Korea since 1988.

This economic miracle is primarily based upon the values of perseverance, commitment, and determination of the Koreans, often characterized as people in the Land of Determination. Such values, norms, behaviors, and expectations began to facilitate the strong commitment of the government to entering into each of the stages of industrialization--import, import-substitution, export-oriented light industries, heavy and chemical industries as fast as possible, with the concurrent enthusiasm from well-trained entrepreneurs and the well-educated general public. This very thesis is indeed reinforced by Scitovsky:

> That, in a nutshell, summarizes how an aggressive economic policy causes the economy to perform beyond its apparent capacity and accommodate the excessive demand made upon it by an overambitious investment plan (Scitovsky, 1986: 180).

The strong determination for export-oriented economic growth on the part of the bureaucracy, as well, is evidenced by the commitment of the MCI (Ministry of commerce and industry) officials:

> If there is a possibility that the target will not be fulfilled, the MCI officials as well as other officials related with export administration work seven days a week and overtime to expedite the administrative process, to strengthen existing export-support schemes, to innovate new subsidy measures, and to exert irresistible pressures on businessmen to accelerate exports even though this may entail losses. If all such efforts fail to achieve the target amount, the MCI officials may even try to adulterate export statistics, e.g., by counting advance export receipts as actual exports. Such overenthusiasm for export expansion has apparently caused some losses, but it has kept fueling the export-oriented growth process in Korea (Hong, 1982: 13).

Jon Woronoff also agreed with the author, highlighting the strong determination of the Koreans:

> The Koreans intensely wanted to develop. They wanted to become a more prosperous people, not only for material reasons but also for moral ones. They wanted to catch up with Japan, or at least make their presence felt, to pay it back for the past. They wanted to prove they were more than a

match for North Korea and that their regime offered more than communism. They even wanted to show the Americans that they had what it takes. And, once economic growth came, their pride returned and they felt able to face any challenges (1983: 175).

The main difference in economic development between Korea and other developing countries in general and between Korea and Taiwan in particular lies not in their aims "but in the much more forceful and aggressive spirit" (Scitovsky, 1986: 151). It was demonstrated in the past by the Koreans against foreign invasions and their exploitations. It was, in turn, later transformed into economic development by policy makers, equally determined entrepreneurs, and the Korean people in general. Nearly every developing country publishes periodically an economic plan with goals and strategies. However, one cannot tell merely by the publication of an economic plan and its big words the extent of success. Only the hard, long-run evidence of record can tell the extent of accomplishments. Table 4-13 shows economic accomplishments of twenty-three "upper middle-income" countries in terms of average annual growth rates (percent) of GDP, agriculture, industry, and services. Table 4-13 clearly indicates that Korea has been exceeding all of the upper middle-income countries consistently in growth rates of agriculture, industry, manufacturing, services, and GDP in both periods of 1965-1980 and 1980-1985.

Conclusion

There are two contending theories that explain economic development. One is the neo-classical economic theory based on "the policy of liberalization." It assumes that the market is, at its best, an automatic, self-adjusting mechanism which ensures an efficient and pro-developmental allocation of resources. Dozens of scholars endorse this theory and emphasize the principle of comparative advantage in the international market as the guiding "invisible hand" of export orientation.[9] The other is the directive state intervention (statist) theory based on "managed liberalization." It assumes that the market, if left unguided, may fail to produce the expected, positive economic outcomes because of lack of its self-adjusting capability.[10]

The argument between the students of these two contending economic theories of development is indeed compared to a chicken-

and-egg game. In reality, no state is fully exposed to international markets. Nor is any state fully committed to state intervention in domestic and international markets, ignoring the principle of supply and demand and comparative advantage. Jones and Sakong clearly support this view of a mixture of market and non-market forces:

> The 'Korean miracle' is not a triumph of *laissez faire*, but of a pragmatic non-ideological mixture of market and non-market forces. Where the market works, fine; where it doesn't, the government shows no hesitation in intervening by means that range from a friendly phone call to public ownership (1980: 294).

After over thirty pages of explanation that the success of the economy in Korea is attributed to the statist theory with specific policies and mechanisms of state intervention in economy, Leudde-Neurath, consciously or unconsciously, admits the mixture of two theories in Korea, too.

> The Koreans adopted a 'two pronged' strategy of foreign exchange-related protection which made a fundamental distinction between products, investments, and technology destined for the domestic market on the one hand, those destined for export production on the other. Whereas the latter were treated in an extremely liberal fashion (to promote exports), the former were tightly controlled (to conserve foreign exchange)(1988: 99).

Nevertheless, Amsden contends that the market-oriented theory is more relevant to "early industrializers, whereas the institutional, market-augmenting state intervention theory to late industrializers" such as "Japan, Korea, Taiwan, Brazil, Turkey, India, Mexico, and possibly Argentina."

> ..... in broad respects the institutions of late industrializers have exhibited the same central tendencies, to the extent that an economic paradigm can be identified that is institutional in character and categorically distinct from the market model. It is suggested here, therefore, that the economies of these late-industrializing countries behave according to economic laws that constitute a new paradigm (1989: 140).

However, admitting disparity in the economic record among the late industrializers, Amsden noticed the presence of discipline in Japan, Taiwan, and Korea for their states to "exact certain performance standards from firms" in return for state subsidies and the absence of discipline elsewhere (1989: 146-47). But she still does not solve the puzzle over why three late industrializers like Japan, Taiwan, and Korea have made significant economic development and why the remaining late industrializers have lagged far behind despite some of the latter having had equally strong state intervention in their respective economies.

Amsden also contended that business groups in late industrializers are more diversified in unrelated products than in the early industrializers. The former are "more centrally coordinated than" the conglomerates of the latter. Her two main reasons were "no technical expertise to build upon in related products or in higher quality product niches" and the subsequent desire "to diffuse risk" (1989: 127). However, not all diversified business firms in the late industrializers perform equally well. Then, we may wonder why *chaebol* in Korea, though more diversified in seemingly unrelated products, outperform their counterparts in other late industrializers. The answers are not only the economy of scope as discussed above but also diversification not in her implicitly implied random and indiscriminate fashion but in relation to the stage of industrial development--first, in the labor-intensive light industries, moving into capital-intensive heavy industries later, and then into technology-intensive intermediate industries recently.

Amsden brushed aside the potential for causality in the regression analysis of the success of labor-intensive light-industries in preparing the ground for heavy industries. She made it clear that:

> there was no natural progression in any tangible, organizational sense from cotton spinning and weaving in particular and light manufactures in general to more complex industrial activity (1989: 155).

I have no dispute with her on the insignificant techno-managerial externalities in Korea, because the technology and management needed for heavy industries are basically different from those for small light industries. By the same token, as she admitted, intersectoral externalities such as raising capital from increase in exports of the products of light industries, improvement in credit ratings, the experiences in exploration of overseas markets together with minimum technological capabilities accumulated from labor-intensive light industries certainly emboldened the government and business firms to carefully examine the dynamic changes in international division of labor, comparative advantages, and their desire for the subsequent increase in exports and profitability. Despite lack of natural statistically significant "progression in any tangible, organizational sense" and despite the failure of the stage theory to "specify the mechanism by which progress from one stage to another is realized" (Amsden, 1989: 244), the relative decline in gains from light industries due to the challenges from other developing countries with much cheaper labor forces, much slower wage increase than the Korean case[11] and yet similar level of skills was by no means ignored. Nor can it be compensated for by a sudden jump into technology-intensive industries without invention and innovation, neither of which Korea and other late-industrializing countries were and are able to immediately accomplish without a long-term investment of human and financial resources. Then, capital-intensive heavy industries became the natural, logical step to explore prior to technology-intensive industries. All major *chaebol* in Korea did not diversify randomly and indiscriminately simply to diffuse risk. Nor did they all diversify "in precisely the same manner" in accordance with the industrial developmental sequence (Kang, 1989: 65). But most of them have followed this sequence of industrial development and investment. Here is a typical case of the Samsung Group, which pursued:

1. Labor-intensive light industries for exports first such as Cheil (meaning first) Sugar Company in 1953, Cheil Wool in 1954, Cheil's production of worsted in 1957, using top-quality machinery, hiring the best salaried managers, and relying on extensive foreign technical assistance;

2. Entering into the insurance business--life, fire, and marine and journalism and mass media in the 1950s;

3. Capital-intensive chemical and heavy industries for exports such as the Hanguk Fertilizer Company in 1963, one of the largest projects of the period, commencing production in early 1967; a real estate development; and construction in the 1960s;

4. Samsong shipbuilding industry, building ships since 1980; and

5. Technology-intensive industries for exports such as Samsung Electronics, the establishment of a central R & D laboratory in

1979, and commitment to R & D and training on in-house training institute (Amsden, 1989: 235-38).

In short, it is not a negative perspective of risk diffusion and the subsequent random and indiscriminate diversification into any enterprises but a positive, enthusiastic, calculated risk in international competition that the Korean government and *chaebol* have engaged themselves in diversification and central coordination in a logical sequence of industrial development.

To the contrary, regardless of domestic differences, Latin American countries in general have experienced the following economic changes: (1) the "mercantalistic" colonial period (1500-1750); (2) the period of "outward growth" dependent on primary exports (1750-1914); (3) the "liberal model" (1914-1950); and (4) the current period of "transnational capitalism" (1950-)(Valenzuela and Valenzuela, 1986: 504).

Striking contrasts, therefore, can be found between Latin American countries and Korea, first, in terms of time span they passed through the first two stages of foreign imports and import substitution. It took about 400 years for the Latin American countries but less than one-tenth of the time span for Korea to have completed these two stages. Moreover, Korea began to enter into the stages of export-oriented labor-intensive light industries in 1963, progressed into the stages of export-oriented capital-intensive heavy industries in 1973 and technology-intensive intermediate industries since 1983-1985, successfully and successively in the shortest possible period.

Latin American countries, on the other hand, did not enter into the stage of labor intensive light industries for exports:

> (1) The investment of centrally (i.e., North America) based corporations in manufactures within the (Latin American) periphery for sales in its internal market or, as Cardoso and Faletto note, the "internationalization of the internal market;" (2) a new international division of labor in which the periphery acquires capital goods, technology, and raw materials from the central nations, and export profits, along with its traditional raw materials and a few manufactured items produced by multinational subsidiaries; and (3) a denationalization of the older import substituting industries established originally (Smith, 1986: 506).

My main thesis in Chapter Four is in what to intervene, how to intervene, and when to intervene for Korea to successfully and successively pass through each of the industrial development stages-- import, import substitution, labor-intensive light industries (LILI), capital-intensive heavy industries (CIHI), technology-intensive intermediary industries (TIII), and the continued, simultaneous application of science and technology to all of LILI, CIHI, and TIII for higher value-added productivity on the basis of the principle of comparative advantage in the international market. Many developing countries, on the contrary, indeed ignore this economic imperative, simply opening indiscriminately for foreign direct investment, unreasonably borrowing foreign loans without carefully examining in what stage they are and therefore on what industries they have to concentrate in investment, reversing from export orientation to domestic markets, stressing more of quality of life right now and therefore spending more on social security and other welfare benefits today than investment for the future, expending a large sum of money by the upper wealthy class on importing luxury items rather than on investment, and colluding those domestic economic elites with foreign investors for domestic market resulting in the dependency economy.

Tony Smith, however, rejects the dependency theory of an all-pervasive and self-perpetuating northern power with respect to the south (1986: 537). The domestic cultural and institutional features of Latin America still can be regarded as the key variables accounting for the relative backwardness of the area. He evidenced that across all of Latin America "the natives invariably wielded significant power at lower levels of the government and in a variety of informal ways" (1986: 517). Even if the natives failed to control the heights of the state, they still "played a fairly powerful role in the colonies." It was "their character and structure that profoundly influenced the process of decolonization." Smith suggested that the Revolution of 1910 in Mexico was achieved not because of the international system, but against it and its local allies. Nor should it be assumed that southern leaders were mere puppets of the international system, even when they were heavily dependent on the North. Conversely, strong American support for Israel has been no way to run an imperial system (1986: 533).

The spectrum of state structures in Latin America also ranges from those that are "clearly paramount power within their society" in terms of both monopolizing means of restrictions on violence and enforcing a set of rules on a vast arena of political, economic, and social activities to those that are "states in little more than name, lacking either the party or the bureaucratic structure" (Smith, 1986: 518). A strong state, however, does not necessarily warrant a viable economic growth, nor does a weak state inhibit economic growth. The real question is whether the state, enterprises, labor, and the general public exert concentrated efforts on identifying in what industrial stage they are and into what next stage they have to plan and aggressively move. The proper measures may include: export orientation, liberalization, restriction, and securing capital by means of increase in domestic saving and foreign loans; learning, apprenticeship, creative application, Theory Y management; strong commitment of labor, long working hours. The state, business firms, labor, and general public need to take these measures to maximize each stage and gear toward entering into the next stage in terms of comparative advantage.

Amsden and Jones and Sakong emphasized the importance of entrepreneurship concerning which ones to penetrate, when, and with what size investment on the basis of economic opportunity and the profitability of the new opportunity (Amsden, 1989: 79-80; Jones and Sakong, 1980: 81) However, it is my understanding that international division of labor and comparative advantage limit and restrict developing nations to indiscriminately move into any enterprises but allow them to pursue a sequential and progressive movement from enterprises related to labor-intensive light industries to heavy industries, then to high-technology intermediate industries on the basis of reinforcement and support by the two previous industries. In essence, entrepreneurship based on the stages of industrial development indeed is a correct model of Korean economic development which developing nations may seriously take into account.[12]

Neither the OECD nor the United States has a grand design for securing and ensuring dependency of developing nations on the North:

> I have never seen it seriously alleged that the countries of the OECD or the United States alone have the cunning or the organization to be able to draw up such a scheme--then the attempt would be a notable failure. Where is the whole-hearted effort to prevent southern industrialization, monopolize southern raw materials, break up domestically

integrated southern markets, oppose southern regional integration schemes, and develop a greater degree of international specialization that would heighten southern reliance on northern goods and markets? Neither the OECD nor the United States gets high marks for imperialist strategy: plans are neither clear nor resolute in purpose; the means whereby to gain the ends have not been specified; interests at home have not been harmonized so that such a strategy would seem enticing. Unlike the influence of Britain in Egypt, India, and Latin America at the end of the 19th century, and unlike Nazi policy toward Southeastern Europe, the impact of the North today would seem to accelerate rather than retard southern industrialization (Smith, 1986: 534).

Even if the OECD and the United States adhere to the dependency theory, it is developing countries themselves that should take proper measures, like Mexico's legislation on foreign investment in July 1970 (Roth and Wilson, 1976: 429). Economic development in a country is the product of cultural, political, and economic causes: therefore, the Korean experience may not be perfectly duplicated in other countries. Nevertheless, the Korean model may provide developing countries with a valuable lesson concerning how each of the successive stages of industrial development has been successfully passed through, what errors, mistakes, and challenges were and are painfully experienced in each stage, and what strategies have been taken.

The years of 1989-1992 witnessed the slowdown in economic growth. Many domestic and foreign media began to raise a question: Is the Korean miracle running on empty? Korea's current problems are five-fold: increase in labor wages of more than sixty percent in the past two years along with rapid democratization; the appreciation of the Korean won by about thirty percent against the dollar since the end of 1985; the subsequent climb of imports faster than exports; loss of interest of investors in manufacturing partly due to labor strikes and partly due to spiraling land speculation for possible higher profits; and the decline of surpluses in balance of payments.

Nevertheless, Jerry Flint predicts that: "Long known as the second Japan, Korea now has the same problems Japan suffered. Chances are the Koreans will solve them as well as the Japanese did (1989: 102).

But again, remember the Japanese example. In 1973 and again in 1979, for instance, when OPEC forced up the price of oil, many smart people thought Japanese industry would be driven into the sea. Instead, the Japanese industry responded by shedding older, labor-intensive businesses and production processes, and replacing them with labor-saving equipment and higher-value-added businesses.

The same kind of process is going on in Korea. "There is a clear trend of each major Korean company building its own lab and recruiting brains, trying to create new ideas. . .

Korea's best bet will be to follow the Japanese model, which emphasizes quality and technological superiority, and not cheap labor (1989: 102-03).

Three major industries such as shipping, overseas construction, and shipbuilding, which experienced serious depression and the subsequent heavy burden to the Korean economy during the 1970s, face the brightest prosperity during the 1990s. All of the Korean ships and containers have already set sail, and not even a single one stays at harbor. Construction companies received orders from Libya for waterway construction, from Iran and Iraq for rehabilitation after the war, from the United States and Japan for urban redevelopment, from the Soviet Union for public housing and a lumber processing facility in Vladivostok. Shipbuilding companies completed a total of 279,000 tons of shipbuilding as of October 1989, which accounted for 47.5 percent increase in volume and 160 percent increase in the dollar gain from the previous year (*Korea Times*, November 20, 1989).

Table 4-14 shows that Japan experienced a relative decrease in new ship orders from 55.9 percent of the total orders in 1984 to 36.0 percent as of May 31, 1990. Korea, on the other hand, continues to receive more orders, reaching 22.6 percent as of May 1990 from 18.9 percent in 1986, and becoming the second largest supplier of new ships. It is estimated that about 50 to 65 percent of the ships on active duty should be retired in ten years due to the substantial increase in insurance costs. About 20,000 new ships will be ordered during the 1990s (*Korea Times*, July 24, 1990).

The emphasis on science and technology by both the government and businesses for higher-value-added goods and services was first evidenced by the integration of sixteen major

Table 4-14 Percent New Ship Orders Placed, 1974-1990

Year	Japan	Korea	EEC	Comecon	Rest of World
1974	38.4	2.8	27.0	2.9	28.9
1976	56.0	2.5	10.6	10.0	21.0
1978	43.2	3.7	14.9	11.5	26.7
1980	52.7	9.0	12.1	4.2	22.0
1982	49.7	9.6	13.5	9.4	17.8
1984	55.9	17.4	10.0	2.5	14.2
1986	37.1	18.9	8.9	8.2	26.9
1990	36.0	22.6	14.5*	4.0	22.9

Source: Lloyd's Registrer of Shipping (various years); data for 1990 from *Korea Times* (7/24/1990)

*Includes 5.0 % of Denmark, 3.8% of Italy, 3.4 % of Spain, and 2.3 % of West Germany.

research institutes into eight large-scale research centers on November 13, 1980. Since then both the public and the private sector have more affirmatively than ever before committed to continuous research and development. The Korean Silicon Valley called the Daeduck Science and Research Center, which started its construction since 1973, has already housed ten state-supported, two state-invested, three private research institutes, and three universities, with a total of 9,115 scientists as of July 1990. The center plans to accommodate 25 additional research institutes with 6,796 additional scientists by 1992. The center covers such research areas as nuclear fuel, explosive group engineering, electronics and telecommunications, chemical technology, ship and ocean engineering, atomic energy, nuclear safety, space, science and astronomy, and a host of other areas (*Korea Times*, July 13, 1990).

Science and technology become of vital importance for technology-intensive intermediate industries. Science and technology also can transform Korea's "labor-intensive" light industries (which still accounted for over forty percent of the total exports as of 1990) into "labor-saving" light industries, and "low-technology" heavy industries into "high-technology" heavy industries by means of automation, robotization, and other technological innovations (KDI, 1986: 16)(see Figure 4-2 and Table 4-2). Korea's simultaneous improvement in all three types of industries by means of science and technology can meet the challenges of the Twenty-first Century from both developed and developing countries in international trade and cooperation. Korea's continued economic development, indeed, depends on the adherence to the principle of international division of labor, proper investment of time, money, and efforts to maximize comparative advantages on the basis of the stages of industrialization.

Notes

1. A few examples on a macro-level approach are: Cole and Lyman (1971); Brown (1973); Frank, et al.(1975); Kuznets (1977).

2. The Korean government enacted the Electronics Industry Promotion Law on January 28, 1969 to lay the foundation for the entering into the high-technology intermediate industries for export. The law stimulated investment in the assembly line plant operations of black-and-white televisions in the beginning and selected fifty-seven items including semiconductors and computers as strategic products for export in the 1980s (The Republic of Korea, 1976).

3. The Blue House Project names after the Korean presidential office equivalent to the White House in the United States. The project was originally conceived in the Blue House, blessed by President Chun as early as in 1983, and urged major *chaebol* including Hyundai, Goldstar, and Samsung to have a long-term plan, R & D, and production to crack the world semiconductor market in the 1990s (*Electronics*, April 2, 1987). The project was enthusiastically pursued. The government soon adopted various specific measures such as organizational support for technology-intensive firms, the selection of 182 research projects of 131 industrial firms with research fund contribution, a low tariff rate on equipment imported for R & D purposes, and tax exemptions to the firms on percentage of their profits for R & D (Amsden, 1989: 81-85).

4. Intersectoral financing in favor of entrepreneurs who later became the *chaebol* (family-based industrial conglomerates) in the 1960s, 1970s, and 1980s is extensively discussed by many scholars.

See Kyong-Dong Kim (1976); Jones and Sakong (1980); Byun and Kim (1978).

5 For further information, Korean Overseas Information Service (KOIS)(1979: 583-618).

6. For further explanation on the last three factors, see Sung Yeung Kwack (1986: 76-79).

7. T. W. Kang introduced an interesting episode on the initiative of business firms as equally or more aggressive and energetic than the government on industrial development and trade promotion. He quoted a corporate-planning director of a major conglomerate, who stated: "The EPB people are nothing more than sophisticated extrapolators. When a private sector company finds success in a particular industry or production area, the planners just write up the success formula and call that a plan. Also, most of the environmental inputs to their plans come from us after the fact" (1989: 30).

8. It is beyond the scope and purpose of this work to have a detailed discussion on the management of large firms in Korea in this section. In fact, Alice H. Amsden did an excellent job on this topic. See Part III in her book (1989).

9. The neo-classical theory for the economic growth of the NICs can be found in Galenson (1985). Its applications to Korea include Krueger (1979), Westphal (1978), Westphal and Kim (1977), Lal (1983), and Frank et al. (1972).

10. The statist theory for the economic growth of the NICs is suggested by White and Wade (1985), and White (1988). Its applications to Korea include Jones and Sakong (1980), Yusuf and Peters (1985), Y.W. Rhee et al. (1984), and Leudde-Neurath (1988).

11. See Amsden's Table 8.1 which compares real wages in Korea, Brazil, Argentina, Mexico, India, Turkey, and Taiwan in the period of 1970-1984. The index of real wages in Korea increased from a base of 100 in 1970 to 276 in 1984, Taiwan from 100 in 1972 to 191 in 1984, Argentina from 100 in 1970 to 112 in 1984, Brazil and Mexico from 100 in 1972 to 84 and 83 in 1984, respectively.

12. The sequential phases of industrial development often referred to as the "flying geese pattern of successive stages," which Korea has successfully and successively passed through, also can be found in Japan (Akamatsu, 1962; Kohama, 1990) and Taiwan (Fei, 1986) as a further empirically verified model for developing countries to seriously take into consideration.

Part II Democratization

Part II aims at exploring and developing a Korean model of democratization. One crucial question on the democratization of Korea is the role and influence of the United States of America. The United States is often credited by some politicians, scholars, media journalists, and intellectuals with democratization in Korea. The United States, on the other hand, is discredited and rather seriously challenged by others for its lukewarm attitude and its alleged policy of cooptation with the authoritarian Chun regime during the Fifth Republic, which became the major stumbling block for democratic activists in Korea (Pae, 1991). Chapter Five, therefore, will examine the American role in democratization in foreign countries, including Korea.

Upon the heels of the American policy of cooptation with the anti-democratic Chun regime, pro-democracy activists in Korea-- opposition politicians, clergymen, journalists, professors, and students--faced another obstacle to democratization, the threat from North Korea being constantly ready for taking advantage of political turmoil resulting from the struggles for democratization in South Korea. In the name of national security, law and order, activists have been vulnerable to the National Security Law, the Anti-Communist Law, and a host of other laws which restricted their struggles for democratization. Nevertheless, Korea led the countries of the Third World during the 1980s as she led them in economic development during the 1960s, 1970s, and 1980s. Chapter Six will examine from a cross-national, comparative perspective to what extent Korea indeed leads the developing countries in democratization.

Chapter Seven will examine to what extent Korea has experienced the cultural characteristics of patron-client politics, which is seen as inhibitive of democratic legacies which have thus far endured as an unextinguished flame. Therefore, Chapter Seven will identify them and suggest the potential for Koreans to struggle for democratization.

Blending a political satellite model and a threshold model, Chapter Eight will suggest a Korean model of democratization which explains how and why the Korean miracle of democratization has finally come true. Chapter Eight will be concluded with what accomplishments have been made and what additional tasks need to be realized for further democratization in Korea.

Chapter 5 The American Role in Democratization

Chapter Five will examine three major questions: (1) What are the origins and political philosophy of the American mission of promoting and protecting democracy in foreign countries?; (2) What model may be offered to explain why the United States has ironically not been faithfully adherent to that noble mission in South Korea?; and (3) To what extent the United States has shifted its policy for democratization in South Korea--from "open diplomacy" (1950s-1960s), to "quiet diplomacy" (1970s), and then to "cooptation" (1980s)?

A main thesis of this chapter is that the firm root of democracy in South Korea upon the inception of the Sixth Republic may be attributed less to the United States and more to the dedication, commitment, and struggles of hundreds of thousands of democracy-aspiring Koreans--opposition party leaders and members, intellectuals, professionals, clergymen, media men, college students, and, above all, middle-class citizens. Democracy is not likely to be transplanted by a foreign power and prosper overnight in developing countries but takes a firm root by determination and commitment "by the native people, of the native people, and for the native people."

American Moral Mission

No country has played so vital a role as the United States in helping the Republic of Korea defend its territorial integrity and accomplish modernization at an unprecedented rate in modern civilization. It was the United States which protected South Korea from the communist invasion with over 30,000 killed and over 100,000 wounded in action among its own forces. A mutual defense pact was signed in 1953. Since then the United States has been the ultimate guarantor of South Korean security by continuously stationing some 40,000 U.S. troops. It was also the United States which provided South Korea with economic aid of $5.7 billion and military aid of $6.8 billion from 1945 to 1976.

The strategic importance of Korea and its subsequent national security interest to the United States may be by no means completely ruled out in explaining American commitment to the defense of South Korea. But there may be a more profound and principal goal of the United States for its commitment and sacrifice for South Korea: the American mission of protecting and promoting democracy not only in the United States but also in foreign countries, including South Korea.

From the shores of the North American continent, American leaders and citizens, deeply committed to the value of democracy, were disgusted at the "struggle for power" continuously unfolding in the continents of Europe, Africa, and Asia. Their detestation of power politics was partly due to lack of interest of the United States in particular advantages in terms of power or of territorial gain. But the deeper, underlying political philosophy behind the detestation was their belief that the internal order of states would be considered a major determinant of a state's external behavior and, hence, world peace. If a state's domestic politics were not characterized by democratic institutions and processes, then that state would have the tendency to threaten world peace. History reinforces the perception that states with undemocratic institutions and processes have almost invariably turned to aggressive behavior for power aggrandizement.

Therefore, to export and promote democracy in foreign countries has been the Americans' noble mission. That very mission was indeed envisioned and emphasized by Thomas Jefferson, John Quincy Adams, Grover Cleveland, and Theodore Roosevelt. The more dedicated and eloquent contemporary spokesmen for this foreign policy are Woodrow Wilson, Franklin D. Roosevelt, Harry S. Truman, Lyndon B. Johnson, and Jimmy Carter.

President Woodrow Wilson's famous war message on April 12, 1917 attributed the cause of World War I to lack of democracy and the subsequent lack of consultations with the German people by their leaders.

> We have no quarrel with the German people.... It was not upon their impulse that their government acted.... It was a war determined as wars used to be determined upon the old, unhappy days when peoples were nowhere consulted by their

rulers and wars were provoked and waged in the interest of dynasties or of little groups of ambitious men who were accustomed to follow their fellow men as pawns or tools (Wilson, 1971: 3-8).

No sooner than fifteen years following World War I did three nondemocratic countries--Nazi Germany, Fascist Italy, and Militarist Japan--begin to dominate the continents of Europe, Africa, and Asia. President Franklin Roosevelt again claimed nondemocratic institutions and processes as the main cause of World War II. Only if democracy is firmly established everywhere would the final curtain fall and the struggle for power in the international arena be alleviated. Therefore, President Roosevelt justified the American involvement in World War II on the same moral mission of protecting democracy in Europe and other continents.

> Every realist knows that the democratic way of life is at this moment being directly assailed in every part of the world--assailed either by arms, or by secret spreading of poisonous propaganda by those who seek to destroy unity and promote discord in nations that are still at peace.

> During sixteen long moments this assail has blotted out the whole pattern of democratic life in an appalling number of independent nations, great and small. The assailants are still on the march, threatening other nations, great and small (1941: 46).

In addition to its contribution to world peace, democracy is seen as a political means by which citizens of foreign countries may as well enjoy life, liberty, the pursuit of happiness, and self-actualization under the guarantee of the same basic freedoms and human rights--civil, political, economic, and social--as Americans enjoy. "Aiding in this achievement" has been conceived to be "America's mission" (Morgenthau, 1982: 10).

Democratization is seen as the core of American foreign policy because it is central to what the United States is and stands for. Former American Ambassador to the United Nations Jean Kirkpatrick admits democratization in developing countries as a major legitimate purpose of American foreign policy:

The emphasis on science and technology by both the government and businesses for higher-value-added goods and services was first evidenced by the integration of sixteen major

I believe that it must be the policy of the United States to support peoples who are resisting attempted subjugation by armed minorities or by outside pressure.

I believe that we must assist free peoples to work out their own destinies in their own ways (Truman, 1947: 178-79).

Many presidents of the United States, in fact, endorsed the American commitment to democracy and human rights. President Eisenhower stated in his address to the American Bar Association on August 24, 1955 that there would be no true peace as long as "we find injustice to many nations, repressions of human beings on a gigantic scale. . . with constructive effort paralyzed in many years by fear." President Kennedy, in his inaugural address, delivered a message to the world that: "let every nation know, whether it wish us well or ill, that we shall pay any price, bear any burden, meet any hardship, support our friends or oppose any foe to assure the survival and success of liberty."

In his inaugural address President Carter called the attention of the American people to the same moral mission, which has long been inherited from the inception of the republic.

Because we are free, we can never be indifferent to the fate of freedom elsewhere. Our moral sense dictates a clear-cut preference for those societies which share with us an abiding respect for individual human rights. We do not seek to intimidate, but it is clear that a world which others can dominate with impunity would be inhospitable to decency and a threat to the well-being of all people (1977: 258-59).

His strong commitment to democracy and human rights was more explicitly stated in his address at the United Nations General Assembly on March 17, 1977. For example, he warned that "no member of the United Nations can claim that mistreatment of its citizens is solely its own business. Equally, no member can avoid its responsibilities to review and to speak when torture or unwarranted deprivation occurs in any part of the world" (1977: 354-56).

President Carter, in his State of the Union address in 1978, reaffirmed human rights as the moral basis for American foreign policy. The essence of his foreign policy can be summarized in the following quotation from his speech: "We stand for human rights because we believe that the purpose of government is to promote the well-being of its citizens. This is true in our domestic and in our foreign policy. The world must know that in support of human rights, the United States will stand firm" (1978: 228).

The U.S. Congress has also demonstrated its commitment to the American moral mission of promoting democracy and respect for human rights worldwide, passing the Foreign Assistance Acts of 1973 and 1974. The acts required the President to "deny any economic or military assistance to the government of any foreign country which practices the internment or imprisonment of that country's citizens for political purposes." The International Development and Food Assistance Act of 1975 and the International Security Assistance and Arms Export Control Act of 1976 required the President to withhold aid to a foreign nation if the nation had a record of gross violations of human rights, with exceptions and escape clauses in the event of undefined "extraordinary circumstances."[1] Congress has passed a variety of country-specific provisions making aid contingent upon human rights practices (Cohen, 1982: 254-56).

The American mission, indeed, has brought about exceptional accomplishments. Among them may be listed a few salient examples: the Marshall Plan, the Truman Doctrine, the Point Four programs, the rebuilding of democracy in West Germany and Japan. The United States also led the United Nations in enshrining these values in legal instruments and international agreements: the Universal Declaration of Human Rights in 1948; the International Convention of the Elimination of Racial Discrimination that was adopted on December 21, 1965; the International Covenant on Economic, Social and Cultural Rights and the International Covenant on Civil and Political Rights which were adopted on December 16, 1966; the Helsinki Agreement by 35 countries assembled in 1975 to give solemn approval to the commitment to implementing the principles of human rights.

Realism: A Model of the American Role

But the U.S. has been facing a dilemma of the ideal principle vs. the harsh reality of power politics in the international arena. The American attempts to accomplish such a manifest mission--the promoting and protecting of democracy in foreign countries--have been challenged by: the Russian government and leaders during the

Russian civil war;[2] the Chinese Communist forces during the Chinese civil war; the North Korean Communists during the Korean War; the North Vietnamese forces during the Indo-China War; and a host of anti-democratic forces in Europe, Asia, Africa, and Latin America. Therefore, the United States has been able to pursue this lofty foreign policy not in a uniform, consistent way but in different ways, taking into account two perspectives: (1) how important a foreign country is in terms of the U.S. national interest; and (2) how dependent that country is upon the United States. Based upon the relationship between these two dimensions, a model is developed.

The very notion of national interests is itself a matter of debate. The geopolitical perspective, for example, defines the national interest in terms of power. Its principal ingredients are military and economic strengths. The traditional geopolitical theory in the contemporary international arena postulates a contest for control of the rimland of Eurasia between the great oceanic powers such as the United States, Great Britain and Japan, and the dominant heartland power of the USSR. Whichever dominates the rimland would control the world (Mahan, 1900; Mackinder, 1904; Spykman, 1944; Jones, 1955: 492-508). Derived from this theory are the following objective national interests of the United States as observed in the report to the Congress by former Secretary of Defense, Mr. Brown:

1. Ensure that the rival superpower, the USSR does not gain a global preponderance of military power;
2. Prevent the Soviet Union from enlarging the territorial extent of its sphere of control;
3. Keep the other advanced, non-Communist industrial countries (the Western European countries, Canada, and Japan) within the United States sphere of influence;
4. Maintain access to foreign sources of critical raw materials (particularly the oil of the Persian Gulf area);
5. Keep hostile forces out of the land, sea, and airspace adjacent to the United States; and
6. (Derivative of all the above) Maintain United States naval superiority in the Atlantic and Pacific Oceans, the Mediterranean Sea, and the Indian Ocean (Brown, 1984: 4-5).

Based upon these criteria, the dimension of U.S. national interest may be divided into "vital," "important," and "indifferent."

Table 5-1 Scores of Key Nations Vital to the U.S. Security Interest Based on Survey from the American Public and Elites by the Chicago Council on Foreign Relations

Countries	Public in General 1982	1986	Countries	Elites 1982	1986
England	80	83	W.Germany	98	98
			Japan	97	98
Canada	82	78	Mexico	98	96
Japan	82	78	Canada	95	96
W.Germany	76	77	England	97	94
Saudi Arabia	77	77			
Israel	75	76	China	87	89
Mexico	74	74	Saudi Arab.	93	88
The Philipp.	--	73	Israel	92	86
			France	84	82
Egypt	66	61	The Philipp	--	81
China (PRC)	64	61	*S Korea	66	80
Nicaragua	--	60			
South Africa	38	59	Nicaragua	--	63
*South Korea	43	58	S Africa	54	63
France	58	56	Brazil	80	63
Taiwan	51	53	India	57	55
Iran	51	50	Taiwan	44	48
Syria	36	48	Egypt	90	61
Brazil	45	44	Italy	79	--
Italy	35	41	Iran	79	--
India	30	36	Nigeria	53	--
Poland	43	35	Poland	47	--
Nigeria	32	31	Syria	46	--

Source: Adapted from John E. Reilley (1988: 45-56); Quoted from *The Dong-A Ilbo,* May 5, 1987
-- Indicates the countries not included as important in the survey of the particular year.

Therefore, some countries become "vital" to the U.S. national interest, whereas others may be either "important" or "indifferent."

Different administrations with different presidents in the United States, however, were subjectively biased and viewed the same foreign country as either vital, important, or indifferent despite the fact that the country's geopolitical variables remained the same. The domestic political process often provided legitimacy to the specific foreign commitments and policies which might otherwise be rejected from the geopolitical perspective as unwarranted in terms of its seemingly objectively defined national interest. A few salient examples are the unequivocal support to the security of Israel, even

Figure 5-1 A Model for U.S. Commitment to Democratization

U.S. National Interest

	a	b	c
Vital	Full Commitment Japan of 1950s W. Germany of 1950s	Open/Quiet Diplomacy Israel(81) The Philippines(81) of 1980s	Cooptation G. Britain(94) Canada(96) Japan(98) W. Germany(98) Saudi Arabia(88) Mexico(96) Korea(80) China(81) France(82) of 1980s
	d	e	f
Important	Open Diplomacy Korea of 1950s & 1960s	Quiet Diplomacy Korea of 1970s Saudi Arabia(63) Nicaragua(63) Egypt(61) of 1980s	Symbolic Support Brazil(63) India(55) Taiwan(48) of 1980s
	g	h	i
Indifferent	Rare Cases	Rare Cases	No Commitment

Dependency on USA

Full   Moderate   Limited or Equal Partnership

*Sample countries are located in the appropriate cells on the basis of the outcome of the 1986 surveys sponsored by the Chicago Council on Foreign Relations on America's vital interest around the world--the public and elites. The scores parenthesized are the scores answered by the elites. For further information, see John E. Reilley (1988: 45-56).

in the face of the Arab control of oil, as vital to the United States; the decision not to bomb Rome during World War II; and the decision to cut off military aid to Turkey in 1975-1976, primarily in response to the domestic demands and sentiments of Jewish Americans, Italian Americans, and Greco-Americans, respectively (Brown, 1984: 7-9).

The perception of a foreign country in terms of the U.S. national interest is by no means fixed once and for all. As the Chicago Council on Foreign Relations presented the outcome of its 1986 survey, Egypt and Brazil, for example, were regarded as "vital" to the U.S. national interest with 90 and 80 scores assigned by American elites in 1982 but declined to 61 and 63 in 1986, respectively (see Table 5-1). This clearly indicates that, depending on the change in the environment surrounding a particular foreign country and depending on the change of power of the country, the United States may change its perception on security interests in that country.

Moreover, the security interest alone does not dictate the action and commitment of the United States. The degree of commitment to promoting and protecting democracy may as well consider the degree of the dependency of the country upon the United States for political, economic, and/or military support and its subsequent compliance with desires and expectations of the United States. The dimension of dependency may be divided into "limited (or equal partnership)," "moderate," and "full."

The interaction of these two dimensions suggests nine combinations, (a) through (i), and their corresponding policy options of the United States for democratization in foreign countries (see Figure 5-1). In cell (a) could be located countries like Japan and West Germany during the American occupation period following World War II. These two countries were considered "vital" to the U.S. national interest and "fully dependent" on the Unites States for their economic rehabilitation and national defense. Therefore, the United States was "willing" and "able" to fully commit itself to helping these two countries develop and implement democracy. In return, they had no options but to comply with the American policy of "full commitment" to democratization.

Korea, however, has experienced changes in the perception of "security interest" and "dependency" on the United States, for example, from cell (d)--"strategically important" and "fully dependent" on the United States during the 1950s and 1960s, to cell (e)--"strategically important" and "moderately dependent" on the United States during the 1970s, and then to cell (c)--"strategically vital" and "equal partnership" with the United States during the 1980s.

During the 1950s and 1960s, when Korea was considered "important" to the U.S. national interest and fully "dependent" on the

United States, the latter was willing to employ "open diplomacy," exerting strong pressure upon the Korean government for reducing violations of human rights, demanding elections to be held as scheduled, and restraining the application of the Anti-Communist Law to opposition politicians. Since South Korea was heavily dependent upon the United States for military defense and economic survival, the Korean government had to comply with the American pressure. However, during the 1970s when Korea had accomplished economic development to a significant extent, explicit American pressure and open diplomacy for democratization and the promotion of human rights began to face resistance from the Korean government. During the 1980s, when Korea was seen as "strategically vital" but "economically strong" enough to enter an "equal partnership" with the United States, the American desire for pressure for democratization in Korea had to be sacrificed for the sake of security interests and economic benefits of the United States. Nor could economic and other kinds of sanctions be employed, either. In short, the model explains why the United States could not exert any significant influence upon the Korean government and its leaders for aggressive movement toward democracy during the 1980s. To the contrary, the United States was seen as a betrayer of democracy and a promoter of cooptation with the authoritarian Korean government in the eyes of opposition leaders, intellectuals, and college students in Korea. They rather credit a giant stride toward democratization upon the embarkation of the Sixth Republic to themselves rather than to the Americans. Let us examine this thesis.

Changes in the American Policy of Democracy in Korea

Open Diplomacy (1950s-1960s)

The American commitment to the defense of South Korea and subsequent military and economic assistance during the 1950s and 1960s were explained and justified not only by Korea's strategic importance to the United States but also by the traditional American mission for democracy.[3] The Joint Chiefs of Staff evaluated as early as 1947 that "from the standpoint of military security, the United States has little strategic interest in maintaining the present troops and bases in Korea" (Miller, 1974: 286-87). Secretary of State Acheson also estimated that "There would be no military aggression in East Asia." What might be expected as the primary threat would be rather "subversion and penetration." But that could "not be stopped by military means" (1950: 116). If military attacks were to come, "the initial reliance must be on the people attacked to resist it and then upon the commitments of the entire civilized world under the Charter of the United Nations" rather than the American forces alone (Acheson, 1950: 116). Therefore, on January 12, 1950, he announced the exclusion of South Korea from the American defensive perimeter in Asia.

Upon the invasion of North Korea, however, President Truman began to perceive South Korea as strategically important to the U.S. security interest and took a decisive action, first of all, to order American air and naval forces to support the retreating South Korean units upon the invasion of North Korean communists and then to deploy American ground troops. Moreover, President Truman and his policy-makers saw the North Korean invasion as the same aggression, the same threat to democracy, and the same subsequent danger as the threats from dictatorship in the past:

> Communism was acting in Korea just as Hitler, Mussolini, and the Japanese had acted ten, fifteen, and twenty years earlier. I felt certain that if South Korea was allowed to fall, Communist leaders would be emboldened to override nations closer to our own shores. If the Communists were permitted to force their war into the Republic of Korea without opposition from the free world, no small nation would have the courage to resist threats and aggression by stronger communist neighbors. If this was allowed to go unchallenged, it would mean the third World War, just as similar incidents had brought on the Second World War (Truman, 1956: 333).

The American commitment resulted in the unexpectedly high human cost, with 33,000 Americans killed and 103,000 wounded in action, and expenditure of $50 billion of direct costs. Upon the conclusion of a truce, the U.S. still committed itself to the defense of South Korea. The Senate, by a vote of 81 to 6, ratified the mutual defense pact with South Korea on January 27, 1954. The vote was far in excess of the required two-thirds majority. The announced purpose of the treaty was to guarantee South Korea against further attack by the communists from North Korea. Moreover, in response to the demand for mutual withdrawal of Chinese and American forces from North and South Korea, respectively, the United States made it clear that the American forces would stay in South Korea until "the conditions for lasting settlement laid down by the United Nations General Assembly be fulfilled" (*NYT*, July 3, 1958).

The United States also provided South Korea with economic aid on the basis of "the economic theory of democracy."[4] The theory holds that democracy can be viable under economic growth and prosperity. When people are made miserable and under constant threat of daily survival, democracy may be less likely to take a firm root. The more economically prosperous a country is, the more stable its democracy becomes. Hence, President Truman's request to Congress for economic aid to South Korea was justified on the same moral mission of the promotion of democracy as the essential American foreign policy.

> Korea has become a testing ground in which the validity and practical value of the ideals and principles of democracy which the Republic is putting into practice are being matched against the practice of communism which has been imposed upon the people of North Korea. The survival and progress of the Republic toward a self-supporting, stable economy will have an immense and far-reaching influence on the people of Asia. Such progress by the young Republic will encourage the people of southern and southeastern Asia and the islands of the Pacific to resist and reject the Communist propaganda with which they are besieged. Moreover, the Korean Republic, by demonstrating the success and tenacity of democracy in resisting communism, will stand as a beacon to the people of northern Asia in resisting the control of the communist forces which have overrun them (U.S. Congress, 1953: 32).

The United States was equally involved in inflation control, tax adjustment, land reform, and rehabilitation of economic infrastructure such as road building, bridge repairs, building schools and hospitals.

When the First Republic of Korea failed to vigorously act against sky-rocketing inflation, the United States issued an unequivocally decisive warning that Korean government leaders should take proper anti-inflationary measures for economic stability and growth. Secretary of State Dean Acheson even threatened to review the entire aid program, if the Rhee Administration continued to ignore the inflation problem. The Aide-memoirs read:

> It is the judgement of this Government that the financial situation in Korea has already reached critical proportions and that, unless this progressive inflation is curbed in the none too distant future, it cannot but seriously impair Korea's ability to utilize effectively the economic assistance (Tewksbury, 1950: 145).

Mr. Paul G. Hoffman, Economic Cooperation Administrator (ECA) offered a specific warning that unless "tax revenues are sharply increased and expenditures are drastically decreased, prices will continue to rise probably at an accelerating rate." Once the inflation reached a critical point, then the American aid would make "no further net contribution to the welfare of the people of Korea" (*NYT*, April 8, 1954).

Land reform was another important, decisive action that the United States called on the Korean government to adopt and implement. Its key rationale was that money and soldiers alone could not maintain a viable democracy in Korea where poverty might be perpetuated among a vast majority of Korean people who were peasants without their own farmland. The American idea was that, while retaining the fundamental principles of private ownership and capitalism, land would be bought from the existing owners with government funds supplied by the United States economic aid. Peasants would then be offered ownership of their own small farms. The ultimate goal would be to create "a middle-class yeomanry, which would become the bulwark of agrarian capitalism" (*NYT*, August 25, 1951). The *New York Times* editorial, excited over the idea, suggested: "Let us exploit it into Korea. Let us take over the supervision of this needed and profitable experiment and control the amount and pace of change" (*NYT*, August 25, 1951).

After the Korean War the American forces in Korea joined rehabilitation projects. American military engineer units began to assist in constructing bridges to restore the flow of commerce, and medical units undertook disease control measures. Ellis O. Briggs, the United States Ambassador to Korea, took a step further, calling on the Korean government to establish "a favorable investment climate" for attracting private capital from the United States.

However, he made it clear that the United States businessmen did not want preferential treatment, only equality (*NYT*, Jan. 13, 1955).

The above listed military and economic aid in fact became only the intermediate goals for America's ultimate objective of democratization in Korea. When democratic institutions and processes were ridiculed in Korea, the United states was willing to pursue "open diplomacy"--"publicly" "criticizing" and "protesting" the Korean government with the "warning" and "threatening" of reconsideration of military and economic aid in case of the repetition of undemocratic practices. Let me identify a few salient examples of "open diplomacy," which the United States had applied to Korea during the 1950s and 1960s, in order to demonstrate how strongly the United States had committed itself to the traditional, moral mission.

In January 1950, under the auspices of the government party, the National Assembly amended the National Security Law primarily for the purpose of re-electing President Rhee. The revised law, however, was subject to intense criticism because of its two notorious provisions. They were the establishment of "re-education camps" and an *ex post facto* provision. The former could eliminate the right to appeal, whereas the latter could make it applicable to offenses committed prior to its enactment. Because of "strong pressure" of the United States, the Korean government introduced amendments to remove these two provisions.

In February 1950, when national emergency was still in effect, the Korean government arrested fifteen opposition National Assemblymen, eliminated an opposition press, and purged the Judicial branch of the so-called "leftist agents" including nine lawyers and prosecutors and six judges. Dr. Philip C. Jessup, United States Ambassador-at-large, on his visit to Korea, "publicly" indicated that he was "not entirely happy with what he had observed" (*NYT*, Feb. 2, 1950).

In March 1950, President Rhee expressed his intention to postpone the date of the general election to June and later suggested that the election should be held as late as November after the Constitution would be amended. Disappointed by President Rhee's violation of the democratic principle of regular election, Secretary of State Dean Acheson "clearly" pointed out that both economic and military aid to Korea was based on the "existence and growth of democratic institutions within the republic" (*NYT*, March 27, 1950). Because of such strong pressure from the United States, President

Rhee reversed his previous decision and said, "opinion seemed to be that the election should be held as scheduled in May" (*NYT*, April 12, 1950).

In May 1952, President Rhee's veto was overridden by 96 to 3 such that martial law had to be lifted for fair competition in the forthcoming presidential election. Nevertheless, martial law was not lifted by the president. Rather, forty-seven opposition Assemblymen were detained on the grounds that they violated martial law still being effective. Although President Rhee insisted that the United Nations Commission for the Unification and Rehabilitation of Korea (UNCURK) had no right to "meddle" in Korea's internal affairs, UNCURK handed the text of a message to President Rhee, "demanding" that martial law in Pusan be lifted "without delay" and the Assemblymen "still under arrest or otherwise detained be released" (*NYT*, May 30, 1952).

President Rhee's removal of Korean troops from the front line to enforce martial law in Pusan led to an unwanted visit of General James A. Van Fleet, Commander of the Eighth Army, and Alan E. Lightner, Counselor of the United States Embassy (*NYT*, May 28, 1952). In that meeting, President Rhee promised not to repeat the Korean troop deployment to support his political purpose (*NYT*, June 3, 1952). President Truman took the unusual step of sending a personal note to President Rhee expressing "shock" at Dr. Rhee's feud with the National Assembly (*NYT*, June 4, 1952). All these actions of "open diplomacy" influenced President Rhee to seek and arrive at a compromise with the National Assembly in the constitutional amendments: permitting the legislative the right to vote dissolution of the Cabinet and favoring President Rhee by replacing the legislative election of the president with a direct popular election.

On April 19, 1960, when student protests against election riggings resulted in 115 dead and 780 injured, Secretary of State Christian A. Hester issued a "stern rebuke" to the Korean government through the Korean Ambassador in Washington, D. C. for "repressive measures." He stated that as a sponsor of the republic, friend, supporter, and ally the United States "felt obliged to speak out" (*NYT*, April 20, 1960).

On May 16, 1961 when the Chang regime was overthrown by a military coup, the United States was strongly opposed to the military government. Right after the military revolutionary group announced that it had seized power from the premier, the United States Embassy in Korea issued a statement opposing the military government and instead expressing strong support for the "freely elected and constitutionally established government" of Premier John M. Chang. General Carter B. Magruder, Commander-in-Chief of the United Nations Command in Korea, took a step further, calling on all military personnel in his command--American and Korean--to "support the only recognized government of the Republic of Korea headed by Prime Minister Chang." He stated, "The chiefs of the Korean armed forces will use their authority and influence to see that control is immediately turned back to the lawful governmental authority and that order is restored in the armed forces." The American government "unequivocally supported" the statement of General Magruder and the American Embassy in Seoul. Washington flatly rejected a suggested meeting between President Kennedy and General Chang Do Young (*NYT*, May 16 & 25, 1961).

Only when President Yun Posun as the *de jure* Commander-in-Chief of the Korean armed forces refused to take any military action with the American assistance against the coup forces did General Magruder realize that there would be no other way to forcefully remove the coup force from the government. A head-on military collision might result in severe casualties of not only military personnel but also innocent civilians in Seoul. The junta, on the other hand, promised to restore political rule to conscientious civilians soon.

America's open diplomacy was evidenced again in March 1963 when General Park announced withdrawal of a referendum originally scheduled in summer of 1965 for the ratification of the constitutional amendments or the extension of military rule for four more years. The United States issued a strong protest and demanded a stable constitutional rule to be restored in South Korea. On April 16, 1963, General Park gave in to the American pressure and stated that he would work toward holding elections in 1963.

Quiet Diplomacy (1970s)

During the 1970s, the United States shifted its foreign policy toward South Korea from "open diplomacy" to "quiet diplomacy." Open diplomacy, which had been implemented during the 1950s and 1960s in Korea, was characterized as 1) "open, formal protests" against the Korean government in violation of democratic institutions and processes, 2) "explicit warnings" against possible repetition of undemocratic practices, and 3) "strong demands" for corrections and improvements. Open diplomacy was usually accompanied by the use of economic and military aid as the leverage to be either threatened or actually increased, decreased, or terminated. Korea, as a client country, because of economic survival and growth and security imperatives, had no other options but to comply with the open diplomacy of the patron country.

Quiet diplomacy, which was implemented in Korea during the 1970s, was characterized as persuasion and recommendations rather than explicit and strong protests and demands. Even persuasion and recommendations were more likely to be made by informal rather than formal, and behind-the-scene rather than open means. Quiet diplomacy may focus on more specific concerns rather than broad, comprehensive ones. Warnings and threats were less likely to be employed. Economic and military aid was no longer effectively utilized as leverage, once the client country had achieved its economic development to a significant extent. Therefore, the amount of economic aid was shrinking in its leverage as its ever-decreasing fraction of the client country's GNP. Moreover, loans began to replace economic aid as the main source for investment. So was the case of military aid. Again, because of rapid economic growth, military aid began to be replaced by military sale. If military sales were not allowed, sales from other export countries could be actively sought. Economic growth and subsequent independence of Korea from foreign economic and military aid were such that the United States was more likely to abstain from resorting to the ever-decreasing amount of aid as leverage on its former client country.

As Table 5-2 indicates, the American military assistance (MA) during the 1950s and 1960s accounted for 100 to 99 percent of the sum (Sum) of both U.S. military assistance (MA) and military sales (MS). But, in 1974, military sales began to increase, reaching about thirteen percent and gradually increased to 95.7 percent of the sum of military aid and sales in 1979. This suggests that by 1979, U.S. military aid was completely phased out and replaced by the military sales of weapons and equipment. The U.S. military aid, for example, accounted for 18.91 percent of Korea's total GNP in 1953 but for only .02 percent in 1979. U.S. nonmilitary government grants and credits explained 12.98 percent of Korea's GNP in 1973 but only .37 percent in 1979. The total amount of U.S. grants and credits--military and nonmilitary--represented 31.9 percent of Korea's GNP in 1953 but 0.6 percent in 1979. In short, American economic and military grants and credits during the 1970s became only 2.25

Table 5-2 Major Elements of the U.S. Leverage on the Korean Government for
Democratization: Military Assistance (MA), Military Sales (MS), Nonmilitary
Government Grants and Credits (NMGGC), Total Military and Nonmilitary
Government Grants and Credits (TMNGGC)*

(units: $millions & %)

Yr	MA	MS	Sum (a)+(b) =(c)	% of MA (a/c)	% of MS (b/c)	% of MA to ROK's GNP (d)	MN-GGC (e)	Its % to GNP	TMNGGC (a+e)	Its % to GNP (f)
	(a) (1)	(b) (2)	(3)	(4)	(5)	(6)	(7)	(8)	(9)	(10)
1953	300.0	.0	300.0	100.0	.0	18.91	206	12.98	506.0	31.9
1954	250.0	.0	250.0	100.0	.0	14.16	169	9.75	419.0	23.7
1955	230.0	.0	230.0	100.0	.0	12.87	276	15.44	506.0	28.3
1956	231.2	.0	231.0	100.0	.0	12.47	307	16.55	538.2	29.0
1957	265.5	.0	265.5	100.0	.0	13.62	373	19.14	638.5	32.7
1958	353.5	.0	353.5	100.0	.0	17.24	311	15.17	664.5	32.4
1959	212.4	.0	212.4	100.0	.0	9.84	232	10.75	444.4	20.6
1960	232.1	.0	232.1	100.0	.0	9.80	261	12.01	474.1	21.8
1961	232.7	.0	232.7	100.0	.0	10.07	230	9.96	462.7	20.0
1962	189.5	.1	189.6	99.9	.0	7.88	238	9.90	427.5	17.7
1963	194.8	.2	195.0	99.8	.1	7.47	240	9.20	434.8	16.6
1964	137.8	.2	138.0	99.8	.1	4.88	158	5.60	295.8	10.4
1965	219.2	.3	219.5	99.8	.1	7.16	167	5.45	386.2	12.6
1966	168.7	.3	169.0	99.8	.2	5.19	168	5.17	336.7	10.3
1967	153.2	.4	153.6	99.7	.2	4.19	193	5.29	346.2	9.4
1968	204.1	.5	204.6	99.7	.2	5.11	191	4.78	395.1	9.8
1969	210.0	.5	210.5	99.7	.2	4.57	260	5.66	470.0	10.2
1970	216.3	1.9	218.2	99.1	.9	2.93	198	2.68	414.3	5.6
1971	140.5	.4	140.9	99.7	.3	1.74	194	2.41	334.5	4.1
1972	164.3	.2	164.5	99.8	.2	1.33	221	1.79	385.3	3.1
1973	96.4	.3	97.7	98.6	1.3	.65	214	1.44	310.4	2.0
1974	91.6	13.3	104.9	87.3	12.7	.56	63	.38	154.6	.9
1975	136.6	57.5	194.1	70.3	29.6	.74	314	1.76	450.6	2.4
1976	91.5	136.5	228.0	40.1	59.8	.33	344	1.27	435.5	1.6
1977	15.3	177.8	193.1	7.9	92.1	.04	250	.72	265.3	.7
1978	26.2	414.1	440.3	5.9	94.0	.05	698	1.47	724.2	1.5
1979	17.6	395.0	412.6	4.2	95.7	.02	228	.37	245.6	.6
1980	160.4	295.2	455.6	35.2	64.8	.27	101	.17	261.4	.4
1981	107.7	295.5	403.2	26.7	73.3	.17	193	.31	300.7	.4
1982	139.1	218.6	357.7	38.8	61.1	.21	337	.51	476.1	.7
1983	.7	299.0	299.7	.2	99.8	.00	448	.60	448.7	.6
1984	1.6	261.0	262.6	.6	99.4	.00	208	.26	209.6	.2

Source: For (a) and (b), *Statistical Abstract of the United States*, various years; U.S. Defense Security Assistance Agency, *Foreign Military Sales and Foreign Military Construction Sales*; Department of Defense, *Military Assistance Facts* (Washington, D.C.: U.S. Government Printing Office), various years; for (e), Department of Commerce, *Foreign Grants and Credits by the U.S. Government*, various years.

*Unable to include in this table the data for 1948-52 due to lack of consistency in the categorization in government documents.

percent of Korea's GNP on average and consequently could not be used as leverage to place any significant pressure on Korea for its democratization.

Moreover, because of increasing economic strength and other environmental factors, South Korea, a former client country, was changed to be more strategically important to U.S. national interest. The collapse of South Vietnam and Cambodia, the potential for spillover on the Korean peninsula, increase in the Soviet naval forces based in Vladivostock, and the subsequent threat to Japan required the United States to reconsider and to perceive South Korea as strategically important.

Former Secretary of State, Cyrus R. Vance, dramatized the American dilemma:

> We know from our national experience that the drive for human freedom has tremendous force and vitality. It is universal. It is resilient. And, ultimately, it is irrepressible.
>
> In a profound sense, then, our ideals and our interests coincide. For we have a stake in the stability that comes when people can express their hopes and build their futures freely.
>
> Yet, certainly the pursuit of human rights must be managed in a practical way. We must constantly weigh how best to encourage progress while maintaining an ability to conduct business with governments--even unpopular ones--in countries where we have important security interests(1980: 569).

Secretary of State George P. Shultz also highlighted the American agony between the moral mission and realism: "How to realize our moral mission without risking the national security interests and without exhausting the national power, how to pursue noble goals in a complex and imperfect world, which disturb the United States in promoting and protecting democracy" (1984: 450).

The answer to Secretaries Vance and Shultz is "quiet diplomacy." So long as a foreign country like South Korea is important to the U.S. national interest and economically strong and less dependent on the United States, quiet diplomacy may be the only option for the U. S. government to employ in promoting democracy in Korea.

Korea of the 1970s witnessed a series of violations of basic freedoms, human rights, and democratic procedural principles. Upon the embarkation of the Fourth Republic in 1972, after the amendment and ratification of the Yushin Constitution, President Park issued a series of nine executive decrees. They prohibited debate on the constitution and proposal of any amendment; restricted press in reporting anything except government views; closed the *Dong-A*, the nation's largest newspaper; dismissed thirteen of its editors and reporters; and imposed a new censorship law which forbade criticism of President Park. Korean armed troops seized the Seoul campus of Korea University and closed some twenty universities in Seoul for 41 days.

Those who were involved in the National Council of Christian Churches, the National Council for Restoration of Democracy, the Urban Industrial Mission, and a host of other organizations, primarily established for civil, political, and economic democracy in Korea, were being arrested and tortured.

Democracy-seeking Koreans sincerely urged the U.S. Government to take open diplomacy to President Park. Similar concern was voiced by American scholars, journalists, congressmen and senators. A delegation of U.S. congressmen led by Representatives Thomas P. O'Neill, Jr.(D: MA), and John B. Anderson (R: IL) said that "South Korea's image is being damaged by Park's political acts" (*NYT*, May 18, 1974). Professor Edwin O. Reischauer urged the United States to rethink its policy because President Park "is making mockery of democratic institutions and undermining loyalty of South Korea" (*NYT*, June 14 & March, 19, 1976). Edwin Reischauer, John King Fairbank, and 35 others signed a petition and protested the "injustice and inhumanity of President Park" (*NYT*, July 15, 1975). Representative Donald M. Fraser (D: MN) called for "an end to American military aid to South Korea until Park's repression ceases" (*NYT*, August 2, 1975). A group of American missionaries staged silent demonstrations in the U.S. Embassy compound in Seoul, "urging the United States to make stronger protest to the South Korean government over the hanging of 8 persons convicted of attempting to overthrow President Park's government" (*NYT*, April 17, 1975). A letter signed by 119 senators and representatives on April 4 and a letter of protest signed by 154 U.S. Congressmen on October 28, 1976 expressed "profound distress over arbitrary action in jailing political critics." They contended that continued American military support for South Korea might "make the United States an accomplice to political repression by President Park" (*NYT*, April 14 & Oct. 28, 1976).

Typical responses of the United States government to the above demands and recommendations ironically were the continued military and economic alliance with South Korea because of its strategic importance to the U.S. national interest, and the subsequent implementation of "quiet" rather "open" diplomacy for the promotion of democracy in Korea.

Former Secretary of State Henry Kissinger, for example, testified before the Senate Appropriations Subcommittee, saying that "the United States has decided to continue economic and military aid to South Korea, although the United States does not approve of South Korea's repressive measures at home." He stated, "South Korea's strategic position in Asian security is crucial to Japan, and Japan shares the United States' view" (*NYT*, July 25, 1974).

Quiet diplomacy was clearly witnessed in the typically well-phrased statements by the U.S. Government such as "carefully watch," "does not feel comfortable about," "expressed concerns about," "privately indicated," "deplored human rights violations," and "privately protested." For example, Assistant Secretary of State Robert Ingersoll, after he reviewed the United States stance on human rights with South Korean Deputy Premier Tae Wan Son, issued a statement: "The United States 'continues to watch' South Korean developments carefully. The Korean government is aware of U.S. views on human rights" (*NYT*, July 17, 1974). In fact, the term "quiet diplomacy" was officially advocated for the first time in 1974 by Deputy Secretary Robert Ingersoll and Acting Assistant State Secretary Arthur W. Hummel, Jr. Both of them "deplored" human rights violations in Korea but stressed its military importance.

Quiet diplomacy was further demonstrated by the then American Ambassador Richard Walker, who showed reservation in promoting democracy in an open and explicit way, while a nationwide Korean police round-up of dissidents indeed ridiculed President Carter's human rights issue as the central theme of the U.S. foreign policy.

Instead Ambassador Walker advocated and implemented "quiet diplomacy," "working quietly behind the scenes to soften Mr. Park's policies without bruising South Korea's growing pride and independent spirit" (*NYT*, April 20, 1977). Amidst strong opposition of Korean dissidents and human rights leaders, President

Carter made a state visit and toasted President Park at a state dinner. This was seen on the one hand as a betrayal of Korean human rights leaders and democracy fighters. On the other hand, he quietly called on the Korean government to release more than 100 political prisoners (*NYT*, July 2, 1977).

Korea of the 1980s: Vital to U.S. National Interest

Domestic changes in the United States and external challenges primarily from the Soviet Union in East Asia in the late 1970s and 1980s called for a critical review of the importance of South Korea. During this period the U.S. began to perceive Korea as "vital" to rather than "important" for U.S. security interest.

From the domestic perspective the United States of the 1980s had taken a respite from the exhaustion of energy and will to defend freedoms and democracy in Vietnam. The United States also had the desire to restore its prestige and credibility as the number one democratic nation and to enthusiastically commit itself to strong defense against the ever-alarming increase of defense expenditures of the Soviet Union and her aggressive nature in Afghanistan, El Salvador, Nicaragua, and other countries.

Soviet challenges in the Northeast Asian region may be seen as a more immediate cause for the U.S. to see the security of South Korea of the 1980s as vital to the security of the United States, Japan, and the overall balance of power in the region. First of all, the United States perceived that since the Soviet Union is not only contiguous to China, Korea, and Japan but also has important strategic stakes in the region,[5] the United States should continue to become a legitimate member and the guardian of the region. This official position was mentioned by former President Gerald R. Ford, who declared on December 1975, that the United States should be a nation of the Pacific basin, (having) "a very vital stake in Asia and a responsibility to take a leading part in lessening, preventing hostilities, and preserving peace" (U.S. DOS, 1975: 1). Secretary of State Cyrus Vance reaffirmed Ford's statement and emphasized President Carter's policy in June 1977, stating that: "We are and will remain a Pacific nation by virtue of our geography, our history, our commerce, and our interests" (U.S. DOS, 1977: 1). In the Reagan-Chun joint communique of February 1981 President Reagan reaffirmed that the United States, as a Pacific power, "will seek to ensure the peace and security of the region" (*Korea Herald*, Feb. 4,

1981). The peace and security of the region, however, should precondition the stabilization of the Korean peninsula. This was clearly evidenced by the fact that the Japanese Prime Minister Yasuhiro Nakasone and U.S. President Reagan confirmed the decade-old, mutually shared view between the two nations that: "peace and stability should be preserved on the Korean peninsula, which has become the crossroad to peace and stability in Northeast Asia and the Pacific" (*NYT*, April 17, 1986).

The heightened concern of the U.S. national security interest in the region in general and the Korean peninsula in particular could be examined in two perspectives. A first one was the Soviet Union's emphasis on the security of the Far East. This was demonstrated by its Far Eastern Theater of War, which encompassed the continental Far Eastern Theater of military operations (TDV) and the Pacific Ocean TDV.

The Far Eastern TDV had 57 divisions, equipped with 15,000 tanks, 17,300 armored personnel carriers (APC/IFVs), 13,400 artillery pieces, 388 tactical surface-to-surface missiles (SSMs), and 1,300 tactical aircraft (U.S. DOD, 1987: 18). The Soviets had recently strengthened ground forces oriented against U.S. allies in the region. Four Soviet divisions, for example, were deployed on the Pacific approaches to the USSR such as the Northern Territories south of the Kuril Islands and to the northeast of the Japanese islands of Hokkaido. The deployment of these forces alarmed the United States and her allies, especially Japan as the target for the offensive nature of Soviet military within the region.

The Pacific Ocean Fleet was the largest of the four Soviet fleets. The priority of the Pacific Ocean might be attributed to "its wartime missions, the increasing importance of the Pacific Basin in trade and commerce, and its geographical isolation from the western fleets and the major shipbuilding centers in the USSR (U.S. DOD, 1986: 63). The fleet had four major missions: 1) To conduct strategic strikes by ballistic missile submarines as its primary mission; 2) To maintain control over contiguous sea areas, including the Sea of Japan, Sea of Okhotsk, along the naval superiority in the Kuril Islands, and off the Kamchatka Peninsula; 3) To maintain control over these areas, in fact, requiring the seaward defense of the Soviet Pacific Fleet; 4) To conduct sea-denial operations hundreds of nautical miles from the shore (U.S. DOD, 1987: 68).

The U.S. Department of Defense worried about the potential that the Soviets would deploy attack submarines for anti-submarine warfare (ASW) and possibly lay mines off the U.S. ballistic missile submarine base at Bangor, Washington. Also, a few submarines might be deployed near military bases and piers off the Hawaiian Islands and the U.S. west coast. Taking advantage of Cam Rahn Bay, Soviet naval forces also would conduct anti-ship strikes against transmitting American and allied forces, harass and interdict sea lines of communication and transportation in the South China Sea, and possibly attack U.S. facilities in the region (U.S. DOD, 1986: 63).

Such American worries became more salient after November 1985, when the Soviet Pacific Ocean Fleet was upgraded by the deployment of: three new principal surface combatants--a KIROV-Class nuclear-powered guided-missile cruiser, a SOVREMENNYY-Class guided-missile destroyer, and an UDALOY-Class guided missile destroyer; two attack submarines--the eighth KILO-Class diesel-powered attack submarine and the second AKULA-Class nuclear-powered attack submarine; and a sea-based combat helicopter, the HELIX B, whose primary functions were the delivery of precision-guided weapons and target designation. Former U.S. Secretary of Defense Caspar Weinberger, in fact, warned that "the 800 ship Soviet Pacific Fleet is in a position to challenge the fewer than 600 ship U.S. Navy in the Pacific" (U.S. DOD, 1987: 68-69).

Professor R. A. Brown attempted to qualify Weinberger's apprehensions and stated that the Russian Pacific Ocean Fleet must be far inferior to its American counterpart. The rationales for Brown's contention were three-fold. First, many ships in the Russian Pacific were substantially smaller ones than those of the American Seventh Fleet. The smaller ships are quicker and cheaper to build, shorter in the commitment of resources, easier to operate, and more difficult to target, but they must be restricted to the mission of "sea-denial" as opposed to that of "sea control" as the primary mission of the American fleet. Second, none of the four Russian fleets (Northern, Baltic, Black Sea, Pacific) had naval bases with year round access to the open sea, "being ice bound part of the year or requiring transit through hostile 'choke point' or both." Third, the Soviet Pacific Fleet was not readily reinforceable from the other three fleets, while the U.S. Third Fleet with 154 ships was only nine steaming days away from the U.S. Seventh Fleet. Last, two Russian "aircraft carriers" based in the Pacific, the KIEV-Class Minsk and Novorossiysk could not match the American aircraft carriers due to the former's limited capabilities for amphibious landing operations. They operated only

32 aircraft, of which nineteen were helicopters and eleven were low performance VTOL Yak 36 Forgers. Their American counterparts, on the other hand, operated 85-95 aircraft, of which two squadrons each consisted of 24 extremely capable and expensive F-14 Tom Cats, two squadrons of either A-7 Corsairs or F-18 Hornets, and one squadron of A-6 Intruders. Moreover, the larger the American carriers, the harsher the range of sea conditions and the safer the flights they could operate (Brown, 1986).

Mr. Brown's excellent qualifications notwithstanding, the recently activated mission of "sea denial" by the Soviet Pacific Fleet from Vladivostok to Da Nang and the Cam Rahn Bay caused an increase in tension to the U.S. Navy, which had long monopolized operations and maneuvers in the Pacific. For decades the Northern Pacific waters had been virtually ignored by the U.S. Navy battle groups as they "steamed from San Diego, San Francisco and Seattle on six month deployments to Hawaii, the Philippines and the Indian Ocean." But in response to the "substantial" Soviet threat, Commander of the Pacific Fleet, Admiral James A. Lyons explained that the fleet began to intercept Soviet surveillance missions of the Alaskan coast, conduct amphibious assault exercises, and test-launch a Tomahawk cruise missile near the Aleutian islands. The U.S. Navy had, for the first time, begun regular deployment of aircraft carrier battle groups in the Pacific theater (*Omaha World Herald*, Sept. 7, 1986).

A second major concern of U.S. security in the Far East was the stability of South Korea, which has been disturbed by the ever-increasing military ties between the Soviet Union and North Korea. The Soviet Union had already secured the right to call at Wonsan on North Korea's eastern coast and was pressing North Korea for the use of Wonsan Port as a permanent Soviet military base like Vietnam's Cam Rahn Bay. They also made additional demands for joint military exercises, the training of North Korean military officers in the Soviet Union, and the establishment of a combined intelligence command for closer information exchange (*Korea Herald*, July 27, 1986). The Soviet Union obtained further concessions for their naval ships to visit Nampo Port on the west coast. Now, ever since the end of 1984, Soviet military planes have been allowed to fly over North Korea (*Korea Herald*, August 27, 1986).

In return for these concessions, Pyongyang was supplied with very sophisticated airplanes and weapons. The subsequent formidable military superiority of North Korea over South Korea in the late 1980s may be highlighted as follows:

1. The deployment of 65 percent of its military strength close to the Demilitarized Zone (DMZ).
2. The construction of two air bases near the truce zone that may enable its combat fighters to reach Seoul in eight minutes.
3. Stockpiling of about 180 to 250 metric tons of chemical weapons including mustard gas and nerve gas, which can be launched at targets by mortars, field cannons, rocket launchers, and Scud-B ground-to-ground missiles over a distance of up to 279 km as far south as the city of Taejon.
4. Operating Soviet-built MIG 23 fighters from an airfield in Pukchang, South Pyongyang Province, which can reach Seoul within seventeen minutes.
5. A quantitative advantage of North Korea's military over South Korea's, which may be measured as 1.2 times the ground troops, 2.7 times the number of tanks, 2.0 times artillery pieces, and 1.4 times the number of airplanes.
6. Pyongyang's 100,000 commando force that can harass and interdict the South Korean rear areas using guerrilla operations, posing a serious threat to the security of South Korea.[6]

The expansion of the Soviet Union's threat in the Western Pacific region and its close military ties with North Korea and Vietnam called for a realistic view of the power struggle, re-evaluating and considering South Korea of the 1980s as one of the three major geo-strategic linchpin states for the United States. Ideological competition, of course, might certainly play a role. But such competition, which was colored by "black and white" and "evil and good" kinds of dichotomous perceptions prevailing during the periods of the Cold War, was gradually eroded. Rather the realistic power struggle between the Soviet Union and the United States indeed was examined predominantly "through the extension of power and influence over territory and people and through acquisition of military might designed to intimidate or contain the opponent" (Brzezinski, 1986a: 32). Although the American-Soviet contest was primarily global, one of three central strategic fronts was the Far Eastern region, in which South Korea together with the Philippines was considered by Zbigniew Brzezinski a "geopolitical linchpin." He believed the Soviet domination over South Korea and the Philippines

Table 5-3 Major Elements of the U.S. Leverage on the Korean Government for Democratization: Imports and Exports

Year	Total Import (g) (11)	Import from USA (h) (12)	Its % to ROK's Total Import (h/g) (13)	Its % to ROK's GNP (i) (14)	Total Export (j) (15)	Export to USA (k) (16)	Its % to ROK's Total Export (k/j) (17)	Its % to ROK's GNP (k) (18)
1953	345	93.5	27.1	5.8	40	29.9	74.8	1.9
1954	243	86.6	35.6	4.9	24	19.7	82.1	1.1
1955	341	127.0	37.2	7.1	18	6.1	33.9	.3
1956	386	257.4	40.7	8.5	25	9.7	38.8	.5
1957	442	127.6	28.8	6.6	19	3.9	20.5	.2
1958	378	236.9	62.6	11.5	17	2.9	17.1	.1
1959	304	142.0	46.7	6.6	20	2.2	11.0	.1
1960`	344	118.3	34.4	5.4	33	3.7	11.2	.2
1961	316	143.3	45.3	6.2	41	6.9	16.9	.3
1962	422	220.3	52.2	9.2	55	12.0	21.9	.5
1963	560	284.1	50.7	10.9	87	24.3	28.0	.9
1964	404	202.1	49.9	7.2	119	36.6	30.7	1.3
1965	463	182.3	39.3	5.9	175	61.7	35.2	2.0
1966	716	253.7	35.4	7.8	250	95.8	38.3	2.9
1967	996	305.2	30.6	8.4	320	137.4	42.9	3.7
1968	1,463	449.0	30.7	11.2	455	237.0	52.0	5.9
1969	1,824	530.2	29.1	11.5	623	315.7	50.7	6.9
1970	1,984	584.8	29.5	7.9	835	395.2	47.3	5.4
1971	2,394	678.3	28.3	8.4	1,067	531.8	49.8	6.6
1972	2,522	647.2	25.7	5.2	1,624	759.0	46.7	6.2
1973	4,240	1,201.9	28.3	8.1	3,225	1,021.2	31.7	6.8
1974	6,852	1,700.8	24.8	10.5	4,460	1,492.1	33.5	9.2
1975	7,274	1,881.1	25.9	10.2	5,081	1,536.3	30.2	8.3
1976	8,774	1,962.9	22.4	7.3	7,715	2,492.5	32.3	9.2
1977	10,815	2,447.4	22.6	7.1	10,046	3,118.6	31.0	8.9
1978	14,976	3,043.0	20.3	6.4	12,711	4,058.3	31.9	8.6
1979	20,313	4,602.6	22.6	7.6	15,756	4,373.9	27.8	7.3
1980	22,292	4,890.0	21.9	8.5	17,505	4,606.6	26.3	8.0
1981	26,131	5,694.7	21.8	9.3	21,254	5,667.7	26.7	9.3
1982	24,251	6,025.7	24.8	9.2	21,583	6,064.6	27.7	9.2
1983	26,192	6,168.8	23.5	8.4	24,445	7,854.8	37.1	10.7
1984	30,631	6,446.4	21.0	8.1	29,245	9,973.6	34.1	12.5
1985	31,500	6,489	20.6	7.8	34,700	10,754.0	30.9	12.9
1986	29,700	6,545	22.0	7.2	33,900	13,880.0	40.9	15.3
1987	41,000	8,578	21.4	7.4	47,300	18,311.0	38.7	15.4
1988	52,500	12,539	23.8	8.1	57,500	20,562.0	35.7	13.3

Source: For (g), (h), (i), & (j), the Bank of Korea, *Economic Statistical Yearbook*, various years; *World Almanac and Book Facts*, various years; *The Korea Herald*, various years.

*Unable to include in this table the data for 1948-1952 due to lack data.

would encircle China, directly threaten Japan's security through Korea, and potentially endanger Japan's main maritime lifeline from the Philippines.[7]

One may suggest a third reason for the change of the status of South Korea from being "important" to becoming "vital" to U.S. security interests of the 1980s on the basis of a hypothesis that: whether the security of a foreign country is vital to U.S. security interest depends on how economically strong the foreign country becomes and how interdependent and reciprocally beneficial the two nations are in terms of trade, investment, and joint venture. South Korea became one of the fastest growing nations throughout the late 1970s and 1980s. Its economic growth is demonstrated by the rapid increase of per capita GNP, for example, from less than $100 in 1962 to $5,000, 70 percent of urbanization, and over 90 percent of literacy in 1990.

As shown in Table 5-3 a total of South Korea's import from the U.S. accounted for $93.5 million in 1953, but increased to $8.7 billion in 1987 and $12.5 billion in 1987. South Korea's export to the U.S. amounted to $29.9 million in 1953, reached $18.3 billion in 1987, and $20.5 billion in 1988. South Korea, indeed, was enhanced enough to be the seventh-ranked nation in terms of a two-way trade volume with the U.S.

Due to a more rapid rate of economic growth, Seoul is very optimistic about the potential that South Korea may be able to achieve a parity with North Korea in overall military strength by the mid-1990s and will exceed North Korea thereafter. But for the time being, both the United States and South Korea estimate that the military balance of power is skewed heavily in favor of North Korea. The geographical proximity of Seoul to the DMZ, vulnerability of industrial and economic centers of Seoul with over one-fourth of the entire population, vulnerability of a dozen nuclear-power plants to North Korea's air strikes, and the small size of the territory of the peninsula with rugged terrain are such that South Korea could be severely effected by a North Korean blitzkrieg.[8]

The American public in general and elites in particular began to perceive South Korea as "vital" to U.S. national interest. Based upon a random sample of 1,585 from average Americans across the nation and 343 from the elites represented by high-ranking bureaucrats, congressmen and senators, leaders in business, the press, labor unions, academic and religious areas during the period from October 20 to November 12 of 1986, the Chicago Council on

Foreign Relations released its survey results. As shown in Table 5-1, the positive American public view on South Korea as "vital to U.S. security interest" increased from 43 percent in 1982 to 58 percent in 1986, whereas the American elites' view increased from 66 percent in 1982 to 80 percent in 1986. To state it differently, South Korea was seen as the thirteenth-ranked nation by the Americans in general and as the tenth-ranking by the American elites (*Dong-A Ilbo*, May 5, 1987). This suggests that American people and elites considered South Korea together with the Philippines as a linchpin nation for the protection of Japan from the Soviet Union in East Asia, next in importance to the protection of West Germany and England in Europe and Saudi Arabia and Israel in the Middle East.

The security of South Korea was becoming so "vital" for the United States that President Carter's initial decision to withdraw 33,000 ground troops by 1982 was cancelled. The American forces authorized in South Korea rather increased from 38,000 in 1976 to 41,718 as of September 30, 1985--29,750 of the U.S. Army including 13,900 of one infantry division (the U.S. Second Division) and 11,200 of the U.S. Air Force including one division consisting of two wings, five squadrons (two with 36 F-4E, two with 48 F-16, and one with 18 A-10), one tactical control group with 18 OA-37 and one search and rescue squadron with six HH-3 (U.S. Air Force Assoc., 1986: 65). Such formidable U.S. Army and Air Force contingents were further reinforced by the U.S. Seventh Fleet.

The security of South Korea, vital to U.S. security interests, was attested by additional evidence. On May 8, 1987, the House of Representatives voted 311-64 against a proposal that would have directed the White House to develop a plan for withdrawing U.S. troops from South Korea (*Korea Herald*, May 10, 1987). Former U.S. Defense Secretary Casper Weinberger stated in May 1987 that the United States was prepared to send "additional assets," if necessary, to South Korea, where over 40,000 U.S. troops and modern weapons were already stationed.

> We have very close cooperation--in the course of the next year so that if at any time it becomes desirable for us to add some additional assets or additional assistance we would both be ready to do that and they could get in position in time to be effective (*Korea Herald*, May 9, 1987).

In order to enhance the security and stability in the Korean peninsula, in-depth cooperation and communications were held between the United States and South Korea at the annual U.S.-South Korea foreign ministers' meeting, the annual security consultative meeting, and the annual joint military exercise called "Team Spirit."[9] From these meetings might be listed many positive outcomes: the replacement of "Honest John" and "Sergeant" missiles in South Korea with Lance missiles capable of carrying nuclear warheads (*Korea Herald*, Nov. 15, 1986); South Korean acquisition of an unspecified number of sophisticated F-16 fighters; the reaffirmation that the "security of the Republic of Korea is pivotal to the peace and stability of the United States" (*Korea Herald*, June 28, 1986); and the subsequent reiteration of the "firm commitment of the United States to render prompt and effective assistance to repel any armed attack against the Republic of Korea in accordance with the U.S.-ROK Mutual Defense Treaty of 1954" (*Korea Herald*, April 5, 1986 & May 10, 1987).

Korea of the 1980s: Equal Partnership with U.S.A.

Some congressmen and senators assert that the United States must forcefully require the South Korean government to pursue democratization. One may wonder, then, to what extent the United States had exercised leverage on the Korean government toward democratization during the 1980s. This question may be examined, first of all, by the overall economic growth of South Korea and its expected future growth.

During the period of the Fifth Five-Year Economic Development Plan (1982-86), Korea achieved an annual average of 7.9 percent economic growth that was 0.4 percentage points higher than the projected growth rate. Its three most significant outcomes were stabilization of prices, control of the chronic double-digit inflationary trend, and improvement of the nation's balance of payment status. The year of 1985 brought about a surplus of $3.2 billion. The surplus reached $4.2 billion in 1986 and $6.3 billion in 1987. Based upon the successful accomplishment of the Fifth Five-Year Plan, the government developed the Sixth Five-Year Plan (1987-1991), projecting annual economic growth rate at 7.2 percent and the inflation rate at 2.3 percent. The plan also helped Korea to join the ranks of top ten world traders and increase its per capita GNP to $5,500 in 1991. However, the Sixth Five-Year Plan that was announced in September 1986 needed readjustment because the Economic Planning Board originally expected to have a $4.0 billion surplus in the current account in 1991, but by the end of 1986 the surplus target had already been secured (*Korea Herald*, Sept. 24, 1986).

The increasing economic power of Korea relative to the United States may as well suggest a thesis that Korea experiences its status to change from nearly "complete dependency" upon the United States (a patron-client relationship) in the 1950s to "equal partnership" in the 1980s (see Figure 5-1).

As shown in Table 5-3, Korea had suffered from a trade deficit with the United States consistently from 1953 to 1982 (except three years of 1976, 1977, and 1978). But since 1983, Korea has managed to have a surplus with the United States, for example, from $1.7 billion in 1983 to $3.5 billion in 1984, $4.3 billion in 1985, $7.4 billion in 1986, and $9 billion in 1987 (*Korea Herald*, July 19, 1987). The ratio of Korea's export to the United States to Korea's total export still shows high percentage points: 37.1 percent on 1983, 34.1 percent in 1984, 38.7 percent in 1987, and 35.7 percent in 1988, but the overall trend shows a gradual decline from 74.9 percent in 1953 to 35.7 percent in 1988. This indicates the corresponding decrease in dependency of Korea upon the United States in trade. The diversification of trade from the U.S.A. to many other countries such as those in the European Community, South Asia, Southeast Asia, and the Middle East as well as Japan becomes the major foreign policy goal. It is because of this priority that President Chun embarked upon a series of foreign trips while substantive coordination and negotiations were followed by his staff. Since the late 1980s the People's Republic of China, the Soviet Union, and the Eastern European states have become Korea's trade-target countries.

The increasing economic power of Korea relative to the United States could be seen, when the U.S. military assistance to South Korea that had prevailed up until 1975 was nearly completely replaced by South Korea's purchase of military weapons and equipment from the USA in the 1980s. Military grants, economic aid, and credits have long been considered as the major means of U.S. leverage on South Korea for the promotion of democratization and human rights during the period of the 1960s and 1970s, but they are lessening in their weight. If they were still employed, the United States would use them more for economic leverage against its own ever-increasing trade deficits than for political leverage. Let us briefly examine to what extent the United States has used economic leverage on Korea for its own economic benefits.

One of the major means of U.S. leverage in Korea is the generalized system of preferences (GSP). The GSP is a system of low or zero tariffs which developed countries have conceded to the developing nations since 1970. The United States adopted the GSP for the first time in 1976, five years later than the EEC and Japan. The U.S. Government decided in 1984 to extend the effective period of the GSP to June 1993. The U.S. Trade and Tariff Act of 1984 provided three major criteria for its implementation: (1) If imports of any single item should exceed $25 million in value or 25 percent of all U.S. imports on that item, it would be removed from the GSP list; (2) If a country's per capita GNP exceeds $8,500, the country should be automatically phased out of GSP eligibility; and (3) The U.S. President was authorized to unilaterally reduce GSP favors or exert pressure to a specific country should the latter be found to engage in a) unfair trade practices such as restrictions of reasonable access to its market for U.S. goods and services, b) inadequate or no protection of U.S. intellectual property rights, c) trade-disturbing investment practices, and d) the violation of internationally recognized rights for its workers (U.S. DOC, 19 : 2948).

Senator Kennedy (D: MA) and some liberal Democrats proposed the use of the GSP as a leverage upon South Korea for democratization. But one has to keep in mind that the GSP favors accounted for only fifteen percent of total Korean shipments to the U.S. worth $10 billion in 1984. Should the U.S. government totally abolish GSP favors to Korean goods, an average five percent in additional tariffs would be levied on Korean-made products (*Korea Herald*, Nov. 19, 1985). This indicates that the impact of the GSP upon South Korea along with its continued economic growth may not be devastating and much less significant in the future.

Liberal Democrats suggested the exercise of a veto power on the part of the United States in multinational credit institutions' decisions to make loans available to Korea. This also becomes less important with the continued economic strength of South Korea and its increased annual current account surplus. In fact, Korea surprised Western and Japanese banks by turning down a $500 million loan. The state-owned Korea Development Bank in the past borrowed heavily to finance industrial development at home and had sought a loan again. But it was overruled by the Ministry of Finance (*Korea

Herald, June 19, 1986). The Korean government rather planned to speed up the payment of foreign debts ahead of the schedule.

Contrary to liberal Democrats, the U.S. government and business firms would rather enhance the opportunities to export more of American goods and to commit further investment and loans to Korea. In response to their demands, Korea began to adopt a liberalization policy with 302 initial items to be imported effective July 1986, 160 more commodities starting from July 1987, and an additional 141 in 1988. With the proposed measures, Korea's import liberalization rose to 91.6 percent in 1986, 93.6 percent in 1987, and further increased to 95.4 percent in 1988. Liberalization promotes not only the import of foreign goods but also direct American investment in South Korea. As the Ministry of Finance officials explained, the measures would be drastic because they would deal a significant blow to a number of local industries, including soft drinks, hotel operations, laundry services, joint investment in construction, mining, and automobile industries, although not more than fifty percent of total shares of a company would be allowed to foreign investors.

The near-complete liberalization of the banking business, for example, results in high profits for foreign banks. The combined net profits of foreign banks increased from 39.8 billion won in 1980 for 33 branches, to 49.8 billion won in 1983 for 46 branches, 59.8 billion won ($69.25 million) in 1984, and further to 80.6 billion won ($90.6 million) for 53 branches in 1985. Among the foreign banks operating in Korea, U.S. banks are the best in business performance. Among many elements to be listed, the three major factors for the advantage of foreign banks over Korean domestic ones are: the adoption of "overnight" forward exchange rates higher than the spot exchange rate of the next day, to which the Korean banks are restricted by the Korean banking laws; the charge of lower rates than the domestic banks in dealing with corporate debenture guarantees to attract more clients; and the advantage of the worldwide networks over local banks in cash management, trade financing and foreign exchange business (*Korea Herald,* June 7, 1986).

U.S. firms as a whole repatriated $389.9 million in returns on investment in South Korea between 1962 and the end of May 1987. The remittance accounted for 33.6 percent of their equity investments of $1,160.1 million in 452 projects. This amounted to 29 percent of the total foreign equity invested in South Korea as opposed to Japan's 51.2 percent with $2,050.8 million (*Korea*

Herald, August 4, 1987). It goes without saying that refusal of the U.S. government guarantee of investments by the American business firms and banks in Korea would hurt the American economy in competition with other countries.

The economic partnership between the United States and South Korea was further expanded by the agreements on trade negotiations in July 1986 into several new areas: 1) the imports of 40 million packs of foreign cigarettes per year into South Korea starting from September 1, 1986; 2) the permission of two American insurance companies--American Home Insurance Co. and Cigna Insurance Co.--to join the "pool"of the Korea's fire insurance companies immediately and the permission of one U.S. firm to join Korea's life insurance market by the end of 1986; 3) the protection of foreign product patents effective July 1, 1987 for fifteen years after public notification. Product patents, on the one hand, require Korean enterprises to pay a considerable amount of royalties to foreign firms for patent rights, and, on the other hand, encourage technological transfers abroad and subsequently increase American investments in Korean chemical and pharmaceutical industries; 4) the protection of copyrights on Korea from July 1987 for up to fifty years on foreign copies published since 1977; and 5) the protection of the foreign-developed software technology (*Korea Herald*, July 22, 1986).

The new round of trade agreements also became greatly beneficial to the United States, but in the short-run perspective the trade deficit on the part of the United States has been increasing. Thereby, the Korean government attempted to alleviate the ever-increasing gap, allowing the purchase of more American products and American business expansion in Korea. For example, in June 1986 the Ministry of Energy announced the postponement of the construction of nuclear power plants Numbers 11 and 12 on the grounds that the existing facilities were able to produce a surplus of energy and the Korean government did not want to incur more than a $1 billion of foreign debt. But less than four months after the announcement, the government reversed its previous decision and entered into a contract with the American firms, Combustion Engineering and General Engineering. The selection of the American firms against other countries' bidding was "justified" by the consent of the American firms for the technology transfer (*Dong-A Ilbo*, October 1, 1986).

In short, the proposal of Senator Kennedy and liberal Democrats for the United States to exercise a veto power on loans to Korea and to refuse to provide American firms with the U.S. government guarantee of their investment in Korea are not acceptable to the Reagan Administration, American business firms, and other legislators both because of the lack of economic soundness and the potential for exacerbating rather than reducing the trade gap.

U.S. Policy of Cooptation (1980s-)

South Korea in the 1980s was changed in its status from "important" to "vital" national interest and from "full dependency" to the "equal partnership" such that the United States began to pursue a policy of cooptation with the authoritarian government of South Korea.

The political rationale behind the adoption of the policy of cooptation is "realism" that calls for evaluation of international relations in terms of a realistic perspective. First of all, authoritarianism is evil, but the totalitarian evil is worse than the authoritarian one. The lessons of modern history are loud and clear on the fact that the authoritarian form of government still may have the potential for becoming democratic like the most recent cases of Spain, Portugal, Greece, Turkey, Brazil, Argentina, Uruguay, Peru, Ecuador, and the Philippines, since 1974 (Huntington, 1988: 7). But once a society is dominated by a Marxist-Leninist party, Western-style democracy is paralized. Alexander Solzhenistsyn stated it well:

> Communism is something new, unprecedented in world history. . . . Communism is unregenerate. . . .
>
> It stops only when it encounters a wall, even if it is only a wall of resolve. . . . It will always present a danger to mankind. . . .
>
> Society is closed; dissidence is not tolerated; the state is all encompassing. Marxists ruthlessly maintain themselves in power (Quoted from Gorman, 1984: 547).

Authoritarian regimes also allow a significantly greater degree of freedom and diversity than totalitarian ones in political, economic, social, cultural, and religious activities. Therefore, protection of friendly authoritarian governments from threats of totalitarian aggression must be the priority of the U.S. foreign policy.

Secondly, democracy lies in the hearts of men and women, namely those who are socialized by the democratic political culture rather than by legal documents of human rights and freedoms. The American open or quiet diplomacy alone, without concurrent socialization of the democratic political culture in the hearts and minds of citizens in foreign countries, is less likely to produce a viable democracy. There is no quick road to democracy. Therefore, external forces, no matter how nobly motivated, cannot and shall not impose justice, human rights, or freedoms on other states.

Thirdly, the American moral mission itself cannot be consistent and coherent. President Carter and his secretaries, for example, had ceaselessly scolded authoritarian governments of countries that were friendly and ignored authoritarian governments of countries that were not. This inconsistency was declared as an act of hypocrisy by Senator Barry Goldwater (R: AZ):

> The American Administration is quick to yell "foul" when appraising human rights in places such as South Africa, Rhodesia and Latin America, but we hear little of anything about the gross repression and violation of human rights in countries like Communist China, Cuba, Uganda, Cambodia, and Vietnam. I, for one, am sick of this hypocrisy (1978: 455).

Moreover, even among friendly authoritarian countries, those vital to the U.S. national interests, like South Korea, were immune from direct and open criticism, whereas those less vital were more seriously blamed and urged for improvement in human rights.

Fourthly, the promotion of democracy and human rights in South Korea is unrealistic because of the limited power of the United States for absolute morality. Therefore, President Reagan called attention to historian Charles Beard, who warned nearly forty years ago that:

> The defect of a foreign policy based on what he called 'the selfless sacrifice required by an absolute morality' was the ability to understand the limited nature of American power to relieve, restore, and maintain life beyond its own sphere

of interest and control--recognition of the hard fact that the United States. . . . did not possess the power. . . . to assure the establishment of democratic and pacific government (Reagan, 1978: 422).

The United States in the 1980s did not rule out quiet diplomacy completely. Once in a while, when human rights violations in Korea seemed to become extreme, the Reagan Administration quietly influenced the Chun Administration. In fact, Senator Kennedy and thirteen members of Congress acknowledged that the Reagan Administration had exerted quiet diplomatic pressure so as to bring about: reduction of sentences of Kim Dae Jung from death in May 1980 to life imprisonment in January 1981 to twenty years in March 1983; amnesty granted to 197 of 419 political prisoners; and restoration of civil rights to 125 involved in the Kwangju uprising (*NYT*, March 3, 1982).

But cooptation with the Korean government on the basis of realism became the dominant foreign policy of the United States in the 1980s. The U.S. policy of cooptation can be witnessed by: (1) lack of open protest against General Chun for his deployment of Korean troops in his revolt against senior generals without prior consultation with General John Wickham; (2) lack of explicit and public demand for the restoration of civilian government after the December 16, 1980 revolt; (3) General Wickham's reticence about the Korean troop deployment to smash Kwangju protesters for democracy; (4) refusal of U.S. officials--the President, the Secretary of State, and the American Ambassador to Korea--to meet with Korean opposition leaders and the subsequent lack of endorsement for democracy; (5) the welcome of President Chun to the White House four times over a relatively short period of time and invitation of the government party presidential candidate, Roh Tae Woo, to the White House in September 1987 prior to the December 1987 presidential election in Korea, while opposition leaders were not invited. In fact, the U.S. policy of cooptation with the authoritarian Korean government became a cause for anti-Americanism from those who perceived that the United states had violated its long cherished, noble mission for democracy abroad (*NYT*, December 16, 1979).

Unlike the coup of May 16, 1960, the United States officials refused to comment on the arrest of martial law commander Chung Sung Hwa, and several other senior generals on December 16, 1979.

General Chun "ignored the Combined Forces Command, main operational military command here under General John A. Wickham of the United States Army," and "moved the Ninth Division and other units to take military control." The Carter Administration expressed, at best, "deep concern" over crisis in the South Korean military. At that time *The New York Times* indicated that the United States "privately" protested the breach of military guidelines on deployment of forces. However, the form of U.S. protest to the South Korean government over General Chun's actions was "unknown" (*NYT*, December 16, 1979). Upon complaints and protests against the lukewarm attitude, the United States responded, "There is nothing Americans can do about the breach of the Combined Forces Command's rules." Rather U.S. officials were concerned over "possible reaction from North Korea to an apparent rift in South Korea's martial law command" (*NYT*, December 16, 1979). That kind of response, in the view of democracy-aspiring Koreans, signaled a green light for military leaders to rise up at any time in the future, but the United States would remain silent and pay attention only to the security matter.

The U.S. Government explained that the Korean Special Forces, which were deployed to Kwangju in May 1980, had never been under General Wickham's command. Only after he learned that the forces had become outrageous, did he and Ambassador Gleysteen arrive at concurrence to permit the transfer of well-trained troops of the 20th R.O.K. Division to restore law and order in Kwangju. Therefore, the United States was not responsible for the Kwnagju incident (*NYT*, July 6, 1982).

This may be an accurate statement, but it must be subject to some critical questions: Why was it not explained on time in 1980? Why did the explanation appear in *The New York Times* belatedly two years later, in 1982, not on a voluntary basis but as a response to Bruce M. Cumings' criticism of the U.S. involvement in the Kwangju incident? How many Korean people residing in Korea had access to *The New York Times* and were able to read it? More than eight years after the incident, the National Assembly of Korea organized an investigation committee and agreed to ask then-Ambassador Gleysteen and General Wickham to appear before the investigation committee hearing. Unfortunately, the U.S. government refused to receive such a request on July 28, 1988 on the grounds that both of them were no longer active U.S. government officials, and requests of American civilians to appear before the Korean

Legislative Committee should be arranged through the formal channels of the two governments.[10]

The American policy of cooptation is further evidenced by the negative attitudes of U.S. officials toward opposition leaders and students. General Wickham, for example, was reported to have stated that the Korean people were "like lemmings that follow anyone who becomes their leader and are not ready for democracy." It was contended that his remarks rather aided General Chun's takeover of governmental power (*L.A. Times*, August 8, 1980). Richard L. Walker, former American Ambassador to Korea, called college students on demonstrations "spoiled brats." Upon the inundation of protests by many angered Koreans who demanded a public apology for his humiliating remarks, he grudgingly acknowledged that: "I frankly admit that the term 'spoiled brats' was a major mistake" (Suh, 1982: 97). His negative attitude was evidenced by repeated refusal to meet with Kim Dae Jung, Kim Young Sam, Moon Ik Hwan, and Cardinal Kim Soo Hwan. Angered by the humiliating remarks, forty-two leaders of the Korean Christian Action Organization issued a statement asking President Reagan to recall both General John A. Wickham and Ambassador Richard L. Walker (*NYT*, April 15, 1982).

Democracy-aspiring Koreans were further disappointed by the betrayal of the American moral mission by President Reagan and his cabinet members. Secretary of State George P. Shultz, for example, upon a visit to Seoul on his way from the Tokyo summit meeting, held a breakfast meeting, but he did not invite to his breakfast gathering two most prominent critics of the South Korean government, Kim Dae Jung and Kim Young Sam, on the grounds that they were "not leaders of their party" (*NYT*, May 8, 1986). On his state visit to Korea, President Reagan acted as a host at a reception for religious and cultural leaders. Among them, several were the opponents of President Chun, but none of the South Korean President's more forceful critics were invited. A U.S. official stated, "The point here is to speak to a representative group but not upsetting or provocative to our hosts (*NYT*, November 12, 1983).

The United States often declared "political neutrality" between the Korean government and opposition side. Assistant Secretary of State Gaston Sigur urged that it would be "Korean efforts that nurture and achieve the open and more consensual political system that all Koreans desire." The United States should not favor one side nor interfere in political debates in Korea (*NYT*, April 3 & 18,

1986). Nevertheless, the American favor for the Korean authoritarian government and disfavor for the opposition side was loud and clear.

Disfavor to the opposition party may be best explained by the frustration and disappointment Mr. Lee Min Woo experienced during his visit to the United States. Amidst intense confrontation between the government and opposition leaders on the issue of constitutional amendments for a direct popular election of the president and other democratic reforms, President Lee Min Woo of the opposition New Korea Democratic Party (NKDP) decided on a four-day visit to the United States in May 1986. His main objective was to secure support from the United States for the constitutional amendments for a direct popular election of the president in Korea.

His objective was based upon the assumption that American officials of today would still have a strong moral mission for democracy abroad. There might be only a few staff members of President Reagan who were favorable toward the Chun regime, but a majority of the U.S. policy makers in the bureaucracy and Congress would endorse the desire of the Korean people for a direct popular election of their president. He also assumed that even those few pro-Chun officials would change their attitude if they were accurately informed of a ten million signature campaign being undertaken in Korea and the readiness of the Korean people for democracy based on economic growth and high levels of literacy, education, and urbanization. However, he was not welcomed nor endorsed by American friends, either.

In response to a ten million signature campaign, the South Korean government confined over 300 opposition party members including eighty NKDP members. The government mobilized fifty buses of reinforcements, several armored cars equipped with tear gas dispensers, hundreds of plainclothesmen, and several thousand riot policemen to stop collection of the signatures. The American support of the Chun regime and its absence of support for democratic change were justified by Secretary of State Shultz: "What we would like to see is the continuation of that movement in a stable, orderly way. The way to have change take place is a nonviolent way and violence is not tolerated as a part of the democratic way of changing things" (*NYT*, April 21, 1986).

Robert E. White, former American Ambassador to El Salvador and President of the International Center for Development Policy deplored the Reagan Administration's policy of cooptation. At the crucial time for Korea under the campaign for constitutional amendment, he saw the Reagan policy come across "as timid and confused." The fundamental error of the Reagan Administration in Korea was "to identify U.S. power and prestige with the survival of a military regime dedicated to hanging onto power regardless of the people's will" (*NYT*, March 5, 1985).

Mr. A. M. Rosenthal, a former executive editor of *The New York Times* lamented:

> Those of us who have been graced by being born into freedom, or have settled within its arms, have the obligation to support as best we can those who struggle for what we possess and cherish. The enemy is dictatorship, left or right. I believe that, where we have the power to change it, we should. Where we do not have the power, we should draw a moral and judgemental political line between us and tyrants, making this plain to oppressor and oppressed (1986: 23).

Unfortunately, he has observed American foreign policy to "stand behind one tyrant or another." He deplored the fact that "Americans who live and flourish under liberty--writers, intellectuals, politicians, journalists, and scientists--decide that freedom is really not all that important--for others." He admitted, "I find myself still puzzled and pained about why my own country so often does not act as it talks" and "why many of my countrymen who demand freedom for themselves don't give much of a damn about it for long to other countries" (1986: 25).

The American policy of cooptation ensured the security interest and secured more economic gains by opening the door of Korea more widely for more American goods and services--banking and credit services, insurance, beef, tobacco, American-made large-size cars, a contract for nuclear power plant numbers 11 and 12--in return for the continued support of the authoritarian government. What the Reagan Administration might not perceive accurately was the potential for greater cooperation between the United States and South Korea, if and when the latter would establish a democratic government. Only under democracy could more Koreans become more creative, energetic, and active in pursuit of enterprise, trade, and security.

Because of the Reagan Administration's deviation from the traditional American moral mission for promoting and protecting

Table 5-4 Violations of Democratic Principles and Subsequent Demonstrations

Year	Arrest (19)	Dismissal (20)	Attack (21)	Jail (22)	Closing (23)	Censorship (24)	Political Ban (25)	Overall Factor Scores ***(26)	Civil Demonstrations (27)
1953	10	1	0	0	0	0	0	.445	0
1954	48	0	2	0	0	0	0	-.492	0
1955	11	0	0	0	1	0	0	-.480	9,300
1956	907	0	1	1	0	0	0	-.634	20,000
1957	0	0	1	1	0	0	0	-.636	0
1958	7	0	0	2	0	2	1	-.778	0
1959	26	0	0	1	1	1	3	-.579	0
1960	232	5,000	0	192	0	1	1,500	-.367	120,150
1961	2,391	0	0	0	0	1	633	.439	120,150
1962	117	0	0	0	0	0	104	-0405	0
1963	0	0	0	0	0	0	0	-.568	930
1964	115	0	15	0	0	2	0	-.374	23,800
1965	4,044	1	0	3	0	50	0	.144	35,866
1966	1	0	1	0	0	0	0	-.532	500
1967	20	0	3,001	0	0	11	0	-0226	39,450
1968	1,743	0	0	0	0	0	0	-.567	0
1969	176	0	0	0	0	0	0	-.570	70,896
1970	5	1	1	2	0	2	0	.275	40
1971	1,891	0	3	0	0	10	0	-.448	21,800
1972	3	0	0	0	1	82	0	-.472	0
1973	417	0	15	0	0	11	5	-.364	60,711
1974	2,934	1	22	5	2	4	1	.715	8,830
1975	127	2	28	17	3	20	8	1.335	3,900
1976	65	400	5	0	0	0	2	-.530	300
1977	117	0	20	0	0	0	0	-.568	4,100
1978	120	0	70	0	0	0	0	-.563	600
1979	955	0	2	0	1	0	1	-.489	8,500
1980	3,072	8,678	8	**304	67	106	82	4.547	153,600
1981	120	0	30	0	0	10	912	.881	830
1982	5,392	2	21	-38	0	0	0	.639	2,620
1983	*-291	1,364	0	23	0	10	-564	1.749	2,650
1984	1,200	-1,300	22	291	0	3	-285	-.520	9,750

Source: *The New York Times Index* from 1953 to 1984
*The minus sign indicates the number of persons who were released from arrest or jail or the number of persons who were lifted from political ban.
**Including 191 persons reported as dead by former Defense Minister Yun in relation to the Kwangju incident. See *The Korea Herald*, June 9, 1985.
***The overall factor scores indicate the level of violations of those democratic principles as a continuum from the highest negative score such as -.778 of 1958 to the highest positive score like 4.547 of 1980.

(19): Number of opposition politicians, clergymen, intellectuals, and students who were arrested for their struggle for human rights and democracy
(20): Expulsion or dismissal from political parties, universities or jobs
(21): Physical threat, torture, or police attack

democracy in Korea, anti-Americanism began to emerge in the 1980s. It was expressed not only by rhetoric but by violent behavior, attacking American facilities in Korea on more than a dozen of occasions.

A Quantitative Approach

Thus far we have examined a main thesis that in a foreign country whose security is "vital" to the U.S. national interest and whose dependency on the United States is limited and shifted to "equal partnership" with the United States, "cooptation" with the foreign government--authoritarian as well as democratic--tends to be the major American foreign policy (Figure 5-1). "Quiet" rather than "open" diplomacy is once in a while pursued to alleviate the excessive violations of democratic principles practiced by the foreign government. But security concern rather prevails over democratization. In a foreign country under these two conditions--vital security and equal partnership--democracy is less likely to be transplanted and superimposed by the United States or any democratic power but more likely to be accomplished by struggles and efforts of the native people--leaders, intellectuals, professionals, college students, and the masses--of themselves, by themselves, for themselves. We may now examine to support the qualitatively examined thesis in terms of a quantitative perspective.

In order to quantitatively examine the thesis, a total of sixteen variables in Tables 5-2 and 5-3 are chosen as the independent variables, which may be considered as major means of the U.S. leverage on South Korea for democratization. They are: the annual amount of the U.S. military assistance to South Korea, its ratio to Korea's GNP, the annual amount of the U.S. military sales to South Korea, its ratio to Korea's GNP, the sum of U.S. military assistance and sales, the U.S. nonmilitary government grants and credits, its ratio to Korea's GNP, the total U.S. military and nonmilitary grants

---

(22): Number of persons jailed
(23): Closing or suspension of organizations
(24): Number of censorship imposed on mass media and publishing companies
(25): Political ban on students, labor workers, media men, and others
(26): The overall factor scores of the annual violations of the democratic principles measured by the factor analysis of seven variables
(27): Number of persons who participated in civil demonstrations.

and credits to Korea, its ratio to Korea's GNP, Korea's import from the United States, its ratio to Korea's total imports, its ratio to Korea's GNP, Korea's export to the United States, its ratio to Korea's total exports, and its ratio to Korea's GNP.

In order to explore to what extent these sixteen variables of the American leverage may have impact on the Korean government to adhere to the democratic principles, nine Korean domestic dependent variables are chosen. They are: 1) the number of Korean people who were "arrested" for protests against the authoritarian regime, 2) "expulsion or dismissal," for example, of opposition politicians from their political parties, opposition legislators from the National Assembly, professors and students from universities, party members from their political parties, journalists from the media, and leaders and members from labor unions, 3) the number of Koreans under "physical threats, torture, and police attack," 4) number of people "put to jail" for their struggles against the authoritarian regime, 5) "closing or suspension" of such organizations as political parties, newspapers, periodicals, labor unions, universities, and other interest groups and associations, 6) "censorship" imposed on mass media, and 7) "prohibition" of interest articulation and aggregation by students, politicians, media men, and other agents against the regime (see Table 5-4).

Added to the data are the overall factor scores (OFS) of one factor that was computed from the factor analysis of the above seven variables by means of the varimax rotation to see the overall level of the violation of basic freedoms and human rights.[11] The high factor score of 1.335 in 1975 shows the time of political turmoil resulting from President Park's extraordinary method of adopting the Yushin Constitution for the perpetuation of his power against intense resistance by opposition leaders and citizens in 1975. A much higher score of 4.547 in 1980 might result from the political turmoil following the assassination of President Park and the Kwangju incident. Thus, the computed OFS seems to reasonably represent the overall level of annual violations of democratic rules in Korea. The last variable included in the analysis is the number of participants in civil demonstrations.

The data for these seven dependent variables were collected from the *New York Times Index* from 1953 to 1984. Main reasons for its selection were the lack of annual index volumes in any daily newspapers in Korea; over one-fourth of the entire span of the republic under martial law, emergency measures and/or extraordinary laws, and the subsequent censorship on the media were such that the choice of any Korean daily newspaper was avoided. *The New York Times* covered all major events in Korea, especially during the 1970s and the 1980s when South Korea was seen as increasingly more powerful and important.[12]

Sixteen (American) independent variables and nine (Korean) dependent variables were employed into stepwise linear regression analysis. The percent explanation of each of the independent variables for each of the dependent variables as well as the overall percent explanation of all sixteen independent variables for each of the dependent variables is presented in Table 5-5.

Table 5-5 suggests a few salient findings. First of all, economic and military means of American leverage on South Korea are more effective and influential on the areas of more explicit violations of the democratic rules such as jail (44.22%), arrest (29.72%), and closing or suspension of organizations (25.53%) than in the more subtle and yet more critical areas such as censorship (17.44%), and the prohibition of interest articulation and aggregation by various groups of people (17.69%), physical threat (12.26%), and expulsion or dismissal of people from their organizations (7.36%).

Second, except in the case of arrest, jail, and closing or suspension of organizations, the American influence on the violation of other democratic rules in Korea is explained by less than twenty percent.

Third, nonmilitary American government grants and credits (NMGGC) do not have any significant impact upon the Korean government in its degree of violation of the democratic rules except in the case of arrest (10.44%). This may be due to the continued decrease in the amount of the American economic aid in terms of its ratio to Korea's rapidly increasing GNP.

Fourth, both the U.S. military assistance and military sales are very limited in their leverage on the violation of these democratic rules. This reinforces the thesis of security imperatives as discussed in the previous section--that the security of South Korea of the 1980s became vital to the U.S. (national) interest. Therefore, the increase or decrease of the American military aid and military sales were not used as the leverage on the Korean government for its democratizations.

The findings in this quantitative research show consistency with what the United States government has been pursuing in South Korea. The change of the relationship from patron-client status to

Table 5-5 Percent Explanation (RSQ) of Major Elements of the American Leverage on South Korea against Violations of the Democratic Principles: 1953-1984

Year	Arrest	Dismissal	Attack	Jail	Closing	Censorship	Political Ban	Overall Factor Scores	Civil Demonstrations
	(19)	(20)	(21)	(22)	(23)	(24)	(25)	(26)	(27)
USA Security:									
MA(1)	--	--	--	--	1.49	0.12	1.56	--	--
MS(2)	--	0.29	0.10	1.94	2.82	1.41	3.16	--	--
Sum(3)	1.66	--	--	10.42	--	--	--	0.01	3.73
(1)/(3) (4)	--	1.42	0.97	--	1.76	1.18	--	--	--
(2)/(3) (5)	1.10	--	--	2.79	--	--	0.07	0.09	0.20
(2)/GNP(6)	5.06	--	0.27	2.35	1018	0.15	--	0.05	1.00
Economy:									
NMGGC(7)	10.44	0.35	0.22	0.86	--	0.66	0.41	0.05	--
(7)/GNP(8)	2.50	0.34	0.06	--	1.92	--	0.43	--	--
(1)+(7) (9)	3.13	0.62	--	--	8.65	--	--	--	1.80
(9)/GNP(10)	--	1.33	--	1.94	--	0.75	2.84	0.14	0.71
Import from USA(12)	2.00	1.68	8.99	4.64	4.10	7.35	2.63	0.02	3.31
(12)/Total Imports(13)	0.19	0.00	0.26	4.95	1.00	0.16	--	--	0.15
(13)/GNP(14)	0.68	0.07	0.08	0.54	1.08	0.36	0.72	0.03	0.20
Export to USA(16)	0.58	0.35	0.40	1.55	0.70	3.79	5.27	0.02	5.04
(16)/Total Exports(17)	0.76	0.45	0.76	0.36	0.16	1.49	0.49	0.02	5.04
(17)/GNP(18)	1.62	0.46	0.15	11.88	0.67	0.02	0.11	0.01	0.36
Sum of RSQ	29.72	7.36	12.26	44.22	25.53	17.44	17.69	0.44	19.42
Domestic:									
Arrest(19)		0.09	0.36	3.54	8.31	--	0.96	0.05	5.36
Dismissal(20)	4.77		5.50	5.75	0.68	0.77	26.91	3.91	30.34
Attack(21)	0.78	56.04		5.14	33.07	64.85	12.30	87.82	1.95
Jail(22)	6.33	1.01	0.51		9.92	3.29	0.71	2.02	1.94
Closing(23)	22.44	3.86	3.42	6.68		0.71	7.04	1.89	3.59
Censorship(24)	0.37	0.86	64.85	6.49	--		7.04	1.89	3.59
Pol. Ban(25)	1.31	24.81	8.52	1.79	1.68	0.80		2.90	10.05
Overall(26) Factor Scores	3.87	0.28	0.60	0.54	2.88	0.25	24.18		0.05
Sum of RSQ	39.87	86.95	83.76	29.93	58.16	70.67	74.66	98.82	54.06

Source: Tables 5-2, 5-3, and 5-4.
* Numbers parenthesized correspond to those in Tables 5-2, 5-3 and 5-4.
--Indicates no percent explanation resulting from a stepwise regression analysis.
Blank indicates the variable was employed as the dependent variable.

that of equal partnership was such that, contrary to Mr. Rosenthal and other liberal Democrats, the United States government showed restraint and exercised no open threat and no direct sanctions against South Korea for its violation of democratic rules and human rights. On June 27, 1987, the U.S. Senate unanimously adopted a resolution warning President Chun Doo Hwan that "failure to agree in timely, democratic changes essential to free elections was endangering the peaceful transfer of power he has promised for 1988." This was indeed a "mildly worded resolution" because it did not have the force of law and did not require the President's signature. The resolution, according to its sponsor, Senator Dennis DeConcici (D: AZ) "was intended to blunt efforts by Senator Edward M. Kennedy and other liberal Democrats to seek economic sanctions against South Korea." The resolution also deleted the original section on "the recognition that torture has no place in a democratic society" (*NYT*, Sept. 6, 1984).

The security imperatives coupled with equal partnership are such that the United States is likely to use the limited means of American leverage on South Korea for its democratization within the framework of silent diplomacy in the 1970s and that of cooptation in the 1980s.

Such moderate and limited exercises of American leverage are manifested as: persuasion to save the lives of key opposition leaders, the expression of concern about the house arrest of several opposition leaders, repeated U.S. endorsements of President Chun's peaceful transfer of power in 1988 as the initial step toward democracy, the firm and decisive refusal to endorse the major opposition political party leaders as witnessed in the case of Lee Min Woo during his visit to the United States, and the refusal of former Ambassador Walker and Secretary of State George P. Shultz to meet with opposition leaders.

Despite the fact that various security measures have been taken against the potential for a blitzkrieg by North Korea, the United States does not rule out the possibility that South Korea's domestic turmoil and disturbances may be escalated by anti-regime demonstrations and protests by opposition politicians, intellectuals, and students for the restoration of democracy. Such turmoil may invite a reckless offensive from North Korea. That kind of risk may be taken in collusion with subversive activities of North Korean spies and/or domestic leftist groups in the South.

Moreover, the major opposition party was seen as deeply embedded in factional strifes from its inception and as unprepared and inexperienced to take over the government. Those college students, who frequently resorted to protests and demonstrations were very radicaly left-wing-oriented and therefore represented a tiny portion of the student population. The American support for these anti-government forces for the sake of the immediate and extensive promotion of democracy in Korea might cause them to escalate political turmoil to overthrow the regime overnight. This might result in devastating impact on the stability of Korea and, in return, become detrimental to U.S. security interests. The grip of power by the opposition party might repeat the nightmare of the Second Republic of Korea under the helmsmanship of the Democratic Party, which was divided into two nearly equally powerful factions and experienced four major cabinet reshuffles over a period of eleven months. Its lack of institutionalization was unable to cope with the mounting demands for near unlimited freedoms in the press, labor unions, and education; unconditional unification based on nationalism; and *ex post facto* laws for political retaliation against the leaders of the former regime.

Table 5-5 suggests that violation of each democratic rule in South Korea is attributable to the Korean government's violations of other democratic rules as a chain reaction. For example, 86.95 percent for the expulsion or dismissal of people from their organizations are explained by protests against physical threats (56.04%), closing or suspension of organizations (3.86%), and the prohibition of interest articulation and aggregation (24.81%) by the government. Eighty-three percent of physical threat, torture, and police attack are attributed to protests against expulsion or dismissal (5.5%), closing or suspension of organizations (3.42%), censorship (64.85%), and political prohibition of interest articulation and aggregation (8.52%).

Nevertheless, hundreds of thousands of Koreans--opposition politicians, intellectuals, college students--were not subjugated by the government's suppression and continued to wage a nationwide campaign for democratization in Korea. Its climax was reached for the last ten days of June 1987, when the middle-class, thus far considered the core of the pro-government coalition, began to forsake the Chun Administration and join the "people's power" for democracy (*Korea Herald*, June 24, 1987).

The scope and extent of enthusiasm of Korean people for democracy and the subsequent escalation into a head-on collision with the government became so serious that the very survival of the regime might be endangered in the eyes of the leaders of the Korean government. The government leaders could not but believe that their initiative for democracy was inevitable for their own survival. In short, democratic movements and the establishment of the Sixth Republic on the basis of democratic spirit were the product "of the Korean people, by the Korean people, for the Korean people."

Interviewed by *Time's* Tokyo bureau chief Barry Hillenbrand concerning the American influence in Roh Tae Woo's July 29 announcement of democratic reforms, Mr. Roh responded:

> Because the U.S. is our closest ally and because American officials do not want only instability in Korea, they have emphasized the importance of sticking to democratic principles but U.S. officials remained within the proper limits. They understand that the decision has to be made by the Korean people, and interfering with our own problems is not their business (*Time*, July 13, 1987).

U.S. envoy Gaston Sigur flatly admitted, "There is an assumption that we can dictate in such cases. But credit the Koreans. The U.S. could not force what's happening" (*US News & World Report*, July 13, 1987).

Conclusion

A U.S. foreign policy model for democratization was developed on the basis of security interests and dependency dimensions (see Figure 5-1). The model suggests the American role for democracy. In cell "A," where the vital security interests and the full patron-client relationship merge like the cases of Japan and West Germany right after World War II, the United States became fully committed to promoting democracy with the American Occupation forces in charge of security and with the vast amounts of economic and military aid, on which the recipient countries were fully dependent for economic recovery as well as their immediate survival. In cell "C," where the vital security interests of the United States merge with full partnership, like the case of South Korea of the 1980s, the American leverage on the country for democratization is limited and becomes moderate. The U.S. security interest may as well not be forsaken, either. Liberal journalists, politicians, and intellectuals, in both the United States and South Korea as well as other countries, may be emotionally upset with American foreign policy if they fail to understand this model.

The failure to understand this model and the subsequent unrealistic commitment of the United States to the protection and promotion of democracy at the expense of U.S. security interests and dependency dimensions may be reanalyzed and corrected only after the exhaustion of the national power and resources, like the case of Vietnam. Premature termination or giving up of the American noble mission without consideration of this model may equally not be recommended because of its importance of democracy, to which the United States has been adhering as the best type of government ever invented for people in foreign countries, as well.

Since there are not many countries whose security is "vital" to the U.S. national interest and whose status is "fully dependent" on the United States, democracy is not and cannot be transplanted and coercively promoted by the United States. Democracy can be expected when the native people in developing countries--leaders, intellectuals, professionals, and the masses--commit themselves to adopting and implementing it "of themselves, by themselves, and for themselves." While democracy has not yet been successful in the absolute majority of the developing countries, Korea has entered into the threshold of democracy upon the embarkation of the Sixth Republic. One may wonder, then, to what extent Korea leads developing countries in democratization. This is the topic of Chapter Six.

Notes

1. For further information on the role of Congress on human rights-aid linkage, see Sandy Vogelgesang (1980: 49-92); Roberta Cohen (1979: 216-46); Steven B. Cohen (1982: 246-79).

2. The United States, together with Great Britain, France, and other countries, sent an international army to join the Russian domestic counterrevolutionary "white armies" that lasted in a struggle against the Bolshevik Revolutionary government from 1918 to 1921. The United States sent 40,000 troops and suffered several thousand casualties. For further information, see Gardner (1984: 170

& 180); Williams (1967: 62); Sayers and Kahn (1946: Chs.. 6, 7, 8 & passim).

3. Strategic consideration of the Korean peninsula was by no means excluded in President Truman's decision to defend South Korea. For further information, see Harry S. Truman (1965).

4. For further information on the theory and its application to South Korea, see Sung M. Pae (1986: Ch. 3).

5. For nearly two decades, and especially in the last decade, the Soviet Union has been strengthening its military forces in the Pacific, particularly its naval assets, for three principal reasons. They are: to influence through intimidation decisions of both friendly and hostile states in the region on the basis of *realpolitik* that force is the ultimate arbiter in international affairs; to maintain the balance of power against the combined strength of its principal adversaries such as the United States, Japan, the PRC, and other U.S. allies; and to guarantee its interests in the entire region in the absence of its significant economic and diplomatic leverages. For further information, see Solarz (1985); Petrov (1978); Primakov (1979); Bok (1986); and Stephan (1982).

6. *The Korea Herald* (March 22, 1986). For a detailed comparative study of military strengths of Seoul and Pyungyang, see International Institute for Strategic Studies (IISS) (1989).

7. Brzezinski (1986a: 32). For full discussion on three strategic fronts of competition between the two superpowers, see his book (1986b).

8. For an excellent discussion on this topic, see Ralph N. Clough (1976).

9. The 18th Annual Security Consultative Meeting was held on April 2-3, 1986 and the 3rd Annual Foreign Ministers' Meeting on May 7-8, 1986. See *The Korea Herald*, (April 3, 1986 and May 10, 1987). The United States announced that the 1990 Team Spirit might be cancelled as a conciliatory gesture for North and South Korea to open dialog for tension reduction and the promotion of cooperation. It was not actually cancelled.

10. Two days later both of them indicated that they were willing to explain the role of the United States upon the official request from the committee. See *The Korea Times* (July 28 & 30, 1988); *The Chung Ang Ilbo* (August 16, 1988).

11. One factor which was chosen had the eigenvalue of 2.68. For further information on factor analysis, see Rudolph J. Rummel (1970: Chs. 15 and 16); SPSS Inc. (1983: Ch. 35).

12. A portion of data for these seven variables were collected originally in my previous research. See Sung M. Pae (1986: 105-107). From this, data collection was extended from 1953-1968 and from 1982-1984.

Chapter 6 Korea: Leader of the Nations in Democratization

Democratization has been studied by many students of comparative politics. However, some students define democracy substantively; others approach it procedurally. Moreover, each student chooses different criteria on either substantive or procedural grounds upon which he/she defines democracy. Consequently, this inconsistency provides us with conflicting findings and suggestions concerning what countries have reached what level of democratization. Simply, many of us feel as if we were wandering around in a jungle without any clear idea on how to compare the level of democratization among different countries.

Chapter Six has four objectives. First, it will examine shortcomings on the concept of democracy defined in terms of a substantive perspective. Second, it will examine the lack of empirical evidence on a clear dichotomy between Lijphart's majoritarian and consensus models of democracy. A critical review will provide readers with a correct understanding of democracy, which can be defined only in terms of a procedural perspective.

Third, Chapter Six will review many comparative studies on democratization of different countries from a procedural perspective. One major shortcoming across all of these studies, however, is that they are based on a one-time, static approach. Therefore, the ultimate objective is to suggest a thesis that Korea leads developing nations in democratization in terms of a multi-year dynamic and longitudinal perspective. Korea belatedly started democratizing, yet has already caught up with most rapidly-democratizing, developing countries, and is now in the forefront.

The Definition of Democracy

The Fallacy of Its Substantive Definition

Democracy, a fascinating concept, attracts all of the nations in the world. In fact, most nations incorporate the term democracy into their respective constitutions. The Constitution of the Union of Soviet Socialist Republics, for example, states in its preamble that after achieving victory in the Civil War and repulsing imperialist intervention, the Soviet government created new opportunities for "democracy" as well as for growth of the forces of socialism, national liberation, and peace throughout the world. The Constitution claims that the Soviet Union is a society of "true democracy, the political system," which ensures effective management of all public affairs, and participation of all of the working people in running the state, together with the guarantee of citizens' real rights and freedoms.[1]

North Korea even incorporates the term "democratic" into the official name of the republic, called the Democratic People's Republic of Korea (DPRK). The DPRK's constitution seems to characterize its republic as "democratic." It stipulates that the state "defends and protects the interests of the workers, peasants, soldiers, and working intellectuals freed from exploitation and oppression" (Article 6). The working people exercise power through their representative organs (Article 7). The organs of state power at all levels are "elected by secret ballot on the principle of universal, equal, and direct suffrage" (Article 8).[2]

When the constitutions of these countries are carefully examined, however, their democracy bases itself upon a "genuine democracy" for equitably distributing wealth among the masses and for raising the people's living standards by socialist ownership of the means of production in the form of state property and collective farm-and-cooperative property (the USSR: Article 10 and the DPRK: Article 11).

Communist countries collectively contend that a "genuine democracy" must emphasize the substantive nature rather than the formal nature of democracy--serving the interests and ultimately enhancing the living standards of the masses. So, they strive to create societies without homeless people, without a waste of intellect because of insufficient tuition for a college education, without suffering, starvation and/or malnutrition because of poverty and unemployment. The true meaning of "genuine democracy" is not a spurious procedural question of how a government should be run but a substantive question on how values and resources should be allocated for the happiness of each member of society. Communists insist, therefore, that since poverty, slums, sickness, ignorance, and unemployment persist in the capitalistic countries, they have no genuine democracy.

The definition of democracy in terms of a substantive perspective, which is endorsed by communist countries, however, does not provide any solution or guideline for resolving the following questions:

> (1) Whether a democratic country should be capitalistic or socialistic; (2) even if the former is preferred, how capitalistic it should be; (3) if the latter is chosen, how socialistic it should be; (4) to what extent capitalistic and socialistic elements should be combined in one democratic country, if a combination of the two is preferred (Pae, 1986: 1).

Take the case of England. Adam Smith (1723-1790) championed the cause for the adoption of capitalist democracy in England of the 18th and 19th Centuries. But under the full swing of communism prevailing across the European continent, the Labor Party played a messianic role for the adoption of socialist democracy. The time period of 1945-1951 showed the first major effort to nationalize The Bank of England, coal production, air transportation, electricity, gas, land transportation, and iron and steel. During the 1960s the second major nationalization of steel, oil, atomic energy, and the partial nationalization of Rolls Royce and Leyland automobile production took place (Macridis, 1986: 113). In the 1970s, the state took control of 95 percent of the British schools.

Rampant entry into socialist democracy in Great Britain resulted in many unexpected dysfunctional consequences. The size of school enrollment based on registration rather than actual attendance became the criterion for the amount of financial aid from the socialistic government and the subsequent justification for inflated staffing and supervisory hierarchical levels. Hence, the teachers' unions supported the raising of the school-leaving age unconditionally without flunking out the students on academic failure. At the same time, university bureaucracies proposed lowering university entrance standards in order to keep up the number of matriculants, the appearance of the schools, and the staffing levels. The academic communities loved to lower these standards uncritically because greater student numbers provide the justification for larger university establishments, chairmanships, and deanships (Sherman, 1986: 654).

Socialized housing in England was by no means less serious than socialized education. For example, public housing costs went up five times as much per unit as homes built by private developers for sale to owner occupiers, when the costs of interest and land were taken into account. Yet many houses had to be demolished after as few as ten years because of shoddy construction, even though the outstanding debts remained to be paid by taxpayers over the unexpired portion of sixty years.

State-owned manufacturing firms were required to guarantee tenure to workers, staff, and management regardless of their performance. Hence, workers lost incentive and many firms went deeper into the red due to lower output.

> Marshalled by corps of social workers, community workers, and salaried workers, their claimant troops enlarged. They were the welfariat of pensioners, the unemployed and the unemployable. The more generous the state became in welfare services, the greater the extent of statistical poverty. "Their latest estimate is that one third of the population of Britain is living on or below the poverty line, a higher proportion than in India" (Sherman, 1986: 652).

Socialist democracy prevailing in England reached a critical point at which the state could no longer continue to bear the ever-mounting costs. It also worsened a zero-sum game between Peter and Paul over the matter of how much taxes were to be levied on each of them and how much welfare was to be expended for each of them by the government. Sherman summarizes the "inflation of rights" and the subsequently intensified "zero-sum game" as follows:

> The lavish promise of rights beyond all possibility of fulfillment creates inflation of rights followed by defaults and devaluation of rights. It can no longer be taken for granted that the right to a decent home, education, safety, medical care, and so forth, will necessarily be honored.

> The war of every man against every man takes place through the state and therefore against the state. Hence, the paradox is that beyond a critical limit the more the state gives, the more

it is hated. And since the state can give Peter only what it takes from Paul, it becomes to be doubly hated as a parsimonious giver and a prodigal taker (1986: 658).

Upon three occasions of attempts and the subsequent frustrations since 1979 by her own ministers and members of parliament under pressure from various interest groups and associations, Prime Minister Margaret Thatcher still refused to give in and steered the ship of England from socialist democracy gradually but boldly toward capitalist democracy.

The British experience raises a critical question on which substantive democracy--a capitalist democracy, a socialist one, or a combined one--may or must be uniformly adopted by all democratic countries regardless of different times and economic circumstances.

Each of these three substantive democracies--capitalistic, socialistic, and combined--is further complicated by its own variation in terms of conservatism and liberalism as a left-to-right ideological continuum. The United States, for example, has long been regarded as a country of capitalist democracy. However, the American capitalist democracy was very conservative in the 18th and 19th Centuries and became liberal during the 1930s and more liberal during the 1960s. But its pendulum began to swing back to conservative capitalist democracy under the Reagan and Bush Administrations during the 1980s and 1990s. The American experience also raises doubts on what substantive capitalist democracy--liberal, moderate, or conservative--should be the correct choice to be imposed upon the United States consistently.

In short, there are democrats who are capitalists and democrats who are socialists. Among them some democrats are liberals and others are conservatives. Moreover, the definition of conservatism and liberalism differ from country to country and from time to time.

> These bothersome problems of conservatism and liberalism differing from place to place and from time to time poses problems for analysis. A Canadian conservative will emphasize something different from a Japanese or Swedish conservative. In addition, a conservative in the United States in the last half of the 20th century does not believe the same thing that a U.S. conservative in 1890 did. The same thing is true of liberals in these different times and places (Sargent, 1981: 65).

Our inability to determine the correctness of substantive goals and policies leads to the conclusion that the definition of democracy and its subsequent measurement of the level of democracy among the nations may be futile from a substantive perspective.

Variety of Democratic Institutions and Practices

Arend Lijphart identified twenty-one countries, primarily in the Western European continent, as being truly democratic. These democratic countries could be fitted into either the Anglo-American model or the consociational model. Later he suggested the majoritarian model and the consensus model without further elaboration on whether the Anglo-American model would be identical with the majoritarian one and the consociational model identical with the consensus model. Given this constraint of conceptualization we may briefly highlight major differences between his latest majoritarian and consensus models (see Figure 6-1 and Table 6-1)(Lijphart, 1984).

Figure 6-1 The Majoritarian vs. the Consensus Model

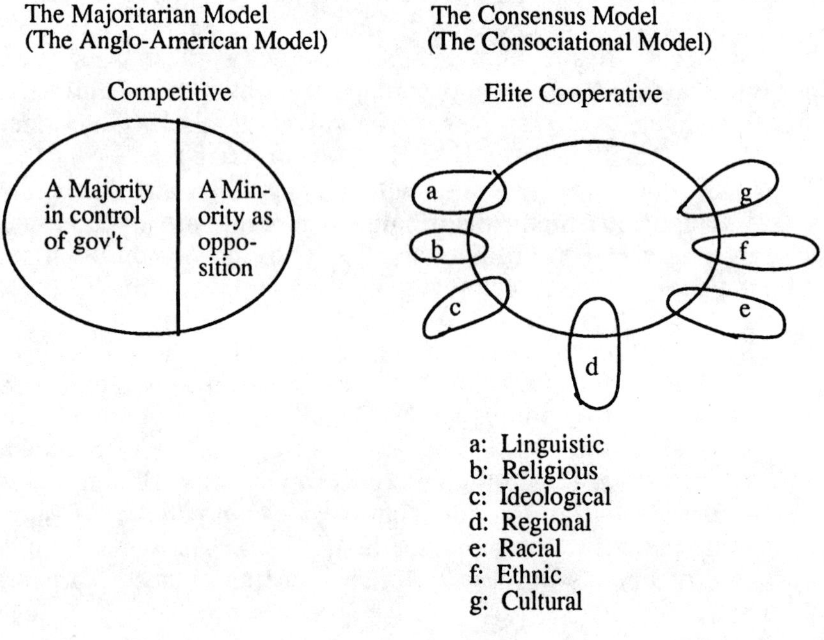

The Majoritarian Model
(The Anglo-American Model)

Competitive

A Majority in control of gov't | A Minority as opposition

The Consensus Model
(The Consociational Model)

Elite Cooperative

a: Linguistic
b: Religious
c: Ideological
d: Regional
e: Racial
f: Ethnic
g: Cultural

Table 6-1 Differences between the Majoritarian and Consensus Models

Major Characteristics: Majoritarian	Consensus
*The government vs opposition	*A grand cooperation
*Homogeneous, secular political culture	*Heterogeneity
*Highly differentiated role structure	*Less differentiated, poor boundary maintenance
*Autonomy of groups and associations	*Less Autonomous
*Linkage between groups and political parties	*Linkage centered around each of the major cleavages
*The concentration of executive power	*The executive power-sharing
*The fusion of power and cabinet dominance	*The separation of power
*Single-member district election based on plurality votes	*Proportional representation *Fair distribution of power
*Unitary/highly centralized government	*Territorial/non-territorial federalism an decentralization
*The potential for polarization and crisis	*Less polarized
*The potential for short-term coalition	*The potential for long-term coalition
*The potential for power turnover due to floating voters	*Less frequent power turnover
*Asymmetrical bicameralism Two-party system	*Balanced bicameralism and minority representation *Multiparty system

Sample Countries:

The United Kingdom, New Zealand, Canada, Japan, Norway, Sweden, Denmark	Belgium, France, Italy, The Netherlands, Switzerland

Source: Lijphart (1977 and 1984)

The majoritarian model of democracy shows a dichotomous division of the leaders and people into the government and its opposition. Political leaders are divided into a government with either a wide or a slim majority. The majoritarian model of democracy is characterized by a "homogeneous, secular political culture" and a "highly differentiated" role structure. Hence, interests of various autonomous groups and associations are articulated and subsequently aggregated by political parties. The association between certain social groups and political parties tends to be stable, with working class people, labor unions, central city residents, Catholics, and low income people tending to be closer to the left-wing party; professionals, managerial, executives, large-size business firms, and Protestants usually siding with the right-wing party. This demonstrates the potential for polarization and subsequent competition. But a short-term grand coalition may be established by mutual concessions and adjustment. Floating voters and groups also may be able to transfer power between political parties.

Nevertheless, both government and opposition leaders and their supporters share the common political culture in adhering to: democratic procedural rules, fair competition between political parties, peaceful transfer of power, importance of issue differences between political parties, and the subsequent popular verdict in the next general election. Membership overlapping further alleviates the potential for extreme adversarial competition.

The majoritarian model is further characterized by the concentration of executive power, the fusion of power and cabinet dominance, asymmetric bicameralism, a two-party system, single-member district election on the basis of plurality votes, and unitary and/or highly centralized government. The United Kingdom, New Zealand, Japan, Norway, Sweden, and the United States are typical of this model.

The consensus model of democracy tends to be identified in a plural society which inherits "segmental cleavages" of a "religious, ideological, linguistic, regional, cultural, racial, or ethnic nature." Moreover, political parties, interest groups, media of communication, schools, and voluntary associations tend to be organized along the lines of segmental cleavages. The groups bound by such cleavages are referred to as "the cleavages of a plural society" (Lijphart, 1977: 3-4).

Segmental cleavages in a plural society tend to make it difficult to achieve and maintain stable democratic government. Nevertheless, many continental Western European countries have been able to shape the cooperative attitudes and behavior by the leaders of the different segments of the population. A variety of grand coalition, in fact, could be identified: a "grand coalition cabinet," which was organized by seven members from four major parties in Switzerland, two overwhelmingly strong parties in Austria (1946-1966), and three major parties in Belgium; a "grand council or committee," which was maintained in the Netherlands and Austria;

and a "grand coalition" or a president and other top officials, which was established in Lebanon. Elite cooperation, the formation of a long-term grand coalition encompassing all of the major cleavages, and the subsequent fair and equitable distribution of costs and benefits among the cleavages make their democracy stable and viable. Those segmental groups are not well differentiated in their roles and structures. They are less autonomous and more centered around the interests of each of their own segmental cleavages. This tends to promote a multi-party system and entail the principles of separation of power, proportional representation, and demand for fair distribution of power among segmental cleavages. Nevertheless, cooperation by the leaders of major different groups to keep democracy viable tends to transcend segmental or subcultural cleavages.

The consensus model of democracy is further characterized by executive power-sharing of different segmental group leaders, proportional representation, territorial/non-territorial federalism, and decentralization. Belgium, the Netherlands, France (of the past), and Switzerland are considered typical examples of this model. In short, twenty-one democracies were clearly distinguished by Lijphart into the majoritarian and consensus models due to different socio-economic factors.

In order to examine whether these twenty-one democratic countries can be clearly identified along two models of democracy, I selected the same seventeen variables which Lijphart himself employed in his book. They are: (1) plurality in terms of ideology and clan conflict--nonplural, semi-plural or plural; (2) plurality in terms of religious and linguistic perspectives--homogeneous or heterogeneous; (3) usual types of cabinet--oversized, minimum-winning or minority cabinet; (4) proportions of time during which minimal winning, oversized, or minority cabinets were in power, 1945-1980; (5) type of government--partliamentary, presidential, or hybrid; (6) dependence of the chief executive on the legislature's confidence--yes or no; (7) average cabinet durability in 1945-1980--more than 5 years, 2.5 to 5 years, or less than 2.5 years; (8) the number of legislative houses--unicameral or bicameral; (9) the congruency and symmetry of the two chambers--strong, weak or insignificant; (10) population size--large or small; (11) unitary or federal government; (12) government centralization measured by the central government's share of total central and noncentral tax receipts in the 1970s (%); (13) effective number of parties; (14)

194   Korea Leading Developing Nations

Table 6-2 Differences in Institutes and Processes of Twenty-One Democratic Countries

	Austral.	Austria	Belgium	Canada	Denmark	Finland	France	West Ger.	Iceland	Ireland	Italy	Japan	Luxembor.l	Netherl.l	New Zeyn.	Sweden	Switzer.	United.K	USA
Types: Majoritarian (M) or Consensus (C)	M	M	C	M	C	C	C	M	C	M	C	C	M	M	C	M	M	M	C	M	M
Plurality: *Ideological & Class(1): Nonplural (NP) Semiplural (SP) Plural (P)	NP	P	P	SP	NP	SP	SP	SP	NP	NP	P	SP	NP	P	P	NP	NP	NP	P	NP	SP
*Religious & Linguistic (2): Homogeneous (Ho) Heterogeneous (He)	He	Ho	He	He	Ho	Ho	Ho	He	Ho	Ho	Ho	Ho	Ho	Ho	He	Ho	Ho	Ho	He	Ho	He
*Cabinet Formation (3): Minimum-Winning (W) Oversized (O) Minority (M)	W	W	W	W	M	O	O	W	W	W	O	O	W	W	O	W	W	M	O	W	O
*Proportion of Time(%)(4)	86	84	75	73	68	50	63	78	86	78	81	46	77	96	71	100	67	68	100	90	--
*Form of Government(5): Parliamentary (Pa) Presidential (Pr) Hybrid (H)	Pa	Pa	Pa	Pa	Pr	Pr	Pa	Pa	Pa	Pa	Pa	Pa	Pa	Pa	Pa	Pa	Pa	Pa	H	Pa	Pr
*Vote of Nonconfidence (6): Yes (Y) No (N)	Y	Y	Y	Y	N	N	Y	Y	Y	Y	Y	Y	Y	Y	Y	Y	Y	Y	Y	N	Y	N
*Average Cabinet Durability (7): Long (L: 5 yrs) Medium (M: 2.5-5 yrs) Short (S: 5 yrs)	L	L	S	L	M	S	S	M	M	L	S	S	M	M	M	L	M	L	-	L	-
*Parliament Number of Houses (8): Unicameral (U) Bicameral (B)	B	B	B	B	U	U	B	B	U	B	U	B	B	U	B	U	U	B	B	B
*Strength (9): Strong (S) Weak (W) Insignificant (I)	S	I	W	W	-	-	W	S	-	I	-	W	W	-	W	-	-	-	S	W	S
*Population Size (10): Large (L) Small (S)	L	S	L	L	S	S	L	L	S	S	L	L	S	S	S	S	S	S	L	L

Korea: Leader of the Nations in Democratization

Table 6-2 Differences in Institutes and Processes of Twenty-One Democratic Countries

	Australia	Austria	Belgium	Canada	Denmark	Finland	France	West Germany	Ireland	Israel	Italy	Japan	Luxembourg	Netherlands	New Zealand	Norway	Sweden	Switzerland	United Kingdom	US	USA·K
Types: Majoritarian (M) or Consensus (C)	M	M	C	M	C	C	C	M	C	M	C	C	M	M	C	M	M	M	C	M	M
*Federal (F)/ Unitary (U)(11)	F	F	U	F	U	U	U	F	U	U	U	U	U	U	U	U	U	F	U	U	F
*Central Government's Tax Share of Total Taxes(%)(12)	80	70	93	50	71	70	88	51	83	92	96	96	65	82	98	93	70	62	41	87	57
*Effective Number of Parties (13)	2.5	2.2	3.7	2.4	4.3	5.0	3.3	2.6	3.5	2.8	4.7	3.5	3.1	3.3	4.9	2.0	3.2	3.2	5.0	2.1	2.0
*Party Issue Salience (14)	2.5	2.0	3.0	1.5	2.5	3.5	3.5	2.0	3.0	1.0	3.0	3.0	3.0	2.0	3.0	1.0	3.5	2.5	3.0	1.5	1.0
*Legislative Electoral Formula (15): Plural (P) Majority (M) Alternative (A) Proportional (Pr) Semi-proportional (S)	A	Pr	Pr	P	Pr	Pr	M	Pr	Pr	Pr	Pr	S	Pr	Pr	P	Pr	Pr	Pr	P	P	P
*Constitutional Amendment (16): Pure Majority (M) Referendum (R) Minority Veto (Mv)	Mv	Mv	Mv	Mv	R	Mv	R	Mv	M	R	M	R	Mv	Mv	Mv	M	Mv	M	Mv	Mv	M
*Judicial Review: Review (17) Yes (Y) No (N)	Y	Y	N	Y	Y	N	Y	Y	Y	N	Y	Y	N	N	Y	Y	N	Y

Source: Adopted from Arend Lijphart (1984). For further information, see Table 3.2 for (1) and (2), Table 4.2 for (3) and (4), Table 5.1 for (5) and (6), Table 5.3 for (7), Table 6-2 for (8), Table 6.4 for (9), Table 6.3 for (10) and (11), Table 10-2 for (12), Table 7.4 for (13), Table 8.6 for (14), Table 9.1 for (15), Table 11.1 for (16), and Table 11.2 for (17).

salience of party issue difference measured by seven indices such as socioeconomic, religious, cultural-ethnic, urban-rural, regime support, foreign policy, and post-materialist. Numerical value is measured by summation of the scores of these seven indices--one point for high salience of each index, one-half point for medium salience, or a zero point for low salience; (15) classification of the electoral formula for the election of the first or only chambers in 1945-1980--plurality (a candidate who receives more popular votes than other candidates becomes the winner), majority (a candidate who must receive 50%+ of the popular votes to be elected), or proportional; (16) procedures for constitutional amendments--pure majority vote, approval by referendum, or minority veto available; and (17) the availability of judicial review--yes or no. Table 6-2 shows the appropriate information and data on each of the seventeen elements for twenty-one democratic countries.

When twenty-one democracies in Table 6-2 are carefully examined and compared on the basis of these seventeen variables, clustering of these countries along the two models of democracy--majoritarian and consensus--is really blurred. I would rather suggest a thesis that there are not just two distinct clusterings but many with different institutes and modes of operation for successfully running twenty-one different democracies. Let me explain my thesis.

According to Lijphart, the consensus model is characterized as heterogeneous, highly decentralized, fragmented, and salient in issue differences among different segmental cleavages. However, two consensus model democratic countries, Denmark and Iceland, are not plural in their socio-economic compositions and not heterogeneous in religious and linguistic perspectives either. On the other hand, two majoritarian democracies, Austria and Luxembourg, are as plural as some consensus model democracies.

Contrary to Lijphart, four consensus model democracies--Belgium, Israel, Italy, and the Netherlands--are not decentralized but highly centralized, when the degree of centralization is measured by their central government's share of total taxes. While the central government's tax share of these four consensus model countries accounted for a whopping 93%, 96%, 96%, and 98%, respectively, three majoritarian model democracies, Canada, Sweden, and the United States ironically had only 50%, 62%, and 57% of the total taxes, collected and expended by their central government in the 1970s, respectively. This finding does not support the Lijphart hypothesis that the consensus model democracies are more likely to promote decentralization perhaps with a larger proportion of tax money to be collected and used for the regional and local governments due to their segmental cleavages and contending interests.

The principle of checks and balances--between the branches of government in a horizontal perspective and between the levels of government in a vertical perspective--may be a critical element for consensus model democracies to protect and promote their segmental interests. One important institution for promoting their segmental interests may be an independent and authoritative judicial review power. Nevertheless, four consensus model democracies--Belgium,

Israel, the Netherlands, and Switzerland--do not have a judicial review system.

Lijphart suggests that consensus model democracies tend to have more salience in party issue differences than the majoritarian counterparts. But a majoritarian democracy, Norway (3.5), shows its party issue salience as high as two consensus democracies, France and Finland; and much higher than all other consensus democracies. A majoritarian democracy, Japan, also has a high score of 3.0 in its party issue salience, which is as high as many consensus model democracies such as Belgium, Iceland, Israel, Italy, and Switzerland (see Table 6-2).

Lijphart's own factor analysis ironically did not show two distinct clusters of his majoritarian and consensual models. Contrary to his hypothesis, he found "two clearly different and unrelated empirical clusters." The first factor virtually coincides with the effective number of parties (factor loading of .99 of the 13th variable in Table 6-2), cabinet formation (.85 of the 3rd variable), party issue salience (.75 of the 14th variable), and parliamentary strength (executive dominance, .72 of the 8th variable). The second factor groups together the characteristics of the number of parliamentary houses (unicameralism, .65 of the 8th variable), centralization (.51 of the 12th variable), and constitutional flexibility (.76 of the 16th variable)(Lijphart, 1984: 214-215). Each of these two factors was further divided into three categories--majoritarian, intermediate, and consensual, resulting in "nine clusters of democratic regimes" instead of two distinct clusters of the majoritarian and consensus models (1984: ch. 13).

Differences are equally salient among the democracies of the same models. Two most often cited model democracies, the United Kingdom (UK) and the United States (USA), which are classified as the same majoritarian model, share commonality on eight elements such as bicameralism, large population, the effective number of political parties, party issue salience and plurality electoral system. But the number of elements that differentiate the two countries is greater than the number in commonality. The UK and the USA are different in eight elements such as ideological and class plurality, religious and linguistic plurality, cabinet formation, form of government, and so on (see Table 6-2).

Sweden and Norway, which are both under the same consensus model, share many elements but are different in at least four areas such as cabinet durability, central government's tax proportion,

Table 6-3 Varimax Rotated Factor Loadings*

Variable Names	Assignment of Weight	Majoritarian Model Factor (Factor 1)	Consensus Model Factor (Factor 2)
1. Ideological & class plurality	Nonplural = 1 Semiplural = 2 Plural = 3	-.079	.480
2. Religious & linguistic plurality	Homogeneous = 1 Heterogeneous = 2	.544	.501
3. Cabinet formation	Oversized= 1 Minimum-Winning = 2 Minority= 3	-.008	-.549
4. Proportion of time of the above cabinet in power	Percentage	-.121	-.337
5. Form of Government	Parliamentary = 1 Presidential = 2 Hybrid = 3	-.079	.782
6. Vote of nonconfidence	Yes = 1 No = 2	-.089	.708
7. Average cabinet durability	Short (<2.5 yrs) = 1 Medium (2.5-5 yrs = 2 Long (>5 yrs) = 3	.191	-.809
8. Number of legislative houses	Unicameral = 1 Bicameral = 2	.740	.094
9. Strength of house(s)	Insignificant = 1 Weak=2 Strong=3	.873	.335
10. Population size	Small = 1 Large = 2	.642	.064
11. Types of government	Unitary = 1 Federal = 2	.490	.532
12. Central government tax share	Percentage	.270	-.406
13. Number of effective parties	Actual number	-.755	.540
14. Party issue salience of seven dimensions	Actual scores computed by Lijphart	-.562	.279
15. Legislative electoral formula	Plural = 1 Majority = 2 Alternative=3 Proportional=4 Semi-proportional=5	-.582	.080
16. Constitutional amendment by	Pure majority =1 Referendum = 2 Minority = 3	.392	.409
17. Judicial review	Yes =1 No = 2	-.090	.072

Source: Table 6-2
*Factor analysis is computed from the SPSS factor analysis program. Factors 1 and 2 have the eigen values of 3.816 and 3.172, respectively.

party issue salience, and the constitutional amendment procedures. Belgium and the Netherlands, which are closest to each other among all the consensus model countries, still demonstrate their differences in four areas such as cabinet formation, cabinet durability, population size, and effective number of political parties.

In order to demonstrate the absence of clear-cut clusterings of twenty-one countries in terms of dichotomy into the majoritarian and consensus models of democracy, seventeen variables in Table 6-2 are employed into factor analysis. Table 6-3 shows factor loadings of two factors resulting from varimax rotated factor analysis.

Factor One is clustered by such variables as the number of legislative houses (as bicameral rather than unicameral) (.740), increase in the strength of legislative houses (.873), a large population (.642), a limited number of effective parties with less salience in party issues, and plural or majoritarian rather than proportional electoral formula of the legislature (-.582). This factor is closely associated with Lijphart's majoritarian model of democracy

Factor Two, on the other hand, is clustered by such variables as a high degree of ideological class plurality (.480), a high degree of religious and linguistic plurality (.501), oversized cabinet form (-.549), more hybrid form of government, (-.337), the absence of a vote of non-confidence (.708) and yet a relatively short durability of cabinet (-.809) perhaps due to demands and negotiations among elites of heterogeneous backgrounds--ideological, class, religious, and/or linguistic. Two other variables are equally important to represent Factor Two. They are: the tendency to have "a federal type rather than a unitary form" (.532) which may meet the needs of conflicting heterogeneity of people; and the "smaller federal tax share out of the total" (-.406) such that local governments have a larger proportion of tax shares for various programs for their respective cleavage members. This factor closely represents Lijphart's consensus model.

Based upon this finding, factor scores of twenty-one countries are generated for each of two factors (see Table 6-4). The factor scores of twenty-one countries are then located along the two dimensions--the majoritarianism factor on the Y-axis and the consensus factor on the X-axis (Figure 6-2).

Findings from Figure 6-2, however, challenge Lijphart's two models of democracy. While Lijphart's six countries of the majoritarian model--Australia, Austria, the United Kingdom, New Zealand, Luxembourg, and Japan--cluster together along the

Table 6-4 Factor Scores of Twenty-One Countries for Two Factors

Countries	Lijphart's Category	Majoritarianism Factor	Consensus Factor
Australia	Majoritarian (M)	2.338	-1.031
Austria	M	.969	1.010
Belgium	Consensus (C)	-1.622	2.052
Canada	M	.327	.518
Denmark	C	-.027	-.288
Finland	C	-2.655	2.491
France	C	.733	.165
Germany (West)	M	1.797	.677
Iceland	C	-.860	-1.232
Ireland	M	-1.096	.658
Israel	C	-1.607	.090
Italy	C	.155	.011
Japan	M	-.101	-1.511
Luxembourg	M	.031	-1.200
Netherlands	C	.454	-.872
New Zealand	M	.440	-1.247
Norway	M	-1.000	.431
Sweden	M	-1.033	-1.201
Switzerland	C	-.130	2.730
United Kingdom	M	.790	-.995
USA	M	2.091	.765

Source: Tables 6-2 and 6-3

Korea: Leader of the Nations in Democratization   201

Figure 6-2 Location of Twenty-One Democracies Along the Majoritarian and Consensus Model Dimensions

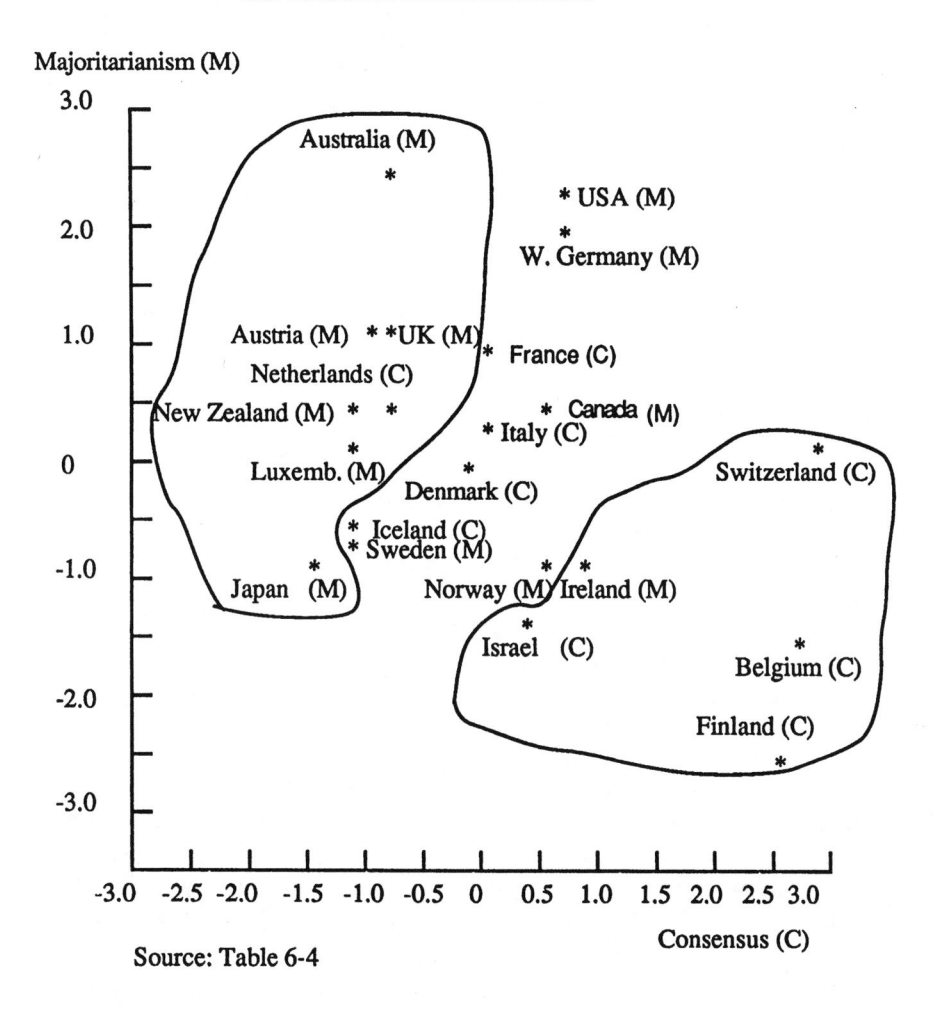

Majoritarianism (M)

[Scatter plot showing 21 democracies plotted on axes of Majoritarianism (M) vertical, ranging from -3.0 to 3.0, and Consensus (C) horizontal, ranging from -3.0 to 3.0. Countries plotted include: Australia (M), USA (M), W. Germany (M), Austria (M), UK (M), Netherlands (C), France (C), New Zealand (M), Canada (M), Italy (C), Luxemb. (M), Denmark (C), Switzerland (C), Iceland (C), Sweden (M), Japan (M), Norway (M), Ireland (M), Israel (C), Belgium (C), Finland (C). Two clusters are outlined.]

Source: Table 6-4

majoritarianism factor, his two majoritarian democracies, Norway and Ireland become the outlanders, being located rather closely to the countries of the consensus cluster. Among Lijphart's nine countries of the consensus model, only four countries--Israel, Belgium, Finland and Switzerland--cluster along the consensus factor. Nevertheless, these four consensus countries are much more widely scattered than their majoritarian counterparts. Lijphart's consensus democratic country, the Netherlands is ironically located within the majoritarian cluster. Moreover, his four majoritarian countries--the United States, West Germany, Canada, and Sweden--and his four consensus countries--France, Italy, Denmark and Iceland--are located along the nearly forty-five degree angle between the two factors. This clearly indicates that these eight countries are oriented to neither the majoritarian nor consensus model, but a combination of both. These nine countries are even more widely scattered.

There is no question, then, that twenty-one democracies do not cluster along Lijphart's majoritarian or consensus model. His model building of two contrasting democratic types primarily on the basis of empirical research presents an empirical puzzle because nearly one half of his selected countries do not fit into either one of his two models. Ironically, Lijphart himself admits that one of the principal messages of his book is that "there are many different ways of successfully running a democracy."

The Procedural Definition of Democracy

Readers may raise a very important question: Are there any common denominators across twenty-one different, yet successfully running democratic countries such that democracy can be still distinguished from nondemocratic countries? An affirmative answer can be made if democracy is examined in terms of its process rather than prescriptions about its substance.

William Ebenstein and his colleagues, for example, have long endorsed preference of process to substance of democracy on the basis of Abraham Lincoln's famous speech at Gettysburg. They contended that the main thrust of Lincoln's democracy was self-government, namely, government "of the people" and "by the people" rather than "for the people." Whether self-government is in the interest of a particular segment of people--average citizens, organized groups, bureaucrats, professionals, or power elites--is important but not decisive. Therefore, they believed that Lincoln put the government "of" the people and "by" the people ahead of "for" the people (Ebenstein et al., 1967: 3).

In fact, many students of democracy have attempted to define democracy in terms of its procedural perspective and suggested procedural principles to distinguish democratic governments from other types. Anthony Downs enumerated eight rules and stated that if they were honored and observed in a political system, its government could be qualified as democratic. They are:

1. popular election of a political party or a coalition of parties to run the governing apparatus;
2. holding such elections within periodic intervals, the duration of which cannot be altered by the party in power acting alone;
3. allowing all adults legal citizens of the society to vote in each such election; one person, one vote;
4. each voter may cast one and only one vote in each election;
5. allowing any party (or coalition) receiving the support of a majority of those voting to take over the powers of government until the next election;
6. prohibiting the losing parties in an election from trying by force or any illegal means to prevent the winning party (or coalition) from taking office;
7. no suppression on political activities of any citizens or other parties as long as they make no attempt to overthrow the government by forces;
8. competition between two or more parties for control of the governing apparatus in every election (1957: 23-24).

Robert Cord and his colleagues also suggested that, if the following procedural rules are followed by a political system, it becomes democratic. They are: the election of representatives by the voters; popular support of government; policy evaluation by the voters in the subsequent elections; free and open political competition between candidates and between political parties; the guarantee of all basic human rights and freedoms; and a majority rule and minority protection (Cord et al., 1985: 62-71).

Public dissent and disobedience have become a highly controversial issue among many students of democracy. Anthony Downs, on the one hand, flatly refused to incorporate public disobedience, especially violent ones, because he emphasized the principles of majority rule, minority protection, and peaceful transfer of power. Robert Cord and his colleagues, rather, endorsed the importance of public dissent and disobedience.

Public dissent and disobedience was accepted by Mahatma Gandhi and Martin L. King within the framework of the constitution and law. On the other hand, John Locke, Henry Thoreau, and Thomas Jefferson endorsed even violent means of public dissent and disobedience. Locke suggested three specific circumstances, under which violent protest and even revolution might be justified. They are:

1. When the people are made miserable, and find themselves subject to the ill usage of arbitrary power. . . .
2. Not upon every little mismanagement in public affairs, [but] great mistakes in the ruling part.
3. Many wrong and inconvenient laws. . . (1969: 235).

While violent public dissent and disobedience become one major disagreement, all other procedural rules are commonly accepted by all the students of democracy. These rules become the criteria to make distinctions between democratic and non-democratic countries. These rules are to be honored, if a government--capitalistic or socialistic, conservative or liberal in terms of a substantive perspective--is to be democratic. They are:

1. Partisan politics
    a) The existence of two or more political parties that freely compete with one another for the governing apparatus, regardless of either under the majoritarian or consensus model of democracy, either party issues being more or less salient.
    b) Selection of a political party under the majoritarian model or formation of a coalition among parties under the consensus model, to run the governing apparatus.
2. A system of popular representation, regardless of either a parliamentary form or a presidential form of representation, either a unitary form or a federal form of government.
3. Regular and periodic elections, regardless of cabinet durability as either long, medium, or short, regardless of legislative electoral formula as plural, majority or proportional.
4. One person one vote principle, regardless of segmental cleavages.
5. Universal suffrage without discrimination to any specific segmental groups.
6. Guarantee of basic human rights and freedoms for equal opportunities.
7. Peaceful transfer of power, regardless of vote of no-confidence granted or denied, and regardless of such no-confidence implemented.
8. Civilian supremacy over the armed forces.

Does democracy viewed from this procedural perspective matter, then? An affirmative answer to this question is given to one entire chapter by Robert A. Dahl in his book, *Polyarchy*. His five reasons may be more than enough to justify the normative preference for democracy. They are: (1) the greater the level of democratization is, the greater the guarantee for the classical liberal freedoms becomes; (2) the more broadened the participation, combined with political competition, the greater the potential for change in the composition of the political leadership; (3) the more competitive or inclusive a political system becomes, the greater support politicians seek from groups who can participate more easily in political life; (4) the greater the opportunities become, the greater the number and variety of preferences and interests represented; and (5) the greater the opportunities, the less the degree and extent of coercion (Dahl, 1972: Ch. 2).

The substance of democracy--the allocation of political, economic, and social values, costs, resources, and benefits--can be decided, adjusted, and readjusted, depending upon the changing environments but still under adherence to the above listed democratic procedural principles. Only under the premise of a procedural perspective, democratization--degree or level of adhering to the procedural democratic principles--can be measured and in fact compared among countries by many students. Let us briefly examine who had attempted to do so by using what criteria and identifying what types or stages of democratization. The ultimate objective is to explore to what extent South Korea, which has been leading all Third World nations in economic development, leads them in democratization now.

Comparative Studies of Democratization

A One-Time Static Approach

Seymour M. Lipset defined democracy as a "political system," which supplies regular constitutional opportunities for changing the governing officials, and a "social mechanism," which permits the largest possible part of the population to influence decisions by choosing among contenders for political office (Lipset, 1963: 27-28). This definition implies three basic procedural principles for stable democracy. The first one is a system of beliefs which allows orderly and peaceful play of power so that the "outs" may adhere to the

Table 6-5 One Time Cross-National Studies of Democratization

Author(s) & Criteria	Types and Number of Countries				Time of Data Collection
	Most Democratic			Least Democratic	
Seymour Lipset 1. Majority rule & minority protection 2. Ruling by a winning party or a coalition 3. Peaceful transfer of power 50 =	European Stable Democracies 13	European Unstable Democracies & Dictatorship 17	Latin-American Democracies & Unstable Dictatorships 7	Latin-American Stable Dictatorships 13	Early 1950s
Robert A. Dahl 1. Freedom to form & join organizations 2. Freedom of expression 3. The right to vote* 4. Eligibility for public office 5. The right of political leaders to compete for support and votes* 6. Alternative sources of information 7. Free and fair elections 8. Institutions for policies based on votes & other expressions of preferences 114 = *The criteria actually employed to classify the countries	 Fully Inclusive 29	 Near-Polyarchies 6		 Non-Polyarchies 79	Late 1960s
Neil J. Mitchell and James M. McCormick 1. Political prisoners taken 2. Use of torture 122 =	Degree of Human Rights Violations				1984
	No Violation 0 1 2 3 4 5			Most Violations 6 7 8	
Robert Wesson et al. No common criteria 159 =	Stable Democracies 28	Insecure Democracies 26	Partial Democracies 18	Limited Democracies 48	Absolutists 39	1985
Thomas Anderson 1. Legal means of gaining powers 2. Peaceful transfer of power 3. Freedom of press	Six Types from Most Free to the Least Free I II III IV V VI				1984-1985

4. Free travel in & out of country						
5. Judicial review						
6. Freedom of assembly						
165 =	9	38	37	41	38	2

Raymond D. Gastil	Free States	Partly Free States	Not Free States	1985-1986
11 Political Rights				
14 Civil Liberties				
167=	57	57	53	

decisions made by the "ins" and that the "ins" may recognize the rights of the "outs." The second one is rule by "one set of political leaders in office," by a winning party or a coalition. The third one is the guarantee of regular constitutional opportunities for a peaceful transfer of power. Based upon these three criteria, Lipset compared fifty European, English-speaking, and Latin American nations using data as of the early 1950s and identified four types of government in terms of democratization: European stable democracies; European unstable democracies and dictatorships; Latin-American democracies and unstable dictatorships; and Latin-American stable dictatorships (see Table 6-5) (1963: 32).

While Lipset focused on European and Latin American countries exclusively on the basis of three criteria, Robert A. Dahl conducted a comparative study covering 122 nations using the data of the late 1960s. Dahl suggested that a reasonably responsive democracy could meet the requirements of "at least eight institutional guarantees." They are: the freedom to form and join organizations, the freedom of expression, the right to vote, the eligibility for public office, the right of political leaders to compete for support and votes, alternative sources of information, free and fair elections, and the institutions for making government policies depending on votes and other expressions of preference (Dahl, 1971: 3).

Dahl, however, admitted the existence of a discrepancy between ideal democracy and actual democracies. Such a gap becomes a source of endless confusions and controversy among scholars; therefore, he suggests the concept of polyarchy, which falls short of ideal democracy.

> This is why the theory of polyarchy adopts a simple terminological distinction: the term democracy is reserved exclusively for an ideal state of affairs. Actual systems that

appear to approach this ideal state of affairs more closely than other systems do, at least in some important aspects, are called polyarchies. The theory of polyarchy assumes that all polyarchies fall short of democracy by a considerable and significant margin (1976: 42).

Since some political systems approach the ideal democracy considerably more than others do, all political systems can then be distinguished and judged according to the above listed eight criteria. As shown in Table 6-5, using the data of the late 1960s, Dahl classified 114 countries into three types. They are "fully inclusive polyarchies" (29 countries), "near- polyarchies" (6 countries), and "non-polyarchies" (79 countries) (1971: 231-245).

However, Dahl's distinction into three types was made not on the basis of his eight procedural rules, but on only two of them without explaining why he excluded his own six remaining criteria. Two procedural rules are: "the opportunity of adult citizens to vote in elections" and "the opportunities available to political oppositions to compete for popular support and public office"(1971: 231). The puzzle still unresolved is his acquiescence on the questions: Are these two rules more comprehensive and important than the remaining six in measuring the level of democracy? Or is his choice of the two limited to the empirical data available to him?

Neil J. Mitchell and James M. McCormick focused on the degree of human rights violations using the number of political prisoners and use of torture. They suggested nine scale values from 0 as no violation to 8 as most violations and their corresponding number of countries (see Table 6-5) (1988: 476-498). Human rights is a very important principle of democracy but falls far short of a comprehensive measurement of the level of democracy among countries.

Robert Wesson and his colleagues also attempted to identify five types of countries in terms of degrees of democracy. They are "stable democracies," "insecure democracies," "partial democracies," "limited authoritarian" regimes, and "absolutist or totalitarian" states. Using the event data of 1985, they identified countries corresponding to each of these types. However, they did not identify and use any specific common criteria to separate the 159 countries into five categories (1987).

Thomas D. Anderson also attempted to rank 165 countries in terms of six civil and political liberties. They are: the adherence to

Korea: Leader of the Nations in Democratization

legal means to gain political powers, peaceful transfer of power, the guarantee of freedom of the press, free travel inside and outside the country of inhabitants, judicial review available, and the freedom of assembly. Using the data of 1984-1985, he classified 165 countries into six types from the most free (Type I) to the least free (Type VI) and suggested the countries corresponding to each type (1988: 143-151).

Perhaps the most comprehensive attempt to measure the level of democracy thus far is Raymond D. Gastil's rating. He used eleven variables related to "political rights," which include partisan competition, open and fair election of the chief executive and the legislative members, peaceful transfer of power based on elections, civilian supremacy over the armed forces, institutionalization of interest groups, and local self-government:

1. Chief authority recently elected by a meaningful process
2. Legislature recently elected by a meaningful process
    Alternatives for (1) and (2):
    a. no choice and possibility of rejection
    b. no choice but some possibility of rejection
    c. government or single-party selected candidates
    d. choice possible only among government-approved candidates
    e. relatively open choices possible only in local elections
    f. open choice possible within a restricted range
    g. relatively open choices possible in all elections
3. Fair election laws, campaigning opportunities, polling and tabulation
4. Fair reflection of voter preference in distribution of power
    Parliament, for example, has effective power.
5. Multiple political parties
    Only dominant party allowed effective opportunity
    Open to rise and fall of competing parties
6. Recent shifts in power through elections
7. Significant opposition vote
8. Free of military or foreign control
9. Major group or groups denied reasonable self-determination
10. Decentralized political power
11. Informal consents: *de facto* opposition power.

He also used fourteen variables related to "basic freedoms and civil liberties:"

1. Media/literature free of political censorship
    a. Press independent of government
    b. Broadcasting independent of government
2. Open public discussion
3. Freedom of assembly and demonstration
4. Freedom of political or quasi-political organization
5. Non-discriminatory rule of law in politically relevant cases
    a. Independent judiciary
    b. Security forces respect individuals.
6. Free from unjustified political terror or imprisonment
    a. free from imprisonment or exile for reasons of conscience
    b. free from torture
    c. free from terror by groups not opposed to the system
    d. free from government-organized terror
7. Free trade unions, peasant organizations, or equivalents
8. Free businesses or cooperatives
9. Free professional or other private organizations
10. Free religious institutions
11. Personal social rights: including those to property, internal and external travel, choice of residence, marriage and family
12 Socioeconomic rights: including freedom from dependency on landlords, bosses, union leaders, or bureaucrats
13. Freedom from gross socioeconomic inequality
14. Freedom from gross government indifference or corruption (1987: 9-10).

Using the 1985-1986 data related to eleven "political and institutional" variables and fourteen "freedom and civil liberties" variables, 167 countries and related territories were assigned the weight of one through seven. Those 57 countries and related territories, whose ratings were one or two for the above procedural principles, were considered "free states." Another 57 countries and related territories whose ratings were three, four, or five, were declared "partially free states." The remaining 53 countries and related territories, whose ratings were six or seven, were labelled as "not free states" (Gastil, 1987: 42-43).

Gastil's (the Freedom House's) measurement attempt has many merits. First of all, he focused on broad interests in "political and institutional rights," and "civil rights and freedoms" rather than on narrow human rights interests as emphasized by Amnesty International or the U.S. Department of State reports (U.S. DOS, 1987). His twenty-five variables, in fact, encompass all democratic procedural principles as illustrated by Downs (1957), Lipset (1963), Cord et al. (1985), Mitchell and McCormick (1988), Wesson (1987), and Anderson (1988). The Freedom House admitted disagreement on some of the comparative ratings among area experts but relied not on the reputation of the countries based on the impression but on actual behaviors. The Freedom House focused on the outputs of actual behaviors, for example, available uncensored literature rather than the inputs such as formal voting and the written constitution and laws which listed many basic rights and freedoms without real implementation.[3]

A Longitudinal, Dynamic Approach

The above scholars are, however, subject to criticism due to their one-time static approach. Ignoring the fallacy of synchronization, which assumes that these countries had started running a race for democratization at the same time, these scholars began to compare the countries at a particular time in terms of the level of progress. But those countries did not start a race together at the same time. A particular point of time as a reference for a comparative study ignores the importance of a longitudinal, dynamic approach concerning what countries have progressed toward or regressed democratization over a reasonably long period of time. Only such a longitudinal, dynamic approach may correct a premature, hasty conclusion on what countries have reached what level of democratization at a particular time.

This section will pursue a dynamic, longitudinal, comparative study, covering the time period of 1973-1987 on the basis of Gastil's variables and data. Gastil considered "political rights" and "civil liberties" as two distinct dimensions. However, it seems to me that they are two sides of the same coin. His "political rights" cannot be made available without the guarantee of "civil liberties." His "civil liberties" cannot be warranted without his "political rights." Moreover, his eleven "political rights" and fourteen "civil liberties" variables encompass all democratic procedural principles. Therefore,

I combined the rating of "political rights" and "civil liberties" together into a broad measurement of the level of democratization for each of 129 countries (Gastil, 1987: 54-65).

First of all, my findings challenge the contentions of Robert Wesson and his colleagues that: "Fascism has been hopelessly discredited and can appeal only to something like a lunatic fringe;" "Communism too has exhausted its revolutionary zeal;" and "radicalism looks desperately for new inspiration." Therefore, their utopian optimism on the universal progress toward democracy is envisioned.

> It seems clear that personal, military, or party dictatorships will have to grant more rights and soften or relinquish political controls in order to keep their societies viable and competitive in the modern world. It may be reasonably assumed that this trend will continue, however, gradually in view of human conservatism and sporadically in view of the unpredictability of politics. The trend toward democracy, that is, will probably continue unless or until there is a major breakdown of the world economic order or a big new explosion of violence to change an authoritarian passion or new antidemocratic ideology (Wesson et al., 1987: 241).

On the contrary, my findings suggest that an absolute majority of 129 countries in the world had remained the same for the past fifteen years without any significant progress or regress. Only five countries regressed and eleven countries progressed toward democratization as shown in Table 6-6 and Figures 6-3 and 6-4.

Some political scientists of comparative politics and politicians exaggerate that the 1970s became the era of many developing countries entering into the threshold of democracy (Wesson et al., 1987: 241; Huntington, 1988: 7). But Table 6-6 and Figure 6-3 show that five countries--El Salvador, Lebanon, Malaysia, Malta, and Nigeria--had regressed rather than progressed toward democracy. Among them El Salvador and Nicaragua had per capita incomes of $820 and $770 as of 1986, respectively. They were in fact in the lowest income bracket of the middle income category. They also had experienced a consistently declining annual average of per capita income of -.2 and -2.1, respectively, over the period of 1965-1986.

Korea: Leader of the Nations in Democratization

Table 6-6 Significant Regress and Progress of Selected Countries Toward Democracy During the Past Fifteen Years of 1973-1986

Countries: Regressed:	Violation of Rights & Freedoms: ('73-'86)	Per Capita GNP ('85-'86)	Economic Development: Middle Income(MI), Upper Middle Income (UMI)	Annual Average Per Capita GNP Growth Rate	Life Expectation (Age) ('85-'86)	Literacy ('85-'86)	Urbanization ('85-'86)
El Salvador	5 --> 7	$820	MI	-.2	64	69	43
Lebanon	4 --> 9	$1,515	MI	-	-	75	-
Malaysia	5 --> 8	$2,000	UMI	4.4	68	75	38
Malta	3 --> 6	$4,057	UMI	1.5	-	83	-
Nicaragua	7 -->11	$770	MI	-2.1	59	87	56
Progressed:							
Argentina	9 --> 3	$2,130	UMI	.2	70	94	84
Brazil	10 --> 4	$1,640	UMI	4.3	65	74	73
Ecuador	10 --> 5	$2,199	MI	3.5	66	84	52
Greece	10 --> 4	$3,500	UMI	3.6	68	95	65
Honduras	10 --> 5	$720	MI	.4	62	56	39
Peru	12 --> 5	$1,285	MI	.2	59	72	68
Philippines	10 --> 6	$580	MI	2.3	63	88	39
Portugal	11 --> 3	$1,970	UMI	3.3	74	80	31
Spain	11 --> 3	$4,290	UMI	2.6	77	97	77
South Korea	11->9->3*	$2,150	UMI	6.6	69	95	64
Uruguay	7 --> 4	$1,665	UMI	1.4	72	96	86

Source: Gastil (1987: 54-65) for the overall scores of democratization; data for other variables were collected from the World Bank (1987) and *The 1989 Almanac*.

*A composite score in the case of South Korea was extended to 1987 and 1988, using the same criteria developed by Gastil.

214 Korea Leading Developing Nations

Figure 6-3 Countries with Significant Regression From Democratization: 1973-1986

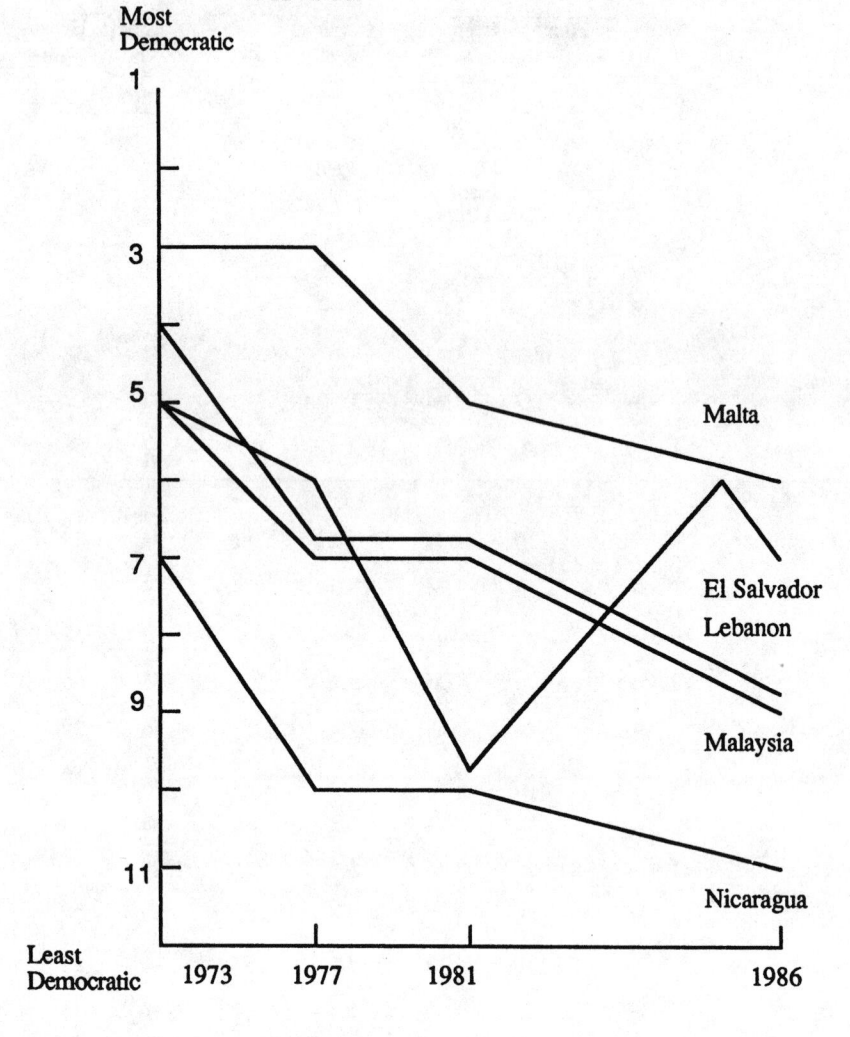

Most Democratic

[Chart showing democracy regression lines for Malta, El Salvador, Lebanon, Malaysia, and Nicaragua from 1973 to 1986, with y-axis from 1 (Most Democratic) to 11 (Least Democratic)]

Least Democratic   1973   1977   1981   1986

Source: Table 6-6

Did low levels of income and declining annual averages per capita GNP rate contribute to a regression from democracy, thereby increasing violations of political rights and civil liberties? The answer is negative, because Malaysia and Malta had high per capita incomes of $2,000 and $4,057, respectively, such that they were in the upper middle incomes category. They also experienced an increase of their annual average per capita GNP of 4.4 and 1.5 percent over the same period, respectively (see Table 6-6). This indicates that no significant difference can be found between middle income and upper middle income countries on the one hand, and between decrease and increase in the annual per capita GNP growth rate, on the other, among the five countries that had experienced regression in democratization.

My finding also challenges Arend Lijphart's thesis that some developing countries, which have many social, religious, ethnic, regional, and/or linguistic segmental cleavages similar to the European Continental countries, may have the potential for establishing and maintaining democracy as viable as that prevailing in the European continental countries. Lijphart stated that "in two of these cases"--Lebanon and Malaysia--"consociationalism" (the consensus model of democracy) "was reasonably successful for an extended period of time. And the conditions for consociational democracy, derived from both its Western and non-Western applications, are by no means overwhelmingly unfavorable elsewhere in the Third World"(1977: 147, 177-81). Lebanon and Malaysia, which were chosen as the two best examples of the successful application of Lijphart's consociational democracy model, in fact, had been able to maintain democracy for 33 years (1943-1975) and fifteen years (1955-1969), respectively. Thereafter, both of them, however, plunged into more violations of the democratic procedural principles from a composite score of 4 in 1973 to 9 in 1986 and from 2 in 1973 to 6 in 1986 in Lebanon and Malaysia, respectively (see Figure 6-3).

Some scholars and politicians, on the other hand, tend to be overly pessimistic about the potential for developing countries to adopt and enjoy Western-style democracy. Ernest W. Lefever claims that full-fledged Western-style democracy, with rare exceptions, has failed to take root in the Third World and is not likely to do so in the future. His main reason is that developing countries do not have cultural, legal, and organizational prerequisites for democracy as European countries have inherited: "a five-thousand-year heritage that embraces the Judeo-Christian ethic of respect for the dignity of the human person, Greek democracy and political theory, Roman law and organization, and the Magna Carta with its implicit guarantee of rights for every citizen" (Lefever, 1988: 621-31).

216   Korea Leading Developing Nations

Figure 6-4 Countries with Significant Progress Toward Democratization: 1973-1986

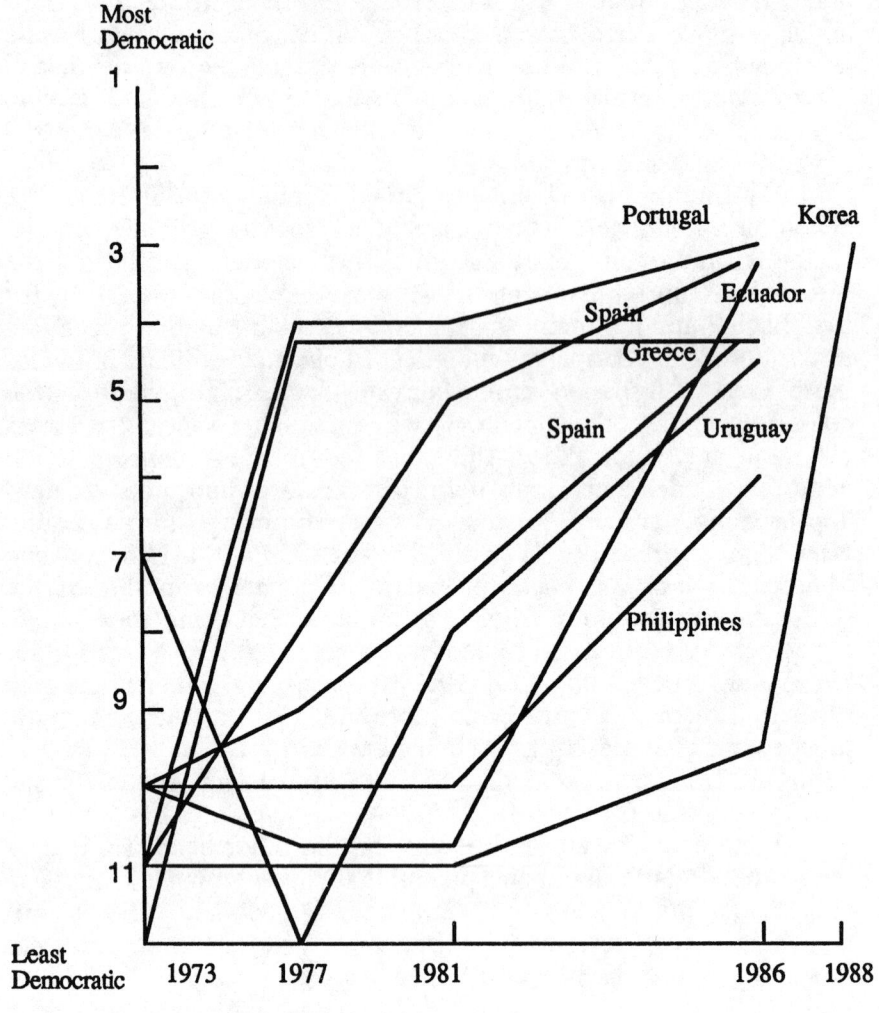

Most Democratic

[Chart showing democratization trends from 1973 to 1988 for countries: Portugal, Korea, Spain, Ecuador, Greece, Uruguay, Philippines. Y-axis ranges from 1 (Most Democratic) to 11 (Least Democratic). X-axis years: 1973, 1977, 1981, 1986, 1988.]

Least Democratic

Source: Table 6-6

But Table 6-6 and Figure 6-4 show that eleven countries have made significant progress toward democracy as close to that of Western European countries. All of these eleven countries had at least a composite score of 9 to 12 in 1973, hence violating political rights and civil liberties to a significant extent. But they all had accomplished truly remarkable levels of democratization, reaching a composite score of 3 to 6 in 1986. Among them Honduras, Peru, and the Philippines had their income bracket in the middle income categories, whereas Argentina, Brazil, Portugal, Spain, South Korea, and Uruguay entered into the upper middle income categories. This indicates that higher income does not necessarily warrant a more viable democracy than lower income. Argentina, Honduras, and Peru had nearly stagnated in their annual average per capita GNP growth rate over the period of 1965-1986, whereas Brazil, Portugal, and South Korea had made a very high rate of growth. This suggests that a higher growth rate does not necessarily bring about more rapid democratization than a lower growth rate. Honduras, the Philippines, and Portugal, whose percentage of urbanization was only in the 30s, still had accomplished the same rate of democratization as Argentina, Brazil, Spain, and Uruguay which reached the 70 to 80 percentage of urbanization.

We may now compare the countries that have regressed and progressed toward democracy on the basis of Table 6-6. Malta and Spain, for example, had almost the same amount of per capita income slightly exceeding $4,000, nearly the same rate of annual average GNP growth throughout the period of 1965-1986, and the equally high rate of urbanization. But Malta had regressed from a composite score of 3 in 1973 to 6 in 1986, while Spain had progressed toward democracy from the score of 11 to 3. Malaysia and Lebanon had almost the same per capita GNP and the same rate of literacy as Argentina, Brazil, and Portugal. But the former had regressed, whereas the latter had progressed. El Salvador and Nicaragua as low income countries had slightly higher income, higher rates of literacy and urbanization than Honduras. But the former showed regression from democracy, while the latter demonstrated significant progress. It goes without saying that no acceptable causal theory can account for all the cases.

Conclusion: Korea Leading the Nations in Democratization

Figure 6-4 shows the time and pace of eleven countries which have made the most rapid and significant progress toward democracy among 129 countries during the period of 1973-1986. We may identify among them four types of progress: 1) rapid but progressive democratization continuously and consistently throughout the period--Brazil, Honduras, and Peru belong to this type; 2) a high degree of upheaval and subsequent significant progress toward democracy--

Argentina represents the second type; 3) very rapid progress in the early phase and the maintenance of stable democracy consistently--Greece (since 1975), Portugal (since 1977), and Spain (since 1978) fit this third type; and 4) late starters of democratization in the 1980s--The Philippines and South Korea represent this type.

South Korea, in fact, is the latest starter of democratization but has most rapidly and dynamically been progressing. When Gastil's eleven "political rights" and fourteen "civil liberties" variables were applied to South Korea in the years of 1987 and 1988, there is no doubt that South Korea had entered into the threshold of near-full and complete democracy, reaching the composite score of 3. It is again the author's thesis that South Korea, which is envied of the most rapid economic development among all the developing countries during the 1970s and the 1980s, has finally progressed toward democratization to a significant extent.

Some students of democracy may raise a question that the author's thesis is premature and his conclusion too hasty. Such a "wait-and-see" attitude is understandable. But Koreans do have an inheritance of many political experiences in conformity with the democratic culture (see Chapter Seven). They too have the determination and commitment to full realization of democracy, indefatigably challenging their authoritarian government. In fact, they have finally realized democracy upon the embarkation of the Sixth Republic, following the compromise among political parties, the adoption of a democratic constitution, a direct popular election of the president and the members of the National Assembly. For the first time in the forty years of the Republic's history, opposition parties experienced to gain a majority of the legislative seats and restored the right to legislative hearing and investigation, thereby probing into illegitimacy of the December 12, 1980 coup for the Fifth Republic, the Kwangju incident, former President Chun's sincere apology and a series of investigations on a variety of corruption incidents committed during the Fifth Republic. All of the basic freedoms of speech, press, assembly, and religion began to be fully restored and all of the basic rights, due process, and equal opportunities continued to be reinstated.

Chapter Seven will examine to what extent Korea had been subject to the patron-client political culture and yet had the inheritance of the democratic political institutions and processes. Chapter Eight will examine how democratization has taken place in Korea on the basis of a political satellite model and a threshold model and how patron-client politics is being replaced by group politics.

Notes

1. For the Constitution of the Union of Soviet Socialist Republics, see Vadim Medish (1984: 318-40).
2. For the Constitution of the Democratic People's Republic of Korea, see Tai Sung An (1983: 213-244).
3. Gastil did an excellent job in defending his research against hasty criticisms of other scholars and explained his rationale for how and why he used those twenty-five political rights and civil liberties variables. See Gastil (1987: 76-96).

Chapter 7 Patron-Client Politics and the Democratic Legacy

Chapter Seven will examine three major theses that: 1) patron-client politics had been prevalent in Korea; 2) nevertheless, no society is completely oriented to either patron-client politics or democratic group politics; both patron-client politics and democratic group politics, in fact, do co-exist in all societies with different degrees of their combination; 3) the prevalence of patron-client politics notwithstanding, Korea has inherited the democratic legacy, which has laid the philosophical and behavioral foundation for struggles for democratization. It is a fallacy to suggest that democratic societies are to complete group politics what non-democratic developing countries are to complete patron-client politics.

Patron-Client Politics

Politics is often viewed as a subsystem of a broad social system. As a subsystem, politics is determined by norms, values, behaviors, and expectations prevailing in the society. When the society is characterized as a patriarchal order, politics is inevitably governed by the patron-client political culture. Korea, which had been pervaded by a patriarchal political order for centuries in the past, had been governed by it upon the inception of its republic in 1948 until the mid-1980s. The patron-client politics at the national level can be explained by the reciprocal and mutually beneficial relationship between the president as the chief patron and relevant others in the bureaucracy, the legislative, the judiciary, the government party, the mass media, industries, and the military as his clients. The relevant others in the major network, in turn, become patrons to the clients in the regional and local network. The entire political system is intricately related to patron-client politics.[1]

The Patriarchal Bureaucracy

The President of Korea as the chief of the Executive Branch, monopolizes the power to appoint his major clients to cabinet secretaries and agency directors. In return for the position, power, and status, they tend to show absolute loyalty to their patron, the president. Dependent on the patronage of executive ministers are their immediate subordinates and aides. The patron-client linkage then goes down all the way to the lowest level of the local administration. This leads to vertical and particular bureaucratic loyalty. Job security is more attributed to satisfying one's superiors than one's loyalty to organization and one's dedication to successful accomplishment of tasks. Promotion is more dependent on the personal considerations of patronage approval than on objective criteria such as merit, skills, and job performance. The patronage-based hiring, firing, and promoting systems tend to ridicule the civil service and merit systems. The power to define, maintain, revise, and respect or ignore the civil service code is "vested in the president rather than in the formal legal system" (Jacobs, 1985: 18-23).

Executive decision-making seems to be sound and rational and carried out by differentiated political and administrative staffs. The cabinet, of course, holds periodic and regular meetings twice a week and "advises" the president along specialized lines. But during the Third and Fourth Republics President Park vetoed or ignored the decisions of both staff and cabinet, absented himself from cabinet meetings, and went over cabinet heads, making his own informal contacts and decisions on an individual, personal patronage basis and thereby ridiculing the entire formal decision-making apparatus.

> The multitude of executive agencies and boards, many imitatives of American decision-making, such as the National Security Council, Audit Boards, and Inspectorate, were under presidential control or review, serving as both buffer and counter to any potentially independent cabinet initiative. Simultaneously, interagency bickering, so typical of patrimonial bureaucracies, dependent as they are on the grace of a patrimonial president for prebends, enabled the Korean President to neutralize potentially meaningful staff opposition to his actions. In sum, presidents, especially Park, have been able to consolidate executive initiative in their own hands on a larger scale and more efficiently--that is, in a more modern way--than was ever possible in the past (Jacobs, 1985: 17).

Nevertheless, cabinet members would not submit resignations from their positions, which provided them with power, prestige, and money. They would rather maintain their positions and power by demonstrating blind loyalty to their patron and by aggressively campaigning for his re-election.

The Minister of Home Affairs becomes the *de facto* campaign director for the elections of the president. The nationwide, organized police force under his command is fully mobilized to disturb opposition party campaigns and to persuade voters to go to the polls for the government party. The Minister of Culture and Information becomes the *de facto* public relations (PR) director for the president. The Minister of the Treasury becomes the *de facto* campaign fund-raising director. The Minister of National Defense mobilizes the military personnel to participate in voting for his patron. The Ministers of Education, Health, and Social Affairs, Construction, Agriculture and Forestries bestow a variety of benefits--scholarships, free medical care, road-building, distribution of fertilizers and other goodies--to secure the victory of their patron.

The guarantee of winning in the election and re-elections of the same president and his political party National Assemblymen had become so paramount that local autonomy and self-government had never been granted and implemented until the year of 1991. For only nine years from 1952 to 1961 the elections of legislative councilmen had been held in the provinces, cities, and counties south of Han River. The elections of their counterparts north of Han River were not allowed until 1956 and lasted until 1961. However, chief executives of all local governments--governors, city mayors, county chiefs--had been consistently appointed by the Minister of Home Affairs of the central government upon the consent of the president except for nine months of the Second Republic (1960-1961).

The preference of the appointment of local heads to popular elections may be traced to President Rhee's embarrassing experience in the presidential election in 1956. As Table 7-1 shows, Syngman Rhee was elected the second-term president of the republic in 1952 with 62.4 percent and 76.8 percent of the urban and rural popular votes, respectively, against three opposition candidates. President Rhee felt so secure in the forthcoming election for his third-term presidency that upon the demand of opposition parties he allowed the Local Autonomy Law to be amended in 1956. The amended law authorized all local chiefs of cities, counties, and towns except

Table 7-1 Preference of the Appointment of Local Heads to Direct Popular Election

	Percent of Votes for Presidential Candidates				Number of Presidential Candidates
	For the Gov't Party (President Rhee)			Opposition Parties	
	Urban	Rural	Total	Total	
2nd term under local chiefs appointed (8/5/1952)	62.4	76.8	74.6	11.3	4
3rd term under local chiefs elected by voters (5/15/1956)	23.5	72.9	69.9	30.0	2
4th term under local chiefs appointed (3/15/1960)	79.6	91.9	88.6	0.0	1

Source: The Central Election Management Committee (CEMC)(1973a)

provincial governors to be directly elected by the voters rather than appointed by himself.

The outcome of the May 15, 1956 presidential election shocked President Rhee because his popular vote in the urban areas declined from 62.4 percent in 1952 to 23.5 percent in 1956, whereas his rural vote declined from 76.8 percent in 1952 to 69.9 percent in 1956. Among many plausible causes for the decline in the percentage of popular votes for the incumbent President Rhee were the direct popular election of all local chiefs and the subsequent lack of their obligations to campaign for President Rhee's re-election.

This was the main reason why President Rhee amended the Local Autonomy Law in preparation for the 1960 presidential election. Reverting back to the appointment of all local chief executives, coupled with the mobilization of police and alleged election riggings helped Rhee to be elected the fourth-term president with a whopping 79.6 percent and 91.9 percent in the urban and rural areas, respectively, in the March 1960 election. It was widely known that the survival and job security of the appointed local chiefs might well be greatly dependent on the higher proportion of popular votes in their constituencies in favor of the president and his political party in the election. This was the main reason why local self-government had not been implemented throughout the Third, Fourth, and Fifth Republics.

Table 7-2 The National Assembly Election Outcomes: 1963-1988

	Number of Registered Voters (1,000)	Percent Popular Votes (%)	Percent Gov't Party (%)	Percent and Number of Seats Received by the Gov't Party Urban	Rural	Percent Population Distribution Urban	Rural	Number of Parties in Competition
1963	13,344	73.7	33.5	54.0 (24)	67.2 (96)	28.3	71.7	12
1967	14,717	78.9	50.6	47.8 (24)	67.1 (96)	33.9	66.1	11
1971	16,616	76.5	48.9	43.6 (25)	58.2(108)	43.1	56.9	8
1973	15,690	75.1	38.7	49.8 (15)	55.8 (54)	48.4	51.6	7
1975	19,489	80.0	31.7	41.6 (15)	56.8 (56)	57.3	42.7	4
1981	20,090	78.4	35.6	NA	NA	62.9	37.1	15
1985	23,987	84.6	35.3	NA	NA	65.0	35.0	9
1988	26,198	75.8	34.0	30.4(121)	40.4(103)	NA	NA	14

Source: The CEMC (1973a, 1973b and 1980)

Article 109 of the Constitution of the Third Republic stipulates that "local self-government bodies shall deal with matters pertaining to the welfare of local residents, manage properties, and may establish, within the limit of laws and ordinances, rules and regulations regarding local self-government. The kinds of local self-government bodies shall be determined by law." Article 110 includes a council as a legislative body of the local self-government. Nevertheless, President Park, as the chief patron, and his clients, government party National Assemblymen in collusion with the cabinet members and local government chief executives, postponed its implementation in clear violation of the constitution of the Third Republic.

The 1972 Yushin constitution of the Fourth Republic explicitly prohibited the restoration of local self-government. Article 30 of the Supplementary Rules reads that "local councils under this Constitution shall not be formed until the unification of the fatherland shall have been achieved." The prohibition of local self-government equally became the imperative for the survival of Chun Doo Whan and his clients, such that upon the inception of the Fifth Republic an excuse for its postponement was justified in the 1980 constitution. Article 10 of the Supplementary Provisions stipulates that "Local councils prescribed by this Constitution shall be established on a phased basis taking into account the degree of financial self-reliance attained by local governments and the dates for their establishment shall be determined by law."

Securing a majority of the National Assembly seats by the government party has been an equally important concern for the chief patron, the president, and his clients. Throughout the history of the National Assembly elections, a salient pattern of voting behavior can be identified. As Table 7-2 indicates, the government party has consistently received more popular votes in the rural areas than in the urban areas, whereas opposition parties gained more popular votes from the urban areas. The more urbanized an election district becomes, the lower the voting turnout is for the government party. Ironically, urbanization in Korea has been rapidly increasing, for example, from 28.3 percent in 1960 to 65.0 percent in 1985.

The survival imperative for the president and the government party members became so desperate that they began to develop several creative devices. One of them was to maintain malapportionment in the National Assembly election districts in favor of pro-government rural counties and towns. Consequently, unequal distribution of population between urban and rural election districts became very salient.

Table 7-3 shows the juxtaposition of some selected larger counties and towns with some smaller ones in population. Duk Hwang Town of Geong Ju city, for example, had a population of 495 that accounted for only 1.0 percent of Ga Zwa town of Inchon city. Pyong Lim Towns One and Two of Chung Mu city had a population equivalent to only 1.4 and 1.8 percent of the population in Suk Nam and Doma Town One of Inchon city, respectively. Six smaller counties in Gang Won, Choong Nam, and Gyong Buk pro-government provinces had a population that was on average only 15 percent that of some larger counties such as Dong Bu, Eui Wang, Mee Gum, and Goon Po of Gyeong Gi province and Song Jung of Jeon Nam province. Inversely speaking, some ten larger towns had a population on average 62.6 times as many as some ten smaller towns as of 1986. Seven large subblocks had populations 7.1 times as many as several smaller ones.

Table 7-3 witnesses the thesis of malapportionment between pro-government rural and anti-government urban National Assembly election districts: over 36 percent of the election districts in the urban areas had populations over 300,000, whereas only 4.8 percent of the rural districts had the same size of population; fifty percent of the urban districts had population of 200,000 to 299,999, while 75.8 percent of the rural districts had population of only 100,000 to 199,999. Urban districts had an average of 279,543 people, whereas

Patron-Client Politics and the Democratic Legacy   227

Table 7-3 Malapportionment in the National Assembly Election Districts in Favor of the Government Party in 1986

	Largest (L)	Smallest (S)		Average Ratio (L/S)
Towns (Dong):	40,000-49,999	Up to 1,000		
Ga Zwa, Inchon	48,467	Duk Hwang, Geong Ju	495	
Suk Nam, Inchon	42,107	Pyong Lim #1, Chung Mu	758	
Doma #1, Inchon	42,095	Pyong Lim #2, Chung Mu	590	62.6
Ung Ahm, Seoul	40,033	Back Shin, Sam Chun Po	915	
Six additional largest towns		Six additional smallest towns		
Sub-blocks (Eup):	50,000-65,000	5,000-9,999		
Dong Bu, Geong Gi	63,271	Him Hwa, Gang Won	5,258	
Eui Wang, Geong Gi	55,003	Chul Won, Gang Won	7,260	
Mee Gum, Geong Gi	53,519	Gan Sung, Gang Won	9,027	
Goon Po Geong Gi	52,710	Sung Gu, Choong Nam	8,300	7.1
Song Jung, Jeon Nam	60,167	Chung Song, Geong Buk	8,843	
Chang Sung Po, Geong Nam	58,715	Ha Yang, Geong Buk	9,074	
Mil Yang, Geong Nam	51,060			

Size of Population	Large Urban Districts (L)		Small Rural Districts (S)		Total
	Number	Percent	Number	Percent	
Over 400,000	2	6.7	1	1.6	3
300,000-399,999	9	30.0	2	3.2	11
200,000-299,999	15	50.0	10	16.1	25
100,000-199,999	4	13.3	47	75.9	51
Below 100,000	0	0.0	2	3.2	2
Total	30	100.0	62	100.0	92
Average popul. per district	279,543		171,188		

Source: Adapted from Pae (1988a: 127)

rural districts had an average of 171,188. Urban underrepresentation and rural overrepresentation have consistently favored the government party and its chief patron, the president of the republic, in their respective elections (Pae, 1988a: 125-126).

A second major creative idea for the president and his chief clients to maintain their power was the establishment of *pan-sang-hoe*, a neighborhood meeting at the lowest governmental level, which consisted of about ten to fifteen rural residential households since 1976. A former Minister of Home Affairs stated that *pan-sang-hoe*, a grassroot local organization, provided a democratic forum for average households to deliver their grievances and other kinds of input to the government. As of May 1986 a total of 1,364,000 petitions and complaints had been suggested to the provincial and central government offices through the *pan-sang-hoe*. Among them as many as 82 percent had been positively taken care of (*Korean Herald*, May 27, 1986). A real objective of *pan-sang-hoe*, however, was the government's deep penetration into rural residential areas with the help of local government administrators to secure rural votes. Impressed by the success of *pan-sang-hoe* operations in mobilizing rural voters for the government party, the Ministry of Home Affairs recently announced that *pan-sang-hoe* should be organized at worksites and factory dormitories in the urban areas, too (*Korea Herald*, May 27, 1986).

A third creative idea for the maintenance of patronage politics is to apply differential allocations of the central government's subsidies to local governments on the basis of which local governments--provinces and cities--are more favorable toward the incumbent president and his political party in the elections and more important for their power maintenance. Table 7-4 supports this thesis. The figures on the left half of the table show per capita expenditures of all the provinces and major cities of 1980-1981, which was computed from the total amount of executed revenues, excluding subsidies of the central government divided by the population of respective local governments. The figures in the center show per capita expenditures of the local governments, this time taking into account the central government's subsidies. The figures on the right side show the financial aid from the central government.

We can identify greater differences among the local governments in the amount of per capita expenditures when the central government's subsidies were included. For example, per capita expenditure of Weon Ju city was 58,814 won, whereas that of Ui Jong Bu city was only 9,305 won. The expenditure gap between these two cities was 49,509 won. When the central government's subsidies were included, the gap between the top and bottom cities showed 68,749 won. This indicates that the central government's subsidies exacerbated rather than alleviated the gap between local governments. Some local governments such as Gan Reung, Weon Ju, Chun Cheon, and Geong Ju gained financial benefits much greater

Table 7-4 Per Capita Expenditures of Major Cities and Provinces with the Central Government's Subsidies: 1980-1981

Major Cities:	Subsidies Excluded	Subsidies Included	Financial Gain (%)
Weon Ju	58,814	65,051	6,237 (10.6%)
Gang Reung	54,441	83,950	29,509 (54.2%)
Seoul	48,222	51,367	3,145 (5.5%)
Mog Po	42,202	51,590	9,388 (22.2%)
Ulsan	40,942	45,033	4,091 (9.1%)
Pusan	40,343	43,208	2,865 (7.1%)
Inchon	35,549	47,746	2,197 (6.1%)
Cheon Ju	35,454	54,264	18,810 (53.0%)
Chun Cheon	35,337	57,181	21,844 (61.8%)
Gun San	32,353	45,676	13,323 (41.1%)
Yeo Su	31,505	50,071	18,566 (58.9%)
Daegu	30,722	35,869	5,147 (16.7%)
Chon Ju	29,026	45,869	16,843 (58.0%)
Che Ju	26,680	44,165	17,485 (65.5%)
Dae Jeon	26,199	34,859	8,660 (33.0%)
Geong Ju	26,031	54,238	28,207(108.3%)
Chung Mu	24,447	29,578	5,131 (20.9%)
Sung Nam	24,121	29,853	5,732 (23.7%)
Chin Ju	22,906	35,891	12,985 (56.6%)
Masan	22,727	30,914	8,187 (36.0%)
Sog Cho	22,575	51,548	28,973(128.3%)
Jin Hae	22,008	40,366	18,358 (83.4%)
Po Hang	14,651	30,938	16,287(111.1%)
Sun Cheon	13,192	33,140	19,948(151.2%)
Gwang Ju	10,850	15,201	4,351 (40.1%)
Ui Jong Bu	9,305	16,898	7,593 (81.6%)
Average	30,023	42,864	12,840 (42.7%)

Provinces:			
Che Ju	22,335	45,869	23,534(105.3%)
S. Gyeong Sang	21,342	41,389	20,047 (93.9%)
Gyeong Gii	20,698	31,618	10,920 (52.7%)
N. Gyeong Sang	17,274	45,325	28,051(162.3%)
Gang Won	16,499	45,447	28,948(175.4%)
N. Jeon Ra	15,538	37,520	21,982(141.4%)
S. Jeon Ra	14,734	38,190	23,456(159.1%)
S. Choong Chung	13,445	29,243	15,798(117.5%)
Average	17,733	39,325	21,592(121.7%)

Source: Adapted from *The Statistical Year Book of 1980/1981* published by each city and province.

than other local governments. Moreover, all the provincial governments on average gained a much higher percentage of subsidies (121.7%) than the cities (42.7%). This clearly indicates that the pro-government rural areas excluding large cities in the provinces gained more benefits from the central government's subsidies than the predominantly anti-government urban areas.

The Patriarchal Legislature

The president of the republic concurrently holds the presidency of the government political party. As the party president, he is empowered to choose and nominate all of his party's candidates for the National Assembly. Aspirants and hopefuls for becoming government party's National Assemblymen are not allowed to compete against one another in primaries, because the primaries are not adopted and implemented. Therefore, they have no opportunities for appealing directly to the voters for popular choice in the primaries. Only those who are chosen and nominated by the president, with a bountiful amount of campaign funds, are allowed to compete with the candidates of opposition political parties who are also nominated by their party bosses without primary competition. In return for nomination, receipt of campaign funds, and subsequent victory in the election, the government party Assemblymen must show complete loyalty and obedience to the president in casting their ballots on their committees and on the floor.

Malapportionment, *pan-sang-hoe*, favorable financial aid to local governments, and a host of subtle strategies could result in the securing of a comfortable majority of the National Assembly seats by the government party. It goes without saying that the government party Assemblymen and the national Assembly as a whole tend to be demoted to legislative maids to the president, blindly passing bills and programs initiated by the Executive.

Table 7-5 shows that the number of bills proposed by the Executive and subsequent legislation exceeds that of the legislative's proposals consistently throughout the entire span of time from the first National Assembly to the eleventh, except in the case of the sixth Assembly. Moreover, the number of bills proposed by the Executive and subsequently legislated by the Assembly increases along the passage of time in each republic. This clearly indicates that the more strongly established the patron-client network becomes with the passage of time centered around the chief patron, the

Table 7-5 Bills Proposed by the National Assembly (NA) and the Executive

Republic	By the Legislative		By the Executive		Total	
	Proposed	Legislated	Proposed	Legislated	Proposed	Legislated
1st Republic:						
1st NA						
5/30/48-	89	43	145	106	234	149
5/30/50	38.0	28.8	61.9	71.1	100%	100%
2nd NA						
6/9/50 -	182	78	216	138	398	216
5/29/54	45.7	36.1	54.3	63.9	100%	100%
3rd NA						
6/9/54 -	169	72	241	85	410	157
5/29/58	41.2	45.8	58.8	54.2	100%	100%
4th NA						
6/7/58 -	120	31	202	44	322	75
7/25/60	37.2	41.3	62.8	58.7	100%	100%
2nd Republic:						
5th NA						
8/8/60 -	137	30	159	40	296	70
5/3/61	42.6	42.8	53.8	57.2	100%	100%
3rd Republic:						
6th NA						
12/17/63 -	416	178	242	154	658	332
3/16/67	63.2	53.6	36.7	46.3	100%	100%
7th NA						
7/10/67 -	244	123	291	234	535	357
4/27/71	45.6	34.4	54.9	65.5	100%	100%
8th NA						
7/26/71 -	43	16	95	23	138	39
10/17/72	31.1	41.0	68.8	58.9	100%	100%
4th Republic:						
9th NA						
3/12/73 -	154	84	479	460	633	544
3/11/79	24.3	15.4	75.6	84.5	100%	100%
10th NA						
3/12/79 -	5	3	124	97	129	100
10/27/80	5.1	3.0	94.8	97.0	100%	100%
5th Republic:*						
11th NA						
4/11/81 -	76	32	77	60	153	92
12/6/84	49.6	34.7	50.3	65.2	100%	100%

Source: General Affairs, *The National Assembly Report* (various years)

*Incomplete in the collection of data for the 11th Assembly

greater the role of the Chief Executive tends to be in the initiative of proposing various government policies and programs. Taking into account the fact that more than half of the bills proposed by the legislature were initiated by the government party Assemblymen on behalf of the Executive, the preponderance of power of the chief executive in the legislation becomes self-evident.

The president's satisfaction with the legislative role of the government party members in the National Assembly was such that he had had no reason to exercise the power of veto and pocket veto against the legislature. A comparative study of the frequency of presidential vetoes of the United States and Korea can demonstrate to what extent the principle of separation between the Executive and the Legislative and the subsequent mutual checks and balances between the two branches have been honored in these two countries.

Table 7-6 shows the number of regular vetoes, pocket vetoes, and total vetoes exercised by the presidents of the United States, and the number of vetoes overridden by Congress. Only six of the thirty-nine presidents did not use the veto power. Five of them were presidents prior to the 1850s. But except for President Garfield, assassinated shortly after the inauguration, all of the presidents since 1853 have resorted to veto power against the legislation passed by Congress in defiance of the recommendation of the presidents. They have exercised a total of 2,449 vetoes, an average of sixty-three vetoes per president. This clearly demonstrates that Congress did not pass legislation at the behest of the presidents in the United States.

On the contrary, Table 7-7 shows an opposite trend in the exercise of veto power in Korea. Former President Rhee used his veto power on forty-two occasions against the National Assembly, which in turn overrode his vetoes twenty-four times (equivalent of 51 percent). But the number of vetoes diminished to only three during the Third Republic under President Park and then to zero from 1972 until 1988.

C. Herman Pritchett suggested five major reasons why the President of the United States is not able to command Congress and therefore has the obligation to exercise veto power against Congress in major legislation in case of conflict with his own legislative versions.

　1. Separation of power makes it possible for the opposition party to be in control of one or both of the houses.

　2. There may be substantial opposition to the president within his own congressional party, and he may not even be on

Table 7-6 Presidential Vetoes of the USA: 1789-1988

Years	President	Regular Vetoes	Pocket Vetoes	Total Vetoes	Vetoes Overridden Number	Overridden Percent
1789-1797	George Washington	2	--	2	--	--
1797-1801	John Adams	--	--	0	--	--
1801-1809	Thomas Jefferson	--	--	0	--	--
1809-1817	James Madison	5	2	7	--	--
1817-1825	James Monroe	1	--	1	--	--
1825-1829	John Quincy Adams	--	--	1	--	--
1829-1837	Andrew Jackson	5	7	12	--	--
1837-1841	Martin Van Buren	--	1	1	--	--
1841	William H. Harrison	--	--	0	--	--
1841-1845	John Tyler	6	4	10	1	10.1
1845-1849	James K. Polk	2	1	3	--	--
1849-1850	Zachary Taylor	--	--	0	--	--
1850-1853	Millard Fillmore	--	--	0	--	--
1853-1857	Franklin Pierce	9	--	9	5	55.5
1857-1861	James Buchanan	4	3	7	--	--
1861-1865	Abraham Lincoln	2	5	7	--	--
1865-1869	Andrew Johnson	21	8	29	15	51.7
1869-1877	Ulysses S. Grant	45	48	93	4	4.3%
1877-1881	Rutherford B. Hayes	12	1	13	1	7.6%
1881	James A. Garfield	--	--	0	--	--
1881-1885	Chester A. Arthur	4	8	12	1	8.3%
1885-1889	Grover Cleveland	304	110	414	2	.5%
1889-1893	Benjamin Harrison	19	25	44	1	2.3%
1892-1897	Grover Cleveland	42	128	170	5	2.9%
1897-1901	William McKinley	6	36	42	--	--
1901-1909	Theodore Roosevelt	42	40	82	1	1.2%
1909-1913	William H. Taft	30	9	39	1	2.5%
1913-1921	Woodrow Wilson	33	11	44	6	13.6%
1921-1923	Warren G. Harding	5	1	6	--	--
1923-1929	Calvin Coolidge	20	30	50	4	8.0%
1929-1933	Herbert Hoover	21	16	37	3	8.1%
1933-1945	Franklin D. Roosevelt	372	263	635	9	1.4%
1945-1953	Harry S. Truman	180	70	250	12	4.8%
1953-1961	Dwight D. Eisenhower	73	108	181	2	1.1%
1961-1963	John F. Kennedy	12	9	21	--	--
1963-1969	Lyndon B. Johnson	16	14	30	--	--
1969-1974	Richard M. Nixon	26	17	43	7	16.3%
1974-1977	Gerald R. Ford	48	18	66	12	18.2%
1977-1981	Jimmy Carter	13	18	31	2	6.4%
1981-1988	Ronald Reagan	35	28	63	9	14.2%
Total		1,410	1,039	2,449	101	4.1%
Average		36	27	63	3	4.7%

Source: *Presidential Vetoes, 1789-1976* compiled by Senate Library (1978: ix); for the case of President Lyndon B. Johnson, *Congressional Quarterly Almanac, 1968* (1968:23); for the data of the remaining presidents from the White House Records Office.

particularly good terms with his party's leadership in Congress.
3. The seniority system gives committee chairmen the powers of small-time monarchies.
4. The unwieldy size of the House and the principle of unlimited debate in the Senate do not facilitate expeditious action.
5. The effectiveness of both majority- and minority-party leadership in both houses is often quite limited (Pritchett, 1979: 17).

Table 7-7 Presidential Vetoes of Korea: 1948-1988

Years	President	Regular Vetoes	Pocket Vetoes	Total Vetoes	Vetoes Number	Overridden Percent
1948-1950	Rhee	14	0	14	6	42.8%
1950-1954	Rhee	25	1	26	18	69.2%
1954-1958	Rhee	3	1	4	0	0.0%
1958-1960	Rhee	0	3	3	0	0.0%
1963-1972	Park	3	0	3	0	0.0%
1972-1974	Park	1	0	1	0	0.0%
1981-1988	Chun	0	0	0	0	0.0%

Source: Data for Rhee and Park from Chung Il Hahn (1969, Tables 1 through 8 in Chapter 8); *The Dong A Daily,* July 15, 1988, p. 3.

None of these factors has been applied to the case of Korea. During the embryonic stage of the republic when political parties were organized, President Rhee had consistently denied the necessity of political parties. His lukewarm attitude toward political parties and lack of leadership in unifying his followers in and out of the National Assembly was such that two parties--In-House and Out-of-House--were chartered and registered with the identical name of Liberal Party. The incompatibility between the two on various issues was too great for them to unite themselves into one. This resulted in securing only 27.5 percent and 11.4 percent of the National Assembly seats by his Liberal Party in the 1948 and 1950 elections, respectively. Lack of party cohesion was also observed in the In-House Liberal Party. On January 18, 1952 when the proposed amendment for direct popular election of the president was voted in the National Assembly, the In-House Liberal Party was split into 19 votes in favor of and 74 in opposition to the proposal. Lack of party cohesion and discipline was such that President Rhee could not help but exercise vetoes on forty-seven occasions during twelve years of his tenure as the president.

From 1963, however, the president began to have a tight control over the government political party in the matters of nomination of the National Assembly candidates, financial aid for their election campaigns, and the party organization. Malapportionment, *pan-sang-hoe*, and tight control of local governments by appointment of all local chief executives, coupled with a bountiful amount of campaign funds, helped the president secure a majority of the National Assembly seats for his loyal lieutenants. They, in return, passed legislation for their patron, the president. This resulted in the sharp decline in the number of presidential vetoes. No incident of presidential veto had been observed from 1972 until 1988.

The Patriarchal Political Parties

Political parties in the Western European countries and the United States are organized and engaged in election competitions primarily on the basis of policies and issues. Political parties in Korea have been organized around the center of party leaders as the patrons and followers as their clients without their commonly agreed policies and issues. Because of lack of the commitment to the mutually accepted policies and programs, leadership competition within each party in Korea often has led to dissolution of the party, or establishment of new contending parties, which began to sling mud at one another whose leaders and members were ironically under the same party label not long ago. Issue differences among political parties may be plotted on the ideological map often referred to as left-center-right. As Table 7-8 demonstrates, Western European democracies like Great Britain, the Federal Republic of Germany, France, and Italy have distinct political parties which fall into either left, center, or right in terms of a left-to-right ideological spectrum.

Parties on the left in the Western European democracies are by no means identical with one another. Roy C. Macridis suggests that even their Socialist parties differ with regards to the pace with which the reforms they advocate are to be implemented and with regard to the kind of socialism they plan to construct.

Table 7-8 Political Parties in Terms of a Left-to-Right Ideological Spectrum

Western European Countries & Election Time	Left	Center	Right	Remarks / Significant Differences
Great Britain (6/1983)	Labour Party 209 of 650 32.2%	Social Democratic Party/Liberal Party Alliance 23 3.5%	Conservative Party 397 61.1%	Conservative Party in Government
Federal Republic of Germany (1/1987)	Social Democratic Party 186 of 490 37.9%	Free Democratic Party (FDP) 46 (9.4%)	Christian Democratic Union(CDU) 174 (35.5%) Christian Social Union (CSU) 49 (10.0%)	A Coalition of CDU/CSU/FDP
France (3/1986)	Socialist Party 276 of 577 47.8% Communist Party 27 (4.7%)	Union of French Democracy (UFD) 126 20.8%	Gaullist Party 129 22.4%	A Coalition of Gaullist and UFD with other Right Parties
Italy (6/1987)	Communist Party 177 of 630 26.6% Socialist Party 94 (14.3%)	Social Movement Party 35 (5.9%) Social Democratic Party 17 (3.0%) Liberal Party 11 (2.1%)	Christian Democratic Party (CDP) 234 (34.3%)	A Five-Party Coalition
USA		Democratic Party Republican Party		Differences Identified
South Korea		Government Party Opposition Parties		A Unimodal Belief system Same Issues

Source: European Publications Limited (1989: Vols. I and II)

> After a long pause the Labor party in England seems to be reasserting a rapid expansion of the socialist sector in the economy, while the French socialists, after a period of drastic nationalizations and income redistribution undertaken in 1981-1983, have reached a pause and reconsideration, while their electoral strength seems to be waning. The German Social Democrats abandoned their commitment to nationalizations and follow an opportunistic path. The Scandinavian Socialist parties emphasize welfare workers' participation in management and ownership, and income redistribution and equalization but not nationalization (Macridis, 1986: 68).

However, political parties in Western European countries demonstrate distinct differences in their socioeconomic positions and especially in the role of the state with respect to the production and distribution of goods and services. To the left, Communist and socialist parties advocate national economic planning, nationalization of major industries and other economic activities, extensive redistribution of the wealth by means of progressive income taxes, and the promotion of various welfare programs. Their ultimate goal is to minimize income inequalities and to maximize income equalities. Communist and Socialist parties appeal to those who would gain significant benefits from such measures. Therefore, the British Labor party, the German Social Democratic party, and the French and Italian Socialist and Communist parties have a strong link with such groups of people as the labor workers, the small farmers, the underprivileged, the poor, the unemployed, and the aged.

The center parties often take an eclectic stance, and their programs are often a cross between the positions espoused by Conservative and Liberal parties. They often vacillate and choose different propositions at different times and "as a result appear to be the least ideological" (Macridis, 1985: 69). But the center parties favor neither radical revolution from the existing political and economic system nor complete individualism and *laissez faire* economy. The center parties in general endorse moderate reforms, thereby strengthening the existing system. The British Social Democratic party and Liberal party, the German Free Democratic party, the Union of French Democracy, and the Italian Liberal party fit this pattern (Table 7-8).

The Western European political parties on the right are not identical in the scope, extent, and pace of programs they endorse, either. But they share a common stance on political, economic, and social issues: the opposition to state intervention in the pursuit of happiness of individuals; the minimizing of taxes as a means for income redistribution so as to oppose the adoption of progressive income taxes; the advocacy of free enterprise and the market economy; the extolling of private initiative and ingenuity; the espousing of individualism rather than collective well-being; less government spending on welfare programs; decentralization; and the preference of the public choice model to the urban reform model for various public services.[2] The Conservative party of England, the Christian Democratic party of West Germany, the Gaullists and their allies of France, and the Christian Democratic party of Italy are the examples on the right.

The American party system is, however, different from its counterparts of the Western European democracies in the scope of class consciousness and ideological conflict. The American parties can be characterized as "moderate, centrist, and pragmatic, with only modest ideological cohesion and voting discipline--especially compared with European political parties" (Burns et al., 1989: 189). Both Democratic and Republican parties are moderate in their policies and leadership, although the Republican party has slightly shifted to the right in the 1980s and 1990s (Chubb and Peterson, 1985).

Danielson and Murphy suggest several factors for the absence of fundamental differences between Democratic and Republican parties in the United States. They are: America's relative lack of class consciousness, perhaps due to the absence of a feudal tradition; the relative prosperity of the economy; the existence of a frontier to absorb dissident elements; the constitutional and legal ideals of egalitarianism without granting noble titles to any citizen; the political castration of radical movements; the diversity of American backgrounds, outlooks, aspirations, and loyalties referred to often as a melting pot; and the ever-increasing number of the middle class whose political standards become the dominant ones widely accepted (1983: 171). As a result, two parties remain closely in the center of the left-to-right ideological spectrum (See Table 7-8).

> Both parties are likely to make appeals to citizens of all social classes and geographical areas. Both accept the basic,

though vague, principles of constitutional democracy. Both reject socialism and endorse a free enterprise system modified by a degree of governmental regulations (Danielson and Murphy, 1983: 170).

Therefore, if the Democratic party begins to drift toward the left too far, its presidential candidate is not likely to win the election. To the contrary, if the Republican party attempts to move farther away from the center toward the right, its presidential candidate is likely to lose the election.

While the two parties remain in the center, the Democratic party is located on the left side, which is impressed as the more liberal and the Republican party on the right side of the center as the more conservative. Differences between the two parties were evidenced by a survey from the delegates to the Democratic and Republican national party conventions--a group that included members of Congress, governors, state and county party leaders, and other political activists. Herbert McCloskey and his colleagues highlighted differences between the two: "Democratic leaders typically display the strongest urge to elevate the lowborn, the uneducated, the deprived minorities, and the poor in general; they are more disposed to employ the nation's collective power to advance humanitarian and social welfare." On the other hand, "Republican leaders subscribe in greater measure to the simple practices of individualism, *laissez faire*, private incentives, frugality, hard working, responsibility and strengthening rather than the diminution of the economic and status distinction" (1960: 426-428).

All of the political parties in Korea are fundamentally different from the parties of Western Europe and the United States. When the party platforms of the government and opposition parties of all six republics of Korea are juxtaposed, two important findings can be identified.

> There is no significant difference between the parties in terms of the content of the platforms; and the party platforms are very broad and comprehensive so as to encompass every member of the society, resulting in no differences in social and economic composition of the parties (Pae, 1986: 175).[3]

Norman Jacobs characterizes the Korean political parties as "collectives of individuals who have banded together to enable a leader to attain and maintain power and reflect advantages for his followers." Party members do not view themselves as "representatives of geopolitical or class interest groups, but as representatives of their political selves" (1985: 26). This results in frequent defection of a patron and his clients from a political party, the establishing of their own separate party, or the merging of different parties into one, not on the basis of consensus on key issues and policies but on convenience and strategies to strengthen their own power and to win the election. A patriarchal party system can be witnessed by both government and opposition parties. Let me illustrate a few cases to see to what extent political parties are patriarchally organized.

Yun Po Sun, the president of the Second Republic, was awarded an honorary doctorate degree from a university in the United States for his "dedication and commitment to the promotion of democracy" in Korea throughout his political life. Of course, he fought President Park of the Third and Fourth Republics against his emergency measures, violations of human rights, and the suppression of basic freedoms. But Yun was equally concerned with keeping and enhancing his patriarchal party system in order to restore his presidency, which was forcefully and unconstitutionally taken away by General Park Chung Hee. During a period of ten years from 1963 to 1973, Yun Po Sun demonstrated an excellent example of patriarchal party politics by establishing his own political parties with his clients three separate times, each time with a different party name, consolidating his party with others on several occasions in vain, actually merging with other parties two times. His outstanding record of patronage politics can be vividly illustrated.

1. On March 22, 1962 Yun Po Sun announced the imperative for the establishment of a single, unified opposition party against the government one.
2. On January 27, 1963 he organized the Civil Rule Party (CRP). Soon the party suffered from factional strifes.
3. On February 6, 1963 the faction of the former Liberal Party defected from the CRP.
4. On July 5, 1963 Yun became aware of the importance of a united front of the opposition camp so as to win General Park in the forthcoming election. He announced no intention to accept his

nomination from the CRP as its presidential candidate. This encouraged the consolidation of other parties into a pan-national, united opposition party--the Party of the People (POP). Ironically, he later sought the party's presidential nomination. The newly merged party was inevitably split into the CRP and the POP.

    5. On March 3, 1965 Yun's CRP and the Democratic Party were consolidated into the Min Joong Party (MJP).

    6. On May 11, 1965 the MJP was split into Yun's CRP faction and anti-Yun faction.

    7. On July 28, 1965 Yun defected from the MJP against his own pledge of "allegiance and unity" to the party. The defection caused him to face automatic disqualification as an Assemblyman.

    8. On August 6, 1965 six additional Assemblymen as his loyal clients followed him in defection.

    9. On March 30, 1966 Yun organized the New Korea Party (NKP) with himself as the party head.

    10. About eight months later Yun reunited his NKP with the MJP into the New Democratic Party (NDP).

    11. On February 2, 1970 Yun defected from the NDP because of his defeat in the election of party leadership.

    12. On January 23, 1971 Yun organized a new political party called the "National Party" (NP). The NP, however, secured only one of the one hundred twenty-one party nominated candidates in the 1971 National Assembly election. The failure in securing less than 1 percent of the Assembly seats, and in maintaining a minimum number of local party branches as prescribed in the Political Party Law caused his party to become extinct on July 2, 1973 (CEMC: 1973a).

The patriarchal party system began to emerge again when martial law was lifted and replaced by the constitution of the Fifth Republic in 1980. President Chun soon began to adopt the "politics of reconciliation" and the "politics of dialogue." While Kim Dae Jung and twenty-three others were still deprived of political and civil rights under the charge of sedition in relation to the Kwangju incident, over five thousand were granted presidential amnesty (Hinton, 1983: 58-70). Client politicians loyal to Kim Dae Jung and Kim Young Sam were then allowed to organize the New Korea Democratic Party (NKDP) under the guidance of their two patron politicians. Twelve incumbent Assemblymen of the Korea Democratic Party under the leadership of Kim Jong Chul soon defected from their party to join the newly established NKDP. Their justification was "to help the more popularly supported NKDP speed up the democratization movement" (*Korea Herald*, December 20, 1984). But the real justification for betrayal of their former patron, Kim Jong Chul, and joining the NKDP was to gain more personal benefits and the guarantee of their winning in the 1985 National Assembly election under two more popular and charismatic patron politicians.

As Table 7-9 indicates, the Democratic Korea and the Korean National, which became the two major opposition parties in the 1981 election, lost a significant number of the Assembly seats in the 1985 election. On the other hand, the NKDP, which was less than three months old, was able to secure 67 seats in the February 12, 1985 election, becoming the second major party. What was more surprising than the outcome of the 1985 election was the defection of 31 out of the 34 incumbent Assemblymen of the Democratic Korea Party to the NKDP in less than three months after the 1985 election. The defected Assemblymen, of course, did not care about the constituents in their respective districts who elected them. Nor did the constituents care about the defection of the Assemblymen of their own choice. The NKDP's relative power in the National Assembly soon rose from 67, 24 percent of the total seats in February 1985, to 102, 36.9 percent in May 1985.

The anti-mainstream members of the NKDP, who did not belong to either one of the two Kim patronage factions, however, could not share the party's key positions and power due to their numerical disadvantages. Like chanting a sutra to cows, they advocated reform in the NKDP and demanded that the party president should announce the abolition of factional strifes and factional lineage and that policies should be adopted following open debate and decision on the floor. Being brushed aside, the party's twelve incumbent anti-mainstream Assemblymen revolted against two patrons and their clients, bolted from their party, and organized a minor party called "The People's Democratic Party" in December 1985 (*Korea Herald*, December 31, 1985). They soon disappeared from the partisan political arena because of their insignificant numerical strength.

The uncomfortable honeymoon between two Kim factions, however, could not keep the NKDP alive for long. Both Kim Dae Jung and Kim Young Sam repeated on several occasions that "the opposition needs to nominate a single presidential candidate at the

Table 7-9 Patriarchal Political Parties and Their Relative Strength in the National Assembly

Fifth Republic								Sixth Republic		
March 25, 1981			Feb. 12, 1985			5/85	12/85	April 26, 1988		
	D*	P*	T*	D	P	T	T	T	D	P	T
DJP	90	61	151	DJP 87	61	148	148	148	DJP 87	38	125
DKP	57	24	81	DKP 26	9	35	4 (-31)	4	PPD 54	16	70
KNP	18	7	25	KNP 15	5	20	20	20	RDP 46	13	59
CRP	2	-	2	NKDP 50	17	67	102 (+35)	90 (-12)	DRP 27	8	35
DSP	2	-	2	PDP				12	One Nation	1	-	1
NPP	2	-	2	Indep. 4	-	4	2	2	Indep. 9	-	9
Others	13	-	13	Others 2	-	2	0	0	-	-	-
Total	184	92	276	184	92	276	276	276	224	75	299

Two-thirds of the Assembly's seats were filled by direct popular election, with each of 92 districts electing two members in the Fifth Republic and with each of 224 districts electing one member in the Sixth Republic. No party could present more than one candidate per district. Of the additional one-third of the seats, two-thirds and one-half were allocated to the party gaining most votes by direct popular election in the Fifth and Sixth Republics, respectively, with the remaining one-third and one-half for other parties in proportion to seats won directly.

*D, P, and T stand for direct, proportional, and total elected seats

    DJP: Democratic Justice Party, the government party (headed by Chun Doo Hwan in the Fifth Republic and by Roh Tae Woo in the Sixth Republic)
    DKP: Democratic Korea Party (Yu Chee Song)
    KNP: Korea National Party (Kim Jong Chul)
    CRP: Civil Rule Party (Kim Eui Taek)
    DSP: Democratic Socialist Party (Ko Jeong Hoon)
    NPP: New Political Party
    NKDP: New Korea Democratic Party (Lee Min Woo)
    PDP: People's Democratic Party
    Indep.: Independents
    PPD: Party for Peace and Democracy (Kim Dae Jung)
    RDP: Reunification Democratic Party (Kim Young Sam)
    DRP: Democratic Republican Party (Kim Jong Pil)

next election" (*Korea Herald*, July 9, 1986). But the competition between the two became clear from the beginning of the NKDP's 1986 pan-national signature campaign for constitutional amendment for a direct popular election of the president in 1988. The two Kims, who led the two largest factions of the major opposition party, the

NKDP, emphasized time and again that they would maintain "cooperative ties with each other even after democratization be achieved." Nevertheless, the more convinced they were that the time favorable for the opposition party was coming due to more enthusiastic popular endorsement for the amendment for a direct popular election of the next president, the greater the intensity of competition between the two Kims became. While Kim Dae Jung's political rights were still suspended under a twenty-year prison term on sedition, his loyal clients attended every campaign rally Kim Young Sam attended, carrying portraits of Kim Dae Jung. Being aware of the inundation of Kim Dae Jung's portraits overwhelming Kim Young Sam, the two factions later had to negotiate on the number of portraits of the two Kims to be displayed during their campaign for the constitutional amendment.

The political ambition of the two Kims became evident with approaching 1988 election. In the first few campaign rallies, Kim Young Sam said that he was "not obsessed with the ambition to become the president." He would "instead devote himself to the development of the nation's democracy." But in later rallies he emphasized "the first and foremost goal of a political party lay in grasping power" (*Korea Herald*, April 30, 1986).

Kim Dae Jung also announced that if the ruling camp would accept the direct presidential election formula, he would not run for the presidency, even if he were granted amnesty and his civil rights restored (*Korea Herald*, November 15, 1986). Being granted amnesty and having his civil and political rights restored in July 1987, Kim Dae Jung grudgingly joined Kim Young Sam as a formal party member on August 8, 1987. Sincerely welcoming Kim Dae Jung into the party, Kim Young Sam proposed the party convention be held for the nomination of the party's presidential candidate by September 1987 so as to have a decent period of time for campaigning. Kim Dae Jung replied, "There will be no competition between the two Kims through a vote. A vote showdown should be avoided in selecting the candidate to prevent an image of intraparty discord" (*Korea Herald*, September 4, 1987). It was Kim Dae Jung, who was nominated the New Democratic Party's presidential candidate by an open competition over Kim Young Sam in 1970. It was not an open competition and a vote showdown but the numerical disadvantage that Kim Dae Jung this time decided not to follow the democratic procedural rule of the election of the party's presidential candidate by means of the party convention.

Nevertheless, Kim Dae Jung repeated, "He will never go against the people's aspirations to have one opposition candidate to challenge Mr. Roh Tae Woo (*Korea Herald*, September 2, 1987). According to a survey conducted by the *Korea Herald*, 69 percent of those answering indicated the importance of a single opposition candidate, and 80.6 percent expressed that the sooner one opposition candidate was chosen, the greater was the chance of winning in the general election (*Korea Herald*, September 26, 1987). Ironically, no less than three months after he joined the opposition party, Kim Dae Jung announced his decision to defect from the party, to organize his own party of Peace and Democracy, and to run for the presidency on October 29, 1987 (*Korea Herald*, October 29, 1987). No sooner than two years and two months after its inception the NKDP and its ninety Assemblymen were split into Kim Young Sam's Reunification Democratic Party and Kim Dae Jung's Peace and Democracy.

Carrot and Stick Techniques

Carrots as political rewards and sticks as punishments are two prominent modes of operation used by patrons of both the opposition and the government parties for the maintenance of their patriarchal systems. The patrons of opposition parties tend to primarily monopolize the power to wield carrot and stick techniques in the nomination of all National Assembly candidates and key positions in their parties. The patron of the government party tends to use a wide variety of carrots in appointments and decisions on various public policies and a wide range of sticks against those who challenge and disturb the patronage system.

A most recent example of the application of sticks in the case of the opposition party involved the election of the National Assembly Vice-Speakership. Kim Dae Jung, while being deprived of civil and political rights, wielded real power behind the scenes in the NKDP and thereby nominated his loyal client, Lee Yong-Hee to be elected as a Vice Speaker of the National Assembly. Representatives Cho Youn-Ha and Kim Ok-Sun, however, ignored the party order not to run, and Cho ironically secured Vice Assembly Speakership over Kim Dae Jung's nominee. Kim Dae Jung decided to mete out the maximum political penalty to Cho Youn-Ha. The party's Executive Disciplinary Committee, consisting of three members from each of the Kim Dae Jung and Kim Young Sam factions, soon decided to expel the two defiants. They were deprived of membership on the

Executive Council, their posts as chief of respective party local chapters, and party membership for two years.

One of the most significant targets of carrots and sticks used by the chief patron of the government is judges of the courts.[4] Contrary to the case of the United States, judges in Korea are subject to appointment and periodic reappointment by the president and to transferral from one court to another. Therefore, those judges who are subservient to the executive are likely to be awarded appointments, reappointments, promotions, and transferral to a more reputable court. One the other hand, those who dare to uphold judicial integrity and independence from the executive in their rulings on sensitive political court cases, tend to face the stick. For example, one-third of the judges lost their jobs in their attempt to assert judicial independence in 1971-1972. Upon the embarkation of the Fourth Republic, all nine Supreme Court justices were deleted from reappointment on March 24, 1973. The period from 1974 to 1976 witnessed several instances of demotion to less reputable, local courts of judges who had failed to rule cases as the Executive wished. In May 1980, six of the fifteen Supreme Court justices expressed dissenting views on the execution of Kim Jae Kyu on the grounds that the case should further explore the objective of Kim's assassination of President Park. On August 9, 1980, all of a sudden it was reported that they submitted "resignations." No reasons for their resignation, however, have been officially made available. Under the constitution of the Fifth Republic (1981-1988) the Chief Justice of the Supreme Court was granted the power of personnel on over 900 judges in the Court of Appeals and District Courts. On behalf of his patron, the Chief Justice wielded the sticks against judges who showed sympathy with those who protested against the authoritarian government: the demotion of Judge Suh Suk-Koo from the Pusan District Court to a local court in 1980 soon after he made the ruling that students involved in campus unrest did not violate the National Security Law; the transferral of Judge Park Shee-Whan from the Inchon District Court to a local court in 1985 about six months after he declared eleven students involved in street demonstrations in Inchon not guilty; the demotion of Judge Chu Soo-Hyun from the Seoul Criminal Court to a local court in 1985 soon after he ruled that the leaders of anti-government opposition groups were not guilty; the transferral of Judge Suh Tae-Young from the Seoul Civil Court to a local court ironically only one day after his appointment to the Seoul court because he had his article on unjust personnel

Table 7-10 Abuses of the Extraordinary Measures in Terms of Objectives, Frequency and Duration

Objectives	Frequency and Duration
Foreign Relations:	
1. War and Armed Conflict	1) 10/17/48 - 12/31/48 6) 11/02/51 - ? 2) 10/21/48 - ? 7) 11/24/51 - ? 3) 07/08/50 - ? 8) 02/03/52 - ? 4) 12/07/50 - 08/13/51 9) 06/07/53 - 07/23/53 5) 08/13/51 - ?
2. Dangerous Situation Arising from Foreign Relations	
Domestic Situations:	
3. Civil War	None. The armed insurrection in Kwang ju developed after opposition politicians were arrested under the nationwide martial law of 05/18/80.
4. Natural Calamity	None.
5. Grave Financial or Economic Crisis	01/14/74 - 12/31/74
6. Public Safety and Order:	
To Amend the Constitution	1) 05/25/52 - 07/26/52 3) 10/17/72 - 12/13/72 2) 05/27/61 - 12/06/62 4) 10/16/80 - 11/21/80
To protect the amended constitutio9n and the regime	1) 04/19/60 - ? 5) 01/08/74 - 08/23/74 2) 04/26/60 - 06/07/60 6) 04/08/75 - 05/13/75 3) 06/03/64 - 07/28/64 7) 05/13/75 - 12/08/79 4) 12/06/71 - ? 8) 10/27/79 - 05/17/80
To secure the regime by military junta	1) 05/16/61 - 12/17/63 3) 10/17/80 - 01/24/81 2) 05/17/80 - 10/17/80

Source: *Dong-A Daily*, various years

Question marks indicate the date of termination of the extraordinary measures as either not available in daily newspapers or not officially announced by the government.

management of court judges published in a judicial newspaper (*Korea Herald*, June 22, 1988).

The anti-government forces--opposition politicians, intellectuals, religious leaders, journalists, labor workers, and college students--are often arrested, house arrested, indicted, and tried. Their offices or organizations are closed or abolished. They are deprived of licences and dismissed from their jobs. When all other restrictive means are exhausted, the last resort of the sticks is the declaration of extraordinary measures by which military officers and court martial replace the civilian counterparts with the president still as the Commander-in-Chief of the armed forces.

Legitimacy of the regime's resort to extraordinary measures is really questioned, because of: abuses of emergency powers by the government leaders beyond the specific objectives implied or specified in the constitution; suppression and/or deprivation of basic freedoms and human rights under the disguise of emergencies; too frequent resort to emergency powers; and the exercise of emergency powers for a prolonged period of time such that the sense of emergency is no longer accepted by the general public.

The Constitution of the Republic of Korea justifies six objectives for declaring extraordinary measures. The first two objectives are involved in foreign relations. They are extraordinary measures to meet: 1) war and armed conflict; and 2) dangerous situations arising from foreign relations. The four remaining objectives are related to domestic situations. They are extraordinary measures to meet: 3) domestic civil war; 4) natural calamity; 5) grave financial or economic crisis; and 6) the maintenance of public safety and order. Table 7-10 shows the arrangement of the extraordinary measures on the basis of these six objectives.

As is shown in Table 7-10, the extraordinary measures taken involving war and armed conflict are mainly attributed to the communists who made uprisings against the government of the Republic of Korea and the direct attack launched by the North Korean Communists into South Korea in 1950 until the end of the Korean War in 1953. Concerning the objective to meet dangerous situations arising from foreign relations we can observe only one case of emergency action taken so far, the National Mobilization Decree declared on January 1, 1971, which was designed to empower the nation's Armed Forces to requisition privately owned land for military operations, especially when it was deemed necessary for the defense of the Seoul area against the North Korean

Communists. These extraordinary measures involving war, armed conflict, and crisis arising from foreign relations are generally accepted as legitimate.

Only a couple of extraordinary measures involving domestic situations may be claimed as legitimate. They are the martial law of 1964 related to the protests against the government's diplomatic normalization with Japan and the executive decree of 1974 involving a grave financial or economic crisis. The absolute number of all other cases was used primarily to amend the constitution for the incumbent president to run for either the third consecutive term or for an unlimited term of service; to protect the amended constitution, its authoritarian regime, and the related patron-client network against challengers; and to secure government power by the military junta.

In fact, more than one-third of the entire history of the Republic of Korea has been under extraordinary measures, under which citizens were deprived of their basic freedoms and rights clearly guaranteed in the constitution. The scope and extent of the deprivation of basic freedoms and human rights may be indirectly examined by the number of those who were released on the amnesties "benevolently" and "gracefully" granted by the president as the chief patron, while the released were outnumbered by those still arrested, put into jail, and yet not reported on time through the mass media due to martial law or other extraordinary measures.

Table 7-11 shows the history of amnesties and reinstatements of civil and political rights of those who were arrested, tried and put into jail from the inception of the republic in 1948 until the end of 1988 of the Sixth Republic. From this table we may deduce a few interesting hypotheses. First, a regime which secures government power in an illegitimate way like military coup tends to arrest more opposition forces in the process of securing power. This is witnessed by the military regime of General Park in the 1961-1963 years and the Fifth Republic of General Chun more saliently than in other republics. Second, such an illegitimate regime tends to arrest more of the so-called hooligans and petty violators of traffic regulations and other minor laws under the guise of correcting social wrongdoing and promoting public security. Third, as soon as the power base is strongly established and the leader is elected the president of the republic, his inauguration ceremony tends to accompany "special" amnesties, "special" reduction of penalties, and "special" reinstatements of civil and political rights to thousands of

Table 7-11 History of Amnesties and Reinstatement of Civil and Political Rights

Date	Amnesties General	Amnesties Special	Reduction of Penalty General	Reduction of Penalty Special	Reinstatement of rights General	Reinstatement of rights Special	Remarks
1st Republic:							
09/28/48	Yes		Yes		Yes		The establishment
12/28/50			Yes				of the Republic
01/01/51		1,901		1,259			
10/17/51				1			
03/01/52		3,616		2,218			
08/15/52			Yes	3,227			
12/31/53		1,467		763			
02/17/54				2			
08/15/54				2			Independence Day
01/01/55		31		49			
03/25/55		20					
01/01/56		1,155		1,062			
08/15/56		1,142		649			Independence Day
08/15/58		984		498			Independence Day
01/01/60		14					
Subtotal		10,330		9,730			
Annual Average		860		811			
Military Regime:							
06/06/61	Yes						May 16 Coup
07/17/61		77					May 16 Coup
08/15/61		4,051		7,088			Independence Day
03/15/62						14	
04/19/62		65		7			
05/16/62		13,158		8,752	Yes		4.19 Anniversary
08/15/62		399		151			5.16 Anniversary
05/16/63		72		41			Independence Day
08/15/63		17			Yes		
Subtotal		17,839		16,039		14	
Annual Average		8,919		8,020		7	
3rd Republic:							
12/16/63	Yes	94		16			
05/16/64		11		80			
12/25/65		37		19			
07/01/67				1,476			
08/15/69		795		1,748			Inauguration of 6th President
08/15/70		308		3,267			
12/25/70		73					
07/01/71		324		3,987			Inauguration of 7th President
10/01/71		4		26			

Patron-Client Politics and the Democratic Legacy   251

Table 7-11 History of Amnesties and Reinstatement of Civil and Political Rights

Date	Amnesties General	Amnesties Special	Reduction of Penalty General	Reduction of Penalty Special	Reinstatement of rights General	Reinstatement of rights Special	Remarks
10/01/72		7		22			
Subtotal		1,653		10,641			
Annual Average		184		1,182			
4th Republic:							
12/27/72		1,203		5,017			Inauguration of 8th President
02/09/73						1	
08/15/73		1		2			
03/01/77				2			
12/27/77		988		3,087	Yes		Inauguration of 9th President
Subtotal		2,192		8,109	1		
Annual Average		313		1,158	0.1		
Interim Regime:							
12/23/79		561		31			Inauguration of 10th President
02/29/80		15			Yes	101	Emergency Measures Lifted
08/15/80		2		1			
Subtotal		578		32		101	
Annual Average		385		21.5		67.3	
5th Republic:							
09/01/80		516					Inauguration of 11th President
11/02/80		2					
01/23/81				12			
03/03/81		2,417		646		167	Inauguration of 12th President
04/03/81		58		23		2	Those involved in the Kwangju Incident
05/11/81		60				5	Buddha's Birthday
08/15/81		1,061		4			Including those involved in the Kwangju
01/01/82		11					
03/03/82		1,419		545		238	1st Anniv. of President Chun
02/25/83						250	1st Major Lifting
03/15/83				2			
08/12/83		1,944		10			Involving Public Safety Law
12/23/83		1,214				551	Independence Day
02/25/84						202	2nd Major Lifting
08/14/84		43		2		671	Independence Day
10/02/84				177			
11/30/84						84	3rd Major Lifting
03/02/85		1,615		512			4th Anniversary of

Table 7-11 History of Amnesties and Reinstatement of Civil and Political Rights

Date	Amnesties General	Amnesties Special	Reduction of Penalty General	Reduction of Penalty Special	Reinstatement of rights General	Reinstatement of rights Special	Remarks
03/06/85						14	President Chun 4th Major Lifting
08/15/85				4			
03/01/87		1,218					
07/09/87		350		270		2,335	6.25 Declaration
08/15/87		1,305					
Subtotal		13,240		2,207		4,519	
Annual Average		1,891		315		646	
6th Republic:							
02/27/88						7,234	Inauguration of President Roh
12/20/88		281				1,581	1,731 as Political Prisoners

Source: *Dong-A Annual (Dong-A Yongam)*, various years

those in jail. The chief patron tends to expect their deep appreciation and cooperation in return for his "benevolent and graceful" grant of amnesties, reduction of penalties, and reinstatement of their civil and political rights. The absence of judicial independence from the Chief Executive and his benevolence bestowed in the name of the presidential clemency clearly demonstrate the patronage politics of carrots and sticks.

Robert E. Gamer suggests a list of coercive techniques against those who attempt to challenge and break the patron-client politics prevailing in developing countries (Gamer, 1976: 142-43). Many of these techniques have been implemented in Korea during the period of the first five republics. They are:

1. Compulsory union membership in government-sponsored union federations; laws against strikes;
2. Security clearance as a precondition for students to go abroad to study; purge of faculty members who criticize the government suppression of freedoms and human rights; the approval of all appointments to university administration positions; the approval of the promotion of faculty members;

3. Registration of all publications, periodical or occasional; restrictions on import of publications;
4. Government liaison with the press to suggest which stories should and should not be covered and broadcast;
5. Suits against newspapers for carrying improper material;
6. Government-owned radio and television;
7. Police clearance of all gatherings of a certain number of persons;
8. Outlawing of political parties founded by individuals who are "pro-communists" or "sympathetic" with North Korea;
9. Outlawing of all opposition parties during the period of power establishment by the coup forces;
10. Co-option of former opposition leaders into the ruling party;
11. Preventive detention without trial for those whom the government deems to be involved in improper activities; torture; deportation;
12. Death or severe penalties for broadly-defined treason;
13. The patron(s) personally selecting all electoral candidates;
14. "Permanent" abolition of parliament and/or cancellation of elections until the power base is firmly established;
15. Public referenda giving the chief executive the power to rule without limitation under a suspended constitution;
16. Military intervention to remove the chief executive from office and assure his swift replacement and the organizing the power bases with his loyal clients;
17. Military takeover of government, involving the killing and deportation of certain key leaders in the previous regime followed by a reorganization incorporating other individuals who had been the faithful clients in the military service.

The Fallacy of Dichotomy Between Patronage and Group Politics

Norman Jacobs contends that all of the advanced countries of Western Europe and Japan were ruled by a feudal social order and its organized group of warriors in the past and are now ruled by independently organized interest groups and associations. On the other hand, developing countries including Korea were characterized as a "patrimonial" (more correctly, patriarchal) society in the past and are now still constrained by a "patrimonial" (patriarchal) social order (Jacobs, 1985: 12). Therefore, the former enjoy democracy, whereas the latter suffer from patron-client politics.

The examples of Japan and the United States, however, attest to the fallacy of a clear dichotomy that developing countries are to patron-client politics what advanced democratic countries are to interest group politics. Japan has been notorious in high-level influence-peddling scandals involving faction leaders of both government and opposition political party leaders and businessmen. Nippon Telegraph & Telephone (NTT) Chairman, Hisashi Shinto, for example, was forced to resign in December 1988 after the disclosure that he received some $80,000 worth of Recruit Cosmos stock for his arrangement for Recruit to buy two supercomputers from an American industry, Cray Research, Inc. Finance Minister Kiichi Miyazawa also stepped down after continuously changing his story about one of his former aides who bought $240,000 worth of stock from Recruit in Miyazawa's name. In an attempt to clean up the mess, Prime Minister Noboru Takeshita appointed a new Justice Minister in January 1989. No sooner was the newly appointed Minister Takashi Hasegawa placed in the Justice Department than he was forced to confess to accepting political donations of more than $46,000 from Recruit.

Prime Minister Noboru Takeshita finally stepped down, after his closest political aide for thirty-year, Ihei Aoki, committed suicide. In fact, Takeshita received more than $1 million in campaign contributions, stocks, and secret loans from the company. The money, of course, was not put into the Prime Minister's personal account but funded campaigns and paid staff salaries. His loyal servant, Aoki might simply have followed a long-standing Japanese patron-client political tradition in which a client accepts all blames for his patron's downfall by even killing himself (MacLeod, 1985: 44). Japanese politicians routinely peddle their influence to businessmen in return for the latter's financial contributions. Former Prime Minister Kakuei Tanaka was convicted in the mid-1970s of accepting bribes from the Lockheed Corporation in return for helping sell Lockheed jets to a Japanese airline. Tanaka's successors have thus far failed to push through effective curbs on influence peddling.

The United States is by no means immune from patronage politics. Machines and bosses are as old as politics. Hamilton, Jefferson, and Burr were bosses, and their factions or caucuses were political machines consisting of members of the gentry. The

Jacksonian democracy, indeed, entered the threshold of full-scale patronage politics, which required ordering and mobilizing a large number of newly enfranchised frontiersmen. The Lincoln Administration finally reached the climax of patronage politics. While patronage politics began to decline in the national political arena after the assassination of President Garfield by an unsatisfied client of his in 1881, local machines continued to prevail in both urban and rural areas at least until after World War II. Since then there has been a decline. Nevertheless, Gottfried contends that machine politics still survives, because:

> There remain large pockets of poverty amid American affluence, where conditions are similar to those who accompanied the rise of the machine. By various estimates 17 percent or 20 percent or 25 percent of the population is poor. Negroes and Puerto Ricans make up a significant portion of the poor, and their problems are somewhat similar to those of the earlier waves of immigrants. Both groups have made important, though insufficient, gains in political representation.
>
> Machine politics is not yet dead, even in invidious sense. There have been major transformations: there will be more. But the need for organizations, for leadership, and for political responsibility has increased in the contemporary world. Some promising new organizational forms are developing side by side with the remaining weakened and modified forms . . . in the troubled Negro, Puerto Rican, and Mexican-American ghettos (Gottfried, 1968: 251-52).

U.S. News and World Report Editor-in-Chief, Mortimer B. Zuckerman deplores that "in the Reagan administration, appointees averaged only two years of service" (Zuckerman, 1989: 71). A short life span of many officials in the Reagan Administration was due to patronage politics such that they were, in fact, indicted, charged, or seriously criticized. His few well-known high-ranking officials involved in patron-client politics are:

1. President Reagan's Assistant for National Security Affairs, Richard V. Allen, who was suspected of receiving $1,000 from Japanese journalists for his arrangement for them to have an

interview with Nancy Reagan, together with the alleged receipt of several wristwatches from one of his former business associates. In the end, Allen grudgingly resigned on January 4, 1982 (*Facts on File*, 1982: 3-4).

2. White House aide Lyn Nofziger, who resigned as head of the White House Office of Political Affairs. A memo signed by him on May 1982 revealed that "he urged a White House official to help persuade the Army to "speedily approve" a $31 million Wedtech contract (*Facts on File*, 1985: 324).

3. Donald J. Levine, who submitted his resignation on May 1, 1985 from a post as a Special Assistant to the President on the grounds that he threatened three Democratic governors with reduction of federal funds for their nonpartisan voter registration in state offices and he campaigned for at least sixteen Republican candidates in the 1984 presidential election. He also politicized the civil service by creating a new top level of appointees and filling them with Republican leaders (*New York Times*, Nov. 4, 1986).

4. Michael K. Deaver, who faced the allegation that his lobbying activities for business firms of foreign countries "had violated federal conflict-of-interest laws." The Deaver firm made twenty-eight contacts in four months with leading Treasury Department enforcement officials. He also met with White House Budget Director, James C. Miller, III and persuaded the administration to buy more of Rockwell's B-1 bombers (*Facts on File*, 1986: 248, 314 and 598).

5. Attorney General Edwin Meese, who "ran afoul of the Federal gratuity law in his friendship with E. Robert Wallach" and his wife Ursula, who got a $40,000-a-year job with the Multiple Sclerosis Society from a grant from Bender Real Estate. The Bender firm soon secured a renewal of a long-term lease for a Justice Department building at triple the previous rent. The building was subsequently sold for a $22 million profit (*Facts on File*, 1988: 286, 696).

A brief examination of the above cases of Japan and the United States demonstrates the fallacy that developing countries are to complete patron-client politics what developed democratic countries are to full interest group politics. Both types--patron-client and group politics--are intermixed in all of the countries. We may, therefore, qualify a thesis of many scholars such as James Scott (1972), Carl Lande (1973), Robert Gamer (1976), and Jacobs (1985) that there is a clear dichotomy between the two. Instead, developing countries are "more subject" to patron-client politics, whereas advanced democratic countries to group politics.

Professor Jacobs suggests another fallacy that patron-client politics is so deeply rooted in Korean politics that the Korean road to modernization is one which accepts change, sometimes hesitantly, sometimes eagerly, but always deliberately "only within certain specified limits." Therefore, if, in the course of the development process, in spite of all precautions, certain values, goals, or procedures which contradict patriarchal characteristics have found their ways into Korean society and in consequence dislocations arise, "the dialectic tension is not necessarily resolved in development's favor" (Jacobs, 1985: 301). The fallacy in his notion of the persistence of patron-client politics in Korea, in fact, is due to his research, which covered the time span up to the end of the Fourth Republic. I would rather postulate that, as will be examined in detail in Chapter Nine, patron-client political culture is not fixed once and for all. From the mid-1980s patron-client politics in Korea began to decline, and pro-democracy forces concomitantly became triumphant.

The Democratic Legacy as an Unextinguished Flame

In the previous section we examined the notion that patron-client politics had prevailed in Korea centered around the president as the chief patron with the key members of the bureaucracy, the legislature, the judiciary, and the government political party as his clients. The patronage also thrives in the linkage of the president as the chief patron to the leaders of major industries, banks and credit institutions, the military, universities, and research institutes as his chief clients. The imperative of maintaining the patron-client network for mutual survival and prosperity became so paramount that the challengers to the patronage network--the opposition leaders, intellectuals, religious leaders, professors, journalists, and students--were deprived of basic freedoms, rights, and equal opportunities for political competition for the government power. It goes without saying that patron-client politics had been the main cause for the failure of democracy to take a firm root in Korea at least until the mid-1980s.

However, the struggles of an ever-snowballing number of participants--hundreds of thousands of Koreans for democratization finally began to toll the death knell of the authoritarian regime centered around the patron-client politics and bear the belated and yet epoch-making fruit of the June 29 Declaration in 1987 for democratic reforms in Korea. The constitution was amended unanimously by both government and opposition parties in the National Assembly and ratified by a referendum. The president of the Sixth Republic was elected by a direct popular election. All basic freedoms and rights began to be established and honored.

It turned out that the American ambassadors to Korea--past and incumbent--repeated in unison in their congressional testimonies that the Confucian culture was so deeply embedded that the changes for democratization in Korea would be very minor (*Korea Herald*, March 2, 1989). However, the struggle for democracy is not new but was prevalent in Korea throughout its history in terms of: 1) political philosophy advocating democracy; 2) literature endorsing democracy and condemning nondemocratic practices; 3) popular protests and campaigns for democracy waged on numerous occasions, and 4) actual implementation of democratic elements. Therefore, the Korean miracle of democracy that finally embarked upon since 1987 would be partly attributed to the flame thus far unextinguished from the democratic legacy inherited throughout the history of Korea, which deserves our attention.

The Legacy of Political Philosophy Advocating Democracy

The most fundamental and the oldest political philosophy advocating democracy in Korea is the Hong-ik In-gan ("Devotion to the Welfare of All Mankind"). This was promulgated at the time when the Tangun Choson was established in 2333 B.C. The philosophy of Hong-ik In-gan emphasizes that humans by nature are basically the same and are born equal. This ideology values human rights and regards politics as a means to the ultimate ends of: guaranteeing the people their basic freedoms and rights; transcending differences of personality and opinions; achieving harmony; and enhancing all private lives. Hong-ik In-gan "respects the will of the majority in terms of politics and endorses the equal distribution of welfare to the majority of the people. The privileged class and maldistribution are not allowed in the spirit of Hong-ik In-gan" (National Unification Board, 1983: 141-42). It was inherited first by the Kija Choson, then by Puya, the three Han states, and the Three Kingdoms. During that period, slavery and the aristocratic system had prevailed with some variations in terms of quality and quantity. But the political philosophy of Hong-ik In-gan had survived. Rulers had been constantly reminded of this democratic philosophy with which Tangun, the progenitor of Korea tried to rule for the well-being of the majority of the people rather than that of the rulers and aristocrats.

The spirit of Hong-ik In-gan influenced scholars of the Sirhak (Practical Learning) during the Yi Dynasty. The Sirhak first appeared during the Seventeenth Century and began to refine its doctrine during the eighteenth century. One of the most important Sirhak scholars was Yun Chung (1629-1714). He contended that "the welfare of the people should be the primary concern." The King "could not exist without the people, but the people could exist without the King." This was a startlingly democratic notion especially at the time when the hereditary and hierarchical principles prevailed. Yun Chung refused the ideas that "men are born unequal" and that "their social status is predetermined" (W. K. Ham, 1987: 325).

Another noted Sirhak philosopher was Yu Hyung-Won (1622-1673). He advocated the principle of equal opportunities regardless of social status. He emphasized the application of equal opportunities to education and employment. His successor Yi Ik (Yulgok)(1681-1763) made a clear distinction between national consensus and "idle prattle," namely, demagoguery in a modern terminology. He then predicted that "demagoguery would be doomed to failure by public resentment."

> Bigger than a mountain and sharper than a blade, demagoguery, once started, shakes the foundation of the kingdom if it is not checked in time, and soon becomes too big to control. No man, however high his stature, can survive once he is involved in demagoguery. No eloquence or courage can save the kingdom once it is enveloped in demagoguery. Public resentment is indirectly attributed to misrule by the leadership. The ruler should take the ruled more seriously (KOIS, 1979: 175).

Yi Ik advocated civil and political rights of democracy based on the abolition of class distinction and of slavery, the importance of public opinions, and consensus. He also endorsed economic and social democracy. Since "the impoverished people are deprived of their true nature, morality crumbles, and penal systems are rendered ineffective under such circumstances." Therefore, any act of reform should "aim at the sole purpose of providing more comfort for the subjects. No injustice will be cured if corrupt officials escape reforms" (KOIS, 1979: 175; H. S. Kim, 1989: Ch. 4).

Added to these philosophers was Chong Yak-Yong (1762-1836). He devoted a great deal of effort to reading and comprehending Western books as well as oriental ones. He detailed his ideas for reform, which included redistribution of land to the farmers, the reorganization of the central government, the establishment of local self-government, and the promotion of technical education.

The Literature Advocating Democracy

While Sirhak scholars were bold enough to openly suggest reforms for civil, political, economic, and social democracy, nondemocratic practices and injustice were exposed in literature by novelists. They, too, intended to shame aristocratic leaders and officials for their discrimination against the artificially established lower social classes such as commoners and low-born slaves, and for their exploitation of the lower class people.

The Tale of Hong Kil-Tong by Ho Kyun (1567-1618), for example, was a satiric novel protesting the discrimination against concubines and their children. The book's hero, Hong Kil-Tong, like the virtuous outlaw Robin Hood, was enraged by corruption and discrimination against lower class people. The author, Ho Kyun, made a bold departure from traditional norms and values and based his democratic morality on the political principle of human equality. He eloquently expressed his conviction that every man is endowed with particular talents to fully explore and develop and, therefore, ought not be exploited by others against his will. The exposure of injustice and exploitation was his major objective in the book. Moreover, it was written in Korean, using Hangul, which could be read by lower class people without difficulty in comprehension. At that time an absolute majority of the lower class people were not able to read the Chinese characters because of lack of education. He

Table 7-12 The Legacy of Democratic Philosophy and Practices

A. Political Philosophy on Democracy

The Thought of Hong-ik In-gan (Devotion to the Welfare of Mankind) which should honor the will of the majority

The Sirhak (Practical Learning)(1650-1900)

Yu Hyong-Won (1622-1673)	Equality of humans; No predestination of social status; Equal opportunities
Yi Ik (Yulgok) (1681-1763)	Serious consideration of the ruled by the rulers; Abolition of class distinction and slavery; The importance of public opinion and consensus
Chong Yag-Yong (1762-1836)	Advocacy of merit system; Redistribution of land; A fair share of crops between landlords and peasants; Decentralization; Abolition of slavery
Chae Hae-Wol (1829-1898)	No distinction of class or origin

B. Literature Advocating Democracy

Ho Kyun (1567-1618)	*The Tale of Hong Kil-Tong* Enraged at corruption and advocated a class-ridden society, equality, and justice
The author Unknown	*The Tale of Chun-Hyang* Described a happy ending with an interclass marriage
Park Chi-Won	*The Tale of Yangban* Discredited the traditional *yangban* (aristocrat) values full of idleness, corruption, and hypocrisy

C. Protests or Campaigns for Democracy

Nationwide slave uprisings (1176-1269)

Uprising of the peasants led by:

Hong Kyong-Nae (1812)	Protests against the discrimination of most Pyongan scholars in the appointment to the central government posts
Peasants in Cheju Islands (1813)	Protests against local nobility, wealthy landlords, oppressive landlords, and the provincial officials

	Kapsin Coup (1884)	For the abolition of the old class system; Equal treatment of all classes; Dismissal of corrupt officials; Revision of the criminal law; Establishment of a policy-making council
	The Tonghak Revolt of 1894	Uprising against the exploitation and oppression of the government officials and the *yangban* class; Uprising for the abolition of the old system of status and destruction of the slave registers; Permission for widows to remarry
	The Kap-O Reform of 1895	Among 14 articles in the new proposed constitution; Merit-based appointment to government posts without regard to social status; Functions and jurisdictions of local governments to be clearly defined; The powers and functions of each central official post to be clearly defined; Civil and criminal law codes to be reformed
	The Independence Association of 1898	Trials for felony should be open to the public

D. Implementation of Democratic Principles

	Ancient Choson's Eight Commandments	Protection of life, property, and compensation for injury or damage
	Koguryo's Taedaero	A system of the election rather than appointment of Tae Daero comparable to the modern Prime Minister
	Silla's Hwabaek	Outlawed the hereditary system and elected the king on the basis of leadership and ability by a unanimous vote of all the important men of the ruling class; Important state affairs were adopted by unanimity of all ministers.
Koryo:		
	King Kwangjong (949-975)	Nobian gumbup, the manumission of slaves; Displacing great landlords from the positions of power; Sons of petty officials and commoners allowed to take military officers examination; Adoption of a civil service system based on the merit basis
	Wonjong (1260-1275)	Slaves whose status was vague were raised to the rank of commoners
Yi Dynasty:		

Taejo (1392-1398)	The establishment of a council of local yangban as an advisory body to prevent disaffection and to detect grievances; The adoption of referendum, directly appealing to the popular vote, bypassing government officials, landlords, and local officials
Sejong (1418-1450)	Development of the Korean alphabet, Hangul to promote literacy and to protect illiterate defendants from forced signing of indictments and other documents without knowing the contents
Yongjo (1724-1776)	The promotion of upward social mobility; Upgrading the commoner status of offsprings of commoner female and mean male; No arbitrary punishment of bondmen by the *yangban*
Sunjo (1800-1834)	Destruction of all bondmen registers in the central government offices and palaces to assure their emancipation
Republic of Korea	Education Law (Chapter 1, Article 1), which emphasizes as main goals "perfecting individual personality, developing the ability for an independent life, and acquiring good citizenship

envisioned that the poor working class, if properly awakened and provoked to action, would become a most powerful force and therefore join in the struggle for the great cause of democracy and social justice.

The Tale of Chun-Hyang was another great novel. It was written anonymously, perhaps for the fear of punishment if the author were known. The tale exposed the corrupt magistracy and the decaying *yangban* (upper class) ethos such as despising lower class people, exploiting them, imposing heavy taxes on them, and arresting and punishing them without due process of law. At the same time, the tale showed the potential for love affairs transcending the barrier of artificially developed social classes. Unlike the case of Romeo and Juliet, the tale led to a happy ending in an interclass marriage. Thereby, the story suggested the promise of a brighter society based on equality and justice in the future. The tale has been reintroduced in prose and verse, drama, and song. It has a special significance for many Koreans even today, who deeply care about political and economic democracy.

In the *Tale of the Yangban*, Park Chi-Won (1737-1805) described a typical *yangban* (a scholar-aristocrat) who had done nothing but read while subsisting on government provender. Because of poverty and debts to the government, the *yangban* had to sell his status to a merchant, who worked hard, accumulated a large sum of wealth, and yearned for a higher social status. Upon the purchase of the *yangban* title, the merchant came to know that the essence of *yangban* life was idleness, corruption, and hypocrisy. Finally, he discarded it. The novel advocated the elimination of artificially established class systems and the equality of all men regardless of different occupations.

Struggles for Democracy

History may evidence not only the promotion of philosophy and literature for democracy but also actual struggles of tens of thousands of Korean people, especially lower status and poor peasants, for democratization. The first significant uprising may be traced back to the year of 1176, when peasants and government slave workers fell into extreme duress due to the depletion of the national treasury resulting from the extravagance of King Uijong (1146-1170) and the court, and the subsequent imposition of excessive taxation. In January 1176, government slave workers waged a serious uprising in the village of Myong-hak-su, near Kongju, Choong Chung Province. After the coup of 1176, the uprisings became nationwide in scope. Slave workers did not comply with the government's partial conciliatory gesture, the promise to raise their status to that of commoners. They rather continued to fight, overrunning most of Choong Chung Province, spilling over into Kyonggi Province by the following year and finally threatening the nation's capital city.

In 1177, a peasant uprising broke out in Pyongan Province. During the 1190s the uprisings also swept north and south Kyongsang Provinces. During the final engagement in 1196, about 7,000 of the farmers fell. Slaves and peasants were, of course, vulnerable to disciplined government troops. However, they were brave enough to risk their lives for freedom, equality, and justice.

The Hong Kyong-Nae uprising of 1812 demonstrates another major struggle for the principle of equal opportunities against the discrimination of the residents of Pyongan Province in the recruitment and promotion in the central government positions. Hong Kyong-Nae came of a *yangban* family but was denied a government post because of his birth province of Pyongan. Being discontented and resentful, he assembled a large group, who shared his grievances and began to wage a rebellion. The year of 1813 witnessed another rebellion, this time by the poor farmers in Cheju Islands against the oppressive landlords and the provincial officials for their exploitation of poor farmers.

While the earlier rebellions became erratic and disorganized, the ensuing rebellions became more specific and articulate. The Kapsin coup of 1884 was an attempt for democratic reforms with the goals of: the abolition of the old social class; the establishment of the principle of equal treatment of all people; the dismissal of corrupt officials; the revision of the criminal law; and the establishment of a policy-making council (Han, 1987: 393). However, such a democratic movement was aborted due to the power struggle between Japan and China over the control of Korea and their subsequent intervention in Korea's domestic politics.

Having exhausted all peaceful and orderly channels of expressing grievances and calling for redress, Chon Pong-Joon led the Tonghak Revolt in 1894 against the government leaders with specific objectives. They were: equitable and fair taxation, and halting of rice exports to Japan that caused many poor peasants and workers in Korea to starve. Added to these two demands, the Tonghak made their cause public in a formal document of twelve items. A few major items for democratization included: no toleration of the oppression from officials and rich *yangban*; the destroying of the slave registers; the abolition of the old system of social class status; the permission for widows to remarry; and the redistribution of land on an equitable basis. Once again, the Tonghak rebellion was doomed to failure because of the intervention of China and Japan in Korea's domestic politics (Han, 1987: 409-411).

Those who were defeated in the Kapsin Coup of 1884 and the Tonghak Rebellion of 1894, however, did not give up their dream for democratization. On January 7, 1895, they established a new form of government under the fourteen articles of the constitution. Its major democratic elements included:

1. The powers and functions of each official post are to be clearly defined.
2. Taxation is to be imposed solely according to the law.
3. The functions and jurisdictions of local administrations are to be clearly defined by law.

4. Talented persons are to be sent abroad for study in order to develop and apply modern science and technology.
5. Reformed civil and criminal law codes are to be enacted.
6. Appointments to government posts are to be made on the basis of merit only, without regard to social status (Han, 1987: 424-425).

Again, the new government failed to take a firm root of democracy due to the financial difficulties involved in the Tonghak Rebellion, the Sino-Japanese War, and Japan's strong grip of domestic economy and politics of Korea.

The Implementation of Democratic Principles

The thesis that democracy is not totally alien to Korea has been examined in terms of the Hong-Ik In-gan and the Sirhak political thoughts, the advocacy of democracy by literature, and various campaigns and struggles for democracy throughout the Korean history. The thesis can be further supported by the actual implementation of various democratic principles at the different time periods, before the Republic of Korea was established in 1948.

The Ancient Choson must be acknowledged for its adoption and implementation of the Eight Commandments. Its three major elements are: Those who kill other humans shall be executed; Those who incur injuries or damage to other people shall make compensation in terms of payment of grains; Those who commit robberies shall be demoted to the status of slaves or should make payment of 500,000 nyang (a unit of money). Historians explain that the Eight Commandments were adopted for "the purpose of the protection of human lives, labor, and properties" (Minister of Education, 1979: 13).

One of the Three Kingdoms, Koryo (37 B.C.-668 A.D.), developed an official hierarchy in the central government with a group of officials with specialized functions. The highest post in this hierarchy, right below the king, was *Tae* ('great') *Daero*, comparable in some ways to the modern prime minister. This post was at first not appointive but elective on the basis of ability and leadership, although the voting qualifications were not clear (Han, 1987: 28).

More democratic than the Tae Daero system of Koguryo was the Hwabaek system of the Silla Kingdom (57 B.C.-935 A.D.). No detailed information on this system is available concerning when it was implemented. But the Hwabaek system required a unanimous voting of all the important men of the ruling class on the selection of the king and important state affairs. The Hwabaek was held at four special meeting places fairly regularly. The selection of kings not on the hereditary basis but on ability and leadership and the full consensus of the ruling class members, coupled with the Hwarangdo ("Flower Knights") military training, became known as the main reasons for the Silla under the competent leadership to unify all three Kingdoms together in the Korean peninsula (Han, 1987: 59-61). The election of kings on the basis of leadership rather than the hereditary method was not practiced even in the Western European countries at the times corresponding to that of the Silla Kingdom.

King Kwangjong (949-975) of Koryo Kingdom (918-1389) must also be acknowledged for his democratic ruling. In 956, he promulgated a law, which freed a large number of people who had been unlawfully enslaved. Added to the manumission of slaves, he adopted an open and competitive examination system for the government posts. This was known as "a good bit more liberal than the Silla had been" and displaced the great landlords from the positions of power. Sons of petty officials and even commoners were given the chance to take the military examinations for becoming officers. The adoption of a civil service system based on a merit system could hire and protect many qualified employees (Han, 1987: 129-130). King Wonjong (1260-1276) took a step further and issued decrees to return land and slaves illegally appropriated to their original owners. Other slaves whose status was vague were raised to the rank of commoners (Han, 1987: 182).

King Taejo (1392-1398) of the Yi Dynasty (1392-1910) wanted to restore local self-government, thereby allowing the establishment of a council of local *yangban*. The council was the basic means of local self-government, which was implemented during the Koryo Dynasty but later abolished during its end period. King Taejo adapted it to the new system of local government, by which his subjects were allowed to voice their opinions and complaints so that grievances could be detected and popular disaffection prevented (Han, 1987: 233).

King Sejong (1418-1450) was respected as a great king because of his adoption and implementation of various measures for political and economic democracy. In response to excessive taxes imposed by landlords and officials on peasants, King Sejong pushed hard to develop a progressive tax system in accordance with the actual yield. Up until that time land-lords and local officials forced the peasants to pay a fixed rate of rent and tax even in times of drought and flood. Against the strong resistance of *yangban* landlords, King Sejong appealed directly to a popular vote and promulgated progressive rent and tax system. The implementation of a referendum adopting a direct popular vote at that time was not conceived even in the Western European countries (KOIS, 1979: 96).

One of his most celebrated achievements was the creation of Hangul, the Korean alphabet. Due to its phonetic characteristics combining consonants and vowels, average people were able to learn how to read and write so as to be participant citizens. Hangul was equally important for the promotion of economic democracy. King Sejong "often pondered the fact that illiterate defendants were forced to sign indictments without knowing the contents" (KOIS, 1979: 96). Once literate, the defendants would be less likely to sign indictments without reading and comprehending false accusations.

King Yongjo (1724-1776) upgraded the commoner status of the offsprings of commoner females and mean males and prohibited any arbitrary punishment of bondmen by the *yangban*. In 1801, King Sunjo (1800-1834), in fact, destroyed over 1,200 volumes of bondmen registers of the central government offices and palaces to assure the emancipation of 36,000 slaves in the palace and 29,000 slaves well in advance of the Civil War in the United States.

With the inception of the republic in 1948, the Education Law emphasizes the following as the goals of education of Korean students. They are: "assisting all people in perfecting individual personality, developing the ability for an independent life, and, above all, acquiring good citizenship needed to serve for the development of a democratic nation and for the realization of human co-prosperity" (Chapter 1, Art. 1). The inculcation of democratic norms, values, and behaviors from the above democratic legacies have influenced the new generation of Koreans to lay the basic foundation of the continued struggles for democratization and the establishment of the Sixth Republic under democratic reforms.

Conclusion

Chapter Seven examined the prevalence of patron-client politics in Korea. However, patron-client politics is not the sole property of non-democratic developing countries. The cases of Japan and the

United States of today reveal that they are not completely immune from patron-client politics. In fact, patron-client and group politics are not fully mutually exclusive but co-exist.

Amidst the prevalence of non-democratic patron-client political practices in Korea, we have identified ample evidence of: 1) the legacy of political philosophy advocating democracy; 2) the literature enhancing the value of democracy; 3) a series of struggles for the adoption of democracy; and 4) the actual implementation of democratic procedural principles.

These evidences suggest that the Western-style democracy based on the promotion of due process of law and equal opportunities is not totally alien to Korea. Therefore, it would be folly to state that democracy and the democratic culture are concepts "totally alien" to developing countries including Korea and that, therefore, no single Third World state has the prospect for democracy taking a firm root in the near future. Korea is one of a few developing countries that demonstrate a rapid rate of democratization. We will now examine how Korea has entered into the threshold of democracy.

Notes

1. For further information on patron-client politics, see Scott (1972) on developing countries in general; Lande (1973) on the Philippines; Jacobs (1985) and Pae (1986) on Korea.

2. For excellent discussion on these contending models, see Ostrom et al. (1961); J. M. Buchanan (1962); and Pae (1986: 132-140).

3. For a detailed analysis of party platforms of all major political parties of the first five republics, see Pae (1986: 173-183); for the case of the Sixth Republic, see *The Korea Herald*. April 29, 1988.

4. For carrot and stick techniques applied to the judges of the courts; see Baker (1983: 136); U.S. Department of State (1982: 642); *The Korea Herald*, June 22, 1988.

Chapter 8 The Korean Model of Democratization

Chapter Eight will introduce the Korean model of democratization on the basis of the combination of a political satellite model and a threshold model. Chapter Eight will, first of all, apply the political satellite model to each of the first five republics of Korea with the aim of explaining how the political satellite was skewed in favor of the anti-democratic, pro-government coalition centered around the president as the chief patron. Each time when the pro-democracy, anti-government coalition began to secure more support from elites, organized groups, intellectuals, students, and average citizens such that their coalition became sufficiently strong so as to challenge the pro-government coalition, the former was seriously restricted and overwhelmed by the latter in violation of all democratic procedural principles, basic freedoms, and rights guaranteed in the constitution. Otherwise, the regime took emergency measures or the military intervened and took over the government power.

Since the mid-1980s, however, owing to the ever-increasing level of education, urbanization, industrialization, and the subsequent inculcation of democratic values and expectations, more elites, organized groups, and middle-class citizens than ever before were determined to risk their lives and join the pro-democracy, anti-government coalition. Thereby, the pro-democracy coalition outnumbered and overpowered the anti-democratic, pro-government coalition, finally reaching the unprecedented, irrevocable threshold of democratization. Their indefatigable struggles forced the anti-democratic, autocratic regime to give in and adopt the June 29, 1987 declaration. Since then Korea has undertaken a series of democratic reforms. Korea, indeed, demonstrates a democratic miracle and suggests a model for the Third World countries.

A Political Satellite Model

One of the central characteristics of any political system is its distribution of power. Concerning the question of who has power and who dominates the allocation of values and resources in a political system, there are several contending models. One of them is a popular rule model, which suggests that each and every citizen participates with more or less equal power in the deliberations of policies and programs. Average citizens have such important political sources of power as voting, campaign, petition, contact with various officials, campaign fund contributions, and the expression of their opinions in a variety of periodic public surveys as negative or positive on various issues and on the evaluation of the elected officials (Mitchell, 1970: 74-76). The voting citizens are often referred to as the Holy Ghost to the Christians. During the regular working days Christians may go astray and commit sins. But at least once a week on Sunday they pay attention to the Holy Ghost and try to be good Christians, abstaining themselves from committing sins and being willing to do good things. At least once every four or five years, when election time comes, the officials flock to their home constituents, listening to their demands and expectations, and appealing to their supporters.

Arthur Bentley, David Truman, and a host of students rather suggest a pluralist group model. Since average individual citizens lack time, knowledge, information, and money, they are more likely to spend their limited, precious time taking care of their own families and devoting their energies to their own affairs. Therefore, individual citizens are not able to have meaningful and significant participation in politics. Organized groups and associations, on the other hand, have such advantages as numerical strength, a large amount of money collected from members as the membership fee, hiring experts, and their lobbying for the benefits of groups and associations (Bentley, 1949; Truman, 1951).

Gaetano Mosca, on the other hand, suggests a power elite theory. He states:

> In all societies--from societies that are very underdeveloped and have largely attained the dawnings of civilization, down to the most advanced and powerful societies--two classes of people appear--a class that rules and a class that is ruled. The first class, always the less numerous, performs all of the

political functions, monopolizes power, and enjoys the advantages that power brings. Whereas the second, the more numerous class, is directed and controlled by the first, in a manner that is now more or less legal, now more or less arbitrary and violent (Mosca, 1939: 50).

Mosca's power elite theory is still endorsed by many scholars even in the most advanced societies of today. In an industrial, scientifically advanced, and technological age, life in a democracy is shaped, just as in a totalitarian society, by a handful of people. They are referred to as high-ranking politicians, business executives, and generals and admirals by C. Wright Mills (1956); underlying economic forces who monopolize the ownership of the means of production (Marx and Engels, 1978: 469-500); bureaucrats at the strategic positions by Max Weber (1948, ch. 8) and Francis E. Rourke (1969); and professionals in the public and private sectors by Frederick C. Mosher (1968). Since they have the monopoly of money, position, education, knowledge, valuable experience in strategic decision-making, and the control of the mass media, "the key political, economic, and social decisions are made by 'tiny minorities'," namely the power elites (Dahl, 1964: 3; Dye and Zeigler, 1981: 3).

The power elite theory is equally challenged by many scholars. In his study of power in New Haven, Connecticut, Robert Dahl admits that community decisions are not made by the citizens of the community as a whole but by "tiny minorities" who are called the power elites. However, Dahl challenges the thesis that the elite system in New Haven is pyramidal, cohesive, and unresponsive to popular demands. His study of major decisions on urban redevelopment, public education, and the nomination for New Haven's mayor in both political parties did not witness Hunter's highly monolithic, centralized, and cohesive power elite structures as identified in Atlanta (Hunter, 1953). Dahl rather found a polycentric and dispersed system of elites in New Haven. The elites exercised differential influences on different issues: urban renewal by business elites and public education by education elites.

> The economic notables, far from being a ruling group, are simply one of many groups of which individuals sporadically emerge to influence the politics and acts of city officials. Almost anything one might say about the influence of the economic notables could be said with equal justice about a

half dozen other groups in the New Haven community (Dahl, 1961: 72).

Elite theorists tend to be preoccupied with who holds what strategic positions but do not claim any interest in what they are doing in terms of concrete behavior and how decisions are made (Bell, 1958: 49-50 and 64-67). Furthermore, even if big decisions, which have "terrible consequences for the underlying populations of the world" are made by tiny power elites (Mills, 1956: 12), "the workings of society are also based on millions of lesser decisions, all of which in total make an enormous difference to the individuals who make and are affected by them" (Mitchell, 1970: 91).

It is, therefore, premature to draw a conclusion that one particular model--the popular rule model, the group politics model, or the power elite model--uniformly and consistently explains who has power and therefore, monopolizes all decision-making processes. In their studies on specific policies in the United States, Gary L. Wamsley (1969), A. Lee Fritschler (1969), and Philip Selznick (1949), to name a few, suggest multiplicity of political arenas and the dispersion of power among various agents in the policy of the Selective Service System, politics on smoking, and TVA, respectively. This is true in the case of various decisions in the New York City:

> Decisions of the municipal government emanate from no single source, but from many centers; conflicts and clashes are referred to no single authority, but are settled at many levels and at many points in the system: no single group can guarantee the success of the proposal it supports, the defeat of every idea it objects to. . . . Each separate decision center consists of a cluster of interested contestants, with a "core group" in the middle, invested by the rules with formal authority to legitimize decisions. . . . and a constellation of related "satellite groups" seeking to influence the authoritative issuances of the core group (Sayne and Kaufman, 1960: 710).

The same holds true in the case of Korea. There is no question that the president as the chief patron wields the greatest amount of power. However, he does not monopolize the power. The chief patron still needs support from the power elites on the major

The Korean Model of Democratization

Figure 8-1 A Political Satellite Model

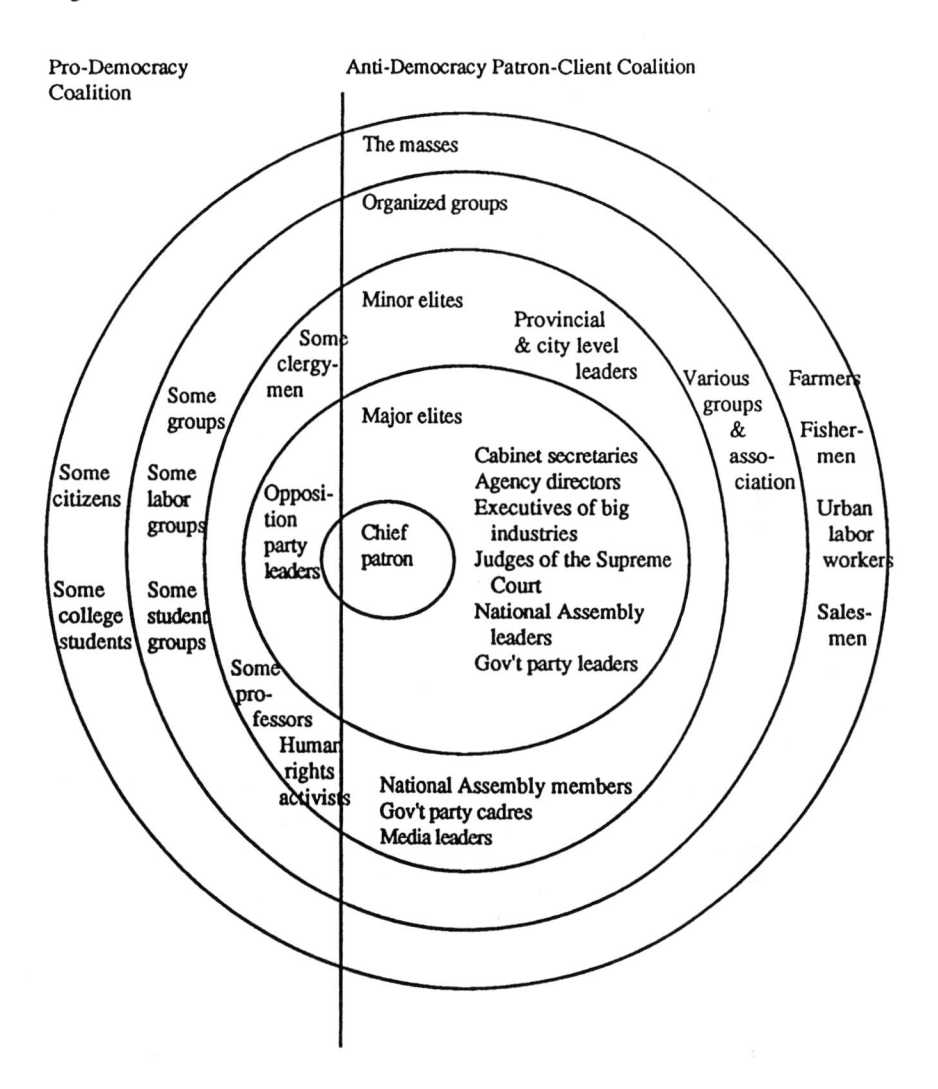

Pro-Democracy Coalition | Anti-Democracy Patron-Client Coalition

- The masses
- Organized groups
- Minor elites
  - Provincial & city level leaders
  - Some clergymen
  - Various groups & association
  - Farmers
  - Fishermen
- Major elites
  - Cabinet secretaries
  - Agency directors
  - Executives of big industries
  - Judges of the Supreme Court
  - National Assembly leaders
  - Gov't party leaders
  - Opposition party leaders
  - Chief patron
  - Some groups
  - Some labor groups
  - Some student groups
  - Some citizens
  - Some college students
  - Urban labor workers
  - Salesmen
  - Some professors
  - Human rights activists
- National Assembly members
- Gov't party cadres
- Media leaders

network of the patron-client politics, the less powerful elites on the minor network, interest groups, and the masses. Multiplicity of political arenas and dispersion of power among various agents are such that the chief patron, power elites, interest groups, and average citizens tend to be organized along the two broad coalitions into allies and hostiles on the struggle "against" and "for" democratization (see Figure 8-1).

A coalition in favor of maintaining the anti-democracy patron-client politics can be identified from the president as the chief patron in the center, the powerful agents of the major network in the inner circle horizontally across cabinet secretaries, leaders of the other two branches, military generals and admirals, the *chaebol*, and the like to those vertically on the minor network in the outer circle of provincial and regional levels and those average citizens in the farthest outer circle of the political satellite.

> A multi-tiered pyramid of a dyadic relationship is organized around the president of the central government: horizontally across cabinet secretaries of the Executive branch, justices of the Supreme Court, leaders of the National Assembly, and the government political party, commanding generals and admirals, and chief executives of the multi-billion dollar industries; and vertically from the central headquarters of those organizations to the local branches and local people such as small traders, commodities middlemen, retail merchants, moneylenders, and voters. The former is called a major network of people and the latter a minor network of people (Pae, 1986: 32-33).

A pro-democracy coalition can also be identified from some key leaders and the National Assemblymen of the opposition political parties in the inner circle to organized groups, intellectuals, professors, university students and religious leaders in the outer circle, and the workers and voters in the farthest outer circle of the political satellite.

Which coalition--pro-democracy or anti-democracy--prevails in a political system depends on extensiveness and intensiveness of participation and commitment of various political agents of the coalition to their cause. The broader the scope and extent of their participation in a pro-democracy coalition and the greater the level of their commitment, the greater the chances become to overpower the anti-democracy coalition and subsequently embark on democratization. From the inception of the republic in 1948 until 1987, pro-democracy coalition was formed in each of the five republics. But when the coalition began to grow strong and sufficiently threaten the authoritarian, patron-client coalition, the former was severely disturbed and weakened by the latter by means of arrest and house arrest, search and seizure by police, martial law, emergency measures, and finally a military coup, if all other carrot and stick techniques were exhausted. Nevertheless, the pro-democracy coalition of 1987 was able to muster more extensive support and more intensive commitment to the cause of democracy so as to reach the threshold, completely paralyzing the anti-democracy patron-client coalition. The Sixth Republic was finally established with the democratic constitution unanimously approved by the National Assembly and ratified by popular referendum. Political prisoners were released. The basic freedoms of speech, press, and assembly were promoted. Wrongdoings which were committed during the Fifth Republic were exposed and proper measures taken. And patron-client politics, nepotism, and favoritism were condemned. The political satellite model which is developed on the basis of empirical evidence in each republic (excluding the Second Republic due to its ill-fated short life expectancy) will explain why the first five republics failed and the Sixth Republic began to take a firm root of democracy.

The First Republic (1948-1960)

The Anti-Democracy Patron-Client Coalition

President Rhee, in the beginning of his administration, appealed to all political leaders and people with the motto that "United we stand, divided we fall." However, he became clearly conscious of the necessity of organizing and maintaining a patron-client network for his power persistence against the opposition forces. First of all, President Rhee made appointments of his loyal clients to the cabinet secretaries. In return for the position, power, and status, the secretaries devoted their loyalty to the President: The Secretary of the Interior Department became the *de facto* campaign manager for the election of both the president and his party Assemblymen with the mobilization of the appointed local government officials and police; the Secretaries of Agriculture, Education, Construction and Welfare provided their clients with the distribution of various services such as fertilizers, subsidies, scholarships, construction of local facilities and projects like bridges and roads. The president also appointed and reappointed the Chief Justice and justices of the

Supreme Court. In return for the position and power, the justices also had the obligation to make various court rulings in favor of their patron. The president provided major business executives with loans with low interest rates, favorable exchange of currency for trade and investment, and government subsidies. In return for these benefits, business executives made bountiful campaign contributions to their patron.

The president began to help organize various interest groups and associations not for the purpose of interest articulation and promotion of their own interests, but for the political mobilization and the securing of their support for the maintenance of his power. Major interest groups which were organized upon the initiative of the president and his immediate clients for a broad coalition of the authoritarian patron-client politics, include:

1. The Korean Association of People (KAP)
2. The Korean Youth Association (KYA)
3. The Korean Farmers Association (KFA)
4. The Korean Women's Association (KWA)
5. The Korean Labor Unions (KLU).
6. The Korean Legion (KL)
7. The Korean Anti-Communist Youth Corps (KACYC)

The KLU, for example, was supposed to protect and promote workers' rights. Similar to the other major associations, the KLU, however, was not voluntarily organized to improve working conditions and to collectively bargain wages and other fringe benefits. It was organized under the guidance and supervision of the central government (Doh, 1964: 68). Coupled with the surplus of labor workers and a limited number of manufacturing firms, the powers of the workers vis-a-vis the employers were so skewed that the workers could not enjoy autonomy. Therefore, the unions were not allowed to become leftist or liberal but rightist and pro-government and financially survive only with the support of the chief patron. The KLU also played a vital role to challenge and suppress left-wing labor unions like the National Council of Korean Workers (NKW)(S. K. Yu, 1983: 159)

The KL was established in 1952 and soon divided in 1953 into two groups on the basis of whether the members joined the Korean War or not. The Korean Legion was, therefore, split into Korean War Veterans and non-Korean War Veterans Association. In 1956, they were integrated into one. (Kook H. Lee, 1962: 82). Regardless of the experience of separation and integration, the legion had consistently supported their chief patron, the president and his coalition.

In preparation for the 1960 presidential election, the Liberal Party began to integrate such national youth organizations as Korean Anti-Communist Corps, United Anti-Communist Youth Association, and Anti-Communist Enlightenment Movement Association into the Korean Anti-Communist Youth Corps (KACYC) on January 23, 1959. It soon organized its subsidiaries in 89 cities and counties across the nation by August 1959. Its chairperson ironically was President Syngman Rhee and Vice Chairman was Leo Kee Boong, President Rhee's vice presidential running mate in the 1960 election (Kee H. Lee, 1961).

In order to maintain political power on the basis of patron-client network, President Rhee as the chief patron developed several creative measures. They were the adoption of interlocking membership of key leaders of the groups and associations into the position of the central committee of the government party (Y.H. Yun, 1987: 147); the election of group leaders from among only those "recommended and endorsed" by the government without open and fair competition for the leadership in the unions; the active campaigns of these groups and associations for the re-election of President Rhee as their chief patron, with Rhee often permitting election rigging (Y.H. Yun, 1987: 148); the prohibition of those working in the private sector from organizing interest groups under the guise of preventing communists and socialists from penetrating into South Korea; and the enactment of a variety of laws such as the Public Official Law to prohibit civil service personnel from participating in interest groups and associations, while they were coercively required to campaign for the re-election of their chief executive, President Rhee (CEMC, 1973a: 200).

As of August 31, 1959 the number of major interest groups and associations reached 780. Numerous as they were, they lacked autonomy in organizational and financial management and, therefore, were not able to perform their primary function of interest articulation (Y.H. Yun, 1987: 146). An absolute majority of them were degraded as clients loyal to their patrons, the president and his political party.

Figure 8-2 shows the political satellite of the First Republic, in which the chief patron, major power elites, minor power elites,

280   Korea Leading Developing Nations

Figure 8-2 A Political Satellite Model of the First Republic: 1948-1960

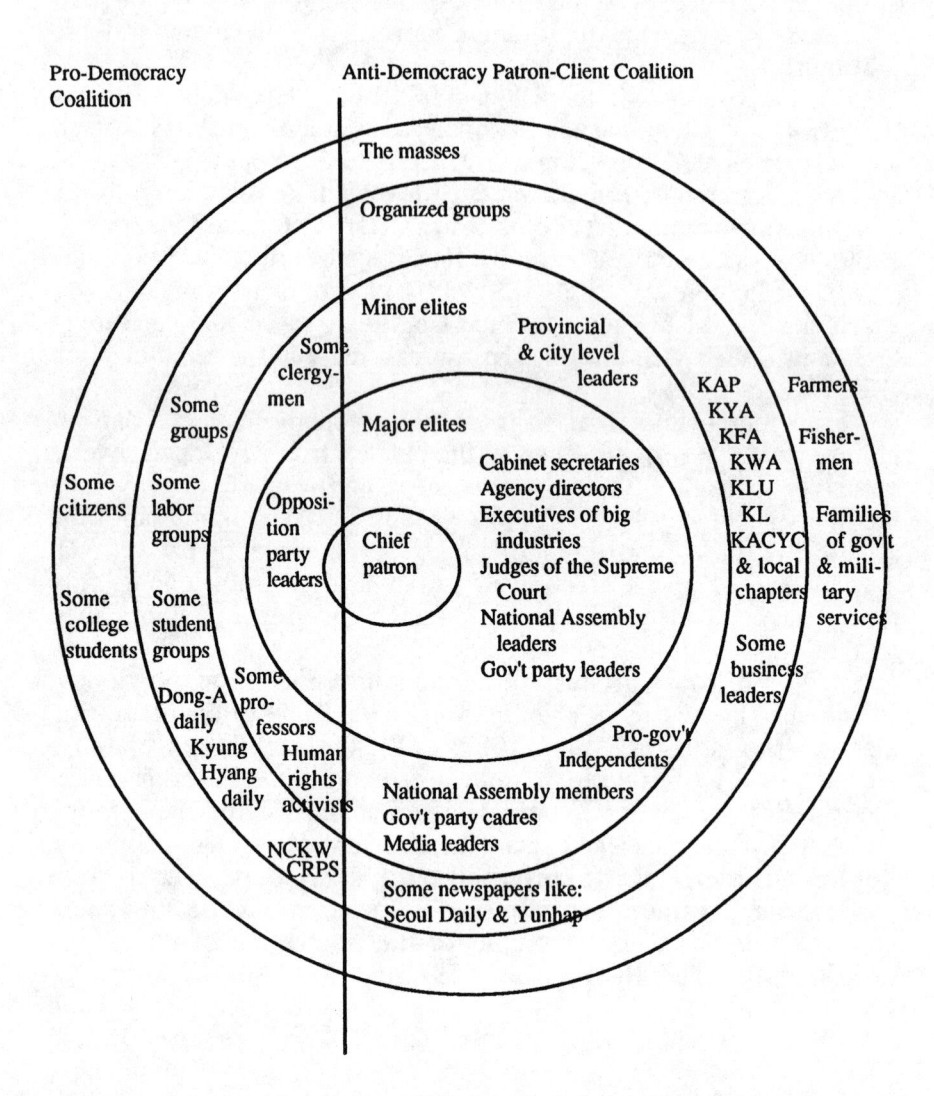

Pro-Democracy Coalition | Anti-Democracy Patron-Client Coalition

- The masses
- Organized groups
- Minor elites
- Major elites
- Chief patron

Pro-Democracy side:
- Some citizens
- Some college students
- Some groups
- Some labor groups
- Some student groups
- Some clergymen
- Opposition party leaders
- Some professors
- Human rights activists
- Dong-A daily
- Kyung Hyang daily
- NCKW
- CRPS

Anti-Democracy side:
- Provincial & city level leaders
- Cabinet secretaries
- Agency directors
- Executives of big industries
- Judges of the Supreme Court
- National Assembly leaders
- Gov't party leaders
- KAP, KYA, KFA, KWA, KLU, KL, KACYC & local chapters
- Some business leaders
- Farmers
- Fishermen
- Families of gov't & military services
- Pro-gov't Independents
- National Assembly members
- Gov't party cadres
- Media leaders
- Some newspapers like: Seoul Daily & Yunhap

various organized groups, and the farmers and fishermen accounted for a majority of the population; all were organized as a broad coalition in favor of the maintenance of President Rhee's anti-democracy patron-client political coalition. A pro-democracy force ironically was organized as a much weaker and smaller coalition consisting of a few opposition political leaders, intellectuals, religious leaders, journalists, college professors, students, and citizens.

President Rhee's Liberal Party, as an embryonic organization, secured only 14.4 percent of the total National Assembly seats in the 1950 election. Therefore, the chances for Rhee to be re-elected by the National Assembly as the second consecutive four-year term president in the 1952 election were very slim. In order for Rhee and his patron-client coalition to maintain government power, they decided to amend the constitution, in which a direct popular presidential election should replace the indirect presidential election by the National Assembly. Since the amendment to the Constitution had to be approved by the National Assembly, which ironically was under the control of the opposition parties and independents, President Rhee declared martial law on May 25, 1952. The opposition Assemblymen were soon coercively taken into the Assembly Hall. Editors of two leading newspapers--*Kyonghyang* and *Dong-A* dailies--were arrested due to their editorials criticizing the martial law. The Assemblymen were not allowed to have debates on the floor and forced to stand up to vote "for" or "against" the amendment such that the democratic principle of secret ballot was blatantly violated. The amendment of a direct popular election of the president was finally approved with 163 to 3 (C.S. Kim, 1981: 53).

In 1954, President Rhee and his Liberal Party again amended the constitution for his third consecutive four-year term re-election with an affirmative vote of 135, which accounted for 66.5 percent, one vote short of the two-thirds majority of the National Assembly.

The Pro-Democracy Coalition

Those on the pro-democracy coalition--opposition leaders, intellectuals, editors and journalists of *Kyonghyang* and *Dong-A* dailies, university professors, and students--declared the amendment illegal. The president and his coalition, on the other hand, claimed that 66.5 percent could be mathematically rounded up to reach the minimally required 67 percent, namely the two-thirds majority and, therefore, insisted the amendment be duly ratified (Y.S. Kwon, 1981: 81).

On August 13, 1956, *Dong-A* and *Kyonghyang* dailies were brave enough to report that policeman Park Chae Kyu observed a ballot box exchanged by other police. Editor Koh Hae Wook and Social News Section Chief Chai Ho, who were responsible for that stormy news, were immediately summoned for investigation. Chang Taek Sang and fifty-eight leaders of the pro-democracy coalition risked their lives, organizing the Committee for the Restoration of Popular Sovereignty (CRPS) in 1957, and protested President Rhee and his anti-democracy coalition against: 1) the coercive way of amending the constitution from the parliamentary election to the direct popular election of the president; 2) the deprivation of basic rights and freedoms of the citizens; 3) the mobilization of police force for both the amendment to the constitution and the presidential election; 4) nepotism and favoritism rampant in both national and local governments; and 5) the Executive's interference with judicial integrity (Y.H. Yun, 1987: 341-342).

In the election of 1954, the government Liberal Party was able to secure 54.1 percent (114 of 203) of the Assembly seats. Utilizing both voluntary persuasion and coercive measures, the Liberal Party was able to secure support from all Independents, who occupied 33.4 percent of the total Assembly seats. Consequently, the opposition parties held only 15 seats, 7.4 percent. A variety of suppressions and restrictions notwithstanding, the pro-democracy coalition gained more popular support in the Fourth National Assembly election in 1958. This helped the opposition Democratic Party gain 33.9 percent, thereby exceeding the one-third of the total seats. Therefore, the President and the Liberal Party were no longer able to dictate the National Assembly even in collusion with all Independents because of the shortage in meeting the constitutional requirements of the two-thirds majority on all major state affairs.

As is shown in Figure 8-3, for the first time in the history of the First Republic, the pro-democracy coalition became strong enough to challenge the anti-democracy patron-client coalition. The chief patron and his clients were so desperate to win the 1960 presidential election that they developed various election riggings such as the close observation of popular ballots by local officials and police, the purchase of ballots, the use of "ghost" voters, and the exchange of ballot boxes via delivery to the ballot counting offices (Y.H. Yun, 1987: 323-324).

The scope and extent of election rigging became so prevalent that university students began to take to the streets, resisting police shootings, repeatedly marching on the Blue House, the presidential office building, shouting slogans to "the downfall of the dictator and his clients," and demanding measures for democratization. Lack of legitimacy and the inability to indiscriminately shoot the student

The Korean Model of Democratization 283

Figure 8-3 Change in the First Republic's Political Satellite Model

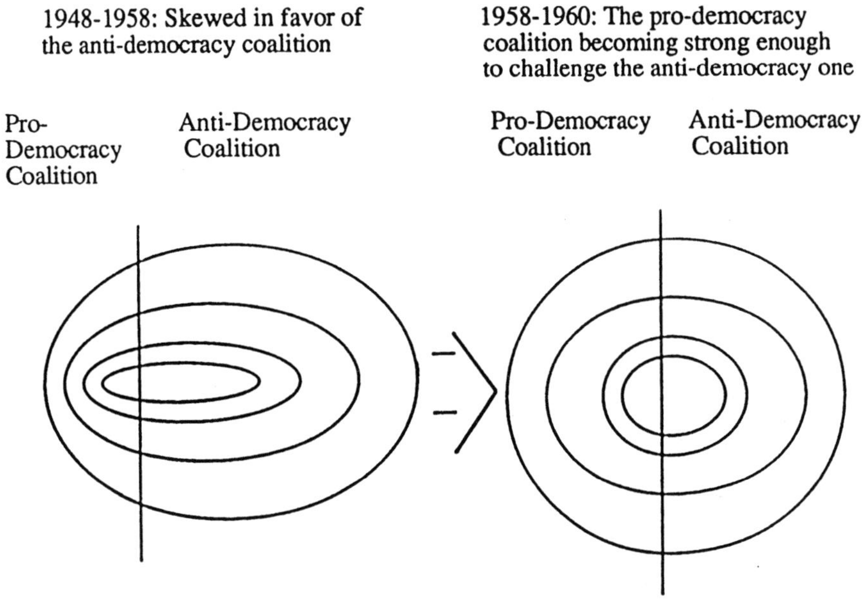

1948-1958: Skewed in favor of the anti-democracy coalition

1958-1960: The pro-democracy coalition becoming strong enough to challenge the anti-democracy one

| Pro-Democracy Coalition | Anti-Democracy Coalition | Pro-Democracy Coalition | Anti-Democracy Coalition |

demonstrators, indeed enfeebled the president, who commanded 600,000 armed forces and tens of thousands of police. President Rhee was forced to resign, and the First Republic collapsed.

The Military Government and Third Republic (1961-1971)

The Anti-Democracy Patron-Client Coalition

The dreams and expectations for democratization right after the April 19 student uprising in 1960 soon evaporated with the military coup on May 16, 1961 led by General Park Chung Hee. This was, indeed, a revolution, which was defined by Robert Gamer as "the replacement of the present patron-client networks by completely new membership from top to bottom" (Gamer, 1976: 171). All of the existing political parties were immediately abolished. All of the "old, corrupt" politicians were deprived of civil and political rights, many of them put into prison and not eligible to run for the government positions. All Cabinet secretaries, justices of the Supreme Court, and military commanding generals were replaced by clients loyal to General Park.

One of President Park's major client groups was the Economic Planning Board (EPB), which took leadership in multi-year economic development planning and subsequent close supervision of major industries, banking and credit institutions, and the infrastructure. Its key members were the Cabinet secretaries and advisors who were specialized in economics, econometrics, and public policy-making. They provided their chief patron with the five-year economic plan and programs which could justify the power maintenance of President Park in the name of economic development and well-being of the people.

To strengthen the newly-organized, anti-democracy patron-client coalition, President Park established the Korean Central Intelligence Agency (KCIA). Its agents began to penetrate into not only various governmental departments and agencies but also various private industries and organizations. In order to secure a majority of the National Assembly seats, the government party system was strengthened with a variety of methods: fifty percent of the at-large Assembly seats to be assigned to the winning party, no matter how marginal the party's winning in the district election became; the allocation of sixty percent of the total financial contributions to the winning party; the requirement for party nomination of its candidates, who would desire to run for the National Assembly; the prohibition of Independents from running for the National Assembly; and automatic loss of the Assembly seat in case of resignation or expulsion from party membership.

President Park, as the chief patron, was very skillful in holding a firm grip on his party leaders and Assemblymen, who were divided into two factions--the pro-Kim Jong Pil faction and the anti-Kim faction. President Park played one faction against the other to secure their loyalty to him and their support for the constitutional amendment for his third consecutive four-year term.

President Park was equally shrewd in organizing, supervising, and controlling various interest groups and associations. Agricultural Cooperatives (AC), for example, were not voluntarily organized by farmers themselves but initiated by the government. The Constitution of the Agricultural Cooperative stipulates in Article 6 that "the association and its central executive committee shall not be involved in politics. Those who join political parties and other political activities shall not be eligible for the position of the association's central executive committee at least until the passage of two years from their previous activities in politics." Nevertheless, the president of the republic appointed a politically involved person the president of the Central Executive Committee of all Agricultural Cooperatives upon the recommendation of its Central Committee (K.H. Lee, 1969: 53). The Minister of Agriculture supervised both the Central Cooperative Committee and all local Agricultural Cooperatives. Local Agricultural Cooperative presidents and key officials were all simultaneously appointed as government employees. In fact, they held two positions concurrently--government employment and the official positions of the cooperatives. They either voluntarily or coercively were forced to play a vital role in the re-election of the president and his National Assembly members. Of course, they lacked autonomy for independent internal operation of their own cooperatives (K.H. Lee, 1969: 86).

The Korean Athletic Association called for a general election and voted for the re-election of the incumbent members of its Board of Directors on January 6, 1964. However, the government forced the association to reverse the January 6 election and ordered its pro-government president to appoint all members of the Board of Directors as well as key members of the association. In preparation for the 1967 National Assembly election, the government again ordered the association to establish Local Encouraging Groups in each of the towns.

All of the groups and associations existing prior to the May 16, 1961 coup became defunct or inactive. New groups and associations began to emerge. Listed here are the examples of a few diverse groups and associations which either voluntarily or coercively became the major client groups for the chief patron, President Park:

1. The Agricultural Cooperatives (AC)
2. The Korean Athletic Association (KAA)
3. Town and Local Athletic Encouraging Groups (TLAEG)
4. The Aquatic Products Association (APA)
5. Industrial Labor Unions (ILU)
6. The Forest Association (FA)
7. The Performing Arts Association (PAA)
8. The Horticultural Association (HA)
9. The Livestock Association (LA)
10. Religious groups such as Catholic, Buddhist, and Protestant Associations

286 Korea Leading Developing Nations

Figure 8-4 A Political Satellite Model of the Third Republic: 1963-1972

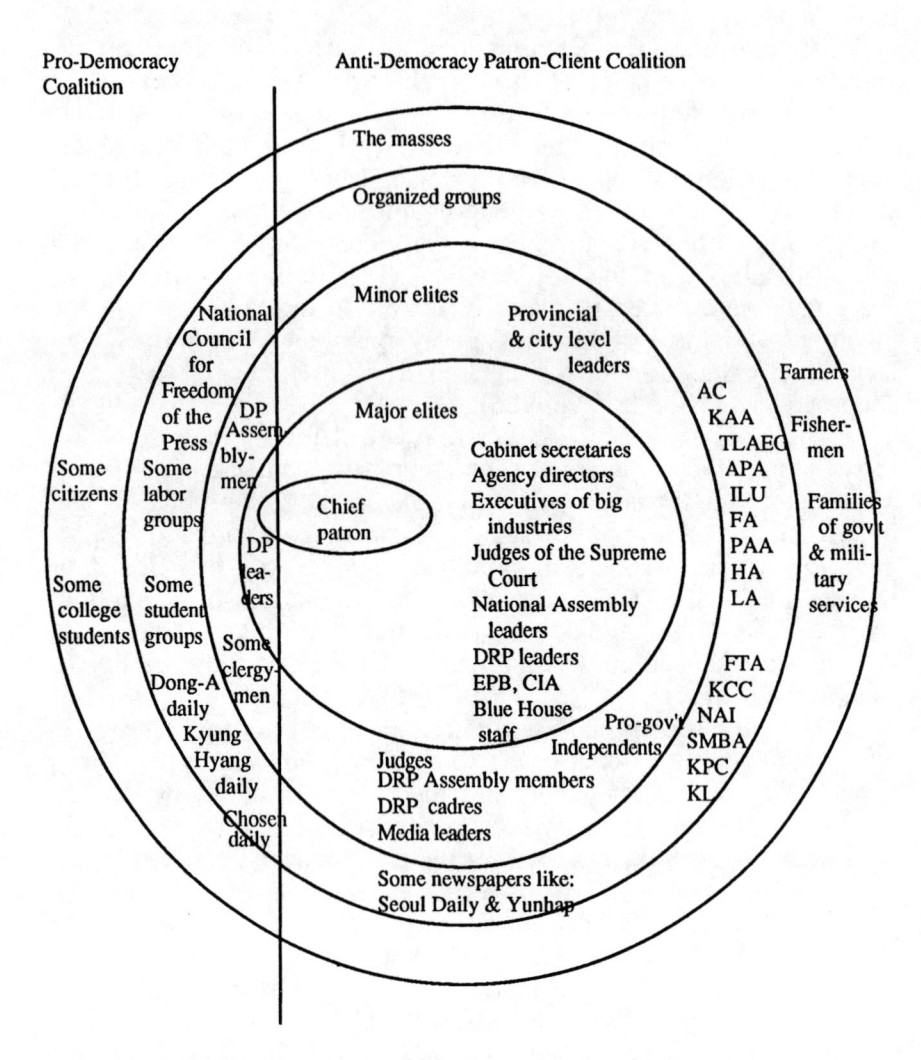

Pro-Democracy Coalition | Anti-Democracy Patron-Client Coalition

The masses
Organized groups
Minor elites
  National Council for Freedom of the Press
  DP Assemblymen
  Some citizens
  Some labor groups
  Some college students
  Some student groups
  Dong-A daily
  Kyung Hyang daily
  Chosen daily
  DP leaders
  Some clergymen

Major elites
  Chief patron
  Cabinet secretaries
  Agency directors
  Executives of big industries
  Judges of the Supreme Court
  National Assembly leaders
  DRP leaders
  EPB, CIA
  Blue House staff
  Judges
  DRP Assembly members
  DRP cadres
  Media leaders
  Some newspapers like: Seoul Daily & Yunhap
  Pro-gov't Independents

Provincial & city level leaders
  AC
  KAA
  TLAEC
  APA
  ILU
  FA
  PAA
  HA
  LA
  FTA
  KCC
  NAI
  SMBA
  KPC
  KL

Farmers
Fishermen
Families of gov't & military services

11. Hotel and Restaurant Business Association (HRBA)
12. The Fortunetellers Association (FTA)
13. The Korean Chamber of Commerce (KCC) and its local organizations
14. The National Association of Industries (NAI)
15. Small and Medium Business Associations (SMBA)(Y.H. Yun, 1987: 158-163)

16. The Korean Press Club (KPC)
17. The Korean Legion (see Figure 8-4).

In 1962, there appeared some 350 groups and associations. By 1966, the number reached some 480. Nevertheless, they were all financially weak and, therefore, dependent on the government. They were not encouraged to articulate their own demands and expectations to the government party and the administration. They were rather forced to blindly obey and follow the instructions of the government in fund-raising, campaigning, mobilizing the members and families, and voting in the next general election for the incumbent president and his National Assembly nominees. For loyalty, dedication, continued campaigning, and keeping the patron-client network in power, these groups and associations were rewarded a variety of favors--financial aid, technical advice, legal protection, and tax exemption.

Figure 8-4 shows the political satellite of the Third Republic along the two coalitions "against" and "for" democratization. The anti-democracy patron-client coalition, which was centered around the chief patron, President Park, became more powerful than that of former President Rhee of the First Republic and dominant over the tiny pro-democracy coalition.

The anti-democracy, patron-client coalition, however, applied the policy of sticks and mounted legal and subtle restrictions, suppression, and even severe punishment on the agents of the small pro-democracy coalition. The Constitution of the Third Republic of Korea stipulates that "the workers' right to association, collective bargaining, and collective actions shall be guaranteed. . . ." The Labor Union Law of 1963 authorized the vertical linkage from the workplace to industry such that region- and nation-wide industry-based labor unions could be organized and share with local unions the power of collective bargaining with management (Article 33, Section 2). But this provision was later deleted. The revised Labor Union Law of 1968 explicitly stipulates that labor unions shall be organized only in each of the unit enterprises. No regional or national unions by industries except federations shall be organized (Art. 13). The Temporary Special Law on Labor Unions and the Adjustment of Labor Disputes in Foreign Enterprises, which became effective on January 1, 1970, limited the right of the workers in foreign invested industries in Korea to bargain collectively and completely suspended the right to collective action. In December

1971, this law was superseded by the Special Measures Law on National Security and Defense, which suspended both the right to collective bargaining and the right to collective action of all workers. The resolution of all potential labor disputes was placed directly on the Department of Labor of the Central Government (Pae, 1986: 86-87).

The government was equally suppressive against the mass media. The Martial Law Command issued an order on May 16, 1961, which stipulated the specific provisions of restrictions on the freedom of the press: no media coverage of any comments "favorable" to the North Korean government; no information and news "in conflict with" the objectives which the Military Revolutionary Command attempted to accomplish; no propaganda conceived as "anti-revolutionary" conspiracy; "no false or distorted" information which might inspire the public to have anti-government attitudes and views; and no comments and news which might "disturb" esprit de corps of the armed forces (SCMR, 1961).

Martial law became effective immediately against the major newspapers such as the *Dong-A Ilbo* in January and March, 1961, the *Hankuk Ilbo* in April, and the *Daehan Ilbo* in May, the *Chosun Ilbo* in July, the *Dong-A* in August, and the *Hankuk Ilbo* in November, 1961. The correspondents, who covered news and comments critical of the Military Revolutionary Command, were soon arrested. Not only the editors but also the publisher of the *Hankuk Ilbo* was subject to severe restraints. *The Hankuk Ilbo* was finally forced to close its publication (Yun, 1987: 258-259).

The Constitution of the Third Republic, which succeeded the military government on December 26, 1962, stipulates in Article 18 that "all citizens shall enjoy freedom of speech and press, and freedom of assembly and association." However, its qualifications were clearly specified in the remaining provisions of the Article: censorship in regard to motion pictures and dramatic plays to be imposed for the maintenance of public morality and social ethics; the requirement for newspapers and the press to meet the publishing facility standards as prescribed by law; neither the press nor any other publication allowed to impugn the personal honor or rights of an individual, nor infringe upon public morality.

In 1963, the government additionally enacted the Law Regarding Registration of the Press, Newspaper, and Communications. Since the government monopolized the power to grant or deny registration, the survival, continuity, and discontinuity of newspapers began to be greatly dependent upon the sole discretion of the Executive Branch of the government. In August 1964, the government party Assemblymen alone on the floor of the Assembly enacted the Law Regarding the Press Ethics Committee, which was empowered to review news and editorial comments on the basis of the ambiguous criteria of "public morality" and "social ethics." The government soon announced that those individuals and organizations which might violate the Press Ethics Law should face punishment from the government. The government also threatened to wage a campaign against the subscription to their publications by the regular customers of both the public and private sectors.

Three major pro-democracy newspapers--the *Kyunghyang*, the *Chosun*, and the *Dong-A*, which were brave enough to criticize patron-client politics and policies--were soon deprived of their editorial independence. Government intelligence agents secured the access to the editorial offices of these three major newspapers for twenty-four hours every day from 1964. In preparation for those on the major patron-client network to amend the constitution of the republic in 1969 for the third consecutive four-year term re-election of President Park, the government took measures to transfer the editorial and production rights from the editors to the publishers. The publishers were, of course, more subject to the government, which could restrict advertisement on the newspapers whose fees accounted for the major financial source for their survival and were, therefore, more compliant with the wishes of the government.

In December 1971, the government declared the Measures Regarding National Security, which stipulated the government's right to restrict the press and publication. The Cabinet Council also enacted the Law Regarding the Protection of Classified Military Affairs and the Law Regarding the Protection of Military Facilities. In response to these three measures adopted "against the threats from North Korea, the Korean Press Association (KPA) gave up the freedom of the press" (Yun, 1987: 263). The KPA was forced by the Ministry of Culture and Information (MCI) to adopt a press card system, which required all correspondents to be annually reviewed for the renewal of their press cards. By February 10, 1972, a total of 3,975 journalists were reviewed and granted press cards, whereas 1,063 were denied the renewal and subsequently forced to quit their jobs (Choi, 1976: 160). Both the national and provincial newspapers were forced to close many local branches. A total of 4,896 were abolished, and only 493 remained intact such that the smaller the number of journalists and local branches became, the more tightly the government could control their access to governmental agencies, and the more efficiently the MCI could supervise the mass media's criticism of the government.

The Pro-Democracy Coalition

Despite tight restrictions by a variety of laws and government measures against the pro-democracy movements, the commitment and dedication of the pro-democracy forces to struggle for the promotion and protection of basic freedoms and rights did not dissipate. They continued to criticize those on the major patron-client network for their imposition of the Political Purification Law on the anti-government, pro-democracy forces and for their scheme to legitimize the Third Republic by means of a popular referendum on the performance of the Third Republic while playing down the military coup and the subsequent unconstitutional means of taking over the government power (J.H. Kim, 1971: 118).

In August 1964, when the government announced the Law Regarding Press Ethics Committee, some opposition National Assemblymen, distinguished men out of office, and media men gathered together in the Seoul Press Hall on August 10, 1964. They organized the National Council for the Protection of the Freedom of the Press, and adopted a resolution for them to fight for the freedom to the last. In 1968, when the government began to have a tight grip on the mass media in order to amend the constitution to extend the restriction of the two consecutive terms of the president to the third consecutive one, university students initiated massive demonstrations against the government scheme and against the acquiescence of mass media on the issue. Being seriously reprimanded for the collusion of the mass media with the government by students, opposition parties, intellectuals, and religious leaders, some thirty junior-level journalists of the *Dong-A Ilbo*, gathered together and announced a Declaration for the Protection of Freedom of the Press on April 5, 1971 (Yun, 1987: 262-263).

President Park and his chief clients were so desperate to maintain power that their ultimate goal in the 1967 National Assembly election was to have their ruling Democratic Republican Party (DRP) secure a minimum of two-thirds or more of the Assembly seats by any means for the constitutional amendment so as to allow President Park to run again. A variety of frauds and riggings, coupled with the mobilization of local administrators and police helped the DRP secure 73.7 percent of the total seats, far exceeding the minimum requirement of 67 percent to amend the constitution. However, the election riggings caused the opposition Assemblymen to boycott the Assembly session for nearly five months.

The National Assembly crisis was further extended into the next year when the Civil Defense Force was organized by an executive order, bypassing the National Assembly. Opposition Assemblymen claimed that deliberation and passage of such a legislation as the Civil Defense should be the sole jurisdiction of the National Assembly instead. In 1969, the DRP openly deliberated an amendment to the constitution and finally prepared the amendment with 122 pro-government Assemblymen, five more than the two-thirds majority needed to pass it. In protest the opposition Assemblymen staged a sit-in strike on the speaker's dais as a move to block the presiding officer from holding the final vote. Opposition Assemblymen, civic and religious leaders, professors, and other intellectuals united, organized the Pan-National Struggle Committee Against the Constitutional Amendment, and waged a nationwide campaign against the amendment. Nevertheless, 122 pro-government Assemblymen secretly walked to the Annex Building located across the street from the National Assembly main building before dawn and passed it without debate. The move plunged the nation into another crisis. The opposition Assemblymen continued their boycott for two additional months. Over seventy thousand college students staged protest demonstrations against President Park.

Angered by the illegitimate way of amending the constitution, ridiculed by the violation of the democratic principle of peaceful transfer of power, and heartened by student demonstrations, more average voters began to join the pro-democracy coalition. This was clearly evidenced in the outcome of the eighth National Assembly election held on May 25, 1971. In the 1967 election, the DRP secured 73.7 percent of the total Assembly seats, 7.7 percent above the level of the two-thirds majority, which could amend the constitution and pass all major legislations and policies without the attendance of opposition Assemblymen on the floor. But in the 1971 election, the DRP received only 55.4 percent of the Assembly seats, whereas the opposition secured 43.6 percent, well above the level of the one-third. Therefore, the opposition Assemblymen could veto the government party's major legislative proposals. The enthusiastic

Figure 8-5 Change in the Third Republic's Political Satellite Model

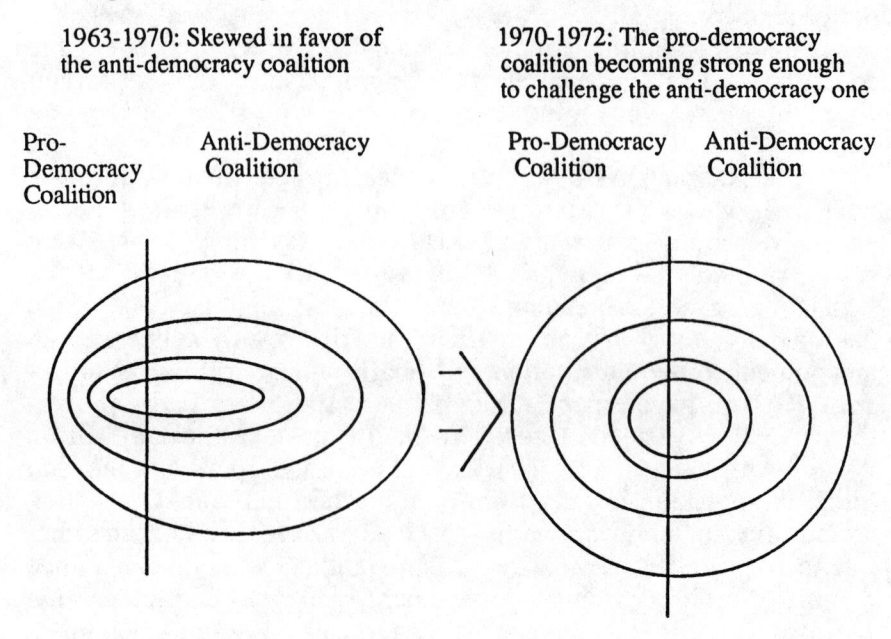

1963-1970: Skewed in favor of the anti-democracy coalition

1970-1972: The pro-democracy coalition becoming strong enough to challenge the anti-democracy one

Pro-Democracy Coalition   Anti-Democracy Coalition

Pro-Democracy Coalition   Anti-Democracy Coalition

popular support for the promotion of democracy and the subsequent securing of 43.6 percent by the opposition were such that President Park could no longer amend the constitution for his fourth consecutive term of service. On the contrary, the opposition Assemblymen began to have louder voices in the Assembly than their predecessors.

Similar to the years of 1958 to 1960 (see Figure 8-3) of the First Republic, the years of 1971-1972 witnessed the pro-democracy coalition as being sufficiently strengthened and significantly threatening the authoritarian, patron-client coalition centered around the chief patron of President Park. Due to increase in education, greater exposure to the mass media, and, ironically, the ever-increasing control over basic freedoms and human rights by the government, the greater number of people--students, intellectuals, religious leaders, opposition--joined the pro-democracy coalition in 1971-1972, which far surpassed the number of participants in the pro-democracy coalition of 1963-1970 (Figure 8-5) in terms of extensiveness (the number of participants) and intensiveness (the degree of commitment to fighting and struggling for democracy).

The Fourth Republic (1972-1979)

The Anti-Democracy Patron-Client Coalition

Being desperate for re-election as a lifelong president and for maintenance of the existing patron-client network, President Park issued martial law and took extraordinary measures on October 17, 1972. He dismissed the members of the National Assembly, dissolved the political parties, and replaced the National Assembly with the Extraordinary State Council. The Constitution of the Third Republic was amended under martial law by the State Council, which consisted of the Cabinet secretaries of President Park's own personal choice. The amendment was finally ratified by a national referendum on November 21, 1972. This was called the Yushin Constitution, which gave birth to the Fourth Republic.

President Park and his clients on the major patron-client network took several steps to strengthen and perpetuate their political power and concurrently weaken the pro-democracy coalition forces in the new constitution. The president of the Fourth Republic was granted all of the powers which the president of the Third Republic had enjoyed. Added to these, the president of the Fourth Republic was empowered to dissolve the National Assembly at his own discretion at any time (1972 Const., Art. 52). Whenever opposition parties might gain more Assembly seats so as to seriously challenge the government party and the president or attempt to postpone or disturb the expedient process of legislation on the floor so as to delay taking proper measures by the National Assembly, the president could dissolve the National Assembly and call for a general National Assembly election. As an alternative he could submit important policies directly to a national referendum at his own discretion without consultation with and approval from the National Assembly (1972, Art. 48). The president also had the power of appointment and dismissal of not only the Chief Justice of the Supreme Court but also all other judges (1972, Art. 104). Moreover, no limit was imposed on the number of terms a president could serve consecutively. Therefore, Park could be a lifelong president (see Figure 8-6).

The president also had the power to take necessary emergency measures "in the whole range of state affairs," which included internal affairs, foreign affairs, national defense, and economic, financial, and judicial affairs. Those emergency measures could be

294 Korea Leading Developing Nations

Figure 8-6 A Political Satellite Model of the Fourth Republic: 1973-1979

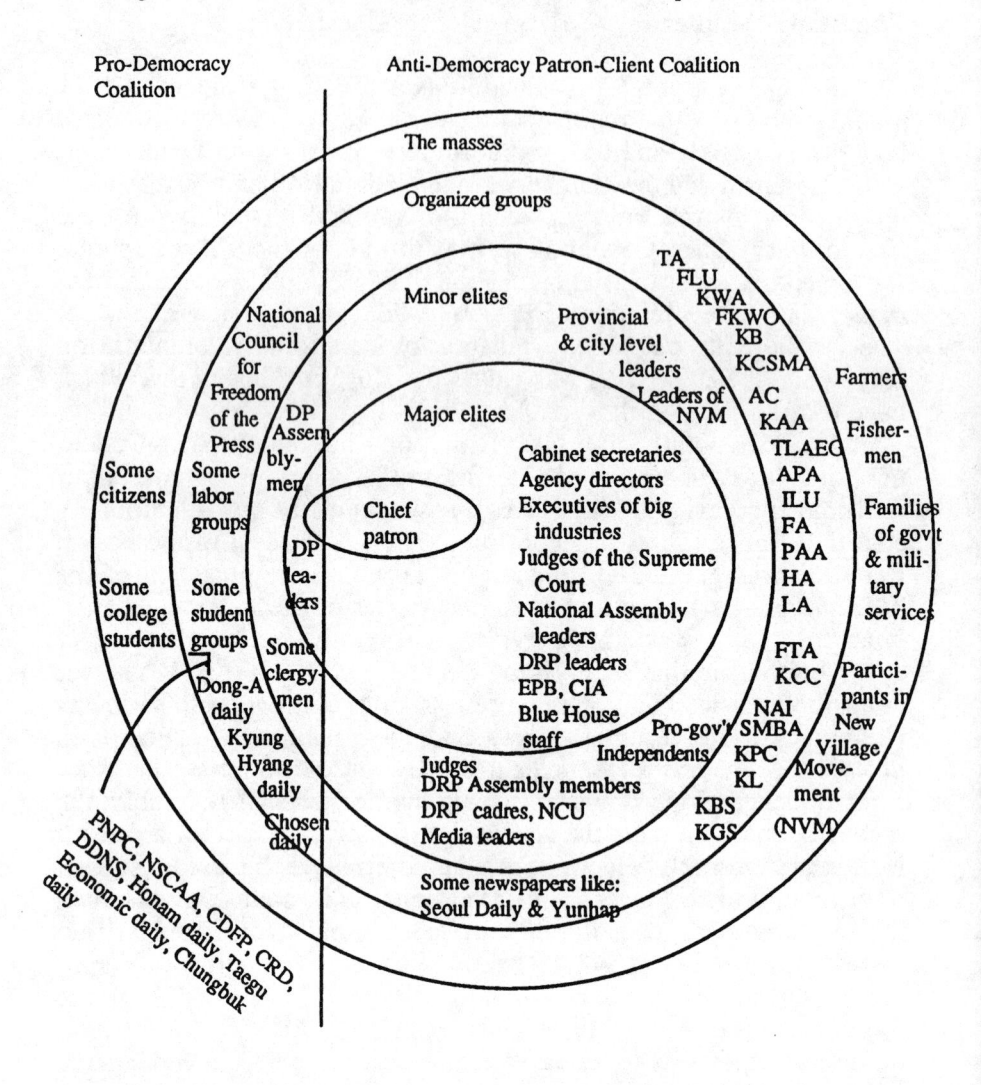

Pro-Democracy Coalition | Anti-Democracy Patron-Client Coalition

The masses
Organized groups
Minor elites
Major elites

National Council for Freedom of the Press
DP Assemblymen
DP leaders
Some citizens
Some labor groups
Some college students
Some student groups
Some clergymen
Dong-A daily
Kyung Hyang daily
Chosen daily

PNPC, NSCAA, CDFP, CRD, DDNS, Honam daily, Taegu Economic daily, Chungbuk daily

Provincial & city level leaders
Leaders of NVM
Cabinet secretaries
Agency directors
Executives of big industries
Judges of the Supreme Court
National Assembly leaders
DRP leaders
EPB, CIA
Blue House staff
Judges
DRP Assembly members
DRP cadres, NCU
Media leaders
Some newspapers like: Seoul Daily & Yunhap

Chief patron

TA FLU KWA FKWO KB KCSMA AC KAA TLAEC APA ILU FA PAA HA LA FTA KCC NAI Pro-gov't SMBA Independents KPC KL KBS KGS

Farmers
Fishermen
Families of gov't & military services
Participants in New Village Movement (NVM)

justified, however, not only for the case of serious threats to national security or public safety but also for the case of even "anticipated" threats. Such a sweeping clause authorized the president to take preemptive measures in anticipation of potential challenge to him and his clients, thereby suspending the freedoms and rights of the people as prescribed in the Constitution and enforcing emergency measures with regard to the powers of the Executive and the Judiciary (1972, Art. 53-(2). His emergency measures were not subject to judicial review nor was the president obligated to terminate them upon the recommendation by the National Assembly even with the concurrence of a majority of its total members (1972, Art. 53-(4) and (6)).

The Constitution of the Fourth Republic established a brand new institution called the National Conference for Unification (NCU), whose members were popularly elected every six years in order to elect the president of the republic. Unlike the electoral college system of the United States, in which a presidential candidate who wins more popular votes in a state takes all electoral votes of the state, the "winner-takes-all" requirement was not honored in Korea. In other words, a range of 2,000 to 5,000 NCU members who were elected by the popular votes were not required to vote for a specific candidate as mandated by their constituencies. Each of the NCU members was allowed instead to cast one vote on the basis of his/her own choice for the election of the president. The NCU, however, was not considered a *de facto* independent and autonomous organization because its members were not allowed to have opportunities to observe open debates between the presidential candidates. Nor were they allowed to exchange their opinions on the competing candidates. They were not guaranteed the secret ballot in their choice. Ironically, the president of the republic became automatically the chairman of the NCU. President Park, in fact, had its members elected himself as the eighth and ninth president in 1972 and 1978 with 99.9 percent (2,357 or 2,359) and 99.8 percent (2,578 of 2,581) of affirmative votes, respectively (CEMC, 1973: 295 and 1980: 381). Moreover, it was the NCU, not a national referendum, that was empowered to ratify amendments to the constitution.

The president of the Fourth Republic was further empowered to have the NCU approve one-third of the members of the National Assembly of his own nomination. The NCU was required to approve or disapprove a list of the one-third candidates nominated by the president. In case of no approval the president should propose another slate with all or some of the nominees replaced (1972, Art. 40-(3)). Accordingly, one-third of the National Assemblymen were those of his own choice. The real objective of this constitutional mechanism was to ensure that the president could secure more than two-thirds of the total members of the National assembly by combining his political party Assemblymen with the one-third of the total Assemblymen of his own choice called the Yujunghoe. Securing two-thirds or more of the members of the National Assembly by the president and his political party was required for: expelling any member of the Assembly (1972, Art. 98-(3)) who would dare to challenge the president or his patron-client coalition; protecting the president from a motion for impeachment (1972, Art. 99-(2)); and proposing amendments to the Constitution by the National Assembly (1972, Art. 125-(2)).

The Constitution of the Fourth Republic also restricted basic civil rights and freedoms to a significant extent. Article 32 justifies that laws which restrict freedoms or rights of citizens shall be enacted "when necessary for the maintenance of national security, order or public welfare" (Art. 32-(2)). The ambiguity on the concepts of national security, order, and public welfare was such that the president's restrictions on civil rights and freedoms could be justified at any time.

The anti-democracy, patron-client coalition centered around President Park of the Fourth Republic included the same participants in his network of the Third Republic. Only those few who dared to express disagreement with President Park on the persistence of his power in violation of the democratic principle of peaceful transfer of power were purged and, therefore, excluded. Added to the coalition were: the National Association of Major Industries, which emphasized the motto of "the undisturbed rapid rate of continued economic growth;" the National Council for Unification; and key policy-makers of the New Village Movement, which planned to enhance the quality of life of the farmers, who had been loyal and obedient to President Park's patron-client network but ironically suffered most from the government's priority of rapid industrialization and the subsequent increase in wage and low grain policies.

The major interest groups and associations, which maintained loyalty to President Park's network, continued to stay in the same network. A few additional groups joined his patronage coalition. They were the Trade Association (TA), the Federation of Labor Unions (FLU), the Korean Women's Association (KWA), the Federation of Korean Women's organizations (FKWO), the Korean Boy Scouts (KBS) and Girl Scouts (KGS), and the Korean College Student Missionary Association (KCSMA) (S.R. Yu, 1977: 22-31).

Those on the anti-democracy patron-client coalition were awarded a variety of benefits upon the benevolence of the chief patron--job security, government grants, government loans with low interest, contracts, tax exemption, and financial support.

On the other hand, those who dared to challenge the pro-government patronage coalition, were severely punished and restrained. As soon as martial law was declared on October 17, 1971, journalists and correspondents were restricted in access to government officials, especially police officers. Legislative activities and procedures in the National Assembly such as the opening ceremony, foreign guest speeches, activities of the Speaker, and committee hearings were not allowed for videotaping, recording, and coverage on daily newspapers and television. On March 30, 1972, upon the advice of the Ministry of Culture and Information (MCI), restrictive measures on the freedom of the press were taken. They were the press self-purification campaign, measures for reorganizing and merging the newspapers and television networks, and a press card system to which correspondents were subject for annual review of their activities and the subsequent renewal or deprivation of their practice as media men. On October 19, 1972, the MCI made a request for press cooperation, which, in fact, meant an order not to cover campus unrest and protests against the government and to minimize the news on college student activities. On December 3, 1973, Prime Minister Kim Jong Pil again made a request for restraints on news coverage of national security matters, the legitimacy of the Fourth Republic, and editorials critical of the government policies because of their negative impact on "public well-being." Finally ordered to close their press were the *Taegu Ilbo* on March 30, 1972, *Taegu Economic Ilbo* on May 31, 1973, the *Chunbuk Ilbo* and *Honam Ilbo* on June 1, 1973, and *Hankuk Economic Ilbo* on March 22, 1973 (Yun, 1987: 273-280).

The Pro-Democracy Coalition

The government's ever-increasing coercive and repressive measures, however, could not force those on the pro-democracy coalition to give in to the authority for long. Various religious organizations began to wage a Pan-National Prayer Campaign for the Rescue of the Republic from the Authoritarian Regime (PNPC). In August 1973, when opposition leader Kim Dae Jung was allegedly kidnapped in Japan by the Korean Central Intelligence Agency, tens of thousands of college students took to the streets, demanding investigation of the kidnapping incident. On January 4, 1974, the Opposition party leader, Yu Jin O began to hold a National Signature Campaign for the amendment of the authoritarian constitution (NSCAA). On January 21, 1974, about 100 leaders, including some forty Christian clergymen made protests for the release of dissident poet Kim Chi Ha, who was arrested for his satirical poetry criticizing the corruption, wrongdoings, and reciprocal benefits gained by those on the major patron-client network centered around President Park. On October 24, 1974, 180 correspondents of the *Dong-A Ilbo* called for a Convention for the Declaration of the Freedoms of the Press (CDFP) and demanded the release of their colleagues in jail. In November 1974, the journalists of the *Dong-A Ilbo* with the support of their colleagues of the *Hankuk Ilbo*, the *Chosun Ilbo*, the *Kyunghyang*, and *Seoul Ilbo*, declared the Implementation of the Freedom of Speech and the Press:

1. No government agents should be allowed to enter into publishing offices of the daily newspapers.
2. No external interference on the editorial independence and integrity.
3. The adherence of correspondents to the principle of accurate reporting.
4. Joint struggles of media men and women against the arrest of their colleagues (Ahn, 1979: 440).

On March 8, 1975, a total of eighteen correspondents of the *Dong-A Ilbo* were laid off. Those who protested against the lay-off of their colleagues were soon dismissed. And additional seventeen reporters were laid off again. On March 17, 1975, a total of 160 correspondents on protest were coercively removed from their indoor campaign site by some 200 mysterious agents. Equally determined and dedicated to the promotion of democracy were about 100 Catholic priests, 100 Protestant clergymen, and another 100 civil leaders who organized a Campaign for the Realization of Democracy (CRD) and held a meeting in the Seoul Myungdong Church (CISJD, 1973: 272-273).

Emergency Measures Number One through Eight and their progressively increasing repressive measures notwithstanding, the Park regime was not able to prohibit the pro-democracy forces from challenging the legitimacy of his power. As the last and most repressive resort, President Park declared Emergency Measure Number Nine on May 13, 1975, which prohibited: the proposing of amendments to the Constitution of the Fourth Republic; the raising of questions on the legitimacy of the Park regime; and anti-government demonstrations and protests. The government announced that those in violation of Emergency Measure Number Nine should be arrested without warrant and without due process of law. It became immediately effective. A total of 139 journalists were denied their press card renewal. Opposition party Assemblywoman Kim Ok Sun was deprived of her membership on the National Assembly on the grounds of the violation of the emergency measure. So was Representative Chung Il-Hyung dismissed from the National Assembly.

The extremely strong presidential powers inherent in the Constitution of the Fourth Republic, however, could not perpetuate President Park and his clients in power. On March 1, 1976, a total of about 100 pro-democracy leaders--priests, university professors who were dismissed from the teaching positions due to their anti-government campaigns and lectures, and other noted civic leaders--gathered together to have a special Mass in commemoration of the March 1 National Independence at the Myungdong Catholic Cathedral. But they instead adopted a Declaration for the Democratic National Salvation (DDNS) in order to restore democracy, and demanded the revocation of Emergency Measure No. 9 and the stepping down of the incumbent President Park and his followers from the government. They also protested against the government's violation of human rights, and demanded the immediate release of the political prisoners who had been arrested for their fight for democracy. Sheer repressive measures to perpetuate control of the government led to ever-increasing popular support for the pro-democracy coalition in the National Assembly elections (see Table 8-1).

The 1973 National Assembly election outcome indicated that President Park's Democratic Republican Party (DRP) received only 38.7 percent of the popular vote despite the maximum employment of all legal and subtle means such as constitutional, legal, and emergency measures together with the mobilization of all local officials and police forces. The New Democratic Party (NDP) and the Democratic Unification Party (DUP), on the other hand, received 32.5 and 10.2 percent, respectively, thus securing a total of 42.7

Table 8-1 The National Assembly Election Outcomes in the Fourth Republic

Political Parties	Percent Popular Votes	Number of Seats Won	Percent of Seats Won	Percent Total of Seats Won with Yujunghoe Included
The Ninth National Assembly Election of 02/27/73				
Democratic-Republican Party (DRP)	38.7%	73	50.0	67.3% (73+77=150)
New Democratic Party (NDP)	32.5%	52	35.6	23.3%
Democratic Unification Party (DUP)	10.2%	2	1.4	0.9%
Independents (I)	18.6%	19	13.0	8.5%
Subtotal	100.0%	146	100.0	
Yujunghoe (YJH) members nominated by the president & approved by the NCU		77		
Total		223	100.0%	
The Tenth National Election on 03/11/79				
Democratic-Republican Party (DRP)	31.7	68	44	62.8% (68+77=145)
New Democratic Party (NDP)	32.8%	61	39.6	26.4%
Democratic Unification Party (DUP)	7.4%	3	1.9	1.3%
Independents (I)	28.1%	22	14.3	9.5%
Subtotal	100.0%	154	100.0	
Yujunghoe (YJH) members nominated by the president & approved by the NCU		77		
Total		231	100.0%	

Source: CEMC (1973b: 279-284; 1980: 365-371)

percent of the popular votes. The districting malapportionment system with the over-representation of pro-government rural voters and the under-representation of pro-opposition urban voters was such that the government DRP with 38.7 percent of the popular votes was able to hold 73 seats, which accounted for fifty percent of the popularly elected Assembly seats. Only because of the reinforcement to the DRP of 77 Yujunghoe Assemblymen who were nominated by the president and automatically confirmed by the NCU, could the Park regime command the National Assembly with 67.3 percent which exceeded the requirement of the two-thirds vote and therefore passed all important domestic issues and foreign affairs without disturbance from the opposition camp. But the 1979 National Assembly election showed the tendency of the ever-decreasing popular support for President Park's authoritarian patron-client coalition and the ever-increasing popular support for the pro-democracy coalition. The government party this time received only 31.7 percent of the popular votes, whereas the major opposition NDP gained 32.8 percent. Taking advantage of the districting malapportionment system, the DRP could secure 68, only 7 more Assemblymen than the NDP. Reinforced by 77 Yujunghoe Assemblymen, the Park regime still was not able to secure the two-thirds majority such that the DRP could no longer command the National Assembly and began to face significant challenges and demands from the opposition camp for democratization.

On June 11, 1979, Kim Young Sam, the major opposition party (NDP) president held a press conference with the *New York Times* correspondent at the Press Club in Seoul and stated that he would be willing to meet with the leaders of North Korea for the unification and that the United States should exercise strong leverage on President Park for democratization in South Korea (*NYT*, 6/11. 1979). On July 19, 1979, he dared to state that the Yushin Constitution of the Fourth Republic was proposed under martial law and ratified coercively against the will of the majority of the Korean voters. Therefore, the Yushin Constitution and the Fourth Republic were declared illegitimate (CEMC, 1980: 382).

President Park and his followers saw Kim Young Sam's statement in the press conference as the defamation to the constitution and the republic in clear violation of Emergency Measure No. 9 and his announcement of willingness and readiness to talk to North Korean leaders as violation of the National Security Law. On October 4, 1979, a total of 159 government party,

Figure 8-7 Change in the Fourth Republic's Political Satellite Model

Transition of the relative powers of the two coalitions from the one heavily skewed in favor of the anti-democracy patron-client coalition in 1972 toward the one relatively balanced in terms of the extensiveness and intensiveness of confrontation between the two coalitions

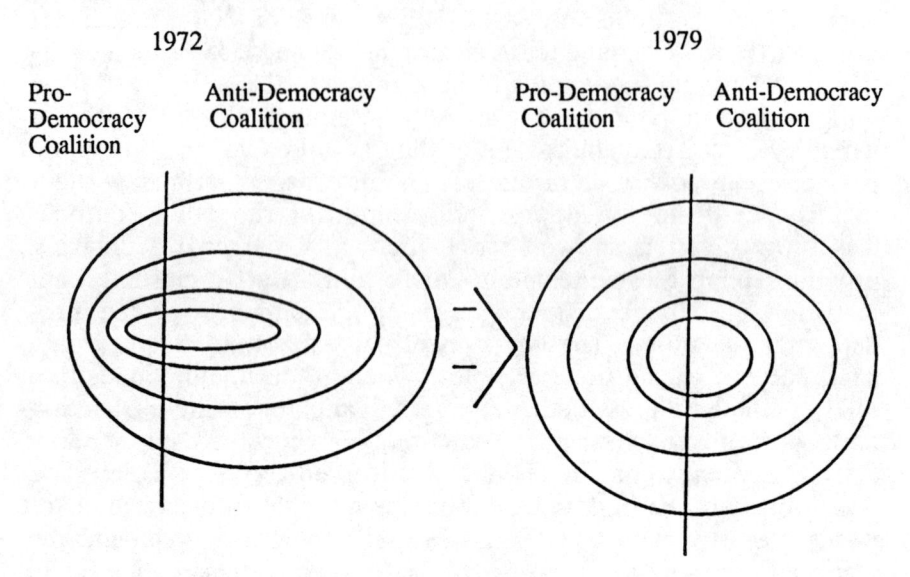

1972

Pro-   Anti-Democracy
Democracy   Coalition
Coalition

1979

Pro-Democracy   Anti-Democracy
Coalition   Coalition

Yujunghoe, and other pro-government Independent Assemblymen attended the Assembly session, adopted a resolution to expel Kim from the National Assembly, and finally passed it with the total absence of the opposition party Assemblymen on the floor. This was the first incident in the history of the legislative branch that a popularly elected Assemblyman as the president of the major opposition party was expelled from the National Assembly by the pro-government Assemblymen. Nine days later sixty-nine opposition Assemblymen *en masse* submitted their letters of resignation. The voters, high school and college students in the city of Pusan, which represented the home constituency of Kim Young Sam, began to rise up against the Park regime. On October 16, 1979, about 5,000 students, unemployed workers, and others took to the streets, shouting the illegitimacy of the Yushin Constitution and the Park regime, and demonstrating for the step-down of President Park and his clients from the government. Next day the demonstrations and protests began to expand beyond the city of Pusan to the city of Masan and its neighboring area.

On October 18, 1979, the government could not help but immediately declare martial law, curfew, and press censorship. But the commitment and struggle of tens of thousands of citizens, students, civic leaders, and opposition leaders for democratization could not be continuously suppressed. The more people were arrested and tortured, the more people joined the campaign for democratization and for the securing of their basic rights and freedoms. At the height of people's demand for democratization, President Park was assassinated on October 26, 1979 by one of his most confident chief clients, the KCIA Director. Kim Jae Kyu allegedly justified his decision of the assassination of President Park for the latter's violation of the constitutional principles of peaceful transfer of power and a series of executive emergency decrees depriving tens of thousands of democracy-aspiring citizens and leaders of their basic freedoms and rights. As Figure 8-7 shows, upon the inception of the Fourth Republic in 1972, the anti-democracy patron-client coalition was becoming bigger and stronger. But the political satellite slowly and gradually experienced the transition of the relative power of the two coalitions from the one heavily skewed in favor of the anti-democracy patron-client coalition toward the one in favor of a pro-democracy coalition and consequently challenging the regime to a critical point.

The Fifth Republic (1980-1988)

The Anti-Democracy Patron-Client Coalition

Democracy and the promotion of human rights were expected upon the death of President Park. Kim Jong Pil immediately succeeded the late President Park as the president of the Democratic Republican party. On December 6, 1979, the then Prime Minister, Choi Kyu Ha, was elected the interim president of the republic. The next day the notorious Emergency Measure No. 9, which was declared and had been effective since May 13, 1975, was finally lifted. About seventy political dissidents including Kim Dae Jung, who were arrested in relation to the decrees, were released. Three major party leaders--Kim Dae Jung, Kim Young Sam, and Kim Jong Pil--began to demand the prompt scrapping of the Yushin Constitution, to establish the Fifth Republic under a truly democratic constitution, and to hold an open, fair presidential election. On February 29, 1980, a total of 687 anti-government politicians, including Kim Dae Jung, were granted the restoration of civil and political freedoms and rights (*Dong-A Annual*, 1986: 702-703).

Amidst the height of the desire and expectation for the establishment of a democratic republic, an alarming incident was reported first on December 12, 1979. It was a military coup waged against Martial Law Commander Chung Sung Hwa and other senior generals by junior generals led by Chung Doo Hwan of the Defense Security Command and alumni of the eleventh Class of the Korean Military Academy, the first four-year class. What disturbed opposition leaders, intellectuals, students, and citizens was the fact that "units of the Ninth Division commanded by General Roh Tae Woo" had been "moved into Seoul in connection with the coup and without the permission of General John Wickham, Commander of the Combined Forces Command" (Hinton, 1983: 50).

The new group lost no time in replacing all military key positions with its own client generals (*CSM*, Dec. 20, 1979). On December 18, 1979, the newly appointed army chief of staff and martial law commander, Lee Hui Sung issued a "special announcement" regarded as a manifesto that "politics is outside the realm of the armed forces" (*WP*, December. 19, 1979). Ironically, he added a "political" statement of denouncing "corruption on the part of civil servants and unethical behavior of those in business, and enjoined the public against any sort of activity that might incite the North Koreans" (Hinton, 1983: 50).

The first major sign of their intervention in politics was the appointment of General Chun Doo Hwan in mid-April of 1980 as the Director of the KCIA. The intervention of the military in politics was most saliently manifested in the Kwangju incident in May 1980. General Chun and his clients illustrated several justifications for their decisive military action in the Kwangju incident and the ensuing matters. Contrary to their official warnings to stop and the efforts by the police to contain demonstrations, the students rather gave the government an "ultimatum to lift martial law by May 22 or face a new wave of demonstrations" on May 17, 1980 (Hinton, 1983: 52). Military leaders also worried about the possible contact and influence of Kim Dae Jung, who might have instigated the students of his home province to demand the government to expedite the transition to a civilian government. North Korea began to take advantage of street demonstrations, urging the students to "wipe out the fascist Yushin system and set up a new democratic regime" (PDSB, April 18, 1989). This propaganda was further reinforced by the rumors that

The Korean Model of Democratization

North Korean troops began to mass near the demilitarized zone. Military leaders also were concerned about a possible strong reaction to the execution of Kim Jae Kyu as scheduled on May 24.

Young generals began to take military action as professionally trained soldiers. First of all, the crackdown took the form of a declaration of extraordinary martial law effective May 17, 1980. The Martial Law Command, the Defense Security Command, and the Special Forces soon took over military and political predominance: arresting Kim Dae Jung and six other politically prominent leaders after charging them with their support for students and labor union strikes; forcing the entire cabinet to resign on May 20 and replacing it with one acceptable to the military; establishing a 25-man Special Committee for National Security, fourteen of whose members were military leaders; and appointing General Chun Doo Hwan the chair of its Standing Committee (Rees, 1981: 19-20).

The Martial Law Command deployed paratroopers to decisively smash a crowd of some 2,000 protesters in Kwangju on May 18. But the paratroopers were soon outnumbered and overpowered by the protesters and forced to withdraw from the center of Kwangju city. The civil riots began to rapidly spread to other towns in South Cholla province and turned out to be an insurrection, demanding the end of martial law, the sacking of general Chun, and the release of Kim Dae Jung. The army's retaking of the city on May 27 finally put an end to the revolt at the terrible cost of about 200 lives and a large number injured.

The Martial Law Command also announced search for the arrest of 329, who were charged with unlawful amassment of fortunes and disturbances of national order on June 17. Kim Jong Pil was arrested and later released only after agreeing to turn over his private fortunes of $36 million to the state, resigning the presidency of the Democratic Republican Party, and, moreover, promising to "stay out of politics." Kim Young Sam was released from house arrest after "voluntarily resigning" from the leadership of the New Democratic party and, more specifically, announcing that he would retire from politics. Kim Dae Jung was arrested and charged with sedition. All three Kims, who were widely considered to be formidable to the political beginner Chun Doo Hwan, suddenly disappeared from the political scene.

Like their predecessors, General Chun and his close clients on the major patron-client network wanted to offer jobs to their clients on their minor network. In the name of corruption and other wrongdoings, some 8,000 civil servants were dismissed in violation of job security guaranteed and protected in the civil service system (Rees, 1981: 22-24). Many executives of state corporations and journalists were expelled, and 172 journals were closed on July 31, 1980.

General Chun soon turned over the directorship of the KCIA to his colleague general, was promoted to full general, received the endorsement of the chiefs of staff and ranking commanding generals of the armed forces for the presidency on August 21, retired from the army the next day, and was finally "elected" the eleventh president of the republic by the National Council for Unification on August 27, 1980, about eight and a half months since he led the coup on December 12, 1979.

In the late summer of 1980, the government began to arrest several hundred students and others who were considered to have played active roles in the turbulence in Seoul and Kwangju. They were "tried, secretly and in groups, by military courts, and given various prison sentences" (*CSM*, 19/15/84). Kim Dae Jung and 23 of his supporters were charged with sedition. He was sentenced to death on September 17, 1980. About eight hundred prominent politicians who were "old and corrupt" under the Third and Fourth Republics-- both government and opposition--were banned from taking part in presidential and National Assembly elections until 1988, when President Chun's term should be completed and the subsequent election which would choose his successor (*Korea Herald*, November 13, 1980). This could guarantee the completion of the seven-year term of Chun as the first president of the Fifth Republic, the assurance of the nominee with his blessing as the succeeding president, and the securing of a majority of the National Assembly seats by his own political party, soon to be organized.

Since the news groups had been the center of criticism of the government, the Chun regime began to "purify the media organizations" on November 14, 1980.[1] The government closed sixty-seven newspapers, six news agencies, and several provincial newspapers in the name of media reorganization. The government also closed private television networks including the Samsung Group's Tongyang Broadcasting Corporation and the Christian Broadcasting Corporation on the grounds that all television networks should be integrated into a single state-run network called the Korean Broadcasting Corporation (*NYT*, 11/29 and 12/12/80). Soon after the ratification of the new (eighth amended) constitution for the

The Korean Model of Democratization 307

Figure 8-8 A Political Satellite Model of the Fifth Republic: 1980-1988

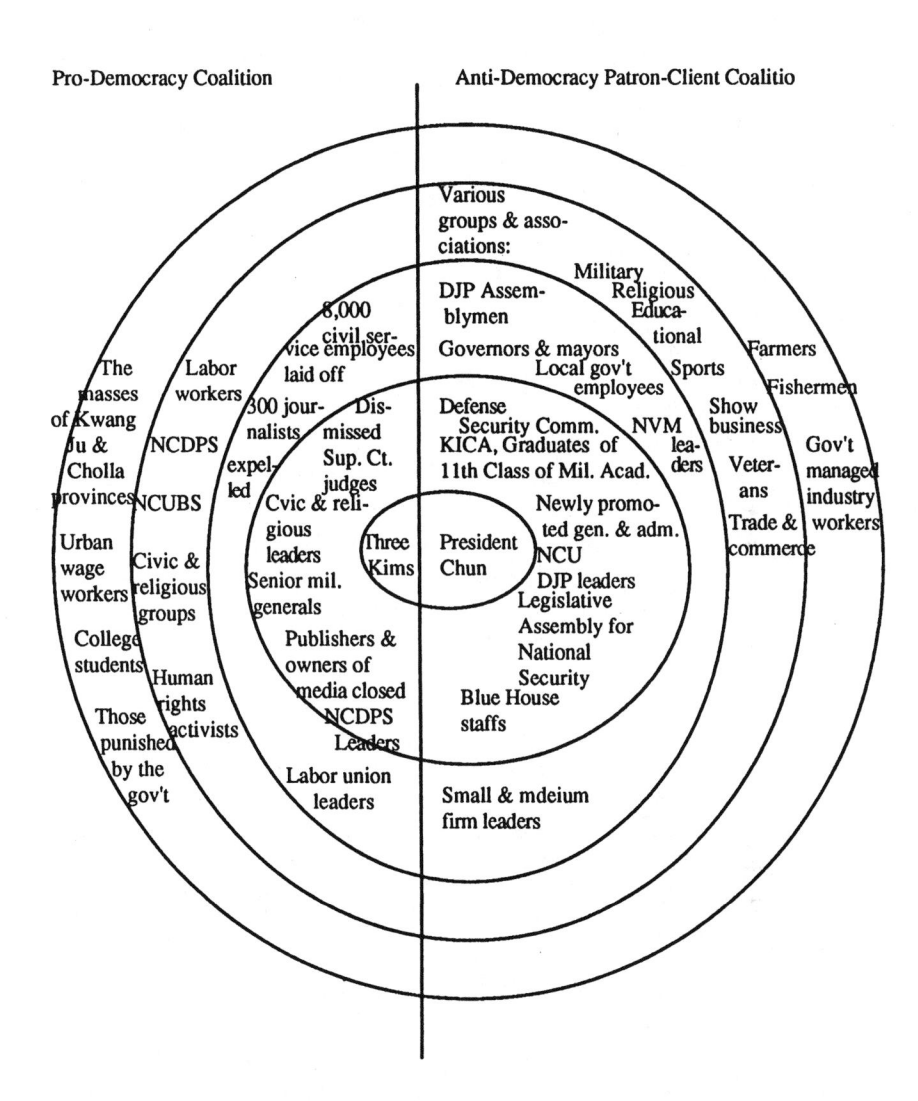

Pro-Democracy Coalition | Anti-Democracy Patron-Client Coalition

[Concentric circle diagram]

Innermost circle: Three Kims | President Chun

Second ring (Pro-Democracy side): Cvic & religious leaders; Senior mil. generals; Publishers & owners of media closed; NCDPS Leaders; Labor union leaders

Second ring (Anti-Democracy side): Newly promoted gen. & adm.; NCU; DJP leaders; Legislative Assembly for National Security; Blue House staffs; Small & mdeium firm leaders

Third ring (Pro-Democracy side): 8,000 civil service employees laid off; 300 journalists dismissed; Sup. Ct. judges expelled

Third ring (Anti-Democracy side): Various groups & associations: DJP Assemblymen; Governors & mayors; Local gov't employees; Defense Security Comm.; KICA, Graduates of 11th Class of Mil. Acad.

Outer ring (Pro-Democracy): The masses of Kwangju & Cholla provinces; NCUBS; Urban wage workers; College students; Those punished by the gov't; Human rights activists; Civic & religious groups; NCDPS; Labor workers

Outer ring (Anti-Democracy): Military; Religious; Educational; Sports; Show business; NVM leaders; Veterans; Trade & commerce; Farmers; Fishermen; Gov't managed industry workers

Fifth Republic, the Basic Press Law was enacted on December 26, 1980. It stipulated severe restrictions on the freedom of the press with the overemphasis of the responsibility of the press for the public interest and underemphasis on the right of the press to news coverage and commentaries.

The Basic Press Law required journalists to be annually reviewed for the renewal of their press card and to abide by the "pool report system" such that types and contents of news, which were screened and released only by the Ministry of Culture and Information (MCI), should be covered on the newspapers. Therefore, many activities and campaigns for the promotion of democracy had been restricted and not available to the general public.

The government enacted another repressive measure against urban wage workers in order to restrict their collective action and collective bargaining. The Law Regarding Labor Disputes Coordination, which was enacted on December 17, 1981, stipulated the prohibition of labor disputes by the employees of the central government, local government, state-run enterprises, and defense-related industries. The law also prohibited labor disputes outside the working place in the private industries and restricted intervention in the labor disputes by a third party--the federation of labor unions, a political party, a religious group or college students. The new labor law also extended both a cooling-off period and a mediation period to iron out differences between management and labor unions without disrupting the normal operation of production (*Dong-A Annual*, 1973: 230-244).

Subject to a variety of repressive techniques employed by the government were political agents, who were yet brave enough to challenge the patron-client network centered around President Chun, and who later began to join one another to form a broad pro-democracy coalition more committed and much larger than that of the previous republics. The agents included: leading opposition politicians, who were banned from politics and coercively resigned from leadership in the party organization; five of the fifteen justices of the Supreme Court, who grudgingly submitted resignation because of their voting against the sustaining of the death sentence ruled by the Court of Appeals decreed to the assassin of the late President Park, Kim Jae Kyu (U.S., DOS, 1982: 642); and many other judges who were fired or demoted to less prestigious local courts because of their recalcitrance and claims for judicial integrity and their subsequent rulings in the courts against the wishes and expectations of the Chun regime; 8,000 civil servants, who were coercively required to perform the tasks specifically assigned and closely supervised by the central government and yet dismissed from their jobs by President Chun and his clients; university administrators and professors, who lost administrative and teaching positions because of their lack of cooperation with and their criticism of the regime; students of many universities, who protested and struggled for democratization and were subsequently expelled from their colleges; hundreds of journalists, who were not offered the renewal of a press card because of their pro-democracy stance and criticism of the authoritarian regime; and labor workers, who demanded the right to unionization and collective bargaining and were subsequently arrested and expelled from their jobs (see Figure 8-8).

Facing formidable challenges from the pro-democracy coalition, President Chun as the chief patron began to strengthen his major patron-client network in order to establish his power base and to fortify it against the pro-democracy forces. First of all, Chun took with him into the Blue House some trusted junior associates from his previous military career as his key staff. Reinforced to those ex-colonels as his loyal assistants were some first-rate civilians with advanced degrees of Ph.D. or equivalent from universities in the United States. President Chun, for example, appointed as his chief of staff, Kim Kyong Won, a political scientist and a Harvard University Ph.D. who also served in staff capacities under former Presidents Park and Choi. Kim Jae Ik, a Stanford University Ph.D. was appointed Chun's chief economist. (*Korean Newsview*, September 30, 1980).

President Chun appointed some of his closest friends and assistants of his previous career noneconomy-related cabinet secretaries such as the Ministers of Interior, Defense, Transportation, and the like. He also took into consideration that undisturbed and continued economic growth should be the most important means for sustaining and legitimizing his power. Therefore, he chose as the Prime Minister Nam Duck Woo, a U.S.-trained economist and a former Deputy Premier and the Minister of the Economic Planning Board under the late President Park (*NYT*, 9/30/1980).

President Chun also appointed to various military and strategic positions his classmates of the Eleventh Class of the Korean Military Academy who continued to be loyal to Chun and support him against the potential of another military coup or protests from the pro-democracy forces. Roh Tae Woo, for example, was appointed the head of the Defense Security Command. Many of his classmates and assistants in his military career began to retire from active service and joined the Democratic Justice Party as party cadres and members of the National Assembly.

The Special Committee for National Security Measures, which took over the functions of the National Assembly, was replaced in late October 1980 by the Legislative Assembly for National Security (LANS). Its eighty-one members, however, were not elected by the voters but all appointed by President Chun. Only ten of them had been the members of its predecessor and 71 were the new legislative appointees of President Chun. Two hundred and twenty-six legislations which were enacted in 156 days by the Legislative Assembly under martial law still in effect (Kihl, 1988: 78) were so sweeping and extensive as to extremely favor the anti-democracy, patron-client Chun coalition and to excessively disfavor the pro-democracy forces.

> During its lifetime of about four months it passed, at the government's initiative, considerable important legislation. Approximately 560 individuals were banned from politics until June 30, 1988 . . . Procedural legislation was passed governing the composition of the National Assembly, the number of legislation districts, and the like. Enabling legislation was passed for the benefits of various ministries. Finally, some legislation, fairly moderate in the eyes of the establishment although too rigorous to suit the opposition, was passed to provide a "storm-barrier" against possible future disorders, especially student unrest, and against anti-government campaigns in the media, or in effect to provide the government with a stronger legal basis for and more effective means of maintaining order without declaring martial law again (Hinton, 1983: 59).

The Constitution of the Fifth Republic, which was ratified by a popular referendum under martial law on October 22, 1980, further reinforced the power of the anti-democracy, patron-client coalition centered around President Chun. Its two major provisions, which were designed to sustain Chun's coalition beyond his one seven-year presidential term, were the election of the next president not by a direct popular vote but by an electoral college, and the power of the president to dissolve the National Assembly. The electoral college could be easily subject to government pressure for the election of the government party's presidential candidate with the blessings of

President Chun, whereas the National Assembly could be vulnerable to the president for his decision to dissolve it in case of serious challenge from the opposition Assemblymen.

To prevent opposition Assemblymen from securing more than half of the total seats, the National Assembly Election Law established two types of Assembly seats--184 seats to be directly elected by the voters in their respective districts and 92 seats to be allocated on the basis of a kind of proportional representation. A party that won more Assembly seats in the district popular election should secure 61 seats, two-thirds of the proportional seats, whereas the remaining 31 seats were to be divided in proportion to the popularly elected seats among other parties with a minimum of five seats each. In the 1981 election, the Democratic Justice Party (DJP) won 90 elected seats as opposed to 57 seats for the major opposition Democratic Korea Party. Therefore, the DJP was qualified to gain 61 proportional seats, resulting in a total of 151 that accounted for 54.7 percent of the total Assembly seats. The Chun regime felt secure with a majority of the Assembly seats under his control (see Figure 8-8 on the anti-democracy patron-client coalition).

A Pro-Democracy Coalition Entering Into the Threshold in 1987

The president and his newly established patron-client network, secure of full control of power, began to show conciliatory gestures to their opponents in the name of "grand reconciliation for national development." On January 24, 1981, President Chun lifted martial law 456 days after its declaration. On March 3, he declared an executive clemency, reduction of penalties, and restoration of civil rights for 5,221. On January 5, 1982, curfew, which had been effective from midnight until 5:00 a.m. every day since the Korean War of 1950, was lifted. On February 25, 250 of 555 political prisoners were released. On March 2, the Ministry of Education relaxed dress codes, dropping the mandatory requirement for junior and senior high school students to wear their school uniforms. The government liberalized overseas travel of citizens and reduced the power of the KCIA, which had been known for the illegitimate abuse of its power, and renamed it the Agency for National Security Planning (ANSP). Moreover, President Chun had his tenure constitutionally limited to a single seven-year term, with no future amendment applicable to this provision for the incumbent chief executive.

The more conciliatory the government leaders became, however, the more vigorously the opposition forces began to escalate their demands for, first, release of more political prisoners, then the complete release of all political prisoners, a full investigation of the Kwangju Incident, direct popular election of the president in the next election by means of an amendment to the constitution, and the full realization of democracy by abolishing all laws which were passed illegitimately by President Chun's appointees to the Legislative Assembly for National Security (LANS).

Kim Young Sam initiated a nonviolent anti-government protest with a hunger strike which started on May 18, 1983, demanding that all political and conscientious prisoners be released and that all opposition politicians should be restored civilian political rights and freedoms. Kim's hunger strike had been blacked out by the government-monopolized mass media. His belatedly known protest, however, began to trigger gradual and ever-increasing nationwide campaigns against the government.

The parents soon began to wage hunger strikes for the release of their sons and daughters under arrest on January 22, 1985. Kim Sang Hyun, the chair of the Council of Steering for Democracy (CSD) joined the parents on February 7. Kim Young Dong, the Secretary General of the New Democratic Party also demanded the release of the arrested on April 2, 1985. The CSD, Korean Student Christian Federation (KSCI) and the Council for Korean Catholic Student Federation (Pax Romana) also protested for the release of the arrested students and opposition leaders. About 360 of 1,000 protesters were taken to the police station.

Demand for full investigation on the Kwangju Incident became another important issue. On February 2, 1985, Lee Min Woo, the NDP President, requested that the government pursue full investigation of the Kwangju Incident. The demand was soon escalated into a series of massive protests by a large number of college students and opposition leaders, who reached 6,000 students from fifteen major universities in Seoul and 11 local universities on May 10, 1985; within a week 7,000 students from eleven Seoul and fourteen local universities, 368 of whom were soon arrested; 15,000 students from fourteen universities in Seoul on May 16, 1985; the entire Council of Mass Movement for Democracy and Unification (CMFDU) led by Reverend Moon Ik Hwan; 38,000 students from thirty Seoul and fifty local universities, about 2,500 of whom remained to wage an all-night protest the next day.

Their demands became militant and began to question the legitimacy of the Chun regime. Lee Min Woo, the NDP president, for example, demanded that the timetable for democratization should be unequivocally made available to the public and that President Chun should resign before the completion of his term by August 1986. The Campaign for Securing a Democratic Political System (CFSDPS), which was headed by civic leader Ham Suk Hun, was forcefully prohibited from its attempt to protest the government. But 1,500 took to the streets in protest.

The government's suppression of unionization and collective bargaining became an equally important concern for urban wage workers and their supporters. The Council of Steering for Democracy demanded the termination of suppression on labor union activities, the revision of the Labor Union Law, and the guarantee of unionization on April 9, 1985. The year of 1985 witnessed a total of 250 incidents of labor disputes by various workers. College students dared to join labor workers for the promotion of collective bargaining. For example, 1,000 students joined the Chunggae Apparel Union on April 12, 1985. About 150 students in the city of Inchon supported workers of the city, together waging a candle strike in commemoration of the May Day. About 200 student representatives of 37 universities in Seoul protested against the government's suppression of labor unions on July 6, 1985. The protest reached the climax when 4,100 students of 21 universities demanded the abolition of the Labor Union Law. The students finally became violent, forcefully occupying the government party building, its Central Political Training Center, on three occasions during the month of November 1985. They also attacked police boxes, throwing homemade fire bombs into police buildings and cars. The year of 1985 witnessed a total of 2,138 incidents of protests and demonstrations with 46,900 student participants in open clashes with a total of 5,400,000 riot police mobilized. The Council on Campaign for Democratic Press (CCDP) and the Literary Association (LA) demanded the abolition of the Basic Press Law and the cancellation of the registration requirement for publications.

The government was equally determined to resist the ever-increasing protests from the pro-democracy forces. Police blocked students from coming out of the campus first and used tear gas to disperse them from street demonstrations once initial blocking from the gate of the campus had failed. Police began to move into the campuses without a request from the university authority. About 6,420 riot police went into the campus of the Seoul National University on November 14, 1984. On June 29, 1985, 467 riot police waged a surprise entrance into nine universities, arresting 66 students and confiscating 80,000 fire bombs and other items. On August 13, 1985, police took a surprise midnight operation of search and seizure of the student unions and the offices of student councils of 85 universities. The government authorized plainclothesmen to enter the universities and arrest the leaders who were expected to lead student demonstrations. The government enacted the Campus Security Law to restrict student anti-government demonstrations and disturbances. The Ministry of Culture and Information (MCI) began to prohibit the publication of the opposition New Democratic Party bulletin, confiscated 665 copies of "radical" ideology-related books and 4,500 copies of 298 different books on May 1 and 4. The MCI cancelled the registration of *Isak* and *Changbee Publishing Companies*, closed the *Silchon Literary Magazine* on August 30, and arrested fourteen staff working on the *Flag* and the *Ewha Press* as pro-Communist journals.

The most important issues, which had been controversial since the inception of the Fifth Republic in 1981 between the anti-democracy patron-client coalition centered around President Chun and the pro-democracy forces, were the amendment to the Constitution, direct election of the next president, and subsequent democratization. Lee Min Woo, the president of the NDP repeatedly called on January 10, April 12, May 4, May 20, and July 31, 1985 for direct popular election of the next president. He proposed the establishment of the Committee of Steering for Constitutional Amendment on August 25, 1985. A month later, a total of 1,800 students from seven Seoul and seven local universities supported the NDP, demanding a direct popular election of the president. On October 16 and November 21, 1985, about 21,000 students from ten universities, demanded the constitutional amendment. Each time the government stonewalled their demands. President Chun announced his adherence to the constitution of the Fifth Republic for the election of his successor. Roh Tae Woo, the Chairman of the DJP, expressed his opposition to the amendment. Roh Shin Young, the Prime Minister, criticized the proposal of the constitutional amendment for the possible political disturbances.

After the Asian Games (September 20-October 5, 1986), the Chun government once again resorted to the Draconian policy of oppression against pro-democracy activists. The most suppressive incident was the case of Konkuk University of October 28-31, 1986. Some 19,000 riot police carried out a combat-style operation and sacked a large body of students assembled on the Konkuk University campus, throwing barrage after barrage of tear gas cannisters, while cutting off the supply of water, food, and heat for four days. The incident ended with over 2,225 students rounded up. According to the government, the student activists were "radical leftists," "pro-communist activists," and "pro-North Korean agitators intent upon destroying the Republic of Korea" (*Korea Herald*, Nov. 1, 1986). On the contrary, the Christian Federation and the Ecumenical Youth Council in Korea asserted that:

> We believe the Konkuk University incident was not the result of a planned occupation by the students, or a riot caused by communist revolutionaries, as claimed by the authorities, but an intended action to provoke the students by the regime. The authorities intentionally forced the students into the buildings and locked them in. Through a blitz of trial by media they distorted the case as one of pro-communist action, and moved in to kill and suppress the students. This is nothing more than a part of the regime's vicious conspiracy to paint the student movement as a pro-communist and destroy it from its root. The authorities knew of the plans for this combined assembly of students. It has, as always, the capacity and chance to prevent the assembly. Instead, however, it carried through a pre-planned operation as part of its thoroughly worked out scheme to destroy the student movement at once (North American Coalition for Human Rights in Korea, 1987: 4).

The National Coalition for a Democratic Constitution (NCDC), which was headed by two Kims and the NDP, finally announced a pan-national campaign for ten million citizen signatures for the constitutional amendment. It was not their bluff but the shifting of many neutral and some pro-government forces into the NCDC that the government was forced to reluctantly moderate its original repressive measures. In the year of 1986, the number and types of various pro-democracy forces, which coalesced to amend the constitution, were extensive in the quantity and intensive in the quality of commitment to the democratization. The agents who recently joined the pro-democracy coalition are as follows (see Figure 8-8):

1. A Campaign for Organizing the Headquarters for the Constitutional Amendment (COHCA) which was sponsored by 1,500 students of 15 universities on February 14.

2. Waging a Campaign for Ten Million Signatures for the Constitutional Amendment by the Council of Steering for Democracy and the NDP on February 12.

3. The announcement on March 19, 1986 of Kim Soo Hwan, the Archbishop as the leader of the entire Catholics in Korea that "democratization is the will of God and, therefore, should be implemented."

4. Local branches for the actual implementation of ten million signatures campaign, which were established in all provinces and major cities like a wild fire by the enthusiastic support of local people. The Seoul branch was established on March 11. That was followed by Pusan on March 23, the South Cholla Province on March 30. By the end of May of the same year, all provinces and major cities had completed the establishment of local branches for the signature campaign.

5. University professors, who voiced the concern over the current state of affairs and began to endorse a direct election of the next president. On March 28, Korea University's 28 professors initiated a declaration for democratization. They were followed by 42 professors of the Korean Theological Seminary and 941 additional professors of some 30 other universities who were willing to risk their research funds, promotion, and tenure.

6. The Council of Korean Catholic Justice and Peace (CKCJP), which declared on March 14 that the voters should have the right to amend the constitution.

7. The Christian Youth Council Struggling for the Democratic Popular Constitution (CYCSDP), which was established to campaign for the constitutional amendment on March 25.

8. The Korean Bar Association (KBA), which demanded the constitutional amendment with the recommendation of its own version on April 7.

The Korean Model of Democratization

9. The Women's Council Struggling for the Democratic Constitution (WKSDC), which endorsed an amendment to the constitution on April 3.
10. The YMCA, which also joined the pro-democracy coalition, supporting constitutional amendments on April 26.
11. The Pan-National Catholic Priests for Social Justice (PCPSJ), which demanded an amendment to the constitution on May 16.
12. One hundred and fifty-two Buddhist monks, who endorsed an amendment on May 19, 1986.

President Chun and his major clients had no option but to change their arrogant stance from the announcement of "the amendment only after the year of 1989" following the indirect election of an heir designated with Chun's blessing as the next president to "his willingness to accommodate himself to the demand of the pro-democracy forces." In other words, no less than two months after President Chun's announcement of no amendment by any means for the 1988 presidential election in his New Year State of Affairs Address on January 16, 1986 he was forced to announce on February 24, 1986 that "the constitution could be amended if that were the wishes of the people." On April 30, 1986, President Chun once again qualified his February statement, saying that the amendment would be favorably considered during his term, if three political parties could reach consensus. About a month later on June 6, President Chun made a more conciliatory statement announcing that the earlier consensus would be made among the political parties on the constitutional amendment, the better it would be for a direct popular election of the next chief executive. On June 21, 1986, Roh Tae Woo proposed the establishment of a Special Legislative Committee for the Constitutional Amendment.

The survival imperative of President Chun and those on his patron-client coalition was so paramount that they proposed a constitutional amendment for the establishment of a cabinet form of government, under which they felt they could continue to have a firm grip on the National Assembly and the subsequent Prime Ministry. But the pro-democracy coalition continued to adhere to the principle of a direct popular election of the president, which became the supreme campaign promise of the 1985 National Assembly election of the NDP. When the disagreement between the two was stonewalled, President Chun reversed his previous endorsement for an amendment to the constitution and instead stated on April 13, 1987 that he would suspend the talks on constitutional amendment until after the 1988 Seoul Olympics and that the next president should be indirectly elected by the electoral college under the Constitution of the Fifth Republic.

The humiliation of President Chun and his major clients and their final surrender to the pro-democracy coalition was possible only when the size and commitment of the latter outnumbered and overpowered the former. On May 27, 1987 about 150 pro-democracy leaders began to launch a Pan-National Campaign for the Constitutional Amendment (PNCCA), whose membership included the leaders of all walks of life:

> Two hundred fifty-three Catholic leaders, 270 Protestants, 160 Buddhist leaders, 35 Min Tongryon (Democratic Unification Coalition) leaders, 162 women leaders, 308 Farmers Association leaders, 171 farmers, 39 labor workers, 43 media leaders, 66 artists, 55 education leaders, 15 youth leaders, 213 politicians, and representatives of all provinces (*Dong-A Annual*, 1988: 47).

The government immediately declared illegal the pan-national campaign for the amendment to the constitution for a direct popular election of the next president and mobilized 60,000 riot police to blockade the campaign. Nevertheless, on June 10, 1987, the pro-democracy forces launched mass demonstrations on the basis of the principles of civil disobedience and passive resistance in eighteen major cities including Seoul, Kwangju, Pusan, and Inchon simultaneously. Taxi drivers of all business and private cars on the streets began to sound the horn all over the cities as a protest against the authoritarian regime and its leaders. Angered by the ever-increasing repressive measures of the police by indiscriminately using tear gas, the demonstrators became violent, destroying one branch office of the city hall, fifteen police boxes, two branch offices of the government political party, and throwing homemade fire bombs and rocks at the riot police. The head-on collision resulted in the injuries of 708 police, 30 civilians, and the arrest of 3,831 (*Dong-A Annual*, 1988: 48). The demonstrators forcefully occupied the Myungdong Catholic Church and refused to vacate it. The building was soon encircled by 1,200 police. University students began to march toward the church to help their colleagues in the building resist the riot police. The confrontation escalated into a matter of survival of the Chun regime.

On June 13, 1987, the government announced its intention to arrest all the participants in the protests. What was ironic was the fact that there were not sufficient numbers of prisons and correctional institutions to accommodate hundreds of thousands of citizen participants in civil demonstrations. Government tanks, howitzers, and rifles, even if they had been mobilized, were not likely to shoot tens of thousands of citizens. Leaders of the patron-client coalition centered around President Chun by no means dared to risk another massacre like the Kwangju incident. The most significant factor in the midst of the struggle between the two coalitions was "the middle class moderates" who "joined students and other opposition activists on the streets of the pro-democracy coalition" (Harrison, 1987: 6).

The affirmative view of the masses for democracy and the negative view toward the military-controlled anti-democracy regime of President Chun were clearly revealed by a series of public surveys. A survey conducted by the pro-government *Kyunghyang Ilbo*, on May 15-19, 1985, indicated that 65.2 percent of 1,037 respondents and 60.7 percent of the above-average income group stated their dissatisfaction with the Chun regime. Among those in their 20s and the college graduates, 73.6 percent and 85.7 percent reported their dissatisfaction with the regime in power, respectively (*Dokrip Shinmun*, Sept. 26, 1986). In January 1987, Selig S. Harrison quoted the result of a secret poll recently taken for the Chun government by a leading newspaper in Korea. The poll indicated 66.4 percent opposed the present anti-democratic regime and 20.5 percent "strongly opposed" it (*Washington Post*, Jan. 25, 1987). A public survey conducted by the *Hankuk Ilbo* on May 4-13, 1987 indicated that 85.7 percent of people interviewed considered "the protection of human rights should be achieved even if it delays economic growth." A whopping 81.4 percent of them dared to answer that "they supported the political reforms towards democracy" (*Hankuk Ilbo*, June 9, 1987).

The Reagan Administration, which had long maintained a honeymoon with the authoritarian Chun regime, belatedly became aware of the fact that the pro-democracy forces had been increasing in their size and commitment and that Korea had finally entered into the threshold for democratization. The United States government indeed became the last agent to belatedly but firmly join the pro-democracy coalition in Korea. President Reagan had his Ambassador Lilly deliver his "personal letter," discouraging President Chun from resorting to another extreme measure which could be suicidal to himself (*Dong-A Annual*, 1988: 48). Selig S. Harrison indeed credited President Reagan and the Department of State for the prevention of martial law in Korea:

> . . . the Reagan Administration did intervene decisively to block the use of the Korean armed forces in suppressing demonstrations. President Reagan's June 19 letter to Chun and the State Department's public appeal to military commanders on June 22 undoubtedly played a major role in preventing the imposition of martial law (Harrison, 1987: 3).

Along the passage of days demonstrations continued to become stronger and the demonstrators more determined to fight to the last minutes. Demonstrations of June 16, 1987, which were held in eight major cities, resulted in the destruction of ten police boxes, one branch office of the government party, and five police cars. The next day demonstrations were waged in 127 different localities of ten major cities, and turned out to be violent again, damaging sixteen police boxes, two party offices, two KBS (Korean Broadcasting Station) local stations, and holding the trains on the Seoul-Daejon railroad for 48 minutes. On June 18, a total of 20,000 took part in demonstrations in 247 localities of fourteen major cities, disarming eighty riot policemen. In Pusan, 30,000 protesters held demonstrations with 200 taxies as their forward guards. The civil demonstrations reached a climax on June 26 with one million participants in protests and resulted in the arrest of 3,467 by police.

Being clearly aware of the insufficiency of Gaston Sigur's June 26 (1987) appeal to both sides "to examine their positions and work toward the middle," Roh Tae Woo issued the June 29 Declaration which represented most dramatic and sweeping reforms for democratization. Selig Harrison and many other journalists, politicians, and scholars in and out of Korea contended that the ruling establishment in Korea made "a tactical retreat, not a strategic retreat" as a temporary expediency for the purpose of power maintenance, not a genuine attitude and commitment to democratization in Korea. Roh and his allies, to the contrary, persuaded the hard-liners in their coalition that "the establishment could retain more of its power by making limited concessions than by risking an all-out confrontation in the streets" (Harrison, 1987: 4).

Roh Tae Woo and his moderate allies clearly understood that Korea had finally entered into the threshold for democracy in 1987 after its experiencing of a series of confrontations between the pro-democracy coalition and the anti-democratic patron-client coalition since 1948. Roh Tae Woo stated in his Korean-version book, *The Age of Great Common Men:*

> Authoritarianism is over in Korea. Authoritarianism has no excuse and no justification for its continuation on the soil of Korea . . . . No matter how important economic development, national security, law and order are, they cannot and shall not substitute for democratization . . . . I became the leader in Korea in the critical stage of transformation from half-century-long authoritarianism into democratization . . . . Yes, I am proud to admit that I surrender to the people power and to their cause for democratization . . . . I am mandated by the people to realize democracy in Korea (Roh, 1987: 11-75).

For the first time in the history of the republic, an absolute majority of the authoritarian patron-client coalition--Roh Tae Woo, the government political party, and moderate military generals, and the like--began to join the pro-democracy coalition.

The pros and cons of the impact of urbanization and modernization in general on the political behavior of the electorate has been a focus of academic debate among social scientists. The Chicago school of thought, on the one hand, minimizes the impact of urbanization on political participation (Fava, 1968: 11-22 and 21-81; White, 1973: 8-12). In a study of six developing nations, Alex Inkeles finds out no significant independent influence of urbanization upon an individual's political behavior (Inkeles, 1969: 1139). Norman Nie, G. Bingham Powell, and Kenneth Prewitt also point out that "living in an urban environment has no significant effect on rates of national participation (Nie, et al., June 1969: 368; Sept. 1969: 819). In a five-nation study, David Cameron and his associates suggest that urbanization is a relatively unimportant influence on the political behavior of the electorate. Urbanization is only one aspect of the continuing process of modernization (Cameron, et al.; 1972: 259-290). The main reasons for the insignificant contribution of urbanization to political participation are the decline of a sense of community (Verba and Nie, 1972: 230-231; Verba, Nie, and Kim, 1978: 259-285), the decrease in a sense of individual effectiveness in highly impersonal urban environment, and the subsequent loss of the incentives for urban people to take part in politics (Dahl and Tufte, 1973: 43).

The Chicago school of thought, however, is challenged by the modernization school of thought. Daniel Lerner, for example, saw urbanization as a vital phase of multi-stage processes for the increase in political participation because urbanization tends to enhance the level of literacy which, in turn, promotes media exposure and level of participation on the part of urban residents (Lerner, 1958: 43-75). Karl W. Deutsch echoes Lerner, suggesting that social mobilization broadens political participation. As a society becomes more urbanized, industrialized, and modernized, the people become more dependent on government and more aware of political self-interest. The increase in political self-interest and "the greater scope and urgency of their needs for political decisions and governmental services" tend to translate themselves into "increased political participation" (Deutsch, 1961: 498). Milbraith's center-periphery theory also supports the thesis of positive contribution of urbanization to political participation. Comparing urban residents to the center of society and rural counterparts to the periphery, Milbraith suggests that urban residents are more integrated into political communication channels and more likely to get involved in politics than their rural counterparts (Milbraith, 1965: 110-140; Milbraith and Goel, 1977: 86-122).

Many political scientists who examined the voting behaviors in Korea reveal that the Chicago school rather than the modernization model fits into the case of Korea. Based on the analysis of voting for the National Assembly from 1963 to 1985 (excluding the 1981 parliamentary election), Hong-Nack Kim pointed out that "the population, density, industrialization, postwar generation, college students, and urban voters" seemingly associated with modernization "show strong negative correlations" with voting participation. Districts characterized by a high level of education and a concentration of the postwar generation do "not score high on voter turnout, as the more modernized sectors are expected to participate more actively in the political process, including electoral process, under the modernization model" (H.N. Kim, 1988: 145). Other scholars also support the Chicago school of thought and attributed the low voting turnout in urban areas to the following several reasons:

1. Little faith in the efficacy of elections (Eugene Kim, et al., 1973: 1069). To the urban voters, elections after elections since the inception of the republic manifest a meaningless contest or a mechanism for the ruling party to mobilize the masses of the rural areas to legitimize its continued rule. The more sophisticated the urban residents became, the greater is their interest in politics. Ironically, the more intense become their feelings about the futility of their electoral participation (Eugene Kim, et al., 1973: 1067; Myong W. Kim, et al., 1971).

2. Freedom from mobilization and from fear of retaliation. Those living in rural villages are more likely to be pressured to "conform to the wishes of the heads of their families, their villages, their clans, or government officials in their districts." Rural voters in Korea are indeed "mobilized voters." To the contrary, urbanites are less likely to be involved in neighborhood affairs and less bounded economically and socially. "Atomized urbanites" are less susceptible to communal pressures for their electoral participation (C.L. Kim, 1988: 136; J.O. Kim and B.C. Koh, 1972: 825-859).

3. A weak sense of obligation and a strong sense of right. While the ruralites tend to regard voting as a civic duty and obligation, the urbanites see voting as a right. Therefore, fewer urban than rural voters feel abstention is wrong (K.T. Kim, 1967: 67).

By rejecting the modernization model the above noted scholars on Korean politics demonstrated that they might have had a correct observation on each isolated case of the elections in the past. However, their findings are not sufficient to explain how and why the miracle of democratization finally came true in Korea. They may be subject to the fallacy of overextension from the findings of a study on a particular election to the generalization of Korean urbanites as alienated, cynical, free from mobilization, free from fear of retaliation by the government authorities, and, therefore, less involved in politics than the rural counterparts. They may be equally subject to the fallacy of overemphasis on differences between urban and rural voters without examining whether urban voters have increased or decreased their participation in politics. Only a dynamic, longitudinal study of urban people in Korea--average

324   Korea Leading Developing Nations

Figure 8-9 The Korean Model of Democratization: Korea Entering
into the Threshold of Democratization

Level of Struggle
for Democratization

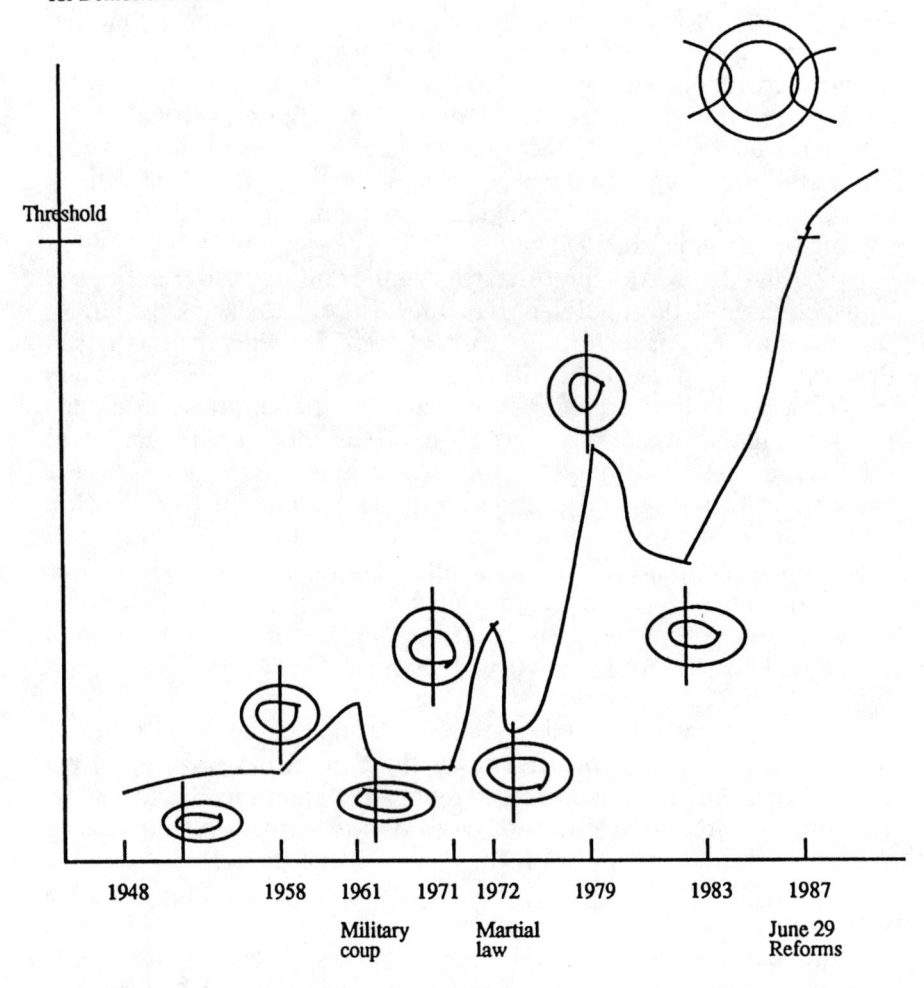

Threshold

1948   1958   1961   1971 1972   1979   1983   1987
                    Military   Martial   June 29
                    coup   law   Reforms

urban voters, college students, intellectuals, religious leaders, opposition party members and leaders--may be able to explain to what extent they have been committing themselves to democratization. We may also pay attention to the fallacy of overexpansion as if citizens' participation in election may truly mean their participation in politics in general. Therefore, no matter how actively and aggressively the urbanites organize interest groups and associations, articulate their interests, join the ten million signatures campaign, and wage civil demonstrations, they are considered alienated, cynical, and inactive in politics, as long as the urbanites show less voting turnout than the ruralites. Even in the case of elections, it is primarily the urban voters who helped the pro-democracy opposition political parties to secure more Assembly seats. Along with modernization--increase in education, industrialization, economic growth, the exposure to mass media, and urbanization, the commitment of more urban citizens to the value of democracy and to the struggle for democratization has been intensified.

A Newly Emerging Political Satellite Model in the Sixth Republic

As Figure 8-9 shows, the first major struggle for democratization was waged in the years of 1958-1961. That was thwarted by the May 16 (1961) military revolution and the subsequent Third Republic. The pro-democracy forces began to challenge the Park regime by securing more than one-third of the National Assembly seats in 1971, which was possible by the participation of more urban voters in the National Assembly election for the opposition party, and by strongly opposing the amendment to the constitution for President Park's third consecutive four-year term. The pro-democracy forces under the second major momentum in 1971-1972 were again dissipated by martial law, under which the constitution was amended and Park became the president of the Fourth Republic in 1972. Lack of regime legitimacy and the ever-increasing suppression of human rights were such that the pro-democracy forces in the urban areas gained the third major momentum with 32.8 percent of popular votes for the opposition party versus 31.7 percent for the government party in 1979, risking their lives and demanding the end of the authoritarian regime.

The greater the level of protests by the pro-democracy forces, the more executive decrees were declared and the more rigid and severe the ensuing decrees became until President Park was assassinated by one of his closest clients in 1979. Martial law was declared again by General Chun and his close clients in the Fifth Republic. Each of these struggles for the movement toward democratization, starting from the year of 1985, gradually escalated and finally reached the threshold in June 1987. Roh Tae Woo and his moderate allies on the government coalition were convinced that reforms for democratization became irreversible and essential for their own survival. They joined the opposition forces for a joint venture for democratization.

The political satellite model in the Sixth Republic shows a fundamental change from a dichotomy into the pro-democracy and anti-democracy coalitions to a trichotomy into a small leftist, a small rightist, and a broad pro-democracy coalition. Let me identify who belongs to what coalitions for what causes.

A Small Left-Wing Coalition

The leftist coalition consists of some radical student groups, labor workers, and opposition forces. It includes: leftist organized groups such as the People's Movement for Democracy and Unification (Min Tong Ryon) consisting of twenty-three separate organizations, the National Teachers Association (Chun Kyo Cho), the Democratic Professors Association (Minju Kyosoo Hyop-Eui-Hoe) and its weekly of College Sound Reasoning (Daehak Chung-Ron), the National Coalition for Democratization (Chun Min Ryon); leftist media and press such as Speech (*Mal*), the Publication of the Council of Campaign for Democratic Speech (*Minju Eulron Wundong Hyop-Eui-Hoe Hoe Gahn*) and One National Daily (*Han Kyorae Shinmun*); leftist university students such as the Council of Representatives of University Students in Seoul Region (Seo Dae Hyop), the National Council of Representatives of University Students (Chun Dae Hyop) and its factions, the National Liberation based on Kim Il Sung's Self-Reliance (Juche) Thought (Pro-Kim NL), and the Anti-Kim Il Sung National Liberation (anti-Kim NL) (C.W. Chung, 1989: 48-55)(See Figure 8-10). The leftist forces are primarily concerned with more salient socio-economic issues such as the widening urban-rural gap, the regional imbalance in distribution, the relative poverty of farmers and slum dwellers, the slow rise in industrial wages, and reunification of the nation. They are rather openly "preaching for a revolution," a socialistic revolution based on the Minjung reform, that is, a government founded on the interests of the workers and peasants (Kihl, 1988: 86).

The Korean Model of Democratization 327

Figure 8-10 A Political Satellite Model of the Sixth Republic: 1988-

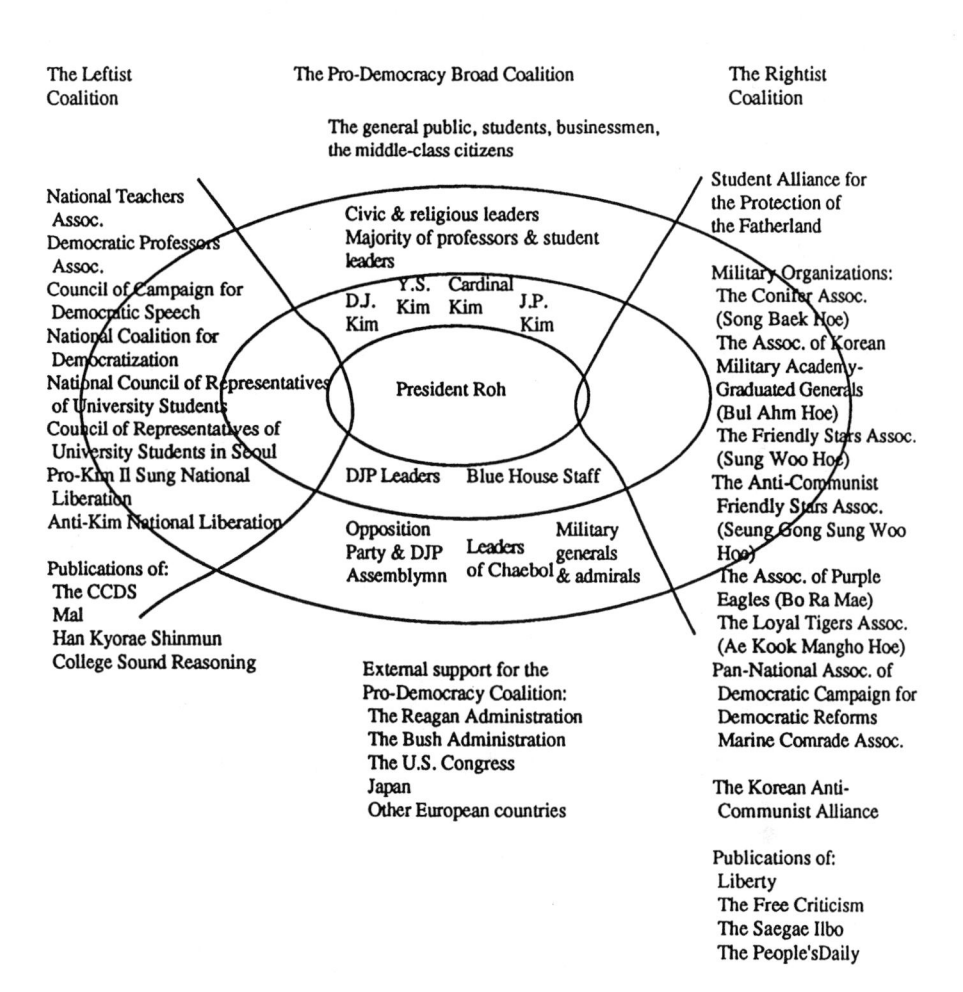

The Leftist Coalition	The Pro-Democracy Broad Coalition	The Rightist Coalition
National Teachers Assoc. Democratic Professors Assoc. Council of Campaign for Democratic Speech National Coalition for Democratization National Council of Representatives of University Students Council of Representatives of University Students in Seoul Pro-Kim Il Sung National Liberation Anti-Kim National Liberation Publications of: The CCDS Mal Han Kyorae Shinmun College Sound Reasoning	The general public, students, businessmen, the middle-class citizens Civic & religious leaders Majority of professors & student leaders Y.S. Cardinal D.J. Kim Kim J.P. Kim Kim President Roh DJP Leaders Blue House Staff Opposition Military Party & DJP Leaders generals Assemblymn of Chaebol & admirals External support for the Pro-Democracy Coalition: The Reagan Administration The Bush Administration The U.S. Congress Japan Other European countries	Student Alliance for the Protection of the Fatherland Military Organizations: The Conifer Assoc. (Song Baek Noe) The Assoc. of Korean Military Academy-Graduated Generals (Bul Ahm Hoe) The Friendly Stars Assoc. (Sung Woo Hoe) The Anti-Communist Friendly Stars Assoc. (Seung Gong Sung Woo Hoe) The Assoc. of Purple Eagles (Bo Ra Mae) The Loyal Tigers Assoc. (Ae Kook Mangho Hoe) Pan-National Assoc. of Democratic Campaign for Democratic Reforms Marine Comrade Assoc. The Korean Anti-Communist Alliance Publications of: Liberty The Free Criticism The Saegae Ilbo The People'sDaily

A Small Right-Wing Coalition

The rightist forces, on the other hand, favor such issues as the preference of a strong government, the primacy of the protection of the fatherland from the North Korean communists and their sympathizers, the imperative of political stability and maintenance of law and order even at the expense of democratic freedoms and rights of anti-government opposition activists, continued economic growth, and the promotion of capitalism, free enterprise, and private ownership. The rightist coalition includes, first of all, the Student Alliance for the Protection of the Fatherland (Hokuk Haksaeng Yunhaphoe), whose fifty members went into the Hanyang University campus and demanded the dissolution of the National Teachers Association (Chun Kyo Cho) and the national Council of Representatives of University Students (Chun Dae Hyop). They opposed radical revolution. They claimed that they could not tolerate the Chun Kyo Cho, which blindly obeyed Kim Il-Sung's Juche Thought and fostered a leftist revolution (*Hankuk Ilbo*, 9/11/1989).

The rightist coalition also includes some active and retired military officers. A very well-known rightist movement was witnessed in the Oh Hong Kun terror incident of 1988. Angered by Oh's editorial titled "The Military Culture to be Liquidated" in the *Chung Ang* (Central) *Economic Daily,* some right-wing officers of the 5616 military unit stabbed and injured Oh on his way home at 7:30 p.m. on August 6, 1988. Angered by the public and embarrassed by the rumor of the involvement of the military in the incident, the Ministry of Defense searched and identified those involved in the incident, and took proper measures: the arrest of six officers and enlisted men including General Lee Kyu Hong for physical violence, the arrest of General Kwon Kie Tae for the destruction of evidence, and the dismissal of Major General Lee Chin Back from the position of Commanding Officer of 5616 military unit for his cover-up of the plot (the Ministry of Defense, 1989: 724-725).

Since the inception of the Sixth Republic, active and retired generals and admirals began to organize rightist groups and associations. Listed below are a few salient examples:

1. The Conifer Association (The Song Baek Hoe), which was organized in September 1987 with Kim Bok Dong as its president. All retired generals and admirals are eligible for its membership as long as they served in the armed forces during the Korean War. The Song Baek Hoe has as its members about 500 of the 1,500 retired generals and admirals with 22 branches engaged in various activities such as fishing, mountaineering, hunting, and breakfast lecture series once every two months.

2. The Bul Ahm Hoe, named after Mt. Bul Ahm behind the Korean Military Academy, which was organized in February 1988 with the membership of 243 retired generals and Chung Ho Yong as its president. It encompasses all retired generals, who graduated from the regular four-year Korean Military Academy from the Eleventh class to the Twentieth class. Those academy graduates without promotion to the rank of general are still eligible to join it as long as they served as the ranks of Secretary, Assistant Secretary of major departments, a National Assembly member, or director general of major private and public corporations. The association raised scholarships of 500,000 won (650 won equivalent to $1.00) for 30 students annually. The key members of this association are those generals involved in the December 12, 1979 revolt against the senior generals.

3. The Friendly Stars Association (Sung Woo Hoe), which was organized with Paik Sun Yup as its president and 180 retired generals and admirals as its charter members. It is open to generals and admirals of all four different branches--the army, the navy, the air force, and the marine corps. However, no general with the regular four-year degree from the military academy has joined it.

4. The Anti-Communist Friendly Stars Association (Seung Gong Sung Woo Hoe), which was established in August 1989 with a membership of 120 retired generals and admirals and Hahn Tae Won as its president.

5. The Association of Purple Eagles, which was chartered in November 1989 by Air Force officers with Chang Chi Ryang as its president.

6. The Loyal Tigers Association, which was organized in September 1989 with a membership of 10,000 officers and enlisted men who have served in the Security Command with Kim Hak Ho as its president.

7. The Federation for Liberty with former Prime Minister Chung Il Kown as its president, the Pan-National Association of Democratic Campaign for Democratic Reforms with Kim Yong Kap as its president, the Marine Comrade Association, and the Nonconventional Forces Association (*Hankuk Ilbo*, Dec. 18, 1989).

All of these associations endorse the protection of democracy and liberty, but prioritize national security and political stability over democracy and the subsequent strong measures against the leftist forces, and oppose indiscreet proposals and attempts for national unification at the expense of national security (*Hankuk Ilbo*, December. 8, 1989).

Professor Dong Ahn Yang represents the rightist groups of the academia. His essay "Is the Right Wing Dead?" deplored the ever-increasing radical leftist movements and called for the establishment of a civilian-based right-wing coalition to check the left wing from arousing the general public and from causing political instability (Yang Dong Ahn, 1988: 724). His article was, in fact, distributed to the Ministry of Interior and all local administrative officials.

Former Minister of General Affairs, Kim Yong Gap led high-ranking officials who represented the right-wing of the administration. On August 13, 1988, he recommended that the government should be more strongly determined than ever before to deal with leftist students and civic leaders after the Seoul Olympic. Because of his strong right-wing stance, he was forced to resign from his post.

Many right wing groups publish periodicals to advocate their views. A few examples are *Cha You* (The Liberty) as the oldest right-wing monthly, *Cha You Kong Ron* (The Free Public Opinion) initiated by the Korean Anti-Communist Alliance (Hankuk Bangong Yonmang) and then resumed by the Korean Alliance for Liberty (Hankuk Cha You Chong Yonmang), *Cha You Pyong Ron* (The Free Criticism) by the Free Criticism Publishing Company (Cha You Pyong Ron Sa), *Cha You Shinmun* (The Free Newspaper) as a weekly, and many daily newspapers such as *Saegae Ilbo* (The World Daily), *Kuk Min Ilbo* (The People's Daily) (C.W. Chung, 1989: 48-55) (See Figure 8-10).

A Broad Moderate Pro-Democracy Coalition

Politicians, journalists, scholars, and middle-class citizens expressed their concern over the fact that President Roh Tae Woo was "elected by less than a simple popular majority vote. This would inject a new element of uncertainty and instability, an image of the minority president trying to depolarize divided South Korean society" (Kihl, 1988: 18). There was no doubt that the government and opposition party leaders had differences on the pace of democratization and related issues. However, they clearly became conscious of the imperative of democratization and determined to share the honor and respect for the democratic procedural principles--peaceful transfer of power, the guarantee of basic freedoms of speech, press, assembly, and religion, the respect for basic rights, the parliamentary way of compromises and negotiations on the basis of the majority rule and the minority protection.[2] The political participants, who joined the moderate, broad pro-democracy coalition, included the government leaders, the government political party, all major opposition parties and their leaders, a majority of military leaders, business executives, university professors and students, mass media, and the middle-class citizens. They began to outnumber and overpower both leftist and rightist coalitions (see Figure 8-10). Therefore, it is safe to suggest that Korea of the late 1980s had finally entered into the threshold of democratization (Figure 8-9).

The Korean model of democratization provides democracy-aspiring developing countries with a valuable lesson that democracy is not given or transplanted overnight by a foreign democratic superpower. But it can be sought and secured by the struggles of the domestic pro-democracy forces that have the commitment and dedication to appeal to the public, organizing a broad pro-democracy coalition, risking their lives, and continuously fighting for democratization. When the pro-democracy forces began to outnumber and overpower the anti-democracy forces--leftist or rightist, democratization began.

Conclusion: Democratic Accomplishments and Unfinished Tasks

Professor Chong Lim Kim deplores that "nearly forty years after the beginning of the Republic, democracy still remains an elusive goal. Despite the persistence with which Korean people have pressed for it, its attainment does not seem anywhere near" (C.L. Kim, 1988: 44). Many students of political culture and political socialization share with him the conviction that the failure of democracy in Korea is due to lack of inculcation of the democratic political culture by the Koreans and the subsequent "political cultural conditions adverse to democracy" (C.L. Kim, 1988: 55; Henderson, 1968: 361-376; John Oh, 1968: 191; Y.H. Lee, 1969; You and Wade, 1981; N.Y. Lee, 1985).

The political culture, which is "adverse" to democracy and yet "prevalent" among Koreans can be highlighted among others the following three characteristics. They are: 1) inconsistent belief systems; 2) norms of political conformity, and 3) norms of conflict resolution.

Inconsistent belief systems are identified by many students of political culture on the basis of their survey research in Korea. Let me introduce a few salient examples of different inconsistent belief systems.

1. A preponderant majority of Koreans, regardless of their status in power and social position, "ardently support the principle of majority rule." Ironically, they prefer, "a rule by an elite" (N.Y. Lee, 1985: 46-89).

2. They believe that individual liberty must be guaranteed at all cost. By the same token, they responded that political competition is undesirable because it causes too much diverse conflict (N.Y. Lee, 1985).

3. About 65 percent of 1,800 citizens surveyed responded that they routinely discussed politics and showed a keen interest in politics. Nevertheless, they were only passive listeners and remained uninvolved spectators. In other words, they were active discussants and yet passive listeners (K.W. Kim, 1985: 111-112).

4. Those who answered that they felt more strongly efficacious ironically voted less frequently than others who had a low sense of efficacy. Therefore, Chong Lim Kim stated that "the best informed, best educated social stratum (equipped presumably with a coherent ideology of democracy) stays away from the key process of democracy, i.e., electoral politics" (1980: 44-45). An inverse relationship was also identified by K. W. Kim that 76 percent of 1,800 respondents participated in recent election "because they felt so strongly about their intrinsic rights." Nevertheless, they showed a low sense of political efficacy (1985: 115).

5. Deprived of basic rights and freedoms and angered at the violation of the democratic procedural principles including peaceful transfer of power, tens of thousands of citizens, nevertheless, paid tribute to the final process of disgraced President Rhee and to the grave of late President Park. The "angry and mounting public outcries" ironically coexist with a "political sentimentalism of respect for autocratic leaders as great heroes (C.L. Kim, 1988: 59-60).

6. Members of the National Assembly equally show inconsistent belief systems. They responded, on the one hand, that they performed their legislative roles as "delegates," which meant that they should consult with their constituents and cast their votes as the

faithful errand boys representing their home voters. On the contrary, they were "generally very vague," when they were asked to identify whose interests they feel they should represent (Kim and Woo, 1972: 626-651).

Norms of political conformity inconsistent with democracy also prevail among Koreans:

1. Professor Nam Y. Lee found out from two nationwide surveys of 1974 and 1984 that: "one of every four adult citizens rejects any form of competition;" politicians should not compete with each other over policies; a multi-party system is harmful because it divides the nation (1985: 84-85). "Fear of division, disagreement, and pluralism stems from the culture of conformity" (C.L. Kim, 1988: 62). Nevertheless, voters supported a multi-party system in the 1987 presidential and 1988 National Assembly elections primarily on the basis of regionalism. Citizens in the Cholla provinces overwhelmingly voted for Kim Dae Jung and the Party for Peace and Democracy (PPD); those in South Kyong Sang province for Kim Young Sam and the Reunification Democratic Party (RDP); those in Choong Chung provinces for Kim Jong Pil and his New Democratic Republican Party (DRP); and those in North Kyong Song and Kang Won provinces for Roh Tae Woo and the Democratic Justice Party (DJP).

2. Asked of their view, a majority responded that the rights of a minority should be protected. Nevertheless, 60 percent and 66 percent of the respondents in the 1974 and 1984 surveys replied, respectively, that the minority should never criticize the views of the majority (N.Y. Lee, 1985: 84-85).

3. Since 1948 the rate of voting has been remarkably high. Nevertheless, the voters responded that they were little informed of politics and issues. "Part of the reason is that a large number of Korean voters are vulnerable to the pressure of mobilization either by the government or by other powerful social groups" (C.L. Kim, 1980: 125-127).

4. Politicians are no exceptions. Opposition politicians have persistently demanded the adoption of a parliamentary form of government because of their sufferings and persecution resulting from a strong presidential form of government. Nevertheless, opposition leaders and members preferred a strong presidential form

of government for the Sixth Republic with the expectation that they could secure the government power.

5. Condemning strong executive power and strong leadership as the primary cause for the violation of democratic practices, opposition party leaders, anti-government groups, and anti-government students as well demand from their members strong conformity or severe punishment. Thereby, the opposition party leaders dismissed their Assembly members, Kim Ok Sun and Cho Yun Ha for their insubordination.

The norms of conflict resolution are a third major cultural characteristic adverse to democracy.

1. Conflicts within an organization are likely to be resolved not by compromises and negotiations but by the inviolate norms of command and dominance on the part of the boss and the norms of obedience and submission on the part of the subordinates. Chong L. Kim and C. W. Park reported that the National Assembly members "would seek an interruption or an arbitration by a political superior of their own faction or party" (C.L. Kim, 1988: 67).

2. It is widely known that one significant mechanism designed to facilitate the process of bargaining and compromises is the role of organized groups. Nevertheless, Woo and Kim revealed that 51 percent of the National Assembly members surveyed denied organized groups any legitimate role in the legislative process (1970: 238).

The cultural requisite for a viable democracy seems loud and clear among the above scholars. Until people and their leaders inculcate the democratic cultural norms, values, and behaviors into their hearts and minds, they are not ready to practice and enjoy democracy.

> The principal obstacles to democracy are cultural: the belief systems and behavioral norms. Until Koreans develop a coherent belief system of democracy, replace their norms of excessive conformity with those of tolerance, and establish a set of legitimate rules of the game for an open and orderly competition, democracy will remain an elusive goal (C.L. Kim, 1988: 70).

The validity and reliability questions on their surveys aside, the overemphasis of these scholars on political culture as the principal obstacle to democracy fails to predict and explain how and why South Korea had finally entered into the threshold of democratization. The cultural requisite is only one of many theories which explain how democracy can take a firm root. Since this question is explained elsewhere in detail with an integrated model of democracy (Pae, 1986), let me identify and briefly explain what accomplishments have been made since June 29, 1987 as giant strides toward democracy in Korea often dubbed as "the Korean miracle of democratization." Major accomplishments include: the amendment to the constitution; open and fair competition and the subsequent direct popular elections of the president and the national Assembly; peaceful transfer of power; increase in the frequency of conferences between the leaders of political parties and their practice of the democratic political game of compromises and cooperation; checks and balances between the legislative and the executive; the promotion of democratic political culture on the basis of no repetition of political retaliation against the leaders of the previous regime, condemnation of the practice of patron-client politics and its replacement with group politics in terms of interest articulation and aggregation; institutionalization of various organizations like the military, the cabinet, and the judiciary; and the guarantee of basic freedoms and rights together with the clemencies and subsequent release of political prisoners.

Soon after the June 29, 1987 declaration an eight-member constitution drafting committee was organized representing both the ruling and major opposition parties. The committee produced the text of a new constitution on August 31, 1987. The new constitution for the Sixth Republic was overwhelmingly approved by both the government and opposition party Assembly members on October 12, 1987 by a vote of 254 to 4. Such a record-breaking high-level compromise among the law-makers indeed enhanced the legitimacy of the constitutional amendment procedure such that the referendum was passed by a record 93.1 percent approval from 78.2 percent of the total 26.6 million eligible voters.

The dream of millions of Koreans for a direct popular election of the president by their own votes came true for the first time in sixteen years. On December 16, 1987, Roh Tae Woo was elected and inaugurated as President of the Sixth Republic on February 25, 1988.

On this day the first peaceful and orderly transfer of power took place from President Chun Doo Hwan to Roh Tae Woo.

The new National Assembly election law was passed through the National Assembly again on the basis of compromise between the government and opposition parties on March 8, 1988. A general election was held on April 26, 1988 to choose 224 of 299 National Assembly seats, the remaining 75 to be apportioned at large. The Thirteenth National Assembly election resulted in a multi-party system. The election was declared "a defeat to the ruling Democratic Justice Party (DJP) as it deprived the Roh Tae Woo government of a majority in the legislature. The ruling DJP, indeed, failed to win the majority of seats in the election, capturing only 87 of the 224 seats" (Y.W. Kihl and I.P. Kim, 1988: 245-246) and 38 of the 75 at-large seats.

The DJP becoming downgraded as a minority and the subsequent emergence of a multi-party system in the Sixth Republic, however, may not be seen as a negative concern alone. The multi-party system and the DJP as a minority party would rather enhance the opportunities for the parties to exercise political compromise and cooperation without the practice of dictatorship as brandished by the government party at the expense of the minority parties in the previous regimes. The thesis that compromise and cooperation are more likely to be feasible under a multi-party system with the government party as a minority one than under a two-party system with the government party as a majority one is clearly witnessed in the history of conferences held and compromises made between the leaders of government and opposition parties. During the First Republic from 1948 to 1960, there had never been any conference between Syngman Rhee, the government party president, and his counterparts of the opposition parties. Dictatorship and unilateral decisions by the government party became the basic rule of the game against the opposition Assembly members. During the Third Republic from 1963 to 1971 there were only two conferences between the government and opposition party leaders. During the Fourth Republic from 1972 to 1979, only three meetings took place. In the first two meetings--one on June 21, 1973 between President Park Chung Hee and opposition leader Yu Chin San and the other on May 21, 1975 between President Park and opposition leader Kim Young Sam--the outcomes of the meetings were not even made available to the public.

The Fifth Republic, under a multi-party system, however, demonstrated eleven occasions of meetings between President Chun Doo Hwan and opposition party leaders. In the first six meetings President Chun dominated the conferences, explaining and briefing the opposition leaders on his visits to the United States, Japan, and Southeast Asia. The remaining five meetings took place after the National Assembly election of 1985, in which the opposition parties became stronger and the government party relatively weaker in the National Assembly. In these meetings President Chun became more compliant with the demands of his counterparts (*Hankuk Ilbo*, October 24, 1989).

Since the DJP became a minority party upon the inception of the Sixth Republic, the spirit of compromise and cooperation became greatly heightened. The past two years meetings have taken place on seven occasions. Leaders of the four political parties agreed in the Blue House meeting on May 28, 1988 the mutual cooperation for the successful accomplishment of the Seoul Summer Olympics, the promotion of political dialogues and compromises, the implementation of democratic reforms, and the reduction of regional animosity. They agreed again in the second separate meeting between President Roh Tae Woo and each of three Kims that partisan political truce should be made during the Seoul Olympics. The most controversial and thorny issue was the rectification of the injustices prevailing during the Fifth Republic, which had been ignored for the past two years until the seventh meeting was held in the Blue House between President Roh and the three Kims. The Grand Compromise of December 15, 1989, resulted in the agreement to call for: (1) the voluntary resignation of former President Chun's several key holdovers from the current offices without political retaliation against them, including Chung Ho Yong, the Special Warfare Commander during the 1980 Kwangju massacre ; (2) a testimony of former presidents Choi Kyu Ha in a written format and Chun Doo Hwan before a joint session of the National Assembly; and (3) the enactment of special laws to compensate the families of the Kwangju victims and to restore their honor. The Grand Compromise indeed could save the faces of the opposition party leaders because these three issues became their outstanding campaign promises in the 1988 election. The DJP and President Roh had "much to gain by settling these issues and heading into the second half of his five-year term relatively free from ties to the past. He also expected more cooperation from the opposition parties, which controlled a majority of the National Assembly" (*Omaha World Herald*, Dec. 17, 1989).

Moreover, checks and balances between the legislative and the executive were practiced within the framework of the constitution, when compromises were not able to be reached. On June 2, 1988, when President Roh submitted his party's nominee, Chung Kee Sung, for the Supreme Court Chief Justice, the nomination failed to obtain the necessary simple majority of votes in the unicameral legislature. President Roh became clearly aware of the constitutional power of the National Assembly and, therefore, complied, submitting the alternative nominee, Lee Il Kyu on July 5.

On the other hand, on July 9, 1988, when the National Assembly enacted new legislation by the coalition of opposition parties to authorize its special investigatory panel to subpoena ex-President Chun Doo Hwan for the investigation of past alleged wrongdoings of the Fifth Republic, President Roh Tae Woo exercised his veto power. The opposition parties' Assembly members, short of the two-thirds requirement for overriding the president's veto, admitted the constitutional limit and dropped the subpoena clause in the revised bill, which was finally signed by President Roh on July 24, 1988. His veto power was able to prohibit the potential for the embarrassment of the former presidents and for possible retaliation against them and their key staff.

Condemnations against and prohibition of the practices of patron-client politics became another important step toward democratization. The National Assembly of the Sixth Republic, fully empowered with the constitutional right to audit the state of affairs together with the legislative committee activities and the Ministry of Justice, began to investigate forty-four major wrongdoings committed during the Fifth Republic. Let me introduce a few examples here to illustrate the scope and extent of patronage-based corruption. They are:

1. The scandal of Ilhae Foundation, which raised 59.8 billion won (about $85 million based on the ratio of 680 won to 1 U.S. dollar) in excess of the original target of 30 billion won. The real concern was the allegedly "coercive and threatening" ways of fund-raising from major industries. However, no evidence was found against any direct fund-raising role by President Chun and his Security Planning Board Director, Chang Sae Dong. But the

expenditures of 2.6 of 4.25 billion won, which was donated by the Dong Kuk Steel Industry, was not explained and became mysterious.

2. The Next Generation Education Foundation, which was founded under the leadership of former First Lady, Lee Soon Ja, raised 23.5 billion won, and received 1.75 billion won of government aid. Again, no evidence was found against the allegedly coercive way of fund-raising. However, the expenditure of 74.7 of 150 million won was not explained.

3. Inhumane treatment in the Sam Chung Military Training Camp, which "trained" and "disciplined" a total of 39,742 civilian trouble-makers, hooligans, and racketeers since its inception in 1980. Inhuman disciplines and torture claimed 54 lives during their concentration camp ordeals (*Dong A Annual*, 1989: 151). The constitutionality of the Chun regime's arresting and putting of civilians--men and women, young and old--into the military training camp without due process of law, inhuman treatment, and torture were fully exposed by the National Assembly investigations in 1988.

4. Wrongdoings of the relatives of President Chun: the embezzlement of public funds of Noryang Chin Marine Products Market by President Chun's older brother, Kee Hwan; receipt of 249 million won by President Chun's cousin, Soon Hwan for his patronage pressure for the government's approval of a golf course; receipt of 176 million won by president Chun's cousin, Woo Hwan for his patronage pressure for the government's approval of the establishment of public rest areas on the highways and other favors; embezzlement of 1.77 billion won by President Chun's brother-in-law (First Lady's younger brother), Lee Chang Suk; receipt of 316 million won by President Chun's brother-in-law (husband of the First Lady's sister), Hong Soon Doo for his pressure for the suspension of tax audit; receipt of 28.5 million won by President Chun's nephew, Kim Young Do for his patronage action for the release of a person charged with a criminal action; receipt of 500 million won by the First Lady's uncle, Lee Kyu Seung for his patronage action for the postponement of the payment of bank loans.

5. Approval of golf courses. During the Fifth Republic a total of 29 golf courses were approved. Those who received the permit from the government were the financial contributors to the Ilhae Foundation, the Next Generation Education Foundation, and the New Village (Sae Ma Ul) Movement.

6. The New Village Movement, a national program for the development of the rural area. President Chun's younger brother,

Kyung Hwan took the successive positions of its Secretary General, its President, and the President Emeritus. He took the embezzlement of 2.55 billion won from the profits running the Sae Ma Ul newspaper, tax evasion of 1.06 billion won, and receipt of 417 million won from various industries for his patronage pressures to the administration for their benefits (*Dong-A Annual*, 1989: 721-736).

A total of 47 persons were subject to punishment following the proper judicial procedure. A thorough investigation, proper judicial review, and subsequent legal punishment provided high-ranking government officials, business executives, the president, and his immediate relatives as well as the general public with a valuable lesson that patronage politics, unfair practices of law, corruption, and abuses of government power and position cannot and will not be tolerated any longer in Korea. Instead, open and public competition in the process of interest articulation by formally and informally organized groups and associations is greatly encouraged and promoted. In fact, as Figure 8-10 shows, more and more interest groups--religious, occupational, ideological, educational, regional, economic, cultural, professional--are being established along with industrialization, increase in education, urbanization, and mass media. They begin to actively articulate their needs and expectations in an open and competitive environment under the full guarantee of basic freedoms of speech, press, assembly, and religion.

Autonomy and freedom also prevail in the academic community, press, literature, and cultural activities. University presidents and deans are no longer appointed but symbolically approved by the Ministry of Education upon the election by the faculty members and endorsement by the Board of Directors in the private universities. Students are allowed to have their own campus activities. Books and literature, which had long been prohibited from the general public because of the authors residing or moving into North Korea, are now on sale in bookstores. Books, articles, and paintings of North Korea and other communist countries are now declassified. North Korea-origin books and documents are made available at the regular bookstores (*Hankuk Ilbo*, December 12, 1989).

Human rights activists in Korea and abroad criticized that more political human rights have been restricted and more political prisoners arrested and detained by the Sixth Republic than the Fifth

Republic. However, their contention is exaggerated and distorted. The Sixth Republic guarantees and honors more civil and political freedoms and rights than any previous republics. After long overdue patience and advice against secret contacts and visits to North Korea and the subsequent, reckless actions against the government's repeated warnings the Sixth Republic began to indict and arrest those who violated the laws. The government proclaims that their discreet and individualistic contacts, visits, and adoption of resolutions for unification would rather hinder the efforts of the government-to-government diplomacy and embarrass the government of South Korea, because the Democratic People's Republic of Korea (North Korea) may continue to not officially recognize the Republic of Korea (South Korea).

Students of political culture as reviewed previously claim the democratic political culture as the independent variable, which determines the success or failure of democracy. However, our discussion thus far clearly indicates the opposite direction: democratic progress--the constitutional amendment, peaceful transfer of power, the practices of checks and balances, the experience in the political game of compromises and cooperations, the condemnations of patron-client politics, the promotion of group politics, and the greater degree of freedom and autonomy to various organizations--also enhances the democratic cultural norms, values, behaviors, and expectations in the hearts and minds of Koreans today more significantly than at any other time in the past.

Finally, we may examine the transformation of the military in terms of its institutionalization and its culture. For the last eight years of the Fifth Republic, a total of 2,765 soldiers died. However, concerning the causes of their death, there were significant differences between the Korean Ministry of Defense and human rights advocates. The Ministry of Defense explained that 86 percent of them passed away primarily because of their disappointment with love affairs and subsequent suicide (*Hankuk Ilbo*, 12/6/1989). Human rights activists rather attributed their deaths to the autocratic political culture inherited from the Japanese militaristic rule during the Japanese colonialism, the antagonistic attitude of the traditionally conservative military toward the drafted college student activists and discriminately severe physical punishment to the drafted anti-government, former student and labor activists (*Washington Post*, March 12, 1989).

The Chicago Tribune, however, reported that the number of deaths was reduced to 239 during 1988. During the first nine months of 1989 the number declined to 52, and only 25 of them died of assault. The Nonsan army training camp for recruits recently began to enforce only eight hours of training a day, made substantial improvements in logistical and food supplies for the recruits, and officially prohibited corporal punishment. A seven-year veteran teaching assistant, who had trained the recruits in the camp under an actual combat simulation, replied that "corporal punishment" was the primary means of teaching the recruits in the past; "explanation" is the principal means of teaching them now. Impressed by the democratic cultural reforms being undertaken and experienced in the Korean army, *the Chicago Tribune* concluded the news coverage with a quotation from an anonymous officer, who said. "The old soldiers in Korea have already perished" (December 1, 1989).

Democratic reforms in the Korean armed forces are vividly evidenced in their official statements on their role. Park Hee Do, former Chief of the General Staff in his farewell address on June 1, 1989, stated that "in the name of democratization and the open-door policy, helmets and army shoes are ridiculed on the podium of the election campaign sites. I cannot help but be greatly angered and anguished over such a humiliation on the army. I also learned a painful lesson that the Korean army shall never be involved in politics for fear of domestic turbulences." Lee Chong Ku, the incoming Chief of the General Staff, also stated that "the armed forces must go back to the barracks for its inherent duty" (*Hankuk Ilbo*, October 17, 1989).

Democratic reforms in the armed forces were further witnessed by various actual behaviors. Lee Sang Hoon, the Army Chief of Staff, for example, broke the forty-year-old precedent of the security imperative of the armed forces, initiating visits to the office of journalists in the Ministry of Defense (MOD) Headquarters, and asking them whether they had any complaints or suggestions for coverage of news on the armed forces. The MOD replaced the previous pattern of handing out a small memo to journalists on major defense policies with briefing them and having face-to-face question and answer sessions. The MOD, for the first time in its history, on March 28, 1989, invited and briefed the presidents of the major opposition political parties on North Korea. The information on military personnel affairs concerning the promotion and appointment to major military posts was no longer classified

(*Hankuk Ilbo*, October 17, 1989). The Army Security Command also experienced major reforms. It closed 196 local branches originally designed to gather intelligence on various local administrative offices. It no longer assumed any special tasks which were in the past assigned by the special order of the president. The Security Command began to suspend intelligence on opposition politicians and political dissidents, and refused to accept any political favoritism. The army also recently made a major personnel shake-up, discharging "political generals" from military service, transferring some, and promoting professional generals and assigning them to strategic positions (*Hankuk Ilbo*, October 18, 1989).

Speculation in the limited land in Korea and the rapid rise of land value depending on the purpose of land use have long been an important public concern. Those who owned a small piece of land became millionaires overnight. Those individuals and giant conglomerates who owed a large quantity of land insisted that the ownership of land must be guaranteed under capitalism and a free market system. Of course, they expected that investment in land would gain higher returns far exceeding the consumer price index and the bank interest rate. While a large amount of land stands idle as a long-term investment, millions of average people have to do without a house or an apartment due to the shortage of construction lots available. The government finally proclaimed the public importance of the land and freed it from its speculation.

Since such a position was clearly made by President Roh, the cabinet members were not supposed to openly challenge their president. However, on two occasions of the cabinet meetings on this controversial issue, on September 2 and 7, 1989, the cabinet members had lively, open, and candid debates among themselves on the pros and cons of the issue (*Hankuk Ilbo*, September 9, 1989). This was the first signal that the cabinet meeting system was no longer dictated by their boss but democratically institutionalized.

Great strides toward democratization have been made. Yet there remain many tasks to be equally affirmatively pursued. Police still have free hands to arrest without judicial due process those who have been previously convicted. Local self-government was declared a major campaign issue of both presidential and National Assembly election of all four political parties in 1987 and 1988. The Local Self-Government Law had long been deadlocked but was deliberated and enacted in an unexpectedly hasty way upon the compromise and cooperation between the government and opposition parties for the election of local legislative councils in 1991 and the election of local chief executives in 1992 *(Hankuk Ilbo,* March 6, 1991). Many outstanding structural and functional issues need to be examined for institutionalization of local self-government (Pae, 1986: Ch. 5). They can be reviewed and improved following its implementation. Local self-government will greatly promote democracy at the grassroots level. Political neutrality of government employees, especially police, has been a major concern. This controversial issue becomes another important agenda item for the competing parties to reach a compromise and enact a law for its enforcement.

All political parties are organized around their leaders, as if the parties were their own personal properties. Structural and functional characteristics of political parties that need institutionalization are examined elsewhere in detail (Pae, 1986: Ch. 6). However, it goes without saying that institutionalization of political parties needs to be made such that the political parties may have competition against one another on the basis of issues and programs commonly shared among the party members in each without personality and regional animosity. Political parties also need to penetrate into the general public and have strong ties with specific groups and associations.

Much legislation, including the national Security and the Anti-Communist Law, which were enacted during the previous regimes and not conducive to democratization, need critical review for revisions. But we should be aware that democracy cannot and shall not be viewed as a dichotomy as to its complete presence or absence but as a continuum progressing from a nondemocratic to a near ideal one in terms of a long-term perspective. The United States has made continued improvement toward a more perfect democracy for two hundred years. There is no doubt that South Korea has already embarked on democratization and continues to progress toward its destination: for the pursuit of happiness and self-actualization of every Korean citizen in the political environment of democracy.

Notes

1. There are no absolutely objective criteria to measure the freedom of speech and press. Therefore, the freedom of communications media must be studied not in terms of an absolute perspective but in terms of its relation to the level of government control in the name of national security and stability. One ultimate

question is: How wide is the zone where the government and communications media may overlap in their respective areas of jurisdiction? The wider the zone is, the greater the degree of conflict between the government and the communications media becomes. For a comparative study of the twilight zone between the United States and the Republic of Korea, see Pae (1988b: 481-502).

2. Four major political parties in the Sixth Republic share a high degree of consensus on all major domestic and foreign policies in contents despite rhetorical differences. For their party platforms for the 1987 presidential and the 1988 National Assembly elections, see *The Dong-A Annual 1989* (1989: 728-729).

Part III Social Welfare Services

No state is fully committed to welfare services such that all its citizens receive perfectly equal quality and quantity of welfare benefits and protection from the cradle to the grave. By the same token no state totally ignores welfare services and thereby abstains from intervention in economic markets and property relations.

Concerning the scope and extent of public commitment to welfare and the subsequent quality of services, Furniss and Tilton contend that the conventional typology of political regimes such as totalitarian or democratic, capitalistic or communistic, industrial or post-industrial obscures and limits the potential range of political possibilities (1977: x). In terms of differences in premises, goals, and related public actions and programs for social welfare, Furniss and Tilton identify three types of states. They are the corporate-oriented positive state, the social security state, and the social welfare state. Among these three, they suggest the social welfare state as the preferred model.

> While we consider each of these perspectives, our sympathies lie with the social welfare state. It alone offers the prospect of satisfying the need for a new political theory commensurate with the demands of a new era, and we stretch the groundwork for this political theory of the social welfare state. We argue explicitly for the values on which it is based: human dignity, equality, liberty, democracy, security, solidarity, and economic efficiency (1977: xi).

Let me briefly explain what are these three types of states and how different they are. This will help us identify major shortcomings and limitations of their models to empirical applicability for a comparative study. Moreover, a cross-national study suggests that welfare programs and services available by the social welfare states do not necessarily contribute to the highest physical quality of life (PQLI), which may be considered the ultimate outcome of the evaluation of welfare services delivered to the people.

My main objective in Chapter Nine is to examine to what extent Korea leads the developing countries in the promotion of physical quality of life with a modicum of state expenditures for social welfare. Chapter Ten will explain how the Korean model of social welfare is developed, what its accomplishments have been, and what additional tasks remain to be pursued.

Chapter 9 Korea: Leader of the Nations in Social Welfare

Liberal Economy as the Root Cause of Welfare Services

Liberal Economy

The liberal economic theory contends that the state is established not to exalt the power of itself but to maximize the opportunity for self-fulfillment by its inhabitants under the guarantee of life, liberty, and property ownership. The liberal theory spans the entire period of human civilization by various economic philosophers and theorists.

Plato (427-347 B.C.) stated in his *Dialogues* the premise that no individual is self-sufficient. Cooperation and mutual interaction are, therefore, the basis of the state as well as of the economy. However, Plato did not equate cooperation and mutual interaction with communism, nor did he endorse it. He rather advocated the existence of an exchange economy and the necessity of a marketplace. Since individuals inherit different innate talents, they may specialize in what they are best fitted for and receive the subsequent differential amount of rewards.

Aristotle (384-322 B.C.) also accepted the existence and the necessity of an exchange economy based on the division of labor and of the institution of private property. He justified the latter on the assumption that people take better care of what is their own rather than what is held in common. His exchange economy ought to be ruled by "corrective justice" on the basis of the "principle of equivalence" in private transactions of buying and selling. His private property ought to be ruled by "distinctive justice" on the basis of "the principle of merit" in the distribution of wealth.

Thomas Aquinas (1225?-1274) did not rule out the potential that in case of extreme necessity all things could "revert to common ownership" and that "superfluities ought to be given to the poor." But he endorsed the principle of private property. People were "entitled to live as befitted their situation in life." "Thus, a poor man on the point of starvation did not steal when he took a piece of bread without the permission of its owner" (De Roover, 1968: 434).

Jean Bodin (1529?-1596) challenged the basic principle of ancient and medieval thought that man is naturally a social, political animal destined to life in society and to the achievement of his bounded tasks within it. Bodin rather insisted that families and their individual members agreed to organize commonwealth, to maintain law and order, thereby to protect individuals' life and liberty, and to secure their properties. Commonwealths were:

> chiefly established to yield to every man that which is his own and to forbid theft, as it is commanded by the word of God who would have every man enjoy the property of his own goods. . . . True popular liberty consists of nothing else, but in the enjoyment of our private goods securely without fear to be wronged. . . . (Bodin, 1959: 675).

John Locke (1632-1703) suggested a theory of social contract that individuals agreed "with other men to join and unite into a community." The main objective of the community was the protection of "life, liberty, and property" inherited as natural rights of individuals: "Their comfortable, safe, and peaceable living one amongst another, in a secure enjoyment of their properties and greater security against any that are not of it" (1969: 168-169).

Of course, Locke was not immune from criticism. Thomas Cook identified several major shortcomings in Locke's theory. It first failed to see the existence of primitive communities--patriarchal or matriarchal--where property was shared among the community members as a collectivity. Production in hunting, fishing, and farming was collectively pursued. More effective and efficient ways of production were greatly attributed to collectively established schools and apprenticeship.[1]

> This [Locke's theory of property] was a dubious step to take, since it rested entirely on the logic of an individualistic state of labor, and failed to see the possibility of primitive co-operation of Communism. It insisted, in short, that initial production was by the individual unaided by his fellows. It insisted also, and much more dangerously, that the conditions of "natural production" were not dependent on society, and that at the beginning values were in no way socially created.

> Nor does Locke subsequently recognize clearly and directly the reality of socially created values: values arising from growth of population, from a commonly inherited stock of knowledge, and from the institutional framework of a growing society. He insisted rather that the individual owns his own labor, and that others, as rational beings, necessarily and tacitly consent to his consequent ownership of produce (1969: xxvii).

Moreover, Cook called special attention to the fact that Locke's original theory of property was stretched from within the limit of the property owner to consume its product to "the very different theory of property in producers' good or capital" (1969: xxvii).

> He in no sense justified the ownership of capital, in land, or otherwise, beyond the ability of the owner to consume its products and to produce them by his own labor; nor did he justify inequality in a world where there is no longer plenty for all (1969: xxix).

The inherent shortcomings in his theory of property and in its interpretation and application beyond his original purpose notwithstanding, Locke's theory still serves as the justification of rational liberalism and constitutionalism.

Another noted scholar on economic liberalism is Adam Smith (1723-1790). It is a fallacy to interpret his *Wealth of Nations* as an equally unqualified eulogy of free enterprise, open market, and property ownership. From a humanitarian perspective Smith accepted as a desirable function of government the public financing of some essential programs as elementary education for the children of the poor. But he did not endorse the lobbying of powerful business groups for special privileges and favors from the government. He was equally concerned about the potential for the emergence of monopoly or oligopoly by a few giant corporations over the means of production and distribution of goods and services. "Where monopoly is unavoidable," Smith "preferred government to private operation" (Viner, 1968: 327). His principle of *laissez-faire* was not a condemnation of all government interference with the activities of private individuals; he endorsed the vital need for the government's measures to adopt standardization of weights and measures, the rules for the commodities to meet quality standards and the establishment of building codes for the safety of properties as well as their residents. He also conceded to the government the provision of raising and maintaining the armed forces for the defense of the community against foreign invasion or internal disorder and of levying taxes to finance these activities.

Smith, however, like the above philosophers and theorists, strongly believed that the basic source of economic progress is the striving of individuals to improve their economic status or their rank in society, namely, "the desire of bettering our condition, a condition which . . . comes with us from the womb, and never leaves us till we go into the grave" (1950: 323). Such desire, according to Viner's highlight of Smith's book, is facilitated by:

> . . . free enterprise; free trade; non-interference of government in the individual's choice of occupation, residence, or investment; freedom for the individual to make his economic decisions of all kinds in response to the price movements of free and fully competitive markets--in short, of "economic liberalism" or "*laissez-faire*," as these terms were used in the nineteenth century--that Smith made his chief mark on the history of economics and on the economic and social history of the Western world (1968: 328).

Problems of Liberal Economy

The liberal economic theory, however, is challenged by its unanticipated economic and political consequences. The market economy takes the form of a series of business cycles of "boom" and "bust," resulting from the discrepancy in the interaction of the supply and demand in the domestic markets and in the exports and imports in the international trade. When the depth of a particular cycle is not severe and the length of the bust not extended, the liberal economy may manage to survive intact. However, when its depth becomes severe and its recession remains for long, many individuals, especially at the bottom of the economic ladder, suffer most "through no fault of their own." They may start condemning the liberal economy. The liberal economy is equally challenged when unregulated capital begins to exploit workers with respect to age, sex, wage, hours of labor, and working conditions. Since the adoption of universal suffrage and the legalized labor movement, those previously helpless workers began to use their political power

Korea: Leader of the Nations in Social Welfare   353

Table 9-1 Economic Changes in the United States: 1920-1939

	1920	1929	1933	1939
Population (million)	106	122	126	131
Gross National Product ($billion, 1929 prices)	73	104	74	111
Per capita GNP (1929 prices)	688	857	590	847
Federal Government Revenues ($billion)	6.7	4.0	2.0	5.0
National debts ($billion)	24.3	17.0	22.5	40.4
Exports of U.S. Merchandise ($billion)	4.4	5.2	1.6	3.1
Unemployed (million & %)	1.7 4%	1.6 3%	12.8 25%	9.5 17%
Volume of Sales on the NYSE (million of shares)	227	1,125	655	262
Bank Suspensions	168	659	4,004	72

Source: Donald B. Cole (1968: 211)

of voting for the promotion of their interests, and form a coalition with their elected representatives. The state inevitably tends to intervene in unregulated markets and property rights.

The worldwide Great Depression of 1929 was the most serious incident which led to state intervention with the liberal economy in the Western European countries and the United States. The scope and extent of economic changes in the United States between 1920 and 1939 resulting from the stock market crash can be partially witnessed in Table 9-1. The decade of the 1920s seemed to show prosperity in the United States: Per capita income rose from $688 in 1920 to $857 in 1929. But the unregulated market economy was not really healthy. The economic premonition was well described by Donald Cole:

> The productivity of industrial workers rose 43 percent, 1919-29, but real wages rose only 25 percent. The unequal distribution of wealth, which grew worse in the 1920s, led to a shortage of consumer purchasing power, and inventories

rose. Corporate profits, meanwhile, shot up 60 percent (1919-29), and many of the profits were reinvested in the stock market. . . . The bull market got underway in 1924 when the index was 91, rose to 125 by 1927, and then roared onward to 260 in 1929. Investors operated on margin and were deeply in debt. The American banking system was unsound as 1929 approached. Over 5,000 banks closed their doors from 1921-28, and banks speculated too freely on the stock market. By 1929 a speculative bubble was ready to burst (Cole, 1968: 212).

The unregulated market economy produced not only the omen of the Great Depression but also the actual collapse of the economy itself in 1929. The per capita income sharply declined from $857 in 1929 to $590 in 1933. The exports of American merchandise fell from $5.2 billion in 1929 to $1.6 billion in 1933. The number of banks which were closed reached from 659 in 1929 to 4,004 in 1933. The number of unemployed increased from three percent of the work force in 1929 to 25 percent in 1933 (see Table 9-1).

The unregulated market was more seriously condemned for the incapacity of "invisible hand" to cope with the economic woes resulting from a deep and extended recession in the 1930s in the Western European countries and the United States. European production of pig-iron and steel ingots in 1939, for example, was not able to regain the level of a decade earlier. The shipbuilding industry was decimated. For the eighteen years from 1921-1938 Sweden and Denmark never lowered their unemployment level below ten percent of the work force. Norway and Great Britain managed this target only once. Germany experienced a series of wild fluctuations--6.9 percent in 1925, 18 percent in 1926, 8 percent in 1928, and 13 percent in 1929 (Furniss and Tilton, 1977: 9). By 1939 the United States unemployment level lingered at seventeen percent.

Unregulated property became not less problematic than the unregulated market. The "men of property," who were encouraged by unconstrained individualism and the desire to accumulate more profits and properties, began to exploit the working class including children and women with cheap wages, long hours of labor, and unsafe working conditions. Many of them were seasonally laid off. Some were too young or too old to continue to carry out physically unbearable toil. Some became victims of industrial accidents; while they were employed, they could survive, but once they were unemployed, disabled, infirm, and/or too old, they were forced to live in destitution. These groups accounted for more than twenty percent of the entire population of London in the 1880s (Booth, 1902). A lifetime of toil in industries notwithstanding, many inhabitants of York in 1900 were unable to acquire "any property of monetary importance" (Rowntree, 1901). Of those retiring in the United States in 1969, "over one-third had a net worth (including home equity) of less than $5,000; almost 60 percent had less than $15,000" (Furniss and Tilton, 1977: 12). Ironically, the concentration of productive property in corporations was galloping such that about sixty percent of the assets of manufacturing firms were controlled by about one thousand of the largest corporations in 1941 but by only two hundred in 1970 (Peterson, 1974: 487).

Unregulated markets and property rights together tend to ignore collective goods and services so long as they do not cause any immediate concerns for survival and safety of the men of property. This results in "private elephant" and "public squalor" in terms of the allocation of financial resources available. Public quality of life may be greatly endangered because of lack of concern and lack of public funds to take care of air and water pollution, toxic waste, and other environmental problems. Public morality may be equally threatened by the principle of free enterprise in drugs, alcoholic beverages, gambling, and prostitution.

Three Types of State Intervention

Unregulated markets, unfettered property ownership, and concern for increasing collective problems sufficiently justified the beginning of state intervention in the liberal economy. Concerning the level of state intervention, Furniss and Tilton suggest three types. They are the corporate state, the social security state, and the social welfare state.

The corporate state has the primary goal of protecting property owners from the failure of invisible hands of unregulated markets. The corporate state tends to maintain a symbiotic relationship between business, bureaucrats, and political communities. Politicians and bureaucrats offer a variety of benefits and privileges such as tax exemptions, subsidies, credits, and contracts to corporations. They in turn offer campaign funds for re-election of politicians and jobs for bureaucrats in case they want to move into the private sector (Miller, 1972: Greenberg, 1974: 3-32; Barnet, 1972).

The corporate state, however, tries to see to it that employment should be maintained high enough so as to assure the high level of consumption for the individuals. On the other hand, the demand for labor should not be strong enough to strengthen labor unions and to cause industries to pay excessive wages. Striking balance between the two issues often characterizes the state role as a "minimalist full-employment policy" (Furniss and Tilton, 1977: 15). The corporate state does not adopt and implement any public welfare programs and services but encourages individuals and families to join private social insurance programs on the basis of actuarial principles with occasional and minor help from general revenues.

According to Furniss and Tilton, the social security state, on the other hand, endorses liberal economic theory based on the values of individualism, open market, free competition, creative ideas, hard work, and private property ownership. As far as social welfare policies are concerned, the social security state adopts a "guaranteed national minimum" for all of the citizens regardless of their income, employment, and physical conditions. The major normative value behind the guaranteed national minimum is the inability of many people to join private social insurance because of seasonal unemployment or wages too small to set aside a portion for the future. Moreover, the chronically sick, the disabled, single parent families with many children, the old, and unskilled workers are not able to join such a private social insurance. A guaranteed national minimum for every citizen "adequate in amount" for the rest of his life for a decent living without other resources and "adequate in time" (Beveridge, 1942:13) becomes the basic political philosophy of the social security state. However, the term "minimum" is not fixed for subsistence but adjusted to advances in the standard of living.

> If the minimum line, "subsistence," is placed at a level commensurate with the minimum expectations of society, and if the level is then raised to conform to advances in the standard of living, and if no one for any reason is permitted to fall below this floor, then decent security "from the cradle to the grave" can be said to have been achieved (Furniss and Tilton, 1977: 17).

The social security state, therefore, adopts and implements such specific programs as the retirement pension, health protection, disability and sickness protection, the protection of survivors and dependents, and unemployment compensation.

Unlike the above two types, the social welfare state of Furniss and Tilton starts from the fundamental assumption of individual human worth and dignity regardless of sex, color, race, religion, language, ethnic origin, education, talents, and physical and genetic differences. Such a basic assumption encourages the social welfare state to promote the values of "equality, freedom, democracy, solidarity, security, and economic efficiency" (Furniss and Tilton, 1977: 28).

1. Equality goes beyond the liberal idea of equal opportunity. Equality does not endorse the equal remuneration for differential contributions. "What equality does require in the economic sphere is the elimination of differentials in reward so large that they create social classes." Furniss and Tilton rather recommend an "income range between twice the national mean and one-half of the national mean." This range would "permit a wide range of life styles, but would make the existence of social classes distinctly harder to maintain" (1977: 30).

2. Freedom "supports the traditional civil liberties supposedly upheld in bourgeoisie society." This includes "free choice of vocation, the opportunity to exercise personal initiative and responsibility, and to organize one's own work activities." However, the "freedom of the marketplace, and particularly the individual's freedom to accumulate wealth, property, and power must yield to more general claims for freedom from concentrated private power" (1977: 34).

3. Economic and social democracy allow men and women to exercise the right to influence their own working conditions, to take part in investment decisions as well as redistribution of goods and services.

4. Solidarity aims "to replace the acquisitive sentiments and exchange relations of capitalism with sympathy and fraternity, the competitive atmosphere with cooperative impulses" (1977: 35).

5. Security, through the development of social insurance and public services, abolishes privation, provides redress to the handicapped for the injustice of nature, and secures the position of the aged, disabled, and bereaved. Security by these "corrective" social policy can be further reinforced by "preventive" social policy with anticipatory measures (1977: 36-37).

6. Economic efficiency is "not the natural result of the free play of market forces" but comes from conscious public efforts to maintain a high and steady level of aggregate demand, to alleviate production "bottlenecks," to restrict oligopolistic inefficiency, and to correct the market's incapacity to deal effectively with externalities such as pollution (1977: 37-38).

The social welfare state, therefore, actively pursues intervention in production, engineers the national economy for full employment and efficiency without full commitment to nationalization or state socialism, promotes solidaristic wage, and adopts Keynesian budgetary planning. The welfare state also takes social welfare programs for every citizen and measures for quality life of the entire community (see Table 9-2).

The Fallacy of the Furniss and Tilton Welfare State

Furniss and Tilton claim that their "ideal-typical constructs are not airy fantasy" but become "the underlying bases of policy choice." For that purpose they identified the United States as a corporate-oriented positive state, Britain as a social security state, and Sweden as a social welfare state. Among these three, they prefer the social welfare state.

> While the fit between these countries and our models is imperfect and approximate at best, Britain does illustrate the accomplishments and limitations of the social security state, Sweden the possibility of a social welfare state, and the United States the moral inadequacy of the positive state. . . . The social welfare state, far from being detrimental to human welfare and political stability as many Americans imagine, actually promotes these two desirable ends (1977: xi).

I have many reservations to wholeheartedly accepting their typology and their practical applicability to the real world. First of all, I wonder whether the United States is an exclusively corporate-oriented positive state, always protecting business and corporations at the expense of individual citizens. The United States, which has long cherished the market economy and private property rights, however, did have no options but to pursue state intervention in the market

Table 9-2 Three Types of State Intervention by Furniss and Tilton

	The Corporate State	The Social Security State	The Social Welfare State
Normative values	Economic growth Protection of corporate interest Individualism	Individualism for higher quality of life Open competition Free enterprise Private property ownership No equality but opportunity The right of every citizen to minimal standard of living Inadequacy of private social insurance	Economic and social democracy Freedom from concentrated private power Solidarity Security Equality, not equal opportunity Economic efficiency
Role of the state	Indirect contribution to promoting national economy Advocacy of private social insurance	Supplement to individuals' social insurance with gov't payments and services	Substitution of public services for social insurance programs Providing public assistance for the needy

Specific actions and programs	Minimalist full employment
	Social insurance program based on actuarial principle
	Job training, regular work habits and savings
		Intervention in redistribution
		Social security programs:
		  Old Age pension
		  Medical care & aid
		  Disability protection
		  Unemployment compensation
			Intervention in production
			Full employment
			Solidaristic wage
			Elimination of wide income gap: a range of two to one half of the national mean
			Progressive taxation
			Keynesian budgetary planning
			Environmental planning

Sample countries	The USA	Great Britain	Sweden

Source: Furniss and Tilton (1977)

economy during the Great Depression. Some of the programs were designed to help business and corporations to survive the depression, but most of the New Deal programs were to promote survival and well-being of the average citizens, offering them employment, income, and security of their savings in the bank. Let me highlight with a few examples the state intervention in the private market in the name of the New Deal policy.

1. Emergency Banking Bill of 1933 for the opening of sound banks under licenses from the Treasury Department.
2. Unemployment Relief Act of 1933 for providing work for men aged 18-25 in reforestation, road-building, and soil erosion control. By 1935, 500,000 young men were employed and received wages of $30 per month.
3. Agricultural Adjustment Act (AAA) of 1933 for restoring the farmers' purchasing power to parity with the period of 1909-1914. The AAA was to maintain price stabilization of farm products through production control with benefit payments to farmers. The act also called for refinancing of farm mortgages through the federal land banks.
4. Tennessee Valley Authority Act of 1933 for accomplishing several major objectives such as construction of dams, establishment of electric power plans, flood control and soil conservation of the Tennessee Valley region, creation of jobs, and the raising of the standard of living in the valley.
5. Home Owners Refinancing Act of 1933 for creating the Home Owners Loan Corporation to issue bonds to refinance non-farm home mortgages.
6. Glass-Steagall Banking Act of 1933 for separating commercial from investment banking, expanding the power of the Federal Reserve Board to enable it to stop speculation, and creating the Federal Deposit Insurance Corporation to insure bank deposits up to $5,000.
7. Civil Works Administration of 1933 for creating jobs for millions of the unemployed. The Civil Works Emergency Relief Act of 1934 had 2,500,000 unemployed at work by January 1935.
8. Emergency Relief Appropriations Act of 1935, which employed three million of the ten million jobless within the year of 1935 and over eight million by 1943. With the expenditure of $11 billion, thousands of buildings, roads, and bridges were constructed.

The state intervention was extended to trade with foreign countries. The Reciprocal Trade Agreements Act of 1934 authorized the U.S. President to negotiate with other nations, raising or reducing tariffs up to fifty percent without the consent of Congress.

Its success could be measured by agreements with fifty-three countries by 1951.

The United States government also committed itself since the implementation of the New Deal policy to intervention in private property rights as well as the protection of workers, labor unions, a minimum wage, and a maximum work week together with the adoption and expansion of a social security system. A few highlights are as follows:

1. National Industrial Recovery Act (NIRA) of 1933, whose Section 7a guaranteed labor workers the right to unionization and collective bargaining on wage, fringe benefits, and improvement in working conditions such that they could no longer become victims of property holders. National Labor Relations Act (Wagner-Connery Act) replaced the NIRA in 1935, required management to collectively deal with labor unions, forbade it to interfere with unions, allowed the closed shop, and created the National Labor Relations Board to judge claims of unfair labor practices.

2. Fair Labor Standards Act of 1938, which established a minimum wage and a maximum work week of forty hours with time-and-a-half for overtime work. It also forbade child labor under the age of 16 years in quarries and mines and under the age of 14 years in mills and manufacturing.

3. Social Security Act of 1935, which adopted a federal system of old-age and survivors' protection. It added the protection of the disabled in 1957, and finally included medical care for the elderly in 1966. State governments administer Aid to Families with Dependent Children (AFDC), Medicaid, food stamps, as well as unemployment compensation.

Compared with the "social security state of Britain" and the "social welfare state of Sweden," the United States as a "corporate state" does not have the coverage of sickness, maternity, medical care, and hospitalization for all citizens (see Table 9-3). Nevertheless, the above list explains the fact that the United States has an extensive range of social security and welfare programs.

Furniss and Tilton suggest that the social welfare state takes measures of state intervention in production, solidaristic wages, progressive taxation, Keynesian budgetary planning, and environmental planning for pollution control and other public safety. However, these specific measures are not the exclusive characteristics of the social welfare state. They are also adopted by the social security state, like Great Britain, and the corporate state, like the United States.

Furniss and Tilton defend the social welfare state which rejects the liberal strategy of free and unregulated markets. They also reject "the traditional socialist nostrum of nationalization because nationalization does not necessarily bring about results suitable for the social welfare state. The experiences of Great Britain and the Soviet Union confirm that "nationalization has proven to be no panacea for the social ills of capitalism" and that "nationalization is not a sufficient means of accomplishing social reforms." It may not even be a necessary one. Furniss and Tilton rather endorse a piecemeal approach.

> The record of contemporary welfare states, and that of Sweden in particular, suggest that the unattractive features of capitalist society must be dismantled piecemeal with as good or better results and with much less tumult than through nationalization (1977: 42).

Concerning who pursues this piecemeal approach toward a social welfare state without revolution and nationalization, Furniss and Tilton suggest a democratic majority of the citizens.

> This, then, is our conviction: that a democratic majority, backed by a committed labor movement, can capture and employ political power to create a more decent society along the lines of social welfare state (1977: 93).

To the contrary, the decade of the 1980s demonstrated that the pendulum was swinging toward the opposite direction. A majority of citizens in Great Britain, the United States, and other Western European countries endorsed reduction in the number of government rules and regulations, less progressive taxation, and the reduction of expenditures on welfare programs; so did their leaders, like Margaret Thatcher and Ronald Reagan. The decade of the 1990s shows a global trend of the same movement, this time sweeping across the Soviet Union, the People's Republic of China, and all of the Eastern European countries (see Figure 9-1).

It goes without saying that the majority of the democratic citizens and the leaders do not, and would not demonstrate such

Figure 9-1 Global Trend of Ideological Changes

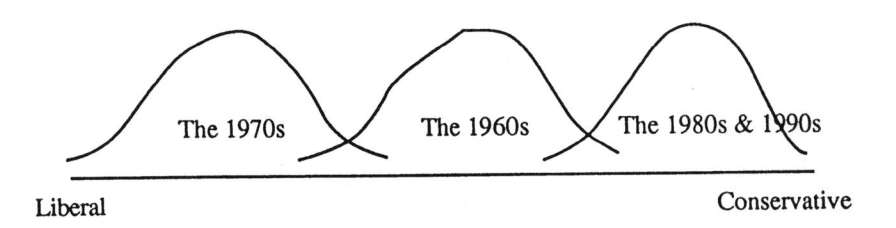

```
         The 1970s        The 1960s        The 1980s & 1990s
Liberal                                                   Conservative
```

wishful thinking and idealism of more commitment to a social welfare state. Nor do incremental and piecemeal changes warrant a right direction of movement toward employing "advanced, economic and solid welfare policy." Amitai Etzioni, indeed, condemns piecemeal incrementalism, because "there is nothing in this approach to guide the accumulation." The steps may be "circular--leading back to where they started or dispersed--leading in many directions at once but leading nowhere" (Etzioni, 1973: 228).

Since Furniss and Tilton fail to suggest how the state can promote welfare services beyond their endorsement of piecemeal approach, they indicate that the "results must become the ultimate measurement of significant difference between three types of the state." They, of course, assume the social welfare state would bring about "as good or better results" than the other two. Different states may prefer different normative values due to different culture, religion, and economic conditions as well as difference in the assumption of human nature and human value; however, actual behavior, commitment, and the subsequent result of services beyond normative values can help to more objectively examine and compare the three types of the state in terms of quality of social welfare services. The United States, Great Britain, and Sweden are chosen by Furniss and Tilton as the model corporate, social security, and social welfare states. Therefore, let me briefly compare these three states on the basis of their results of social services.

Furniss and Tilton contend that full employment is a "preeminent objective of social-welfare statist economic policy" (1977: 43). As of 1983-1984, Sweden, as a social welfare state, had a 3.5 percent unemployment rate, which was well below the overall average of 7.7 percent among the nineteen Western European states. However, Sweden experienced an increase in the unemployment rate

Table 9-3 A Comparative Study of Three Different Types of States

	U.S.A. as a Corporate State	Great Britain as a Social Security State	Sweden as a Social Welfare State	Average Among 19 Western European States
Social Security Program:				
Old Age, Survivors, and Invalidity	Yes	Yes	Yes	
Sickness and Maternity, Medical care/ Hospitalization coverage	No	Yes	Yes	
Work Injury	Yes	Yes	Yes	
Unemployment	Yes	Yes	Yes	
Family Allowances	Yes	Yes	Yes	
Income Distribution Year 1980-1981:				
Lowest 20%	5.3	7.0	7.4	6.6
Second Quintile	11.9	11.5	13.1	12.3
Third Quintile	17.9	17.0	16.8	17.4
Fourth Quintile	25.0	24.8	21.0	23.7
Highest 20%	39.9	39.7	31.7	40.0
Highest 10%	23.3	23.4	28.1	24.8
Population per: Physician				
1965	670	870	910	875
1981	500	680	410	515
Daily Calorie Supply				
1965	3292	3346	2922	3188
1981	3663	3131	3097	3384
Number Enrolled in School as Percentage of Age Group in 1984:				
Primary	101	101	98	101
Secondary	95	83	83	90
Higher Education	57	20	38	30
Average Annual Growth Rate: GDP				
1965-80	2.9	2.2	2.7	3.8
1980-85	2.5	2.0	2.0	1.9
Unemployment Rate:				
1975	7.7	5.8	1.6	
1983-84	6.8	13.8	3.5	7.7

Source: World Bank (1987: various tables); U.S. Department of Health and Human Services (1987: xxviii-xxxi).

more than twice that, for example, from 1.6 percent in 1975 to 3.5 percent in 1983-1984, primarily due to decline of maritime industries resulting from high costs and overseas competition. But the United States reduced the unemployment rate from 7.7 percent in 1975 to 6.8 percent in 1983-1984 (see Table 9-3).

Furniss and Tilton also claim that the social welfare state provides better health care of all of the citizens, offers them higher education, and more significantly reduces income inequality than the other two types of state. The more doctors available, the shorter time the patient waits and the more readily the doctor is available to the patient. Sweden indicates a significant accomplishment in increasing the number of doctors such that 910 persons per physician on average in 1965 declined to 410 in 1981. However, the United States equally shows an impressive record. The statistics of its 500 persons per physician in 1981 suggests that the United States as a corporate state has more doctors than nineteen Western European non-corporate, social security or social welfare states on average.

Furniss and Tilton quote a 1975 study that "in the United States 40 percent of full-time wage and salary workers making less than $5,000 (20 percent of the employed population) had no group health insurance; eight percent of those earning more than $25,000 were in a similar position" (1977: 174). What they ignore is the fact that the absence of national health programs in the United States by no means denies any American hospitalization and medical treatment by any doctor or hospital. Although American students are required to pay tuition for college, they are by no means denied admission and enrollment in many expensive private colleges for financial problems. The free or no free tuition controversy notwithstanding, the United States leads Great Britain, Sweden, and all other Western European countries in terms of the number of students enrolled in primary, secondary, and college education as measured by the percentage of the respective age groups in 1984. As Table 9-3 shows, the gap between the United States and all Western European countries including Sweden is wider in the enrollment in secondary schools and much wider in college enrollment. The United States had one and a half times as many college students as Sweden.

Furniss and Tilton state that most European states have more extensive welfare provisions and higher rates of productivity and the potential to modernize the industrial structure (1977: 51, 121). But Table 9-3 does not warrant their contention. Sweden as a social welfare state had accomplished 2.7 percent and 2.0 percent of average annual GDP growth rate in 1965-1980 and 1980-1985, respectively. But the United States as a corporate state shows 2.9 percent and 2.5 percent, showing higher percentages of growth than Sweden.

The thesis of reduction of income inequality in the social welfare state is not evidenced, either. They rather admit the "persistence of substantial inequalities in the ownership of property in Sweden. At one extreme approximately 55 percent of the adult population lack any substantial property" (1977: 148). At the other extreme, Furniss and Tilton identify the concentration of wealth and property by some 250 people as the wielders of decisive power in Swedish society. Table 9-3 confirms that as of 1980-1981 Sweden had higher percentages of income by both the highest twenty percent and the highest ten percent income earners than the United States. Sweden had higher concentration of income on the highest twenty percent and the highest ten percent of the population than the nineteen other Western European countries on average. Sweden again had higher percentages of income earners falling into both the lowest twenty percent and the lowest ten percent income brackets than the United States and nineteen other Western European countries. This clearly contradicts the contention of Furniss and Tilton. Sweden ironically shows more unequal distribution of income among the different income brackets than nineteen Western European countries on average, which still indicates higher unequal distribution of income than the United States.

The Outcome-Based Evaluation of Welfare Services: PQLI

It is not types of the states but the quality of life of their people as the ultimate criteria by which social welfare services can be truly evaluated. This thesis justifies further inquiry into a cross-national comparative study on the welfare outcomes regardless of the types of the states. A few critical questions which will be examined are: (1) what is the objective of social welfare services?; (2) what are the criteria that truly measure the ultimate objective, whose data may be readily available among all of the states regardless of different ideologies and different types of the states?; (3) supposing the ultimate objective of social welfare services is the promotion of physical quality of life, what countries have higher or lower level of quality of life?; (4) is it due to different economic system, different political system, and different forms of government?; (5) to what extent does the physical quality of life increase, decrease, or remain the same within each of the states in terms of a dynamic, longitudinal perspective?; (6) what causes the increase or the decrease of the physical quality of life?; and (7) to what extent does Korea lead the developing countries in terms of the physical quality of life and what model does Korea suggest for developing countries?

The INSP

There have been various attempts to formulate a common concept of outcome-based evaluation of the quality of life of the social welfare services of different countries. One is the Index of Net Social Progress (INSP), which was devised by Richard Estes (1984) as a composite measure of the quality of life of nations. The INSP is based on eleven subindexes, which have a total of 44 indicators. They are listed as follows:

I. Education Subindex
School enrollment ration, first level (+)
Pupil Teacher ratio, first level (-)
Percent adult literacy (-)
Percent GNP in education (+)

II. Health Status Subindex
Rate infant mortality per 1,000 live-born (-)
Population in thousands per physician (-)
Male life expectation at 1 year (+)

III. Women Status Subindex
Percentage eligible girls attending first level schools (+)
Percent children in primary school girls (+)
Percent adult female illiteracy (-)
Years since women literacy (+)
Years since women suffrage equal to men (+)

IV. Defense Effort Subindex
Percent GNP in defense spending (-)

V. Economic Subindex
Economic growth rate (+)
Per capita estimated income($) (+)

Average annual rate of inflation (-)
Per capita food production index (1970=100) (+)

VI. Demography Subindex
Total population (thousands) (-)
Crude birth rate per 1,000 population (-)
Crude death rate per 1,000 population (-)
Rate of population increase (-)

VII. Geography Subindex
Percent arable land mass (+)
Number major natural disaster impacts (-)
Lives lost in major disasters per million population (-)

VIII. Political Stability Subindex
Number of political protest demonstrations (-)
Number of political riots (-)
Number of political strikers (-)
Number of armed attacks (-)
Number of deaths from domestic violence (-)

IX. Political Participation Subindex
Years since independence (+)
Years since most recent constitution (+)
Presence of functioning parliamentary system (+)
Presence of functioning political party system (+)
Degree of influence of military (-)
Number of popular elections held (+)

X. Cultural Diversity Subindex
Largest percent sharing same mother tongue (+)
Largest percent sharing same religious beliefs (+)
Ethnic-linguistic fractionalization index (-)

XI. Welfare Effort Subindex
Years since first law--Old age, invalidity, death (+)
Years since first law--Sickness and maternity (+)
Years since first law--Work injury (+)
Years since first law--Unemployment (+)
Years since first law--Family allowances (+)

The INSP scores relate to a constant of 100 units, which is the score for all countries, regions, and continents. Professor Estes actually utilized the INSP and computed the scores of 107 countries.

Estes's INSP, however, does not truly represent the outcome of the social welfare services provided by different states because it includes geographical indices such as natural disasters, related loss of lives, and percent of arable land mass. These indices are beyond the human control by social welfare services. Estes is biased against increase of population in general and especially those under fifteen years. His indicators of "years since independence (+)" assumes that the longer a nation-state becomes independent, the less depriving and suffering its citizens are. His indicator of "years since most recent constitution (+)" assumes that the older the constitution is, the more favorable it becomes toward social progress. His political participation subindex is equally biased in favor of a democratic form of government, which does not necessarily warrant better quality of welfare services. Estes also assumes that heterogeneity--ethnic, linguistic, religious--is negative because of its potential cause for fractionalization and confrontation.

Estes's INSP misses some essential indicators for the quality of life such as sanitation facilities, drinking water, and other infrastructural elements. His economic subindex fails to include such important indicators as the balance of payment, income gap between different income brackets, and unemployment rate. His welfare effort subindex is overly concerned with a sheer number of years since the adoption of first laws on pension, unemployment compensation, and others without examining to what extent welfare services are actually implemented. It does not indicate the time lag between the first written law and its actual implementation, nor does the number of years of the commitment of the states to welfare programs show a linear-additive increase of services along the mere passage of time; rather a reverse trend is identified. Estes's INSP is, in fact, designed to measure not the outcome of welfare services but "differential levels of human deprivation and suffering experienced by people living anywhere in the world" (1984: 17).

The Physical Quality of Life Index (PQLI)

Ascertaining and measuring the outcome of social welfare services in any nation is a highly subjective enterprise, but there are certain essential physical elements that are universal and can be quantitatively used as neutral indices under any political system. The Overseas Development Council (ODC), which is a Washington-based, nonprofit, public educational organization, has recently developed a composite index to measure the physical quality of life (PQLI). The PQLI is calculated by averaging three indices--life expectancy, infant mortality, and literacy, giving an equal weight to each of the three indicators. Each is rated on a scale from 1 to 100. For life expectancy, the upper limit of 100 is assigned to a particular country which has the highest level, whereas the lower limit of 1 is assigned to a nation which has the lowest level. The same rule applies to two other indices. The relative scores of these three indices are summed and divided by three to indicate the PQLI of each country.

Robert Parke, director of Washington Council doing research on social indicators, for example, challenged the validity of combining life expectancy, infant mortality, and literacy into a single number as "nothing more than a parlor game" (*Washington Post*, 4/14/1977: A9). Irish and Frank also express a concern that the PQLI "falls something short of Thomas Jefferson's life, liberty, and the pursuit of happiness. It leaves out of the index many important elements of the good life: individual freedom, social justice, family stability, economic security, leisure, and recreation" (1978: 422).

The PQLI, however, is a simple index to construct and easy to compare different countries. It measures how states--capitalistic or socialistic, democratic, totalitarian or authoritarian, developed or developing, presidential or parliamentarian, civil or military--are meeting basic human needs. The PQLI indirectly sums up the results of the whole social welfare and public services: "food, sanitation, medical care, education, income, environment, all of which determine life expectancy, infant mortality, and literacy" (Irish and Frank, 1978: 422). Morris claims that the index measures universal human needs. It is "about as non-ethnocentric as it is possible to get" (1976: 6). People everywhere prefer long lives for themselves and for their new-born children and find literacy a key to their personal growth and self-actualization.

The PQLI suggests that bigger and more are not always better and that an expanding GNP is not a sure indicator of the health and wealth of a nation's citizens. A swollen GNP can even mean lowering the quality of life--pollution of air and water, migration of people from the country to city slums, and a surplus of the unemployed amidst the shortage of skilled laborers. For example, per capita income of Kuwait as of 1988 shows $14,800 due to oil wealth, but its

PQLI is only 81. Sri Lanka with a per capita of only $380 demonstrates an equally high PQLI of 79. United Arab Emirates, with a per capita of $18,900 shows a PQLI of 74, whereas the Philippines with a per capita of $580 still shows a PQLI of 75. Cuba, ranked as a lower middle income country with a per capita of $1,590 shows a PQLI of 96, which is as high as that of most advanced industrial countries. This suggests that the increase in GNP does not bring about an automatic increase in the physical quality of life.

There is no doubt that the above listed advantages of PQLI far outweigh its inherent weaknesses. Therefore, I will use the PQLI as the common criteria to relatively measure the outcome of social welfare services--private and public--of different countries regardless of types of states--corporate, social security, or social welfare.

Korea Leading the Third World in the PQLI

The PQLIs of 131 countries are computed for the years of 1973 and 1985 (see Appendix A). Table 9-4 shows their overall average PQLIs and major social welfare indicators. The PQLIs of 1973 and 1985 suggest that the higher the level of economic development as measured by the per capita GNP, the higher the level of the PQLI tends to become. Twenty-one advanced countries show the PQLI of 97 on average in 1985. That is followed by 78 among 24 upper middle income countries, 57 among 36 lower middle income countries, and 33 among 37 low income countries.

Table 9-4 indicates that there is no significant difference between nine communist countries and 24 upper middle income countries in terms of the PQLI. The former represent an average PQLI of 79 and the latter indicate 78, respectively. This suggests that communist countries with seemingly comprehensive welfare services for the people on the basis of "their needs rather than contributions" do not warrant higher physical quality of life than the upper middle income countries. Even if the principle of distribution of welfare services on the basis of "needs rather than contributions" prevails in the communist countries, the quality of their welfare services cannot be improved without the concurrent economic growth and the subsequent increase of the expenditures for welfare services. This suggests a thesis that it is not types of government such as communist, socialist, or capitalist, nor types of welfare states such as corporate, social security, or social welfare state but quality of

Table 9-4 Social Welfare Indicators and Physical Quality of Life as the Ultimate Evaluator of Welfare Services: 1984-1985

131 Countries	Per Capita GNP ($)	TV per 1000	Number of MDs per 1000	Number enrolled in secondary schools	Number enrolled in colleges	Central Gov't's % expenditure Education & economic services	Social security Health Housing S/S	Social security factor scores (1)	POLI '73 (2)	POLI '85 (2)	Life expectancy	Infant mortality	Literacy
Low Income Countries (37)	253	5.2	1.0	19.2	1.8	36.5	10.8	-.12	31	33	49	119	38
Lower Middle Income Countries (36)	902	54.8	3.7	37.1	11.1	35.6	14.7	-.08	51	57	59	77	58
Upper Middle Income Countries (24)	3,060	159.9	12.2	62.1	16.0	29.3	23.9	.22	76	78	68	31	82
Korea	2,150	200.0	7.2	91.0	26.0	35.9	9.7	.05	80	86	69	27	92
High Income Oil Exporter Countries (4)	12,350	206.9	12.4	59.3	11.2	21.5	17.4	-.65	45	68	66	52	62
High Income Industrial Market Countries (21)	10,486	349.2	20.6	89.8	30.1	20.9	50.0	.85	96	97	76	8	98
Communist Countries* (9)	4,337	136.0	18.8	69.6	17.3	NA	NA	.56	79	79	67	38	82
Overall Countries (131)	2,675	117.0	8.5	47.9	12.8	31.6	21.5	.14	59	62	61	66	65

Source: World Bank (1987); U.S. Department of Health and Human Services (1987).

(1) Factor scores were computed from varimax rotation using five elements of social security programs such as 1) old age, survivors, and invalidity, with the value of 1 if available and 0 if not available, 2) sickness and maternity with the value of 1 if available, 0 if not available or 2 if medical care concurrently available, 3) work injury, 4) unemployment, and 5) family allowances with either the numerical value of 1 or 0.

(2) PQLI is computed using the highest scores for each of life expectancy, infant mortality, and literacy of the specific nations as 100 and their lowest scores as 0. The three scores are summed and divided into three.

*Include Albania, Angola, Bulgaria, Cuba, Czechoslovakia, Democratic Republic of Germany, Denmark, Democratic People's Republic of Korea, Mongolia and the USSR.

welfare services--private, public or combined--that determines the physical quality of life.

The thesis of the welfare priority of the government and its subsequent commitment to the expenditures for social welfare services as the major determinant of the physical quality of life requires an examination of cross-national budget allocation. It is widely understood that there is a zero-sum between the welfare expenditures for the physical quality of life of today and the expenditures for education and economic services as a long-term investment for the quality of life of the future. The more appropriations allocated for the social welfare services, the less expenditures are available for economic services. Inversely, the less expenditures for the social welfare services, the more expenditures are likely to be allocated for educational and economic services. Therefore, different states have made a hard choice and differentially allocated their budget for welfare and economic services as a proper combination.

Figure 9-2 shows the location of some seventy countries as of 1973 in terms of percent expenditures of their central governments for the social welfare services including housing, amenities, health and social security on the X-Axis and education and the economic services for long-term economic development on the Y-Axis. Figure 9-2 demonstrates the appearance of two major clusterings among the countries--the welfare-priority states (WPSs) and the economy-priority states (EPSs). The WPSs are primarily economically advanced states such that they are likely to spend a disproportionately higher percentage of their government expenditures for social welfare services than economic development services. The EPSs are mainly economically developing countries so that they are likely to play down the importance of welfare services and rather to spend a much higher percentage of their central government expenditures with the range of over 25 to seventy percent for economic development services.

In order to examine which states--the WPSs or the EPSs--are likely to have a higher PQLI, the welfare (X-Axis) and economic (Y-Axis) expenditure dimensions are related to the third dimension of the PQLI. Figure 9-3 shows the three-dimensional schematic presentation. It goes without saying that 13 WPSs have an average PQLI of 93, whereas 49 EPSs show only 52. This clearly indicates that the higher the welfare expenditures, the higher the level of the PQLI becomes.

Korea Leading Developing Nations

Figure 9-2 Percent Central Gov't's Expenditures for Economic Development and Social Welfare Services, and Related PQLIs of 62 Countries: 1972/73

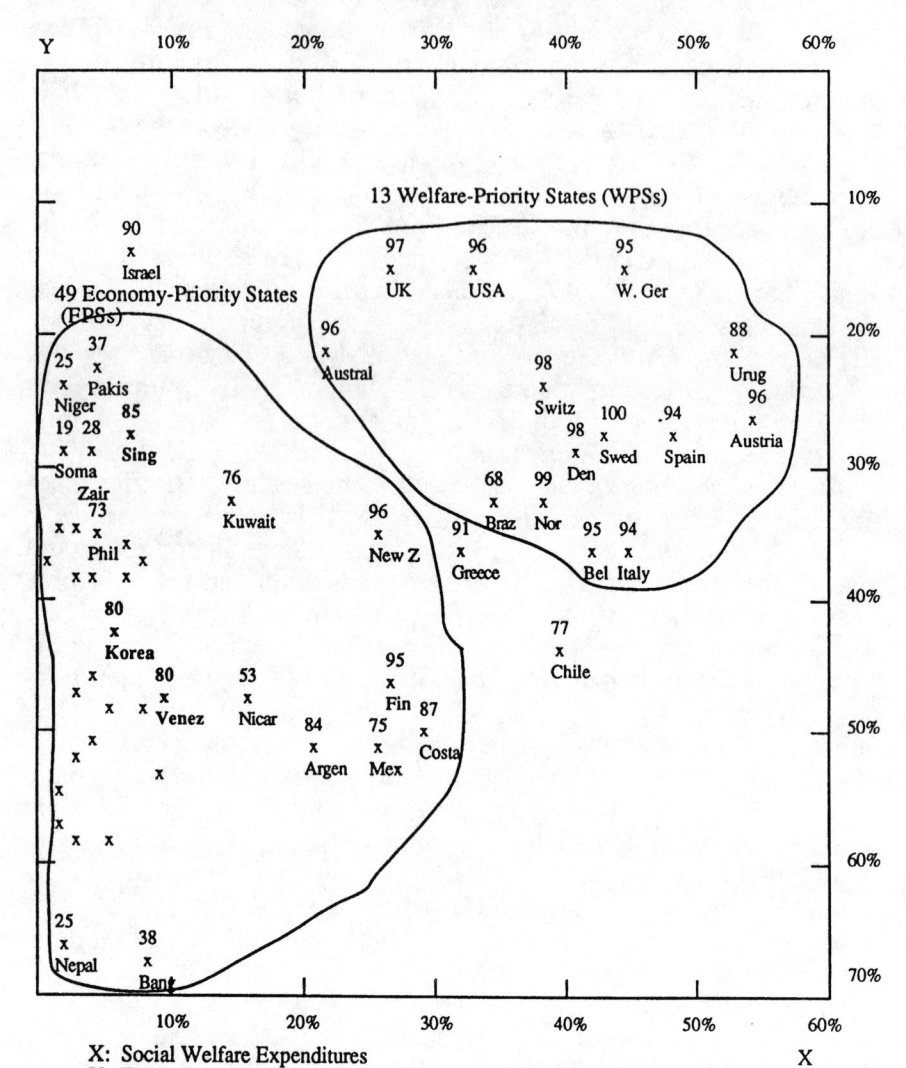

13 Welfare-Priority States (WPSs)

49 Economy-Priority States (EPSs)

X: Social Welfare Expenditures
Y: Expenditures for Economic and Educational Services
x: Indicates the location of countries in relation to X and Y. The names of many countries, however, are not specified due to space limitation.

Source: Appendix A

Korea: Leader of the Nations in Social Welfare 375

Figure 9-3 Korea Leading the Third World in PQLI: 1972/1973

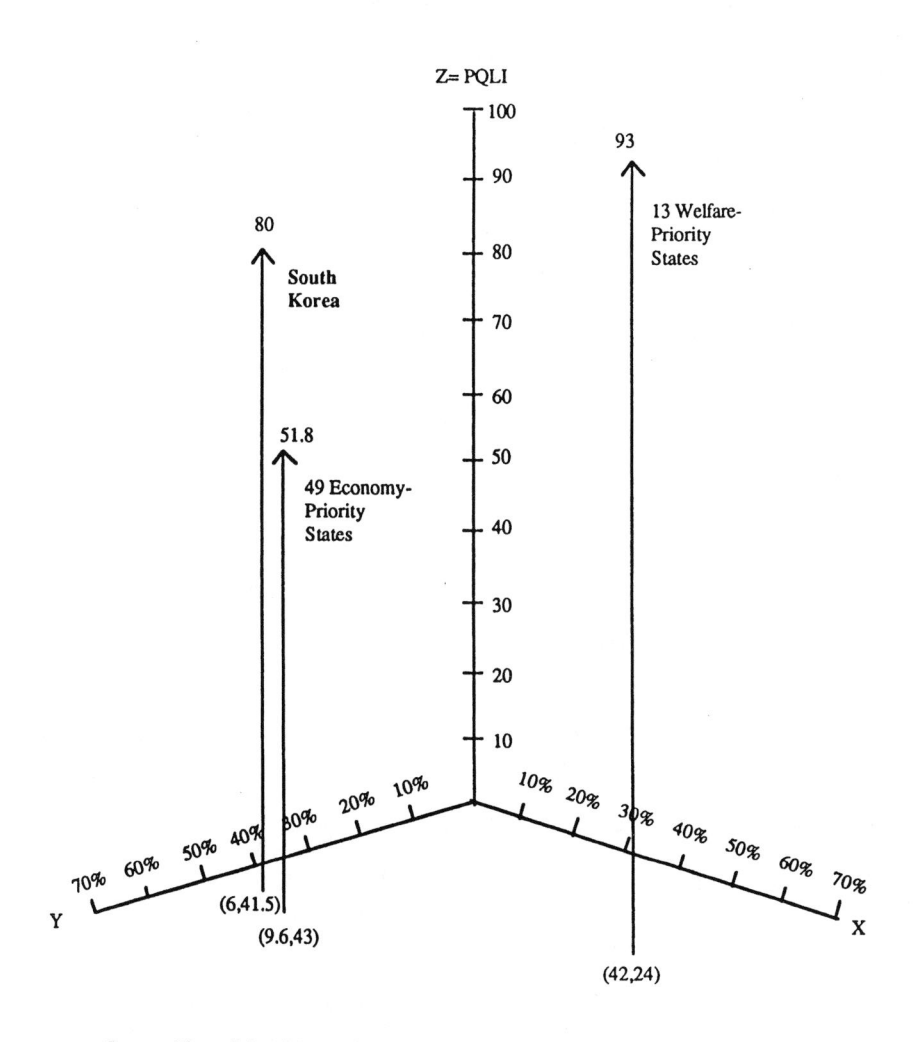

Source: Figure 9-2 and Appendix A
X: Percent Central Government's Expenditures for Social Welfare Services
Y: Percent Central Government's Expenditures for Economic and Educational Services

Figure 9-4 Percent Central Gov't's Expenditures for Economic Development and Social Welfare Services, and Related PQLIs of 87 Countries: 1985

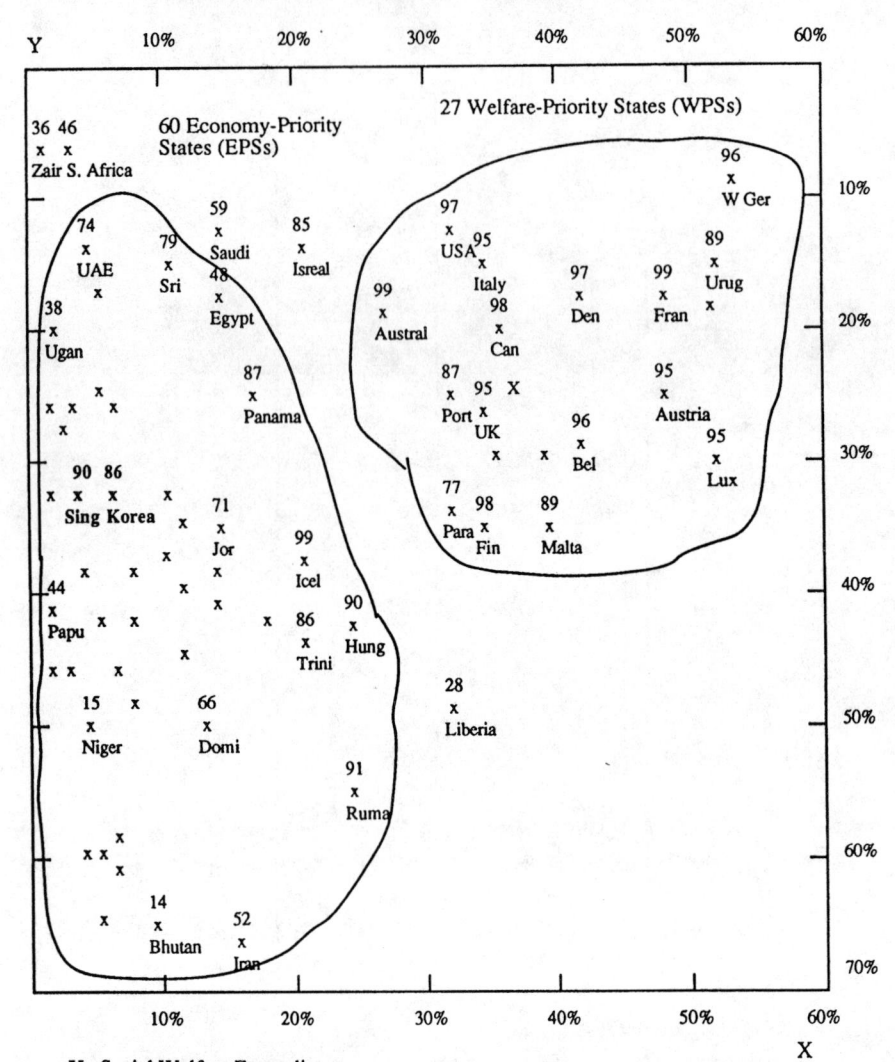

	10%	20%	30%	40%	50%	60%
Y						

```
            10%        20%        30%         40%          50%         60%
     Y      |          |          |           |            |           |
            ┌──────────────────────────────────────────────────────────┐
            │                                    27 Welfare-Priority States (WPSs)
      36 46 │  60 Economy-Priority
      x  x  │  States (EPSs)                                    96
  Zair S. Africa                                                x
            │                                                 W Ger      — 10%
            │  74          59             97
            │  x           x              x   95                89
            │ UAE   79   Saudi   85      USA  x                 x
            │      x      48    x              Italy   97    99 Urug
            │     Sri     x    Isreal   99      98     x     x   x
            │           Egypt           x       x     Den  Fran       — 20%
            │                         Austral  Can
            │             87            87
            │             x             x   95  X           95
            │          Panama         Port     UK           x
            │  x  x  x                 x   x    x   96    Austria
            │   x                              x   x        95       — 30%
            │  90 86                                Bel      x
            │  x x x   x     71         77                  Lux
            │ Sing Korea  x             x   98   89
            │           x  Jor    99   Para x    x
            │  x   x    x  x      x          Fin Malta                — 40%
            │ 44        x x      Icel
            │  x             90
            │ Papu  x  x    x   86  x
            │                x  Hung
            │ x x       x    Trini          28
            │                                x
            │  15      x    66              Liberia                   — 50%
            │  x            x
            │ Niger       Domi
            │                      91
            │                      x
            │                     Ruma
            │  x                                                       — 60%
            │ x x
            │    x
            │      14
            │      x     52
            │   Bhutan   x
            │           Iran                                           — 70%
            └──────────────────────────────────────────────────────────┘
            10%        20%        30%         40%          50%         60%
                                                                          X
```

X: Social Welfare Expenditures
Y: Expenditures for Economic and Educational Services
x: Indicates the location of countries in relations to X and Y. The names of many countries are not specified due to space limitation.

Source: Appendix A

Korea: Leader of the Nations in Social Welfare 377

Figure 9-5 Korea Leading the Third World in PQLI: 1985

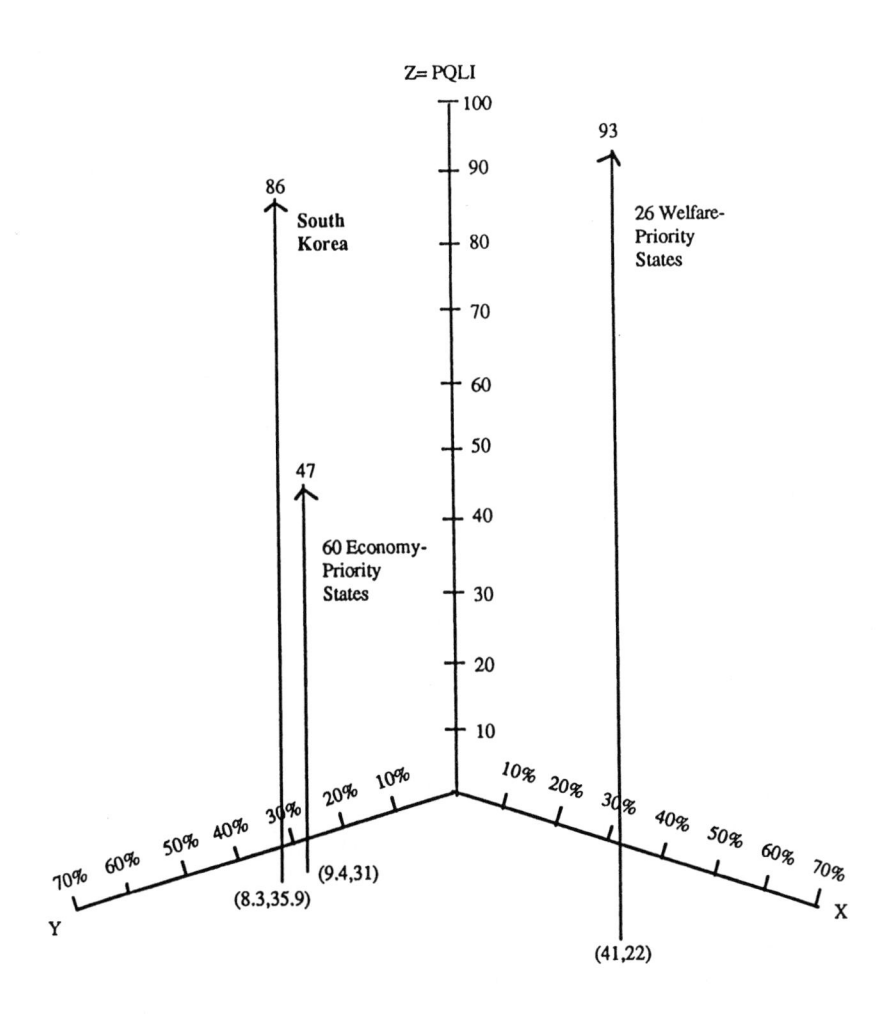

Source: Figures 9-3 and Appendix A
X: Percent Central Government's Expenditures for Social Welfare Services
Y: Percent Central Government's Expenditures for Economic and Educational Services

South Korea, however, with a whopping 41.5 percent of its central government expenditures for educational and economic services and only 5.8 percent for social welfare services, shows the PQLI of 80 and thereby together with Singapore (its PQLI of 85) and Venezuela (its PQLI of 80) led all developing EPSs whose welfare expenditures accounted for less than ten percent of the total expenditures. Four EPSs such as Argentina (PQLI of 84), Costa Rica (87), New Zealand (96), and Sri Lanka (83) show a higher PQLI than that of Korea, but they spent more than three times as much of the expenditures for welfare services (Figure 9-2). With such a modicum of the government's welfare expenditures, South Korea's PQLI of 80 could be a surprise for 49 EPSs whose average percent expenditures for economic and welfare services--42.8 and 9.6--were higher than those of Korea, and yet whose PQLI was only 52. Korea's PQLI of 80 became a surprise for thirteen economically advanced WPSs which spent seven times as many percentages of welfare expenditures to reach the average PQLI of 93.

The thesis of Korea leading the Third World in the physical quality of life with a modicum of government expenditures on social welfare services is equally obvious in a comparative cross-national study as of 1985, about twelve years after my first attempt at a longitudinal perspective. Figures 9-4 and 9-5 show that as of 1985, 27 WPSs accepted social welfare services as the priority of their central government, appropriating a range of 30 to 65 percent of the central government expenditures. Thereby, the WPSs had an average PQLI of 93. Some sixty EPSs, on the other hand, were primarily concerned with economic development, allocating proportionally a much higher percentage of the government expenditures for economic and educational services than welfare services. Such priority in the expenditures caused the EPSs to have an average PQLI of 47, which became about half that of the WPSs.

Korea as an EPS, however, with a whopping 35.9 percent of its central government expenditures for economic and educational services and only 8.3 percent for social welfare services, showed a surprisingly high PQLI of 86. Korea together with Singapore (its PQLI of 90) led all developing EPSs, which expended less than ten percent of their government expenditures on welfare services. Seven EPSs such as Panama (87), Iceland (99), Hungary (90), Costa Rica (92), Trinidad and Tobago (86), Jamaica (89), and Rumania (91) had their PQLI equal to or slightly higher than that of Korea, but they spent at least two to three times as many percentages for social welfare services as Korea. There is no doubt that with a moderate percentage of the government expenditures for welfare services, Korea's PQLI of 86 became a model for all EPSs to be envious of.

Korea: Leader of the Nations in Social Welfare 379

Table 9-5 Nine Welfare-Priority Upper Middle-Income States Compared with Two Economy-Priority Upper Middle-Income States of South Korea and Singapore in PQLI, Economic Growth, and Welfare Expenditures

Countries	PQLI 1973 1985	Per Capita GNP 1985	Central Government's Expenditures: 1985 Education Economic Services %	Health Housing Social Security Welfare %	GDP Growth Rate 1965-80 1980-85
Uruguay (1)	88 89	$1,650	14.5	50.4	2.4 -3.9
Portugal (1)	79 87	$1,970	21.6	31.0	5.3 0.9
Argentina (2)	84 87	$2,130	39.8	38.3	3.3 -1.4
Panama (1)	81 87	$2,100	24.9	33.2	5.5 2.4
Greece (1)	91 94	$3,550	26.7	35.1	5.8 1.0
Spain (1)	94 97	$3,068	16.1	64.2	4.8 1.6
Chile (1)	77 85	$1,430	20.3	43.8	1.9 -1.1
Paraguay (1)	74 77	$ 860	32.9	32.9	7.0 1.4
Brazil (2)	68 69	$1,640	27.0	35.4	9.0 1.3
Average	81.7 85.6	$1,969	23.7	40.5	5.0 0.4
Singapore (1)	85 90	$7,420	35.2	6.5	10.2 6.5
S. Korea (1)	80 86	$2,150	35.9	8.3	9.5 7.9

Source: Appendix A

(1) Represents a unitary form of government.
(2) Represents a federal form of government.

What is more striking than the above finding of Korea leading some fifty developing EPSs is the fact that Korea's PQLI of 86 with only 8.3 percent of government expenditures for social welfare services is not significantly behind the average PQLI of 93 prevailing among 26 welfare-priority states despite their welfare expenditures four to seven times as many percentages as that of Korea. Moreover, among 26 welfare-priority states, nine states fall into the category of the so-called upper middle-income countries as Korea does. Table 9-5 is, therefore, prepared for a comparative study among them.

As Table 9-5 indicates, these nine welfare-priority upper middle-income states spent an average of 40.5 percent of their central government expenditures for social welfare services. Since Argentina and Brazil had a federal form of government, additional expenditures for social welfare services were contributed by their state and local governments. Nevertheless, the average PQLI of 85.6 among these nine welfare-priority states did not exceed the PQLI of

Korea (86), which spent only 8.3 percent. This suggests that the government's commitment to and the subsequent lavish expenditures for social welfare services are not the only panacea for enhancement of the physical quality of life of people. There is no doubt that the increase in welfare expenditures can enhance the PQLI. Because of the expenditures of a disproportionate amount of the government expenditures for social welfare, Chile, Panama, and Portugal, for example, were able to promote their PQLI to a significant extent. Portugal gained 8 points of PQLI from 79 in 1973 to 87 in 1985, Panama added 6 points from 81 in 1973 to 87 in 1985. Chile enhanced 8 points to their PQLI during the same period of time (see Table 9-5).

These nine upper middle income WPSs placed the priority of the state expenditures on social welfare of people "today" probably as "an answer to the increasing demands for socioeconomic equality in the context of the evolution of mass democracies" and as "an answer to growing needs and demands for socioeconomic security in the context of an increasing division of labor, the expansion of markets, and the loss of 'security functions' by families and other communities" (Flora and Heidenheimer, 1981: 8). Consequently, they appropriated less of the government expenditures for long-term investment in education and economic services. The outcome became clear. Their average GDP growth rate was 5.0 in 1965-1980 and declined to 0.4 in 1980-1985. On the other hand, Korea and Singapore, which invested over 35 percent of their central government expenditures in education and economic services and spent less than ten percent in welfare services, brought about almost twice as much of the GDP growth rate as the nine WPSs in 1965-1980. The gap in the GDP growth rate between these nine WPSs and the two EPSs like Korea and Singapore became wider in 1980-1985 with 0.4 and over six percent, respectively.

With such a sustained, stagnant economic condition, these WPSs would not be able to continue to have the same high level of commitment to social welfare services and the subsequent same rate of promotion of the PQLI. They faced a harsh reality of budget constraints and the abuses of "free lunches" made available by the state expenditures. This trend was already identified among some WPSs. During the period of 1972-1985, many WPSs had invigorated the state expenditures for social welfare services (see Figure 9-6). However, some WPSs such as the United States, Austria, and Norway ironically reduced the amount of the expenditures for social welfare

Korea: Leader of the Nations in Social Welfare 381

Figure 9-6 Change in Percent Expenditures of the Central Gov'ts of Selected Countries from 1972/73 to 1985

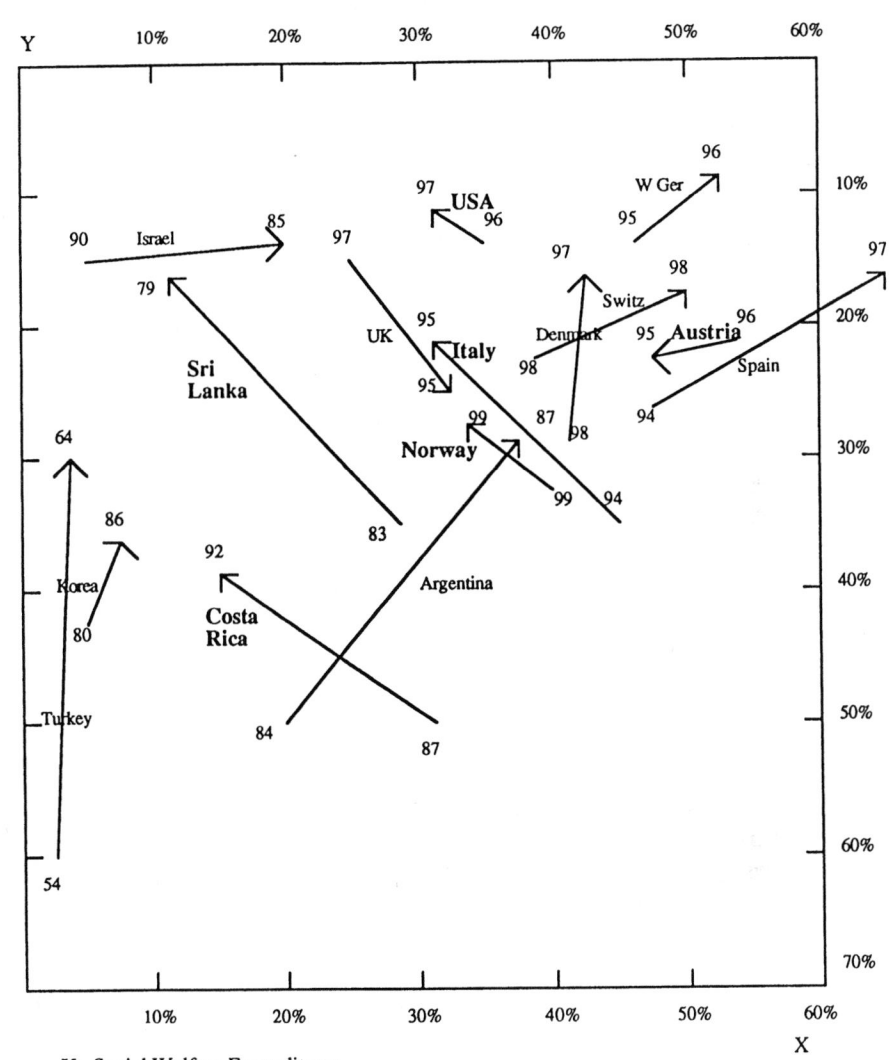

[Figure 9-6: Scatter plot with X axis "Social Welfare Expenditures" (10%–60%) and Y axis "Expenditures for Economic and Educational Services" (10%–70%). Arrows show change from 1972/73 to 1985 for selected countries: Israel (90→85), Sri Lanka (79→97), USA (97→96), W Ger (95→96), UK (95→97), Italy (95→95), Denmark (98→97), Switz (98→97), Austria (95→96), Spain (96→94), Norway (99→99), Korea (80→64), Costa Rica (92→84), Turkey (54→86), Argentina (83→87).]

X: Social Welfare Expenditures
Y: Expenditures for Economic and Educational Services
Sources: Figures 9-2 and 9-4 and Appendix A

services. The United States central government reduced 3.7 percent from 35.3 to 31.6 in 1985; Austria cut 6 percent from 53.7 to 47.7; and Norway cut 3.6 percent from 39.9 to 36.3.

The year of 1990 witnessed the same trend of ever-increasing lavish expenditures for social welfare services and the subsequent economic constraints in Sweden, which had long been envied as the best social welfare state with the perfect 100 scores of the PQLI alone. Sweden expended 44.3 percent of the expenditures for social welfare services in 1973 and increased to 50.1 percent in 1985. Until 1990 its welfare state had been a model for all of the states--developing as well as the Western European and other advanced. Nevertheless, Sweden underestimated the importance of long-term investment in education and economic services. She spent 25.4 percent in economic services in 1973 but only 15.4 percent in 1985. An anaemic set of economic indicators in the year of 1990 augurs the future of the Swedish welfare state model.

1. Inflation was moving toward double digits.
2. An annual growth rate fell well below the Western European average.
3. Interest rates reached sixteen percent.
4. The acute labor shortage had led Sweden's labor unions to press confrontational wage demands. Consequently, wages went too high. So did production costs rise. Sweden lost its competitive edge over the rest of Europe.
5. Sweden's aggressive conglomerates poured $4 billion per year into investment overseas far exceeding the amount they put into their own country.
6. Social welfare services such as the national health system, day care, education, and old age care, which had been very generous by Western standards, began to deteriorate and became subject to shortage and long waiting lists. Here was frustration of Kjell and Margareta Ostrand who have two small children and an affluent lifestyle.

> Yet they have crammed into Kjell's 2 1/2 room bachelor flat for three years because of Stockholm's housing shortage.

> There is a three-year waiting list for day care in their neighborhood, which is one of the reasons Mrs. Ostrand has not yet returned to her job as a financial manager in Stockholm's social-services department despite the fact that her youngest child is now a year old.

"It is your right to have free education, health care, and an apartment, but it's not that simple," Mrs. Ostrand said. "If there's no child care and a housing shortage, you can't manage" (*Omaha World Herald*, 4/1/90).

7. Sweden's progressive income tax system, which imposed excessive tax, for example, the rates of 72 percent and more on the highest income, discouraged the Swedish from working more than 40 hours a week and encouraged many to have absenteeism. In fact, one out of every four Swedes stayed home from work each day.

Magnus Lemmel, president of the Federation of Swedish Industry stated: "The Swedish model is nearing the end of the road." "Reality has finally hit us. We are beginning a period of adaptation, and from any aspects it will be a very painful process" (*Omaha World Herald*, 4/1/90). The Swedish social welfare state, which mandates the state to actively and aggressively assume the responsibility for welfare services, may follow the same trend as the United States, Austria, Norway, and other European socialist welfare priority states have gone through.

Economic theory has not progressed far enough to suggest any firm evidence of a clear relationship between the extent of state ownership of industries and national economic growth. As Figure 9-7 and Table 9-6 indicate, some states whose economies grew very slowly from 1980 to 1985, had substantial public ownership, whereas others had relatively little. Austria, France, India, Italy and Mexico represent the former, while West Germany and Belgium represent the latter. However, four states like South Korea, Canada, Japan, and the United States, which had the least amount of state ownership, gained more economic growth than the majority of the states with more public ownership. This suggests a thesis that "business organizations are more attuned to profit and loss and that their management enjoys greater freedom of action and incentives to perform.

Thus, they are alleged to be "more efficient and better contributors to national economic growth" (Levine, et al., 1990: 8). Privatization, therefore, has been a resonant echo across private industries and the governments and hence energetically implemented in Korea. It may be premature to confirm this thesis; however, it is clear that state ownership, bureaucratization, and centralization, depriving the individual citizens of the incentive to work hard and to

Figure 9-7 Extent of State Ownership

	Posts	Tele-commu-nication	Electri-city	Gas	Oil Produc-tion	Coal	Rail-ways	Air-lines	Motor indus-tries	Steel	Ship build-ing	% owner-ship*	GDP growth rate	PQLI
Austria	●	●	●	●	●	●	●	●	●	●	NA	100.0	1.7	95
India	●	●	●	●	●	●	●	●	○	3/4	●	88.6	5.2	44
Mexico	●	●	●	●	●	●	●	1/2	1/4	3/4	●	83.3	0.8	78
Italy	●	●	3/4	●	NA	NA	●	●	1/4 3/4	3/4	3/4	83.3	0.8	95
France	●	●	●	●	NA	●	●	3/4	1/2	3/4	○	80.0	1.0	99
Brazil	●	●	●	●	●	●	●	1/4	○	3/4	○	72.7	1.3	69
Sweden	●	●	1/2	●	NA	NA	●	1/2	○	3/4	3/4	72.2	2.0	99
Holland	●	●	3/4	3/4	NA	NA	●	3/4	○	1/2	1/4	66.6	2.7	98
Britain	●	1/4	●	1/4	1/4	●	●	3/4	1/2	3/4	●	65.9	2.0	95
Switzer	●	●	●	●	NA	NA	●	1/4	○	○	NA	65.6	1.2	98
Spain	●	1/2	●	3/4	NA	1/2	●	●	○	1/2	3/4	60.0	1.6	97
W. Ger	●	3/4	●	1/2	1/4	1/2	●	●	1/4	○	1/4	59.0	1.3	96
Austral	●	●	●	●	●	●	●	●	○	3/4	NA	57.5	2.5	99
Belgium	●	1/4	●	1/4	NA	●	●	●	○	1/2	○	50.0	0.7	96
S. Korea	●	●	3/4	●	NA	●	●	1/4	○	3/4	○	47.5	7.9	86
Canada	●	1/4	●	●	●	●	3/4	3/4	○	○	○	34.0	2.4	98
Japan	●	●	●	●	NA	●	3/4	1/4	○	○	○	30.0	3.8	100
USA	●	●	1/4	●	●	●	1/4	○	○	○	○	13.6	2.5	97

● : 100% publicly owned   ◐(3/4) : 75%   ◐(1/2) : 50%   ◔(1/4) : 25%   ○ : 0%

*Numerical value assignment of 100 for ●, 75 for ◐(3/4), 50 for ◐(1/2), 25 for ◔(1/4), 0 for ○. The scores are summed and divided by the number of cases.

Source: Adapted from Thomas K. McCraw (1984: 34)

Table 9-6 State Ownership and Economic Growth

GDP Growth Rate: 1980-1985

	0.1- 2.0 %	2.1- 5.0 %	5.1 + %
80-100 %	Austria Mexico Italy France		India
50-79 %	Brazil Sweden Britain Switzerland Spain W. Germany Belgium	Holland Australia	
10-49 %		Canada Japan USA	S. Korea

State Ownership (row label)

Source: Figure 9-7

take care of themselves in the open market system, may not be the only answer to welfare benefits and the physical quality of life.

The case of South Korea suggests another thesis: that immediate, extensive, state-sponsored welfare services may not be a viable option for developing countries. Coercive redistribution by the state without corresponding economic growth results in the sharing of poverty among the people. Rather the sustained, rapid economic growth as a bit longer-term priority may bring about a spillover of prosperity from the wealthy business executives onto their own employees and into the entire population.

Those who are overly concerned with income distribution in Korea tend to assert that during the period of 1965-1980 income inequality had been heightened. As Table 9-7 indicates, the bottom forty percent of the income brackets among the entire households earned 13.34 percent of the income in 1965. Their income in 1985 increased to only 17.71 percent. On the other hand, the top twenty percent earned 41.81 percent of the total income in 1965, increased to 43.71 percent in 1985. This clearly indicates a disproportionate

Table 9-7 Percent Share of Household Income in Korea

Ten Income Strata	1965	1970	1976	1980	1982	1985
1	1.32	2.78	1.84	1.57	2.56	2.06
2	4.43	4.56	3.86	3.52	4.30	4.02
3	6.47	5.81	4.93	4.86	5.46	5.24
4	7.12	6.48	6.22	6.11	6.48	6.39
5	7.21	7.63	7.07	7.33	7.51	7.47
6	8.32	8.71	8.34	8.63	8.73	8.76
7	11.31	10.24	9.91	10.21	10.03	10.21
8	12.00	12.17	12.49	12.38	11.94	12.14
9	16.03	16.21	17.84	15.93	14.94	15.42
10	25.78	25.41	27.50	29.46	28.05	28.29
Sum	100.00	100.00	100.00	100.00	100.00	100.00
Gini Coefficient	0.3439	0.3222	0.3808	0.3891	0.3574	0.3631
Bottom 40% (A)	13.34	19.63	16.85	16.06	18.08	17.71
Top 20% (B)	41.81	41.62	45.34	45.39	42.99	43.71
(A) - (B)	(0.46)	(0.47)	(0.37)	(0.35)	(0.44)	(0.41)

Source: Yung Euy Chung (1989: 284)

distribution of income and the income gap between the rich and the poor have not been declining. The Gini Coefficient, which measures the level of unequal distribution, indicates .3439 in 1965 but increased to .3631 in 1985, demonstrating that the rich became richer and the poor poorer in Korea.

Table 9-8, however, demonstrates that the income gap in Korea became less serious than most of the welfare-priority and Western European countries. The absolute majority of eighteen advanced welfare-priority states, sixteen of the eighteen states which seemed to have consistently reduced the income gap between rich and poor with a variety of welfare services, ironically had a much higher percentage of their households in both the lowest twenty percent and the second quartile income brackets than Korea. On the other hand,

Korea: Leader of the Nations in Social Welfare

Table 9-8 Percent Share of Household Income of Advanced Welfare-Priority States: 1984-1985

	Lowest 20 Percent (a)	Second Quartile (b)	Bottom 40 Percent (a + b)	Top 10 Percent
Netherlands (1981)	8.3	14.1	22.4	21.5
Japan (1979)	8.7	13.2	21.9	22.4
Belgium (1978-79)	7.9	13.7	21.6	21.5
Sweden (1981)	7.4	13.1	20.5	28.1
W. Germany (1978)	7.9	12.5	20.4	24.0
Ireland (1973)	7.2	13.1	20.3	25.1
Switzerland (1978)	6.6	13.5	20.1	23.7
Spain (1980-81)	6.9	12.5	19.4	24.5
Norway (1982)	6.0	12.9	18.9	22.8
Britain (1979)	7.0	11.5	18.5	23.4
Finland (1981)	6.3	12.1	18.4	21.7
Italy (1977)	6.2	11.3	17.5	28.1
Denmark (1981)	5.4	12.0	17.4	22.3
U.S.A. (1981)	5.3	11.9	17.2	23.8
Canada (1981)	5.3	11.8	17.1	23.8
France (1975)	5.5	11.5	17.0	26.4
S. Korea (1980)	5.1	11.0	16.1	27.5
New Zealand (1981-82)	5.1	10.8	15.9	28.7
Australia (1975-76)	5.4	10.0	15.4	30.5

Source: The World Bank (1987: 252-253)

New Zealand had the higher percentage of the households in the top ten percent income bracket than Korea.

Furthermore, the income inequality and the Gini Coefficient index do not provide any clue on the question of how wide the income gap becomes between the bottom ten and the top ten percent income brackets and how many of people are below the poverty and subsistence level. To examine this question, Table 9-9 shows percent change in economic class structure in Korea over the period of 1955-1985 together with the percentage of the marginal class. Lack of perfect accuracy on the data is beyond dispute due to discrepancy among the sources of data available. Nevertheless, it is clear that there were about forty percent of the entire population in 1960 whose income was below the subsistence level. It goes without saying that the government could not afford to allocate the limited revenues entirely for welfare services, simply feeding them and standing idle without investment for economic development.

Table 9-9 Percent Change in Economic Class Structure in Korea

	1955	1960	1970	1975	1980	1985
Upper Class	0.3	0.5	0.6	0.9	1.1	1.4
Middle Class						
White Collar Employees						
Public	1.7	1.7	1.8	1.8	2.0	2.1
Private	0.5	0.7	1.5	2.2	3.3	5.2
Subtotal	2.2	2.4	3.3	4.0	5.3	7.3
Professionals and Intelligentsia	1.8	1.9	2.5	2.9	3.4	3.7
Middle Income Farmers (a)	N/A	N/A	17.3	14.3	11.7	8.2
Middle Income Labor Workers	N/A	N/A	8.6	10.9	11.8	12.3
Self-Employed	7.5	9.1	10.7	11.7	14.3	18.0
Subtotal	N/A	N/A	42.4	43.8	46.5	49.5
Lower Middle Class						
Farmers	N/A	N/A	26.8	20.1	17.1	13.5
Labor Workers	N/A	N/A	6.8	15.6	18.3	23.2
Subtotal	N/A	N/A	33.6	35.7	35.4	36.7
Marginal Class	N/A	40.9*	23.4	19.6	17.0	12.4
Total Households Percent	100%	100%	100%	100%	100%	100%
Number**	6,390	7,522	10,543	11,638	12,708	15,350

Source: Adapted from Kwan Mo Suh (1987: 66), S. M. Pae (1986: 94, 97, and 102), Young Ho Park (1987: 71), the Committee in Honor of Dr. Doh Hee Joon on His Retirement (1988: 133), and *Dong-A Annual* (1989: 581, 587, 611 and 617).
N/A: Not available
*As of 1965
**Unit = 1,000

The rapid, sustained economic development dubbed as the "Korean miracle" as demonstrated by the per capita income from less than $100 in 1960 to $5,000 in 1990 becomes a viable option to reduce the number of people below the poverty level within the shortest possible period of time, for example, from over forty percent in 1960 to 12.4 percent in 1985. The Korean government and the private sector, of course, feel more comfortable to take care of twelve percent of the population below the subsistence level now than over forty percent of the population in 1960.

Korea: Leader of the Nations in Social Welfare

Figure 9-8 Rice Production and Consumption: The Agony of Rice Surplus

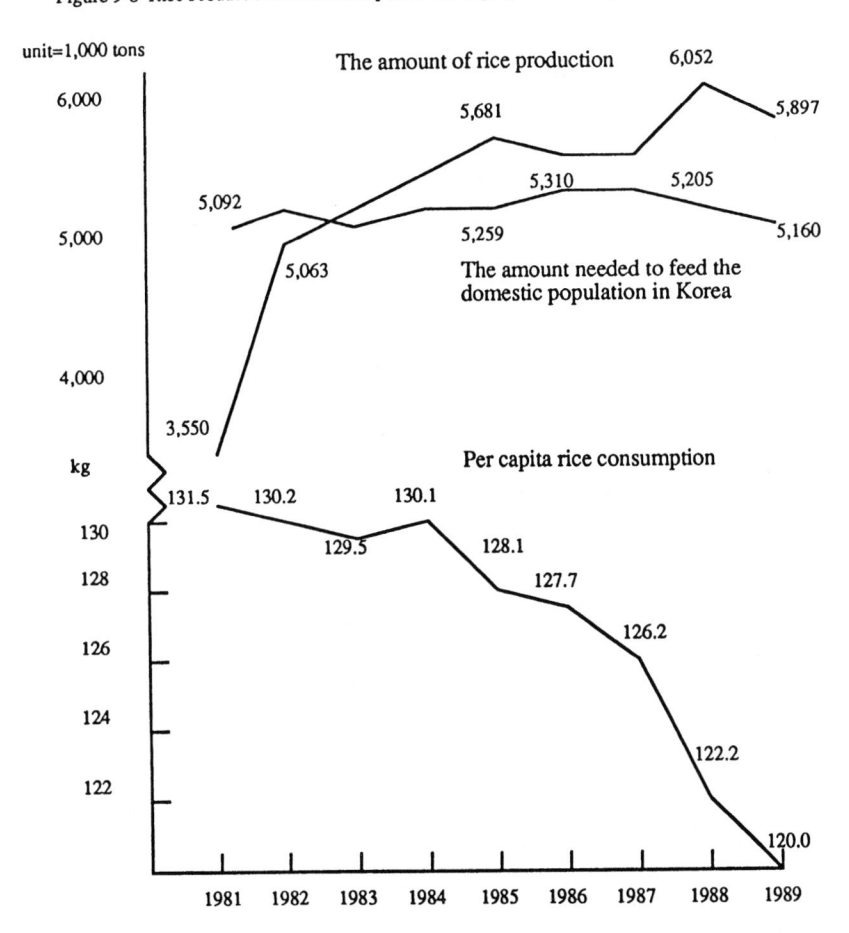

[Chart showing:
- The amount of rice production (1,000 tons): 3,550 (1981), 5,063 (1982), 5,681 (1983), 5,310 (1984), 5,205 (1985), 5,310 (1986), 6,052 (1987), 5,897 (1988)
- The amount needed to feed the domestic population in Korea: 5,092, ..., 5,259, ..., 5,160
- Per capita rice consumption (kg): 131.5 (1981), 130.2 (1982), 129.5 (1983), 130.1 (1984), 128.1 (1985), 127.7 (1986), 126.2 (1987), 122.2 (1988), 120.0 (1989)]

Source: The Hankuk Ilbo, Sept. 19, 26, & 30, 1989

The rapid economic development is primarily due to investment in expert-oriented manufacturing plants. The green revolution in the agricultural sector also followed industrialization. Famine had long haunted every spring before the barley harvest, and a large percentage of the population--urban and rural--suffered from the food shortage and malnutrition. The shortage of rice production had been so serious that in order to realize the dream of self-sufficiency of rice as the staple food, the production of minor grains was forsaken. Therefore, the production of wheat and corn, which accounted for 27.0 and 36.1 percent of self-sufficiency in 1965, respectively, declined to 0.01 and 2.5 percent in 1988. The production of beans, which was 100 percent self-sufficient in 1965, could meet only 15.7 percent of the domestic demands in 1988 (*The Korea Times*, 9/26/1989).

Improvement in seed, land reclamation, irrigation, fertilization, and farm mechanization, coupled with the concentration of rice production and the subsequent renunciation of minor cereals, were all together able to produce a sufficient amount of rice in 1982. As Figure 9-8 shows, for the first time in the history of the republic, the amount of rice production began to exceed the total amount to feed the entire population in 1982. For eight straight years from 1982 on, the amount of rice production has increased more than sixty percent, whereas the amount of rice consumption has consistently declined, for example, from 131.5 kg per person in 1981 to 120 kg in 1989. The more economically prosperous the Koreans become, the more food like meat, fruit, and vegetables they take. Consequently, the total amount of rice consumption despite the increase of population has not increased. The outcome is the ever-increasing stock of surplus rice had to be kept in the storage house. As of September 1989, 1.44 billion kg of rice in the storage whose annual maintenance cost alone amounted to $430 million.

The government, farmers, and the entire population finally faced a happy agony of resolving the surplus rice headache. Listed are a few major programs to dispose of the surplus.

1. A school lunch program which began to provide 260 thousand students, namely 18.4 percent of the entire students in a total of 6,500 elementary schools with more than three free lunch meals per week (*The Korea Times*, 9/26/1989).
2. The encouragement of processing of rice into rice wine, rice juice, rice cake, rice cans, rice flake and other commercial products.
3. A two-tier price system, by which the government purchases the rice from the farmers at a price higher than the production cost and sells it for the urban people at a cheaper price. The government, for example, established a grain special account of $4.7 billion in 1988 for this purpose.
4. The conversion of a large amount of rice producing farmland into non-rice farm production of wheat, corn and beans, whose foreign imports amounted to 4.2, 5.23, and 1.13 million tons, respectively in 1988.

Table 9-10 Surplus of Other Food Production

Items	Production 1988	1989	Percent Increase 1988-1989	Percent Change in Price 1988-1989
Tangerines	410,000 Tons	700,000 Tons	+70.0%	-45.0% per box (15 kg)
Pork	4.8 Million Heads	5.3 Million Heads	+10.4%	-30.0% per unit (90 kg)
Milk	1.63 Million Tons	1.76 Million Tons	+7.9%	Surplus stock of 210,000 tons: 3 times as high as the recommended level of stock
Seaweed	78,000 M/T	100,000 M/T	+28.2%	-50.0%
Vegetables: Radishes	N/A	N/A	+3.0%	-50.0%
Chinese	N/A	N/A	+9.0%	-50.0%

Source: *The Korea Times*, 12/22/1989.

5. Campaigns for increasing the consumption of rice by raising the price of flour and other substitutes for rice from 20 percent the price of rice to up to 50 percent. The relative price increase of flour and other substitutes may encourage people to shift their consumption pattern from flour and other substitutes to rice.

6. Campaign for raising the fund for the purchase of surplus rice to feed the urban poor in Korea and to lead foreign countries in the contribution to the world hunger. Leaders in industry, government officials, university professors and students, urban workers, farmers, even overseas Koreans, foreign diplomatic officials in Seoul, and indeed all walks of life have enthusiastically and voluntarily participated in the cause. The fund is still snowballing.

Surplus does not apply to rice alone (see Table 9-10). Added to rice are tangerine, pork, milk, seaweed, radish, and Chinese cabbage. Surplus became worse after 1989, when the government adopted liberalization of such import items as grapes, pineapples, corn, potatoes, peaches, bananas, dairy products, and a host of agricultural products (*The Korea Times,* 3/27/1990). There is no question that the surplus of rice and other grocery items and the subsequent decline in their prices have significantly contributed to the enhancement of the physical quality of life.

Conclusion

We have examined two main theses in Chapter Nine. First, it is not the types of the states such as communist, socialist, or capitalist nor corporate, social security, or social welfare state as classified by Furniss and Tilton that determines the commitment of the states to social welfare services. Rather, the actual amount of the expenditures for social welfare services can determine the scope and extent of the commitment of different states to welfare services. To examine the actual amount of the expenditures for welfare services, the index of percent central government's expenditures for social welfare services (including social security, housing, health, and other amenities) and for economic services (including infrastructure, investment in machinery and equipment and investment in educating and training human resources) was employed.

As Figures 9-2 and 9-4 show, 62 countries in the year of 1972-1973 and 87 countries in the year of 1985 clustered into two distinct areas, respectively. One cluster includes some developing countries like Argentina, Brazil, Chile, Uruguay (in 1985), the United States as a corporate state, the United Kingdom as a social security state, and Sweden as a social welfare state as classified by Furniss and Tilton. This group of countries cluster together to demonstrate their higher commitment to the expenditures for social welfare services with much less percent of their central government expenditures for economic services. Therefore, these countries are classified as the welfare-priority states (WPSs) due to their priority of social welfare services.

The other cluster includes most of the developing countries regardless of their types of the states as communist, socialist, or capitalist. This group of countries allocated disproportionately higher percent of their central government expenditures for economic services with much lower percentage of the expenditures for social welfare services. These countries are classified as the economy-priority states (EPSs) due to their priority of economic development for future prosperity over the welfare expenditures for today.

However, it is not the actual amount of welfare expenditures but the actual physical quality of life of people that determines the outcome of social welfare services. Since the outcome-based evaluation of welfare services can correctly compare the nations in their endeavors, the physical quality of life index (PQLI) was selected for a longitudinal cross-national comparative study.

The PQLI is calculated by averaging three indices such as life expectancy, infant mortality, and literacy. Irish and Frank state that the PQLI indeed "indirectly sums up the results of the whole social welfare and public services," because food, sanitation, medical care, education, income, housing, environment, and a host of other welfare services ultimately determine life expectancy, infant mortality, and literacy.

The X-dimension of percent expenditures for social welfare services and the Y-dimension of percent expenditures for economic services are finally related to the third Z-dimension of PQLI. Figures 9-3 and 9-5 show a schematic presentation of the cases of 1972-1973 and 1985. Figures 9-3 and 9-5 support a hypothesis that the welfare-priority states, which allocate higher percentage of the expenditures for welfare services (an average of 42 percent of the central government expenditure in 1972-1973) tend to have the higher PQLI than the economy-priority states which spend the lower percentage of the expenditures for welfare services (an average of 9.6 percent).

Nevertheless, Figures 9-2 and 9-3 suggest that Korea spent lower percent of the expenditures than 49 economy-priority states for social welfare services on average and yet its PQLI of 80 far exceeded the average PQLI of 51.8 among those states in 1973. Therefore, Korea led all of the economy-priority states in the PQLI. Moreover, Korea with less than ten percent of the state expenditures for social welfare services was able to have its PQLI of 80.

Figures 9-4 and 9-5 show a much more positive improvement in the case of Korea, because Korea gained six more points of PQLI from 80 in 1972 to 86 in 1985, while it continued to maintain less than ten percent of the expenditures for welfare services. Korea, of course, led all sixty economy-priority states in 1985. Korea's relative improvement in PQLI was such that the gap between Korea and 26 welfare-priority states was ever decreasing. This finding supports another hypothesis that Korea with less than ten percent of its expenditures for welfare services still is able to maintain PQLI of 86 as closely high as that of 93 prevailing among the welfare-priority states with an average of over forty percent of their expenditures for the welfare services. There is no doubt that the Korean model of welfare services can be a good reference for other countries, because of its high PQLI, yet not drifting into aggressive and lavish expenditures for welfare services, and gearing toward continued economic development on the basis of the principles of the government's energetic role for export promotion/market economy, individualism, private enterprise, and privatization.

Notes

1. The dominance of communalism and collective effort in the Third World is explained by many scholars such as Chowning (1977), Constantino (1977), Davidson (1967), Gamer (1976), Kayongo-Male and Onyanago (1984).

Chapter 10 The Korean Model of Social Welfare Services

Chapter Ten will examine how the Korean model, with a small percentage of the government's expenditures for welfare services, maintains one of the highest PQLIs among the developing economy-priority states, and how it pursues high PQLI as envisioned by the advanced welfare-priority states, which on average allocate over forty percent of their expenditures for welfare services (see Figure 10-1).

The Korean model of welfare services suggests three main theses. First, the Korean government has thus far allocated less than ten percent of its budget for welfare services so as to expend a much higher percentage (over 35 percent) of its budget for continued economic development by investing in human and material resources, facilities and machines, and R & D. The rationale is that economic stagnation or recession means no gain or mere distribution of poverty among people.

Second, a small percentage of budget mandates that the state prioritize welfare services--comprehensive national medical care protection, pension for those who are able to and willing to join, state support for the handicapped, the poor and the old, and housing, in order.

Third, a limited amount of budget also requires private and quasi-public institutes--church, business firms, hospitals, medical doctors and students, philanthropists--to voluntarily join the government in planning, adopting, implementing, and delivering various welfare services.

Chapter Ten will examine these theses in five areas of welfare services such as 1) pension, 2) medical care, 3) support for the old, the handicapped, and the poor, 4) education, and 5) housing.

Pensions

Pension for old age, disability, and survival of the spouse upon the death of the main pension recipient is considered one of the most

396   Korea Leading Developing Nations

Figure 10-1 The Korean Model of Social Welfare Services: 1973 & 1985

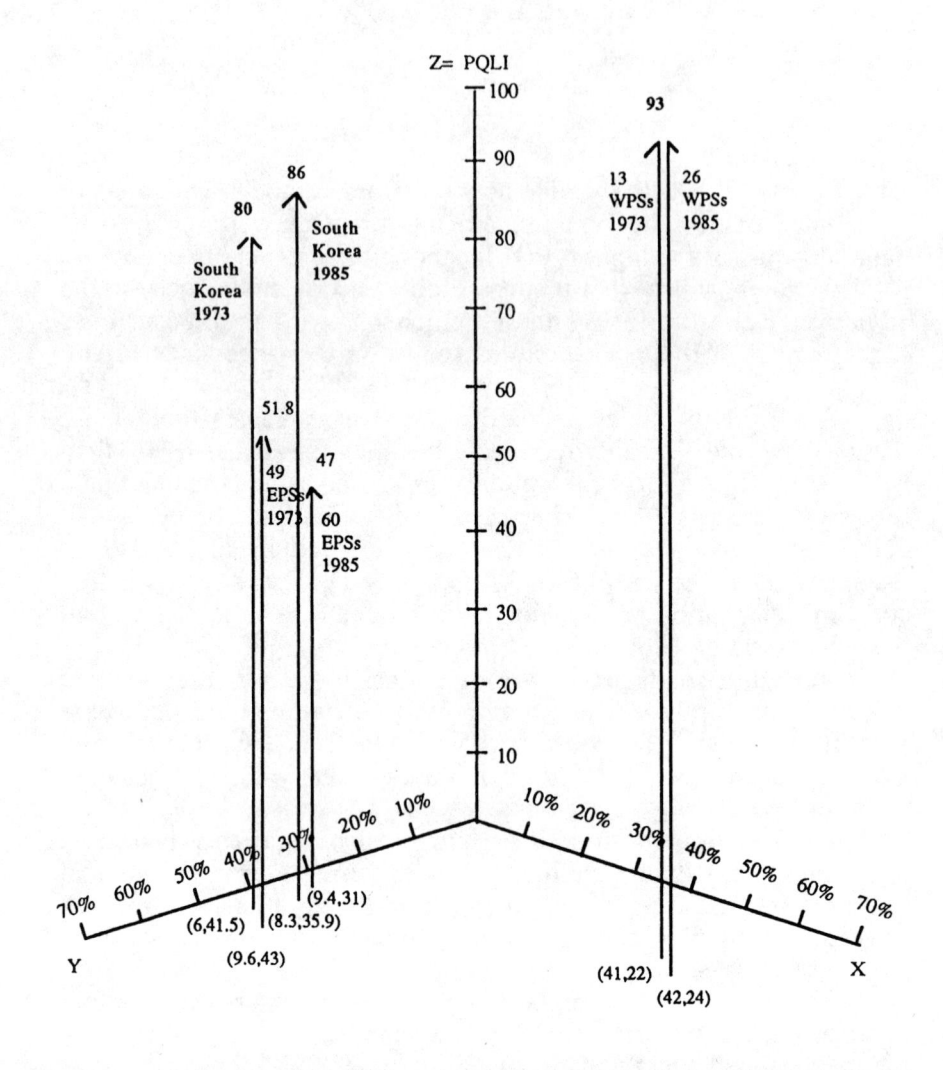

Source: Figures 9-3 and 9-5
X: Percent Central Government's Expenditures for Social Selfare Services
Y: Percent Central Government's Expenditures for Economic and
   Educational Services

important elements of the social security system. Article 1 of the Public Welfare Pension Law of 1973 reads that "the pension system shall meet the objectives of the securing of stable living and the improving of welfare of the public by providing pension benefits in case of old age, disability, and death."

Expansion of Pensions Based on Financial Feasibility

The pension plan in Korea, however, is not comprehensive and mandatory for all working people but is limited and gradually expanded within the frameworks of financial feasibility of both the employees and their employers, and the financial neutrality of the state. The government civilian employees working at both national and local levels became the first special occupational group who began to secure the pension protection in 1962. The government employees were required to contribute 5.5 percent of their annual salaries to the pension. Their employer, the state, was mandated to equally contribute 5.5 percent. A total of 11 percent began to be put up with the pension. The Office of General Affairs was charged with the administration and management of the plan. Military personnel soon joined their civilian counterparts in the pension plan in 1963 with the same percentage of contribution by themselves and the state, respectively. Therefore, by 1963 all government employees--civilian and military--became the first selected group for the pension. Since they received their monthly salary regularly and, therefore, the Office of General Affairs and the Ministry of Defense were able to deduct 5.5 percent from their monthly salaries, the implementation of the pension plans was feasible (Table 10-1).

About ten years later in 1973 the private school teachers and their employers were required to contribute 5.5 percent and 3.5 percent, respectively, to the pension. The state decided to contribute 2.0 percent to their pension, resulting in a total of 11 percent equivalent to the percentage of the pension premium for the government employees. The private school teachers have been the only group up until 1990 to which the state has committed its pension contribution. The government's decision to contribute to private school teachers might be three-fold: President Park of the Fourth Republic, who approved the plan, was a school teacher himself; school teachers--public and private--play a vital role in educating the next generation and, therefore, should be well respected and financially secure after retirement. The number of private school

Table 10-1 The Pension System

Social Insurance	Law enacted	Agency responsible	% Income-Based Contribution				Total	Year Implemented
			The insured	The Employer or corporation	The State	Transfer from retirement allowance		
Pension								
1. Special Occupations (Mandatory)								
a. Gov't Employees	8/1962	General Affairs	5.5%	0.0%	5.5%	0.0%	11.0%	1962
b. Military Personnel	1/1963	Defense Dept.	5.5%	0.0%	5.5%	0.0%	11.0%	1963
c. Private School Teachers	12/1973	Education Dept.	5.5%	3.5%	2.0%	0.0%	11.0%	1973
2. Workers of Firms with size of 10 or more (Mandatory)	12/1973 1986	Health & Welfare	'88-'92 1.5% '93-'97 2.0% '98- 3.0%	1.5% 2.0% 3.0%	0.0% 0.0% 0.0%	0.0% 2.0% 3.0%	3.0% 6.0% 9.0%	1988 1993 1998
3. Workers of Firms with less than 10 (By 2/3 workers)	1986	"	'88-'92 1.5% '93-'97 2.0% '98- 3.0%	1.5% 2.0% 3.0%	0.0% 0.0% 0.0%	0.0% 2.0% 3.0%	3.0% 6.0% 9.0%	1988 1993 1998
4. Local Participants (Voluntary): Self-Employed: a. Farmers b. Fishermen	1986	"	Full	0.0%	0.0%	0.0%	The amount of self contribution	1988
Small business with less than 10	"	"	Same as the self-employed					
5. Extended from 60 to 65 yrs of age to meet pension requirement	"	"	Same as the self-employed					

Source: *The Dong-A Annual* (1988: 203-205; 1989: 251-253)

teachers was not so excessive as to incur heavy financial burden by the state. In fact, the total number of those three special occupational groups--the government civilian employees, military personnel, and private school teachers, who were protected under the pension plan, accounted for only 2.1 percent of the entire population (Y.M. Kim, 1986: 83).

The Public Welfare Pension Law, which was enacted in 1973 and scheduled to expand to other groups in 1974, was suspended in 1974 by Emergency Measure Number 3, which was issued by President Park. The government used various domestic and international unfavorable economic conditions such as the energy crisis, chronic inflation, and economic recession as the rationale for the postponement of implementation of the pension plan for over ten years. The government again rescinded the revised plan for the implementation of the pension during the Fifth Five-Year Economic Development period (1982-1986) due to its discrepancy from the original growth targets to be accomplished.

In preparation for a twelfth National Assembly election in 1985, a Presidential Preliminary Committee (PPC) for the implementation of a public pension system, whose membership consisted of the Minister of Health and Welfare as its chairperson, seven related vice-ministers, two labor union representatives, and five commissioners, was established in September, 1984 by an Executive Order. In October 1985, the Minister of Health and Welfare (MHW) prepared a public pension system which would be incorporated into the Sixth Five-Year Economic Development Plan in 1987-1991. In June 1986, the Korea Development Institute (KDI) also published a basic plan for pension and analysis of its socio-economic impact upon the request of the PPC.

These three plans--the PPC, the MHW and the KDI--provided the government with a basic framework for the expansion of the pension from the original special groups to the general public. The PPC's rationales for the recommendation for the adoption of a pension system included: continued economic growth, price stability, the decline of the unemployed, the improvement of living standards, the increase in the frequency and scope of industrial accidents, and industrialization and the subsequent urgency for protection of the disabled. The promotion of well-being of the retired with the guaranteed income for living also helps Korea join internationalization of pension plan.

Table 10-2 Plans Recommended for the Expansion of Pension System

PPC's (Presidential Preliminary Committee) Plan for the Implementation of the Public Welfare Pension by the Executive Order (9/1984)	MHW's (Ministry of Health & Welfare) Pension Plan in 6th 5-Year (1987-91) Economic Development Plan (10/1985)	KDI's (Korea Development Institute) Basic Plan for and Analysis of Its Socio-Economic Impact (6/1986)
Rationale for the adoption of pension: 1. Price stability 2. Continued economic growth 3. Decline of the unemployed 4. Improvement of living standards 5. Increase in industrial accidents along industrialization 6. Compliance with internalization of pension 7. Well-being of the retired	1. The same as left 2. The same 3. The same 4. The same 5. The same 6. Urbanization and increase in nuclear families 7. Meeting the popular expectations along with democratization 8. Increase in the number of the elderly	1. The same as left 2. The same 3. The same 4. The same 5. The same 6. Inadequacy of the existing programs 7. The same
Basic Premises 1. Minimal state contribution 2. Within financial feasibility and gradual implementation from those capable of making contributions 3. Gradual increase of the contribution rate 4. Long-term financial stability 5. Healthy investment of the premiums in economic & social enterprises for proceeds	1. State neutrality in financial commitment 2. Within financial feasibility; not to impair the incentive to work or to invest 3. Pension expansion compatible with the existing programs 4. Optimum plan conducive to economic development	1. Maintaining the pension level necessary for basic living cost 2. A pension plan to sustain long-term financial stability 3. Conducive to income redistribution for low-income classes 4. Healthy investment of the premiums in such areas as public housing highly profitable, safe, and conducive to public welfare
Year(s) recommended for implementation 1987-1991	Three options for the year of 1987, 1988 or 1989	1988

Expansion from the existing plan:		
Age 18-60 Type I	18-60	18-60
1. Expansion of workers in firms from 16 to a minimum of 10 or more employees 2. Contribution of 1% by the state for those below a specified amount of income	1. The same as left 2. Contribution of 7% of the monthly income: 3% by the insured 4% by the employers 3. 1% set aside for unemployment compensation 4. Graded rate of premium for those below a specified amount of income	1. The same as left 2. From 2.5% in the initial stage to 10% in the year of 2000: The ratio of 4 to 6 by the insured & the employers 3. Its replacement of the the retirement plan 4. The administrative expenses by the state 5. Voluntary participation of the self-employed, farmers & fishermen with full payment for themselves

Source: Y. M. Kim (1986: 127-141)

The PPC's blueprint, however, was based upon the same traditional premise that the state should have a minimum contribution to the pension. The pension should be expanded to the general public on the premise of financial feasibility of the insured and their employers. The pension should be implemented from those who are capable of making contribution to it. Their contribution rate should be gradually increased. Long-term financial stability should be an imperative for ensuring continued payment from the time of retirement to the grave; therefore, investment of the premiums should be made in healthy economic and social enterprises.

The PPC recommended the implementation of its own plan during the Sixth Five-Year Development period for those between ages 18-60 by expanding the workers in the firms with an employment size of sixteen to the minimum size of ten. The state should contribute one percent of the monthly income of those with the income below a specified amount (Table 10-2).

The MHW identified almost the same factors as the PPC as the rationale for the adoption of a pension plan but added three other reasons such as urbanization and increase in the number of nuclear families, the urgency to meet the popular expectations of pension protection along with democratization, and the increase in the number of the elderly. However, the MHW was equally concerned with the potential of pension and other welfare programs to impair the incentive for working people to work hard and to save. The MHW's pension plan also was based on the premises of state neutrality in financial contribution, the keeping of the pension program to be compatible with the existing one, and the gradual expansion within the imperative of financial feasibility and with the aim of conducing to continued economic development.

Based upon these premises the MHW suggested three options for its implementation in the year of either 1987, 1988, or 1989, but without fail during the Sixth Five-year Economic Development Plan period in 1987-1991. The MHW plan suggested that the pension should cover working people between the ages of eighteen and sixty. The insured and their employers should contribute three percent and four percent of the monthly income, respectively, resulting in a total of seven percent. Among them one percent should be set aside for unemployment compensation. Those with income below a specified amount should be required to contribute to their pension on the basis of a graded rate of premium (Table 10-2).

The KDI suggested its own pension plan, which sounded more radical than the above two proposals because of its strong endorsement of such premises as maintaining the pension level "necessary for basic living cost," sustaining "long-term financial stability," and "conducing to income redistribution for the benefits of low-income classes," and making healthy investment of the premium in such areas as public housing "highly profitable, safe, and conducive to public welfare" (Y. M. Kim, 1986: 133).

Nevertheless, the KDI's pension plan was equally conservative as the two previous proposals because of its recommendation for the mandatory expansion of pension from the workers in the firms with the employment size of sixteen to those of ten, in which statistics on employment and salary could be obtained. In the initial year of 1988, only 2.5 percent should be contributed together by both the insured and their employers in the respective ratio of four to six. The premium should be increased to ten percent in the year of 2000. The KDI also recommended the pension plan to replace the retirement allowance currently under implementation. The self-employed, farmers, and fishermen were allowed to voluntarily join the plan with the full payment of the premium for themselves. The state was to be responsible for financial expenses incurred from the administration of the pension plan (Table 10-2).

Taking into consideration the above proposals and recommendations, the government began to deliberate the Public Welfare Pension Law (PWPL) as a part of the comprehensive public welfare plan. In 1987, the government finally completed the PWPL and its related regulations for the implementation of pension starting from the year of 1988. While endorsing the existing pension program for three special occupational groups such as the government employees, military personnel, and private school teachers, the law requires both the workers and their employers in the firms with the employment size of minimum ten or more to mandatorily contribute 1.5 percent, respectively, resulting in three percent total for the initial period of 1988-1992. During the second period of 1993-1997, the workers and the employers shall be required to contribute two percent each with additional two percent to be transferred from their retirement allowance to the pension. In the third final stage starting from 1998, the premium shall be increased by one percent each, resulting in a total of nine percent of the monthly salary for the pension to be paid in fifteen years from the year of 2003 (Table 10-1).

The small firms with the employment size of less than ten are not required to join the pension system mandatorily but voluntarily upon the agreement of two-thirds of the employees with the same percentage contribution to the pension as the case of the firms with ten or more employees. The pension plan also allows the so-called local participants, such as the self-employed like farmers and fishermen and the employees in the small firms with less than ten workers without the firm-wide collective voluntary pension participation, to individually, voluntarily, and fully contribute to the pension for themselves (Table 10-1).

Pension Types and Amount of Benefits

The Public Pension Law of 1986 has four types of pension such as old age, disability, survivors, and payment in a lump sum. As Table 10-3 shows, the Old Age Pension provides different amounts of allowance to the recipients, depending on the number of years of their contribution. Those who reach the age of sixty after twenty years of contribution (age of 55 for miners and seamen) are eligible to receive full 100 percent of the basic pension allowance and the added allowance calculated on the basis of the number of family. Those who reach the age of sixty but have contributed for fifteen to nineteen years shall receive a range of 72.5 to 92.5 percent of the basic pension allowance plus added allowance. Those who reach the ages of sixty but continue to contribute to the pension between the age of sixty to 65 to meet the pension requirement, may receive a range of fifty to ninety percent of the basic allowance. Those who continue to contribute until the age of 65, however, become eligible to receive full 100 percent of the basic allowance, even though they have not contributed for tweenty years. In addition, a special pension provision was established for those with the age of 45 to 60 as of January 1, 1988 at the time of the implementation of the Public Pension Law, who could not contribute for fifteen years until their retirement but at least five or more years. Then they are eligible to receive 25-75 percent of the basic pension allowance plus the added allowance.

Disability pension is available to those who become physically or mentally disabled resulting from sickness or injury at least after one year of contribution to the pension. The disabled shall receive a range of 60-100 percent of the basic allowance on the basis of the level of disability plus the added allowance. Survivors are equally protected from their spouses who contribute for more than one year. Equally protected are the survivors whose spouses become the recipients of full old age pension or the handicapped recipients with Status II or higher. For those who become ineligible for pension due to early retirement or death with less than fifteen years of contribution and for their survivors, a lump sum payment is to be made on the basis of the computation from the amount of contributions multiplied by a designated interest rate for a specific number of years (Table 10-3).

Criticism on the Pension Program

Since the pension program was adopted for the government civilian employees for the first time in 1962 and expanded to the firms with the employment size of ten or more mandatorily and to other citizens voluntarily in 1988, it has been subject to a variety of criticisms. We will examine major objections to the pension plan on the basis of its implementation of the Public Pension Law as of the year of 1988.

The first and most serious complaint on the pension system is that the government employees--civilian and military--are favored more than any other groups. The favor to the government employees

Table 10-3 Types and Levels of Pension Allowance

Type	Eligibility	Level of Allowance
Old Age Pension		
1. Full allowance	Age of 60 after 20 years of contribution (Age of 55 for miners and seamen)	100% of Basic Pension Allowance plus Added Allowance based on number of family
2. Reduced allowance	Age of 60 after 15-19 years of contribution	72.5-92.5% of Basic Pension Allowance plus Added Allowance
3. Extended allowance	Age of 60-65 to meet 20 years of contribution (Age of 55-60 for miners and seamen)	50-90% of Basic Allowance or 100% of Basic Allowance at the age of 65 regardless of income
4. Early retirement allowance	Those not earning income earlier than age of 55 (miners and seamen) or 60 after 20 years of contribution	75-95% of Basic Allowance plus Added Allowance
5. Special allowance	Those of age of 45-60 unable to meet 15 years of contribution but payment for at least 5 or more years	25-75% of Basic Allowance plus Added Allowance
Disability Pension	The physically or mentally handicapped by sickness and injury after 1 year of contribution	60-100% of Basic Allowance (based on the level of handicap) plus Added Allowance
Survivors Pension	For survivors of: 1. Contributor for more than one year 2. Recipient of full old age pension 3. Recipient of handicap status II or higher	40-60% of Basic Allowance plus Added Allowance
Payment in a Lump Sum	Those who become ineligible because of retirement or death with less than 15 years of contribution or their survivors	Contribution of firms: (Amount of self-contribution x 3 years compound interest saving rate) + (Amount of employer contribution x 1 year fixed interest rate)
		Local participants: (1/2 x premium x 3 years compound interest rate) + (1/2 x premium x 1 year fixed rate)

Source: *Dong-A Annual* (1988: 203-205; 1989: 251-253)

is two-fold: time and the amount of pension benefits. The government employees began to receive pension protection since 1962 and 1963, about ten years ahead of private school teachers and about 25 years earlier than all other groups. Moreover, from the first year of pension protection in 1962 and 1963, the government civilian and military employees were able to make a total of eleven percent annual contribution to the pension (Table 10-1).

The workers in the firms with the employment size of ten or more began to join the pension in 1988. However, their total contribution is only 3.0 percent--1.5 percent from their salaries and 1.5 percent from their employers, which amounts to less than one-third that of the government employees. The premium to be gradually increased as the final stage of their pension starting from 1998 still accounts for only nine percent, which is equivalent to 81 percent of that of the government employees. The nine percent total premium in 1998, however, becomes feasible by phasing out the retirement allowance and its transfer to the pension plan by the employers against the opposition of the employees and labor unions (Table 10-1).

What is more disappointing than the above two concerns is the exclusion from the mandatory participation in the pension of those workers in the firms with the employment size of less than ten and the self-employed such as farmers, fishermen, and small shopkeepers. They are allowed to join the pension system, if they would, with the payment of full premium for themselves without contribution by the state.

Table 10-4 indicates, the smaller the size of firms is, the smaller the amount of remuneration of the employees becomes. Moreover, despite the fact that during the period of fourteen years from 1968 to 1981 the salaries in large firms with the employment size of 200 and over experienced the decrease of ten percent, their salaries were still above 100 percent of the average salary of all of the firms. On the other hand, the salary of small firms with the size of 5-20 employees gained only 1.9 percent, thereby continuously hovering around 65.5 percent of the average salary of all of the firms. If we focus on much smaller firms with less than ten employees, the salary might be much less than 65.5 percent.

Therefore, the contribution of 1.5 percent of the salary to the pension during the initial stage of 1988-1992, 2.0 percent for 1993-1997, and 3.0 percent from the year of 1998 on becomes relatively easier and lighter for the employees of large firms but ironically

Table 10-4 Percent Remuneration per Employee in Firms with Different Size of Employment

Year	Employment Size of Firms					
	5-20	21-50	51-100	101-200	201-500	500+
1968	67.4	79.2	88.1	98.9	113.4	127.3
1970	60.8	72.3	95.2	100.0	106.2	127.8
1971	60.5	73.5	92.3	96.0	107.3	124.9
1972	61.5	77.5	91.6	99.1	111.4	118.1
1974	64.5	79.2	90.2	94.3	103.4	113.5
1975	63.8	77.1	88.4	94.6	97.3	116.1
1976	63.4	79.0	88.2	90.5	99.4	115.4
1977	67.5	81.4	88.5	88.7	98.9	114.6
1978	70.1	82.4	89.2	90.8	98.3	114.3
1979	74.3	86.6	92.7	95.8	99.4	110.8
1981	68.7	86.2	91.3	94.3	101.7	114.3
Percent Average	65.5	79.5	90.5	94.8	103.3	117.9
% Change from 1968 to 1981	+1.9	+8.8	+3.6	-4.6	-10.3	-10.2

Source: Pae (1986: 94-95)

harder and heavier for those of small firms. For those employed in the firms with fewer than ten, their contribution becomes much more difficult than their counterparts of the firms with over ten. Nevertheless, the employees in firms with fewer than ten must bear full responsibility for paying the premium for themselves, whereas those in large firms are offered half in 1988-1992 and two-thirds of the premium in 1993 on by their employers.

Readers may wonder, then, precisely how many firms and their total employees may fall into the category of fewer than ten employees and what percent of the total economically active they account for. Table 10-5 provides statistical information on these two questions of two different years of 1981 and 1986. As of 1981, there were 1,195,000 out of 1,264,000 firms which hired fewer than ten. They amount to 94.6 percent of the total firms (with 2.4 million employees). These small firms hired 37.2 percent of the total employees of all firms. This accounted for 17.6 percent of a total of 47.5 percent of the total population as the economically active. Therefore, the number of the employees in firms with fewer than ten

Table 10-5 Number of Firms and Employees by the Size and Percent Economically Active
(Unit=1,000)

Employment Size of Firms	1981 Firm	1981 Employees	1981 Percent Economically Active	1986 Firms	1986 Employees	1986 Percent Economically Active
Total	1,263.9 100.0%	6,603.3 100.0%	47.5%	1,676.6 100.0%	8,856.6 100.0%	58.4%
1-2	949.4 75.1%	1,377.3 20.9%	9.9%	1,194.6 71.2%	1,773.8 20.0%	11.7%
3-4	159.3 12.6%	533.7 8.1%	3.8%	250.9 15.0%	839.2 9.5%	5.5%
5-9	86.7 6.9%	544.2 8.2%	3.9%	126.5 7.6%	793.3 9.0%	5.2%
1-9	1,195.4 94.6%	2,455.2 37.2%	17.6% 37.0 % of the active	1,572.0 93.8%	3,406.3 38.5%	22.4% 38.4% of the active
10-19	32.8 2.6%	439.9 6.7%	3.1%	51.9 3.1%	688.8 7.8%	4.5%
20-29	11.2 0.9%	268.0 4.0%	1.9%	17.7 1.1%	421.6 4.8%	2.8%
30-49	10.6 0.8%	403.8 6.1%	2.9%	15.8 0.9%	602.1 6.8%	3.9%
40-99	7.5 0.6%	518.9 7.9%	3.7%	10.8 0.6%	739.7 8.3%	4.8%
100-299	4.4 0.4%	725.9 11.0%	5.2%	5.8 0.4%	955.7 10.8%	6.3%
300+	1.7 0.1%	1,791.3 27.1%	12.9%	2.2 0.1%	2,0421.1 23.0%	13.5%

Source: The EPB (1986); *The Dong-A Annual* (1988: 574)

was equivalent to 37.0 percent of the total economically active. About five years later in 1986, the number of small firms with fewer than ten and their employees vis-a-vis the firms with ten or over were by no means reduced but rather increased. There were 1,572,000 small firms, which represented 92.8 percent of the total firms. They hired 1.4 percent more, reaching 38.4 percent of the total economically active (Table 10-5).

Among such a large number of small firms and their employees, there were only 4,363 firms which voluntarily joined the pension plan with the agreement by two-thirds of their employees in January 1988. In November 1988, 8,710 firms participated in the pension plan. This accounted for only 0.1 percent of the total small firms with fewer than ten hired. Therefore, 99.9 percent of such small firms and their employees were not able to join the pension program (Table 10-7). The only option available is the participation of the employees individually with full payment of the premium from themselves without contribution from their firms. Because of the disproportionally smaller amount of salary by such small firms (Table 10-4), their employees are less likely to join the pension plan within the foreseeable future.

Equally responsible for individually participating in the pension plan with full payment of the premium from themselves are farmers and fishermen. We wonder how many of them can really afford to join the pension plan. Here, we may examine income status of the farmers on the basis of the size of their farmland among the farmers themselves and their average household income vis-a-vis that of urban households. Table 10-6 provides three types of statistical data: (1) the number of all farm households and their average income, (2) the number of farm households and the average incomes for each of the four categories on the basis of the size of their farmland such as less than .5 hectare, .5-1.0, 1.0-2.0, and greater than 2.0 hectare, and (3) the average farm household income vis-a-vis that of urban households.

Table 10-6 suggests that the income of farmers is greatly attributable to the size of their farmland. In other words, the larger the farmland, the greater the amount of income. As of 1969, the farmers with less than .5 hectare earned only 64.2 percent of the average income. Farmers with .5-1.0 hectare still made only 83.5 percent. On the other hand, farmer with greater than 2.0 hectare of farmland earned 196.8 percent, almost twice as much income as the average farmers. The trend remained the same almost ten years later in 1978. The average income of the farm households with less than .5 and .5-1.0 hectare, showed a range of 65 to 85 percent of the overall average income of the farmers. Yet, they accounted for 67 percent of the total farmers in 1971 and slightly declined but remained above sixty percent of the total farm households in 1987.

Table 10-6 Average Monthly Income (I) and Number of Households (H) by Size of Farmland (Unit: Household=Million, Income=1,000 Won)

Year	Overall H Average I	Less than .5 hectare	.5-1.0	1.0-2.0	Greater than 2.0 hectare	Rural (a)	Urban (b)	a/b
1969 Household (H: 6.1)* Income (I)	18.0(100.0%)	12.0(64.2%)	15.0(83.5%)	23.0(126.3%)	36.0(196.8%)	18	28	64
1971 H(5.9)	2.5(100.0%)	.8(33.8%)	.8(32.8%)	.7(26.9%)	.2(6.5%)			
I	30.0(100.0%)	18.0(59.1%)	25.0(82.7%)	39.0(131.4%)	57.0(191.6%)	30	38	79
1973 H(5.7)	2.4(100.0%)	--	--	--	--			
I	40.0(100.0%)	24.0(59.1%)	33.0(83.3%)	51.0(127.8%)	81.0(202.1%)	40	49	82
1975 H(5.6)	2.4(100.0%)	.7(30.2%)	.8(36.2%)	.6(27.1%)	.2(6.5%)			
I	73.0(100.0%)	44.0(61.0%)	65.0(88.9%)	92.0(126.1%)	145.0(198.7%)	73	72	101
1977 H(5.3)	2.3(100.0%)	.7(28.3%)	.9(37.9%)	.7(27.3%)	.2(6.5%)			
I	119.0(100.0%)	73.0(60.9%)	99.0(83.8%)	159.0(133.5%)	250.0(208.9%)	119	117	102
1978 H(5.2)	2.2(100.0%)	--	--	--	--			
I	157.0(100.0%)	102.0(65.1%)	133(84.9%)	200.0(127.2%)	302.0(192.5%)	157	160	98
1979 H(5.0)	2.16(100.0%)	.64(30.0%)	.76(35.0%)	.55(26.0%)	.12(5.2%)	185	281	66%
1980 H(5.1)	2.15(100.0%)	.61(28.0%)	.74(35.0%)	.63(29.0%)	.14(1.4%)	224	344	65%
1981 H(5.1)	2.03(100.0%)	.60(30.0%)	.74(37.0%)	.54(27.0%)	.11(5.2%)	307	408	75%
1982 H(4.9)	1.99(100.0%)	.57(29.0%)	.72(36.0%)	.55(27.0%)	.11(5.2%)	372	460	81%
1983 H(4.9)	2.00(100.0%)	.57(28.0%)	.71(36.0%)	.55(28.0%)	.11(5.1%)	427	528	81%
1984 H(4.8)	1.97(100.0%)	.55(28.0%)	.70(36.0%)	.55(28.0%)	.11(5.2%)	462	583	79%
1985 H(4.2)	1.92(100.0%)	.53(28.0%)	.68(36.0%)	.55(29.0%)	.11(6.2%)	478	622	77%
1986 H(4.3)	1.90(100.0%)	.54(29.0%)	.66(35.0%)	.55(29.0%)	.11(6.2%)	499	694	72%
1987 H(4.2)	1.87(100.0%)	.52(28.0%)	.65(35.0%)	.55(29.0%)	.12(6.4%)	544	841	65%

Source: For 1969-1978, The Christian Institute for the Study of Justice and Development (CISJD) (1980: 124-126); for 1979-1987, *Dong-A Annual* (1986: 598) and 1989: 587).
*Indicates the number of average members per farm household.

Their incomes were, of course, less than that of the average urban households. Moreover, the income gap between rural farmers and urban wage workers has not been reduced in 1969-1987.

The Korean Model of Social Welfare Services   411

Given such a relatively small income, a large number of small farmers were not able to join the pension plan. To make the matter worse, large farmers with two or more hectares of farmland, who earned almost twice as much income as the average farmers, did not show an enthusiastic participation in the pension plan. In short, as of the end of November, 1988, only 1,001 out of 3.3 million economically active farmers, fishermen, and the self-employed joined the pension (Table 10-7).

Table 10-7 Percent Economically Active Under the Pension Protection

Type	1/1988 (a)	11/1988	Gains %	Economically Active 11/1988(b)	Percent Active Under each Pension (a/b)	Percent Total Economically active	Year of Implementation
1. Special Occupations							
a. Gov't Employees	1,039,375	1,049,375	+10,000 (+0.9%)	1,049,735	100.0%	6.12%	a. 1962 b. 1963 c. 1973
b. Military Personnel							
c. Private School Teachers (All mandatory)							
2. Firms with 10 or more employees (mandatory)	4,197,524	4,343,610	+146,086 (+3.5%)	4,343,610	100.0%	25.36%	1983
3. Firms with fewer than 10 employee (Agreement by 2/3 Workers)	4,363	8,710	+4,347 (+99.6%)	7,327,015	0.17%	0.05%	1988
4. Local Self-Employed:	91	1,001	+910 (+1,000%)	3,326,640	0.0003%	0.19%	1988
5. Extended Contribution from 60 to 65 years of age to meet pension requirement (Voluntary)	0	147	+147 (+147%)	1,076,000	0.014%	0.001%	1988
Sum	5,241,353	5,402,843	+161,490 (+3.1%)	17,123,000		31.54%	1988

Source: *Dong-A Annual* (1988: 203-205; 1989: 251-253)

It goes without saying that daily workers, temporary employees, and seasonal workers are by no means able to join the pension plan. Ironically the state provides contribution of two percent to only private school teachers, whose income is relatively higher than most urban wage earners and rural farmers who are still ironically much more stable and secure in living than the daily workers and temporary employees. Therefore, it is widely known that the existing pension plan does not aim at contribution to reducing income inequality and progressively redistributing the income.

Due to lack of contributions by the state and lack of the requirement for mandatory participation, as of November 1988, only 31.55 percent of the economically active joined the pension. Therefore, a vast majority of people are left without the pension protection. Even for those insured, the pension payment starts at the age of sixty, whereas the absolute majority of the insured are forced to retire at the age of 55.

Merits of the Pension

The Public Pension Law of 1986, however, laid the foundation for the expansion of the pension program from three special occupational groups such as the government civilian and military personnel and school teachers to all of the workers in the firms with a minimum of ten employees primarily on the basis of financial feasibility and private pension insurance without financial burden on the state. As a result, the number of the pension-insured had increased from only two percent of the economically active in 1962, four percent in 1963, 6.12 percent in 1973 to a whopping 31.54 percent in 1988 (Table 10-7).

While the voluntary system for the self-employed slows down the expedient, immediate, and comprehensive implementation of the pension program, the pace of voluntary participation during eleven months from January to November 1988 was impressive. Only 4,363 workers in the firms with fewer than ten originally joined the pension plan voluntarily in January, 1988. But ten months later in November 1988, 8,710 participated in the pension plan. That accounted for a 99.6 percent increase over a relatively short period of eleven months (Table 10-7).

The more impressive is the case of the self-employed such as farmers, fishermen, small storekeepers, and others. As of January

1988, only 91 persons joined the pension. But in November 1988, 1,001 participated in it. This represented ten times as many as those in January 1988 (Table 10-7).

The government announced its plan to implement a national comprehensive pension program incorporating the entire working people by 1991 (*Dong-A Annual*, 1989: 251). Even if the plan may not be implemented as scheduled, the number of pension participants will continue to increase. The government, of course, would like to see as many citizens as possible to participate in the pension protection mandatorily and/or voluntarily. The fewer people left out of the pension protection and remain stragglers for self-sufficiency, the more financially able the state becomes to provide them--the handicapped, the elderly, the dependent, and so on--with public support for living and survival.

Medical Care Security

The Korean government boasts of medical care as the most comprehensive social welfare program, covering all citizens on the basis of three types of service by 1989. They are medical "insurance," medical "protection," and medical "assistance" (Table 10-8). The medical "insurance" is designed to help those with regular income and financial ability to join medical insurance. The medical care "protection" is to take care of almost all medical expenses of the poor who can't afford to pay. The medical care "assistance" is to partially assist low-income people in paying their medical expenses.

Medical Insurance

Medical Insurance Law (MIL) originally was legislated in December 1963. But it was not implemented due to lack of financial feasibility. About thirteen years later in 1976, when the national economy had progressed to a significant extent, implementation of medical insurance became a reality. Therefore, in December 1976, the MIL was completely revised and its enforcement decree was enacted in 1977. For the first time in the history of the republic, the medical insurance was mandatorily enforced for those hired in the firms with the employment size of 500 or more in 1977. It was extended to those in firms with 100 or more in 1981, to those in firms with a minimum of sixteen or more mandatorily, and to those in firms with five or more voluntarily in 1983 (Y.M. Im, 1986:

Table 10-8 The Medical Care Security

	Law enacted	Agency responsible	Percent Contribution The insured	The employers	The state	Total	Types of allowance	Year implemented	Administrative expenses	Self expenses*
Medical Insurance										
1. Employees in firms	12/'63 12/'76 revised	Employee Association	1/2	1/2	0	3-8% monthly income	a. Recuperation b. Delivery c. Added allowance for family d. Medical examination	1977 for firms with 500 or more. 1977 for 300 or more, 1983 for 16 or	Part by the state	a. Expenses over 1,000 won: 1) In-patient 20% 2) Out-patient 30% (50% in hospital, 55% in medical center)
2. Gov't employees & private school teachers	12/'77	Medical Insurance Mgt Corp. (MIMC)						1979 1988 for military personnel	Part by the state	b. A fixed amount less than 10,000 won: 1) 2,000 won in clinic 2) 6,184 won in medical center
a. Gov't employees			1/2	--	1/2	3-8%	Same as above	Same as above	Same as above	Same as above
b. Private school teachers (Voluntary)			1/2	3/10	1/5	3-8%	Same	Same	Same	Same
3. Type II a. Local self-employed farmers & fishermen	12/'76	Local Insurance Assoc.	50-75% 4 grades	--	25-50%	3-7%	Same	1981 1988 for farmers & fishermen	Full by the gov't	
b. Urban self-employed & occupational groups (From voluntary to mandatory)		Occupational Insurance Asso.	50-75% 4 grades	--	25-50%	3-7%	Same	1989 for urban self-employed	Same	

Medical Care Protection	Law enacted	Agency responsible	Percent Contribution Nat'l Gov't	Local Gov't	Medical Expenses Outpatient	Inpatient City	Rural	Year implemented	Administration Expenses	Treatment by
The absolutely poor in private or public facilities (Yellow card)	12/'77	Local Gov't	80%	20%	100% paid by local gov't, Supervised by local gov't	50% by gov't, 50% by self	80% by gov't, 20% by self	1977	Full by gov't	1st by clinics & health center, 2nd by hospital & medical center, 3rd by special hospital like mental hospitals
The poor (Green card)	Same	Same	Same	Same	Same	Same Supervised by MIMC	Same	1981	Same	

Medical Care Assistance									
Low income people	Same	Same	Same	Same	1/3 by gov't, 2/3 by self	40-60% by gov't, 60-40% by self	60% by gov't, 40% by self	1984	Same	Same

Source: Y. M. Kim (1986: 142-154); *Dong-A Annual* (1986-1989)

*Subject to adjustment

142). The employees under this category of protection is called Typed I medical insurance recipients.

Type I insurance is based on the contribution of fifty percent and fifty percent by the insured employees and their employers, respectively, amounting to three percent of the employee's monthly income initially but gradual increase to eight percent on the basis of financial feasibility. Type I provides the insured employees with recuperation allowance, delivery allowance, and added allowance for their family (Table 10-8). Employee associations become responsible for the management of Type I insurance.

A separate Medical Insurance Law for Government Officials and Private School Teachers and Staff was enacted in 1972 and began to be implemented in 1979. Military personnel soon joined the medical insurance in 1980. The government civilian and military employees put up fifty percent of the insurance premium, while the state contributed the remaining fifty percent. The total premium accounted for three percent of the insured's monthly income but will be increased gradually up to eight percent. Private school teachers and staff were required to contribute the half of the premium, which was matched by three-tenths and two-tenths by their schools and the state, respectively. The insurance covers recuperation and delivery allowances together with the added allowance based on the size of the family (Table 10-8).

Medical insurance for occupational groups and the self-employed such as rural farmers, fishermen, and urban storekeepers, which was called the Type II insurance, was implemented originally in 1981 on the voluntary basis with the full payment of the entire premium by themselves without support from the state. In 1981, three counties--Hong Chun County in Kang Won Province, Koon Wee County in North Gyung Sang Province and Ok Ku County in

North Jeon Ra Province--with 192,000 residents were selected to experiment the feasibility of medical care insurance for farmers, fishermen, and urban storekeepers. Surprisingly, 464 billion Won ($67.4 million) of deficit was incurred during one year of its implementation due to the failure of over thirty percent of the beneficiaries to pay one hundred percent of the insurance premium and yet receive medical care (Pae, 1986: 104-105).

In 1982, the experimentation was further expanded into three additional areas--Kang Wha County in Gyong Gi Province, Po Eun County in North Choong Chung Province, and Mok Po City in South Jeon Ra Province. The collection rate of premiums from the residents of these five counties improved to be 84 percent in 1982 and 96.7 percent in 1985. Therefore, deficits incurred amounted to only 1,187 million Won ($1.5 million) in 1983, and further decreased to 720 million Won in ($813,559) in 1985. At least four of the five counties were estimated to turn out in the black soon (*Dong-A Annual*, 1987: 191).

Occupational groups also began to voluntarily join Type II medical insurance with one hundred percent of payment of the premium from their own pocket. The members of the Korea Artistic and Cultural Organization joined the insurance on December 10, 1981. The members of the National Association of Barbers and Cosmeticians took part in it on January 1, 1982. They were soon followed by grain salesmen, national taxi drivers, those engaged in livestock, insurance, overseas merchant seamen, and even the Medical Doctors Association (*Dong-A Annual*, 1986: 200).

Nevertheless, many occupational groups and self-employed, like farmers, fishermen, and urban residents, who could not afford paying one hundred percent of the premiums, left out of Type II medical insurance. Therefore, as of 1984, only 41 percent of the total population could join the medical insurance (Table 10-9). On September 1, 1986, the government finally announced its comprehensive medical insurance program, encompassing all of the farmers and fishermen as of January 1988 and all of the urban low income and self-employed as of January 1989 into Type II insurance.

To implement this plan, farmers and fishermen were required to pay their medical insurance premium on the basis of four income grades: Grade One for about twenty percent lowest income farmers to pay 3,000 Won ($4.40 as of 1988) per month; Grade Two for the next thirty percent low income farmers to pay 6,000 Won ($8.17); Grade Three for the next higher thirty percent to pay 9,000 Won

Table 10-9 Number of Persons Under the Medical Care System (unit=1,000)

Type of Medical Care	1977 Insured (I) Family (F) Total (T)	1979 I F T	1981 I F T	1984 I F T	1986 T	1987 T	1988 T	1989 T
Medical Insurance	1,185	1,820	2,637	3,754				
*Type I	1,955	2,864	4,624	7,582				
Employees in firms	3,140	4,684	7,261	11,336	100%	100%	100%	100%
*Gov't employees & private school teachers		741 2,303 3,044	873 2,990 3,863	885 3,085 3,980	100%	100%	100%	100%
*Type II Self-employed:	14 49 63	12 49 61	72 211 283	328 1,111 1,439	3,636	5,265	13,525	23,215
Farmers, fishermen & urban shoppers							8,260	9,690
State financial support					Admin. expenses Insurance		$57.8m. $70.0m.	$52m. $241m.
Subtotal	3,203	7,789	11,407	16,755	18,952	20,581	28,847	38,531
% total population	9%	21%	29%	41%	46%	50%	69%	91%
Medical Care Protection: *The absolutely poor *The poor			2,100 480 2,580 7%	2,258 5.5%	2,462 6%	2,634 6%	About same	About same
Medical Care Assistance for Low income people				3,245 8%	1,924 5%	1,752 1%	About same	About same
State financial support					$59m.	$86m.		
Total Participants	3,203	7,789	13,987	22,258	23,338	24,967	33,227	42,381
% total population	9%	21%	36%	55%	57%	60%	79%	100%

Source: Y. M. Kim (1986: 127-141); *Dong-A Annual* (1986-1989)

($13.15); and Grade Four for the top twenty percent highest income group to pay 11,000 Won ($16.08)(*Dong-A Annual*, 1987: 190).

Graded premium clearly indicates a progressive and redistributive system among the insured of Type II such that the higher the income, the higher their premium becomes. To meet the premium level still far below the medical costs due to disproportionate small amount of premiums to be payable by Grades

One, Two, and Three, the government decided to contribute 395 billion Won ($57.8 mission) for the entire insurance administration expenses and additional 479 billion Won ($70 million) to cover fifty percent of the total insurance premiums, starting from 1988. A total of 874 billion Won ($127.8 million)(*Dong-A Annual*, 1989: 252) was the largest amount in the Korean history and yet a modest one in the international standard for the adoption of a comprehensive medical insurance. As of January 1988, 8.26 million farmers and fishermen were added to Type II, resulting in the coverage of a total of 13.525 million. This accounted for 69 percent of the entire population protected under the medical insurance (Table 10-9).

To incorporate the urban self-employed and other occupational groups into the comprehensive medical insurance as the last 21 percent of the total population starting from January 1989, the government again divided them into four grades on the basis of their income for the collection of the different amount of premium to pay: Grade One for the payment of 4,000 Won ($5.71); Grade Two for 7,000 Won ($10.00); Grade Three for 12,000 Won ($17.14); and Grade Four for 14,000 Won ($20.00), per month (*Dong-A Annual*, 1987: 190). In 1989, the government committed its contribution of fifty percent of the total Type II insurance premium for urban self-employed with 734 billion Won ($104.8 million) and 100 percent of the total administration expenses with 163 billion Won ($23.2 million). The total amount of the state contribution for both rural farmers and fishermen and urban self-employed in 1989 amounted to 2,056 billion Won ($293.6 million), which explained an almost 130 percent increase, as that of 1988 (Table 10-10).

The original four grades for differential amounts of premiums to be paid for Type II insurance were re-arranged into fifteen grades and further divided into thirty grades on the basis of income, real estate, and type of automobile owned by the insured. The revised policy of the thirty grades, which was scheduled to be implemented from July 1990, indicated a much greater progressive system. Those whose income and real estate values exceeded the average of the middle grade were required to pay much higher premium than in the case of the previous fifteen grades. On the contrary, those whose income and real estate value fell far below the middle grade were greatly relieved of the burden and paid much less than under the previous fifteen grades. Moreover, those who owned automobiles were required to pay a higher premium than those who did not own

Table 10-10 Type II Medical Insurance Premium and State Support (unit=Korean won)

	1988		1989	
	The insured	State contribution for:	The insured	State contribution for:
Farmers & fishermen				
Grade One	3,000($4.40)	A* 395billion	3,000	A 204billion
Grade Two	6,000($8.17)	($57.8m.)	6,000	($29.1m.)
Grade Three	9,000($13.15)	P* 479billion	9,000	P 955billion
Grade Four	11,000($16.08)	($70.0m.)	11,000	($136.4m.)
		T* 874billion		T 1,159billion
		($127.8m.)		($165.5m.)
Urban Self-Employed				
Grade One			4,000	A 163billion
Grade Two			7,000	($23.2m.)
Grade Three			12,000	P 734billion
Grade Four			14,000	($128.1m.)
Total		874billion		2,056billion
		($127.8m.)		($293.6m.)

Source: *Dong-A Annual* (1989: 252)

*A stands for the administration expenses; P for the insurance premium; T for the total expenses.

a car. The larger the size of an automobile, the higher the premium level (*Korea Daily*, 6/29/1990).

Until 1985, the insured were required to pay thirty percent of the medical expenses from their pocket in the case of the medical expenses in excess of 10,000 Won ($11.61). In case of less than 10,000 Won ($11.61) of the medical expenses, the insured were to pay rather a fixed amount: 2,000 Won for the first visit and 1,500 Won for each of the subsequent visits to a clinic or health center. In case of the medical expenses in excess of 10,000 Won, the insured should have the obligation to pay thirty percent of the total fee. When they visited the next higher level facilities such as a hospital or a medical center, the payment from the insured themselves increased to fifty percent and fifty-five percent, respectively (*Dong-A Annual*, 1986: 199).

The so-called partial fixed amount of self-payment system involving less than 10,000 Won of medical expenses incurred from clinics and health centers became a product of creative ideas through trial and error on the implementation of the medical insurance program. The fixed rate, on the one hand, would help the patients and medical doctors reduce the potential for disputes over the computations on the amount of self payment from the insured.

Since the relatively small fixed amount is charged by clinics and health centers, patients who suffer from minor pains such as cold, fever, illness from fatigue are encouraged to visit clinics or health centers. This also relieves large hospitals and medical centers of traffic congestions primarily resulting from long lines of patients. In fact, the fixed rate system helps screen the patients and promotes the quality of the delivery of medical services on the basis of graded medical facilities from clinics for minor patients to medical center for operation and treatment of the most critical patients.

According to a statistical analysis of the Ministry of Health and Welfare, the fixed amount system saved 540 billion Won ($63.5 million) at the levels of hospitals and medical centers, resulting in a total of 830 billion Won ($97.3 million) in 1986 (*Dong-A Annual*, 1986: 199). The medical insurance program, which embarked with the coverage of only nine percent of the population in 1977, finally began to encompass 91 percent in 1989. About nine percent remaining citizens who were not included in the medical insurance still began to receive medical care by the state-sponsored medical protection and medical assistance programs.

Criticisms of the Medical Insurance

The medical insurance program has long been a major target of criticism. The medical insurance is seen as a zero-sum or a variable-sum game both within each type and between different types of insurance programs. The Type I insurance program, for example, demonstrates the fact that the higher income firm employees such as those engaged in management pay relatively lower amount of insurance premium than the low income firm employees such as those on the production and assembly lines see Table 10-11).

A variable-sum game is also identified due to lack of a uniform national medical insurance among the (Type I) firm employees, the government employees, and the (Type II) self-employed. For example, the amount of insurance premium for the Type I insured to contribute is solely based on their monthly salary. Therefore, their annual bonus equivalent to one hundred, two hundred, or three hundred percent of their annual salary is totally excluded in the computation for their contribution to the insurance. On the other hand, the premium for the government employees and private school

Table 10-11 Differential Amounts of Premiums and Allowances by Occupations for Type I Insurance

Occupation	Remuneration	Actual Amount of Premium	Its Percent	Premium (a)	Allowance (b)	Allowance Rate (b/a)
Management	651,728	405,100	62.1	12,153	8,085	66.4
Office	137,528	90,766	66.0	2,723	2,460	90.3
Production	30,768	25,600	83.2	768	117	15.2
Others	26,368	19,933	7536	598	325	54.4
Total	846,392	541,400	63.9	16,242	10,978	67.6

Source: Choi Sung Kyu (1988)

teachers to contribute is based on both salary and bonus. The Type II insured such as farmers, fishermen, and urban self-employed are also required to make contributions to the insurance on the basis of their overall income. In fact, they are not able to separate part of their income as bonus. Therefore, the self-employed, government employees, and school teachers complain that their relative amount of premium is much more burdensome than the Type I insured.

The Type I insured, on the other hand, argue that, while they receive only part of the insurance administration expenses by the state, the Type II self-employed received one hundred percent of the insurance administration expenses by the state. In addition, the former do not receive contribution to their premium by the state at all, whereas the latter receive fifty percent of the total premium by the state.

Type I insured, government employees, and private school teachers are required to pay a fixed percent of their salary rate to their insurance. But Type II insured have to differentially contribute to their premiums on the basis of their income, real estate values, and family size. Therefore, the medical insurance program is based on a mixture of regressive and progressive redistributive systems. Moreover, the complaint becomes louder from the higher graded rural and urban self-employed because of their relatively higher burden of premium than their lower graded counterparts and because of the progressive nature of Type II insurance which benefits the lower graded insured at the expense of the higher graded insured.

The fairness in the graded amount of premium to be contributed by the Type II insured is, indeed, based on the assumption that their income and wealth should be accurately measured. However, bank deposits, the subsequent interest, transaction of real estate, and proceeds from stocks and bonds are all practiced with false names. To make the matter worse, those who are responsible for measuring the level of income and wealth are not professionally trained administrators but local governmental unit heads. Their nonprofessional judgment may raise the question of fairness and justice. They may abuse their powers, exerting significant influence and pressure to the local residents in the presidential and National Assembly elections for the government party.

Employee Associations for Type I, medical insurance management corporations for the government employees and private school teachers, and local insurance association for Type II complain that they are all intervened by the state in the sound investment of the premiums for long-term financial stability and internal management autonomy on the grounds that the state provides them with part or full administration expenses.

The government, on the other hand, contends that, while those management agencies were originally established for politically independent and autonomous administration of their own premiums for their own insurance members, they lack sophisticated administrative skills and experience. Moreover, employee associations in medium and small firms may be less effective and efficient in management than their counterparts in large firms. Many local and occupational insurance associations may face similar problems of shortage of well-trained management. This is evidenced by the fact that Type II insurance management associations in both rural and urban areas are dominated by Directors General, over ninety percent of whom are the government-appointed, former high-ranking officials, the government political party officials, ex-military officers, and the Peaceful Unification Advisory Committee members. They receive a monthly salary of 1 million Won ($1,462), a sedan, and other benefits (Association of Physicians for Humanity, 10/15/88: 6). They are not specialized in medical care delivery services, nor are they delegates or trustees of their local insurance members. Appointed by the central government, these Directors

General play a vital role in the presidential and National Assembly elections for the government party (K. S. Koh: 1989: 10-13). Even if these management agencies and associations may be capable and energetic, many of them may be too small to maintain or promote effectiveness and efficiency because of their economies of scale as too small.

Table 10-12 Ratio of Dependents Insured by Three Types of Medical Insurance

	1977	1979	1981	1984
Type I Employees in firms	1.65	1.65	1.76	2.07
Gov't employees & private school teachers		3.11	3.02	3.06
Type II Self-employed	3.42	2.75	3.57	3.06

Source: Y. M. Kim (1986: 146)

Medical insurance coverage of dependents becomes an equally controversial issue among three types of the insured. As Table 10-12 indicates, government employees, private school teachers, and the self-employed have their children and their parents, who reside in their homes and, therefore, become eligible for receiving medical insurance. On the other hand, many employees in firms migrated from their rural homes and reside alone in or near manufacturing firms in the industrial areas. Therefore, their parents and dependents, who do not physically reside with them but remained in the countryside, are not eligible for insurance coverage. Having paid the same percent of premium, Type I insured feel that the existing insurance policy definitely favors the government employees, school teachers, and Type II insured at the expense of themselves. To make the matter worse, parents-in-law recently became eligible for medical insurance. Hence, the relative deprivation of Type I employees seems further aggravated.

The greater the desire for medical care is, the greater the frequency of the insured's visit to medical facilities becomes. Subsequently, medical costs have increased continuously. For the five years from 1980 to 1984, the annual medical cost increased four times on average per one insured (Y. M. Kim, 1986: 148). The medical insurance at the present time does not cover preventive medical treatment for liver cancer, the examination for uterus cancer, chemical and fertilizer intoxication, pollution, and other similar cases due to the financial limit (K. S. Koh, 1989: 13). It becomes controversial for the medical insurance to cover preventive medical care. Moreover, the medical insurance coverage for high blood-pressure, diabetes, and other chronic diseases was limited up until 1983 to a maximum of 180 days for such patients throughout their entire life but extended to 180 days per year for the rest of their lives. Therefore, the overall medical coverage began to substantially increase. The consequence was that government employees and private school teachers experienced deficits in their insurance because of the expenditure (1,513.3 billion Won equivalent to $183.2 million) exceeding the contribution (1,424.6 billion Won equivalent to $172.5 million).

Merits of the Medical Insurance

Different types of insurance participants express complaints against others as if they were situated in a zero-sum game. However, when the above complaints are carefully examined, no one gains everything. Type II receive the fifty percent of their premium from the state, whereas Type I, government employees, and school teachers have to pay their premium only from their own salaries excluding their bonus. The former have to pay their premiums on the basis of their income. Therefore, the higher the income, the greater the premium. The latter, however, have the advantage to pay a fixed rate of their income. In short, no one group gains or loses everything. What distinguishes Korea from many developing countries is the fact that Korea has accomplished the goal of comprehensive national health insurance within the earliest possible period. As Table 10-9 indicates, only nine percent of the population received the medical insurance coverage in 1977. Eleven years later, a whopping 91 percent of the population were protected under the insurance program, while the remaining nine percent, who were below the poverty level, were under the state medical protection and assistance program. Therefore, 100 percent of the population began to be provided medical care security by 1989.

The Korean model of medical insurance also suggests the least amount of government contribution to the premium and the least amount of government intervention in the management of the insurance. The Korean model, in fact, endorses the concept of the public choice model (Ostrom, 1974; Bish, 1971; Buchanan and Tullock, 1962; Pae, 1986: 133-140) in which insurance participants are granted the privilege to locally and occupationally organize and manage their own insurance, independent and autonomous of other management associations as well as the government.

Many scholars, social security research institutes, social workers, and practitioners contend that there should be a single, uniform, comprehensive national medical insurance by encompassing all existing fragmented management associations and corporations (Korea Social Security Research Institute, 1984 and 1986). They contend that only one national comprehensive insurance can promote a progressive system, thereby collecting more premiums from the pockets of wealthy people, returning some of the premium to the protection of low-income participants, and equalizing the quality of medical services for all citizens. They insist that the only one national comprehensive insurance program may reduce the gap between urban and rural residents, between public and private sector employees, and between the regions, and promote social integration. However, they rule out the obstacles and difficulties in ironing out many contending policies on: (1) how to raise financial sources for the adoption of a comprehensive, uniform national insurance; (2) what types of taxes to be levied and how; (3) how to reconcile the controversies over the choice of a progressive, proportional, or regressive tax among different income brackets; (4) what is to be the maximum amount as the ideal amount for quality medical treatment of all people; (5) how to grade the differential amount of payment required to pay by the patients; (6) how to resolve a variable-sum game between those who gain more benefits and those who gain less benefits and the subsequent lack of fairness among different groups of the insured in terms of the linkage between their contribution and medical benefits (B. I. Kim, 10/15/1988: 20-28).

The existing separate management associations and corporations rather share the same assumptions with the public choice model that each insured person is "free and rational" to choose public medical insurance service in his own self-interest. Free and rational individuals desire to influence the delivery of medical services whenever "the benefits they anticipate exceed their costs" (Bish, 1971: 5-6). By the same token, they care that their insurance should not go broke. Therefore, they want to take part in sound management of their own insurance by investing their premiums in a long, healthy term. They also make sure that the closer the contribution of their premium paid corresponds to the service received, the more efficient the public economy of medical insurance is likely to be. Individuality and self-interest for each of the different types of insurance are such that a free ride for others on their own insurance is discouraged and sound management of their own associations or corporations is greatly encouraged. Each of the different management associations and corporations, on the one hand, tries to meet the specific needs of its own insured. Each of them, on the other hand, provides other management associations with sound experimentation and valuable lessons from trials and errors for their reference.

Table 10-13 Medical Facilities and Their Number and Percentage Gain: 1978-1987 (1978 as 100%)

Year	Total	Medical Center	Hospitals	Physician's Office (PO)	PO's Local Branch	Special Hospitals	Dental Hospitals & Clinics	Herb Doctor's Office	Midwife's Clinics	Health Center & Branch	Clinics
1978	12,791	61	218	6,044	249	5	1,790	2,306	572	1,538	--
1979	12,868	70	233	6,110	268	5	1,905	2,174	555	1,540	--
1980	13,324	80	240	6,344	266	5	2,028	2,328	488	1,535	--
1981	14,167	89	256	6,604	278	12	2,158	2,356	480	1,538	396
1982	15,138	111	263	6,824	240	12	2,320	2,461	576	1,579	752
1983	16,419	156	282	7,252	236	11	2,522	2,519	696	1,605	1,140
1984	17,053	170	310	7,584	256	13	2,752	2,628	503	1,527	1,310
1985	18,322	183	317	8,069	279	13	2,998	2,791	504	1,528	1,640
1986	19,623	195	316	8,580	262	15	3,278	2,957	502	1,528	2,000
1987	20,889	205	305	9,089	356	18	3,599	3,235	504	1,540	2,038
% Gain 1978-1987	+38	+70	+28	+34	+30	+72	+50	+29	-13	+0.1	+81
% Gain Population 1978-87	+10										

Source: *Dong-A Annual,* various years

The government claim of the comprehensive national insurance program is evidenced not only by its coverage of over ninety percent of the entire population but also by its emphasis on the quality of its delivery by means of the fastest rate of the expansion of medical facilities and medical personnel over the period of 1978 to 1989 in the Korean history. As Table 10-13 demonstrates, midwives clinics and health centers and their branches either declined or remained the same from 1978 to 1987. But the number of all other medical facilities had increased to a significant extent, far exceeding the rate of population increase. Over the past ten years from 1978 to 1987, population increased by ten percent, while medical centers, which should be vital for major operations and treatment for the quality of medical care, increased by seventy percent. Special hospitals, like mental and rehabilitation hospitals, which were considered marginal for medical care until 1977, gained recognition of their contributions to medical care. Subsequently, they increased by 72 percent from 1978 to 1987. Medical centers and hospitals, of course, began to be scattered around different provinces rather than in a few major cities alone.

The quality of medical care along the comprehensive nationwide medical insurance is also evidenced by a fifty percent increase of dental hospitals and clinics and 34 percent increase of physicians offices. Of most remarkable significance is the fact that the number of clinics, which provide rural patients with lowest level initial medical service, increased by 81 percent.

Table 10-14 Medical Care Personnel: 1978-1987

Year	Total	Medical doctors	Dentists	Herb doctors	Mid-wives	Nurses	Nurse aides	Medical technicians	Pharmacists
1978	140,062	20,079	3,102	2,852	4,455	33,672	47,019	6,512	22,371
1979	153,320	21,279	3,326	2,913	4,641	36,975	53,288	7,517	23,381
1980	168,798	22,564	3,620	3,015	4,833	40,373	61,072	8,955	24,366
1981	183,877	23,742	3,947	3,133	5,115	43,605	68,517	10,447	25,311
1982	196,429	25,097	4,266	3,268	5,403	46,651	73,159	12,278	26,307
1983	217,987	26,473	4,611	3,409	5,681	49,587	85,910	14,921	27,395
1984	234,946	28,015	4,972	3,591	5,991	54,081	92,264	17,501	28,531
1985	262,455	29,596	5,436	3,789	6,247	59,104	106,340	22,077	29,866
1986	278,526	31,616	5,995	4,041	6,513	64,270	107,672	27,085	31,334
1987	303,669	34,185	6,761	4,426	6,849	69,829	116,348	32,416	32,855
% Gain 1978-1987	+54	+41	+54	+36	+35	+52	+60	+80	+32

Number of population per one health specialist

1978	264	1,841	11,918	12,962	8,298	1,098	786	5,677	1,652
1987	137	1,216	6,149	9,393	6,070	595	357	1,283	1,265
% Change	-48	-34	-48	-28	-27	-46	-55	-78	-23

Source: *Dong-A Annual,* various years

Quantitative and qualitative medical care under the comprehensive medical insurance may necessitate more medical personnel like doctors, dentists, and nurses. Table 10-14 clearly demonstrates that nationwide medical insurance is not mere lip-service but reinforced by a substantial increase in the number of medical personnel. While the entire population increased by only ten percent during the period of 1978-1987, the number of medical doctors and dentists increased by 41 percent and 54 percent, respectively. More impressive is the increase in the number of nurses, nurse aides, and medical technicians as evidenced by 52 percent, 60 percent, and 80 percent, respectively.

Quantitative and qualitative medical care can also be measured by the number of persons per medical doctor, dentist, nurse, and pharmacist. In 1978, there were 1,841 persons per one medical doctor, but in 1987 there were 1,216 persons. This indicates the decline of 34 percent in the work load of medical doctors. A similar high percentage of decline in the medical care load can be found in case of dentists, nurses, and nurse aides. The overall number of persons per one medical staff as a whole was 264 in 1978 but declined to 137 in 1987. Such a fast rate of increase in medical facilities and medical personnel clearly indicates that Korea indeed leads all of the nations--advanced and developing.

As indicated above, the arrangement of medical facilities such as clinics, health centers, hospitals and medical centers into a hierarchy greatly contributed to screening the patients in terms of types of medical care and in turn saved a significant amount of costs. Computerization equally enhanced saving of the insurance administration expenses. As Table 10-9 indicates, the government contributed 395 billion Won ($57.8 million) to the administration expenses vis-a-vis 479.6 billion Won ($70 million) to the premium of Type II insurance in 1988. The government's contribution to the administration expenses indeed accounted for 82.4 percent of its contribution to the insurance premium. But due to the expansion of computerization, the amount of the government contribution to the administration expenses in 1989 for Type II was 367 billion Won ($52 million), only 21.7 percent of the amount of the state contribution of 1,689 billion Won ($241 million) to the premium. Further computerization and the promotion of management efficiency continue to reduce the insurance administration expenses.

Medical Protection and Assistance

Excluded from the medical insurance are about nine percent of the population, some of whom were "absolutely poor" residing at either public or private residential facilities. Since 1977, local governments such as provinces and cities have been responsible for identifying them, issuing them a yellow card, and providing them with medical care protection. The national and local governments share eighty percent and twenty percent of the total medical premiums, respectively.

Since 1981, the government began to extend the medical care protection to "the poor." Local governments again became responsible for identifying "the poor," issuing them a green card, and ensuring them the same quality of medical protection as the absolutely poor. The patients are required to visit a clinic and health center first and then allowed to visit a hospital, and then a medical center on the basis of doctor's recommendation. The expenses for the out-patients are fully paid by the local government. In case of in-patients, the local government and the patient are required to pay fifty percent and fifty percent of the total expenses, respectively, in cities, and eighty percent and twenty percent, respectively, in the rural areas (Table 10-8).

The medical protection program is by no means perfect but subject to criticisms on the selection of those below the poverty level, relatively heavier financial burden on the poor themselves, difficulty in collecting the patient's share of the total costs, and the subsequent increase in the medical protection expenses. The criteria for identifying the impoverished include the amount of monthly income, family size, the amount of wealth in possession of farmland and/or cash in savings or rental premium, and the geographical location (Y. M. Kim, 1986: 150-153). Due to lack of adequate information on these criteria, coupled with lack of expertise of non-welfare local government administrators on the objective and fair application of the criteria, it was contended that about ten to forty percent of yellow and green card holders were not really poor. In fact, they were overqualified and therefore should be excluded from the medical protection (Y. M. Kim, 1986: 153).

The ever-increasing financial burden on the part of the government is another concern. Due to poverty, poor nutrition, and lack of preventive medical care, the number of yellow and green card holders, who received medical treatment, was doubled in case of out-patients and quintupled in the case of in-patients over the period of 1977-1983 (Y. M. Kim, 1986: 153). Because of their failure to pay fifty percent of the medical expenses by the patients in the cities and twenty percent in the rural areas, the uncollected amount accounted for 62 percent of the total expenses. Nevertheless, the government has continued to medically protect the absolutely poor and the poor, who were about seven percent of the total population in 1981, but declined to about six percent since 1986.

In-between those under the medical insurance and the poor under the medical protection were located about eight to ten percent of the population, who were called "low-income people" such as daily employees, temporary employees, and seasonal employees. In 1984, the government began to provide them with medical assistance, in which the state covered one-third of the total medical expenses in case of out-patients, while the patients were required to pay the remaining two-thirds of the expenses. For in-patients, the state contributed forty percent of the expenses in the urban areas and sixty percent in the rural areas. The patients should pay the remaining percentage of the expenses from themselves (Table 10-8).

Due to continued economic growth, increase in income, and the expansion of the medical insurance program, the number of recipients for medical care protection and assistance has consistently decreased. There were originally about eight percent of the population who received medical assistance in 1984. But the number of recipients declined to five percent in 1986, one percent to 1987, and remains unchanged thereafter (Table 10-9).

By means of the medical insurance for 91 percent of the population and medical protection and assistance for the remaining nine percent, as of January 1989, the entire population began to be included in the medical care security.

Public (State) Support for the Elderly, the Handicapped and the Poor

In the name of public support, the state identified three different groups of recipients of state financial support. Those in the first group are the recipients of state support for "institutional care," who reside in orphanages, nursing homes and rehabilitation centers. This group also includes those of state support for "residential care," who reside in their own homes, both 65 or older and 18 or younger,

Table 10-15 State Support for the Elderly, Handicapped, and Other Low Income People

Type of Recipients	Eligibility	State	Other Support	Number of Recipients 1982	1987
1. Support for					
a. Institutional Care	Those in orphanage, nursing home, rehab. center	Food, Utility fee, Medical protection, Funeral expenses,	Tuition fee for junior high school of children	.05mil.	.06million.
b. Residential Care	65 or older, 18 or younger Those incapable to work or support family	Food, Utility fee, Medical protection (100%)	Same as above	.28mil.	.29mil.
2. Support for the poor				2.95mil.	1.98mil.
a. The poor	Income below 26,000 won per month	Utility fee, Medical assistance (50%),	Same as		
b. The semi-poor		Food during winter, Medical assistance (50%)			
3. Support for disabled veterans & bereaved families		Same as		0.13mil.	0.12mil.
Total number of recipients				3.55mil.	2.51mil.
% Total population				9.0	6.0

Source: Y. M. Kim (1986: 32 and 315); *Dong-A Annual* (1989: 631)

and who are incapable of working and therefore unable to support their families. They all together accounted for 230,000 in 1982 and 350,000 in 1987. They receive state support for food, utility fee, medical protection, and tuition for junior high school education of their children (Table 10-15).

Those in the second group are about 3 million in 1982 but declined to about two million in 1987, who were the poor, and the semi-poor. They received state support for utility fees, medical assistance, and food during the winter, when jobs might be seasonally less available. Those in the third group were disabled veterans and bereaved families, who received the same amount and the same types of state support as those of the second group. Again, continued economic growth, increase in employment, and the subsequent increase of income helped reduce the number of those on the state support, for example, from about nine percent in 1982 to six percent in 1987 (Table 10-14). The Economic Planning Board reported that as of July 1990, the number of the absolutely poor who received the state support for living further declined to 2.25 million who accounted for 5.24 percent, while 2.45 additional percent of the population as the low income people received the medical assistance from the state (*Korea Daily*, 7/5/1990).

Private Sector Contributions

A high PQLI and a high rate of increase of PQLI in Korea over a short period of time with less than ten percent of the government expenditures for welfare services (Figure 10-1) could not be accomplished without energetic voluntary contributions to the medical care, the promotion of education, and housing construction and improvement by various participants from the private sector. This section, first of all, will examine a few samples, one from each of various private medical associations, hospitals, and doctors to explain extensiveness and intensiveness of voluntary contributions to quality of medical care.

Medical Professionals and Organizations

There are many private, voluntary organizations related to medicine, whose members are willing to donate their time, money, and professional expertise for taking care of the patients who cannot afford visiting medical doctors for proper medical care and treatment. A few well-known examples include the Association of Pharmacists for Realization of Healthy Society (APRHS), the Association of Church-Sponsored Medical Services for the Poor (ACSMSP), the Association of Christian Youth Medical Services (ACYMS), the Institute for Health and Society (IHS), the Association of Yonsei (University) Democratic Dentists (AYDD), and the Association of Youth Dentists (AYD). The last two dentist groups were combined and emerged as the Association of Dentists for Healthy Society (ADHS). They all deserve attention. But due to space limitations the Association of Physicians for Humanism (APH) is selected as an example to explain its major goals and activities.

The Association of Physicians for Humanism (APH)

The APH was chartered on November 21, 1987 as a non-registered, voluntary organization with three major goals: 1) the promotion of preventive medical care for tuberculosis, AIDS, other epidemic diseases, industrial accidents, and occupational diseases such as black lungs, and other occupation-related intoxication; 2) taking care of low-income patients who were legally insured or protected for medical treatment and yet unwilling to visit the doctor's office because of the inability to pay an amount of their own expenses (see Table 10-8 on the last column of Self-Expenses); and 3) positive rather than passive medical treatment of the patients such that the APH was willing to aggressively pursue public health education, visitation to the poor neighborhood, and providing medical care for the patients.

Table 10-16 Association of Physicians for Humanism: Age, Area & Specialty of Its Members

Age	Number of Doctors	Area	Number of Doctors	Employment	Number of Doctors
Younger than 25	5(2%)	Seoul	159(58%)	Professors	27(10%)
25-29	108(39%)	Kyong Gi & Inchon	35(13%)	Own clinics	52(19%)
30-34	59(22%)			Private hospitals	124(45%)
35-39	42(15%)	Kang Won	15(5%)		
40-44	11(4%)	Choong Chung	17(6%)	Public health services	51(18%)
45-49	5(3%)	Jeon Ra & Kwangju	14(5%)		
50-54	5(3%)			Not Specified	20(7%)
55-59	2(1%)	Gyong Sang, Taegu, & Pusan	6(2%)		
60-	0(0%)				
Not specified	35(12%)				
Total	274(100%)		274(100%)		274(100%)

Source: *Bulletin for the Association of Physicians for Humanism*, December 3, 1988: 35-37.

As of October 21, 1988, there were a total of 274 doctors who joined the APH. As Table 10-16 indicates, 39 percent of the members are in their twenties. About 37 percent are in their thirties. This suggests that an absolute majority of doctors who are willing to join the APH for their voluntary contribution of their time and efforts are in the twenties and the thirties. The younger the medical doctors, the greater their idealistic sense of mission and dedication to other humans becomes. Over seventy percent of them are concentrated in the areas of Seoul, Gyong Gi province, and Inchon. About 45 percent of the members are working in the private hospitals. About eighteen percent are hired in the public health service. About nineteen percent have their own clinics. Ten percent of them are medical school professors.

Despite heavy work loads in their respective jobs, the member doctors of the APH have engaged themselves in a variety of voluntary activities:

1. Medical Consultation

During the eleven-month period from December 1987 to October 1988, a total of 1,772 cases of medical consultations were made available. Among them 1,579 cases were telephone consultations, 127 were correspondence consultations, 63 cases were visiting ones. The APH identified 22 types of consultation on the basis of International Classification of Health Problems in Primary Care. They are virus-caused liver infection, stomach ache, sciaticas, tuberculosis, arthritis, high blood pressure, diabetes, etc. (*Bulletin of the APH*, Dec. 3, 1988: 12-16).

2. Black Lung Investigation

Upon the request from the residents in the neighborhood of a briquet manufacturing company, the APH conducted a black lung investigation on the basis of five percent of 497 households as a random sample and found six suffering from black lung and nine threatened. The APH reported these findings to an academic journal, notified the victims of the investigation outcomes, and conducted public education lecture series (*Bulletin of the APH*, Dec. 3, 1988: 17-19).

The APH called the attention of the Seoul City government authority to immediate, proper actions for the re-location of black lung-causing companies from the residential areas, mandatory anti-pollution measures to be imposed on them, periodic medical check-ups of the residents in the neighborhood of such manufacturing companies, and proper medical treatment for the victims. Upon the recommendations from the APH, the Seoul City government authorized the public health clinics to have a total of 2,070 residents in the neighborhood of such companies X-rayed from June 24 to July 14, 1988, and an independent medical team to read the X-ray results. Among the residents, fifty persons were given a second, detailed X-ray examination for possible black lung contamination. Five of them were identified as positive for treatment.

3. Studies on the Medical Care Insurance

On the occasion of the expansion of the medical care insurance program to farmers and fishermen from January 1988, the APH established a Committee on Medical Insurance. The committee conducted conferences, lectures, and symposiums. A few major topics include "A Political-Economic Perspective of Social Security," "Understanding and Critiques on a Welfare State," "A Comparative Study of National Health Services and National Health Insurance," "National Health Services Systems of England, Japan, and China," "Problems of the Korean Medical Insurance System and Policy Recommendations for its Improvement" (*Bulletin of the APH*, Dec. 3, 1988: 20-21).

4. Industrial Accidents and Occupational Diseases

Due to rapid industrialization and increase in the demands for exports and domestic consumption, industrial accidents and occupational diseases in Korea may be highest among all of the developing countries. During the year of 1988, about 114,000 workers were injured, 26,000 became physically handicapped, and 1,925 were killed. As Table 10-17 indicates, industrial accidents increased from .68 percent of the total workers in 1975 to .84 percent in 1988.

The APH attributed the high frequency of industrial accidents and increase in the number of victims to excessive work load exceeding forty hours of work per week, insufficient wage and malnutrition, lack of safe measures and facilities in the work sites, lack of training and education for safety and health, lack of periodic examination of environmental pollution, and ignoring the importance of period medical check-ups.

Table 10-17 Industrial Accidents

Year	The Employed (1,000)	Number of Industrial Accidents	Dead	Injured	Handicapped	Total
1975	11,692	79,819	1,006	73,074	6,490	80,570(.68%)
1976	12,412	94,844	887	86,598	7,804	95,289(.76%)
1977	12,812	117,077	1,174	105,501	11,336	118,011(.92%)
1978	13,412	138,182	1,947	124,832	13,013	139,247(1.03%)
1979	13,602	128,457	1,537	111,523	17,247	128,457(.94%)
1980	13,683	112,111	1,273	97,229	14,873	113,375(.82%)
1981	14,023	116,698	1,295	101,837	14,806	117,938(.84%)
1982	14,379	136,952	1,230	120,704	15,882	137,816(.95%)
1983	14,505	156,116	1,452	138,652	16,868	156,972(1.08%)
1984	14,429	156,479	1,667	139,478	16,655	157,800(1.09%)
1985	14,970	140,218	1,718	120,267	19,824	141,809(.94%)
1986	15,505	140,404	1,660	118,505	21,923	142,088(.91%)
1987	16,354	141,495	1,761	115,591	25,244	142,596(.87%)
1988	16,870	141,517	1,925	114,165	26,239	142,329(.84%)

Source: Lee Byung Tae, et al. (1988: 53); *Dong-A Annual* (1990: 560)

On the occasion of the death from mercurialism on July 15, 1988 of Mr. Moon Song-Myon, a fifteen-year-old boy who worked for less than two months to pay tuition for his senior high school education, the APH conducted on-the-spot investigation and data analysis and concluded that mercurialism was the cause of his death. The APH immediately began to participate in a protest, demanded compensation for his family, and recommended the government take proper safety measures for workers in various industries such as manufacturing, construction, mining, and others. The government soon adopted long-term and short-term measures regarding industrial safety and health.

The APH conducted medical check-ups on the people in the neighborhood of Young Kwang Nuclear Power Plant on July 16-17, 1989 and toured Kori Nuclear Power Plant on August 27-28, 1989, to observe the safety measures. The APH organized a special medical care team and sent it to the flood-victim area of Raju. From July 29-August 2, 1989, 20 doctors and nurses took care of 1,064 victims. The APH also sent a medical team every other weekend for three consecutive times to take care of patients in the recently relocated area of Don Am Dong, Seoul, in the month of July, 1989 (*Bulletin of the APH*, September 19, 1989: 22-23).

Medical Students

No less significant than the APH are non-registered voluntary organizations by the students in each of the medical schools in Korea. They open small clinics, mainly using church buildings in cooperation with various Protestant and Catholic churches. The clinics play a vital role in taking care of many patients, who cannot afford paying their own expenses of visiting the officially designated clinics, although their health insurance program covers the remaining, large amount of the total medical bill.

Due to lack of vertical and horizontal coordination between the students, no exact number of medical students, their clinics, and other services across the nation is available, but Eunju Lee in Seoul, Korea could identify more than twenty clinics in the cities of Seoul and Inchon without difficulty. These clinics can be found in all major cities including Seoul, Pusan, Taegu, Inchon, and Kwangju, where medical schools are located. One has to keep in mind that these students donate their time and money for the needy patients, raise funds for themselves, run their clinics, and provide the patients with medical care without charge. During summer vacation, medical students organize clinical teams and visit many local and rural areas, where there are no hospitals and doctors readily available although they are not able to tour during the regular school year. Some medical schools establish and maintain sisterhood relations with specific rural areas for long-term assistance.

Keimyung University Medical Center

Among many hospitals and medical centers which have made significant contributions to free medical treatment is the Keimyung University Medical Center. Its predecessor, the Dongsan Presbyterian (missionary) Hospital was founded in 1899. In 1981, the hospital was incorporated into Keimyung University as its medical center. Table 10-18 shows the number of in-patients, who received free medical treatment from June 1988 to May 1989 by different departments, together with the amount of medical expenses. The Department of Orthopedics had taken care of the largest number of the in-patients. That is followed by the departments of neurosurgery and general surgery. This clearly indicates that a majority of the patients, who received free medical treatment, were low-income blue-collar wage earners injured on the worksite. A total of 743 in-patients were treated without charge. This amounted to 275 million Won (equivalent to $393,100).

Table 10-18 Number of Inpatients Under Free Medical Treatment by the Keimyung University Medical Center (former Dong-San Presbyterian Hospital): June 1988 to May 1989

Department	1988 June	July	Aug.	Sept.	Oct.	Nov.	Dec.	1989 Jan.	Feb.	Mar.	April	May	Total
Internal Medicine	2	2	3	5	2	0	1	1	4	4	7	6	37
Neurology	2	0	4	1	1	2	1	1	1	1	0	1	15
Psychiatry	0	1	2	0	0	0	0	0	1	0	0	0	4
General Surgery	5	7	6	7	3	5	7	8	5	4	7	8	72
Thoracic Surgery	2	1	1	6	2	3	2	4	1	1	5	0	28
Orthopedics	28	21	14	32	27	20	36	20	24	13	22	17	274
Neuro Surgery	8	21	9	20	12	21	14	10	12	12	12	14	165
Plastic Surgery	1	6	1	4	2	1	3	7	4	2	5	4	40
Obstetrics & Gynecology	3	4	4	3	6	3	3	3	5	3	1	4	42
Pediatrics	4	2	2	1	1	2	3	0	1	1	1	1	19
Ophthalmology	1	3	1	0	0	1	0	1	1	1	0	1	10
Ear, Nose & Throat	1	1	3	2	2	1	1	0	0	1	3	1	16
Dermatology	0	0	0	1	0	0	0	0	0	0	0	0	1
Urology	1	1	2	0	1	0	3	4	0	0	0	1	13
Occupational Medicine	0	0	0	0	0	0	0	0	0	0	0	0	0
Dentistry	1	1	1	0	0	0	1	0	1	1	1	0	7
Total	59	71	53	82	59	59	75	58	60	44	64	58	734
Medical fee: Million won	18.3	23.2	11.5	31.5	19.4	21.2	31.5	17.9	22.1	34.5	20.0	24.1	275
U.S.$1,000	26.2	33.2	16.4	44.9	27.7	30.3	45.0	25.5	31.5	49.3	28.6	34.5	393

Source: Provided by the Finance Department of the University Medical Center

The center also took care of in-patients, without charge on the medical costs in excess of the amount covered by their medical insurance. A total of 601 in-patients received such benefits, whose medical costs amounted to 27.8 million Won (equivalent to $39,900).

Table 10-19 Number of Inpatients Treated by the Keimyung University Medical Center Without Charge on the Costs in Excess of the Medical Insurance Payment: June 1988 to May 1989

Department	1988 June	July	Aug.	Sept.	Oct.	Nov.	Dec.	1989 Jan.	Feb.	Mar.	April	May	Total
Internal Medicine	14	5	4	4	18	30	4	6	6	6	8	11	116
Neurology	1	0	2	2	10	5	0	2	1	0	2	4	29
Psychiatry	1	0	0	5	4	0	0	0	0	0	0	0	10
General Surgery	6	8	5	7	2	4	3	7	5	3	2	5	57
Thoracic Surgery	0	0	0	1	3	2	2	0	0	0	0	0	8
Orthopedics	1	2	0	4	9	1	1	1	2	2	4	2	29
Neuro Surgery	2	2	0	1	6	2	1	5	1	2	1	1	24
Plastic Surgery	0	0	0	0	0	3	1	0	0	0	1	0	5
Obstetrics & Gynecology	14	7	4	15	15	15	5	13	15	7	11	13	134
Pediatrics	6	3	3	2	1	2	1	8	3	3	5	4	41
Ophthalmology	0	1	1	2	8	5	5	2	1	1	1	1	28
Ear, Nose & Throat	3	2	1	2	8	3	0	4	6	0	1	1	31
Dermatology	0	1	0	1	11	13	0	0	0	0	0	0	26
Urology	1	1	1	1	2	2	1	1	0	1	0	4	15
Occupational Medicine	0	0	0	0	14	15	0	0	0	0	0	0	29
Dentistry	0	0	0	0	7	11	0	0	0	0	0	0	18
Radiology	0	0	0	0	0	1	0	0	0	0	0	0	1
Total	48	33	21	42	119	118	24	49	40	25	36	46	601
Medical Fee:													
Million won	2.4	2.8	1.3	2.9	0.8	1.0	1.7	2.4	1.8	2.2	2.3	6.2	27.8
U.S. $1,000	3.5	4.0	1.9	4.1	1.2	1.5	2.5	3.4	2.6	3.1	3.2	8.9	39.9

Departments of obstetrics and gynecology and internal medicine had treated the largest number of such in-patients. However, all seventeen departments participated in medical treatment of the in-patients (Table 10-19).

Table 10-20 Number of Outpatients Under Free Medical Treatment by the Keimyung University Medical Center: June 1988 to May 1989

Department	1988 June	July	Aug.	Sept.	Oct.	Nov.	Dec.	1989 Jan.	Feb.	Mar.	April	May	Total
Internal Medicine	32	21	24	24	3	7	25	21	18	28	28	20	251
Neurology	4	4	7	5	5	0	7	3	7	10	5	7	64
Psychiatry	2	2	8	3	0	1	2	2	1	5	5	2	33
General Surgery	2	5	3	2	3	4	1	5	0	85	3	1	34
Thoracic Surgery	1	1	2	3	0	0	2	0	0	0	0	0	9
Orthopedics	8	17	12	9	2	1	2	7	9	5	20	10	102
Neuro Surgery	3	2	4	1	2	1	2	1	2	4	4	5	31
Plastic Surgery	2	1	1	0	0	0	2	0	2	3	1	0	12
Obstetrics & Gynecology	16	14	15	19	5	7	16	29	25	22	8	22	198
Pediatrics	14	12	8	3	3	2	3	2	1	0	3	5	56
Ophthalmology	8	5	6	11	0	2	6	11	3	4	7	10	73
Ear, Nose & Throat	15	6	16	13	1	2	10	12	6	3	3	8	95
Dermatology	11	10	6	15	1	0	11	10	3	11	6	7	94
Urology	3	4	0	0	0	0	2	1	2	2	2	3	19
Occupational Medicine	24	13	8	6	0	0	3	24	64	18	29	145	337
Dentistry	1	1	18	13	0	0	5	9	10	11	4	2	74
Radiology	0	0	0	1	0	0	0	0	1	0	0	1	3
Total	146	118	141	128	25	27	102	137	154	131	128	248	1,485
Medical Fee: Million won	1.0	1.1	1.1	1.0	1.4	2.4	1.7	1.3	1.8	1.3	1.6	1.5	17.2
U.S. $1,000	1.4	1.5	1.5	1.4	2.0	3.4	2.5	1.8	2.6	1.9	2.3	2.2	24.5

During the same period of time, the center had taken care of 1,485 out-patients. Among them 337 received free medical treatment from the department of Occupational Medicine, 251 from the department of Internal Medicine, and 102 from the Orthopedic department. Table 10-20 again implies that the largest proportion of the out-patients who received free medical treatment were low-income wage earners injured during their work. The third largest number of out-patients were women who visited obstetrics and gynecology.

These three tables suggest that during the period of June 1988 to May 1989, when the nationwide health insurance program was being undertaken, the Keimyung University Medical Center still had provided a total of 2,829 in-patients and out-patients with free medical treatment, being willing to assume the medical costs amounting to 320 million Won (equivalent to $457,500). It goes without saying that, prior to the years of 1988 and 1989 when the nationwide health insurance program was not implemented for all Koreans, the Keimyung University Medical Center had made a much greater contribution to medical treatment of more poor patients because of lack of medical insurance. Keimyung is just one of many other private hospitals and medical centers in Korea which shared the same humanitarian obligations.

Dr. Yeo Sung-Sook

So far our discussion has focused on organized associations, groups of medical students, and hospitals. However, we may equally pay attention to significant contributions of many individual medical doctors to their voluntary medical services. Among them is Yeo Sung-Sook. She is in her seventies and yet continues to run a hospital which was established some thirty years ago in the city of Mokpu located in the southwestern tip of the Korean peninsula. She is the first recipient of the APH award as the Humanitarian Practitioner for her dedication to taking care of tuberculosis patients by establishing Hahn Sahn Village, a sanatorium.

She attests to the fact that tuberculosis patients in Korea account for about 2.2 to 2.5 percent of the total population. About one-fourth of them are positive patients. As of the late 1980s, one-fourth of 200,000 positive patients have been taken care of. The remaining three-fourths of the positive patients are not aggressively treated. If the patients visited public health clinics for help and treatment, they were inhumanely treated and dismissed with a modicum of medicine. Moreover, the patients soon stop taking medicine, when they feel better.

Table 10-21 Students Enrolled in Higher Educational Institutions

Year	Number of Students Enrolled	Number of Students per 100,000	Percent Increase	Remarks
1945	7,879	30	100	As of 1989,
1950	11,358	56	186	Korea exceeds
1955	78,649	365	1,216	W. Germany,
1960	101,041	404	1,350	France,
1965	131,600	452	1,506	England, &
1970	180,389	574	1,913	Japan. Only
1975	234,767	676	2,253	second to
1980	568,045	1,490	4,966	the USA
1985	1,209,647	2,950	9,833	
1989	1,353,088	3,161	10,536	

Source: *Korea Times* (*Hankuk Ilbo*), June 29, 1990

Dr. Yeo believes that hospitalization and humane and professional medical treatment are the best ways to cure the tuberculosis patients. Soon, DIAKONIA joined her. DIAKONIA, meaning "servicemen" in Greek, was established in the Hahn-Sahn Village as a public corporation, consisting of Protestant bachelor brothers equivalent to Catholic sisters of charity.

Education by the Private and Public Contributions

Korea Times had a special editorial on a statistical trend of the number of students enrolled in higher educational institutions in Korea from 1945 to 1989 (6/29/1990). Table 10-21 suggests that the enrollment in 1945 numbered 7,879, equivalent to thirty for every 100,000 population. But the enrollment had geometrically increased to 1.35 million in 1989. This figure was equivalent to 3,161 for every 100,000. This demonstrates that the enrollment in 1989 increased 105 times as many students per 100,000 as in the year of 1945. Such a geometrical increase of the enrollment in the higher educational institutions helps Korea exceed all of the Western European countries and Japan, and become second only to the United States.

Since the United States and Korea lead all other nations, we may examine to what extent public and private institutions have

Table 10-22 Number of Colleges (NC) in the USA: 1949-50 to 1985-86

Year	Public 4-Year	Public 2-Year	Public Total	Private 4-Year	Private 2-Year	Private Total	All 4-Year	All 2-Year	All Total
1949-50	344	297	641 34.6%	983	227	1,210 65.4%	1,327	524	1,851 100%
1954-55	353	295	648 35.0%	980	221	1,201 65.0%	1,333	516	1,849 100%
1959-60	367	328	695 34.7%	1,055	254	1,309 65.3%	1,422	582	2,004 100%
1964-65	393	406	799 36.7%	1,128	248	1,376 63.3%	1,521	654	2,175 100%
1969-70	426	634	1,060 41.9%	1,213	252	1,465 58.1%	1,639	886	2,525 100%
1974-75	447	763	1,214 44.2%	1,297	236	1,533 55.8	1,744	1,003	2,747 100%
Number of Students enrolled (NS)	4.9m.	3.8m.	8.8m.	2.2m.	.1m.	2.3m.	7.2m.	3.9m.	100%
1979-80	464	846	1,310 44.0%	1,399	266	1,665 56.0%	1,863	1,112	2,975 100%
NS	5.1m.	4.3m.	9.4m. 78.2%	2.4m.	.2m.	2.6m. 21.8%	7.6m.	4.5m.	12.1m. 100%
1985-86	461	865	1,326 42.0%	1,450	367	4,817 58.0%	1,915	1,240	3,155 100%
NS	5.2m.	4.3m.	9.5m. 72.4%	2.5m.	.3m.	2.8m. 22.6%	7.7m.	4.5m.	12.2m. 100%
% Change: 1949-50 to 1985-86	+34	+191	+107	+47	+62	+50	+44	+137	+70

Source: U.S. Department of Education (1988: 144, 182)

contributed to higher education in these two countries. Table 10-22 shows the number of private and public two-year and four-year colleges and their respective enrollment of students from 1949-1950 to 1985-1986 in the United States. The number of four-year public colleges and universities increased from 344 to 461, whereas that of the private ones increased from 983 in 1945-50 to 1,450 in 1985-86. This explains that four-year public colleges and universities increased by 34 percent, while the private ones increased by 48 percent. The number of private four-year colleges and universities was 2.85 times as many as that of public ones in 1949-1950 but increased more rapidly to reach 3.14 times as many as that of the public ones in 1985-1986. This clearly indicates that private colleges and universities outnumber the public ones. However, private colleges altogether have 2.5 million students enrolled which indicates less than half the number of students enrolled in the public ones.

Concerning two-year community colleges, the public ones far surpass the private ones both in terms of the rate of increase in the number of colleges and the number of student enrollment. The public community colleges increased from 297 in 1949-1950 to 865 in 1985-1986, whereas the private ones increased from 227 to 367. The discrepancy between public and private colleges becomes more salient in the enrollment. The public ones have an enrollment of 4.3 million students, while the private ones only .3 million. The two-year and four-year private colleges and universities all together, which account for 58.0 percent of the total colleges and universities in the Unites States, have 22.6 percent of the total students enrolled. The remaining 42 percent are the public colleges and universities with 77.4 percent of the total students. This clearly demonstrates that public colleges and universities in the United States educate over two-thirds of the entire students.

The Korean case is almost opposite to that of the United States. As Table 10-23 indicates, the national and other public colleges and universities in Korea accounted for only 22 percent of the total and accommodated about 25 percent of the total students in 1988. On the other hand, the private undergraduate colleges and universities explain 78 percent of the total and have an enrollment of 75 percent of the total students. A similar trend can be observed in the case of graduate programs. In 1988, the national and other public graduate schools account for only 20.8 percent of the total enrollment. They have 27.4 percent and 36.2 percent of the students in the masters and doctoral degrees programs, respectively. About 79 percent of the total graduate schools are the private ones, which enroll 73 percent and 64 percent of the total masters and doctoral degree programs.

The higher educational institutions in Korea face several major challenges. First of all, private colleges and universities depend on student tuition for about 70-93 percent of the overall operating expenses. Therefore, in order to meet the financial needs, eighteen private colleges and universities had admitted a total of 557 students for the past four academic years in violation of admissions criteria in

Table 10-23 Number of Colleges (NC), Departments (ND), and Students (NS) Enrolled in Korea

	Undergraduate Programs					Graduate Programs			
	National	Public	Private	Total		National	Public	Private	Total
1985									
NC	21	1	78	100		41	2	158	201
%	21%	1%	78%	100%		20%	1%	79%	100%
ND	888	22	2,216	3,126	MA/S	490	18	1,416	1,924
%	28%	.7%	71%	100%		25%	.9%	74%	100%
					Ph.D.	330	5	680	1,015
						32%	.5%	68%	100%
NS	181,346	3,631	521,344	706,321	MA/S	15,340	196	42,162	57,698
%	26%	.5%	74%	100%		26%	.3%	74%	100%
					Ph.D.	3,815	11	6,654	10,480
						36%	.1%	64%	100%
1988									
NC	22	1	81	104		51	2	198	251
	21%	1%	78%	100%		20%	.8%	79%	100%
ND	1,055	25	2,546	3,626	MA/S	647	23	1,863	2,533
	29%	.7%	70%	100%		25%	.9%	74%	100%
					Ph.D.	372	5	760	1,137
						33%	.4%	66%	100%
NS	179,556	3,747	552,098	735,401	MA/S	15,213	219	41,456	56,888
	24%	.5%	75%	100%		27%	.4%	73%	100%
					Ph.D.	3,907	21	7,073	11,001
						36%	.2%	64%	100%
% Change 1985 to 1988									
NC	4.7%	0.0%	3.8%	4.0%		24.4%	0.0%	25.3%	24.8%
ND	18.8%	13.6%	14.8%	15.9%	MA/S	32.0%	27.7%	31.5%	31.6%
					Ph.D.	12.7%	0.0%	11.2%	12.0%
NS	-0.9%	3.2%	5.9%	4.1%	MA/S	-0.8%	11.7%	-1.6%	-1.4%
					Ph.D.	2.4%	90.9%	6.3%	4.9%

Source: *The Dong-A Annual* (1989: 552-553)

return for their financial contribution of 64.3 billion Won ($9,18 million)(see Table 10-24). Illegal admission of the students resulted in the dismissal or voluntary resignation of nine presidents, warnings

Table 10-24 Private Colleges, the Number of Students Illegally Admitted, and Their Financial Contributions: 1986-1988

Colleges & Universities	Number of Students Illegally Accepted	The Amount of Financial Contribution : Billion won ($million)
Woo Suk	233	23.73 ($3.39)
Ho Nam	37	.73 ($ .10)
Han Kuk Medical School	61	8.19 ($1.17)
Dong Kuk	45	19.8 ($2.83)
Young Nam	30	4.3 ($ .61)
Korea Theological Seminary	15	7.56 ($1.08)
Inha	43	
Kyong Gi	46	
Korea	21	
Hang Gong (Aeronautical)	6	
Hahn Lim	8	
Sae Jong	2	
Kyong Sung	5	
Jeon Ju	3	
Hahn Yang	4	
Kyong Hee	4	
Sook Myung	3	
Joong Ang	1	
Total	557	64.3 ($9.18)

Source: *The Korea Times* (Sept. 19, 1989)

to two presidents, and reprimanding one president by the Ministry of Education.

Financial shortages were such that the student-to-faculty ratio in all of the private colleges and universities on average as of 1990 was 36 versus 23.8 in the public and state colleges. Both national and other public colleges in Korea show more students per faculty member than the cases of the United States and Japan.

A third concern is the lack of clear separation between the ownership of private colleges centered around the Board of Directors and the administrators. The founders and their Board of Directors tend to encroach upon university administrators concerning the academic decisions, the personnel decisions on the hiring, firing, and promoting of faculty members and the appointing of all major administrators including university president, vice president for academic affairs, and college deans. The monopolistic and dictatorial control and supervision of private universities by the founders and their second-generation owners rather discourage other private industries and philanthropists from financial contribution.

Student participation for the university affairs under the full swing of "democracy on the campus" since 1988 shows a mixed blessing. In the case of Chosun University, long-held student protests and demonstrations brought about the resignation of the founder, Park Chul Woong, from the presidency. On the other hand, Lee Chong Chul, who was elected the president of Saejong University, was not confirmed by the Ministry of Education because of the unacceptable level of student involvement in the election of the university president. The Ministry of Education contends that the ideal of campus democracy by no means should allow the students to choose the university president, overpowering the Board of Directors and the presidential search committee (*The Korea Times*, 9/6/1989).

One very significant challenge which universities--private and public--face today in Korea is the traditional Confucian-biased preference of social sciences and humanities to science and engineering and the preference of four-year college education to two-year technical and skill training. Such preferences are further reinforced by differential amounts of wages based on the level of education.

A recent survey report by the Korea Employers Federation (KEF) from 544 nationwide firms indicates that despite more difficult and time-consuming load, four-year engineering major graduates received only 3.4 percent higher starting salaries than their humanities and social sciences counterparts. This discourages many bright students from pursuing engineering degrees (Table 10-25).

Table 10-25 also suggests that junior technical college graduates receive 81.1 percent of the four-year college-graduate salary. The starting salary for high school male graduates accounts for about 69 percent, whereas that of female counterparts was only 52.1 percent.

Industries and universities, however, become clearly aware of the fact that once Korea had successfully passed through the first three stages of economic development (such as importation, import-substitution, and labor-intensive industries), entered into capital-intensive heavy and chemical industries, and finally into high-technology medium industries, two-year trained technicians, four-year educated engineers, and researchers with advanced degrees are in greater demand than at any previous time in history. Since 1985,

Table 10-25 Monthly Payment of Beginning Employees by Occupation and Level of Education

Types of Occupations	4-Year College Business	4-Year College Engineer	2-Year Technical College	High School Education Technical	High School Education A&S(M)	High School Education A&S(F)	Junior High Male (M)	Junior High Female (F)
Mining	301,984	318,079	275,808	253,684	227,876	167,218	236,561	154,543
Manufacturing	305,543	314,724	246,886	213,540	210,985	160,366	164,876	129,764
Food Processing	304,376	314,401	259,221	230,802	228,274	168,321	179,145	132,377
Textile	297,578	305,355	241,795	208,261	208,032	153,939	161,189	124,993
Lumber & Furniture	276,290	301,162	231,349	200,003	197,079	144,617	161,562	133,185
Paper & Publishing	310,194	322,232	242,945	208,671	207,310	153,751	164,843	123,411
Chemical	329,531	332,107	254,350	225,593	226,092	170,185	167,123	130,942
Metalloid Mining	305,293	321,604	240,805	203,021	201,744	154,722	151,499	122,947
Primary Metal	290,115	303,316	249,802	208,095	204,372	155,309	162,811	130,273
Machine	307,396	317,146	244,524	196,658	196,579	163,362	171,951	135,518
Construction	318,832	335,884	277,366	230,311	224,132	164,085	118,576	--
Others	278,848	301,882	236,993	199,076	190,785	156,619	167,620	129,118
Average	303,779	314,172	246,535	212,145	208,889	158,254	165,438	129,069
% with 4-yr business as 100	100.0%	103.4%	81.2%	69.8%	68.7%	52.1%	54.4%	45.5%

Source: *Korea Time* (August 20, 1987)

technicians and engineers have been in great demand, whereas those majoring in humanities and social sciences over-supplied. This is the major reason why only about 64 percent of the annual four-year bachelor's degree graduates were able to get a job in 1985, which declined to 60.3 percent in 1989. On the other hand, the percentage of the two-year associate technical degree graduates who secured jobs (Figure 10-2) had been increasing from 66.8 percent in 1985 to 79.4 percent in 1989.

Figure 10-2 Percent Yearly Employment: 2-Year Technical and 4-Year College Graduates

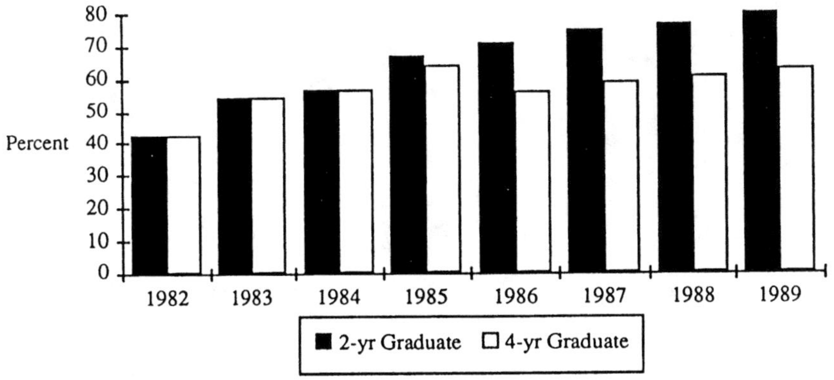

Source: *The Korea Times* (March/30/1990)

Figure 10-3 Annual Enrollment as Freshmen in 2-Yr and 4-Yr Colleges

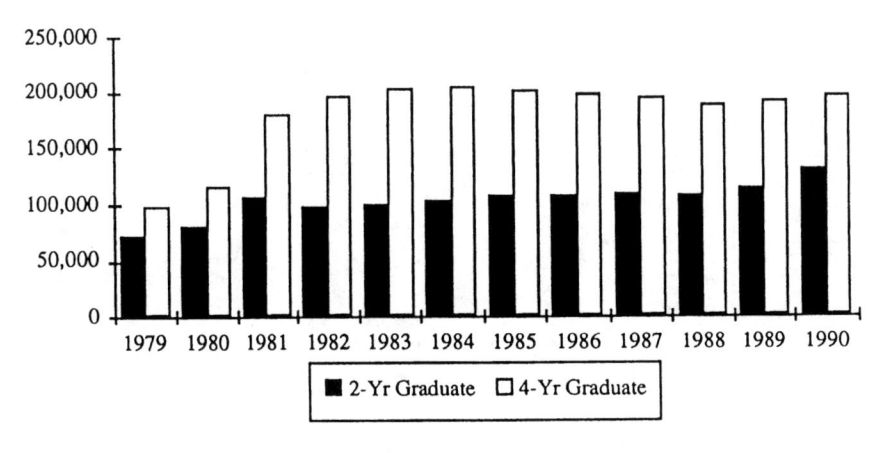

Source: *The Korea Times* (March/30/1990)

    The high rate of employment, the cost of about seventy percent that of four-year college in tuition, the offering of evening classes for those who are working in the industries during the day, and the gradual decline in the wage gap between the two-year technical and

Figure 10-4 Shortage of Human Resources

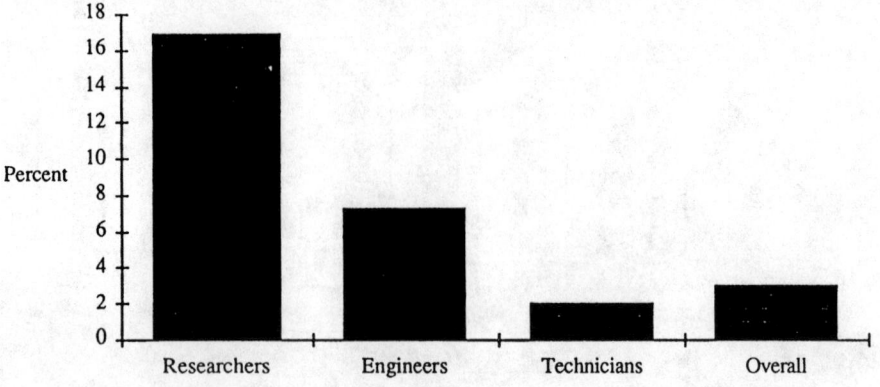

Figure 10-5 Percent International Competitiveness in Various Technological Areas

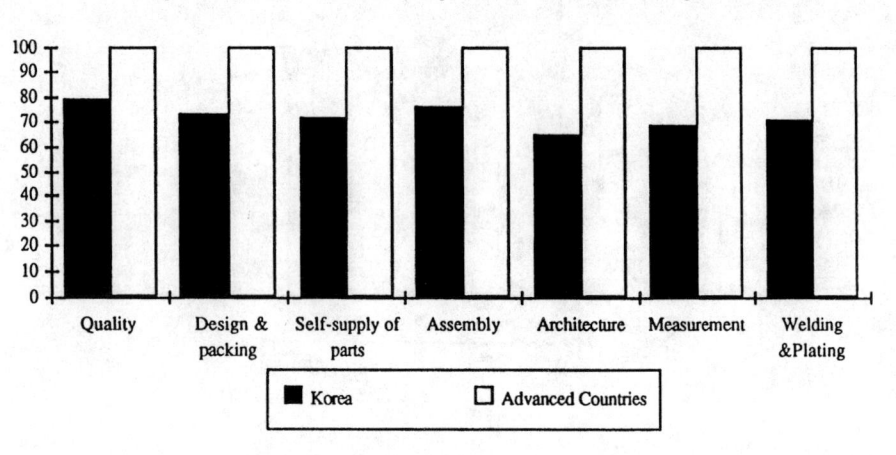

Source: *The Korea Times* (Sept./5/1990)

four-year colleges become the major reasons for the increase in the enrollment as freshmen in two-year technical college. Therefore, enrollment in two-year colleges, for example, increased from 100,270 accounting for 49 percent that of the four-year college enrollment in 1983 to 130,505 amounting to 66 percent that of the four-year college students in 1990 (Figure 10-3).

Industries began to face the shortage in supply of technicians, engineers, and researchers in such specialized areas as electronic, mechanical, electrical, chemical, and biomedical engineering, and other high-tech areas. Figure 10-4 indicates the shortages of 1.99 percent of two-year trained technicians, and 7.23 percent of four-year educated engineers. The most serious shortage is in the number of researchers with an advanced degree (16.27 percent) for long-term research and development so as to enhance international competition and reduce the ever-increasing royalties for foreign copy rights. The short supply of technicians, engineers, and researchers, clearly witnesses the fact that Korea's level of international technological competitiveness ranges from 65 percent that of the advanced countries in design engineering to 79 percent in quality and performance of the Korean-made products (Figure 10-5). The shortage causes an intense competition among giant corporations and the scouting of many experienced technicians to large corporations from small and medium industries, whose skilled labor shortage numbered 198,382 as of January 1990 (*The Korea Times*, 2/1/1990).

The future trend of decrease in the demand for unskilled labor and the corresponding increase in the demand for two-year trained technicians, four-year educated engineers, and researchers with an advanced degree in Korea is clearly manifested in a report on the Prospect for Changes in the Occupational Composition in the Industrial Human Resources by the Industrial Research Institute. Figure 10-6 shows that the unskilled labor workers accounted for 69 percent in 1989 but will decline to 65 in 1994. Four-year trained engineers and researchers with an advanced degree should also increase from 9.83 percent and 2.98 percent in 1989 to 11.24 percent and 4.57 percent in 1994, respectively. The two-year trained technicians will increase from 65 percent to 68 percent in 1990.

The most serious challenge in the area of higher education in Korea is the ever-widening gap between the number of applicants for colleges and the number of freshmen actually admitted to the colleges. The gap is attributed to two main reasons. The first one is the number of college applicants far surpassing the maximum number of students to be admitted. Therefore, every year, more than half of the total applicants since the mid-1970s have not been admitted. This results in a geometrical increase in the number of

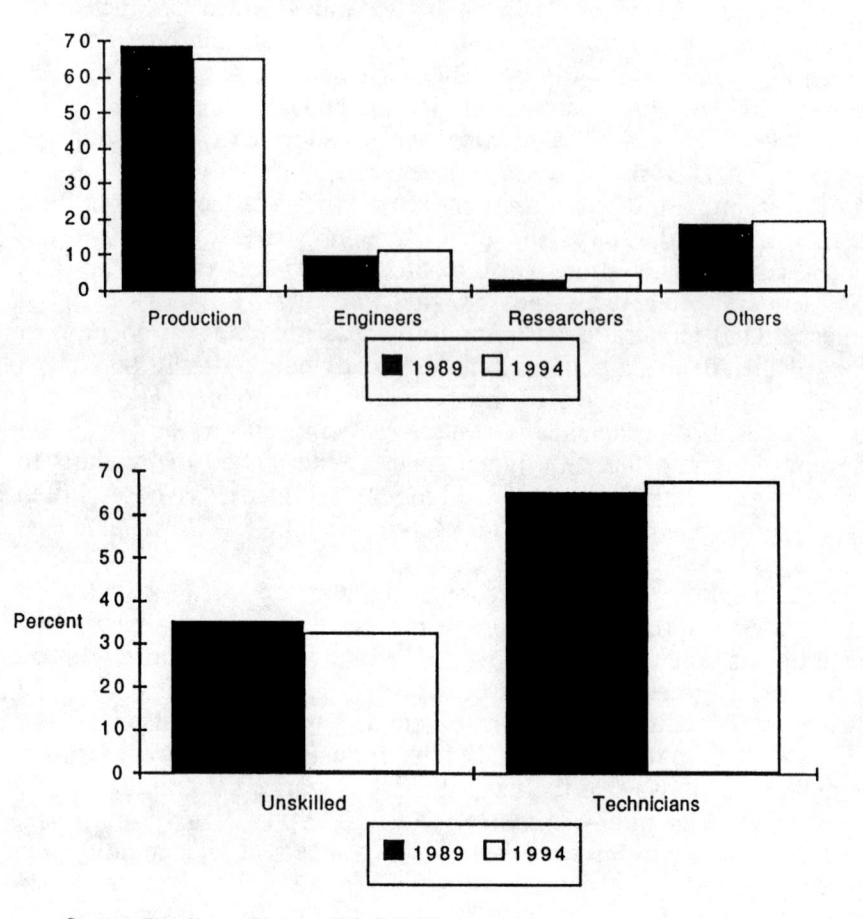

Figure 10-6 Prospect for Change in Occupational Composition in Industrial Human Resources

applicants who were not admitted in the previous academic years and continue to take the entrance examination for possible admission. The so-called delinquent applicants add a mounting pressure to the upcoming high school seniors for the admissions into the colleges. As Figure 10-7 indicates, the absolute number of freshmen admitted to the colleges has increased 89 percent from 172,472 in 1979 to

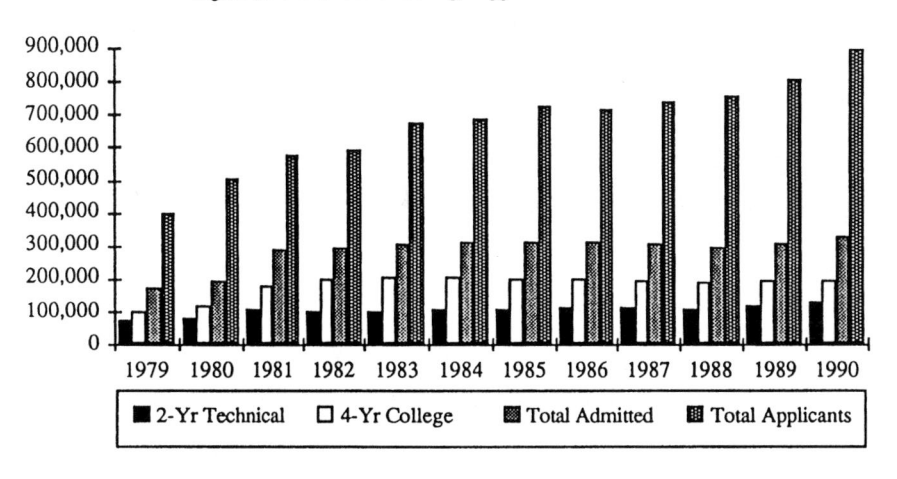

Figure 10-7 Number of College Applicants and Freshmen Admitted*

[Bar chart showing number of college applicants and freshmen admitted from 1979 to 1990, with categories: 2-Yr Technical, 4-Yr College, Total Admitted, Total Applicants. Y-axis ranges from 0 to 900,000.]

Source: Adapted from *The Korea Times* (March 3/1990)
*Excluding nontraditional and teachers' colleges

327,035 in 1990. But the number of applicants increased by more than 122 percent during the same period. Therefore, the percentage of applicants who were admitted to the colleges rather decreased from 43 percent in 1979 to only 36 percent in 1990. Therefore, 64 percent of them in 1990 were denied admission.

To meet the demands of the ever-increasing applicants for college educational opportunities and to meet the shortage of technicians and engineers, the Ministry of Education accredited two technical colleges in 1991 and decided to accredit three additional four-year colleges, nine two-year technical colleges, and allow two colleges to be universities in 1992 (*The KoreaTimes*, 9/15/1990). The increase in the number of private colleges and universities in Korea has still matched the increased number of applicants. However, Korea exceeds all advanced countries in the rate of increase in the number of private colleges.

The traditional Confucian value of education continues to influence many wealthy landlords and businessmen to establish private colleges and universities not only in the capital but in all major cities across the nation. The rapid increase in the number of private colleges is just the tip of a huge iceberg of the contribution of the private sector to higher education in Korea in the name of scholarships for both need base and academic merits, funds for library collection of books and journals, for example, from Korea Gunpowder, Inc.'s pledge of 25 billion Won ($35.7 million) to the Seoul National University (*The Korea Times*, 8/21/1990) and the construction of university buildings.

As Tables 10-22 and 10-23 demonstrate, there is no doubt that private colleges and universities have played and continue to play a more significant role in Korea than in any advanced countries. The vital contribution of the private sector to higher education in Korea, which in turn becomes the basic foundation for rapid economic development, democratization, and welfare of the people, cannot be overemphasized.

Housing by the Private and Public contributions

Housing Status

Housing status becomes the most serious concern for both the government, industries and citizens in Korea. As Table 10-26 indicates, for the past ten years from 1975 to 1985, the number of housing units, which had been constructed, accounts for 28.9 percent of increase, whereas the number of households increased by 42.3 percent. Therefore, the percentage of housing units to the total households had steadily declined from 70.4 in 1975 to 66.7 in 1980 to 63.7 in 1985. This suggests that as of 1985 there were only 6.1 million housing units for 9.57 million households.

Due to rapid industrialization, urbanization, and the emphasis of the nuclear family value, housing shortage becomes more serious in the cities than in the rural counties. When percent housing supply is compiled by the number of the total housing units divided by the total households, the rural counties as a whole had about 85 percent of housing supplies, while the cities in general had only 52.8 percent in 1980 and remained the same in 1985. A similar gap can be observed between four major cities and the provinces.

The supply of 6.1 million housing units in 1985, however, does not mean that 6.1 million households owned these units separately. Table 10-27 rather suggests that only 5.1 million households resided in their own housing units. The remaining 1 million housing units were then owned and rented rather than resided for themselves. Therefore, the actual percentage of the owner households that resided in their own housing units is 53.3 percent, while 46.7 percent

Table 10-26 Number of Households, Housing Units, and Percent Housing Supply

		1975 (unit=1,000)	1980 (unit=1,000)	1985 (unit=1,000)	% Increase: 1975-1985
Total:	Households (1)	6,722	7,969	9,571	142.3
	Housing Units (2)	4,734	5,319	6,104	128.9
	% Housing Supply (3)	53.7	66.7	63.7	10.0
All Cities	(1)	3,364	4,670	6,331	188.1
	(2)	1,809	2,468	3,349	185.1
	(3)	53.7	52.8	52.8	-0.9
All Counties	(1)	3,334	3,299	3,240	97.1
	(2)	2,925	2,851	2,755	94.1
	(3)	87.7	86.4	85.0	-2.7
Special Cities:					
Seoul	(1)	1,384	1,837	2,324	167.9
	(2)	744	948	1,176	158.0
	(3)	53.7	52.6	50.6	-3.1
Pusan	(1)	498	688	839	168.4
	(2)	254	343	427	168.1
	(3)	51.0	49.8	50.8	-0.2
Taegu	(1)	273	362	500	183.1
	(2)	129	174	246	190.6
	(3)	47.2	48.0	49.2	2.0
Inchon	(1)	160	244	339	211.8
	(2)	87	132	194	222.9
	(3)	54.3	54.1	57.2	2.9
Provinces:					
Gyong Gi	(1)	647	839	1,165	180.0
	(2)	462	546	719	15536
	(3)	71.4	65.0	61.7	-9.7
Kang Won	(1)	360	375	403	111.9
	(2)	284	294	31.5	110.9
	(3)	78.8	78.4	78.1	-0.7
Chung Buk	(1)	280	291	321	114.6
	(2)	228	233	245	107.4
	(3)	81.4	80.0	76.3	-5.1
Chung Nam	(1)	532	582	654	122.9
	(2)	440	466	501	113.8
	(3)	82.7	80.0	76.6	-5.1
Jeon Buk	(1)	444	452	490	110.3
	(2)	364	368	386	106.0
	(3)	81.9	79.7	76.8	-5.1
Jeon Nam	(1)	696	765	834	119.8
	(2)	570	610	641	112.4
	(3)	81.8	79.7	76.8	-5.0
Kyung Buk	(1)	674	930	731	108.4
	(2)	567	750	576	101.5
	(3)	84.1	80.6	78.7	-5.4
Kyung Nam	(1)	625	711	851	136.1
	(2)	504	532	596	118.2
	(3)	80.6	74.8	70.0	-10.6
Cheju	(1)	92	105	118	128.2
	(2)	70	73.3	81	115.7
	(3)	76.0	73.3	68.6	-7.4

Source: Adapted from the *Dong-A Annual* (1990: 507-508)

Table 10-27 Occupancy Status of Housing Units by the Households (units=1,000 & %)

	Year	Number	Residential (including Apartments) Units Ownership	Lending with Premium to be repaid back	Monthly Rental	Others	Residing at non-residential Units
Total	1980	7,969	4,659(58.4)	1,898(23.8)	1,219(15.3)	153(1.9)	43(0.6)
	1985	9,571	5,107(53.3)	2,163(22.6)	1,918(20.0)	345(3.6)	42(0.4)
All Cities	1980	4,670	1,995(42.7)	1,651(35.4)	921(19.7)	67(1.4)	36(0.8)
	1985	6,331	2,595(41.0)	1,935(30.5)	1,582(25.0)	186(2.9)	36(0.6)
All Counties	1980	3,299	2,661(80.7)	247(7.5)	298(9.0)	86(2.6)	7(0.2)
	1985	3,240	2,512(77.5)	228(7.0)	336(10.4)	159(4.9)	6(0.2)
Special Cities:							
Seoul	1980	1,837	811(44.2)	691(37.6)	298(16.2)	2(1.1)	16(0.9)
	1985	2,324	952(40.9)	829(35.6)	469(20.2)	62(2.7)	13(0.6)
Pusan	1980	688	271(39.4)	263(38.2)	143(20.8)	6(0.9)	5(0.7)
	1985	839	322(38.4)	211(25.1)	281(33.5)	20(2.4)	5(0.6)
Taegu	1980	362	132(36.5)	126(34.8)	95(26.2)	5(1.4)	4(1.1)
	1985	500	188(37.6)	140(28.0)	154(30.8)	14(2.8)	4(0.8)
Inchon	1980	244	110(45.1)	88(36.1)	41(16.8)	3(1.2)	2(0.8)
	1985	339	154(45.4)	114(33.6)	61(18.0)	8(2.4)	2(0.6)
Provinces:							
Kyung Gi	1980	839	479(57.1)	178(21.2)	159(19.0)	18(2.1)	5(0.6)
	1985	1,165	593(50.9)	279(23.9)	242(20.8)	45(3.9)	6(0.5)
Kang Won	1980	375	259(69.1)	34(9.1)	65(17.3)	16(4.3)	1(0.3)
	1985	403	250(62.0)	39(9.7)	75(18.6)	38(9.4)	1(0.3)
Chung Buk	1980	291	212(72.7)	37(12.7)	34(11.7)	7(2.4)	1(0.3)
	1985	322	218(67.7)	40(12.4)	50(15.6)	12(3.7)	2(0.6)
Chung Nam	1980	582	424(72.8)	88(15.1)	57(9.8)	12(2.1)	1(0.2)
	1985	655	440(67.2)	104(15.9)	87(13.3)	22(3.3)	2(0.3)
Jeon Buk	1980	452	338(74.8)	72(15.9)	33(7.3)	8(1.3)	1(0.2)
	1985	490	344(70.2)	72(14.7)	58(11.8)	15(3.1)	1(0.2)
Jeon Nam	1980	765	561(73.3)	120(15.7)	68(8.9)	15(2.0)	1(0.1)
	1985	835	566(67.8)	138(16.5)	98(11.8)	31(3.7)	2(0.2)
Kyung Buk	1980	718	522(72.7)	78(10.9)	94(13.1)	22(3.1)	2(0.3)
	1985	733	510(69.6)	72(9.8)	115(15.7)	35(4.8)	1(0.1)
Kyung Nam	1980	711	470(66.1)	107(15.1)	114(16.0)	17(2.4)	2(0.2)
	1985	851	503(59.1)	117(13.8)	195(22.9)	34(4.0)	2(0.2)
Cheju	1980	105	67(63.8)	16(15.2)	18(17.1)	3(2.9)	1(1.0)
	1985	118	67(56.8)	8(6.8)	33(28.0)	9(7.6)	1(0.8)

Source: *The Dong-A Annual* (1987: 560)

of the households did not have their own and had to rent housing units. Again, the situation became more serious in the cities than in the rural counties. All major cities including Seoul, Pusan, Taegu, and Inchon had 41 percent of housing supplies on average. Hence, there were more than two households per housing unit. Since many wealthy house owners can afford and prefer to occupy their own housing unit alone, there are three or more than three households that had to share each housing unit. Loss of privacy had long been forsaken. The overcrowded conditions and the sharing of one or two bedrooms by the members of one household made it difficult to have conjugal privacy. Sharing the same kitchen, bathroom, and shower room by different households caused immense inconvenience and embarrassment.

The quality of the existing housing units, of course, was improved. For example, traditional kitchens, which were usually located outside the main residential areas and therefore did not have piped water, heat in winter, air conditioning in summer, electric or gas ovens, accounted for 81.8 percent of the total existing housing in 1980. But about 16.4 percent of them were remodeled so as to have a modern kitchen by 1985. About fifteen percent of them improved to have flush toilet in their bathroom. About twelve percent of them began to have hot water and/or cold piped water, respectively. Nevertheless, as of 1985, 65 percent still did not have modern kitchens, flush toilets, and piped water in the shower room (Table 10-28).

Table 10-28 Quality of Housing Units

Year	Total units	Kitchen Modern	Traditional	Bathroom Flush	Traditional	Shower Room Hot Water	Cold Water	No Water
Total 1980	5,319	966 (18.2)	4,353 (81.8)	977 (18.4)	4,342 (81.6)	531 (10.0)	642 (12.1)	4,146 (77.9)
1985	6,104	2,109 (34.6)	3,995 (65.4)	2,018 (33.1)	4,086 (66.9)	1,221 (20.0)	855 (14.0)	4,028 (66.0)
Change		1,143	-358	1,041	-256	690	213	-118
All Cities 1985	3,349	1,840 (54.9)	1,509 (45.1)	1,821 (54.4)	1,528 (45.6)	1,009 (32.8)	675 20.2)	1,575 (47.0)
All Counties 1985	2,755	269 (9.8)	2,486 (90.2)	197 (7.2)	2,558 (92.8)	122 (4.4)	180 (6.5)	2,453 (89.1)

Source: *The Dong-A Annual* (1990: 510)

Frustration over the inability to make purchase of their own residential units, and the subsequent loss of privacy, overcrowded conditions, inconvenience, and embarrassment, however, became no longer a major concern for 4.46 million household tenants who accounted for 46.3 percent (22.6% + 20.0% + 3.6%) of the total households in 1985. Their primary concern today is whether they can continue to reside at the current rental housing unit or will be forced to move out of it because of their failure to put up a geometrically galloping additional amount of the lease premium. As Figure 10-8 indicates, the average housing price increased by 26.2 percent in general from 1983 to 1989. But the lease (deposit) premium which the tenants have to put up as a large sum, sufficient to generate an interest that can offset monthly rental fee for the landlords, and therefore to be paid back at the time of release of a lease contract, increased by 90.1 percent.

Figure 10-8 Percent Increase in Sale and Rental Prices in 1989: The Prices of 1983 as 100% *

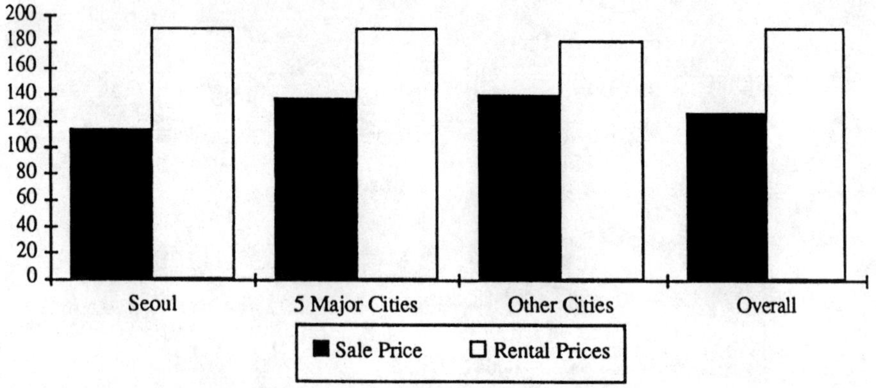

Source: *The Korea Times* (October/17/1990)
*The housing price as of December 1983 as the base with 100 scores

Since the housing price increased faster than the saving by the tenants, the dream of the average Korean households to own their own housing unit, no matter how small and humble it may be, evaporated. Their only hope is to stay in their rental housing unit by saving and putting up a lease premium so that the lump sum premium paid at the time of the lease contract and an additional amount added each year should remain intact. Almost every year, landlords demand fifteen to twenty percent increase of the premium, with a certified notice as an alternative to vacate the rental housing unit for other tenants.

The consequence is the demotion of more and more of households from the status of being able to save and put up a premium for lease without losing their money and without paying the sinking monthly rental fee to that of paying and the subsequent giving away of their monthly rental fee. Table 10-27 illustrates that the increase of the lease premium four times as much and as fast as that of the housing prices began to force the lower middle-income class and the poor households to move from the status of premium payment to that of monthly payment. Over the five years from 1980 to 1985, about 1.2 percent of the total households amounting to 265,000 households were forced to move out of their premium status residential units to monthly rental units. About five percent of households across all cities experienced such painful demotion. The gradual demotion reaching the level of utter humiliation starts from the premium housing units to the monthly rental units, from the city residence to the outskirt residence, from the above-ground residence to the underground residence, from the underground residence to the refugee areas with tin, tent, or vinyl makeshifts near the garbage dumping sites (*The Korea Times*, 10/17/1989, 4/10/1990, 4/14/1990).

Housing Development by Joint Efforts

Making one's fortune at one stroke by speculative investment in land has been the simplest and most basic economic principle in such a territorially small country like Korea. Land speculation is indeed fanned by over seventy percent of land covered with steep mountains, the remaining small size of arable land, a high density of population in the urban areas in particular, the increase in the number of households centered around the nuclear families, the desire of the youngsters to separate themselves from their parents, and the rapid rate of urbanization. These become the root causes for the geometrically increasing price of land, far surpassing the inflation rate and the wage increase rate. The higher the land value goes, the higher the price of housing units.

Land speculation becomes a full-time job for many wealthy homemakers with enough cash-in-hand from their savings, their spouses' incomes, or bank loans and also access to inside information on development plans. The purchase of any size of land speculated for model city and/or housing development helps them become *nouveau riche* overnight.

During the height of the rumor that the development of a new international airport was planned in the areas of Young Jong Do and Yong Yu Do, research was conducted to examine the ownership of the land in that area. To great dismay of the public, the ownership of about 72 percent of the land was already in the hands of non-residents of the area. When the development of a new model city in the area of Ilsan was announced, it was revealed that 32 percent of its land was owned by the non-residents. When Seo Gwee Po, Cheju Island was chosen for a new model city, 77 percent of the land was also under the ownership of non-residents. It was known that two Seoul youngsters--twelve and nine years old--owned 630,000 pyong (514 acres) of the forest area. About thirty percent of the land in Gyong Gi province and 55 percent of the forest area of Ahn San were known to be owned by the Seoulites (*The Korea Times* , 6/28/1990). To put it in another way, unbridled land speculation, gobbling up of more and more land, and the subsequent gaining of fortune without productive labor can be illustrated by the statistics that the top five percent of the total land owners hold 59.7 percent of the total housing construction land. The geometric increase of land value for the year of 1989 alone incurred the profit of 68 trillion Won ($97 billion), which accounted for 180 percent as much as the wages the total labor workers earned in Korea.

The relative deprivation of a vast number of wage earners who were not able to purchase their own housing units and who could not afford to pay the ever-increasing lease premium for the mere renewal of the rental of their current housing units, heightened the question of social justice in land speculation. The culmination of democratization on the inception of the Sixth Republic and the ever-widening reverberating voice of the grassroots supported by opposition politicians, intellectuals, and the mass media finally began to suggest the concept of "public ownership" as far as land and housing were concerned despite their overall endorsement of the principles of free enterprise and market system in Korea.

The government was subject to criticism for its reluctant and grudging acceptance and enforcement of the concept of "public ownership of land and housing." The National Tax Bureau's (NTB) lukewarm attitude and the postponement of its report for longer than one and one-half months than was originally scheduled cast doubts on the credibility and sincerity of the investigation. The frequent visitation of the bureau's staff to the giant conglomerates was seen as a collusion between the two and the subsequent betrayal to the general public by allegedly minimizing the magnitude of the non-business purpose land owned by the industries. The public's alarm was further reinforced by: the inconsistent and different criteria to distinguish between the business and non-business purposes of the invested land; tacit admission of corporate land whose deeds were registered by their key staffs with disguise; the alleviation of tax on the speculative land to a much less extent than the original tax standard; and no coercive enforcement of the disposal of the land within six months once it was declared non-business speculative investment purposes (*The Korea Times*, 7/30/1990).

Nevertheless, the government ordered the NTB to examine the potential for the purchase of land for non-business speculative purposes by giant conglomerates whose bank loans exceeded 1,500 billion Won ($214.3 million). As Table 10-28 shows, the NTB declared that 72.8 million pyong (89,215 acres) out of 215.3 million pyong (263,897 acres), which accounted for 33.8 percent of their total land, were not for business expansion but for speculative investment purposes. The NTB urged them to dispose of the non-business land soon. However, the government refrained from fully enforcing the "public ownership of land," which prevents the business and individuals from purchasing the land for the speculative purpose. The government also stopped short of the full-scale implementation of the concept of "public housing," which puts a ceiling on the number of housing units per individual and prohibits the wealthy and speculative businessmen from purchasing housing units by registering the deeds with the names of other persons or their relatives.

Public Ownership of Housing and Land

The government belatedly but firmly began to take a series of actions to place restraints in rampant land speculation and to alleviate the housing shortage. First of all, the National Bank Supervision Bureau (NBSB) fired Lee Byung Sun, President of Han-il Bank for his tacit admission and his aiding and abetting of giant conglomerates in borrowing and purchasing the land, not for the purpose of business expansion, but for the purpose of speculation. The NBSB also suspended three of his key staff from duties. President Lee and his staff were aware of the misuse of their banks loans for the land speculative purposes and were clearly in violation of the bank loan policy and yet approved an excessive amount of loan to Sam Sung Conglomerate. The NBSB issued warnings to the presidents of four additional national banks: Chae-il (First National Bank), Sahng-up (Commercial Bank), Cho-hung (Korea Rehabilitation) and Seoul Shin-tak (Seoul Trustee Bank). The NBSB announced its plan to pursue investigation of other major banks in the capital and local cities for possible violation and commission of similar practices of illegal loans to other business firms or individuals (*The Korea Times*, 5/11/1990).

In addition to tight control over banks and other lending institutions, in 1990, the government combined the land property tax and the tax on the ownership of an excessive size of land together into a comprehensive land progressive tax system. The government imposed a relatively smaller tax on small size of land, and a proportionally much higher tax on excessive size of land owned by a few wealthy.

As Table 10-29 shows, about 63 percent of the land owners held a small size of land such that their annual property tax amounted to only $14. A total of 96 percent of the land owners were declared as small-size owners. Therefore, their annual tax became less than $143. On the other hand, the amount of property tax was geometrically increased for those few wealthy, who were less than one percent of the total landowners. The progressive tax system evidenced the tremendous increase of property tax for large landowners, for example, from a range of $714 to $1,428 to above $1.4 million. The government justified the adoption and implementation of a comprehensive land progressive tax system on the grounds that the substantial increase in the number of large-size land owners from 47,619 in 1989 to 70,487 in 1990 clearly indicated the evidence of speculative investment on land by the wealthy, fanning and aggravating the price of land and the price of housing units.

Furthermore, the government enacted a law which required land owners to mandatorily report land ownership and buildings on the land and to mandatorily request the permission for future land transactions from the government. The report requirement applies to the ownership of the size of land of 330m^2 or above for residential and commercial purpose, 1,000m^2 or above for manufacturing plant construction, and 660m^2 or above of green area

Table 10-29 Progressive Land Property Tax System: 1990   (unit=Korean won)

Amount of Tax	Number of Persons	Percent Total Owners	Number of Persons Increased from 1989 to 1990
Smaller Amount of Tax			
Less than 10,000 ($14)	5,130,000	63%	NA
10,000-30,000 ($14) - ($43)	2,420,000	25%	NA
30,000-50,000 ($43) - ($71)	510,000	5%	NA
50,000-100,000 ($71) - ($143)	330,000	3%	NA
Subtotal	8,390,000	96%	NA
Larger Amount of Tax			
500,000-1 million ($715) - ($1,428)	35,580	0.4%	8,215
1 million-10 million ($1,428)-($14,286)	31,429	0.3%	12,354
10 million-50 million ($14,286)-($71,429)	2,826	0.03	1,831
50 million-100 million ($71,429)-($142,857)	372	0.004%	261
100 million-1,000million ($142,857)-($1,428,571)	242	0.0026%	170
Subtotal	70,489	.737%	22,870

Source: *The Korea Time* (October 13, 1990)

in the case of within-the-city limit. The ownership report also applied to the size of 5,000m² or above of farm land, and 10,000m² or above of forests and fields in the case of outside-the-city limit. The ownership report should apply to the specifically designated cities and counties of several major provinces (Table 10-30).

The law also requires the land owners to request permission from the government on the future transaction of land, its rental, or its lease in excess of: 90m² of residential and commercial zone; 200m² of manufacturing plant construction zone; 660m² of the green area in the case of within-the-city limit. In case of outside-the-city limit, the permission applies to the size of land in excess of 1,000m² of farm land, and 2,000m² of forests and fields.

The government expects that the ownership report and transaction permission would prohibit the potential for large-scale, monopolistic ownership of land by giant conglomerates and a few

Table 10-30 Requirement for Mandatory Ownership Report and Transaction Permission

Objectives			
1. To prohibit large-scale, monopolistic ownership of land by giant corporations and the wealthy			
2. To prohibit land investment on speculation			
3. To maintain housing price stability			

Type	Ownership Report of: Land Buildings on the land		Transaction Permission of: Land ownership, Buildings on the land, Rental, Lease
Size		(m^2)	(m^2)
Within the city limit	Residence & commerce	330	90+
	Manufacturing plant	1,000	200+
	Green area	600	660+
Outside the city limit	Farm land	5,000	1,000+
	Forest and field	10,000	2,000+
	Others	1,000	500+
Areas to be included			
Six major cities			The entire green areas: <u>64.4% of the total areas</u>
			(km^2)
Kang won	9 cities and counties		1,554
Kyong Gi			13 cities and counties: 584
Chung Buk			6 cities and counties: 670
Chung Nam			7 cities and counties: 824
Jeon Buk	2 cities and counties		5 cities and counties: 462
Jeon Nam	4 cities and counties		4 cities and counties: 125
Kyung Buk	1 county		15 cities and counties: 1,770
Kyung Nam			18 cities and counties: 2,483
Cheju			3 cities and counties: 319

Source: *The Korea Time*, September 6, 1988

wealthy. The government also would restrict the potential for excessive speculative investment on land so as to maintain housing price stability (Table 10-30).

The Korean Model of Social Welfare Services 465

Table 10-31 Non-Business Related Land Owned by Forty-Five Giant Corporations
(units= acres and $million)

Corporations	National Tax Bureau's Report				Ratio (1)/(2)		Voluntary Disposal	
	Total Size of Land(1)		Land on Speculation(2)					
	Size	Value	Size	Value	Size	Value	Size	Value
Total	175,717	25,068	59,403	1,448	32.8	5.7	25,538	14.5
Top Ten:	88,179	15,892	21,192	1,016	24.0	6.3	12,770	14.4
Sam Sung	24,493	3,595	1,237	222	5.1	6.2	4,708	*19.2
Korea Gun Powder	14,146	1,125	9,060	181	64.0	16.2	522	3.7
Sun Gyung	13,832	1,268	492	63	3.6	5.0	2,578	*18.6
Ssang Yong	8,546	581	2,013	65	23.6	11.3	922	9.4
Han Jin	6,094	632	4,456	71	73.1	11.4	538	8.8
Lucky Kum Sung	5,935	2,281	1,294	52	21.8	2.3	1,142	19.2
Dae Woo	3,964	2,098	354	25	8.9	1.2	122	3.0
Lotte	1,572	1,456	362	172	23.0	11.9	718	*45.6
Dong A	965	459	302	42	31.4	9.3	709	*73.5
35 Additional Ones	87,538	9,175	38,211	432	436	47.0	12,767	14.5
Doo San	5,298	604	528	35	10.0	5.8	777	*14.6
Dong Kuk Steel	4,627	407	3,875	52	83.7	2.3	36	0.7
Kum Ho	4,469	627	2,887	51	64.6	8.2	384	8.5
Ko Oh Rong	2,994	280	2,111	13	70.5	4.6	506	16.9
Kuk Dong Const.	1,501	218	1,394	23	92.9	10.7	248	16.5
Dong Bu	1,550	367	403	20	26.1	5.4	287	18.5
Dong Yang Cement	3,254	162	1,330	15	40.9	9.8	42.3	13.0
Kuk Dong Refineries	638	902	97	6	15.2	0.7	57	9.0
Tong Il	8,386	211	105	15	13.4	7.2	3,762	*44.8
Han Ra	2,902	240	1,410	5	48.6	2.1	767	26.4
Dong Yang Chem.	4,321	187	317	7	7.4	4.0	1,202	*27.8
Jin Ro	1,656	254	401	2	24.2	0.9	328	19.8
Woo Sung Const.	1,089	479	28	37	2.6	7.9	488	*44.8
22 Others	44,853	4,237	23,325	151	51.9	3.5	3,502	7.8

Source: *The Korea Time* (May 11, May 30, and July 30, 1990)

*Indicates voluntary disposal of land exceeding the size designated by the government.

Public and Private Partnership

When the government exerted pressure for the top ten conglomerates to dispose of their non-business speculative land, only four of them--Sam Sung, Sun Gyung, Lotte, and Dong-A--disposed of more of their land than was suggested by the government. But the six remaining corporations showed a strong resistance and grudgingly announced the disposal of their land, far less than demanded by the government. Ten conglomerates got rid of only

14.4 percent of their land contrary to 24.0 percent as demanded by the government (Table 10-31).

The concept of the "public ownership of housing units" refers to the government's adherence to: the principle of one household-one housing unit; a progressive property tax as discouragement for excessive ownership; and the enforcing of the housing units as the sole purpose of residence but not that of speculative investment. The government, however, shows restraint from the full adoption and implementation of the "public ownership of housing units" and the "public ownership of land." A first and most important reason for the restraint is the potential for the stagnation of the housing construction business, if and when the government would rigidly prohibit the prevailing free market permissiveness of one household-multiple housing units and subsequently impose a tight grip on the hands of the wealthy who only can afford to purchase housing units beyond their own residential one. This may cause newly constructed housing units to remain unsold and empty. This may slow down the increase in the price of housing units in terms of a short-run perspective. But the housing construction businesses are not able to continue to build more houses. This may cause a significant decline of housing supplies and worsen the housing shortage because of the continued increase in the number of households in the long-run. The subsequent gap between the supply and demand of housing units in the long-term perspective accelerates the price of housing units and dissipate the dream of many households to have their own housing units.

The sharp increase in the price of housing units from 1987 until 1990 in fact results from the sharp decrease in the supply of new housing units starting from 1983 due to the stagnation of housing businesses whose construction funds were frozen in the newly built houses. The only potential buyers, who were able and willing to buy were then all prohibited from the purchase because of the government's rigid restriction on the ownership of multiple housing units per household. Therefore, housing demand fell more sharply than the supply since 1983. The housing shortage in the long run became aggravated and fanned the housing price increase since 1989 (see Figure 10-9). The Institute for National Land Development (INLD) predicts the vicious cycle of another housing construction stagnation to occur in 1992, if and when the government would reinvigorate the "public ownership of housing units" and the "public ownership of land" (*The Korea Times*, 10/15/1990).

Table 10-32 Housing Construction Plan   (unit=1,000)

Construction by: The Gov't:	1988-1989	1990	1992	Total	Eligible for
Permanent	40	60	150	250	Those under gov't financial & medical support
Long-Term lease	90	40	120	250	Low income households
Low Income	130	100	170	400	Sale for low income labor workers
Subtotal	260 (33.7%)	200 (44.4%)	430 (55.1%)	900 (45.0%)	
The Private Sector	510 (66.3%)	250 (55.5%)	340 (43.9%)	1,100 (55.0)	
Total	770 (100.0%)	450 (100.0%)	780 (100.0%)	2,000 (100.0%)	Allocation of 10 trillion won ($14.3 billion)
Households	9,913	10,188	10,748		
Housing Units	6,869	7,399	8,179		
% Housing Supply	69.3%	72.6%	76.1%		

Source: *The Dong-A Annual* (1990: 168-169; 507-509)

The government's second major concern is that the concept of "public ownership" clearly violates the constitution of the republic, which guarantees the "freedom of residence" and "the right to move at will" (Article 14), the "right of property of all citizens" (Article 23-(1)), and the "private enterprises and ownership" (Article 126).

The government finally attempted to strike a balance, moving short of full implementation of the concept of "public ownership" and yet taking the proper measures for the housing problems. Being subject to complaints and critiques by the conglomerates for the coercive disposal of their land, the government this time encouraged thirty-nine remaining giant corporations to dispose of their non-business speculatively owned land voluntarily for the sake of the reduction of monopolistic tendency of land ownership and the subsequent stability of land value. Private interest groups and associations soon began to play an intermediary role to encourage such voluntary disposal of land and real estate properties owned by corporations: The National Enterprise Association for the thirty-nine conglomerates; The National Chamber of Commerce for large corporations; The Central Committee of the National Enterprise Association for small and medium-size business firms in Seoul; the Local Committees of the National Enterprise Association for local small and medium-size business firms. These private groups and associations voluntarily began to take initiative on: the disposal of non-business land and other properties; the enhancement of "the cultural value for healthy society;" the condemnation of unfair and unjust business transactions; the prevention of illegal labor-management disputes; the supply of housing units for labor workers; and the encouragement of investment in business expansion and modernization rather than on speculation (*The Korea Times*, 5/14/1990). The government's appeal to voluntary actions and the private sector's intermediary role in fact encouraged thirty-five conglomerates to voluntarily dispose of their real estate properties 29.1 percent less than initially demanded by the government but four times as much as the government expected them to get rid of. The size of their voluntary disposal was equivalent to the percentage of land disposal by the top ten conglomerates as otherwise coercively enforced by the government (Table 10-31).

The government finally announced the five-year housing development plan with the expenditure of 10 trillion won ($14.3 billion) with the cooperation from the private sector housing construction firms (Table 10-32). The five-year plan revealed that in the year of 1988-1989, the private sector planned to contribute to about 66 percent of the total housing construction, whereas the state 34 percent. Moreover, the public and private sectors set up different priorities in their housing plans. The government, on the one hand, focused on low-income families, who currently received financial support and medical protection from the government mainly due to their income being below the poverty level. President Roh Tae Woo explained that the government planned to build a total of 250,000 housing units for low income families, who depended on financial and medical support from the government and another 250,000 for other low income families. The government would require them to put up a range of one to two million won ($1,428-$2,857) and a very modest rental fee of 30,000 to 40,000 won ($42.8-$57.1) per month for one or two bedroom housing units. Then they can have a near permanent or a long-term lease. The housing complexes were to be equipped with schools, playgrounds, nurseries, hospitals, placement centers, and the like. Another 400,000 housing units were planned for sale to low income families with sixty percent of the total price as a 20-30 year low interest rate loan. The home buyers would be required to pay 7 million won ($10,000) as a down payment and 90,000 won ($128.57) as a monthly mortgage (*The Korea Times*, 2/25/1989).

The private sector, on the other hand, planned to contribute to 55 percent of the total housing construction primarily for middle and upper middle-income families who want to move to a bigger and better house and from one or two bedroom to three or more bedroom house. There is no question that the government's five-year housing development plan would not accomplish the target number of housing units without the energetic participation of private housing construction firms. The plan does not have a magic power to solve the housing shortage within five years, but housing supply would be significantly improved from 69.3 percent in 1988 to a whopping 76.1 percent in 1992. The government plans to reach 90 percent by 2000.

The government also allocated 900 billion won ($128.5 million) to make loans available to low income families under the lease of housing units with less than 7 million won ($10,000) who recently faced the demand of an additional significant amount of the lease premium from their landlords far exceeding wage increase and inflation rates. They were eligible for up to 3 million won ($4,285.70) of loan, payable by the end of two years in a lump sum or to be extended for two additional years in case of the extension of current lease. The annual interest rate should be determined by the chief executives of the local governments not exceeding 7.5 percent. Due to housing shortages more serious in Seoul, the government allocated 600 billion won ($85.7 million) for those residents in Seoul and 300 billion Won ($42.9 million) for other cities (*The Korea Times*, 5/19/1990). A slow, but steady increase in the housing supply will be continuously expected when the government skillfully strikes the balance between the speculative investment of land and housing by giant corporations and the wealthy and the public ownership of land and housing for the homeless, low income families.

Conclusion

The Korean model of social welfare services is based upon several major premises. First, lavish expenditures in social welfare services tend to cause middle- and low-income people to have ever-increasing dependency on the state. Second, this, in turn, causes them to lose the incentive to voluntarily and energetically help themselves find jobs, improve their skills, and pursue higher levels of income. Third, once a state has deeply committed to socialistic programs, assuming full responsibility for all social welfare services, the state is less likely to swing the pendulum toward a capitalistic system and to drastically cut welfare expenditures. Fourth, developing countries like Korea have limited government budget; therefore, they are not able to adopt and implement all types of welfare services fully and simultaneously. The welfare services inevitably should be prioritized. Fifth, welfare services with economic stagnation or recession means no improvement or the equalizing of the ever-shrinking size of a pie, namely, the equal distribution of poverty. Hence, welfare expenditures for the quality of life of today shall not impair the continued economic growth, which needs investment in human and material resources, equipment, machines, and R & D. Sixth, a state alone is not financially able to take care of all welfare services. Therefore, affirmative and proactive role of the private sector in the delivery of welfare services is sincerely encouraged and welcomed.

Based upon these premises, the government provides its employees--civilian and military--with pension whereas business firms contribute fifty percent of the premiums for their employees to join the pension protection. As of 1988, the pension participants accounted for about 32 percent of the total population. More of the self-employed such as farmers, fishermen, and small shop owners continue to join the pension every year (Table 10-7).

Covering only nine percent of the people in the year of 1977, medical protection was finally able to encompass 100 percent of the Korean people by 1989. Again, the state takes care of all government employees, public and private school teachers. The state also provides the poor and the low-income with medical care protection and medical care assistance, respectively. But the private sector plays a vital role, because business firms, which hire about three times as many as the government employees and private school teachers, contribute to medical protection of their employees. Farmers, fishermen, and urban self-employed were finally included into the protection in 1988 and 1989 respectively, with the state contribution to their premium on the basis of four income grades (Table 10-9 and 10-10).

The state support for the old, the handicapped, and the poor accounted for about nine percent of the total population in 1982, but rapidly declined to only six percent in 1987 due to the continued economic growth, the increase in the employment, and the overall enhancement in the level of income (Table 10-15).

In the United States, about 78 percent of the college students receive education from the public institutions and only 22 percent of them from the private ones (Table 10-12). In contrast, in Korea, 74 percent of all the students receive education from 71 percent of all departments of the private colleges. There is no doubt that private colleges and universities play a major role in higher education of the Korean students (Table 10-23).

The high physical quality of life which Koreans enjoy, despite less than ten percent of the state expenditures for social welfare services, indeed can be explained by the enthusiastic participation in and contribution to welfare services by various private agents. They include medical doctors and students, various professional associations, hospitals, philanthropists, educators, church, and the like. There is no question, then, that the Korean model of social welfare services can be carefully examined for both developing economy-priority states and advanced welfare-priority states.

Chapter 11 Life, Liberty and the Pursuit of Happiness

Interdependence Among Economy, Democracy and Welfare

There are a plethora of books and articles on Korea. Some focus on economic development, whereas others exclusively examine democracy or welfare. Life, liberty, and the pursuit of happiness of individual citizens, however, cannot be conceived by economic growth, democratization, or welfare services alone, but by all three. They are indeed highly interdependent, sometimes positively and other times negatively. The interdependence and the subsequent impact of one on the other two, the two on the one, or the three on the three can be illustrated with many scenarios.

Economic growth, in the long run, can enhance the overall living standard of the citizens as a whole. Demand and supply of goods and services and various mutual supports by means of contracts, transfer of technological know-how, financial help for the opening or the expansion of plants, and prepayment may promote a sense of the common destiny between the firms of different sizes. The sharing of stocks by the workers and other employees may heighten a sense of joint ownership of the firms by labor and management such that the concerted efforts--hard work, commitment, learning, apprenticeship, and creativity--from both sides may increase productivity, value added, export, and the subsequent sharing of the profits.

Economic growth, in the short-run, however, may widen the gap between rich and poor, between the *chaebol* and other small firms in their financial strength and in the amount of loans available, and between management and labor concerning how to share the profits. The mutually conflicting interests and the ensued zero-sum games may ultimately enter into the political arena, where political participants, thanks to tremendous progress toward democratization, may enjoy greater degree of freedoms, exercise more of their rights, and feel freer to wield more political power than ever before to uphold the values of their own preference (for example, either more socialistic or capitalistic, more pro-business or pro-labor) and to get a larger piece of pie on the table of the allocation of resources. The more democratized a state becomes, the louder the voice of its different political agents, the greater the potential for a highly disharmonious political orchestra tends to be. The necessity of political support from different agents for securing and maintaining the government power may inevitably force the political parties and their leaders to reluctantly succumb to the demands of "political inflation"--more loans, more houses, more wages, and more welfare services.

By the same token, the more allocation of resources to satisfy the needs of the agents today for various welfare services may result in the less allocation of the remaining resources in investment, R & D, and subsequent impairment of export and economic growth. This may have a further chain reaction to the imperative of economic decline and the retrenchment of welfare services.

Continued Democratization

Given these scenarios--negative and positive--the interdependence among polity, economy, and welfare in Korea continues to show progress toward a positive end. Among these three, polity leads the other two, strides toward further democratization, and steers the economy and welfare.

Ever since the embarkation of the Sixth Republic in 1988 with the guarantee of basic freedoms and rights, five major political tasks involving further democratization have been the important concerns. They are: 1) the preference of either a presidential form or a parliamentary form of government and the related proposals for the amendments to the constitution for the implementation of the selected form of government; 2) the restoration of local self-government; 3) democratization within the armed forces often seen as the last bastion, the only remnant and the specter of the former authoritarian legacy; 4) the abolition of corruption; and 5) the elimination or major revision of the Anti-Communist Law, the National Security Law, and other related legislations and institutions as the legacy of the Cold War, which have long been inhibiting both democratic movements and the opening of dialog between North and South Korea in the private sector.

The preference of a presidential or a parliamentary form of government, which had been a major controversial issue between the leaders in power and those out of power, seemed to have settled down first in 1987. The ever-increasing size of the pro-democracy, anti-regime coalition finally reached the critical point for the matter of survival of the Fifth Republic such that on June 29, 1987, Roh Tae Woo had no options but to declare "democratic reforms" together with yielding to the popular demand of the continuation of a presidential form of government.

The Sixth Republic, which was established upon a direct popular presidential and legislative elections, however, from its embarkation, had to face a multi-party system with the government Democratic Justice Party (DJP) being downgraded to be one of the four minor parties. The consequence was lack of power of the DJP and the subsequent humiliation and embarrassment by three major opposition parties on the floor of the National Assembly. The perception of weak leadership of Roh Tae Woo caused his regime to fail to resolve injustices and wrongdoings committed by the Fifth Republic and to fail to take measures for proper compensation to the victims in an expedient way. In addition, labor disputes and violent demonstrations began to prevail across major business firms.

President Roh was becoming desperate for possible alternatives to the existing weak leadership. He still believed a parliamentary form of government, which he reluctantly had to discard in 1987, would be favorable for him and his party to maintain power. In collusion with the New Democratic Party and the New Democratic Republican Party, after a series of secret negotiations behind the scenes, a new party called the Democratic Liberal Party (DLP) was established on February 15, 1990. The core of the agreements made among the top leaders of the three parties was the adoption of a parliamentary form of government upon the amendment to the constitution and the maintaining of the government power by sharing the power among themselves. The DLP, however, is not a new political party but a loose coalition party with three distinct factions and faction leaders of their original parties.

Thanks to the freedom of speech and the press, the news on the DLP's collusion spread. University students, professors, clergymen, and the Peace and Unification Party (PUP), the only left-out formerly second major opposition party, began to wage protests against the DLP. The entire PUP National Assemblymen submitted resignations of their Assembly seats *en masse* on July 14, 1990. This caused the legislative branch to be practically defunct and to be in recess despite its many urgent outstanding issues, including the budget approval prior to the beginning of the new fiscal year. The PUP president, Kim Dae Jung, began a hunger strike for an unlimited period of time with the two outstanding demands to the DLP: 1) the renunciation of the conspiracy to attempt to adopt a parliamentary form of government because of the continued desire of the absolute majority of the Koreans to elect their president directly; and 2) the restoration of local self-government. Deterioration of Kim Dae Jung from his hunger strike and the mounting pressure from all walks of life forced President Roh Tae Woo and the DLP to admit that, so long as the majority of voters would like to uphold a presidential form of government, a parliamentary form of government seemingly superior for a stable democracy should not be considered for its implementation at the present time.

President Roh and the DLP violated their original timetable of the implementation of local self-government by April 30, 1988 as mandated by their own legislation and delayed it again against the agreement among the then four political parties, which scheduled the election of the members of legislative councils for local government at least within the first half of the year of 1990. The main cause for the long overdue delay of its implementation was the intricate relation of local politics to the control of the power of the central government. In fact, "the competition between the political parties for the control of local governments" was seen as "a microcosm of the competition for the control of the central government" (Pae, 1988a: 137).

The opposition party demanded a partisan competition in local government election, a medium-size district system, where at least two should be elected local council members, the permission of nationally-known party leaders to campaign for their party's local candidates, and an unrestricted frequency and scope of campaigns by the candidates. The DLP, on the other hand, was equally concerned with winning as many local council members by its own party as possible. Contending views and strategies notwithstanding, the PUP made it clear that the legislation for the implementation of local self-government should be passed prior to the deliberation of the budget for FY 1991. Both parties reached an agreement on the agenda. Hence, the PUP Assemblymen returned to the National Assembly on November 19, 1990, four months and five days after their mass resignation, to deliberate these urgent issues (*The Korea Times*, Nov.

20, 1990). The Local Self-Government Election Law was finally enacted and the election was held in 1992.

Democratization in the armed forces can also be clearly witnessed. A twenty-four years old army private, Yoon Suk Yang deserted from the barrack on September 23, 1990 with confidential papers, computer disks, and data which the Defense Security Command compiled by spying on more than 1,300 civilians and politicians including all opposition party politicians including Kim Dae Jung and excluding all government party leaders. Opposition politicians, citizen groups, lawmakers, and dissidents reacted in outrage and made protests, calling for the dissolution of the intelligence units, and claiming that the scandal indeed proved the "undemocratic nature of Roh Tae Woo government." President Roh immediately fired his Defense Minister, Lee Sang Hoon, the Commander of the Defense Security Command, Lt. Gen. Cho Nam Pung, and replaced them with former Army Chief of Staff, Lee Jong Koo and Lt. Gen. Koo Chang Hoe, respectively. President Roh said that "the government would enact reforms to meet with circumstances befitting the new era," although he did not elaborate his plan (*Omaha World Herald*, Oct. 8, 1990).

The Ministry of Defense also adopted military service regulations and barrack life regulations with the aims of democratization and rationalization of the soldiers in their barrack life. Their few outstanding characteristics include: 1) the political neutrality against the long-practiced coercive requirement of officers and the enlisted to campaign for the government party and its candidates; 2) the prohibition to support or challenge a political party or a political interest group; 3) no coercive voting in the ballot; 4) no physical assault and other inhumane treatment of the enlisted in the barracks. These and other written rules and regulations specify proper disciplines and punishment on those who commit the violations (*The Korea Times*, Sept. 11, 1990). Democratization can be clearly observed in the army training camps for recruits. The camps have had a long reputation for their near complete isolation from the society and severe punishment and inhumane treatments of the recruits. However, since 1989, the major objectives of the training camps were changed from punishment, threats, and inhumane physical hardship to rational, voluntary participation, and willingness of the recruits to gain training, confidence, and combat readiness with *esprit de corps* and patriotism. The training camps were subsequently open to the parents and relatives of the recruits to have on-the-spot observation of the training programs, the quality of meals and barrack life, and the democratic environment (*The Korea Times*, Sept. 20, 1990).

Corruption and embezzlement have long been an important issue of the concerned citizens and leaders. Lack of hard evidence has often become a good excuse for the prosecutors to not promptly exercise law enforcement. There had spread a rumor that the National Assemblymen serving on the Commerce Committee took an overseas trip with $57,000 contributed by the automobile manufacturing association lobbyists for lenience on emission standards and for the restrictions on foreign car imports. The hard evidence secured this time by the prosecutors finally obligated the opposition parties to belatedly accept a legislative ethics bill proposed by the government party to abolish illegal lobbying and corruption (*The Korea Times*, Jan. 25, 1991).

The last obstacle for further democratization--the Anti-Communist Law, the National Security Law, other related laws and institutions--may have a less promising prospect for their immediate abolition and/or radical changes, so long as the threats from North Korea do not dissipate with mutual force reduction, the renunciation of the use of nuclear and other fatal weapons, and the replacement of the contemporary truce by a peace treaty. Despite criticism by Amnesty International and Asia Watch on Korean government's violations of human rights involving unification activists, the complete abrogation of these laws may enfeeble the government to regulate and supervise indiscriminate and discrete interactions and exchanges of humans and materials with North Korea by students, professors, the media, business, and a host of others in the private sector. This may hinder the government in pursuing a coherent unification policy and even endanger the national security of South Korea. Therefore, more judicious, time-consuming effort and wisdom need to be exchanged and examined on this question. However, there is no question that the adherence to a presidential form of government, the deliberation of local self-government legislation, reforms in the armed forces, and the efforts to minimize corruption and embezzlement clearly evidence the continued democratization in Korea by a pro-democracy, moderate majority coalition consisting of both government and opposition parties against the minority coalitions, which still advocate a radical leftist and a radical rightist alternatives.

Continued Economic Development

It is this pro-democracy, moderate majority coalition that has fought and secured and continues to steer democratization in Korea. It is the same coalition that simultaneously and strongly believes that the state should continue to steer the helmsmanship of economy, providing business and entrepreneurs with a variety of incentives, and requiring good performance from them in return for their benefits. The Seventh Five-Year Economic Development Plan covering the period of 1992-1996, which the state recently announced with ambition and excitement, still demonstrates the potential for continued growth, for example, from $6,767 of per capita GNP in 1992 to $10,190 in 1996 and the target of $5.5 billion of surplus in account balance of trade in 1996 (see Table 11-1).

Table 11-1 The Seventh Five-Year Economic Development Plan ($1=715 Korean won)

Category	1992	1993	1994	1995	1996
GNP (10 billion won)	210,634	234,521	263,348	294,462	392,253
($ million)	294,593	328,001	368,318	411,834	548,605
Per capita GNP	6,767	7,495	8,302	9,197	10,190
Growth Rate (%)	7	7	7	7	7
Gross Savings Rate (%)	34.6	35.3	35.8	36.0	36.0
Gross Investment Rate (%)	34.6	34.7	34.8	34.9	35.0
Current Account Balance ($billion)	0.0	1.0	3.0	4.0	5.5
Exports ($ billion)	76.5	84.5	94.0	102.5	112.0
Imports ($ billion)	81.0	88.5	96.5	104.5	113.0
Debt Service ($billion)	-4.5	-4.0	-2.5	-2.0	-1.0
Foreign Debts ($ billion)	-5.5	-4.5	-1.5	2.5	8.0
Percent Manufacturing	31.9	32.2	32.6	32.9	33.3
Percent Agriculture	8.5	8.1	7.8	7.4	7.0

Source: *The Korea Times* (October 27, 1990; July 13, 1991)

As Figures 4-2 and 4-5 and Tables 4-2 and 4-7 demonstrate, Korea has successively and successfully passed through the stages of import, import substitution of daily necessities, export-oriented labor-intensive light industry, export-oriented capital-intensive heavy and chemical industries, and export-oriented technology-intensive intermediate industries. Korea continues to pay attention to the imperative of science and technology and the subsequent investment in R and D and its application to all light, heavy, and intermediate industries for higher value-added productivity and comparative advantage.

One major target of quality improvement in the technology-intensive intermediate industries is automobile manufacturing. Making debut with Pony in 1974, three automobile manufacturers in Korea continued to increase the production of automobiles for domestic demands and exports. The number of production, domestic sales, and exports had exponentially increased from 1980 to 1988 (see Table 11-2). Korea took the tenth and the eighth ranks in the quantity of cars produced and exported, respectively. As Table 11-3 indicates, Korea is the only developing country which competes with the advanced Western European countries and Japan, and exported 11.6 percent of the 2.4 million cars imported in the American automobile market

However, Korea's automobile export does not have a continued rosy prospect. The year of 1989 (see Table 11-2) showed a significant decline of export, for example, from 576,000 cars in 1988 to 356,000 in 1989. Both the government and automobile industries attributed the 38 percent decline of export to Korean won devaluation, a long overdue labor-management dispute, the subsequent shut-down of plants, an unprecedented wage increase, loss of price competition in the overseas market, and the decline in the demand of overseas consumers for automobiles. However, despite the improvement in these areas of concern in 1990, no corresponding increase was evidenced in the export.

The government and automobile industries belatedly became aware of the imperative of quality of automobiles as the preponderant key to the success in export. While they boasted of over ninety percent of all parts domestically self-sufficient, the auto industries still had to pay as of 1990 58.6 percent of the total sale amount of auto export to the foreign suppliers of the major parts. About 1,100 domestic firms provided the automobile industries with 20,000 parts of 5,000 different types. However, 95.1 percent of them were small and medium-size firms. Among them only 57 firms had their own research. The majority of them were not able to financially allocate a certain percentage of profits for research due to the economy of scale. It was ironic that the industries with the production of over 1 million automobiles had no major research institutes, while steel, shipbuilding, electronics, communications, and

Table 11-2 Automobile Production in Korea

Year	Total Number		Domestic Sales		Export	
	Number	% Increase	Number	% Increase	Number	% Increase
1980	123,000	100 %	102,000	100 %	25,000	100 %
1985	378,000	307 %	239,000	234 %	123,000	100 %
1986	601,000	488 %	284,000	278 %	306,000	1,224 %
1987	978,000	795 %	417,000	408 %	546,000	2,184 %
1988	1,082,000	879 %	521,000	510 %	576,000	2,304 %
1989	1,129,000	918 %	762,000	747 %	356,000	1,424 %

Source: *The Korea Times* (April 4, 1990)

Table 11-3 Automobile Sales in the USA: January -October 1989

Supply	Producers	Number Sold	Percent Sale	% Total Import
Domestic	GM	2,862,289		
	Ford	1,840,677		
	Chrysler	798,213		
	Foreign Manufacturers	647,393		
	Subtotal	1,708,200	71.8 %	
Imports from:				
Japan	Toyota	426,016		
	Nissan	369,690		
	Honda	188,184		
	Mitsubishi	141,175		
	Four others	251,598		
	Subtotal	1,708,200	19.9 %	70.9 %
Europe	Volkswagen	110,309		
	Others	313,071		
	Subtotal	423,380	4.9 %	17.6 %
Korea	Hyundai	175,027		
	Daewoo	42,605		
	Others	61,105		
	Subtotal	278,737	3.2 %	11.6 %
	Import Subtotal	2,410,317	28.2 %	
	Total	8,558,889	100.0 %	100.0 %

Source: *The Korea Times* (November 21, 1989)

all other major industries had government-supported research institutes. Nevertheless, continued research recently brought the exciting news that Korea-made engines would have their own debut. This proved to be more powerful and efficient than the engines thus far imported from Japan and other countries. Therefore, all Korea-made automobiles will have their own Korea-made engines installed. This will greatly reduce the royalties for foreign technology and dependence on foreign countries in automobile industries.

Gary Marchant highlighted Korea's current status and its future prospect for continued high technology research and development in the following areas:

1. Korea is the world's sixth greatest producer of electronic goods.

2. She is the third (after the USA and Japan) to produce a supercomputer.

3. Korean industries have developed a number of unique products. One of them is a fingerprint recognition device, which is faster and less expensive than the existing US and Japanese systems. Cross Engineering will market the system known as "The Magic Finger" to police forces and other investigation offices around the world.

4. In July 1990, Samsung Electronics announced a plan to launch the world's first double, video machine called "the GV 2000." This can play audeotape and record another program simultaneously. The company is now manufacturing 30,000 of the machines for Arizona-based Go-Video Corporation.

5. Hewlett Packard and Samsung began to operate a joint venture in Seoul in 1989 to develop a low-cost, high-volume workstation for less than $5,000 within two years.

6. HDTV (High-definition television) is another area Korean scientists and engineers are working to improve movie-quality television reproduction. Goldstar, Daewoo, and Samsung Electronics plan to manufacture HDTV sets for $100 billion market overseas. The domestic broadcasting of HDTV sets is also planned by 1996.

7. Korea also planned its plan in 1990 to launch its first satellite into orbit aboard its own rockets by 1993 with sixty percent of both rocket and satellite parts Korean made (Marchant, Sept. 17, 1990).

Life, Liberty and the Pursuit of Happiness 483

There is no doubt that technology-intensive intermediate and heavy industries will be continuously enhanced. Due to the ever-increasing orders for new ships during the 1980s and 1990s and the increase in demand of a variety of quality steel products from heavy and intermediate industries, Pohang Steel Corporation (POSCO), for example, invested 18,146 billion won in 1988 and 20,056 billion won in 1989 for the facility improvement, and expanded 19,271 billion won for the construction of the Third Kwang Yang Steel facilities. They amounted to a total of 57,473 billion won, which were equivalent to $8.04 billion. This accounted for about twelve percent of Korea's total annual investment in the manufacturing sector for the past three years. The Third Kwang Yang, completed on December 4, 1990, has the capacity to produce 2.7 million tons of steel and was equipped with the world's most sophisticated state-of-art facilities, which could enhance much higher value-added productivity and comparative advantage (*The Korea Times*, December 5, 1990).

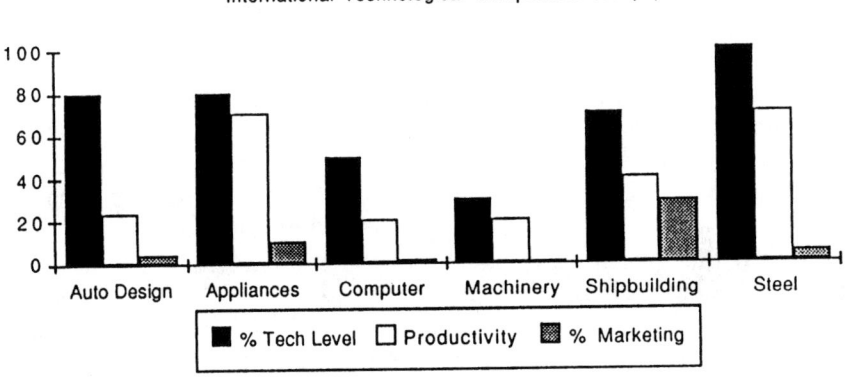

Figure 11-1 The Status of Major Industries in Korea in terms of International Technological Competitiveness (%)

Source: *The Korea Times*, March 15, 1991

The Korean government and the private sector are clearly aware of the current status of their major industries in the international technological competitiveness. As Figure 11-1 shows, only the steel industry has recently reached 100 percent of technological advance as equally competitive as the most advanced countries. On the other hand, automobile design, appliances, textile, and shipbuilding have about 80-100 percent of competitiveness. Korea is far behind the advanced countries in electronics and machinery manufacturing with only fifty and thirty percent of competitiveness, respectively.

To accomplish technological independence and enhance the international competitive edge, the government and the private sector in Korea announced on March 15, 1991 an ambitious plan to contribute fifty percent each, amounting to $2.1 billion to investment in R and D on 919 strategically important targets over the period of 1991-1995. To meet the needs of the ever-increasing demand for engineers and scientists, major universities plan to expand facilities and equipment and enroll 16,000 additional engineer students and 10,000 additional science students during the same time period. To meet the need of additional manufacturing plant sites, the government announced converging of about 1.1 million acres of the recently reclaimed land along the coast in the Chung Nam and Jeon Nam provinces into commercial and manufacturing zones (*The Korea Times*, March 15, 1991).

The prospect for Korea's continued economic growth also can be identified in the light industries. In the long-run economic perspective in Korea, the relative weight of the light industries in terms of their contribution to the overall trade in particular and economic growth in general has been declining, for example, from 55.5 percent of the total amount of export in 1975 to 43.9 percent in 1988. However, the absolute amount of the light industries in their contribution to the overall exports and economic growth still exceeded that of capital-intensive heavy industries and technology-intensive intermediate industries during the late 1980s (see Table 4-7 and Figure 4-5). There is no question, then, that healthy light industries, further enhanced by the application of science and technology and the subsequent higher value-added productivity, become of continued importance. Thanks to the strenuous efforts for quality improvement, Korea-made shoes continue to overwhelm the world shoe markets. Another light industry in Korea for the greater future prospect is golf-related items such golf clubs, golf balls, golf shoes, golf gloves, golf socks, and golf hats. Their total amount of export was $20.6 million in 1988, increased 23.5 percent in 1989, reaching $25.5 million. As of the end of May 1990, the export reached $15.8 million. This explained as much as 44.1 percent increase from the same period of the last year. The success is primarily attributable to the application of technology and engineering explored and developed by Korean World Sports and ten other firms which have had intense competition for quality improvement.

Korea's policy of *nordpolitik*, which was originally intended to pursue political tension reduction and the subsequent peace in the Northeastern region, brought about positive economic outcomes, as well. Diplomatic normalization or progress with one country after another in the Eastern European region, the Soviet Union, and the PRC began to expand economic cooperation and trade. Korea's exports to these countries accounted for $180 million in 1984, but steadily increased to $2,381 million in 1990 and $2,902 million to be expected in 1991. This indicates 0.64 percent of Korea's total exports in 1984, but will be 4.32 percent in 1991 (see Table 11-4).

Table 11-4 Increase in Exports following Korea's Nordpolitik   (unit: $million)

Major Countries	1984	1985	1986	1987	1989	1990	1991
PRC	160	605	736	813	1,437.8	1,462.7	1,601.2
USSR	26	60	50	67	207.7	485.0	804.0
Eastern European Countries	---	97	118	172	249.5	433.7	496.6
Sum (A)	186	762	904	1,052	1,895.0	2,381.4	2,901.8
Total Exports (B)	29,245	34,900	33,900	47,300	62,380.0	64,900.0	67,200.0
A/B	0.64%	2.18%	2.66%	2.22%	3.04%	3.67%	4.32%

Source: For the data from 1984 to 1987, Sung Chul Yang (1989: 545); for the remaining years, *The Korea Times* (December 14, 1990)

Continued Welfare Services

The pro-democracy, moderate majority coalition in Korea continues to endorse a political philosophy of adhering to providing and expanding welfare services in terms of: 1) the financial ability of the state; 2) abstaining from drastic and radical commitment to welfare services as witnessed among the welfare-priority states; 3) encouragement for business firms and the private sector to take active parts in welfare services to the fullest and voluntary extent in cooperation with the state ; 4) increase in welfare services on the basis of the continued economic development such that the continued investment for economic growth should not be disturbed; 5) providing welfare services less in the amount of cash but more indirect, long-term benefits and amenities such as education, health care, and housing, which, in turn, further enhance the spirit of self-help, independence, and economic development.

This is clearly illustrated in Figure 10-1. For the past twelve-year period from 1973 to 1985, the amount of expenditures for social welfare services in Korea did not exceed ten percent of the central government budget. Since Korea is a unitary form of government, its central government's expenditures were tantamount to the total expenditures of the state for welfare services. On the other hand, two dozen states like the USA, Canada, Nigeria, Mexico, West Germany, and the like have a federal type of government. Thereby, their state and local level governments should have made additional contributions to welfare services.

Table 11-5 Sharing Rice with Love

Countries	Tons of Rice	Amount ($million)
Domestic	909	$1.31
North Korea	800	$1.16
Bangladesh	999	$1.45
The Philippines	520,000	$752.23
Cambodia	102	$0.15
India	17	$0.02
Total	522,827	$756.32

Source: *The Korea Times* (Dec. 20 and 21, 1990)

Given such a disadvantage, the Korean model (Figure 10-1) still shows that Korea, with less than ten percent of the total government expenditures, was able to provide all Korean citizens with comprehensive health protection, a pension for those who were hired in the firms with the size of five or more employees, public support for low income, and continued housing expansion with the cooperation of the private sector. Labor and management had experienced sustained unfortunate clashes over the wage as their primary cause of friction. Both of them, however, became belatedly aware of the wage issue as mutually self-defeating, since the increase in housing prices continued to exceed that of the wage. No matter how rapidly the wage may increase, the housing prices continue to far exceed the wage increase. This became a turning point for both of them to look for an alternative in ensuing labor management disputes. Finally, both of them agreed to turn to the issue of housing construction by business firms for either subsidized purchase or lease of the housings for the employees. The contribution of firms in the private sector to welfare services may be exemplified by the case of the POSCO, which provides the employees with schools and scholarships, medical facilities, pollution control, and housing (*The Korea Times*, Dec. 5, 1990).

These welfare services--health, aid to those below poverty income, pension, education, and housing--with a modicum of state welfare expenditures--resulted in Korea's PQLI increasing from the score of 80 in 1973 to 86 in 1985, which led all economy-priority developing states and continued to progress closer toward the overall average PQLI of 93 scores for the welfare-priority advanced countries.

A private sector voluntary campaign for "Sharing Rice with Love," which started on March 1, 1990 with the modest objective to help the underprivileged, gained enthusiastic support and participation from all walks of life. Its headquarters were flooded day and night with the donations from all walks of life, resulting in $756.32 million by the end of 1990. About 900 tons of rice from seven consecutive years of surplus production was purchased and donated to the families without the parents, flood victims, school lunch programs for the low-income students, nursing homes, and welfare service institutes in Korea with $1.31 million.

What was astonishing many citizens and leaders in Korea and abroad was to allocate 99.8 percent of the total amount and donate 800 tons of rice to North Korea, 999 tons to Bangladesh, 520,000 tons to the Philippines, 102 tons to Cambodia, and seventeen tons to India with a total of $755 million. Korea, for the first time in its history, was able to become a giver of financial aid, sharing its blessings with foreign countries in the international community solely for the humanitarian purposes.

Conclusion

The Korean model of rapid economic development as explained in Chapter Four and as summarized in Figures 4-2 and 4-5 and

Tables 4-2 and 4-7 may provide developing countries with a valuable paradigm for their careful examination. The Korean model of rapid democratization as explained in Chapter Eight and as summarized in Figure 8-9 may awaken and enlighten leaders and citizens of many developing nations as to how pro-democracy Koreans were determined and united together to inculcate the democratic procedural principles into the hearts and minds of more Koreans and to subsequently form a broad, pro-democracy coalition so as to outnumber and overpower the anti-democracy, authoritarian, patron-client coalition. Finally, Korea has reached the threshold of democratization. The Korean model of welfare services as introduced in Chapter Ten equally provides a valuable lesson not only for developing countries, which face the agony of how to expand welfare services with a relatively small percentage of their government expenditures, but also the advanced countries, which experience a completely opposite agony of how to reduce the over-promised welfare services having escalated beyond the ceiling of what they can afford. What is more exciting than each of the above three models is the Korean challenge to developing and advanced countries, which wonder how these three--economic development, democratization, and the expansion of welfare services--can be accomplished simultaneously.

Appendix A

Percent Government Expenditures for Economic Development Services, Welfare Services, and Physical Qaulity of Life Index

Countries	Economic & Educational Services 1972-73	1985	Social Welfare Services: Housing, Social Security & Welfare 1972-73	1985	Physical Quality of Life Index 1973	1985
Ethiopia	37.3	31.3	4.4	4.9	16	16
Bangladesh	68.9	58.4	9.8	5.3	33	24
Burkina Faso	36.1	31.3	6.6	7.0	--	15
Bhutan	--	63.9	--	9.1	--	14
Nepal	64.4	60.6	0.7	6.8	25	17
Malawi	48.9	47.4	5.8	2.5	29	18
Zair	28.5	6.1	2.0	0.6	28	36
Burma	35.1	46.9	7.5	9.3	51	51
Burundi	57.3	--	2.7	--	28	--
Togo	--	35.1	--	9.2	28	29
Madagascar	49.6	--	9.9	--	23	44
Niger	--	50.2	--	6.0	14	15
Benin	--	41.3	--	11.7	23	23
Central African Rep. (CAR)	--	37.2	--	7.5	18	18
India	--	28.9	--	4.4	41	44
Rwanda	44.2	60.4	2.6	4.9	27	25
Somolia	27.1	19.7	1.9	--	19	31
Kenya	52.0	44.6	3.9	0.6	40	45
Tanzania	56.3	31.2	2.1	1.4	33	51
Sudan	25.1	29.6	1.4	3.7	33	23
Sierra Leon	--	36.3	--	2.6	29	6
Senegal	--	36.8	--	10.8	22	18
Ghana	35.2	41.8	4.1	7.0	31	38
Pakistan	22.6	30.7	3.2	10.2	37	30
Sri Lanka	33.1	16.6	19.5	11.5	83	79

Appendix A

Countries	Economic & Educational Services 1972-73	1985	Social Welfare Services: Housing, Social Security & Welfare 1972-73	1985	Physical Quality of Life Index 1973	1985
Zambia	45.7	38.9	1.3	6.3	28	47
Chad	36.6	--	1.7	--	20	19
Uganda	37.7	20.3	7.3	2.8	33	38
Mauritania	--	23.9	--	5.4	15	21
Bolivia	43.8	17.5	--	5.4	45	45
Lesotho	44.0	60.4	6.0	3.4	50	49
Liberia	--	44.7	--	31.8	26	28
Indonesia	37.9	49.2	0.9	1.4	50	50
Yemen, PDR	--	30.3	--	--	27	20
Yemen Ara Rep.	--	29.3	--	2.7	27	15
Morocco	44.8	45.0	8.4	7.0	40	43
Philippines	33.9	65.0	4.3	4.0	73	75
Egypt, Arab Rep	--	18.5	--	14.4	46	48
Irory Coast	--	29.7	--	5.7	28	34
Papua N. G.	--	39.6	--	1.4	34	44
Zimbabwe	--	42.3	--	9.3	42	52
Honduras	50.6	39.5	8.7	8.2	50	58
Nicaragua	43.8	--	16.4	--	53	60
Dominican Rep.	49.6	50.3	11.8	15.2	64	66
Nigeria	13.0	--	0.8	9.2	25	33
Thailand	45.5	42.1	7.0	4.6	70	76
Cameroon	--	48.2	--	11.4	28	53
El Salvador	35.8	34.0	7.6	5.7	67	64
Botswana	38.0	47.4	21.7	9.0	38	60
Paraguay	31.7	32.9	18.3	32.9	74	77
Jamaica	--	43.9	--	12.9	87	89
Peru	53.2	--	2.9	2.3	58	60
Turkey	59.9	29.6	3.1	3.6	54	64
Mauritius	27.4	26.6	18.0	17.3	75	75
Ecuador	56.4	44.3	0.8	1.1	68	75
Tunisai	53.8	47.4	8.8	12.4	44	61
Guatemala	43.2	--	10.4	--	53	57
Costa Rica	50.1	39.6	26.7	17.1	87	92

Central Gov't's Expenditures for:

	Central Gov't's Expenditures for:					
	Economic & Educational Services		Social Welfare Services: Housing, Social Security & Welfare		Physical Quality of Life Index	
Countries	1972-73	1985	1972-73	1985	1973	1985
Chile	42.5	20.3	40.0	43.8	77	85
Syria	51.2	38.0	3.6	12.7	52	61
Lebanon	--	15.8	--	--	80	76
Brazil	31.6	27.0	35.0	35.4	68	69
Uruguay	19.3	14.5	52.3	50.4	88	89
Hungary	--	40.4	--	25.7	92	90
Portugal	--	21.6	--	31.0	79	87
Malaysia	37.6	--	4.4	--	59	75
South Africa	--	5.1	--	1.8	48	47
Poland	--	--	--	--	94	92
Yugoslavia	--	--	35.6	6.8	85	87
Mexico	50.6	39.6	25.0	11.9	75	78
Panama	--	24.9	10.8	17.4	81	87
Argentina	50.0	29.8	20.0	38.3	84	87
Korea, Rep. of	41.5	35.9	5.8	8.3	80	86
Venezuela	44.0	40.5	9.2	14.7	80	83
Greece	35.5	26.7	30.6	35.1	91	94
Israel	14.2	12.5	7.1	20.3	90	85
Trinidad & Tog.	--	42.3	--	18.6	88	86
Oman	28.1	31.0	3.0	1.5	--	33
Singapore	35.6	35.2	3.9	6.5	85	90
Iran	46.4	66.6	6.1	13.3	38	53
Iraq	--	--	--	--	46	57
Rumania	--	52.9	--	25.2	92	91
Libya	--	--	--	--	42	58
Saudi Arabia	--	11.6	--	15.4	29	59
Kuwait	31.6	38.2	14.2	17.9	76	81
United Arab E.	34.8	14.8	6.1	5.0	34	74
Spain	25.8	16.1	49.8	64.2	94	97
Ireland	--	26.7	--	30.1	96	95
Italy	34.5	15.2	44.8	32.5	94	95
New Zeland	33.4	23.2	25.6	32.3	96	95
Belgium	34.4	26.7	41.0	42.7	95	96

Appendix A

	Central Gov't's Expenditures for:					
	Economic & Educational Services		Social Welfare Services: Housing, Social Security & Welfare		Physical Quality of Life Index	
Countries	1972-73	1985	1972-73	1985	1973	1985
United Kingdom	13.7	26.7	26.5	35.1	97	95
Austria	21.5	23.0	53.7	47.7	96	95
Netherlands	--	20.8	--	41.0	99	98
France	--	15.3	--	47.9	97	99
Australia	18.5	15.8	20.8	29.4	96	99
Finland	43.2	35.4	28.4	35.0	95	98
Germany	12.8	7.8	46.9	50.5	95	96
Denmark	27.3	16.7	41.6	41.7	98	97
Japan	--	--	--	--	98	100
Sweden	25.4	15.4	44.3	50.1	100	99
Canada	--	20.7	--	35.8	97	98
Norway	30.1	29.0	39.9	36.3	97	98
Switzerland	22.6	15.3	39.5	50.6	98	98
United States	13.8	10.1	35.3	31.6	96	97
Iceland	--	37.2	--	20.2	99	99
Luxemboug	--	26.5	--	51.6	96	95
Malta	--	34.8	--	39.7	89	89
Albania	--	--	--	--	76	78
Angola	--	--	--	--	15	18
Bulgaria	--	--	--	--	94	90
Cuba	--	--	--	--	86	94
Czechosl.	--	--	--	--	95	91
German Dem.	--	--	--	--	96	94
Korea, Dem.	--	--	--	--	--	86
Mongolia	--	--	--	--	--	72
USSR	--	--	--	--	94	88

Source: Government expenditures data from Schumacher et al. (1989) and data for the comutation of the PQLIs from the World Bank (1989)

Bibliography

Acheson, Dean. 1950. "Crisis in Asia--An Examination of U.S. Policy." *Department of State Bulletin*, Vol. 22 (January 23): 111-118.

Ahn, Hae Kyun. 1979. "An Analysis of the Administrative Structures of the Fourth Republic" (in Korean). *Sung Gok Journal* (in Korean), Vol. 19.

Akamatsu, Tsutomu. 1962. "A Historical Pattern of Economic Growth in Developing Countries." *Developing Economies*, 1 (March-August): 3-25.

Almond, Gabriel A. and Sidney Verba. 1963. *The Civic Culture*. Princeton, N.J.: Princeton University Press.

Amin, Samir. 1976. *Unequal Development*. New York: Monthly Review Press.

Amsden, Alice H. 1989. *Asia's Next Giant: South Korea and Late Industrialization*. N.Y., N.Y.: Oxford University Press, Inc.

An, Tai Sung. 1983. *North Korea: A Political Handbook*. Wilmington, Delaware: Scholarly Resources, Inc.

Anderson, Thomas D. 1988. "Civil and Political Liberties in the World: A Geographical Analysis," in Jim Norwine and Alfonso Conzalez, eds. *The Third World: States of Mind and Being*. Boston: Unwin Hyman.

Association of Physicians for Humanism (APH). 1989. *Bulletin of the APH Monthly, 1988-1989*. Seoul, Korea: APH.

Baker, Edward J. 1983. "Edward J. Baker's Testimony," in U.S. Department of State. *Reconciling Human rights and United States Security Interests in Asia*. Washington, D.C.: U.S. Government

Baran, Paul A. 1968. *The Political Economy of Growth*. New York: Monthly Review Press.

Baran, Paul A. and Paul M. Sweezy. 1969. *Monopoly Capital*. Balitmore: Penguin.

_____. 1971. "Notes on the Theory of Imperialism," in K. T. Fann and D. Hodges, eds. *Reading in U.S. Imperialism*. Boston, MA: Porter Sargent.

Barnet, Richard J. 1972. *Roots of War*. New York: Atheneum.

Bell, Daniel. 1958. "Is There a Ruling Class in America? The Power Elite Reconsidered." *American Journal of Sociology,* Vol LXIV (November): 238-258.
Bentley, Arthur F. 1949. *The Process of Government.* Evanston, Ill.: The Principia Press of Illinois.
Bergensen, Albert. 1980. "From Utilitarianism to Globology: The Shift from Individual to the World as a Whole as the Primordial Unit of Analysis," in Albert Bergensen, ed. *Studies of the Modern World-System.* New York: Academic Press.
Beveridge, William. 1942. *Social Insurance and Allied Services.* New York: Macmillan.
Bish, Robert L. 1971. *The Public Economy of Metropolitan Areas.* Chicago: Markham Publishing Company.
Bodin, Jean. 1959. *Six Books of a Commonwealth.* Cambridge, Mass.: Harvard University Press.
Bok, Georges T. E. 1986. *The USSR in East Asia.* Paris: The Atlantic Institute for International Affairs.
Booth, Charles. 1902. *Life and Labor of the People in London.* London: Macmillan.
Browm Gilbert T. 1973. *Korean Pricing and Economic Development in the 1960s.* Baltimore, MD: Johns Hopkins University Press.
Brown, R. A. 1986. "Soviet Navy in East Asia." *The Korea Herald* (June 5).
Brown, Seyom. 1984. *On the Front Burner: Issues in U.S. Foreign Policy.* Boston: Little, Brown.
Brzezinski, Zbignew. 1986a. "My Game Plan for the U.S." *U.S. News & World Report,* June 30.
_____. 1986b. *Game Plan.* Atlanta, Georgia: Atlanta Monthly Press.
Buchanan, J. M. and Gordon Tullock. 1962. *The Calculus of Consent: Logical Foundations of Constitutional Democracy.* Ann Arbor: The University of Michigan Press.
Burki, Shahid Jared. 1983. "UNCTAD VI: For Better or for Worse." *Finance and Development,* 20 (December): 16-19.
Burney, Mahumud A. 1979. "A Recognition of Interdependence: UNCTAD V." *Finance and Development,* 16 (September): 15-18.
Burns, James McGregor, J. W. Peltason, and Thomas E. Cronin. 1989. *Government By the People: Bicentennial Edition, 1987-1989.* Englewood Cliffs, N.J.: Prentice-Hall, Inc.
Byun, H. Y. and S. H. Kim. 1978. *Modernization of Private Enterprises in the Republic of Korea: A Study of the Fifty Groups'*

Developing Pattern. Institute of Developing Economies (IDE), Joint Research Program Series No. 7. Tokyo, Japan: IDE.
Cameron, David R., J. Stephen Hendrichs, and Richard I. Hofferbert. 1972. "Urbanization, Social Structure and Mass Politics: A Comparison of Five Nations." *Comparative Political Studies,* Vol. 5 (October): 259-290.
Caporaso, James A. 1978. "Dependence and Dependency in the Global System." *Special Issue of International Organization,* 32 (Winter): 1-300.
Carter, Jimmy. 1977a. "Inaugural Address of President Jimmy Carter." *Vital Speeches of the Day,* Vol. XXXIII (February 18): 258-59.
_____. 1977b. "President's Address at the United Nations." *Vital Speeches of the Day,* Vol. XXXIII (April 1): 354-356.
_____. 1978. "State of the Union." Delivered to the Joint Session of Congress on January 19, 1978. *Vital Speeches of the Day,* Vol. XLIV (February 1): 226-230.
Chenery Hollis, Sherman Robinson, and Moshe Syrgiun. 1986. *Industrialization and Growth: A Comparative Study.* New York: Oxford University Press.
Cho, Soon Sung. 1967. *Korea in World Politics 1940-1950.* Los Angeles: University of California Press.
Choi, Jae Wook. 1978. "Press Card" (in Korean). *Journalism* (in Korean) (Fall).
Choi, Sung Kyu. 1988. *A Study on Unfairness of Premium Contribution for Type-I Insurance Program* (in Korean). Korean University. Unpublished Master's Degree Thesis.
Chowning, A. 1977. *An Introduction to the Peoples and Cultures of Melanesia.* Menlo Park, CA: Cummings.
Christian Science Monitor (CSM)
Chubb, John and Paul Peterson, eds. 1985. *The New Direction in American Politcs.* Washington, D.C.: Brookings.
Chung, Chee-Wun. 1989. "A Thorough Analysis of Studies on Right-Wing Media" (in Korean). *The Unified Korea* (in Korean), Vol. 6 (November): 48-55.
Chung, Yung Euy. 1989. "A Study of the Relationship Between Korean Tax Policy and Income Redistribution Effects: Focused on the Income Tax and Property Tax." *The Annals of Public Administration Research* (in Korean). The Research Institute for Public Administration, Hanyang University, Vol. 9 (Dec. 1989): 267-307.

Clough, Ralph N. 1976. *Deterrence and Defense in Korea: The Role of U.S. Forces.* Washington, D.C.: Brookings Institution.

Cohen, Roberta. 1979. "Human Rights Decision-Making in the Executive Branch: Some Proposals for a Coordinated Strategy," in Donald F. Kommers and Gilbert D. Loescher, eds. *Human Rights and American Foreign Policy.* Notre Dame, Ind.: University of Notre Dame Press.

Cohen, Steven B. 1982. "Conditioning U.S. Security Assistance on Human Rights Practices." *American Journal of International Law,* 76 (April): 246-79.

Cole, David C. and Princeton L. Lyman. 1971. *Korean Development: The Interplay of Politics and Economics.* Cambridge, Mass.: Harvard University Press.

Cole, Donald B. 1968. *Handbook of American History.* New York: Harcourt, Brace & World, Inc.

Constantino, R. 1977. *Philippines: A Past Revisited.* New York: Monthly Review Press.

Cord, Robert, et al. 1985. *Political Science: An Introduction.* Englewood Cliffs, N.J.: Prentice-Hall, Inc.

Dahl, Robert A. 1964. "Power, Pluralism, and Democracy: A Modest Proposal." A paper delivered at the American Political Science Association Annual Meeting.

_____. 1971. *Polyarchy: Participation and Oppostion.* New Haven, Conn.: Yale University Press.

_____. 1976. *Democracy in the United States: Promise and Performance.* Chicago: Randy McNally.

Dahl, Robert A. and Edward R. Tufte. 1973. *Size and Democracy.* Stanford, CA: Stanford University Press.

Dahl, Robert. 1969. *Who Governs?* New Haven, Conn.: Yale University Press.

Dam, Kenneth W. 1970. *The GATT: Law and International Economic Organization.* Chicago: Chicago University Press.

Danielson, Michael N. and Walter F. Murphy. 1983. *American Democracy.* New York: Holmes & Meier Publishers, Inc.

Davidson, B. 1967. *The Growth of African Civilisation.* London: Longman.

De Roover, Raymond. 1968. "Ancient and Medieval Thought," in David L. Sills, ed. *International Encyclopedia of the Social Sciences.* New York: The Free Press.

Deutsch, Karl W. 1961. "Social Mobilization and Political Development." *American Political Science Review*, Vol. LV, No. 3 (September): 493-515.

Doerner, William R. 1988. "Too Far, Too Fast? ReForm's Price: A Moscow Shake-up and a Beijing Slowdown." *Time*, (October 10): 50-52.

Doh, Hee Joon. 1964. "Realization and Normalization of Democratic Labor Unions" (in Korean). *Sa Sang Gae* (Thought), January.

Dongrip Shimmum

Downs, Anthony. 1957. *An Economic Theory of Democracy*. New York: Harper & Row, Publishers.

Dye, Thomas R. and L. Harmon Zeigler. 1981. *The Irony of Democracy: An Uncommon Introduction to American Politics*. Monterey, CA: Duxbury Press.

Ebenstein, William, et al. 1967. *American Democracy in World Perspective*. New York: Harper & Row, Publishers.

Economic Planning Board (EPB), R.O.K. 1986. *Report on Statistical Analysis of Business Firms in 1986* (Korean). Seoul, Korea: The EPB.

Electronics. 1987. "Korea Aims for the Top VLSI by 1991." April 2.

Emmanuel, Arghire. 1972. *Unequal Exchange: The Imperialism for International Trade*. New York: Monthly Review Press.

Estes, R. J. 1984. *The Social Progress of Nations*. New York: Praeger.

Etzioni, Amitai. 1973. "Mixed Scanning: A 'Third' Approach to Decision-Making," in Jong S. Jun and William B. Storm, eds. *Tomorrow's Organizations: Challenges and Strategies*. Glenview, Ill.: Scott, Foresman and Co.

European Publications Limited. 1989. *The Europe World Year Book 1989*, Vols. I and II: London, England.

Facts on Files, 1982-1988.

Fairbank, John K. and Ssu-yu Teng, eds. 1954. *China's Response to the West: A Documentary Survey*. Cambridge, MA: Harvard University Press.

Fanon, Frantz. 1971. "The Pitfalls of National Consciousness--Africa," in K. T. Fann and D. Hodges, eds. *Reading in U.S. Imperialism*. Boston, MA: Porter Sargent.

Fava, Sylvia Fleis. 1968. *Urbanism in the World Perspective*. New York: T. Y. Crowell.

Fei, John C. H. 1986. "The Economic Development of Taiwan, 1950-1980," in Ilpyong J. Kim, ed. *Development and Cultural Change:*

Cross-Cultural Perpspective. New York: Paragon House Publishers.
Flint, Jerry. 1984. "No More Mr. Cheap Guy." *Forbes* (October, 30): 102-103.
Flora, Peter and Arnold J. Heidenheimer. 1981. *The Development of Welfare States in Europe and America.* New Brunswick, N.J.: Transaction Books.
Frank, Andre G. and Dale Johnson. 1972. *Dependence and Underdevelopment.* Garden City, N.Y.: Anchor.
Frank, Charles R. Jr., et al. 1975. *Foreign Trade Regimes and Economic Development: South Korea.* New York: Columbia University Press.
Fritschler, A. Lee. 1975. *Smoking and Politics.* Englewood Cliffs, N.J.: Prentice-Hall.
Furniss, Norman, and Timothy Tilton. 1977. *The Case for the Welfare State: From Social Security to Social Equality.* Bloomington, Indiana: Indiana University Press.
Gamer, Robert E. 1976. *The Developing Nations: A Comparative Perspective.* Boston, Mass.: Allyn and Bacon, Inc.
Gardner, Lloyd. 1984. *Safe for Democracy, The Anglo-American Response to Revolution, 1913-1923.* New York: Oxford University Press.
Gastil, Raymond D. 1987. *Freedom in the World: Political Rights and Civil Liberties 1986-1987.* New York: Greenwood Press.
General Affairs, National Assembly, The Republic of Korea. Various years. *Report of the National Assembly* (in Korean). Seoul, Korea: The National Assembly.
Goldwater, Barry. 1978. "Mankind's Slow Painful Path." *Vital Speeches of the Day*, Vol. XLIV, No. 15 (May 15): 455-456.
Gordenker, Leon. 1959. *The United Nations and the Peaceful Unification of Korea: The Politics of Field Operations, 1947-1950.* Hague, Netherlands: Martinus Nijhott.
Gorman, P. E. 1984. "The Caribbean Basin: U.S. National Interest." *Vital Speeches of the Day*, Vol. L, No. 18 (July): 546-547.
Gottfried, Alex. 1968. "Political Machine," in David L. Sills, ed. *International Encyclopedia of Social Sciences.* New York: The Macmillan Company.
Government of the Republic of Korea. 1976. *Che Sacha O Gaenyon Kyungje Kyehoek, 1977-81 (The Fourth Five-Year Economic Development Plan, 1977-1981).* Seoul, Korea: The Economic Planning Board.

Bibliography

Greenberg, Edward. 1974. *Serving the Few: Corporate Capitalism and the Basis of Government Policy.* New York: John Wiley.

Guh, Kwan Mo. 1987. *A Study on Economic Class Composition in Korea* (in Korean). Unpublished Ph.D. Dissertation. Seoul, Korea: Seoul National University.

Haggard, Stephan and Chung-In Moon. 1990. "Institutions and Economic Policy: Theory and a Korea Case Study." *World Politics*, Vol. XLII, No. 2 (January): 210-237.

Hahn, Chung Il. 1969. *Korean Politics and Administration: A Study of Legislative Process and Political Development* (in Korean). Seoul, Korea: Park Young Publishing Company.

Han, Woo-Keun. 1971. *The History of Korea.* Honolulu, Hawaii: The East-West Center Press.

_____. 1987. *The History of Korea.* Seoul, Korea: The Eul-Yoo Publishing Company.

Hansen, Roger D. 1976. *The U.S. and World Development: Agenda for Action 1976.* New York: Praeger.

Harrison, Selig S. 1987. *The South Korean Political Crisis and American Policy Options.* Washington, D.C.: The Washington Institute Press.

Henderson, Gregory. 1968. *Korea: The Politics of Vortex.* Cambridge, Mass.: Harvard University Press.

Higgins, Benjamin and Jean Downing Higgins. 1979. *Economic Development of a Small Planet.* New York: Norton.

Hinton, Harold. 1983. *Korea Under New Leadership: The Fifth Republic.* New York: Praeger Publishers.

Hong, Won Tack. 1982. "Economic Growth and Transformation of Industrial Structure." Seoul, Korea: A paper presented at Korea Development Institute's International Forum on Industrial Planning in June.

Hunter, Floyd. 1953. *Community Power Structure.* Chapel Hill, N.C.: University of North Carolina Press.

Huntington, Samuel P. 1988. "One Soul at a Time: Political Science and Political Reform." *American Political Science Review*, Vol. 82, No. 1 (March): 3-10.

Il Yun. 1969. *Samguk Yusa (Memorabilia of the Three Kingdoms).* Byung Dow Lee, translated and annotated. Seoul, Korea: Dong Guk Munhwasa.

Inkeles, Alex. 1969. "Participant Citizenship in Six Developing Countries." *American Political Science Review*, Vol. LXIII, No 4 (December): 1120-1141.

International Institute for Strategic Studies (IISS). 1986. *The Military Balance, 1986-1987*. London: IISS.
International Monetary Fund. 1983. *World Economic Outlook*. Washington, D.C.: International Monetary Fund.
_____. 1990. *World Economic Outlook*.
Irish, Marian D. and Elke Frank. 1978. *Introduction to Comparative Politics: Thirteen Nation-States*. Englewood Cliffs, New Jersey: Prentice-Hall, Inc.
Jacobs, Norman. 1985. *The Korean Road to Modernization and Development*. Urbana, Ill.: University of Illinois Press.
Jones, Leroy and Il SaKong. 1980. *Government, Business and Entrepreneurship in Economic Development: The Korean Case*. Cambridge, Mass.: Harvard University Press.
Jones, Stephen B. 1955. "Global Strategic Views." *Geographical Review*, Vol. 45: 492-508.
Jones, Walter S. 1985. *The Logic of International Relations*. Boston, MA: Little, Brown and Company.
Kang, T. W. 1989. *Is Korea the Next Japan? Understanding the Structure, Strategy, and Tactics of America's Next Competitor*. The Free Press.
Kayongo-Male, D. and P. Onyanago. 1984. *Sociology of the African Family*. London: Longman.
Kihl, Young Whan. 1988. "Party Politics on the Eve of a Gathering Storm: The Constitutional Revision Politics of 1986," in Ilpyong Kim and Young Whan Kihl, eds. *Political Change in South Korea*. New York: Paragon House Publishers.
Kim, Byung Ik. 1988. "Direction Toward Our Country's Medical Security System" (in Korean). *Association of Physicians for Humanism Bulletin* (in Korean), No. 8 (October): 20-28.
Kim, C. I. Eugene, Young Whan Kihl, and Doock-Kyou Chung. 1973. "Voter Turnout and the Meaning of Elections in South Korea." *Asian Survey*, Vol. 23 (November): 1062-74.
Kim, Chong Lim. 1980. "Political Participation and Mobilized Voting," in Chong Lim Kim, ed. *Political Participation in Korea: Democracy, Mobilization and Stability*. Santa Barbara, CA: ABC-CLIO.
_____. 1988. "Potential for Democratic Change in a Divided Nation," in Llpyong J. Kim and Young Whan Kihl, eds. *Political Change in South Korea*. New York: Paragon House Publishers.

Kim, Chong Lim, and B. K. Woo. 1972. "Political Representation in the Korean National Assembly." *American Journal of Political Science* (formerly Midwest Journal of Political Science), Vol. 16.
Kim, Chul Soo. 1981. *Introduction of the Constitution* (in Korean). Seoul, Korea: Park Young Sa.
Kim, Ho Sung. 1989. *Korean Nationalism: A Historical Perspective of Korean Philosophical Thought*. Seoul: Woo-Num Publishing Co.
Kim, Hong Nack. 1988. "Urbanization and Changing Voting Patterns," in Ilpyong J. Kim and Young Whan Kihl, eds. *Political Change in South Korea*. New York: Paragon House Publishers.
Kim, Ilpyong J. 1986. "Introduction," in Ilpyong J. Kim, ed. *Development and Cultural Change: Cross-Cultural Perspectives*. New York: Paragon House Publishers.
Kim, Jae Hong. 1971. "A Study of Restrictions on the Freedom of the Press in Korea" (in Korean). *Journal of the Seoul National University Institute for Studies on Journalism* (in Korean), Vol. 8.
Kim, Jae-On and B. C. Koh. 1972. "Electoral Behavior and Social Development in South Korea: An Aggregate Data Analysis of Presidential Elections." *Journal of Politics*, Vol. 34 (August): 825-859.
Kim, K. W. 1985. "Democratic Consciousness and Voting Behaviors." Seoul, Korea: A paper presented at the Sixth Meeting of Korean Political Science Association and the Association of Korean Political Scientists in North America on August 5-7.
Kim, Kwang Suk, and Michael Roemer. 1979. *Growth and Structural Transformation: Studies in the Modernization of the Republic of Korea: 1945-1975*. Cambridge, Mass.: Harvard University Press.
Kim, Kyong-Dong. 1976. "Political Factors in the Formation of Entrepreneurial Elite in South Korea." *Asian Survey*, Vol. XVI, No. 5 (May): 465-477.
Kim, Kyu-Taik. 1967. "A Statistical Analysis of the Elections in Korea." *Koreana Quarterly*, Vol. 19 (Summer).
Kim, Ung Soo. 1986. "Comments," in Ilpyong J. Kim, ed. *Development and Cultural Change: Cross-Cultural Perspectives*. New York: Paragon House Publishers.
Kim, Young Mo. 1986. *Problems of Korean Social Welfare* (in Korean). Seoul, Korea: Institute for Study on Korean Social Welfare.
Kim, Young-soo. 1983. "Legitimacy: Freedom Fighters and the Succession to Independence Spirit," in National Unification Board, The Ministry of Culture and Information, ed. *The Identity of the*

Korean People: A History of Legitimacy on the Korean Peninsula. Seoul, Korea: Rsearch Center for Peace and Unification.

Kim. Myong-Whai, Eui-Young Ham, and Hyong-Sup Yoon. 1971. "Korean Voting Behavior and Political Orientation." *Korea Observer*, Vol 3 (January): 51-81.

Kirkpatrick, Jeanne. 1981. "Human Rights and American Foreign Policy." *Commentary* (November).

Klein, Sidney. 1986. "Economic Development in Hong Kong and Singapore," in Ilpyong J. Kim, ed. *Development in Cultural Change: Cross-Cultural Perspective.* New York: Paragon House Publishers.

Koh, Kyong Sim. 1989. "Problems of Urban Area Medical Insurance." *Association of Physicians for Humanism Bulletin* (in Korean), No. 15 (June): 10-13.

Kohama, Hirohisa. 1990. "Japan's Economic Development and Foreign Trade," in Chung H. Lee and Ippei Yamazawa, eds. *The Economic Development of Japan and Korea: A Parallel with Lessons.* New York: Praeger.

Koo, S. M., S. Y. Hong, and J. M. Shin. 1982. *A Study in Informal Financial Market in Korea.* Seoul, Korea: Korea Economic Institute.

Korea Institute for Educational Development (KIED). 1983. "Study on the Demand and Supply of Science and Engineering Manpower at Master's and Ph.D. Levels." Mimeo. Seoul: KIED.

Korea News Review.

Korea Social Security Research Institute (KSSRI), ed. 1984. *Medical Care Under the Social Security, What is the Problem?* (in Korean). Seoul, Korea: KSSRI.

_____, ed. 1986. *Medical Care Insurance System, What is the Problem?* (in Korean). Seoul, Korea: KSSRI.

Korean Overseas Information Services (KOIS), Military of Culture and Information. 1979. *A Handbook of Korea.* Seoul, Korea: Samhwa Printing Company.

Krasner, Steven D. 1974. "Oil Is the Exception." *Foreign Policy,* (Spring): 68-90.

Krueger, A. D. 1979. The Developmental Role of the Foreign Sector and Aid." Cambridge, Mass.: Council on East Asian Studies, Harvard University Press.

Kuznets, Paul W. 1977. *Economic Growth and Structure in the Republic of Korea.* New Haven, Conn.: Yale University Press.

_____. 1986. "Economic Development in South Korea," in Ilpyong J. Kim, ed. *Development and Cultural Change: Cross-Cultural Perspective.* New York: Paragon House Publishers.

Kwack, Sung Yeung. 1986. "Economic Development in South Korea," in Lawrnece J. Lau, ed. *Models of Development: A Comparative Study of Economic Growth in South Korea and Taiwan.* San Francisco, CA: Institute for Contemporary Studies.

Kwon, Young Sung. 1981. *Introduction of the Constitution* (in Korean). Seoul, Korea: Bup Mun Sa.

Lal, D. 1983. *The Poverty of 'Development Economics'.* Hobart Paperback 16. London: Institute of Economic Affairs.

Lande, Carl. 1973. "Networks and Groups in Southeast Asia: Some Observations on the Group Theory of Politics." *American Political Science Review,* Vol. LXVII, No. 1 (March): 103-127.

Lee, Byung Tae, et al. 1988. *Industrialization and Labor Management Relations in Korea: Essays in Honor of Retirement of Dr. Doh Hee Jun* (in Korean). Seoul, Korea: Chung Am Sa.

Lee, Cheong Soo. 1983. "Legitimacy on the History of the Korean People," in National Unification Baord, The Republic of Korea, ed. *The Identity of the Korean People: A Hitory of Legitimacy on the korean Peninsula.* Seoul, Korea: Research Center for Peace and Unification.

Lee, Kee Ha. 1961. *History of the Development of Political Parties in Korea* (in Korean). Seoul, Korea: Representative Politics Press.

Lee, Kook Hun. 1969. *A Study on Interest Group Politics in Korea* (in Korean). Unpublished MA thesis. Seoul, Korea: Korea University.

Lee, Nam Y. 1985. "Industrialization and Political Culture: Focused on Change of Political Consensus" (in Korean). *Korean Political Science Review,* Vol. 19.

Lee, Young Ho. 1969. *The Political Culture of Modernizing Society: Political Attitudes and Democracy in Korea.* Unpublished Ph.D. Dissertation. New Haven, Conn.: Yale University.

Lefever, Ernest W. 1988. "Observations on the Cultural Diversity of Non-Western Governments." *World & I,* Vol. 3, No. 1 (January): 621-631.

Lenin, V. I. 1969. *Imperialism: The Highest Stage of Capitalism.* New York: International Pub.

Lerner, Daniel. 1958. *The Passing of Traditional Society.* New York: The Free Press.

Leudde-Neurath, Richard. 1988. "State Intervention in South Korea," in Gordon White, ed. *Developmental States in East Asia.* New York: St. Martin's Press.

Levine, Charles M., B. Guy Peters and Frank J. Thompson. 1980. *Public Administration: Challenges, Choices, Consequences.* Glenview, Illinois: Scott, Foresman/Little, Brown Higher Education.

Lewis, John P. and Valeriana Kallab. 1983. *U.S. Foreign Policy and the Third World: Agenda 1983.* New York: Praeger for the Overseas Development.

Lipset, Seymour M. 1963. *Political Man: The Social Bases of Politics.* Garden City, New York: Doubleday & Co., Inc.

Little, Ian N. D. 1979. "An Economic Reconnaissance," in Walter Galenson, ed. *Economic Growth and Structural Change in Taiwan.* Ithaca, N.Y.: Cornell University Press.

Lizphart, Arend. 1977. *Democracy in Plural Societies: A Comparative Exploration.* New Haven, Conn.: Yale University Press.

_____. 1984. *Democracies: Patterns of Majoritarian and Consensus Government in Twenty-One Countries.* New Haven, Conn.: Yale University Press.

Lloyd's Register of Shipping. Various years. Shipping Economist. London.

Locke, John. 1969. *Two Treatises of Government,* Edited with an Introduction by Thomas Cook. New York: Hafner Publishing Company.

MacKinden, Halford J. 1904. "The Geographical Pivot of History." *Geographical Journal,* Vol. 23: 421-441.

MacLeod, Scott. 1989. "Sand in a Well-Oiled Machine." *Time* (May 8): 44.

Macridis, Roy C. 1986. *Modern Political Regimes: Patterns and Institutions.* Boston, Mass.: Little, Brown and Company.

Magdoff, Harry, and Paul Sweezy. 1971. "Notes on Multinational Corporations," in K. T. Fann and D. Hodges, eds. *Reading in U.S. Imperialism.* Boston, MA: Proter Sargent.

Mahan, Alfred T. 1900. *The Problem of Asia and its Effects upon International Relations.* Boston: Little, Brown.

Marchant, Gary. 1990. "Fast Forward: Korea's High-Tech Future." *Time* (Sept. 17: Special Advertising Section).

Marley, Brian D. 1970. *Wild Flowers of the World.* New York: Crescent Books.

Marx, Karl and Friedrich Engels. 1978. "The Manifesto of the Communist Party," in Robert C. Tucker, ed. *The Marx-Engels Reader*. New York: Norton.
Mason, Edward S., et al. 1980. *Economic and Social Modernization of the Republic of Korea*. Cambridge, Mass.: harvard University Press.
McCloskey, Herbert J., et al. 1960. "Issue Conflict and Consensus Among Leaders and Followers." *American Political Science Review*, Vol. LIV: 409-427.
McCraw, Thomas K. 1984. "Business of Government: The Origins of the Adversary Relationship." *California Management Review*, Vol. 26 (Winter): 33-52.
Medish, Vadim. 1984. *The Soviet Union*. Englewood Cliffs, N.J.: Prentice-Hall, Inc.
Milbraith, Lester, and M. L. Goel. 1977. *Political Participation*. Chicago: Rand McNally.
Milbraith, Lester. 1965. *Political Participation: How and Why Do People Get Involved in Politics*. Chicago: Rand McNally.
Miller, Arthur. 1972. "The Legal Foundations of the Corporate State." *Journal of Economic Issues*, Vol. 6, No. 1 (March): 60-73.
Miller, Merle. 1974. *Plain Speaking: An Oral Biography of Harry S. Truman*. Berkeley, New York: Medallion.
Mills, C. Wright. 1956. *The Power Elite*. New York: Oxford University Press.
Ministry of Education (MOE), Republic of Korea (ROK). 1979. *Kuk-Sa (History for Junior High Schools)*.
Ministry of Health and Welfare (MHW), Republic of Korea. 1982. *Five-Year Helath and Medical Plan with Fifth Five-Year Economic and Social Development Plan: 1982-1986*. Seoul, Korea: The MHW.
Ministry of Science and Technology (MOST), Republic of Korea. 1988. *Introduction to Science and Technology, Republic of Korea, 1988*. Seoul, Korea: The MOST.
Mitchell, Neil K. and James M. McCormick. 1988. "Economic and Political Explorations of Human rights Violations." *World Politics*, Vol. XL, No. 4 (July): 476-498.
Mitchell, William C. 1970. *The American Policy: A Social and Cultural Interpretation*. New York: The Free Press.
Morgenthau, Hans J. 1982. *In Defense of the National Interest: A Critical Examination of American Foreign Policy*. Washington, D.C.: University Press of America.

Morris, Morris D. 1976. "A Quality of Life Index." Washington, D.C.: The Overseas Development Council (a Washington-based nonprofit, public education organization)(mimeo, December).

Mosca, Graetana. 1939. *The Ruling Class*. New York: McGraw-Hill.

Mosher, Frederick E. 1968. *Democracy and the Public Service*. New York: Oxford University Press.

Myrdal, Gunnar. 1972. *Against the Stream: Critical Essays on Economcs*. New York: Vintage.

Nagle, John D. 1987. *Introduction to Comparative Politics: Political System Performance in Three Worlds*. Chicago: Nelson-Hall.

Nie, Norman H., G. Bingham Powell, Jr., and Kenneth Prewitt. 1969. "Social Structure and Political Participation: Developmental Relationship." *American Political Science Review*, Vol. LXIII, No. 2 (June and September): 361-378; 808-832.

North American Coalition for Human Rights in Korea (NACHRK). 1987. "Korea: A Statement of Situation." *Korea/Update*, No. 81 (January): 4-8.

O'Connor, James. 1971. "The Meaning of U.S. Imperialism," in K. T. Fann and D. Hodges, eds. *Reading in U.S. Imperialism*. Boston, MA: Porter Sargent.

Oh, John K. C. 1968. *Korea: Democracy on Trial*. Ithaca, N.Y.: Cornell University Press.

Ostrom, Vincent. 1974. *The Intellectual Crisis in American Public Administration*. University of Alabama Press.

Ostrom, Vincent, et al. 1961. "Organization of Government in Metropolitan Areas: A Theoretical Inquiry." *American Political Science Review*, Vol. LV, No. 4 (December): 831-842.

Pae, Sung Moon. 1986. *Testing Democratic Theories in Korea*. Lanham, Maryland: University Press of America.

_____. 1988a. "Institutionalized Local Self-Government in South Korea," in Ilpyong J. Kim and Young Whan Kihl, eds. *Political Change in South Korea*. New York: Paragon House Publishers.

_____. 1988b. "The Twilight Zone between Government and Communications Media: A Comparative Study of the U.S.A. and the Republic of Korea" (in Korean), in the Korean Public Administration, *Public Administration for Democratic Society* (In Korean). Seoul, Korea: Go-See Won.

_____. 1991. "Korean Perspectives on American Democracy: American Policy Changes, Anti-Americanism, and Policy Recommendations," in Ilpyong Kim, ed. *Korean Challenges and American Policy*. New York: Paragon House Publishers.

Parenti, Michael. 1989. *The Sword and the Dollar: Imperialism, Revolution, and the Arms Race.* New York: St. Martin's Press.

Park, Young Ho. 1987. "Economic Development and Social Inequality in Korea: 1960-1980," in Korean Political Science Association (KPSA). *Korean Politics in the Period of Transition* (Proceedings of the Seventh Joint Conference, July 27-29, 1987). Seoul, Korea: KPSA.

Payer, Cheryl. 1972. *The Debt Trap: The IMF and the Third World.* New York: Monthly Review Press.

Peterson, Wallace C. 1974. "The Corporate State, Economic Performance, and Social Policy." *Journal of Economic Issues*, Vol. 8, No. 2 (June): 483-507.

Petrov, D. V. 1978. *International Relations of the Soviet Union in East Asia.* Moscow: International Press.

Pirages, Dennis. 1978. *The New Context for International Relations: Global Ecopolitics.* North Scituate, MA: Duxbury.

Prebisch, Raul. 1964. *Toward a New Trade Policy for Development.* New York: United Nations.

Primakov, E. M. 1979. *International Situation in the Asian Pacific Region: Basic Trends and Developments.* Fourteenth Pacific Science Congress, Khabarovsk, August 1979. Moscow: Nanka.

Pritchett, C. Herman. 1979. "The President's Constitutional Problems," in Thomas E. Cronin and Rex G. Tugwell, eds. *The Presidency Reappraised.* New York: Praeger Publishers.

Pye, Lucian W. 1990. "Political Science and the Crisis of Authoritarianism." *American Political Science Review*, Vol. 84 (March): 3-17.

Pyongyang Domestic Service Broadcasting (PDSB).

Reagan, Ronald. 1978. "Foreign Affairs: The Need for Leadership." *Vital Speeches of the Day*, Vol. XLIV (May 1): 421-425.

Rees, David. 1981. "Crisis and Continuity in South Korea." London: Institute for the Study of Conflict. *Conflict Studies*, No. 128 (March).

Reilley, John E. 1988. "America's State of Mind: Trends in Public Attitudes Toward Foriegn Policy," in Charles W. Kegley, Jr. and Eugene R. Wittkopf, eds. *The Domestic Sources of American Foreign Policy: Insights and Evidence.* New York: St. Martin's Press.

Rhee, Yung Whee, Bruce Ross-Larson, and Gary Pursell. 1984. *Korea's Competitive Edge.* Baltimore: The Johns Hopkins University.

Roh, Tae Woo. 1987. *The Age of Great Common Men: Plans and Programs for the 1990s* (in Korean). Seoul, Korea: Eul-You Publishing Company.

Roosevelt, Franklin. 1941. "Address of the President of the United States." *Congressional Record,* 87. Washington, D.C.: U.S. Government Printing Office (January 6): 44-47.

Rosenthal, A. M. 1986. "Journey Among Tyrants." *The New York Times,* March 23, 1986.

Rostow, Walt W. 1960. *The Stages of Economic Growth: A Non-Communist Manifesto.* London: Cambridge University Press.

_____. 1971. *Politics and Stages of Growth.* London: Cambridge University Press.

Roth, David F. and Frank L. Wilson. 1976. *The Comparative Study of Politics.* Boston, Mass.: Houghton Mifflin Company.

Rourke, Francis E. 1969. *Bureaucracy, Politics and Public Policy.* Boston, Mass.: Little, Brown and Company.

Rowntree, B. Seebohm. 1901. *York: Poverty, A Study of Town Life.* London: Macmillan.

Rudolph, Barbara. 1988. "Forgive Us Our Debts: A Concensus Emerges in Favor of Easing the Developing Nations' Trillion-Dollar Burden." *Time* (October 10): 86-87.

Rummel, Rudolph J. 1970. *Applied Factor Analysis.* Evanston, Ill.: Northwestern University Press.

Sargent, Lyman T. 1981. *Contemporary Political Ideologies: A Comparative Analysis.* Homewood, Ill.: The Dorsey Press.

Sayers, Michael and Albert Kahn. 1946. *The Great Conspiracy, The Secret War Against the Soviet Union.* San Francisco: Proletarian Publishers.

Sayre, Wallace S. and Herbert Kaufman. 1960. *Governing New York City.* New York: Russell Sage Foundation.

Schumacher, Rose, et al. eds. 1989. *World Quality of Life Indicators: A compendium of Current Information for All Countries of the World 1989.* Santa Barbara, CA: ABC-CLIO.

Scitovsk, Tibor. 1986. "Economic Development in Taiwan and South Korea," in Lawrence J. Lau, ed. *Models of Development: A Comparative Study of Economic Growth in South Korea and Taiwan.* San Francisco, CA: Institute for Contemporary Studies.

Scott, James. 1972. "Patron-Client Politics and Political Change in Southeast Asia." *American Political Science Review,* Vol. XVI, No. 1 (March): 91-113.

Selznick, Philip. 1949. *TVA and the Grass Roots.* New York: Harper & Row.

Senate Library. 1969. *Presidential Vetoes.* Washington, D.C.: U.S. Government Printing Office.

Sherman, Sir Alfred. 1986. "Can Democracy Survive an Omnilateral Conflict of Rights?" *World & I,* Vol. I, No. 11 (November): 647-660.

Shim, Jae Ryong. 1987. "Korean Traditional Thought and Intersecting Clture." Washington, D.C.: A paper presented at the Fourth Annual Conference of Overseas Koreans on December 17-20.

Shultz, Geroge P. 1984. "Power and Diplomacy in the 1980s: Facing the Future." *Vital Speeches of the Day.* Vol. L, No. 15 (May 15): 450-453.

Simon, Herbert A. 1966. *Administrative Behavior: A Study of Decision-Making Processes in Administration Organization.* New York: The Free Press.

Smith, Tony. 1979. "The Underdevelopment of Development Literature: The Case of Dependency Theory." *World Politics.* 31 (January): 247-88.

_____. 1986. "The Underdevelopment of Dependency Theory," in Roy C. Macridis and Bernard E. Brown, eds. *Comparative Politics: Notes and Readings.* Chicago, Illinois: The Dorsey Press.

Snape, R. J., ed. 1986. *Issues in World Trade Policy: GATT at the Crossroads.* New York: St. Martin's Press.

Solarz, Stephan. 1985. "The Soviet Challenge in East Asia." *Asia-Pacific Community,* No. 25 (Summer): 4.

Spero, Joan Edelman. 1985. *The Politcs of International Economic Relations.* New York: St. Martin's Press.

SPSS Inc. 1983. *SPSS User's Guide.* New York: McGraw-Hill Book Company.

Spykman, Nicholas. 1944. *The Geography of the Peace.* New York: Harcourt Brace.

Steinberg, David I. 1988. "U.S. Assistance to Korea: A Policy Dialogue Retrospective." Washington, D.C.: A paper presented at a conference on Korean Challenges and American Policy on December 6-8.

Stephan, John J. 1982. "Asia in the Soviet Conception," in Donald Zagaria, ed. *Soviet Policy in East Asia.* New Haven, Conn.: Yale University Press.

Suh, Dae Sook. 1982. "South Korea in 1981: The First Year of the Fifth Republic." *Asian Survey,* vol. xxii (January): 107-115.

Suttmeier, Richard. 1988. "The Role of Science and Technology in South Korean Development." Washington, D.C.: A paper presented at a conference on Korean Challenges and American Policy on December 6-8.

Tewksbury, Donald, ed. 1950. *Source Material on Korean Politics and Ideologies.* New York: Institute of Pacific Relations.

The Central Election Management Committee (CEMC), The Republic of Korea. 1973a. *The History of Elections in the Republic of Korea* (in Korean), Vol. 1, Seoul, Korea: The CEMC.

_____. 1973b. *The History of Elections in the Republic of Korea* (in Korean), Vol. 2. Seoul, Korea: The CEMC.

_____. 1980. *The History of Elections in the Republic of Korea* (in Korean), Vol 3. Seoul, Korea: The CEMC.

The Christian Institute for Study of Justice and Development (CISJD). 1980. *A Report on Korean Economic Status* (in Korean). Seoul, Korea: CISJD.

The Christian Institute for the Study of Justice and Development (CISJD) (in Korean). 1983. *Press and Society: History and Christianity* (in Korean). Seoul, Korea: Min Eum Sa.

The Europa World Year Book, 1990.

The Korea Development Institute (KDI). 1986. *Korean Year 2000: Prospects and Issues for Long-Term Development Summary Report.* Seoul, Korea: KDI.

The Ministry of Defense, The Republic of Korea. 1989. "The Oh Hong Kun Terror Incidents" (in Korean). *Dong-A Annual, 1989*: 724-725.

The Ministry of Education (MOE), The Republic of Korea. 1979. *The History of Korea.* Seoul, Korea: MOE.

The National Unification Board (NUB), The Republic of Korea. 1983. *The Identity of the Korean People.* Seoul, Korea: NUB.

The South Commission. 1990. *The Challenge to the South: The Report of the South Commission.* Oxford University Press.

The Supreme Council for National Reconstruction (SCNR), The Republic of Korea. 1961. *Military Revolution in Korea.* Seoul, Korea: The Ministry of Foreign Affairs.

The U.S. Air Force Association, 1986. "The Military Balance 1985-1986." *Air Force*, Vol. 69, No. 2 (February): 65.

The U.S. Department of State. 1982. *Country Reports on Human Rights Practices.* Washington, D.C.: U.S. Government Printing Office.

Bibliography

_____. 1987. *Country Reports on Human Rights Practices of 1987.* Washington, D.C.: U.S. Government Printing Office.

The United Nations Centre on Transnational Corporations. 1981. *Transnational Corporations in World Development: Re-Examination.* New York: United Nations.

_____. 1988. *Transnational Corporations in World Development: Trends and Prospects.*

The United Nations Conference on Trade and Development. 1964. *Toward a New Trade Policy for Development.* New York: United Nations.

The Wall Street Journal. January 29, 1981.

The Washington Post. September 25, 1983.

The World Almanac and Book of Facts, various years.

Todaro, Michale P. 1971. *Economic Development in the Third World.* New York: Longman.

Truman, David. 1951. *The Governmental Process.* New York: Alfred A. Knopf.

Truman, Harry S. 1947. "The Truman Doctrine: Special Message to the Congress on Greece and Turkey, March 12, 1947." In *Public Papers of the Presidents of the United States.* Washington, D.C.: U.S. Government Printing Office.

_____. 1956. *Memoirs: Years of Trial and Hope.* Garden City, New Jersey: Doubleday.

_____. 1965. *Memoirs.* New York: New American Library.

U. S. Congress. 1968. *Congressional Quarterly Almanac, 1968.* Washington, D.C.: Congressional Quarterly News Features.

U.S. Congress, House Committee on Foreign Affairs, 81st Congress, First Session. 1949. *Hearing on H.R. 5330 Korean Aid.* Washington, D.C.: U.S. Government Printing Office.

U.S. Congress, Senate, Committee on Foreign Relations. 1953. *The United States and the Korean Problems: Documents 1943-1953.* 83rd Congress, 1st Session. Washington, D.C.: U.S. Government Printing Office.

U.S. Defense Security Assistance Agency. 1986. *Foreign Military Sales and Foreign Military Construction Sales. 1982-1985.* Washington, D.C.: U.S. Government Printing Office.

U.S. Department of Commerce. Various years. *Foreign Grants and Credits by the U.S. Government.* Washington, D.C.: U.S. Government Printing Office.

U.S. Department of Commerce. 1984. *U.S. Statutes at Large*, Vol. 98. Washington, D.C.: U.S. Government Printing Office.

U.S. Department of Commerce. 1986. *Statistical Abstract of the United States, 1986*. Washington, D.C.: U.S. Government Printing Office.

U.S. Department of Defense (DOD). 1986. *Soviet Military Power 1986*. Washington, D.C.: U.S. Government Printing Office.

_____. 1987. *Soviet Military Power 1987*. Washington, D.C.: U.S. Government Printing Office.

_____. 1978. *Foreign Military Sales and Military Assistance Facts*. Washington, D.C.: U.S. Government Printing Office.

U.S. Department of Education, Office of Educational Research and Improvement. 1988. *Digest of Education Statistics*. Washington, D.C.: U.S. Government Printing Office.

U.S. Department of State (DOS). 1947. *Foreign Affairs Background Summary: Korea*. Washington, D.C.: U.S. Government Printing Office.

_____. 1951. *In Quest of Peace and Security: Selected Documents on American Foreign Policy: 1941-1951*. Washington, D.C.: U.S. Government Printing Office.

_____. 1975. "President Ford's Pacific Doctrine." News Release, December 7, 1975, Honolulu, Hawaii. Washington, D.C.: Department of State, Bureau of Public Affairs, Office of Media Services.

_____. 1977. "United States and Asia." Speech by Cyrus Vance before the Asian Society, June 29, 1972, New York. Washington, D.C.: Department of State, Bureau of Public Affairs, Office of Media Services.

U.S. News & World Report. July 24, 1989.

Valenzuela, J. Samuel and Arturo Valenzuela. 1986. "Modernization and Dependency," in Roy C. Macridis and Bernard E. Brown, eds. *Comparative Politics: Notes and Readings*. Chicago, Illinois: The Dorsey Press.

Vance, Cyrus. 1980. "U.S. Foreign Policy: Constructive Change." *Vital Speeches of the Day.* Vol. XLVI, No. 18 (July 1): 568-572.

Yerba, Sidney and Norman H. Nie. 1972. *Participation in America*. New York: Harper & Row.

Verba, Sidney, Norman H. Nie, and Jae-On Kim. 1978. *Participation and Political Equality: A Seven Nation Study*. Cambridge, Mass.: Cambridge University Press.

Viner, Jacob. 1968. "Smith, Adam," in David L. Sills, ed. *International Encyclopedia of the Social Sciences*. New York: The Free Press.

Vogelgesang, Sandy. 1980. "Democratic Politics Behind Human Rights Diplomacy," in Tam J. Farer, ed. *Toward a Humanitarian Diplomacy: A Primer for Policy.* New York: New York University Press.

Wade, Robert. 1988. "State Intervention in 'Outward-Looking' Development: Neoclassical Theory and Taiwanese Practice," in Gordon White, ed. *Developmental States in East Asia.* New York: St. Martin's Press.

Wamsley, Gary. 1969. *Selective Service and A Changing America.* Columbus, Ohio: Charles E. Merrill Company.

Ward, Barbara, Lenore D'Anjou, and J. D. Runnals, eds. 1971. *The Widening Gap.* New York: Columbia University Press.

_____. 1979. *The Radical Economic World View.* New York: Basic Books.

Washington Post (WP)

Weber, Max. 1948. *From Max Weber: Essays in Sociology.* Translated and edited by H. H. Garth and C. Wright Mills. London: Routledge and Kegan Paul.

Wesson, Robert, ed. 1987. *Democracy: A Worldwide Survey.* New York: Praeger Publishers.

Westhal, L. E. and Kwang Suk Kim. 1977. "Industrial Policy and Development in Korea." World Bank Staff Working Paper, No. 263. Washington, D.C.: IBRD.

Westphal, L. E. 1978. "The Republic of Korea's Experience with Export-led Industrial Development." *World Development*, Vol. 6, No. 3: 347-82.

White, Gordon and Robert Wade, eds. 1985. *Developmental States in East Asia.* Brighton, England: Institute of Development Studies, Research Report No. 16.

White, Gordon, ed. 1988. *Developmental States in East Asia.* New York: St. Martin's Press.

White, James W. 1973. *Political Implications of Cityward Migration.* Beverly Hills, CA: Sage Publications.

Williams, William Appleman. 1967. "American Intervention in Russia: 1917-1920," in David Horowitz, ed. *Containment and Revolution.* Boston: Bacon Press.

Wilson, Woodrow. 1971. "War Message." 65th Congress, first session, Senate Document No. 5. Washington, D.C.: U.S. Government Printing Office: 3-8.

Woo, B. K. and C. L. Kim. 1970. *Various Issues on the Legislative Process in Korea* (in Korean). Seoul, Korea. The National Assembly.
World Bank. 1983. *World Development Report 1983*.
_____. 1987. *World Development Report 1987*.
Woronoff, Jon. 1983. *Korea's Economy: Man-Made Miracle.* Seoul, Korea: The Si-sa-yong-o-sa Publishers, Inc., and Arch Cape, Oregon: Pace International Research, Inc.
Yang, Dong Ahn. 1989. "Is the Right Wing Dead?" *Dong-A Annual*, 1989: 724.
Yang, Sung Chul. 1989. "The Status of North and South Korean Diplomatic Relations and the Future Prospects: Search for New Direction and Policies," in Korean Political Science Assiciation (KPSA). *The Korean National Community and State Department.* Seoul, Korea: KPSA.
Yoo, J. and L. L. Wade. 1981. "A Study on Current Political Culture: An Interpretative Perspective." *The Journal of East Asian Affairs.*
Yoo, Yushin. 1987. *Korea the Beautiful: Treasures of the Hermit Kingdom.* Los Angeles, CA: The Golden Pond Press.
Yu, Suk R. 1976-1977. "Relationships of Interest Group to Government and Political Parties in South Korea." *Korean Affairs*, Vol. VI, No. 3-4 (October 1976-January 1977): 22-31.
Yu, Suk Yul. 1983. "The Role of Interest Groups Following the Inception of the Republic" (in Korean). *Korean Political Science Review,* Vol. 17.
Yun, Nae Hyun. 1980. "Restoration of the Ancient Chosun History." Washington, D.C.: Presented at the Fourth Annual Overseas Korean Conference held on December 17-20.
Yun, Yong Hee. 1987. *A Systems Analysis of Korean Politics* (in Korean). Seoul, Korea: Bup Mun Sa.
Yusuf, Shahid and R. Kyle Peters. 1985. "Capital Accumulation and Economic Growth: The Korean Paradigm." Washington, D.C.: World Bank Staff Working Paper No. 712.
Zuckerman, Mortimer B. 1988. "The Kingdom of Distorting Mirrors." *U.S. News & World Report,* (October 3): 74.
_____. 1989. "What Should Make Bush Run Now." *U.S. News & World Report* (February): 7.

Index

America's mission 135
Amsden, Alice H. 70, 98, 110, 111, 113, 118, 119, 120, 121, 123, 127, 128
Anti-Communist Law 141
anti-democracy coalition 276, 282, 283, 292, 326
Basic Press Law 307, 308, 313
belief system 331, 332, 334
Bodin, Jean 350
Buddhism 35, 67, 68
Buddhist Tripitaka 5
Cairo Conference 11
carrot and stick techniques 245, 269, 277
Ch'ang 13
cheap money policy 97
Chicago Council on Foreign Relations 140, 159
Choi Kyu Ha 303, 337
Christianity 35, 67, 68
Chun Doo Hwan 180, 304, 305, 336, 337, 338
comparative advantage 38, 46, 64, 69, 73, 85, 88, 89, 95, 111, 117, 118, 120, 122, 123, 127
Confucianism 35, 67, 68
consensus model 185, 190, 192, 193, 196, 197, 199, 201, 202, 204, 215
consociationalism 215
Daeduck Science and Research Center 102, 126
Dahl, Robert 205, 207, 208, 273, 274, 322
Declaration of Independence 28

demand inelasticity 38, 42
dimension of dependency 140
 limited 140, 142, 167, 174, 176, 179, 181
 moderate 140
 full 140
diplomacy
 open 131, 141, 145, 146, 147, 148, 151
 quiet 131, 147, 148, 150, 152, 167, 168
Dye, Thomas and Zeigler, L. Harmon 273
Economic Development Plan
 Fifth Five-Year Plan 161
 Sixth Five-Year Plan 163
 Seventh Five-Year Plan 479
economic development theories
 the conventional theory 37, 38
 the radical theory 38, 53, 54, 57, 65
Economic Planning Board (EPB) 284
economic theory of democracy 145
economies of scale 109, 110, 112
economies of scope 113, 119
Extraordinary Measures 247, 248, 249, 293
factor analysis 175, 182
Far Eastern Gang of Four 57, 65
Flint, Jerry 124
foreign direct investment (FDI) 55, 56, 57, 99, 122
foreign debts 46, 48, 50, 58, 60, 97, 110, 112
Fritschler, A. Lee 274
Furniss, Norman and Tilton, Timothy

347, 354, 355, 356, 357, 358, 361, 362, 363, 365, 366, 392
Gamer, Robert 252, 257, 283
Gastil, Raymond D. 209, 210, 211, 212, 218, 219
General Agreement on Tariff and Trade (GATT) 72, 73
General John Wickham 170, 304
General Ulchi Mun-dok 21
General Yon Kae-so-mun 21
Generalized System of Preferences (GSP) 73
geopolitical theory 139
Gottfried, Alex 255
group politics 219, 221, 253, 254, 257, 269, 274, 335, 341
Han Yong-un 15
Harrison, Selig S. 319, 320, 321
Hong Kong 54, 57, 60, 64, 84, 105
Hong-ik In-gan 258, 259, 261, 266
human rights 133, 135, 136, 141, 150, 151, 152, 162, 167, 168, 175, 178, 181
Hwabaek 262, 266
Hwarangdo 68, 267
Index of Net Social Progress (INSP) 367, 369
industries for economic development
  import substituting industries 121
  labor-intensive light industries 73, 76, 83, 85, 88, 89, 91, 97, 98, 99, 103, 119, 120, 122, 123
  capital-intensive heavy industries 76, 89, 91, 96, 98, 119, 120, 121, 122
  technology-intensive intermediate 76, 78, 98, 99, 103, 104, 119, 121, 126
intersectoral
  externalities 119
  financing 81, 127
  transfer 82
Jacobs, Norman 222, 240, 253, 254, 257, 269
Woronoff, Jon 35, 116
Kanghwa Treaty 6, 7
Keimyung University Medical Center 437, 441
Kim, Chong Lim 331, 332
Kim Dae Jung 241, 242, 244, 245, 297, 303, 304, 305, 306, 333
Kim Jong Pil 284, 297, 303, 305, 333
Kim So-wol 13, 14
Kim, Ung Soo 112
Kim Young Sam 241, 242, 244, 245, 301, 302, 303, 305, 312, 333, 336
Kim Yu-sin 22
King Muyol 22
King Sejong 267, 268
Kirkpatrick, Jean 133, 134
Kobukson 24
Korea Development Institute (KDI) 114, 127
Korean Advanced Institute of Science and Technology (KAIST) 101
Korean-Japanese Protocol 8
Kuznets, Paul 61, 91, 127
Kwack, Sung Yeung 92, 93, 128
Kwang-gaeto Wang 20
Kwangju uprising 170
Labor Union Law of
  1963 287
  1968 287
laissez faire economy 237
Land of Determination 17, 18, 19, 20, 23, 24
Land of Morning Calm 3, 4, 13
land reform 145, 146
law of diminishing relative marginal utility 73
left-to-right ideological spectrum 235, 238
liberal economy 349, 352, 353, 355
Lijphart, Arend 185, 190, 191, 192,

193, 196, 197, 199, 201, 202, 215
Lipset, Seymour M. 205, 207, 211
Locke, John 350, 351
Macridis, Roy C. 187, 235, 237
Maitreya Buddha 23
majoritarian model 190, 191, 192, 196, 197, 199, 204
malapportionment 226, 230, 235, 301
manumission 262, 267
Marchant, Gary 482
market economy 352, 353, 354, 359, 394
Martial Law Command 288, 304, 305
McCloskey, Herbert 239
Ministry of Culture and Information (MCI) 289, 290, 297, 308, 314
medical care assistance 470
medical care protection 395, 429, 430, 470
medical insurance 413, 415, 416, 418, 419, 420, 421, 422, 423, 424, 425, 426, 427, 428, 429, 430, 435, 438, 441
multinational corporations (MNCs) 50, 51, 52, 57
National Security Law 145
National Council for Unification (NCU) 295, 301
neo-imperialism 50, 56, 65
New Community Movement 90
nordpolitik 485
Pae, Sung M. 187, 227, 239, 269, 276, 288, 335, 344, 345
pan-sang-hoe 227, 228, 230, 235
Park Chung Hee 240, 283, 336
patriarchal
  bureaucracy 221
  legislature 230
  political parties 235
patron-client politics 131, 219, 221, 252, 254, 255, 256, 257, 268, 269,
275, 276, 277, 278, 289, 335, 338, 341
Physical Quality of Life Index (PQLI) 347, 366, 369, 370, 371, 373, 374, 378, 379, 380, 382, 393, 394, 395, 432, 487
pluralist group model 272
political satellite model 218, 271, 272, 277, 283, 292, 302, 325, 326
political system 186, 202, 203, 205, 208, 221, 272, 276, 313
popular rule model 272, 274
Potsdam Conference 11
power elite model 274
presidential veto 232, 234, 235
price decay 40, 42
Pritchett, C. Herman 232, 234
pro-democracy coalition 271, 276, 277, 281, 282, 287, 290, 291, 292, 293, 297, 299, 301, 303, 308, 309, 311, 316, 317, 318, 319, 321, 326, 330, 331
progressive tax 361, 362, 462
Public Pension Law of 1986 403, 412
public choice model 425
public ownership of housing units 466
Research and Development (R & D) 99, 101, 102, 103, 113, 120, 127
Roh Tae Woo 245, 304, 309, 314, 317, 320, 321, 326, 330, 333, 335, 336, 337, 338
Rose of Sharon 19, 20
Rosenthal, A. M. 174, 180
Rostow, Walt W. 37
Russo-Japanese War 8, 11
Samguk Yusa 16
Samsung 107, 120, 127
Scitovsky, Tibor 105, 107, 108, 109, 110, 111, 112, 116, 117
Seoul Olympics 31, 33, 318, 337
shop floor management 111

Singapore 54, 57, 60, 64, 105
Sino-Japanese War 7, 11
Sirhak 259, 260, 261, 266
Standard International Trade Classification (SITC) 87
Son In 13
state ownership 383, 384
states
  economy-priority states (EPSs) 373, 378, 379, 380, 392
  welfare-priority states (WPSs) 373, 378, 380, 392
Steinberg, David I. 70, 72
stepwise linear regression analysis 176
Tae Daero system 266
Tae Kwondo 20
Taft-Katsura Agreement 8
Taiwan 105, 106, 107, 108
Tale of
  Chun-Hyang 261, 263
  Hong Kil-Tong 260, 261
  the Yangban 263
Tangun mythology 35, 67
Taoism 35, 67, 68
Theory Y management 123
threshold model 218, 271
Tonghak rebellion 265, 266
total factor
  input 64
  productivity 64
Tripitaka Koreana 23
U.S. national interest 137, 138, 140, 150, 152, 153, 159, 167, 174, 181
  indifferent 137, 138
  important 137, 138, 140, 142, 150, 153, 159, 163, 166, 172, 176
  vital 131, 137, 138, 139, 140, 141, 153, 159, 160, 166, 167, 174, 176, 180, 181
U.S. Trade and Tariff Act of 1984 163
U.S.-ROK Mutual Defense Treaty 161

United Nations Conference on Trade and Development (UNCTAD) 50, 65, 73
Wamsley, Gary L. 274
Wesson, Robert 211, 212
Wilson, Woodrow 27, 132
Yalta Conference 11
Yeo, Sung-Sook 441
Yi Sun-shin 24
Yujunghoe 296, 301, 302
Yun Po Sun 240
Yushin Constitution 151, 175
zero-sum game 188